Knowledge Worlds

Reinhold Martin

Knowledge Worlds

MEDIA, MATERIALITY,

AND THE MAKING OF

THE MODERN UNIVERSITY

Columbia University Press / *New York*

Columbia University Press
Publishers Since 1893
New York   Chichester, West Sussex
cup.columbia.edu
Copyright © 2021 Columbia University Press
Library of Congress Cataloging-in-Publication Data
Names: Martin, Reinhold, 1964– author.
Title: Knowledge worlds : media, materiality, and the making of the modern
university / Reinhold Martin.
Description: New York City : Columbia University Press, 2021. |
Includes bibliographical references and index.
Identifiers: LCCN 2020028433 (print) | LCCN 2020028434 (ebook) |
ISBN 9780231189828 (hardback) | ISBN 9780231189835 (trade paperback) |
ISBN 9780231548571 (ebook)
Subjects: LCSH: Education, Higher—Philosophy. |
Classification: LCC LB2322.2 .M3677 2021 (print) | LCC LB2322.2 (ebook) |
DDC 378.001—dc23
LC record available at https://lccn.loc.gov/2020028433
LC ebook record available at https://lccn.loc.gov/2020028434

Cover image: William Hallock and Charles F. McKim, Illumination of main
reading room, Low Memorial Library, Columbia University, c. 1897.
"Plan Showing Position of Lamps, Dome, and Globe." From Hallock,
"Diffused Illumination," *Progressive Age* 16, no. 3 (1 March 1 1898): 109.

For Neelan, and in memory of Reinhold Ilmar Martin
(Baltic University, 1946–1949) ∽

CONTENTS

Preface   ix

Introduction: Knowledge and Technics   1
Prologue, c. 1800   21

PART 1: FIGURES

1. Student Bodies and Corporate Persons   29
2. Greek Lines: The Geometry of Thought   52

PART 2: TEMPORALITIES

3. Bricks and Stones: Time-Based Media   77
4. Sources: A Political Ecology of Cultivation   104
   Interlude, c. 1900   130

PART 3: VOICES

5. Diffuse Illumination: The Silence of the Universal   139
6. The Dialectic of the University: His Master's Voice   170

PART 4: SYMBOLS

7. Frontier as Symbolic Form   195
8. Technopoesis: Human Capital and the Spirit of Research   223
   Epilogue, c. 2000   250

Notes   257

Selected Bibliography   323

Index   351

PREFACE

How to understand the long, recursive passage in university discourse from liberal to neoliberal reason? Within what material infrastructures, what ways of organizing space and time, regulated by what representations, what poetics, have systems of academic knowledge formed? To what regimes of power, what dialectics of mastery and subordination, what distributions of value, do these infrastructures belong? By what symbolic and political economy of media, technics, and intellectual life, in short, has the modern university been governed?

Animated by such questions, this book opens in several directions. The first, signaled in the subtitle, puts the accent on media. This identifies *Knowledge Worlds* as a contribution to the history of infrastructural media, or media complexes, with the modern university as its central object. Over the decade or so during which I have researched and written the book, I have conceived of it primarily in these terms, and I still do. Media, broadly construed, take center stage as social and technological systems. Writing from in-between fixed topoi like academic disciplines, institutions, and their guiding concepts, I have tried to show how specific media complexes have enabled, constrained, and otherwise defined the freedom to know, the freedom to learn, and the freedom to teach.

A second reading places the accent slightly differently, on *university*, as in the "making of the modern university." This locates the book among works of intellectual and institutional history and in the history of higher education, especially those that have taken universities or particular aspects of universities or colleges as their subject matter. Many of the books that have filled my shelves during this time belong to these areas, and I have frequently relied on the foundations these works have laid. I hope that this book will take its place among them, if only (in some cases) as a rejoinder.

A third reading concerns what is modern about universities and the media by which they are shaped. A provincialism masked in the subtitle—"the" modern university—is that the colleges and universities that *Knowledge Worlds* considers are all located in the United States, and most of the hardware that constitutes their media complexes is American-made. This might lend credence to the metonymic fallacy that allows "America" (or Euro-America) and all things "American" (or Western) to stand for modernity as such.

My hypothesis instead is that the hegemonic microcosm I study here—the American university—refracts the variegated macrocosm, which includes its counterparts around the world. Putting U.S. colleges and universities under the microscope highlights the boundary problems that have defined them, the recurrent efforts to make worlds inside their walls distinct from those outside even while connecting the two. For what is modern about colleges and universities in the United States from about 1800 to about 1975 is so by virtue of the particular ways in which their numerous gates, passages, and thresholds—both spatial and temporal—have secured knowledge, consolidated power, and laid claim on universality through the regular, carefully orchestrated opening and closing of doors.

Lurking within these readings of the book is the difference between a university and a college, each of which generally serves different constituents to different ends. Rather than accept this difference as categorical, I have tried to show it in formation. In the United States, colleges most often preceded universities and sometimes grew into them. But the transformation of one into the other was rarely straightforward, just as the persistence of some traits and the introduction of others rarely followed a predictable path. In all cases, my main concern has been the line that distinguishes and joins the two, diachronically and synchronically. Whether it is a history of media or of universities, then, this book is a history of differences, inequalities, connections, and continuities in the production, storage, and transmission of knowledge.

Finally, there is the matter of the subjects who make this history even as they are made by it. Throughout I emphasize the making, which like all construction requires tools. From books to buildings, material things mediate countless acts of knowledge-making that—in each case—recursively define their makers. *Knowledge Worlds* is about these human agents and their degrees of agency, just as much as it is about the hardware that enables them to know, and to be recognized in turn as knowing subjects who operate that hardware.

For a book like this, the author's disciplinary orientation should be especially consequential. Mine begins with the history of architecture. Despite its institutional location in schools of architecture and in departments of art history, the history of architecture—or "architectural" history—is, as I conceive it, of a piece with historical scholarship in general, not a separate domain. Media history is a history of such connections. Still, the architectural historian brings certain tools to the job site. Time spent walking around campuses, poking around their buildings, and examining visual documents has been especially important. Unmentioned in the title, architecture is everywhere in the book. Yet what I have written about is frequently unseen: the infrastructures that pass through more visible or legible structures. Historians of architecture may therefore find some expectations of their craft unmet. My hope nonetheless is that a patient reading will show how doing history with architecture reanimates the languages of space, form, utility, and meaning that have been refined by generations of scholars to whom I am silently indebted.

Writing media history also means writing media theory. In this regard, my project is a strictly experimental effort—using the laboratory equipment supplied by the historical sciences—to verify the hypotheses that I outline in the introduction, if not entirely to resolve the conceptual dilemmas from which these hypotheses derive. Theory here is something like Friedrich Nietzsche's philosophical hammer: an instrument with which to tap gently the idols of academe, not to smash them but to test their durability and their resonance. Today, critical thought is under direct assault in the United States and in much of the world, as are those intellectuals and students deemed exterior to the social body. Colleges and universities—despite their contradictions—still offer precariously sheltered islands of sanctuary and dissent, even as cynical powers attack academic freedoms and cast aside hard won scientific truths. I therefore want to state unambiguously at the outset: the university must be defended, as well as transformed.

In this and other respects, every day, every academic experience, from the classroom to the committee meeting, has been instructive in one way or the other. Each has entailed a bit of informal field work that has left an impression, conscious or not, circumscribed by limitations and distortions that I have not always been able to overcome. This book and its author therefore owe intellectual and personal debts far too numerous and to far too many individuals and institutions to name here. I will restrict my acknowledgements to those in contexts and circumstances most directly related to the actual writing, in the hope that those unmentioned will recognize the unrecorded debt as well as the dialogue. Errors and omissions, however, are entirely mine.

Directly and indirectly, in person and virtually, my research would have been impossible without the work and assistance of archivists and staff at these institutions: the University of Arizona, the Billings Family Archives, Bryn Mawr College, the University of California at Berkeley, the University of Chicago, Columbia University, Dartmouth College, Harvard University, the Massachusetts Institute of Technology, the New York Historical Society, the University of Pennsylvania, Stanford University, Tuskegee University, Vassar College, the University of Vermont, the University of Virginia, Washington University in St. Louis, the University of Wisconsin, and Yale University. At Columbia, I am especially grateful to my colleagues at the Avery Architectural & Fine Arts Library, as well as to those at Butler Library's Rare Books & Manuscripts Library. I am also grateful to those who, as students, provided invaluable research assistance along the way: Maya Ephrem, James Graham, Hilary Huckins-Weidner, and Mayrah Udvardi. As always, my gratitude to Jacob Moore and Jordan Steingard at Columbia University's Temple Hoyne Buell Center for the Study of American Architecture must be repeated. So too for Dean Amale Andraos of Columbia's Graduate School of Architecture, Planning and Preservation (GSAPP), from whose generous support I have regularly benefitted, as well as GSAPP dean emeritus Mark Wigley. Early on, the chance to coteach a design studio/seminar on the "new university" with Jonathan Cole and Laurie Hawkinson at GSAPP proved an especially welcome stimulus.

At Columbia's Society of Fellows / Heyman Center for the Humanities, Eileen Gillooly has nurtured a truly singular environment for scholarly exchange; my special gratitude goes to her and to all of the postdoctoral fellows from whose work I have been privileged to learn. Also at Columbia, numerous colleagues at the Center for Comparative Media and at the Institute for Comparative Literature and Society (ICLS) have helped to define this book's points of departure. Those reading between the lines will recognize the debt that *Knowledge Worlds* owes to the boundary problems posed so productively by these two institutions, and to the camaraderie that has come from collaborative work; likewise for colleagues at Columbia's Committee on Global Thought. In a related vein, my project was informed in fundamental ways by the intellectual intensity and warm hospitality at the Internationales Kolleg für Kulturtechnikforschung und Medienphilosophie (IKKM) in Weimar, under the guidance of Lorenz Engell and Bernhard Siegert, where I was honored to spend time as a fellow during the early stages of writing and research.

Over the course of about a decade, numerous colleagues have provided advice and criticism, asked questions, or offered invitations to speak, while showing in their own work how to think about questions I have thought about here. I am especially grateful to Lucia Allais, Zeynep Çelik Alexander, Stefan Andriopoulos, Weihong Bao, Timon Beyes, Irene Cheng, Wendy Hui Kong Chun, Lisa Conrad, Jonathan Crary, Charles Davis, Arindam Dutta, Ed Eigen, Noam Elcott, Maria González Pendás, Bernard Harcourt, John Harwood, Andreas Huyssen, Fabian Krämer, Andres Kurg, Laura Kurgan, Brian Larkin, Ayala Levin, Helena Mattsson, Rosalind Morris, Eric Mumford, Ginger Nolan, Michael Osman, Carsten Ruhl, Robin Schuldenfrei, Felicity Scott, Joshua Shannon, Bernhard Siegert, Gayatri Chakravorty Spivak, Laurent Stalder, Jesús Velasco, Aurélie Vialette, Mabel Wilson, and Claire Zimmerman. I particularly want to thank Harlan Chambers, Fabian Krämer, Bruce Robbins, and Dorothea von Mücke for their thoughtful, constructive responses to parts of this work presented at Columbia on four separate occasions. Among the many extraordinary graduate students—most unnamed here, alas—from whom I have been lucky enough to learn over the years, more than a few have made important contributions that are directly related to material covered here: Caitlin Blanchfield, Erik Carver, Irene Cheng, Christopher Cowell, Maur Dessauvage, Leslie Herman, Alexander Hilton Wood, Hollyamber Kennedy, Maura Lucking, Diana Martinez, Jonah Rowen, Ife Salema Vanable, Manuel Shvartzberg Carrió, and Elliott Sturtevant. To all of the students at every level with whom I have been fortunate enough to discuss ideas shared in this book, and especially to participants in several seminars related to this topic: Thank you.

Parts of chapters have found their first expression or further development thanks to speaking invitations in conferences or as public lectures at the following institutions: the Courtauld Institute of Art, London; the Department of Film and Media, University of California, Berkeley; the Deutsches Architekturmuseum, Frankfurt am Main; the Estonian Museum of Architecture and the Estonian Academy of Arts, Tallinn; the Graduate School of Design, Harvard University; IKKM, Weimar; the Institute for History and Theory of Architecture, ETH Zürich; the Malcolm S. Forbes Center for Culture and Media Studies and the Cogut Center for the Humanities, Brown University; the Netherlands Institute for Advanced Study in the Humanities and Social Sciences; the Potomac Center for the Study of Modernity; the Sam Fox School of Design & Visual Arts, Washington University in St. Louis; and the Society of Architectural Historians; and at Columbia: Casa Hispanica, the Center for Science and Society, ICLS, and the Race + Modern Architecture Project.

I especially want to express my appreciation to the Schoff Fund at the University Seminars at Columbia University for their help in publication. Material in this work was presented to the University Seminar: Theory and History of Media. I also thank Columbia's Society of Fellows / Heyman Center for the Humanities for related support.

Parts of several chapters have been published along the way. A version of chapter 6 appeared in *Grey Room* 60 (2015) under its current title; part of the prologue is included in my essay "Drawing the Color Line: From Jefferson to Mumford," in Irene Cheng, Charles L. Davis II, and Mabel O. Wilson, eds., *Race and Modern Architecture: A Critical History from the Enlightenment to the Present*, (Pittsburgh, PA: University of Pittsburgh Press, 2020); a portion of chapter 1 appeared in early form in Moritz Gleich and Laurent Stalder, eds., *Architecture/Machine: Programs, Processes, and Performance* (ETH Zürich, 2017); a modified excerpt from that chapter also appears in Timon Beyes, Lisa Conrad, and Reinhold Martin, *Organize* (Minneapolis: University of Minnesota Press, 2020); and a section of chapter 8 appeared, also in an early form, as "The MIT Chapel: An Interdiscursive

History," in Arindam Dutta, ed., *A Second Modernism: MIT, Architecture, and the "Techno-Social" Moment* (Cambridge, MA: MIT Press, 2013).

At Columbia University Press, my very special thanks to Philip Leventhal for his trust and thoughtful stewardship from start to finish, and to Monique Briones and Marielle Poss for guiding the book through production, to Ben Kolstad and Karen Stocz Oemler at Cenveo for their expert editing, and to Kitty Chibnik for the index. I am also honored by the care shown by the two anonymous readers who generously took time from their own work to review the manuscript. Their considered and precise readings and especially, their criticisms and suggestions shared in a language of common, thought-provoking purpose, reconfirmed the preciousness of peer review.

The public, formal side of academia is balanced, of course, by the fact that we live our lives historically in the most personal ways. I write in uncertain times, every moment of which I have treasured sharing with Kadambari Baxi, a gifted teacher from whose calm insight and uncompromising imagination I continue to learn each day. A generation earlier than ours my mother, Josephine Martin, did not have access to higher education for structural reasons, though her penetrating alertness would stand out in any classroom. My father, Reinhold Ilmar Martin, an Estonian "displaced person" in more ways than one, had his education interrupted by war, resumed it at the fleetingly utopian Baltic University in postwar Hamburg, and then later, courtesy of the American land-grant system, at the University of Western Illinois. Education—enlightenment—is an untimely thing. Facing in history's other direction, every word in this book is dedicated to Neelan Baxi Martin, a fearless custodian of the future whose actions and convictions reawaken the old, luminous imperative: "Dare to know!"

New York, March 1, 2020

NB: *These prefatory words were written just prior to the global shutdown of all but "essential services" due to the COVID-19 pandemic. At that time, educators and their students around the world embarked on unprecedented, profoundly uneven efforts to transfer what they could of their work online, to various remote-learning platforms. Research, when it was not halted or severely curtailed, withdrew from libraries, laboratories, and field sites. What these processes have revealed, the countless ways in which media have mattered to them, and the countless material infrastructures involved, will no doubt be examined intensively by scholars studying a world order shaken to its foundations.*

Knowledge Worlds

INTRODUCTION

Knowledge and Technics

O n the evening of October 31, 1974, from eight to ten o'clock, attendees at the sixteenth annual meeting of the Midwest Modern Language Association (MMLA) gathered in the Chase Club at the Chase-Park Plaza Hotel in St. Louis to hear, see, and discuss two presentations on "The Worldliness of Literary Criticism." The conference program listed the featured speakers as "Frederic [*sic*] R. Jameson, University of California at San Diego," and "Edward W. Said, Columbia University."[1] Jameson's talk was published the following spring in the MMLA *Bulletin* as "Beyond the Cave: Demystifying the Ideology of Modernism." Said's appeared in the next issue as "The Text, the World, and the Critic."[2]

Media Complexes

Here already is the university as a media complex, *extra muros*: printed texts, a professional meeting, a schedule, speakers and auditors, institutional affiliations, a room with chairs, a city. We will gather elements like these throughout the book. Our recurring problem will be when, where, and how to draw the line separating inside from outside, a broken, twisted line that puts the university in the world—to some degree by setting it apart.

A media complex is a network of material infrastructures, operations, and techniques through which human beings know themselves and their world. Each such complex combines formats and translates between them. Each scales up and down, linking with others into networks of networks that make worlds intelligible. A world is, in this sense, both a knowable thing and a cognitive environment, a sphere of knowledge and of action. Media are socially produced objects and systems that bring worlds into view, admitting and excluding subjects like any entrance exam.[3] To write, read, speak, or hear something is to know that it can be known. All academic knowledge is, by this definition, worldly knowledge: the output and input of media complexes.

We therefore pick up where old debates about text and world, cognition and exclusion, left off, with Said as our introductory speaker. Several versions of his MMLA text reside with the Edward W. Said Papers, in Columbia University's Rare Book & Manuscript Library, on the sixth floor of Butler Library. It is fascinating to see there the future author of *Beginnings*, an extended meditation on what it means to begin a text, outline his own in pencil and blue ink on two pairs of stapled-together note cards, point by tentative point.[4] What scholars will likely regard as the definitive version appeared eventually as the title chapter of *The World, the Text, and the Critic* (published by Harvard University Press in 1983), which was awarded the American Comparative Literature Association's René Wellek Prize in 1984.[5] As happens sometimes, the MMLA conference program listed both Said's and Jameson's presentations under different titles than those of the later publications: for Jameson, "Criticizing Criticism: Repression in Literary Scholarship Today," and for Said, simply, "The Worldliness of Literary Criticism."[6]

To what did this "worldliness" refer? In his letter of invitation to Said, Gerald L. Bruns, the MMLA's general secretary and a scholar of English literature at Notre Dame, indicated his wish to publish Said's address in the *Bulletin* and enclosed a two-page description of the panel's theme. A handwritten postscript enjoins: "Fred Jameson will be the other speaker, so by all means come if at all possible!"[7] Already then we have a kind of postal hailing from the addressee's discipline, via certified messenger, to appear in public with a peer and to publish the results. The Said Papers contain two copies of Bruns's session description, one a barely readable xerographic reproduction, the other apparently retyped with Said's scribbled annotations in the margins. In this memorandum we find many of the concerns of literary theory at the time regarding the interplay of speech and writing. The centerpiece is a long quotation from the philosopher Paul Ricoeur, later re-cited by Said in its entirety, that argues for the priority of "living speech" over a text that, in its disembodied virtuality, "obliterates" its world, meaning its "circumstantial setting" and "cultural background." The profession's Midwestern general secretary asks in his invitation whether it is the task of the critic to rebuild that world, in the process redeeming the otherwise "merely textual cosmos" of interpretive writing.[8] One unmentioned detail being that, beginning in 1970 the MMLA required participants to precirculate their texts, with most panels "given over entirely to discussion rather than oral delivery of papers," as a published announcement put it.[9] At the 1974 meeting, this procedure applied to all forums and sections, but evidently not to Said's and Jameson's "General Session," which was effectively a keynote. The session thus stood in intermedial relief against the others, anticipating in its worldly circumstance—which, unlike the others, put speech before writing—the very question to which it was thematically addressed.[10]

Worlds

In both published versions as well as in the several archived drafts, Said begins his text with a tableau. The classical pianist Glenn Gould has abandoned the stage. Gould has subsequently issued a studio recording of Liszt's piano transcription of Beethoven's Fifth Symphony, along with a recorded interview in which he explains to his interlocutor, a record company executive, that one reason he has forsaken live performance is that, when touring the Soviet Union, he tended to "distort" the phrasing of Bach "so that," as Said puts it, "he could more effectively 'catch' and address his listeners in the eighth balcony."[11] Lingering on the special irony of Gould compromising his self-imposed musical asceticism with a commercial interview, a mock-astonished Said exclaims: "And finally all this fixed on a mechanically repeatable object, which controlled the most obvious signs of immediacy (Gould's voice, the peacock-like style of the Liszt transcription, the brash informality of an interview packed along with a disembodied performance) beneath, or inside (or was it outside?) a dumb, anonymous, and disposable disc of black plastic."[12]

The book you are reading is about the plastic; it is also about the eighth (or, in the later version, third) balcony, and the people in it, and those on the stage, and the stage itself. Said's text about texts in the world invites us to consider what a media history of university discourse could entail. Exiting his tableau, the Palestinian American literary critic draws parallels that align Gould's recording with what Said calls "written performance." "First of all," he says, "there is the reproducible material existence of a text. Both a recording and a printed object are subject to similar legal, political, economic and social constraints, so far as their sustained production and distribution are concerned," and so on. Then there is "style," wherein "the paradox is that something as impersonal as a text, or a record, can nevertheless deliver an imprint or a trace of something as lively, immediate and transitory as a 'voice.' "[13] Said's "worldliness," then, is a veritable media circus, if by media we understand not only the means of a text's recording and transmission but also the infrastructures within which it becomes readable and its lived world becomes knowable.[14]

Despite its author's resistance to prioritizing speech over writing, and despite acknowledging the subtending "paradox," Said's text also smuggles in, through the literary-critical concept of "style," the precritical immediacy of "voice." A small historical irony attending the premiere of Said's text in St. Louis is that on the following afternoon, November 1, 1974, "Gayatri Spivak, Univ. of Iowa" chaired what the conference program called a "seminar," titled "On Jacques Derrida."[15] While diverging on the matter of deconstruction, within a decade Said and Spivak would become leading figures in the new field of postcolonial studies, a loosely defined but powerful attack on the career and legacies of the Eurocentric imagination, which was especially influential in literature departments in U.S. colleges and universities during the 1980s and 1990s. Whereas for his part, Said's copanelist Jameson would go on to become a leader in the study of what became known, during the same period, as postmodernism.

In other words, the historical foundations of the world in question were already trembling, and the edges of its primary texts had begun to fray. Learning from Said, we know immediately that the text with which we have begun cannot be isolated as if in some otherworldly laboratory. To its multiple versions, from conference paper to journal article to book chapter, we have already added the conference program, the letter of invitation from Bruns, and the memorandum describing the panel's theme. Now follow Said all the way down to the black plastic on which Gould's performance of the Liszt transcription was recorded, in what amounts to a return of the repressed, Soviet-scaled "eighth balcony." By this point, the separation between text and world has become so fragile, so contingent that we must also include the archive in which Said's papers are held, the university library that holds the archive, the campus on which that library sits, and even, moving outward in space and backward in time, the conference hotel in St. Louis in which the paper was first delivered.

Asymptotically, we approach the absurd extension of the text's world into the totality of history, as well as into all possible versions and all possible interpretations (including this one), which Jorge Luis Borges documented so vertiginously in "The Library of Babel." But Columbia University's Butler Library, where the Said Papers reside, is not, to borrow from Jameson (borrowing earlier from Friedrich Nietzsche), a "prison-house of language."[16] Like others of its kind, the library is a selection mechanism, an ordering device designed to make sense of the intertextual babble toward which its contents otherwise tend. I therefore want only to take Said's argument more literally than perhaps he was willing, to include among the knowledge worlds of the university the paper on which words are written and the spaces in which they are spoken, read, and stored.

My concern is, in short, to reconstruct in the domain of technical media like university libraries what Gerald L. Bruns, general secretary of the MMLA, called in his memo "worldliness." Said, sensitive to the Liszt transcription's cultural politics, acknowledges its storage and playback system as part of the musical text's material conditions of existence and circulation, and he even highlights the studio recording as a medium through which to discern an author's voice amid the din of the world. Still, he ultimately allows his three interrelated figures—text, world, critic—to settle in as echoes, shadows flickering across "dumb" base materials like black plastic through which their relations are conveyed.

The university environments in which arguments like these circulate belong to media complexes that make knowledge, and knowledge about knowledge, possible. In this case, the complex includes not only Said's "home" institution (Columbia University, which is also my own) but also the system of academic conferences and their venues, like the Chase-Park Plaza Hotel and its affordances, and the instruments of academic publishing such as the MMLA *Bulletin*, and later Harvard University Press (and the Wellek Prize), through which Said's text moved from writing to speech to writing. Although the 1974 MMLA conference did not include any panels devoted explicitly to the subject, media were ubiquitous there, too.[17] Since then, Gould's withdrawal from performance has become a subject for the new field of sound studies which, unlike most musicological treatments Said would have known, calls attention to the social and technical features of the studios in which piano recordings are made.[18]

Walls and Gates

During what the philosopher of media Friedrich Kittler, employing a customary periodization, called the "age of Goethe" (*Goethezeit*, circa 1800), the archetypally male scholar's studio was his study. By 1974, scholars at the MMLA conference could attend a number of sessions on feminist topics, including a meeting of the Coalition of Women in *Germanistik*, Kittler's field.[19] Kittler began *Discourse Networks*, his oblique study of German university discourse, with an excursus on the textual, typeset origins of the "mother's mouth," the paradigmatic site of what the media philosopher and theologian Walter J. Ong called "primary orality," as literacy's domestic, paradoxically aural point of transmission.[20] My account of the American scene begins around the same time but extends past where Kittler ends, circa 1900, to about the time of the sixteenth MMLA conference, circa 1975. Though my periodization is comparable to Kittler's, I trace continuities as well as discontinuities. My analysis also revises the Kittlerian doxa by, among other things, noticing women in lecture halls, behind telescopes, and in classrooms doing much more than taking dictation as components of what Kittler's German title, translated literally, calls "writing-down systems" (*Aufschreibesysteme*).[21]

Kittler's discipline, literature, is among Immanuel Kant's philosophically elevated "lower" faculties, or today's faculties of arts and sciences. Mine, architecture, takes its place among the morally and intellectually suspect "higher" faculties, or professional schools, closer to the sovereign.[22] As a science of walls, lines, and foundations, architecture rests both inside and outside the university, drawing distinctions and inserting doors, windows, and gates. In this way, architecture puts knowledge in the world.

I therefore add a few prosaic details. The Chase-Park Plaza Hotel in St. Louis was the site of the MMLA annual meeting for at least three years running, from 1972 to 1974. The hotel was actually two amalgamated into one: the Chase, a staid Beaux-Arts palazzo similar to many American campus buildings, and the adjacent Park Plaza, a soaring Art Deco tower.[23] The 1974 annual meeting had, in fact, originally been planned for the Detroit Hilton, and it was only relocated to St. Louis, it seems, at the last minute after Hilton Hotels pulled out of its management contract for the Detroit property, which closed the following year.[24] The timing is telling. Coming as it did in the midst of that city's long, wrenching period of deindustrialization, the Detroit hotel's closing is not surprising. Nor should we be surprised to find that in 2006, at the other end of the Midwest's neoliberal turn, the Chase-Park Plaza Hotel, located within sight of the Washington University campus, was converted into luxury condominium apartments.[25]

So this is one way to begin a media history of the American university: with a theoretical discussion beyond the university's gates, inside a hotel near a campus. Jotting notes on stationery from Ithaca's (and Cornell's) Statler Inn, Said was not the first or last academic to write in transit.[26] Turning inward, toward the university archive that secures these jottings, and translating to the historian's métier, we might take this inside-outside confusion as an invitation to pause for a moment at the archive's threshold, laptop or tablet (or pencil and paper) in hand, as we place our belongings in the locker, turn the key, sit down, and open the cardboard box. Not all college and university archives are so well appointed; most are understaffed. But if there are boxes, someone has brought them, while someone else probably organized their contents. Given the special tendency of colleges and universities to write their own histories, or rather, the tendency of university administrators to commission scholars to do so online or in print, the protocols of acquisition and organization—of a faculty member's papers, a department's records—draw a horizon of interpretation in advance. Even what Brian Larkin has called the "media system of empire" may not have attended quite so carefully as have U.S. colleges and universities to chronicling their traditions and documenting the lives and output of their officers.[27] To a greater extent than with most domains, university history comes prewritten in the archival finding aid. As elements in a media complex, university archives form microcosmic windows—worlds—that artfully refract the macrocosm, unevenly and with inherent distortion and data loss.

Whether seen from within or from without, the modern university is constituted by a series of material, institutional, and epistemological boundary problems. Of these, the best known is the one described by Kant as a conflict over academic freedom between the "lower faculty," philosophy, and the "higher" professions of theology, law, and medicine. Conflicts of interest and political hierarchies, Kant argues, draw boundaries between these faculties, assigning to each its "legal" position with respect to governmental authority. The higher faculties serve the sovereign with their interested knowledge; the lower faculties, guardians of disinterest, offer respectful critique.[28] The nineteenth century saw related conflicts in debates over classical versus modern learning, and by the twentieth century, similar disputes arose around the competing priorities of basic versus applied research.

Already in the antebellum years, what distinguished American institutions from their German counterparts (while connecting them with their British predecessors) was that underneath all of this lay the university's uncomfortable partnership with the residential college, which brought boundary disputes and power struggles of its own. Recognizing the ambiguities that have defined this partnership, my account underscores relations between the two. The difficulties of managing this internal threshold were comparable in scope and scale with the difficulties encountered by colleges and universities in setting themselves apart from society even as they remained integral to it, a tension that recurred in their efforts to define and relate disciplines and fields. Each scale and each set of relations—of university to society, of college to university, and among academic disciplines—is materially based. The modern university is, in short, a world of gates, screens, departments, papers, reports, and other media. Far more complex topologically than they might appear, its interfaces and its boundaries belong to a plastic economy of insides turning out and outsides turning in.

Other Worlds

Said's text begins with Glenn Gould and ends with Frantz Fanon, followed by a coda on literary criticism. My opening with it signals both the ambitions and the limits of my contribution. The formidable literature on the history of universities tends to stress one of two things: epistemological changes, or changes in the political economy of knowledge; some scholars lean toward intellectual history, others toward the history of institutions.[29] One important exception is William Clark's *Academic Charisma*, which shows scholars, students, and their institutions changing as both epistemic things and as worldly beings. As Clark explains, academic charisma is not innate; it is a historical product of learning environments and their material practices.[30] Edward W. Said was an unquestionably charismatic figure, in his style of dress and in his writing as much as in the contours of his thought or the rigors of his unflinchingly public defense of the Palestinian cause.[31] As a media practice, academic charisma (or more commonly, its absence) is also a matter of drawing distinctions, of marking boundaries and bodies, including those of universities and of their distinguished professors.

The deepest distinction recorded by Said's text operates at another, more evidently worldly level with which he was intimately and passionately connected and which, as he shows, has shadowed European modernity. This line separates the bright, paved streets of the well-fed "settlers' town" from the squalor of the "native town" in Fanon's celebrated passage from *The Wretched of the Earth*, which Said compares with the ethno-social exclusions mapped by James Joyce. "Despite Ricoeur's disastrous simplification of it," Said observes, still replying to Bruns's internal memo on worldliness, the discursive situation "is more usually of a kind typified by colonizer and colonized, the oppressor and the oppressed." Such a world "places one interlocutor above another" and in the process, "re-enacts the geography of the colonial city" per Fanon.[32] Translated into the language of this book, such lines connect with others, like the recurrent line separating "town" from "gown" or like W. E. B. Du Bois's "color line," to oppress and to exclude.

Since the first decades of industrialization, in U.S. colleges and universities these boundaries have typically followed class lines, reinforced by gender, with near-absolute racial correlations. They have also measured levels of achievement within an uneven, ideologically determined meritocracy. Distinctions among types of knowledge have further divided college from university discourse, in reciprocal correspondence with the dynamics of capital, of civil society, and of the state. Although not all of these divisions reproduce unjust hierarchies, all store powers great and small in their pockets and their purses. The restricted scope of my inquiry prevents me from approaching the full cultural and political geography implied by Said's reference to Fanon and in his own scholarship, as well as in his political actions. Where Said drew insight from Arabic philology, I make little detailed reference to primary textual sources outside of Europe or North America, examining instead (in one case) their vegetal equivalents in agricultural colleges. Nor do I make any pretense of coming close to decolonizing the university, if by this we mean making reparations, long overdue, to those systematically excluded, or to those made to experience directly the brute force of imperial knowledge.[33] Nor do I offer plans for a more democratic, more just, more peaceful alternative, urgent as that task is; instead, I only consider one instance when something like this was attempted, by the Indian economist B. R. Ambedkar, under formally postcolonial conditions with reference to American educational philosophy.

I do, however, follow Said when he comments offhandedly, in his introduction to *Reflections on Exile* (2000), on "the American university generally being for its academic staff and some of its students the last remaining utopia."[34]

This has become daily more true in antidemocratic times, particularly as a site of oppositional thought. But the literary critic chooses words carefully, designating only "some" students as beneficiaries, omitting administrative staff and maintenance workers entirely. In the chapters that follow, I name one or two service workers for whom university life was decidedly less than utopian, who nevertheless performed crucial tasks in maintaining utopian order and who stand here for countless others unnamed. Others have studied more deeply the American college and university system's dependence upon, and perpetuation of, slavery and of racial oppression, exploitation, and exclusion.[35] But even without these caveats and compensatory gestures, Said's comment marks an outer limit to worldliness, the moment when what he calls "paradox" (Gould's singular "style" on reproducible black plastic) becomes contradiction.

On this, Gayatri Chakravorty Spivak elaborates in a 1979 talk on "marginalia" and scholarly explanation delivered at a humanities center symposium. Thinking critically from the margins, Spivak argues, means thinking about "the production of the universities," including "the subdivision of their curricula, the hierarchy of the management-labor sandwich with its peculiarly flavored filling of the faculty, the specialization emphases, the grants and in-house financial distributions that affect choice of research and specialty, faculty life-and class-style." These, she says, "are often brushed aside as we perform our appointed task of producing explanations from our seemingly isolated scholarly study with its well-worn track to the library."[36] A muted, conservative version of this critique was made around 1830 by defenders of the classical curriculum. Virtually all of it applies today. This does not mean that nothing has changed. Among other things, the "track to the library" has become wired, a process that began, as we shall see, around 1890. At the MMLA conference, Said contrasted what he called the "eccentricity" of Western culture with dominant narratives of its "concentricity."[37] Five years later Spivak, with a strong feminist base line, spoke of "margins."

Writing closer to the edges of humanities scholarship, off-center, I address such questions in several cases through mathematical and scientific subjects. For humanities discourse, too, can inhibit worldliness. As Spivak shows elsewhere, a literary, artistic, or historical "world" can become so ideologically bracketed that its subjects are unable to recognize, much less process, its most basic contradictions. Among her examples is the cultivation among the male faculty of the Riyadh University Faculty of Arts, with American support and under the sign of modernization, of a " 'humanist' intellectual elite that will be unable to read the relationship between its own production and the flow of oil, money, and arms."[38]

I therefore begin here, at the historical moment when the book's chapters roughly end, to show how the reading of texts, and of the world as text and text as world, entails relations among media. A young woman, a student in Riyadh, asks Spivak what it means to "live like a book." Spivak replies: "Everyone reads life and the world like a book. Even the so-called 'illiterate.' " And especially "politicians and businessmen," the leaders, "the ones who make plans," who "read the world in terms of rationality and averages, as if it were a textbook."[39] The book you are reading is written from beneath the words on the page. It is about the table on which the textbook of the world sits, the floor on which that table stands, the lighting in the room, and the silence necessary to read. It is about pamphlets, paper, electricity, fire, libraries, card catalogues, and other material things that enable us to speak of reading the world in this way.

I have chosen to limit my inquiry to the United States, then, for two reasons. First, because the American university system, which became crucial to U.S. political and economic hegemony during the later twentieth century, offers a revealing study in what I describe below as a mediapolitics of knowledge. Second, because this seemingly coherent, nationally bounded case is so internally differentiated, and so full of connections to others, that its worldliness merits close examination on its own. Owing much to German reforms of the early nineteenth century mixed with the inheritance of English and Scottish precedent, research universities and residential colleges in the United States resolved inside-outside, higher-lower problems in new and varied ways.[40] Their modernity is neither simply one among many nor universal. Rather, what is modern about these institutions lies in specific, mediapolitical claims on universality made by material and intellectual forces that these institutions and their discourses have, in their turn, helped to create.

For at least half of the period covered by this book the United States was a "developing country."[41] Across the antebellum and post-Civil War periods, the country's colleges and later, universities, were integral to its economic growth and to its imperial project. They were equally integral to the process of building mediascapes that extended well beyond an elite Republic of Letters.[42] For these and other reasons, I do not presuppose anything like an essentially American model of higher education. Throughout, whatever national peculiarities we may detect derive from the college's and the university's border-drawing functions rather than from cultural determinants. With this in mind, my aim is modestly to provincialize America by documenting a few exemplary border crossings in order to cast a sideways glance at the field of global relations and their contradictions out of which anything like an "American" university came to be.

Technics and Mediapolitics

Ties and tensions among collegiate learning, university-based scholarship, and capital ran long and deep through the later nineteenth century in the United States and were consolidated during the twentieth. Christopher Newfield has argued eloquently for an historical understanding of conflicts between human-istic inquiry and industrial reason ("ivy" and "industry") that rejects the scenario of a winner-take-all, zero-sum game. Recasting the professoriate as members of the professional-managerial class, Newfield parses liberalism's post-Civil War crosscurrents to make room for the disalienated "craft" of scholarship and teaching.[43] In place of craft I offer technics, a concept that retains the instrumentality of *technē* without relinquishing a sense of artfulness, to evoke a matrix of meaning, a cultural system built out of technologically mediated social relations. Technics is a matter of making things and being made by them, of reciprocally shaping and being shaped by technological environments. *Mediapolitics*, a term I use sparingly below, names the power relations of ordering and knowing, as the human, social subjects of technics make worlds appear through media. Media operate between things. Mediapolitics is a politics and a technics of the in-between.

Technics also forms a succinct English companion to the German *Kultur-techniken*, or "cultural techniques," defined persuasively by Cornelia Vismann as the verb form of media.[44] Vismann's groundbreaking work on early modern bureaucracy and the law, and Bernhard Siegert's on European postal systems, have helped call attention to an infrastructural, cultural technics that, more than any philosophical or historical epoch, defines what, in my account, is "modern" about the university. So too has Siegert's virtuosic study of "artic-ulations of the real" through grids, doors, and other ontic operators.[45] Most expansively, John Durham Peters uses "technics" to evoke the epic prose of Lewis Mumford, who appears alternately below as an historical actor and an interlocutor.[46] In conversation with these and other thinkers, I have tried to write a media history that revises what Mumford dramatized as the interplay of "technics and civilization," by bringing civilization down to earth through its equally whitewashed proxy, academe.

German "cultural studies" (*Kulturwissenschaften*), from which the study of "cultural techniques" derives, does not translate cleanly into anglophone cul-tural studies.[47] As Vismann points out, the study of cultural techniques is the study of cultivation. "A plough drawing a line in the ground," she writes, "deter-mines the political act [of sovereignty]; and the operation itself produces the subject, who will then claim mastery over both the tool and the action associ-ated with it."[48] From cultivation, social relations including relations of property arise. Although Vismann's source is imperial Roman law, her argument recalls Jean-Jacques Rousseau's claim, in the *Discourse on the Origin and Foundations of Inequality among Men* (1755), that—as a recent translation puts it—"the first man who fenced in [*ayant enclos*] a plot of land and dared to say, 'This is mine,' found people who were sufficiently simple to believe him, was the true founder of civil society." To which we must immediately add, however, Rousseau's cry: "How many crimes, wars, murders, how much misery and horror, could have been spared the human race if someone would have pulled up the stakes or filled in the ditch and called out to his fellow men: 'Beware! Do not listen to this imposter. You will be lost if you forget that the fruits of the earth belong to all, and that the land belongs to no one.' "[49] Land becomes property, then, through a combination of speech act ("this is mine," at once constative and performative) and enclosure, as words and things are fenced in as "culture," and the feedback system of unequal cultivation proceeds.

Siegert elaborates on Vismann's example, adding corrals and calendars as elementary techniques of hominization derived from the earlier sense of *Kulturtechnik* as agricultural engineering. My chapters below on agricultural research and on the political economy of the frontier reply to this proposition. Siegert adds: "Every culture begins with the introduction of distinctions," such as inside versus outside. Doors, gates (including logic gates), and other operators actively process these binaries.[50] My discussion, in a chapter on the pedagogical acoustics of "his master's voice," of the chain that binds bondsman to lord (or slave to master) in G. W. F. Hegel's dialectic, emphasizes the power differentials built into every binary. Pedagogical concepts like *Bildung* (self-fashioning), Siegert points out, adhere to the "sovereignty of the book" as the preferred medium of "middle-class" (i.e., bourgeois) culture.[51] Mediapolitics names the sociohistorical practices and struggles that link technics with forces beyond those of knowledge narrowly construed as cultural, in the ground wars for which terms like *cultivation*, *Kultur*, and *Bildung* too often provide polite cover.

Returning to the language of architecture, then, there remains the matter of evaluating this *technē* in relation to its *archē*; that is, in relation to metaphysical postulates naturalized as foundations, and the ordering systems built upon them, including the architectonics of the university. Consistent with the Kittlerian hypothesis, I propose here the study of technē as archē, or ordering principle, and of technological details as elemental ordering systems, or what Michel Foucault called *dispositifs* (apparatuses).[52] It has long been said of architecture that its details harbor gods. Doing media history with architecture, let us say instead that these details are where knowledge and power meet. So Kittler notwithstanding, this is not just another materialist inquiry into what Derrida called "arche-writing," or the writing that comes before writing.[53] Nor is it an essay in technological determinism. Even media archaeology, an antifoundational science of the archē conceived as a sort of primordial command issuing from technical things, remains, like the "cultural" study of cultural techniques, only indirectly attentive to power in its two senses, of energetics (including labor, and physical force) and of hegemony.[54] Technology is social, and therefore subject to the daily struggles of human agents. In this sense, the foundation of any edifice (or discipline, or institution) is just another wall. To modify slightly the insight of John Durham Peters who, playing on Marshall McLuhan's *Understanding Media* (1964), writes that "infrastructural media are media that stand under," we can say, rather, that infrastructural media are media that stand between, like any foundation. The study of mediapolitics is therefore one way of understanding media historically and politically, at once.[55]

In a related vein Jameson, in his published MMLA talk, enjoined his readers to consider Plato's allegory of the cave "in the most *literal* sense."[56] In the 1955 translation of *The Republic* on which Jameson relies, this means prisoners so bound as to face inward, fire, a road on which bodies move, a "curtain-wall" (a 1950s architectural figure), the cave itself, shadows—again, a media complex.[57] We might call further attention to the stone surface of the cave's interior, to the artful craft of the "curtain-wall's" builders and of those who forged the prisoners' chains, and to the bright, hot energy of the shadow-casting fire. Transposed onto other scenes of knowledge-making and of learning, this media complex brings us closer to a history of the process of producing ideas than to a history of those ideas per se, including the storied "idea" of the university itself.[58] That is, thinking literally about the architecture of Plato's cave brings us closer to a technics of thinking and learning as material, social practices. Returning to Newfield's appeal to professional craft, Mumford's was among the most strident voices calling for a return to architectural handwork to offset the rationalized utilitarianism of the Gilded Age and its progeny. His standard bearer was the Boston architect Henry Hobson Richardson, an architect of sensitive caves if there ever was one, who designed rough-hewn stone houses for railroad executives, capital's most loyal representatives, and in one important case that we will consider, a memorial campus library.

So think of Plato's cave as a quotidian thing, where ideas are technical matters rather than blinding abstractions. Media history differs from intellectual history in its focus on the material complexes that make ideas possible. It also treats intellectuals differently, as bound to the worldliness of technics to a degree that even Said's world-text-critic nexus minimizes. The first published version of Said's text ends, for example, with a minor typographic error. Uncannily Said's error, or rather, that of his typesetter, misspelled "criticism" as "ciriticism."[59] This was likely due to some combination of the typesetter's time, the proofreader's inattention, and the author's distraction. It comes in a concluding sentence that brandishes worldly criticism as a weapon against monocentrism, which for Said is synonymous with ethnocentrism. In the essay's later version, Said abbreviated this section slightly, retaining the opposition of worldly to monocentric but ending with Matthew Arnold's *Culture and Anarchy* and Nietzsche's *The Birth of Tragedy* as joint testimony to culture's "dark side."[60] Subtly, "criticism" has expanded outward, from the professional literary sort addressed by the original conference panel and paper, to a more sweeping sort associated with the two figures with whom Said ends.

The literary critic, whose profession was at the time barely a century old, had become a critical intellectual. The small typo in his text tells us nothing about

Said's idea of criticism, but it does tell us something about what an intellectual is. The text's materiality, marked by the misplaced letters, ties it back to a whole division of labor seen and unseen, and a whole domain of scholarly practice from which the intellectual, stepping out of her study, is born. That domain includes classrooms, libraries, and laboratories. It also includes the mechanics of typesetting, the purchase and maintenance of laboratory equipment, and other technical matters that even university discourse as worldly as Said's trains us to consider as prescholarly, preideational. It was Said's great achievement to challenge scholars with the effects of their equipment, their typed and printed words, their syllabi and their curricula. By concentrating on the line that separates oppressor from oppressed, and on the chain in Hegel's dialectic that binds lord to bondsman, media history, too, can do the work of critical history, albeit of a different sort. Media history attends to the cloaks, veils, and screens that allegedly impede our access to the truth of culture's "dark side." It does so by studying these as technical things out of which the idea that there is something behind the screen—the idea that there is an idea—arises. Like historical materialism, media history recognizes a material a priori, but in an underdetermined and underdetermining sense.

A Dialectic of Dialectics

Zig-zagging across two centuries, the chapters in this book trace genealogies that may seem to find their apotheosis in today's "corporate" (or perhaps "global") university. Reading Nietzsche, Foucault famously described historical genealogy as "grey, meticulous, and patiently documentary." Genealogy eschews the search for origins, reconstructing instead dotted lines of descent, deviations, births and deaths, processes of emergence rather than immaculate conceptions.[61] The genealogies I have traced cast certain features of the present conjuncture in an uncomfortable light. In recent decades, for example, burgeoning university administrations, the subordination of academic freedom to market pressures and to political force, and the encroachments made by commercial ventures have become growing concerns.[62] Mention is rarely made, however, of the vexing fact that residential colleges centered on liberal learning were among the nation's first corporations. Though these were devoted to the reproduction of a clergy and of a governing class rather than to furthering business interests, the instrumentality of even the most disinterested classical curricula cannot be overlooked.

Paradigmatic institutions of an "information age," universities today are also easily cast as "knowledge factories," machines for producing utility at the expense of critical reflection. But what knowledge is useful and what is not is, to a considerable extent, an affordance of media complexes that link universities to industry. Equally, universities have been celebrated as vehicles of social mobility and for their democratizing potential, or scorned for their exclusivity.[63] The pretensions to universality that echo through the name—*university*—have led to fierce contests over inclusiveness and equity, both in curricula and among constituents. These processes, too, come under selective scrutiny in the histories I have pieced together. In all cases, what matters most is a reckoning with difference, a drawing of distinctions that is also a rehearsal of identities, of inequalities masquerading as ontologies, including the mythic archetypes (embalmed in alumni associations) that still stalk the halls of social privilege. This calculus changes over time, and I have periodically had recourse to step-by-step narration to demonstrate its development and its consequences.

To place the governing contradictions in perspective, and to consider them from the side of the subject as well as from object relations, the book follows a broad arc that moves from the cultivation of liberal to neoliberal reason.[64] We will not seek, however, a fixed standpoint (an origin) for our perspective, from which to discern a reliable vanishing point—liberal, neoliberal, or otherwise. The reader may be caught off guard by the premature emergence of certain traits and the delayed development of others. We will favor processes over finished products, incomplete liberalizations and returns thereof, rather than epochal closure.

I use "liberal" to suggest a crossing, a place and a set of practices where several projected freedoms meet. Liberal education sits at the thoroughly engineered intersection of free will, free expression, and free markets.[65] Passing through the university, each of these follows its own line of development. "Neoliberal" denotes more than just their climax, or their farcical exaggeration. Neoliberalism here entails a series of returns and rebirths, like that of a superintending alma mater reborn as an online "friend" in the networks of multinational capital. This halting, stuttering phase change, in which the neoliberal university awkwardly but uncannily repeats the social relations of the liberal colleges, belongs to one of several long-term passages that I have tried to reconstruct. Each is dialectical, but with no one set of antinomies complete, and none entirely regulating the others. As with a student hesitatingly reciting Latin verse under the tutor's stern eye, every stutter transforms, and each attempt to conserve produces something new. Consequently, the environments we will explore are more like molecular compounds than mechanical assemblies; they are full of agents and reagents, alloys, mixtures, and cocktails, including the unstable compound of political economy and culture. In the foggy, particulate-filled haze of industrial and postindustrial modernity that issues from their chemical reactions, where there is one dialectic there are always many: a dialectic of dialectics.

Dialectics all the way down, then, or at least their possibility. Unsynthesized material spins off; new difficulties arise. Just as we will find no final synthesis, no ultimate end, and only temporary beginnings, we will settle on no prime mover, no unified technological a priori, no implacable drive toward enlightenment in its best or worst senses, no simple backstage to capital that is most mystified when demystified, nor a grinning will to power operating levers behind the lectern. All of these do appear, but they appear as factors in conflicts and paradoxes that sometimes become contradictions. Immediately, an objection arises: absent determination in the last instance if not clear causal chains, is this not mere formalism, or worse, cover for the compliant empiricism that has, for the most part, shaped the writing of university histories in the United States? Or, more worryingly still, do not the suspect slogans of media studies—"the medium is the message," "media determine our situation," and so on—lurk on the margins waiting to pounce when we recast the university as a media complex in an effort to peel back the histories of ideas in which self-study has cloaked it?[66]

No. Staying with technics brings us closer to a genealogy of knowledge but far short of a history of knowledge systems in their fullest breadth and depth.[67] The reader will find nothing so grand here as those "systems of thought" that named the chair into which Foucault settled with his archaeologies and his genealogies at the Collège de France. Cautiously, I have tried to write from the in-between, from the moment when it looks like a border is forming, and with it, possibly a system. The chapters therefore follow false starts, do-overs, forks in the road, and tentative distinctions by which the modern university and its progeny came to be. Mixing sources, and generally subordinating formally archival material to other primary and secondary documents, each tracks boundaries in formation as these delimit and stabilize the academic body before the university's architecture comes fully into view.

"Architecture" here means a given institution's material structures, from campus grounds to buildings to furniture, as well as the virtual diagram or ordering infrastructure that holds these together and gives them meaning.[68] Architecturally speaking, universities and colleges are several things at once: heterotopias, memorials, monuments, and machines. But architecture here is also one among many media.[69] Its twin outputs, organization and representation, are enabled by material properties that are shaped by organizational and representational inputs. Within the reciprocities of modern technics, any building is also a media environment. Each of its technical systems, from the walls to the wiring, manifests cultural and social relations. This applies at all scales in a kaleidoscopic rather than telescopic fashion, which is what allows the bits and pieces gathered here to do their metonymic work without prematurely forming wholes. Carrying all the other scales with them, the pieces of buildings we will consider require us, like Plato's cave, to take as literally as possible the university's "universal" pretensions.

Proceeding cautiously, we pick up one attribute here and another there. Learning from Stefan Andriopoulos's study of fictional "possessions," for example, we notice that what matters most about the spirited, corporate character of the collegiate body is not its business or nonbusiness interests but its legal immortality, even early on.[70] Corporate immortality of this sort accounts for and is enabled by the loyalty of alumni and the generosity of donors. We witness two ongoing embodiments at once, of the student and of the corporate organism, stage-managed by the faculty. These embodiments would not occur but for a seeming conspiracy of technical systems, from the construction of edifices to the ringing of bells. Interruption and repetition are integral to these systems; buildings are built, burn, and are rebuilt, campuses relocate or multiply, students graduate and return. Correspondingly, we find ourselves repeatedly starting over rather than faithfully following a prescribed route that leads, in its most conveniently laid historical passage, from the pious residential college to the secular research university.

Scholars have usefully complicated the traditional story of the research university's transatlantic origins as a synthesis of German idealism with Anglo-American utilitarianism.[71] Most of these accounts, however, still evince a deep-seated desire to resolve dialectical tensions with narrative closure. Most also retain the premise that these institutions, as unified bodies, are intentional things, objects of premeditated planning rather than of awesome and almost comic historical accident. Measuring their contingency while attending to their determinations is therefore no mere historiographical correction. Each effort to stand apart, to draw a line that separates this from that, repeated daily and differently in every admissions office and classroom, has a history that amounts to a genealogy of the border rather than an autobiography of what lies within.

By now it should be clear that my beginning with Said's published conference paper addresses a tendency among scholars to assimilate academic knowledge to the vague generalities of "print culture." In a later chapter, I will consider in more detail sources like technical bulletins and pamphlets, a grey literature that helps to build the background world of what Lisa Gitelman has suggestively called "paper knowledge."[72] Following on from my opening example, I approach the modern university's worldliness by calling attention to the bricks from which students built the campus of the Tuskegee Institute, the diary entries of Vassar's early matriculants, the ringing of bells at Virginia, lighting in Columbia's library, site planning at Berkeley, and competing antebellum geometry textbooks, among numerous other technical considerations. If the reader is persuaded that such details bring the media complexes into sufficient focus, then the diversions from the straight-and-narrow path will have been worthwhile.

Four Parts, Eight Chapters

The book divides into four parts, each comprising two chapters, arranged in overlapping, loose chronology. The chapters are both self-contained and interconnected. The four genealogies into which I have grouped them may be compared synchronically for their connections. They may also be compared diachronically, for the more general processes that each exemplifies. Each centers a different intermedial function: figuration, timekeeping, speech, and signification. A brief prologue and interlude punctuate two phases through which the genealogies pass. An epilogue reviews the argument and considers a third. Excerpting details from colleges and universities across the United States, the chapters draw a map that documents changes and continuities within each context and over time. Though this map is necessarily incomplete, I have tried to select cases that, when seen together, portray the American university system's scope and its key internal differences and changes across time and space. The whole proceeds irregularly from the very late eighteenth century to about three-quarters through the twentieth, with a few backward glances along the way.

The prologue introduces the mediapolitical dialectic of mastery and subordination that organized the republican public sphere around 1800, through two extramural details: Thomas Jefferson's unrealized plan for public education, and the silence-producing dumbwaiters in his Monticello dining room.

The two chapters in part 1 reconstruct complementary genealogies of the collegiate subject since around 1800. During the early decades of industrialization, two different types of figure, corporeal and geometrical, uneasily related humans and machines in legal, economic, literary, scientific, mathematical, and pedagogical discourse. Associated teaching and learning practices reproduced these figures through both repetition and interruption.

Part 2 picks up a mixed genealogy of time in two chapters dealing with industrial life, social mobility, and resource extraction beginning around 1850. These chapters show how, prior to the consolidation of research universities, moving upward entailed looking backward, and how technological development drew on ancient sources. Together, the chapters elucidate a temporality in which race, gender, and colonialism located subjects within coincident systems of production and of deferral.

The interlude interjects the Wisconsin historian Frederick Jackson Turner's "frontier thesis," which was based on data compiled on punched cards, to exemplify an emergent mediapolitics derived from territorial conquest and its limits.

Part 3 reconstructs two genealogies of voice from around 1900. As the university's media complex reoriented toward research and its transmission in lectures, seminars, and libraries, political sovereignty moved from enforced, reflective silence to the clamor of an overconfident literary and philosophical canon. There, at the interface of writing and reading with speech and audition, arose a cascade of conflicts that defined the new research universities.

The two chapters in part 4 take up genealogies of signification from around 1950. One important problem for those working at new, techno-scientific "frontiers," from metallurgy to nuclear physics, was that of verifying their own humanity by making signs into symbols. The first case, previewed in the interlude, finds in the redrawn American "frontier" a new signifying infrastructure. The second outlines an entrepreneurial neoliberalism born out of a techno-scientific sublime serviced by the humanities.

The epilogue reviews the main arguments and examples, takes stock of connections across the chapters, and links these to more recent developments. Today, continuities with what has come before accompany dramatic changes at the human-machine interface, where capital has always done its work. Realignments at this interface, side by side with changes in university discourse, bring into focus the book's long historical arc as corporate persons become human capital. In order to draw out relevant threads, some chapters reach farther back than others, and some follow their implications farther forward. Each connects earlier inputs with later outputs, which then become inputs of their own, in a controlled spiral. This nonlinear causality, which is reflected in each chapter's narrative structure, is more like that of a feedback loop than of a mechanically determining "last instance."

Wars of the Worlds

If my account appears to underestimate the modern university's sublime promise, or to undervalue academic ideals at their moment of greatest peril, it is because nothing less than the production of truth—and access to it—is on the line. In the U.S. academy, the past several decades have seen a seemingly unending series of "wars": culture wars, science wars, history wars, knowledge wars of all sorts. To these, the current conjuncture has ominously added deep-pocketed attacks on climate science and racist assaults on political sanctuary and on the freedom to know, to learn, and to oppose.

Almost a century ago, the political philosopher Antonio Gramsci distinguished between two types of historically transformative action: "wars of maneuver" led by a revolutionary vanguard, and "wars of position," or the slow, unremarkable struggle for cultural and social hegemony. Within academia, we might add a specific form of the latter: what Donna Haraway has called "border wars," including wars conducted, as the saying goes, behind enemy lines.[73] Student movements aside, this language might seem especially out of place on a university campus, removed as it is from more theatrical sites of conflict, whether battlefields or boardrooms. Kant made a point of noting that the conflict of the faculties "is not a *war* [*Krieg*]" since the aim of the "higher" and "lower" faculties is ultimately the same: "*freedom* [*Freiheit*]" and "*property* [*Eigenthum*]"; that is, a liberal society responsive to critique.[74] But property is power, and efforts to avoid or temper worldly conflict by withdrawing into secluded study frequently reproduce that conflict's premises, however unwittingly. That is why I have not abandoned the dialectical critique of ideology and of capital for the genial study of actors in networks or limited my work to the strategic reconstruction of biopolitical landscapes or epistemes.[75] Each of these finds its place among the dialectics, but now and then the tables turn and, in the language of social media, friends become adversaries.

Gathering fragments, I have tried to show how knowledge, power, value, and meaning converged and changed over the course of two centuries. In the end, readers expecting a synthetic overview may be disappointed by an account that stays with the making and remaking of media complexes. Caught in a process of founding and refounding, birth and rebirth, the university and its partner, the residential college, come in and out of focus throughout this book as historically contingent, contradictory formations rather than as internally consistent institutions. Innovation and stability have been their two opposing drives. Measuring contours, tracing edges, and picking up braided threads, I have tried to follow these knowledge worlds, their subjects, and their protocols from place to place, again and again. My aim has been a map assembled from particulars, rather than a typology drawn from the annals of the institutions themselves.

Reconstructing these worlds, I have also sought to indicate the conflicts—epistemological, social, political, and economic—that have defined them and the lines around which these conflicts have formed. Today, the university must be both defended and rethought; I therefore hope that my efforts will be useful in negotiating those old conflicts that remain and new ones recently arisen. If my argument persuades, that the modern university is a mediapolitical boundary problem, even the skeptical reader may come to see the border wars that shape our knowledge as less academic and more worldly, from inside and from out.

PROLOGUE, c. 1800

Who was the liberal individual, paradigmatically? During the early republic in the United States, Thomas Jefferson's white yeoman farmer was one candidate, as was Jefferson himself. Another was the college student. All of these and more came together figuratively around the dining table at Jefferson's Virginia plantation, Monticello. Uniting them was a technics that enabled these figures to do the discursive and practical work of representative democracy and liberal capitalism. A good part of that work involved speaking, publicly and privately, which also meant regulating speech procedures. Another involved reading; the liberal individual was someone who read silently. Still another involved writing; like Jefferson's Northern alter ego, Benjamin Franklin, the liberal individual wrote with and for the printing press. At Monticello, all of this took place upstairs, atop a hill.

The coordinating terraced Lawn at the University of Virginia also sits on the crest of a gentle slope. Chartered in 1819 under Jefferson's leadership as a secular university rather than an ecclesiastical college, the University of Virginia was somewhat exceptional among institutions of higher learning at the time. Still, we find there a contradiction that came to define the research university in relation to the residential college, and both in relation to their world. That contradiction, in which the exercise of universal reason depended upon specific, technologically mediated exclusions and oppression, reproduced above-and-below relations along two axes, one horizontal and the other vertical. Horizontally, a pedagogical Republic of Letters grew out of territorial expansion and administration prefigured in Jefferson's unrealized proposals for public education. Vertically, a dialectics of mastery and subordination exemplified at Monticello derived words spoken upstairs from enslaved silence below, to enable the work of scholars, statesmen, and students to proceed. The following details stand here for the media complex out of which liberal individuals of all kinds were born prior to the Civil War and the mediapolitical practices from which this complex was assembled.

Divisions

In 1779, in the midst of the rebellion against the British Crown, Jefferson proposed to the legislature of the Virginia Commonwealth a "Bill for the More General Diffusion of Knowledge."[1] The bill outlined a system of public education that culminated, for a selected few, in matriculation at the College of William and Mary, where Jefferson studied. Though it failed to pass, the bill is an important document in the eventual establishment of free and universal secondary education in the United States.[2] In it, Jefferson imagined a pyramidal administrative landscape, at the top of which sat the college. Perched above this landscape, the William and Mary faculty was to be joined at several levels by various political bodies in overseeing the public school curriculum, in a republican decentralization of governmental functions.[3]

The system proposed by Jefferson's bill was based on a division of the land into hundreds, a unit of territory larger than a town but smaller than a county. Each hundred was to contain one primary school, for white male and female students. These would aggregate into districts comprising several counties and be served by a secondary boarding school, or grammar school, in which ten or twelve male students, chosen by examination, would take up residence. The most accomplished students would then be given scholarships to study at the college, in an ascending ratio of territory to population. Some two decades later, after a brief involvement with several projects to establish a national university, Jefferson revisited the unrealized plan when, as a private citizen, he drafted a "Bill for Establishing a System of Public Education" in Virginia. Put before the Virginia legislature by his friend Joseph C. Cabell, the bill passed in February 1818, formally establishing the University of Virginia. The following year Jefferson was appointed the new university's rector, a position he occupied for the rest of his life.[4]

In the preamble to the original bill, Jefferson took pains to acknowledge the risk of tyranny even in those forms of government that "are better calculated than others to protect individuals in the free exercise of their rights." To prevent this, he argued, it was best "to illuminate, as far as practicable, the minds of the people at large, and more especially to give them knowledge of those facts, which history exhibiteth." A legitimate social and political hierarchy might then form, "whence it becomes expedient for promoting the publick happiness that those persons, whom nature hath endowed with genius and virtue, should be rendered by liberal education worthy to receive, and able to guard the sacred deposit of the rights and liberties of their fellow citizens."[5] Proposed for a settler colony and based on an agrarian order of property that scaled the division of labor up from the plantation, this system presupposed chattel slavery among its conditions. In providing for free public education "fore the children of all the citizens of this Commonwealth," it excluded enslaved persons and their children.[6] The University of Virginia did the same, as did the university's central organ for illuminating the minds of young white men in order that they may govern—the library.

Like most librarians then and now, Jefferson was keenly aware of the fragility of books, including their flammability, a property that eventually connected his personal library with that of the early republic. On February 1, 1770, Shadwell, the Jefferson family home where a twenty-six year old Thomas lived with his mother and sisters, was destroyed by fire. Anecdote has it that upon being informed of the fire by an enslaved person, Jefferson replied by asking whether his four hundred or so books had been saved. They had not.[7] The books had disintegrated into the first installment of what we can call (to borrow an expression from Manfredo Tafuri) the still accumulating "ashes of Jefferson."[8] Hastening Jefferson's existing plans for building a house on the Monticello site, the Shadwell fire also necessitated rebuilding his library. Between 1770 and 1815, Jefferson developed an eclectic collection of about seven thousand volumes of which he kept a careful inventory. This library, and not his published writings, has most decisively earned him an honored position in the Euro-American Republic of Letters.[9] It was a medium of everyday life integrated into the public sphere that constituted the very fabric of the Monticello household. Silently attended by enslaved persons, Jefferson took pleasure there in introducing his many guests to his many books, often to the accompaniment of French wine or Chinese tea.

Dumbwaiters

In the Monticello dining room, wine was made available by dumbwaiters that connected that room to the wine cellar below, where an enslaved person stood ready to supply the bottles. As its name suggests, the purpose of the dumbwaiter was to exclude enslaved voices and enslaved ears from the conversation above. The dumbwaiter, then, did not merely regulate the boundaries of a sphere that was reserved, in the Kantian sense, for the public exercise of reason; it helped to produce that sphere by minimizing interference and distortion, and restricting transmission and communication in a manner that, as in Georg

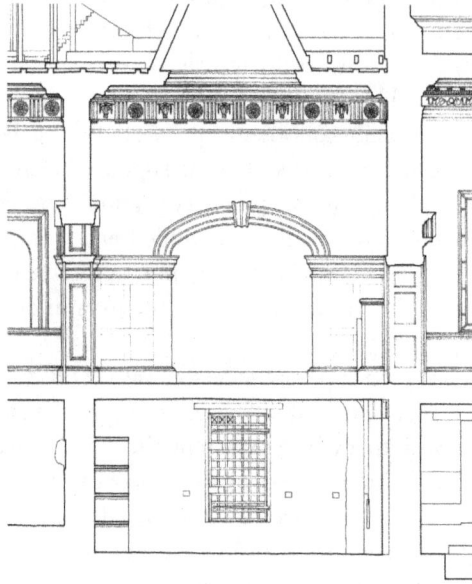

P.1 Thomas Jefferson, Monticello, 1770–1809. Longitudinal section (detail) showing dining room and wine cellar. The dumbwaiter is built into the fireplace on the right and is visible below. Drawn by Timothy A. Buehner, Isabel C. Yang, Hugh D. Hughes, Sandra M. Moore, and Jonathan C. Spodek, Historic American Buildings Survey, 1989–1992. Library of Congress, Prints and Photographs Division.

Wilhelm Friedrich Hegel's dialectic of lordship and bondage, ontically differentiated master from slave.

Like the noise in the channel of a communications circuit, the hearing, speaking bodies of enslaved Black persons were therefore not external to the system of enlightened public reason practiced at Monticello. But nor were they simply Enlightenment's invisible, muted operators, confined below decks, as Max Horkheimer and Theodor W. Adorno might have had it, while Jefferson-as-Odysseus strained with his guests toward the sirens' enchanting call.[10] For Jefferson and his world, these enslaved persons were the system's predialectical, constitutive inside, which, like a body's internal, background noise, had to be made silent with every pull on the dumbwaiter in order for that system to function. Each pull drew their bodies into the dialectic, enslaving them—constituting them as slaves—again. Their material silence, which was produced rather than merely enforced by the space and its hardware, was just as integral to the Jeffersonian Republic of Letters as was the wine in the glasses, the books in the library, the chatter of the dinner guests, and the oral recitations performed by students at the nearby University of Virginia aspiring to a place at the table.

The dumbwaiters that connected the Monticello dining room with the wine cellar were probably installed sometime around 1809, during the last phase of construction on the estate prior to Jefferson's death in 1826. Their design may have been based on similar devices built into table legs in the Parisian Café Mécanique, which Jefferson most likely visited during his stay as minister to France from 1784 to 1789.[11] Monticello's dining room door, which turned on a central pivot, was equipped with shelves on one side so that enslaved persons could discreetly ascend the narrow staircase from the kitchen, located in the basement of the southern dependency wing, and deliver plated food without entering the room. Another enslaved person would then place the dishes on another type of dumbwaiter, a wheeled cart with a stack of four shelves (which may have been adapted from a French *étagère*), and leave the room.[12] Wine could be retrieved at any time by the host, a member of his immediate family, or if necessary, by Jefferson's enslaved personal valet, Burwell Colbert. All of which was designed to encourage in Jefferson's carefully chosen dinner guests something very close to what Immanuel Kant called in his remarks on Enlightenment, "the inclination and the vocation for *free thinking*" intrinsic to "man, who is now *more than a machine*, in accord with his dignity."[13]

Among those guests was the literary portraitist of Washington society, Margaret Bayard Smith, who reported as follows:

> When [Jefferson] had any persons dining with him, with whom he wished to enjoy a free and unrestricted flow of conversation, the number of persons at table never exceeded four, and by each individual was placed a *dumb-waiter*, containing everything necessary for the progress of the dinner from beginning to end, so as to make the attendance of servants [slaves] entirely unnecessary, believing as he did, that much of the domestic and public discord was produced by the mutilated and misconstructed repetition of free conversation at dinner tables, by these mute but not inattentive listeners.[14]

It is no small irony that at least one of the moveable dumbwaiters was probably made by an enslaved woodworker, John Hemmings.[15] Much has been written about the lives of enslaved persons at Monticello, including those fathered by Jefferson with Sally Hemings (unrelated to John), and several first-person testimonies have survived. In one of these, Isaac Jefferson, an enslaved tinsmith and a blacksmith, further associated this white man who, as Kant would have had it, was "more than a machine," with mechanically-aided reading and writing:

> When writing he had a copyin machine: while he was a-writin he wouldn't suffer nobody to come in his room: had a dumb-waiter: when he wanted anything

he had nothin to do but turn a crank and the dumb-waiter would bring him water or fruit on a plate or anything he wanted. Old Master had an abundance of books: sometimes would have twenty of 'em down on the floor at once: read fust one, then tother.[16]

Machines, that is, made the man. As Isaac Jefferson observed, the "Old Master" was a function of his apparatuses, a reading and writing system—a liberal individual—sitting silently atop a hill, fed by enslaved persons bound to daily brutalities below that supported "free conversation at dinner tables," above.

Part I

FIGURES

Cornice.

Frieze.

Architrave

Capital.

Shaft.

Base.
Cornice.

Die.

Plinth.

ATURE

OLUMN

ATE or
STAL

1

STUDENT BODIES AND CORPORATE PERSONS

By 1800, corporations were regularly formed in the United States to enable collective action semi-independently from the state, which many viewed with suspicion. The decades immediately following U.S. independence saw the proliferating incorporation of towns, turnpike authorities, bridge companies, religious associations, colleges, schools, and many other institutions. Most of these were eleemosynary, or charitable, corporations; business corporations were more rare.[1] During the long nineteenth century, all of these corporations shifted under the law from being conceived as mere vehicles for collective activity to being recognized as active agents with rights and responsibilities of their own.

The basis for this agency is often called the legal fiction of corporate personhood. Around 1900, this modern fiction was expounded by, among others, the German medievalist Otto von Gierke and his British and American counterparts. It derived in significant measure from what the historian Ernst Kantorowicz much later called the "heuristic fiction" of "the king's two bodies" characteristic of medieval English jurisprudence, a political theology that distinguished an immortal, immaterial Crown from a mortal king and the physical body politic, or *universitas*, of which he was the "head."[2] Like the christological aporia on which, according to Kantorowicz, it was ultimately based, this fiction has enjoyed a long career well beyond the discourse to which it first belonged. By the end of the nineteenth century, the research university had definitively joined the list of double-bodied corporate persons. But in the United States, the birth of corporate personhood in this modern sense is most clearly visible in the university's precursor, the residential college.

Collegiate Persons

In 1819, in *Trustees of Dartmouth College v. Woodward*, the United States Supreme Court ruled that privately chartered institutions held contract rights comparable to those of private persons. Dartmouth College had been incorporated in 1769 by means of a charter granted by Britain's King George III, as was typical at the time.[3] The charter provided for the establishment of a college in New Hampshire named for an influential English benefactor, "for the education and instruction of the youth of the Indian tribes in this land . . . and also of English youth and any others. And the trustees of said college may and shall be one body corporate and politic in deed, action and name."[4] Since 1754, Dartmouth's founder Eleazar Wheelock had run Moor's Indian Charity School, in Lebanon, Connecticut, which he relocated to Hanover, New Hampshire and expanded into a college. By 1800, three Indigenous students had graduated from Dartmouth; in the whole of the next century only eight followed.[5]

In 1816, in order to resolve a long-running conflict between the Dartmouth trustees and Wheelock's son and successor, John Wheelock, the state of New Hampshire sought to revise the college's charter to render its trustees answerable to state government. The trustees objected, arguing that this violated the contract clause of the U.S. Constitution, which prevents the state from impairing "the Obligations of Contracts" among private individuals, or among individuals and the state. In 1819, the court found that the charter amounted to such a contract, and that the actions of the state were in violation of this constitutional clause.[6] This was an important step toward the doctrine that privately held corporations were, in the eyes of the court, persons capable of entering into contracts who possessed many if not all of the rights and obligations held by their biological or natural counterparts.

Most of the remaining steps were taken in the later nineteenth century, and in 1886, in *Santa Clara County v. Southern Pacific Railroad Co.*, the Supreme Court ruled that corporations were entitled to equal protection under the law as provided to natural persons under the Constitution's Fourteenth Amendment, which had been ratified in 1868 to secure equal treatment for freed slaves.[7] Finally in 1910, in *Southern Railway Co. v. Greene*, the court confirmed that the proposition "that a corporation is a person, within the meaning of the Fourteenth Amendment, is no longer open to discussion."[8] Legal historians have supplied partial explanations as to how this came about. Most, however, presuppose an ontological distinction between natural and artificial persons that is abrogated by force of law, a presupposition that does not explain how a legal fiction—corporate personhood—can have real effects. Moreover, most such accounts give little sense of how the corporate person was or is materially constituted.[9] On both of these counts, the antebellum college offers some clues.

Corporate Behavior

In his closing argument before the U.S. Supreme Court on behalf of Dartmouth College, the lawyer, orator, and Dartmouth alumnus Daniel Webster is said to have exclaimed of his alma mater to the presiding justice, John Marshall, that it is "a small college. And yet *there are those who love it.*"[10] At which point Webster reportedly choked up, tears filling his eyes. Marshall's colleague on the court, Joseph Story, described the effect of Webster's emotional peroration as "almost superhuman," and the Yale professor of rhetoric and oratory Chauncey Allen Goodrich, who attended the proceedings, recalled how, unable to withhold an "unmanly burst of feeling," Webster's "voice choked" with "the words of tenderness in which he went on to speak of his attachment to the college."[11] In his majority opinion, Marshall found Dartmouth to be a "private corporation" but with limited rights, since "a corporation is an artificial being, invisible, intangible, and existing only in contemplation of law."[12] Strategically successful as it was, Webster's declaration of filial love for Dartmouth College was believable, not because his apparent spontaneity testified to true feeling rather than calculation—that we cannot know—but because, as the court's decision bore out, his words recognized Dartmouth as an object worthy of what his society considered a singularly human emotion: love. That is, Webster's avowal of love for Dartmouth helped performatively to call an otherwise impersonal corporation into reciprocal being, as a person.

At the time Dartmouth was indeed small, consisting of about ninety-five students taught by a handful of faculty overseen by a president and a board of twelve trustees.[13] Its campus comprised a single building, Dartmouth Hall, an early example of the all-purpose, double-loaded phalanx- or phalanstery-like residential and educational hall typical of American colonial colleges.[14] The original Dartmouth Hall, which was constructed between 1770 and 1791, the designer of which is unknown, burned in a fire in 1904 and was rebuilt in whitewashed brick as the enlarged quasi-replica that stands today.[15] Webster's love for Dartmouth was likely forged in that original hall, where he lived for three years from 1797 to 1800, and where he and his thirty classmates performed daily recitations of classical verse.[16] That love would have been further secured in the after-hours antics in which he and his cohabitants no doubt indulged, as well as in his enthusiasm for public speaking, which on one occasion included a funeral oration for a classmate, although the young Webster was duly slighted by not being chosen to deliver the valedictory oration at the commencement ceremony.[17]

1.1 Dartmouth Hall, Dartmouth College, 1784–1791. Photograph, c. 1880. Courtesy of Dartmouth College Library.

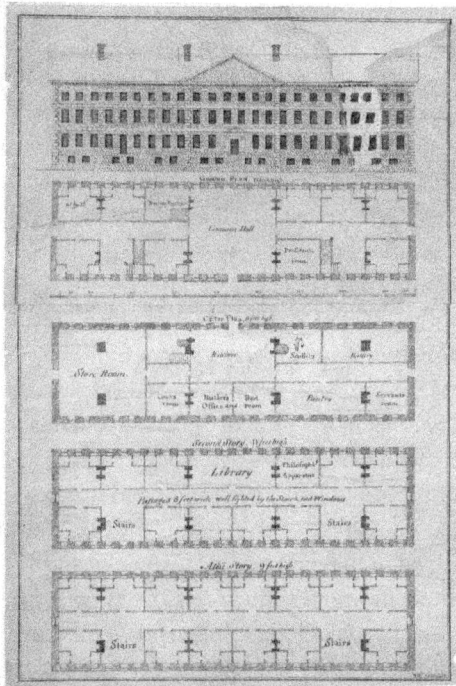

1.2 Dartmouth Hall, Dartmouth College, 1784–1791, as drawn by William Gamble, 1773. Courtesy of Dartmouth College Library.

Accounts of college life in the early republic remind us of the relative youth of the exclusively male students like Webster, who was not from a family of great means, as well as the relative lack of discipline reigning over their world. Among the most infamous examples of collegiate indiscipline was life at Princeton's Nassau Hall from about 1800 to 1820. Nassau Hall, a long, three-story phalanx-like building, was probably designed by Robert Smith, a Philadelphia builder, together with Dr. William Shippen, between 1755 and 1757, and it became a model for Dartmouth Hall and many others. In 1802, Nassau Hall burned, leaving only the stone exterior walls. Immediately thereafter, the hall was entirely rebuilt within these walls, with sturdier construction, a larger cupola, and small classicizing details, to designs by Benjamin Henry Latrobe.[18] Although not among his most distinguished works, Latrobe's Nassau Hall elicited a number of incidents of performative misbehavior, which played its own part in the incorporation of the collegiate body.

As Michel Foucault showed, delinquency is a product of disciplinary systems rather than their antithesis, and failure is among a system's prerequisites for proper functioning.[19] In the sphere of education, a principal instrument for the proper distribution of failure is the examination. Upon arriving in Hanover, New Hampshire in 1797, the fifteen-year old Daniel Webster had his knowledge of English, Greek, Latin, and arithmetic tested orally before being allowed to enroll at Dartmouth College. Such on-the-spot entrance exams were common practice at the time. During those years, young men coming from throughout the Northeast and from parts of the South had to do the same upon arrival in Princeton, as they sought admission to what was still called (until 1896) the College of New Jersey.

In the early decades of the nineteenth century, the Princeton grounds—the country's first campus—consisted of four buildings: the president's house, a professor's house, Geological Hall (now Stanhope, also designed by Latrobe), Philosophical Hall (also by Latrobe, now demolished), and Nassau Hall. Originally, Nassau Hall comprised approximately forty living chambers (some of which were used as recitation rooms), a prayer hall, library, and basement kitchen and dining room.[20] Though not formally panoptic, the edifice had virtually all of the attributes of what Foucault called a disciplinary *dispositif*, or apparatus: enclosure, or confinement; a system of cellular partitioning; distinctly marked "functional sites"; and "ranks," both within rooms (rows of beds, or desks) and among them (by year, etc.). Likewise class schedules, daily recitations, the teaching of proper handwriting, with proper posture, the student-pen-paper-chair-desk interface, various prohibitions on time wasting, and so on.[21]

Foucault influentially argued that when joined together into a disciplinary system, these properties combine to produce supple, trainable, "docile bodies."[22] But the bodies trained in Nassau Hall were hardly docile. On the contrary, the presidency of Ashbel Green in particular, which began in 1812 after a period

1.3 Robert Smith and Dr. William Shippen. Nassau Hall, College of New Jersey (later Princeton University), 1757. Engraving reproduced in *New American Magazine*, (March 1760). *New American Magazine, Reproductions*; Nassau Hall Iconography, AC177, Princeton University Archives, Department of Special Collections, Princeton University Library.

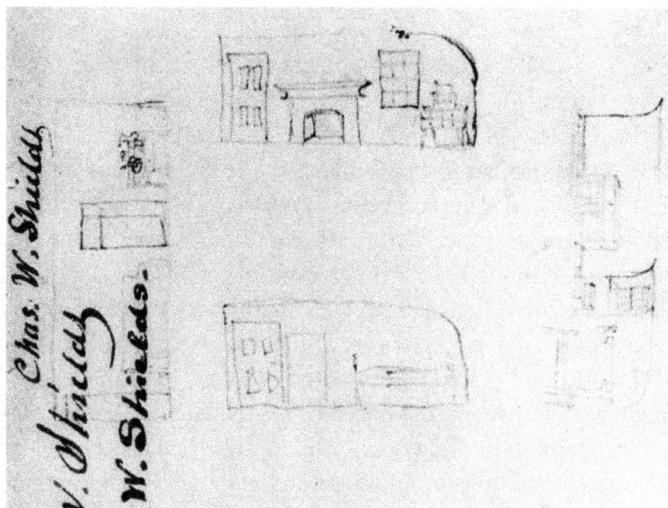

1.4 Benjamin H. Latrobe, Nassau Hall, College of New Jersey (later Princeton University). Student room of Chas. W. Shields. Sketch, 1844 (author unknown). Henry Lyttleton Savage, *Nassau Hall, 1756–1956* (Princeton, NJ: Princeton University, 1956), plate XI (b).

of severely declining enrollments and what some considered declining piety, was punctuated by what Green called "every kind of insubordination."[23] During Green's first term, three students were expelled after gunpowder exploded in Nassau Hall; another was expelled for climbing the belfry and ringing the bell at three o'clock in the morning; yet another broke into the prayer hall and vandalized a Bible by cutting a deck of playing cards into its leaves. The following year, 1813–1814, saw firecrackers set off in the building and graffiti scrawled on its walls. Then, on the night of January 9, 1814, in the words of one historian, "a cracker, consisting of a hollow log charged with two pounds of gunpowder, was set off behind the central door of Nassau Hall." Windows shattered, walls cracked, and a piece of the log crashed through the prayer hall door.[24]

One former student was brought to civil trial and others were expelled. Still, further mayhem ensued, particularly in the building's long hallways before and after evening meals. One evening President Green, who referred in his memoir to the giant firecracker (or bomb) as an "infernal machine," performed the duly panoptic ritual of standing outside the refectory with a lit candle. He recalled: "They passed me in perfect silence and respect, but as soon as they had got out of sight" some "began the usual yell."[25] Exasperated, the faculty voted to dismiss two students. On April 6, 1814, Green wrote ominously in his diary: "I took the examination of the senior class on belles lettres and wrote letters to the parents of the two dismissed students. The Faculty met in the evening and a pistol was fired at the door of one of the tutors." And then again, on April 7: "Attended examination. We had a cracker in the college today and in the evening a company of students in front of the campus behaved in a very improper manner."[26] If that was not enough, in 1817 students nailed all the building's entry doors shut, shouted "Rebellion!" and "Fire," broke windows, and generally ran amok.[27]

The College of New Jersey was far from alone in its troubles. Dartmouth and Yale experienced similar disturbances, and in 1823, there were explosions in Harvard Yard, with forty-three students expelled just prior to commencement.[28] A widely circulated report to the Yale Corporation by its president and faculty—the Yale Report of 1828—responded to the pervasive indiscipline, as well as to the devaluation of classical learning and declining religious piety to which many attributed it, by calling for the "*discipline* and *furniture* [or furnishing] of the mind," dedicated to "the art of fixing the attention, directing the train of thought."[29] Among the requirements for this discipline was "a substitute . . . for *parental superintendence*." That is, according to the Yale faculty, "The parental character of college government, requires that the students should be so collected together, as to constitute one family; that the intercourse between them and their instructors may be frequent and familiar. This renders it necessary that suitable *buildings* be provided, for the residence of the students."[30] Nassau Hall and Dartmouth Hall were typical of such buildings; others included: at

Yale, Connecticut Hall (1750), at Harvard, Massachusetts Hall (1718–1720), and at the College of Rhode Island (later Brown University), University Hall (1770). Though they seem neatly to fit into the encompassing grids of Foucault's apparatuses, the acts of indiscipline and of love that occurred in the halls of these edifices were among the conditions necessary for corporate personhood. Not only because disciplinary failure inscribed a vicious circle in which docility and delinquency were two sides of a coin, but because the apparatus itself elicited familial as well as libidinal affect.

Love Machines

In 1825 there was a masked, drunken, fourteen-person "riot" on the Lawn of the recently opened, public but still incorporated University of Virginia.[31] The following year, a seventeen-year-old Edgar Allan Poe enrolled at the university and took up residence on the Lawn, moving shortly thereafter to a room on the Western Range, in a section known as "Rowdy Row."[32] From his perfectly carceral cell, Poe witnessed fights (including the biting of an arm, which led to an expulsion), gambled away what little he had, and read classics.[33] Although not himself a troublemaker, Poe was indigent, and he withdrew after only a year, resentful of the wealthier, drunken classmates to whose company he was condemned.[34] A few years later, he eulogized, in the persona of Helen,

The beauty of fair Greece / And the grandeur of old Rome.[35]

Scholars have speculated that Poe's gaze in this ode to antique beauty remained fixed on Thomas Jefferson's neo-Palladian, though not exactly Roman and certainly not Hellenic, campus architecture.[36] Regardless, *its* gaze was fixed upon *him*. If we follow Lewis Mumford, we might ascribe what Mumford considered the near madness that stalked Poe and the hallucinatory explosiveness of his writings to the implacable, inversely productive logic of the apparatus, a lifelong rage against the machine. That would make Poe's 1847 short story "The Domain of Arnheim" the literary shadow of Jefferson's Monticello, but also, as Mumford suggests, of the University of Virginia. Mumford celebrated Jefferson's design for the Virginia campus as "perhaps [the] most perfect consummation" of the "classical order" in the early American republic, an order that, according to Mumford, rapidly disintegrated "under the combined influence of pioneer enterprise, mechanical invention, overseas commerce, and the almost religious cult of utilitarianism."[37] Poe bore witness to this process, converting its signs to symbols. Here is Mumford on Poe's metallic melancholy:

1.5 Thomas Jefferson, University of Virginia (1826), engraving by Benjamin Tanner. Detail from Herman Böye et al., *A Map of the State of Virginia: Constructed in Conformity to Law from the Late Surveys Authorized by the Legislature and Other Original and Authentic Documents*, 1827. Albert and Shirley Small Special Collections Library, University of Virginia.

In him, the springs of human desire had not so much frozen up as turned to metal: his world was, in one of his favorite words, plutonian, like that of Watt and Fulton and Gradgrind [a Charles Dickens character]: the tears that he dropped were steel beads, and his mind worked like a mechanical hopper, even when there were no appropriate materials to throw into it.[38]

In the "Domain of Arnheim," Poe conjured a picturesque landscape garden engulfing "a mass of semi-Gothic, semi-Saracenic architecture" built to gratify his wealthy protagonist's aesthetic-erotic dreams.[39] "Desire is real!" exclaimed Mumford, who associated earthly desires, honestly expressed rather than alienated dreams of the sort he found in Poe, with a full-fledged humanity able to confront the despairing nullity of machines, and asked, "But if sexual desire, why not every human desire?"[40]

Alongside Poe's Arnheim, ranged against mechanical nullity was also, according to Mumford, the stylized eclecticism of John Haviland's Tombs prison in New York (1838), the nickname of which derives, Mumford explains, from "the Egyptian character of its façade."[41] The Tombs, to which Herman Melville's intransigent scrivener Bartleby was ultimately dispatched, was the very epitome of the Benthamite utilitarianism by which Mumford felt overwhelmed. It was also an exemplary instance of what Foucault referred to as "carcerality."[42]

Understood this way, machines, as components of larger socio-technical apparatuses, participated in the molding of human subjectivity. But in the process,
as we have seen, the impersonal apparatuses also began acquiring human attributes, becoming legal subjects in their own right. The early republican relation of
collegian to college was not short on libidinal energies. Quite possibly then, Poe's
"Helen" was one name for the corporate person, a figure shaped by the insub-
ordinate love—and fear—of those subjected to its will, even as it shaped them.

An "'Architektonick' Thing"

Matters at Yale were only slightly different. As one of Yale's early historians, the
minister and theologian Leonard Bacon, put it in 1879, "the history of the college
is itself the history of the corporation."[43] Chartered by the colonial legislature in
1701 as a group of ten trustees, all Congregationalist ministers empowered with
the "full liberty and privilege" of "founding, suitably endowing, and ordering a
collegiate school," the social body of the Yale Corporation underwent considerable turmoil during the process of determining the school's ultimate location.[44]
Like the trustees themselves, the pupils and tutors of the Collegiate School
were originally scattered among several towns throughout the state. A number
of these towns sought to host the fledgling institution. In 1716, amid internal
disagreement, the trustees voted to locate the college in New Haven. The Yale
Corporation, entrusted with the care of this new Collegiate School, had also
been dispersed across the colony into the individual bodies and locations of the
ten founding trustees who, often with local, extra-academic interests in mind,
competed to determine the school's site. It was not until the building of Yale
College that the Yale Corporation can be said to have also been located definitively in New Haven.

During the process of debating the school's location, a number of dissident
trustees appealed to the colonial governor and general assembly to intervene.
Though the officials did not, historians have interpreted the incident to suggest
a mix of public and private interests in the founding of the college, potentially
undermining its status as a fully autonomous institution.[45] This is the principal
issue that would come before the court a century later in the Dartmouth case.
Bacon's later account resolves the ambiguity by distinguishing between colonial
(and later, state) patronage and the founders' sovereign exercise of their "liberty." In 1701, the founding trustees (or "undertakers") achieved this liberty via
a speech act that, in Bacon's view, secured Yale's independence by declaring at
their first recorded meeting that: "We do order and appoint that there shall be,
and hereby is erected and formed a collegiate school."[46]

It was not, however, until 1718 that this verbal "erecting" and "forming" was
followed by a physical act of construction in New Haven that would result in

1.6 John Inigo Greenwood, *Johnston's View of Yale College*, etching and engraving after a painting by Thomas Johnston, c. 1742–1745. Yale University Art Gallery.

the completion of the *building* named Yale College, in recognition of a signifi-cant gift of books and other valuables from the British colonial merchant Elihu Yale. Only when the question of location had been settled, construction had begun, and a building committee (among others) had been organized could Bacon retrospectively judge that: "Evidently the corporation was at last in work-ing condition."[47] Triumphantly citing the corporation's formal record book, Bacon reports that by the next meeting,

> The work of the college building, which, a year before, was to "be undertaken with all convenient speed," was now in progress; the huge frame—huge for those days, being a hundred and seventy feet long, and three stories in height— had been for three weeks the most conspicuous "architektonick" thing in New Haven or in the colony of Connecticut.[48]

The New Haven trustees had purchased land on the town green for this pur-pose. In October 1717, under the supervision of the master carpenter Henry Caner, construction began on a three-story wooden building with three evenly spaced entrances, leaded casement windows (subsequently replaced by weighted sash), and a hipped roof with attic dormers capped by what was most likely a central belfry.[49] According to a later description, the narrow structure, about twenty feet wide and one-hundred seventy feet long, contained a dining hall, chapel, and library, and twenty-two rooms (including the attic) that accommodated two and later three students each.[50] Both bell and windows were immediate targets of student mischief; unauthorized bell-ringing (along with "unseasonably Firing Gunns") being the frequent cause of "publick Disturbance" punishable by a fine established by the trustees, with the similarly punishable breaking of windows listed by the young theologian Jonathan Edwards, class of 1721, among the "monstrous impieties" that marred collegiate life.[51]

Fathers and Mothers

According to the collegiate historian Bacon, it was not until 1725, after the matter of physical location for instruction was settled and the building was erected, that the superintending corporate body was finally united and, as Bacon put it, "the trustees were as one man in caring for the college."[52] Their union was, he explains, secured with the appointment of Elisha Williams of Wethersfield (the most persistently dissenting municipality), as rector of Yale College and member of the corporation. On its face, the territorial symbolism in Williams's appointment comports well with the rest of the story, but Bacon's language says more about the career of the corporate person than it does about the Yale trustees. By 1879, when he wrote, there was nothing unusual about personifying an administrative body as "one man" entrusted with the pastoral care of its structures and of its students. In 1876, Daniel Coit Gilman used the phrase "in loco parentis," which had entered Anglophone legal parlance a century earlier, to describe the limitations of collegiate life and learning in his inaugural address as president of Johns Hopkins University.[53] Tacitly favoring mothers over fathers, the figure of Alma Mater, the nurturing mother, was as old as the European university itself, having been written into the motto of the Bologna *studiorum* at its founding in 1088. What changed between 1725 and 1875 was the technics of embodiment, beginning with the head.

Standing on the fatherly side, the Yale College president was the Janus-faced lynchpin that secured the institution's personhood. The conversion of rector to president in emulation of Harvard formalized the Yale presidency's two-sidedness, which was typical of most: facing inward toward the integrated collegiate body and outward toward the dispersed body of trustees. De facto identification of college with corporation is therefore imprecise. It was only through the medium of the president, resident in New Haven, who was at once the corporation's appointed representative, the head of the college and its chief instructor, that corporation and college were recognized as one.

Although President Williams stabilized the Yale administration and proved a successful fundraiser, his successor, the Reverend Thomas Clap, became the model for mediation of this sort. Appointed in 1739, the turning point in Clap's long tenure came in 1745 when, with the adoption of a new charter, his rector-ship formally became a presidency.[54] Yale College now named the institution as well as the building, and the body of trustees was now formally a corporation. The charter of 1745 named Clap and the ten trustees as an "INCORPORATE SOCIETY or BODY CORPORATE AND POLITICK."[55]

Having established the incorporated body's legal personhood, including the immortality of "perpetual Succession," the charter expressly established Clap as president and the other ten as fellows, going so far as to schedule their annual meetings. It also required each, along with any and all professors and tutors, to swear an oath of loyalty to the British Crown publicly in the "college hall," and entrusted to the incorporated body the "Government Care and Management" of all matters and affairs pertaining to the college and its students.[56]

The corporate person that emerged from this document and its context was anything but singular, but neither was it (or he, or she) exactly plural. Comprising both president and trustees, who in turn appointed professors, tutors, and all other officers, the corporation was reducible to none of these while encompassing all. Nor were corporation and college identical, or corporation, college, and collegiate buildings. Multiply embodied, the Yale Corporation faced both toward and away from the state, since personhood, though granted legislatively by the Crown, meant administrative, fiscal, and curricular autonomy from Crown and colony. This contradiction, whereby only the sovereign can recognize a corporate person and thereby bring it into being as an autonomous, rights-bearing entity, was constitutive rather than contingent. In 1792, the situation at Yale was further complicated when, in return for providing state funds for a new building and other needs, six state senators along with the governor and the lieutenant governor of the new state of Connecticut joined the board as ex officio corporate members. Thus state and corporation renewed their bond. In recognition, the student dormitory that opened in 1794, a hundred-foot long four-story brick structure with a cornerstone bearing the name of the learned Ezra Stiles, president, was named Union Hall.[57]

An Aesthetic Education

In 1827, one of those ex officio members of the Yale Corporation, State Senator Noyes Darling, criticized the Yale curriculum for its emphasis on the "dead languages" at the expense of more evidently useful knowledge.[58] By the opening decades of the century, this was a common complaint against both the elitism and the rote character of the classical learning predominant in the early republican colleges. Much more than glorified seminaries for the training of a conservative clergy, colleges like Yale had become important sites for reproducing a governing class. The question facing officers of the corporation like Darling, a Yale alumnus, was how best to do so. Although disagreements surrounding the matter are most easily portrayed as a variation on the longstanding quarrel among ancients and moderns, the details of the Yale case suggest that the classical languages played an unexpected role in securing the distinct modernity of the corporate person. We should therefore read the Yale Report of 1828 with the dialectics of corporate personhood in mind.

Commissioned by a subcommittee of Yale Corporation members including Darling and President Jeremiah Day, the report, which was said to represent the views of the faculty on the study of Greek and Latin, was written by Day and professor of Hebrew, Greek, and Latin James L. Kingsley, with professor of chemistry and mineralogy Benjamin Silliman contributing sections on the teaching of mathematics.[59] Calls from educational reformers to curtail the study of dead languages had been met enthusiastically by some Yale students with the rolling of cannonballs down stairs, the breaking of windows, and the barricading of faculty apartments, acts aimed especially at those faculty judged responsible for the oppressive enforcement of classical tradition.[60] In the fall of 1827, the corporation—that is, president and trustees—responded by appointing a faculty committee to review the curriculum. Even so, student disobedience continued and the faculty was called upon to enforce discipline, supported by the president as the corporation's agent of institutional care.

Also in 1828, discontent at the quality of food provided in the newly enlarged commons led to a college-wide student boycott, the four leaders of which were summarily expelled. Numerous others deserted in solidarity, only to be welcomed back weeks later, minus the original four, provided that they pledged unconditional obedience to collegiate regulations. Having thus put down what became known as the Bread and Butter Rebellion, the Yale faculty was less lenient when, in 1830, members of the sophomore class petitioned for changes in recitation method such that the instructor, presumably Denison Olmsted, professor of mathematics and natural philosophy, might "explain Conic Sections from the book, and not demonstrate them from figures."[61] The request was refused, and oral recitation with hand-drawn figures prevailed over printed text. The students again boycotted, which resulted in the expulsion of forty-four from their number. Such was the solidarity among faculties nationwide on the matter that few other colleges agreed to admit any of the expelled forty-four. Thus the Conic Sections Rebellion was quashed, and, according to an 1879 retelling by William Kingsley, son of one of the Yale Report's coauthors, Yale students began "to understand that mental discipline is to be obtained only by hard work."[62]

Most interpretations of the Yale Report have focused on its authors' efforts to balance classical learning against growing demands to prepare college graduates to operate the levers of industrial capitalism.[63] The two-part report's most quoted passage reads in full:

> The two great points to be gained in intellectual culture, are the *discipline* and the *furniture* of the mind; expanding its powers, and storing it with knowledge. The former of these is, perhaps, the more important of the two. A commanding object, therefore, in a collegiate course, should be, to call into daily and vigorous exercise the faculties of the student.[64]

Coming in the first, more general section of the report, written by President Day as both faculty member and member of the corporation, the passage neatly summarizes a pedagogy of "faculty psychology," for which "culture" (cultivation), "discipline" (disciplining), and "furniture" (furnishing) were meant in the active sense, as pedagogical techniques pertaining to distinct mental capacities in the service of what the lines immediate prior to these call "*parental superintendence*."[65] Day continued by specifying each faculty addressed by the curriculum: attention, direction, analysis, discrimination, judgment, imagination, memory, and genius.[66] The aim was a balanced foundation for future learning, in which each curricular subject had its place as an instrument of both mental and social discipline. Alongside the arts of demonstrative reasoning acquired from mathematics, inductive reasoning from the physical sciences, language from English, thinking from logic, and speaking from rhetoric, in "ancient literature" the student was said to have found "some of the most finished models of taste." Repetitive written exercises were complemented by extemporaneous discussion, with the conviction that "he who has accumulated the richest treasures of thought, should possess the highest powers of oratory." What the report sought, then, was "a union of science with literature; of solid attainment with skill in the art of persuasion."[67]

Young men typically entered Yale College at the age of sixteen, some as early as fourteen. So it is no surprise that the curriculum emphasized the acquisition of basic analytic and expressive skills. Nor was it especially notable that both sections of the report associated Greek and Latin with the faculty of taste. In his more specific defense of the classical curriculum in the second section, professor of Hebrew, Greek and Latin James Kingsley was most explicit, arguing that, "familiarity with the Greek and Roman writers is especially adapted to form the taste, and to discipline the mind, both in thought and diction, to the relish of what is elevated, chaste, and simple."[68] Ancient writers, according to Kingsley, set a standard of literary excellence that could be adduced by analogy to other aspects of classical culture, including architecture and sculpture. Following the contours of transatlantic Hellenism, which American scholars were in the process of updating through acquaintance with German writers like Gotthold Ephraim Lessing and Johann Joachim Winckelmann, Kingsley stressed that the goal was not imitation, but emulation. So often was this claim made, says Kingsley, that he need not belabor it. In sum, in studying the classics, "every faculty of the mind is employed; not only the memory, judgment, and reasoning powers, but the taste and fancy are occupied and improved."[69]

The discourse to which Kingsley alluded, known as faculty psychology, was most prominently associated with the eighteenth-century Scots philosopher Thomas Reid. If, as Caroline Winterer has suggested, the Yale Report was "a dated document, a fossil of eighteenth-century classicism," it was therefore also a fossil of eighteenth-century aesthetic philosophy, but like the dead languages it defended, one with a significant afterlife.[70] Reid divided mind into a series of functions, or "powers," of which what the Yale Report called "taste" was one.[71] For Reid, taste was "that power of the mind by which we are capable of discerning and relishing the beauties of nature, and whatever is excellent in the fine arts."[72] The Yale Report is saturated with a related language of "excellence" which, again for Reid, is a characteristic of objects that is only accessible to the senses as what he calls a "secondary quality," or a sign, that points inward toward the intellect that recognizes it and outward toward the object that, as he puts it, "reflects" that quality. Meditating on the aesthetic property of grandeur, or the sublime, Reid asks rhetorically: "May it not *borrow this quality from something intellectual*, of which it is the effect, or sign, or instrument, or to which it bears some analogy?"[73]

The science of aesthetics to which Reid's "common sense" philosophy of taste and his version of faculty psychology belonged was premised on the contingency of signification. Signs, including natural signs, did not necessarily resemble what they signified; they related to intrinsic excellence only by analogy. There was no way of knowing that the qualities perceived in ancient poetic form, or for that matter, ancient sculpture or architecture, were a direct impression left by the work's excellence or that of its author, only that they stood as a sign for that excellence. Hence, aesthetic principles could best be discerned from classical sources through differential, tabular comparisons: this next to this next to that. The same held for typological distinctions among objects of taste, such as the difference between the emotions elicited by signs of beauty and those of grandeur. For example, Reid argued that unlike grandeur, which inspires either fear or admiration, "as we ascribe beauty, not only to persons, but to inanimate things, we give the name of *love* or *liking* to the emotion which beauty, in both of these kinds of objects, produces."[74]

More surprisingly, among the beautiful objects to which works of art could be compared were machines. According to Reid machines, like paintings, birds, or human beings, were capable of exhibiting signs of intellectual "excellence," and hence of eliciting love. He called this sense of beauty "rational" rather than instinctive, for its correspondence with "some latent perfection of which that beauty in the object is a sign." Sensing it required training, like that of an expert mechanic. Confronted with an apparatus suited in every detail to the purpose for which it was designed, the mechanic "pronounces it to be a beautiful machine."[75] Translated back to the terms of the Yale Report, the mechanic's mind had been suitably "disciplined" and "furnished" to perceive the machine's beauty as though instinctively, the way a child wonders at a butterfly.

Could the techniques for disciplining, furnishing, and incorporating young minds at colleges like Yale themselves be objects of taste and therefore of love? As a mechanism for crafting citizens, the Yale faculty argued, the collegiate curriculum, though not perfect, was uniquely suited. In themselves, these technical details of a philosophy that, at best, loosely underlies the convictions expressed by the Yale administration and faculty in their report explain little about that report's content. But they do allow us to see how the pedagogy that the report defends and seeks to adapt to changing circumstances may not have been so ancient a fossil after all, but a modern machine capable of eliciting an emotional response, like love. Seen from within the dialectics of corporate personhood, the Yale Report's aesthetics, a relic of the eighteenth century, also constituted its modernity.

Technology

We see this more clearly when we compare the Yale document to one of its seeming antitheses. The Yale faculty were reacting in their report not only to internal criticism from members of the corporation like Noyes Darling, or to similar criticisms in the popular press, but to challenges coming from other colleges, notably Harvard. In the 1820s, at the instigation of several new faculty recently returned from graduate education in the German universities led by the scholar of Spanish literature George Ticknor, the Harvard Corporation instituted a partial elective course that included modern languages, lectures with syllabi and tutorials, and separate departments of study. Although the effort foundered, among its important legacies were the modern system of academic departments and faculty control over curriculum.[76] As at Yale, the attempted changes at Harvard were partly linked to the pressures of an industrializing society. Machines had formally entered the Harvard curriculum already by 1815, when that corporation hired Jacob Bigelow as its first Rumford Professor on the Application of Science to the Useful Arts. Bigelow was a botanist and medical doctor with a side interest in mechanics. The conditions of his appointment were quite specific and quite at odds with the dominant recitation-based method of instruction. The stipulations of the fellowship required Bigelow to perform "demonstrations and experiments" in "the Mathematical and Physical Sciences," including those related to the applied arts, and "to describe, with illustrations by the exhibition of experiments and models, valuable improvements, inventions, and discoveries, not generally known or introduced into use."[77] The Rumford professor was also expected to act as an emissary for the useful arts, publicizing his work in the press and introducing his "hearers" to new developments. That is, Harvard's Rumford professor was above all a lecturer. In 1829, after performing this task for over a decade, Bigelow published *Elements of Technology*, by most measures the first treatise on the mechanical arts in the United States, based on his Harvard lectures and intended, as his subtitle put it, "for the use of seminaries and students," a book that we can read as a companion to the Yale Report from the previous year.

Bigelow began his treatise with a boundary problem: "Wherever we attempt to draw a line between the *sciences*, usually so called, and the *arts*, it results in distinctions, which are comparative rather than absolute."[78] One emphasizes discovery, the other, invention. As the endowment of his professorship indicated, by "arts" Bigelow generally meant the applied or "useful" arts rather than the "liberal" ones of humanist classicism, though his words did not distinguish between the two. For Bigelow had no quarrel with the classics; on the contrary:

> The imitative arts, and those which required only boldness and beauty of design, or perseverance in execution, were carried in antiquity to the most signal perfection. Their sculpture has been the admiration of subsequent ages, and their architecture has furnished models which we now strive to imitate, but do not pretend to excel. We might, if this were the place, add their poetry, and their oratory, to the list of arts which flourished in perfection during the youthfulness of intellectual cultivation.[79]

Compare these lines to those in the Yale Report extolling the excellence of classical architecture and sculpture:

> Architecture and sculpture, in their most approved forms, not only had their origin, but received their perfection in Greece. These arts may have been, in certain respects, modified in the progress of time; changes may have been introduced to accommodate their productions to the necessities and manners of a later age; yet the original works of Grecian genius are the models by which artists, even at the present time, direct their labors. . . .
>
> If, then, sculpture and architecture, after the revolution of so many centuries, still derive aid from the remains of ancient skill, it ought not to excite surprise, that in other departments of taste, antiquity should exhibit the same excellence.[80]

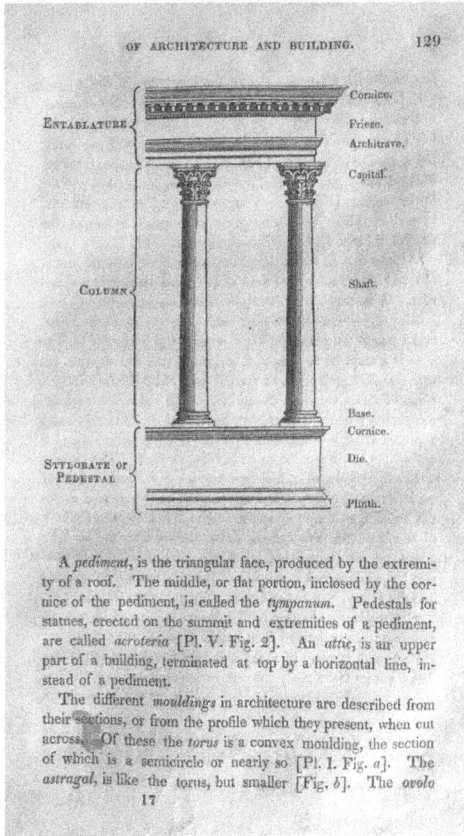

OF ARCHITECTURE AND BUILDING.   129

ENTABLATURE { ... Cornice.
Frieze.
Architrave.

Capital.

COLUMN { ... Shaft.

Base.
Cornice.

STYLOBATE or
PEDESTAL { ... Die.

Plinth.

17

A *pediment*, is the triangular face, produced by the extremi-
ty of a roof. The middle, or flat portion, inclosed by the cornice of the pediment, is called the *tympanum*. Pedestals for
statues, erected on the summit and extremities of a pediment,
are called *acroteria* [Pl. V. Fig. 2]. An *attic*, is an upper
part of a building, terminated at top by a horizontal line, instead of a pediment.
    The different *mouldings* in architecture are described from
their sections, or from the profile which they present, when cut
across. Of these the *torus* is a convex moulding, the section
of which is a semicircle or nearly so [Pl. I. Fig. *a*]. The
astragal, is like the torus, but smaller [Fig. *b*]. The *ovolo*

1.7 Jacob Bigelow, Elements of the classical orders, in *Elements of Technology, Taken Chiefly from a Course of Lectures at Cambridge on the Application of the Sciences to the Useful Arts now Published for the Use of Seminaries and Students* (Boston: Hilliard, Gray, Little, and Wilkins, 1829), 129.

Machines as such do not appear in the Yale Report, but we can read architecture here as their proxy among the useful arts, furnishing signifiers of taste
and "excellence" that can be set beside others, like the well-designed machine
appreciated by Reid's trained mechanic. On this, the Yale authors do seem at
odds with Bigelow. In what may well be the first formal entrance of architecture
into an American college curriculum, Bigelow included a full chapter on "architecture and building" in his published Harvard lectures. While he acknowledged architecture's standing among the fine arts, like his French contemporary
Jean-Nicolas-Louis Durand, whom he listed among his sources, Bigelow seems

to cast architecture in a utilitarian light. Favoring the Greco-Roman, he adds Egyptian, Chinese, and Gothic examples to his matter-of-fact, synoptic inventory of styles and construction methods. Strikingly, the chapter's concluding sequence begins with "The Arts of Writing and Printing," from papyrus to the mechanized printing press, moves on to techniques for drawing and painting, then to engraving and lithography, and to sculpture and casting techniques—a cascade of media.

Bigelow's preferred pedagogic medium was the lecture supplemented with "philosophical apparatus," or scientific instruments and models used in the classroom for demonstration purposes. In keeping with the lecture's linearity, his narrative is developmental and progressive, a tale of obsolescence and maturation. In contrast, the Yale authors identified taste with the kind of repetition that was practiced daily in the recitations. The corporate person to whom these authors reported was born not just from the trustees' circle but from the superposition of that circle onto the student body, mediated in the first instance by the faculty and its techniques, like recitations, and in the second instance by the president, who joined college and corporation together while also holding them apart. Transferred to the Yale context in this more technological sense stressed by Bigelow, architecture—what Bigelow called the "art of erecting buildings"—furnished a pedagogical medium for the disciplining of taste alongside other mental faculties. Moving, then, from the conventional faculty psychology that colors the Yale Report to its authors' offhand reference to classical architecture, we arrive at the report's central contradiction: that the very material conditions reluctantly accommodated if not resisted by the Yale authors, what they call the "business character of the nation" and the correlate subordination of the fine arts to the useful arts, are the basis from which both college and corporation were born, beginning with the erection of Yale College in 1718. This contradiction could only be resolved lovingly and with care.

Persons of Taste

Bigelow's lectures on technology aside, colleges around 1820 typically produced orators of the more classical sort, like Daniel Webster.[81] At Yale, Bigelow's closest peer was Benjamin Silliman, who had been lecturing on chemistry since 1804, and who was the college's first professor of chemistry and natural history and among the report's contributing authors. In 1818, Silliman founded *The American Journal of Science and Arts*, under an extended subtitle advertising "Mineralogy, Geology, and the Other Branches of Natural History; Including Also Agriculture and the Ornamental as Well as Useful Arts." One year after the publication of the Yale Report as a standalone pamphlet, Silliman republished the document in this journal, sandwiching the encomium to classical discipline between a tabulation of "Ferns and Mosses of the United States" and an extract on "The History of Sea-Serpentism."[82] Silliman's brief editorial remarks warn his readers about the "diversity of opinion" surrounding its subject, while recommending the document's attention to "the interests of sound learning, in relation both to literature and science, and to professional and active life."[83]

When recontextualized in this way by one of its authors, in a setting that disseminated the latest scientific knowledge in relation to the "useful arts," the Yale Report appears less as a defense against modern learning than a contribution to it. Silliman probably wrote those of its lines that characterized mathematics as "especially adapted to sharpen the intellect, to strengthen the faculty of reason, and to induce a general habit of mind favorable to the discovery of truth and the detection of error." Anticipating the objection that, the usefulness of mathematics aside, mere arithmetic would do for most professional pursuits, this section of the report argued that familiarity with the principles of mathematics and the sciences constituted a kind of literacy in its own right.[84]

When lecturing publicly on science, Silliman borrowed from classical oratory even when hinting at curricular modification.[85] His Yale lectures on chemistry, on the other hand, were of a somewhat different type. Silliman gave the first of these in April 1804 in a rented space across from South College, since the laboratory then under construction in the new Lyceum building to the designs of the English architect Peter Banner was not yet ready. Lecturing from notes taken from the most recent textbooks, Silliman performed experiments with the college's newly acquired chemistry "apparatus," for which he needed the laboratory space. Evidently, Banner was indifferent to the laboratory's dual function as classroom, since he located it in the Lyceum's basement amid a forest of piers and arches that had to be cleared before the building opened later that year. Silliman's lectures, which were optional and also open to the public, and for which the corporation charged a separate fee, continued in the Lyceum basement until 1829 when a new laboratory building better suited to their needs was designed.[86] Their success depended on Silliman's ability to engage his audience with the demonstrations. So effective were they that a Yale Corporation fellow, the Reverend Dr. David Ely, worriedly asked whether there was not "danger that with these physical attractions you will overtop the Latin and the Greek?"[87]

Yet in 1831, the Yale Corporation established a new professorship in the dead languages with help of the Centum Milla Fund, provided by the newly formed Yale alumni society. James Kingsley's professorship in Greek and Latin, which he had held for twenty-six years, was divided in two, with Kingsley retaining the chair in Latin and Theodore D. Woolsey appointed in Greek.[88] In 1879, Kingsley's son, William Lathrop Kingsley, editor and chronicler of Yale's history, remarked on the 1830s as a turning point in both student "esprit de corps" (his term) and distinction, noting the prominent alumni who issued from the class of 1837 alone: a secretary of state, a Supreme Court chief justice, the U.S. ambassador to England, and, briefly, Samuel J. Tilden, the Democratic presidential candidate who made the deal that ended Reconstruction during the disputed election of 1876. Thus the younger Kingsley was able to exclaim: "Never before had the students been known to manifest such affection for their *alma mater* or to take such pride in the ability and reputation of their instructors."[89] Meanwhile, in the early 1840s, the elder Kingsley's newly hired junior colleague, Thomas A. Thatcher, was obliged to combat the easy availability of cheap Latin translations on which students now surreptitiously relied for their recitations. Where a printed text was previously an original to be read, memorized, and recited, not interpreted, students were now reading one reproduction to translate another. Thatcher's recourse was to require students to defend their recited Latin translations chiefly on grammatical grounds, which could not be derived from the cheap editions.[90] This was classical learning *with* mechanization, not merely against it.

Corporate Veils

Thus was the corporate person manufactured as a person of disciplined taste capable of eliciting and expressing both love and affection—a student body that doubled as the body of the corporation, which, via charters, presidents, and alumni, doubled-up with capital and with the state. But did this make the corporate person real? Deciding a corporate rights case in 1927, the future Supreme Court justice Benjamin Cardozo wrote that this area of the law was "enveloped in the mists of metaphor." Although Cardozo was referring to the relation of "parent" to subsidiary corporations, the principal metaphor in question was the jurisprudential figure of the "corporate veil," which covered parents and subsidiaries, or bodies and their organs.[91] Although there are traces of such language in earlier discourse, the figure was not stabilized until the early twentieth century when, in 1912, Maurice Wormser, a law professor at the University of Illinois, summarized the doctrine of "piercing the corporate veil," or seeing past the "fiction" of corporate personhood to the entity's constituent human agents.[92] In a subsequent article, Wormser further distinguished the theory of the corporation as an organic association of individuals, the real aggregate person endowed with an independent will theorized by Otto von Gierke, from the *persona ficta* codified in U.S. case law and exemplified by Chief Justice John Marshall's opinion in the Dartmouth case, while acknowledging the practical utility of both. Citing jurisprudence, however, that recognized the performative effects of fictive beings, Wormser despaired that the latter form of corporate personhood "is a fiction which is not a fiction,—a thought my mind finds it difficult to follow."[93]

Wormser, who dismissed the extrapolation of Gierke's thesis such "that a corporation could marry or be given in marriage, or that it could vote at an election," resolved the dilemma by arguing that the corporation is a person in law but not in fact.[94] In one English precedent of interest to media history, *Gramophone and Typewriter, Ltd. v. Stanley* (1906), where an English corporation (Gramophone and Typewriter) fully owned a German company (Deutsche Grammophon Aktiengesellschaft), Wormser returned veil piercing to the level of parent and subsidiary by explaining how English courts rejected even the family resemblance of signifier to signified secured by financial control, not to say an organic bond, to preserve the dependent entity's legal autonomy.[95] In this and other cases, Wormser argued, corporate personhood was a "useful" metaphor, nothing more, and should not be misused to deceive or defraud.[96]

Noting its author's rejection of organicist "excesses" like assigning corporate genders (male for the state, female for the church), Stefan Andriopoulos has shown the interdependence of Gierke's theory of real aggregate personality and literary fiction. By arguing that they were "possessed" by a kind of corporate demon, individual corporate agents could claim innocence before the court; thus personified, corporations were comparable to those "invisible supernatural agents" conjured by fantastical literature and spirit photography.[97] Like demons but also like colleges, corporations outlived their mortal members. Nonetheless, behind the corporate veil was gender, and before it stood race. In the American doctrine, the "veil" feminized the figure, leaving the "piercing" to be done by a jurisprudential patriarchy, which in Wormser's telling was unmistakably white.[98] In 1927, a year after Judge Cardozo warned against misty metaphors, John Dewey recommended that readers of the *Yale Law Journal* dispense with the metaphor altogether and, heeding the advice of Charles Sanders Peirce, consider only the corporate person's "effects"; or, as Dewey put it, "what—it—does."[99] What does the corporate person do? As we have seen, it loves and is loved. For this reason, under antebellum historical conditions the figure bifurcated into *both* Poe's Helen and Alma Mater. Just as the metaphor of "piercing the corporate veil" performatively reinscribed the patriarch, so too was the fictional corporate person a real being conjured by collegiate readers of the ancient classics—young white men in love with machines.

2

GREEK LINES

The Geometry of Thought

The preceding chapter examined the chasm that opened up in early colleges between the study of classical languages and literatures and the demands of technological literacy. This chapter turns to the study of geometry at around the same time. With the gradual formalization of technical education during the middle of the nineteenth century came distinctions between alphanumeric and visual knowledge formats. A close look at one such distinction finds art and technics interacting to differentiate corporate bodies, as textual lines drew geometrical figures, and colleges became universities.

Scholars and teachers understood Euclidean geometry, too, as a classical language. At times, techniques for teaching geometry drew on techniques, like faculty psychology, associated with the study of Greek and Latin. At other times, especially when the design of machines was the object, the two sets of techniques diverged. The American descendants of Euclid thereby split into two distinct branches. Those trained to reason with text and number were aesthetes, tasteful citizen-subjects belonging to a governing class reproduced in the colleges. Others, trained to reason with visual figures, were technologists or engineers who designed instruments with grammars of their own. With few exceptions, prior to the Civil War women were denied formal access to either branch; instead they practiced visual taste in society and in the home. Architecture and its discourses provided one bridge.

Classical Architectures

The frontispiece of Louisa Caroline Tuthill's *History of Architecture from the Earliest Times; Its Present Condition in Europe and the United States* (1848) shows an engraved perspectival view of Girard Hall, the central building of the Girard College for Orphans, in Philadelphia, designed in a classical manner by Thomas Ustick Walter and completed that year in emulation of the Athenian Parthenon. On the title page, an epigraph opines: "Some pretend to judge of an individual by his handwriting; but I would rather say, 'show me his house.' "[1] The book, which Tuthill dedicated "To the Ladies of the United States of America, The Acknowledged Arbiters of Taste," is generally regarded as the first survey of architectural history written by an American author.[2] Apologizing for the limitations imposed by the vast scale of the enterprise, Tuthill asserts in her preface that "the study of ancient Architecture is the study of history." Historical study should be useful, she adds. Drawing on the authority of an "able writer" in the *Foreign Quarterly Review*, Tuthill avers that "*ladies* should cultivate a taste for Architecture" and inscribes her book to them. For painters, poets, sculptors, novelists, travel writers, and historians, "acquaintance with Architecture is "indispensable."[3]

2.1 Thomas Ustick Walter, Girard Hall, Girard College for Orphans, 1848. In Louisa Caroline Tuthill, *History of Architecture from the Earliest Times; Its Present Condition in Europe and the United States; with a Biography of Eminent Architects and a Glossary of Architectural Terms* (Philadelphia: Lindsay and Blakiston, 1848), frontis. Avery Architectural & Fine Arts Library, Columbia University.

For others still—specifically, "the young men of our country"—the recently codified architectural profession represents a respectable, even "lucrative" alternative to the traditionally learned professions of law, medicine, and the clergy.[4] To
these professionals, their patrons, and their wives, Tuthill provides abundant
examples for emulation, finely illustrated in the 102 small woodcuts for which
the text periodically makes way, and the forty-six larger engravings printed on
interleaved plates. Nonetheless, she admits that practical limitations prevent her
from offering a full selection of worthy buildings from the American context.
Instead, "the few specimens given, may be compared to those which a lecturer
on science collects upon his table, merely for illustration."[5]

We can recognize this "lecturer on science" as Benjamin Silliman, whose
demonstrations at New Haven's Franklin Institute Tuthill, a prolific author of
etiquette manuals who ran a "French and English School" for "Young Ladies,"
required her own students to attend. But the pedagogical orientation of
Tuthill's treatise is qualified by that fact that, as she acknowledged, portions of
it had been published anonymously some years earlier as *Architecture: Part I,
Ancient Architecture* (1831), a book that is sometimes misattributed to its publisher, Hezekiah Howe. Introducing that volume to a "youthful reader," Tuthill
suggested that, though not originally intended as a "school-book," it "would
be a suitable class-book for older scholars to read in school."[6] This might be
enough to conclude that the ultimate version was dedicated simply to cultivating the tastes of elite male and female readers under the supervision of their
mothers. But the earlier work's characterization as a "class-book" introduces
a new possibility. Referring to the rote procedures for acquiring literacy still
dominant at the time, Tuthill argued that, while class-books used in this way
might aid in developing "pronunciation, emphasis, tone, &c.," they ought also
to impart "valuable information" that could be reinforced by questions posed by
the instructor, a list of which she helpfully provided as an appendix.[7]

In this regard, Tuthill's *History of Architecture from the Earliest Times* is an
object lesson, a demonstration that trains its readers in nonalphabetic, synthetic visual literacy rather than simply taste. In its linearity, its historicism, and
its reliance on narrative, such literacy differs from that presupposed by architectural pattern books of the time, which builders consulted for construction
details and ornament.[8] Nor are its techniques identical with a literacy that for
men would culminate in the recitation of classical verse at Yale, or for women,
in the New Haven parlors frequented by Tuthill and her circle.[9] Nor does the
Hellenic austerity of Walter's Girard Hall appear solely as an ideal to be emu-
lated. More structurally, visual literacy appears at the provisional end of a developmental sequence, as a telos.

The "earliest times" in Tuthill's title indicate that this is an origin story
linked to other stories with which its author likely became familiar in her

days spent researching the book in the personal library of the New Haven architect Ithiel Town.[10] The *History's* first chapter, on the "origin and progress of architecture," cites the art of building as proxy for the enigmas of human development: "It matters not, in this connexion, indeed it is out of our province, to discuss the vexed question of man's progress. Art is progressive."[11] Tuthill's *History* plots a line, point by point, through a series of stages that, in her reading, will have been self-evident. She begins where she is, in a settler colony refigured as a North American version of the abbé Laugier's Eden, with Native American wigwams reproducing the natural shelter of the forest. From there, "the primitive huts of the [African] Caffres, advance one step farther." Thence to tents, "among the earliest habitations," providing shelter to the exiled Israelites and monumentalized in the Tabernacle, the apotheosis of which in a further American variation on Laugier was the Indigenous oblong house, or log cabin, where trabeated frame construction finally converted trees into posts with a roof pitched over them: "The most splendid Grecian temple is only an ornamented copy of the oblong house with its upright posts."[12]

Periclean Athens is just another step along the way, albeit a decisive one. Its normative status is masked by Tuthill's concluding stylistic recommendations: Gothic for churches, Greek for civic buildings, Egyptian for cemeteries. Drawing mainly on the published correspondence of travelers and conquerors along with some archaeological sources, Tuthill arrives in Athens only after an epistolary tour of the monuments of Egypt, India, Persia, Palestine, China, and aboriginal North America, followed by a brief Etruscan sojourn. Her chapter on Greece (nine out of twenty-eight) begins with an exclamation: "Greece—pride of the world!" This she follows incongruously with the concluding lines of John Gardiner Calkins Brainard's "Jerusalem" of 1824:

> Though broken is each consecrated shrine,
> Though crushed and ruined all

Tuthill interrupts the poem's conclusion regarding the divinity of broken shrines (Solomon's Temple) to add that, "yet, every age shall own thee as the *alma mater* of poetry, eloquence, sculpture, and architecture."[13]

The American travel writer Clara Erskine Clement Waters later corrected Tuthill's elision in her own history of architecture "for beginners and students" by reproducing the two concluding stanzas of Brainard's poem in their entirety as she plotted a pedagogical line from Judea to Greece through the Mediterranean ruins.[14] But already for Tuthill writing for young readers, Greece was a nourishing mother, an alma mater: a medium of learning, lineages, and story lines.

Tuthill's book combined the moral tenor of her own education at one or more New Haven private schools for girls with the lyceum-inspired utilitarianism of the home school she later set up for her own children and others.[15] In this regard, the book reproduced the syntax of the eight instruction manuals for an American *Bildung* that Tuthill published prior to writing her *History*, aimed at school-age girls and boys, with titles like *I Will Be a Lady* (1844), *I Will Be a Gentleman* (1845), and *The Boarding School Girl* (1848).[16] These etiquette manuals generally tell fictional coming-of-age tales that instruct by example. Their protagonists, usually young, well-to-do New Englanders, undergo life experiences large and small that set them on the path to a morally sound, socially acceptable usefulness. In all, Tuthill's books, like others of their time and genre, described and implemented a gendered division of intellectual and cultural labor among New England's governing classes. They reproduced in the finest detail the social norms of Protestant probity over which antebellum nation-building was draped. But they also subtly transformed those norms according to a teleology that, for all the eclecticism of her examples, began and ended with Greece. For the female readers of Tuthill's treatise on architecture, whose journey typically led from school to the literate household, taste remained a matter of exemplifying and reproducing moral lessons based on classical models. For those male readers for whom the journey led from school to college, taste became a matter of discerning between competing classical ideals.

Euclid

The most compelling historical writing on classical pedagogy and scholarship in antebellum American colleges and universities, such as Caroline Winterer's *The Culture of Classicism* (2002), has mainly to do with the study and teaching of Greek and Latin letters.[17] Comparatively little has been written about the study and teaching of another form of classical learning lurking within Tuthill's illustrations, Euclidean geometry, prior knowledge of which became a requirement for admission to Harvard College in 1844.[18] In particular, the role played by visual figures as well as by their suppression in the cultivation of deductive reasoning deserves our attention, especially when considering what Winterer calls a midcentury transition from "words to worlds," or from a textual to a cultural approach to the ancients in the midst, as she says, "of troubling economic changes that demoted classical learning in favor of utilitarian knowledge."[19] Tuthill's *History* belonged to this context, and beside its treatment of ancient Greece as the alma mater of artistic taste, typical for its time, lies an encounter with Euclid that elucidates tensions in collegiate education related to the moral training required by industrial capital.

Euclid's *Elements*, which had been used in translation at Harvard and Yale since the early eighteenth century, entered American colleges as training in deductive, propositional reasoning for a male governing class conditioned, as J. G. A. Pocock has shown for ancient letters, into a civic humanism based on Machiavellian virtue.[20] As a figure like Thomas Jefferson suggests, this classical humanism had a strong utilitarian cast, to the extent that by the early nineteenth century what amounts to an epistemic breach between virtue and utility had opened up on college campuses. Euclidean geometry, once the very model of humanistic, logical deduction but also a source of ethno-national, racial pathos (for Jefferson, comprehension of Euclid was a measure of racial superiority), now became identified with mechanistic instrumentality.[21] Toward the end of this process, a minor document of architectural Hellenism seemingly unrelated to Tuthill's treatise offers an indication of the pertinent give-and-take.

In June and July of 1861, at the outset of the Civil War, the Harvard educated architect Henry Van Brunt published a two-part article in the *Atlantic Monthly* titled "Greek Lines," which argued for the superiority of ancient Greek architecture over later imitations on the basis of its suppleness and restrained fluidity of line.[22] In the wake of eighteenth-century archaeological reconstructions, Van Brunt writes, "a fever arose to reproduce Greek temples" that aroused hopes of renewal but devolved into "mere imitation."[23] Nevertheless, he argues, stimulated by the neoclassical innovations of the Prussian architect Karl Friedrich Schinkel, and especially of the dissident French academician and connoisseur of ancient polychromy, Henri Labrouste, by the late 1850s "refining tendencies of the abstract lines of Greece" had begun to propagate along the new boulevards of Baron von Haussmann's Paris.[24]

Van Brunt's distinction between "cold" academic Hellenism and vitalist élan conforms to a dichotomy in classical studies that Friedrich Nietzsche would shortly characterize as a struggle between Apollonian and Dionysian modes.[25] In Van Brunt's version, "true Lines of Grace and Beauty," which Van Brunt described repeatedly as "abstract" and which allude to the painter William Hogarth's "lines of beauty" (1753), could only be derived from the Greek archetype. This, he emphasized, was "not a *precise* and *exact* line, like a formula of mathematics" ready to be mechanically reproduced, as with the all-purpose ellipses that had been proposed by the Scottish decorator David Ramsey Hay. As Van Brunt put it, sardonically: "Ideal Beauty can be hatched from no geometrical eggs."[26]

Textbooks

Van Brunt was enrolled at Harvard from 1850 to 1854, after which he apprenticed in the architectural atelier of Richard Morris Hunt. There, he became intimately acquainted with the architecture of the French École des Beaux-Arts, where Hunt had trained. It was primarily in reaction against this architecture that Van Brunt sought to recover the Greek ideal. But arguably, it was during his earlier Harvard years that Van Brunt, who was only twenty-nine years of age when he wrote "Greek Lines," acquired his vitalist appreciation of Hellenic lineaments through an encounter with the institutionalization of mathematics as an academic discipline.

Having taken a leave of absence from Harvard in his second semester due to a serious football injury, Van Brunt was bedridden for almost a year in the family home at the Portsmouth Navy Yard, where his father was commander. There he began a diary, in which he reported that, to keep up with his course-work, the Harvard registrar had recommended that he master material in Greek (Sophocles), Latin (Cicero), Geometry (Peirce), Natural History (Gray), History (Tytler), as well as French.[27] All of these were standard texts for sophomore year recitations and lectures at Harvard in the early 1850s.[28] Receiving them, Van Brunt singled out an "awfully mysterious work, rejoicing in the euphonious though awful appellation of 'Pierce's [sic] Curves, Functions, and Forces.' "[29] Faced with this work, he confessed that straightaway he took up A. F. Tytler's history instead. Nonetheless, with a tutor's help Van Brunt covered all the required texts and returned to Harvard for examination that fall. Describing the oral mathematics exam with self-deprecating humor, he expressed relief that it was the mathematics tutor, Charles Francis Choate, and not Benjamin Peirce, the formidable author of *Curves, Functions, and Forces*, who examined him. Of Peirce's textbook, Van Brunt noted in his diary: "How often it is that sublime and magnificent exordiums are but the introducers of mean & insignificant conclusions."[30] Later, when informed that he had passed his exams, Van Brunt responded with a request for more Greek literary works in lieu of what he called the "muddy fen of Curves and Functions."[31]

Back at Harvard in November 1853, Van Brunt began his turn toward architecture with a different sort of reading, of the just-published *The History and Rudiments of Architecture* edited by the "architect, engineer, and mechanician" John Bullock.[32] Van Brunt's pathway toward this text, which advertised itself to "Architects, Builders, Draughtsmen, Machinists, Engineers, and Mechanics," most likely did not pass through the Harvard curriculum. The history of the visual arts and architecture was not formally taught at Harvard until two decades later, when Charles Eliot Norton became the university's first lecturer in the fine arts in 1873. Nor did Van Brunt have any options for professional study in architecture upon graduation, as formal academic training in the field would not be instituted until over a decade later.

As was customary for architecture chapbooks and builder's manuals at the time, the edited volume that Van Brunt read began with a treatment of the classical orders, in this case by the English architectural critic William Henry Leeds, who had published his own popular treatise on the orders, *Rudimentary*

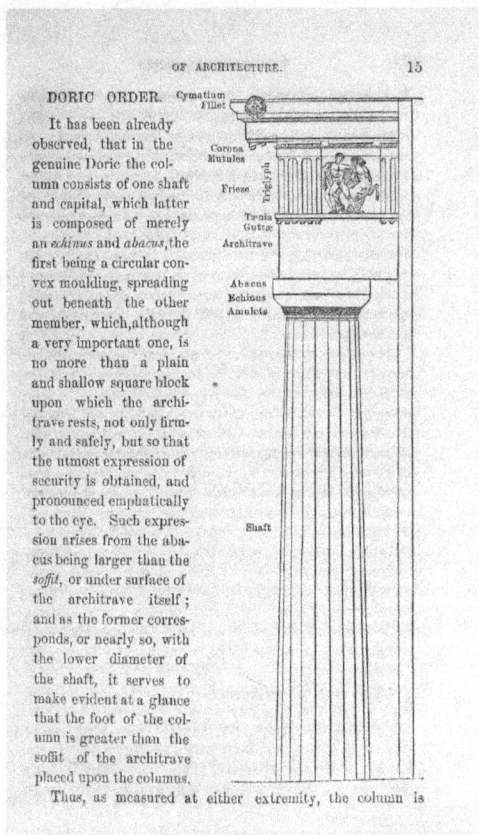

The figure reproduces a printed book page reading:

> OF ARCHITECTURE. 15
>
> DORIC ORDER. Cymatium Fillet
>
> It has been already observed, that in the genuine Doric the column consists of one shaft and capital, which latter is composed of merely an *echinus* and *abacus*, the first being a circular convex moulding, spreading out beneath the other member, which, although a very important one, is no more than a plain and shallow square block upon which the architrave rests, not only firmly and safely, but so that the utmost expression of security is obtained, and pronounced emphatically to the eye. Such expression arises from the abacus being larger than the *soffit*, or under surface of the architrave itself; and as the former corresponds, or nearly so, with the lower diameter of the shaft, it serves to make evident at a glance that the foot of the column is greater than the soffit of the architrave placed upon the column.
>
> Thus, as measured at either extremity, the column is
>
> (labels: Corona, Mutules, Frieze, Triglyph, Trenia, Guttæ, Architrave, Abacus, Echinus, Annulets, Shaft)

2.2 William Henry Leeds, "Doric Order," in *The History and Rudiments of Architecture*, ed. John Bullock, (New York: Stringer & Townsend, 1853), 15.

Architecture: For the Use of Beginners, in London in 1848. When it appeared in 1853, Bullock's edited volume was only the second treatise on architectural history published in the United States, having been preceded five years earlier by Tuthill's *History*.[33]

Of Bullock's volume, Van Brunt wryly noted "the usual display of pedantry and affectation that accompanies treatises on art, especially this art" (architecture), which suggests that this was not the first architectural treatise he had read. While conceivable, it is unlikely that Van Brunt had read Tuthill's history, addressed as it was to "To the Ladies of the United States of America." Reproducing the division of labor by gender, Bullock emphasized practical application and Tuthill, taste. Nevertheless, the two books were connected. When Tuthill asserted in her preface that "*ladies* should cultivate a taste for Architecture," the unnamed "able writer" on whom she drew was none other than Bullock's lead author, W. H. Leeds.[34] Van Brunt, a Victorian New Englander whose diary suggests that he regarded women as ornamental service providers and Harriet Beecher Stowe's *Uncle Tom's Cabin* as a betrayal, was not an emancipated reader.[35] Even so, his reading and Tuthill's writing belong to a larger modulation in antebellum classicism than we might expect.

Primers in the history and principles of architecture published by authors like Tuthill's and Bullock's shared source, Leeds, were intended to educate the tastes and inform the patronage of a lay public according to gender. Where Tuthill addressed a feminized reading public, Bullock's edited volume, to which Leeds contributed and which Van Brunt read, was addressed to implicitly male architects, builders, and engineers. It therefore belonged to a different group of introductory texts circulating in the anglophone Republic of Letters. This group split further into two branches that corresponded with the breach opening up between the moral and instrumental use of classical reason: textbooks addressed to high school or college students, including future academics, and treatises and manuals addressed to professionals, like architects and engineers, and their apprentices. Around 1850, these two readerships were generally separated by social class. Sometimes they coexisted in a single individual, as in the case of Van Brunt. Like Van Brunt, one group were students or future students in the liberal colleges, and the other were practitioners and apprentices, like the "architects, builders, draughtsmen, machinists, engineers, and mechanics" to whom Bullock addressed his volume. Even while enrolled at Harvard and studying classical languages, Van Brunt was also among this latter group, as were his future partner William Ware and the architect Henry Hobson Richardson, both of whom graduated from Harvard shortly after Van Brunt did. With these differences and overlaps in mind, we could follow the popular cultivation of taste and patronage alongside the training of professionals, as the historical study of architecture as one among the fine arts was institutionalized as an academic discipline in the United States. But remembering those books that the Harvard curriculum placed before Van Brunt that he *did not* read, or read only reluctantly, takes us in a notably different direction.

As a freshman, Van Brunt likely did receive mathematics instruction from Benjamin Peirce, the stern author of *Curves, Functions, and Forces.* Peirce, the father of the philosopher Charles Sanders Peirce, was a distinguished mathematician and beginning in 1842 he was Perkins Professor of Astronomy and Mathematics at Harvard. Since 1838, Harvard freshmen had begun their mathematics instruction with recitations from Peirce's *Elementary Treatise on Plane and Solid Geometry* (1837), which Van Brunt would have used both at college and early in his convalescence.[36] Though Peirce writes of the superiority of the differential calculus over the "ancient rigor of demonstration," including the "rigor of ancient Geometry," he does not introduce the calculus until the second half of the second, sophomore textbook.[37] Still, both of Peirce's geometry textbooks sought to modernize the mathematics curriculum. As the Brown University mathematician Raymond Clare Archibald later put it: "Mathematical research in American universities began with Benjamin Peirce."[38] To which Archibald added the observation of Peirce's student, the astronomer and mathematician Simon Newcomb, that "in the geometry, especially, the short and terse forms of mathematical thought and expression, natural to the mathematician, were substituted for the minute demonstrations of Euclid."[39] In other words, Peirce's geometry textbooks replaced Euclidean deduction, which was formerly among the governing languages of civic reason, with a form of algebraic reasoning more suited, it was thought, to training mathematicians.

When first assigned in 1838, Peirce's freshman geometry textbook took the place of Timothy Walker's *Elements of Geometry with Practical Applications, for the Use of Schools* (1829), which was required of Harvard freshmen beginning in 1832. Unlike Peirce, Walker was not a specialist, and where Peirce linked his textbook to higher mathematics, Walker intended his only for "young pupils" and included "practical applications" in his appendix. Both, however, expressed geometric relationships in algebraic terms. Unlike most existing editions of Euclid, both relegated visual figures, which are referenced systematically in the text, to fold-out appendices at the back of their respective volumes.

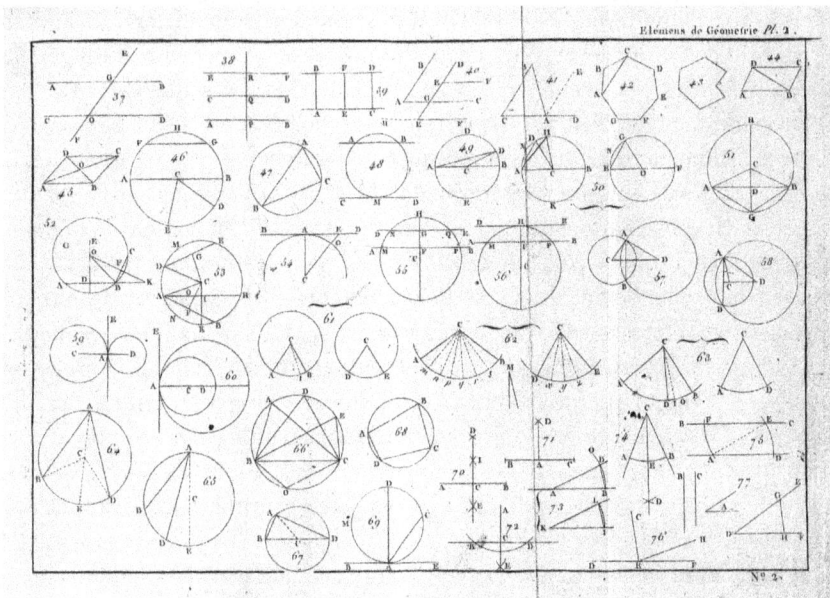

2.3 Adrien-Marie Legendre, *Éléments de géometrie, avec des notes* (Paris: Formin Didot, 1794). Plate 2.

This preference for algebraic expression, Walker wrote, had been a sign of modernity since Descartes: "The ancients were unacquainted with Algebra. Accordingly Euclid was obliged to demonstrate the laws of proportion *geometrically.*"[40]

Opposing alphanumeric, algebraic expression to mixed textual-visual "geometric" expression, both Walker and Peirce were following the revision of Euclid by the French mathematician Adrien-Marie Legendre, in *Éléments de Géométrie* of 1794, which had been translated in 1819 by Harvard mathematics professor John Farrar and was required for freshmen during the 1820s. Legendre, too, took algebraic expression to be a mark of modernity and an improvement over the Euclidean original. His *Éléments*, which also grouped diagrams referenced textually in an appendix, was probably the most influential revision of Euclid since the latter began to circulate in print during the late fifteenth century.[41] Although the nineteenth century saw its share of illustrated Euclids, including a color-coded 1847 edition by Oliver Byrne, college and university curricula increasingly favored the alphanumeric format inaugurated by Legendre, which replaced Euclid's "geometric" demonstrations with their algebraic equivalents.

The Military-Geometrical Complex: West Point and Rensselaer

Preceded by reprints of two recent Euclids by Scots mathematicians Robert Simson and John Playfair, both of which included figures in the text, Legendre's revision did not, however, only enter the American curriculum through the classical colleges. It also entered through the United States Military Academy at West Point, founded in 1802.[42] In 1815, just as scholars like Edward Everett and George Ticknor were traveling to Göttingen in search of the new German classicism, U.S. President James Madison and Secretary of War James Monroe dispatched Sylvanus Thayer, an engineer officer and West Point graduate, to France to study French military technologies and to purchase books for the academy. There, Thayer studied at the École Polytechnique and visited French military installations, returning to West Point a year later with about a thousand books on technical subjects, along with five hundred charts and maps. Among those books was a French edition of Legendre.[43] This was probably the edition used by Claudius Crozet, an artillery officer under Napoléon and graduate of the École, who introduced Legendre's Euclid and other French mathematics treatises, including Gaspard Monge's descriptive geometry, into the West Point curriculum as part of an effort to balance practical application with reasoned, public argumentation. But although the West Point curriculum also required instruction in the French language to facilitate such learning, Crozet found the students unable to read what few textbooks were available. As one of his students later recalled, "geometry is not a thing to be taught orally."[44] An exasperated Crozet therefore had recourse to the French technique of drawing figures with chalk on a painted blackboard made by a local carpenter, in the first documented use of these materials in American collegiate mathematics teaching.[45]

In 1828 Charles Davies, an Academy graduate, professor of mathematics, and prolific textbook author, adapted an earlier translation of Legendre for use at West Point and in the process, restored figures to the text. Davies's reasoning was not that these offered short cuts for practically minded officers-in-training. Rather, it was that Legendre and his translators, in referring textually to the diagrammatic figures appended to their works, undertook a regrettable "departure from the method of Euclid" that, he claimed, eased comprehension for beginning students. "But," as Davies put it, "in avoiding this difficulty, and thus lessening, at first, the intellectual labour, the faculty of abstraction, which is one of the primary objects of the study of Geometry to strengthen, remains, to a certain extent, unimproved."[46] His solution was to state each proposition without reference to any figure and follow that statement with a visual demonstration.

2.4 Adrien-Marie Legendre, *Elements of Geometry and Trigonometry*, 5th ed., ed. Charles Davies, trans. David Brewster [1828] (New York: Wiley & Long; Collins, Keene, 1835). Page spread from Book 3, "The Circle, and the Measurement of Angles," 48–49.

For example, where Farrar's Euclid presents the theorem that the sum of two adjacent angles, ACD and BCD, produced by the intersection of two straight lines, AB and CD, is equal to two right angles, Davies refers only to the "two adjacent angles" resulting from "one straight line" meeting "another."[47] But where Farrar located the visual figures referenced in an appendix at the back of his volume, Davies incorporated them into the text of the demonstrations that follow each proposition.

In his 1862 edition of Legendre's *Elements*, which by now appeared under his own name, Davies explained that in contrast to the French original (and by extension, previous English translations) "each proposition is first enunciated in general terms, and afterwards, with reference to a particular figure, that figure being taken to represent any one of the class to which it belongs. By this arrangement, the difficulty experienced by beginners in comprehending abstract truths, is lessened, without in any manner impairing the generality of the truths evolved."[48] As Amy Ackerberg-Hastings has shown, Davies, like many early-nineteenth-century educators, aimed his teaching at the cultivation of "mental discipline" also valued by the authors of the 1828 Yale Report. His late (1862) acknowledgement of the role of the figures that had been there all along may have been a compromise. Davies repeatedly argued that the verbal statement of general principles represented the utmost in abstraction, hence its mastery entails the utmost discipline.[49] Pedagogically, he argued that such abstract reasoning must be achieved incrementally and so included the diagrams as an enabling step. But the reverse is also possible. Since their introduction, geometry textbooks had orchestrated daily classroom performances in which students redrew their figures from memory on blackboards. By all accounts, as a teacher Davies was also a "clear and logical demonstrator" and an adept user of blackboards. In restoring the Euclidean diagrams to the alphabetized, algebraic texts of high school and college geometry, far from providing a merely utilitarian stepping stone to the abstract, humanistic reasoning of Hellenic classicism, Davies was giving visual expression to what Edward W. Stevens has called the "grammar of the machine."[50]

Stevens has shown how visual literacy formed an important basis for technical education in the early nineteenth century. He has also shown how visually mediated geometrical learning was understood among feminists as a means of "proving the equality of men and women in mental discipline."[51] In restoring diagrams to Euclid's text Davies encouraged, intentionally or not, a form of abstract reasoning unavailable through the rote memorization still practiced in most college recitations but also distinct from the abstraction favored by professional mathematicians like Peirce, for whom algebra, not geometry, led to the calculus. The quest for abstraction, then, appears on both sides. On the one side it was a motive for rendering geometrical figures algebraically and thus subordinating diagrams to text. While on the other, greater abstraction was a reason to restore those diagrams to the geometrical text, to recover Euclidean rigor through the visual demonstration of proofs on West Point's blackboards. The first approach, analytic in form, centered on colleges like Harvard that were gradually becoming universities, where mathematics was being professionalized as an academic discipline; the second, more "synthetic" pedagogy, which balanced reasoned argument *against* instrumentality, derived from the more utilitarian context of the engineering school and later, polytechnic, as a form of humanistic learning in translation.[52]

By 1854, when Van Brunt graduated from Harvard, Davies's illustrated Legendre, which Davies would eventually label as belonging to his "West Point Course," was required for the new degree in civil engineering at the recently reorganized Rensselaer Polytechnic Institute.[53] Led by the geologist and naturalist Amos Eaton, the institute had been established in Troy, New York in 1825 as the Rensselaer School for the practical education of, as its by-laws put it, "the sons and daughters of Farmers and Mechanics," in the *"application of science to the common purposes of life."*[54] By midcentury Rensselaer had become the country's first polytechnic, well before the establishment of the Massachusetts Institute of Technology and at roughly the same time that Harvard opened its practically oriented Lawrence Scientific School. Rensselaer's pedagogical model, which was indebted to the Rousseauian object lessons elaborated by the Swiss pedagogical reformer Johan Pestalozzi, became known as the "Rensselaerean plan." Following professorial lectures from textbooks like Davies, students were required to teach one another extemporaneously from notes in break-out sessions led by their seniors, who were known as "Repeaters."[55] This hands-on repetition favored inductive learning over strict memorization. Inherently visual, it grew into the ample use of blackboard demonstrations, as blackboards, now available commercially in natural or painted ("liquid") slate, became ubiquitous features of mathematics and engineering classrooms, often encircling the room to allow for a running narrative.[56] In these new formats for technical education, geometrical diagrams returned as visual keys to the "grammar of the machine." Understood first as the very mark of the reasoning, classical mind, only to be displaced by algebraic, alphanumeric expression seeking the abstractions of professionalized mathematics, classical learning, far from being opposed to utilitarian knowledge, had now become central to it, visually rather than verbally.

The media that matter most here are printed books and chalk-marked blackboards, alphanumeric characters and geometrical diagrams. But there are also those elusive "Greek lines" that Van Brunt called "abstract," which, as we will now see from his architecture, were transferrable across the historical styles inventoried by writers like Louisa Tuthill. Repeating the language of the mathematics that he shunned, which alternated between algebraic (or verbal) abstraction and geometric (or visual) abstraction, Van Brunt took abstraction as such

2.5 Descriptive geometry class, main building, Rensselaer Polytechnic Institute, 1870s. Institute Archives and Special Collections, Rensselaer Polytechnic Institute, Troy, NY.

for granted. In this, the supple, non-Euclidean lines he sought traced a dialectical alliance with the mechanized world of industrial capitalism. For what else were these incalculable, living lines but lines drawn by an *architect*, not yet consecrated by the university but differentiated institutionally, socially, and economically from the engineers, "sons and daughters of Farmers and Mechanics," drawing and redrawing geometrical figures on polytechnic blackboards? Even as those same engineers, borrowing lines from textbooks descended from Euclid, drew machines unthinkable in purely textual form until, that is, digital scripts took over.

Commemoration

In 1865, Henry Van Brunt returned to Harvard with his partner William Ware (class of 1852) to participate in a competition for the design of the building that would become Memorial Hall. There was very little that was Greek about Ware and Van Brunt's winning design, an eclectic mix of Gothic and Victorian motifs assembled around a tall, off-center bell tower to which a clock was later added. Nor were the austerely sinuous, non-Euclidean lines that Van Brunt had celebrated in his essay a few years earlier very much in evidence. A closer look at the building's details, however, suggests surprising continuity with the geometrical imaginary that Van Brunt cultivated against the grain of his student years.

2.6 Ware and Van Brunt, Memorial Hall, Harvard University, 1878. Detroit Publishing, 1904. Harvard University Archives.

Distinguishing Greek architects from Greek philosophers, Van Brunt had complained to readers of the *Atlantic Monthly* in 1861 that:

The porches where Callicrates, Hermogenes, and Callimachus walked were guarded by no such Cerberus as the disciples of Plato encountered at the entrance of the groves of the Academy,—

"Οὐδεὶς ἀγεωμέτρητος εἰσίτω,"

"Let no one ignorant of Geometry enter here";

but the divine Aphrodite welcomed all mankind to the tender teachings of the Wild Acanthus, the Honeysuckle, and the Sea-Shell, and all the deep utterances of boundless Beauty.

Truly, it is sad and dispiriting to the artist to find that all modern aesthetical writings limit and straiten the free walks of highest Art with strict laws deduced from rigid science, with mathematical proportions and the formal restrictions of fixed lines and curves, nicely adapted from the frigidities of Euclid. The line A B must equal the line C D; somewhere in space must be found the centre or the focus of every curve; and every angle must subtend a certain arc, to be easily found on reference to the tables of the text-books.[57]

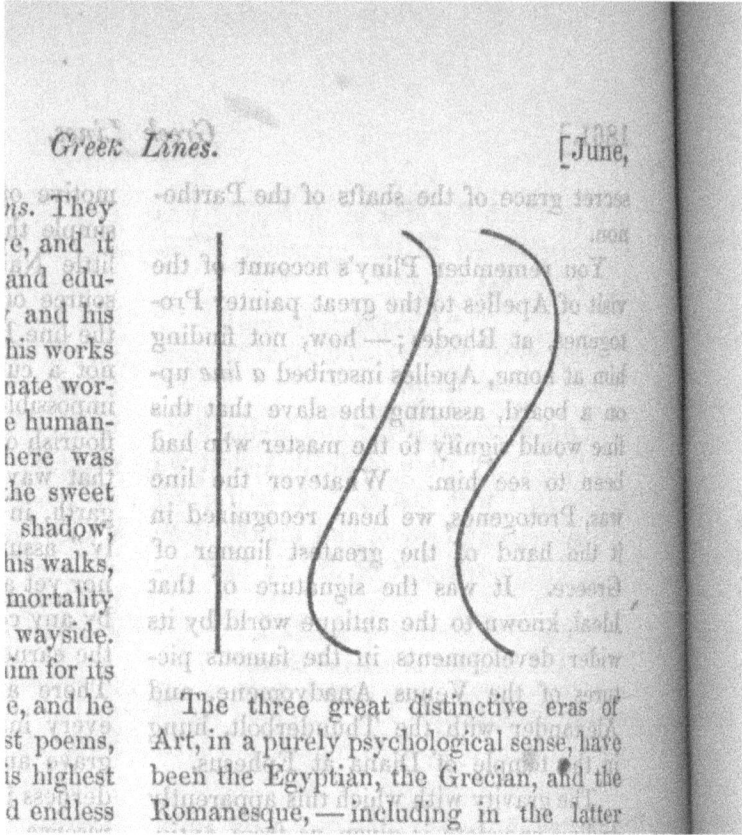

2.7 Henry Van Brunt, "Greek Lines," part 1, *Atlantic Monthly* 7, no. 44 (June 1861), diagram, 662.

In practice, accessing Aphrodite's "boundless Beauty" did not mean reviving the ancient Greek forms drawn from "text-books," their laws and proportions deduced from "the frigidities of Euclid." Like Tuthill's, Van Brunt's aesthetic discourse was historicist; artistic styles were for him relative expressions of epochal tendencies and constraints rather than absolute models. "Greek Lines" summarized this with a succinct diagram showing three types of lines, one straight and two curved. These corresponded, Van Brunt argued, with three epochs of art: Egyptian, in its deathly stillness; Greek, in its graceful restraint; and Romanesque, in its impulsive sensuousness. To each of these epochs Van Brunt assigned an ethos: "destiny," "love," and "life" respectively.[58] Where in the Greek he found an awakening from the Egyptian resignation to mortality, in the Romanesque, beginning with ancient Rome and extending through the medieval period and into the Renaissance, he found both licentious indulgence and slavish reduction to academic formulae. The modern task, therefore, was to reanimate the line, to rescue it from formalization without succumbing to arbitrariness. The twofold problem was academic systematization and an eclecticism stemming from an excess of archaeological information, an easily accessible, widely published inventory of architectural forms "which undeniably have more *knowledge* than *love* in them."[59] Finding hope in the German Romantics Schinkel and Leo Von Klenze, and in their French counterpart Labrouste, Van Brunt ruminated over the circumstances that might give birth to the synthesis of love and life that he sought.

He found these on the Parisian boulevards but also in funerary monuments.[60] Of the latter, the most satisfactory example according to Van Brunt was the tomb designed in 1844 by Labrouste's colleague, Simon-Claude Constant-Dufeux, for the admiral and explorer Jules Dumont d'Urville in the Parisian Cimetière du Sud (Montparnasse). Widely admired for its daring anti-academicism, Constant-Dufeux's figural, phallic monument contained, for his American interpreter, "in its outlines a symbolic expression of human life, death, and immortality, and in its details an architectural version of the character and public services of the distinguished deceased." Tipped by a parabolic cone, the monument's "outlines" and other formal properties were as important as were its representational motifs. The "symbolic expression" Van Brunt sought was therefore not strictly based on iconographical conventions accessible to the learned viewer. Rather, the d'Urville tomb was a symbol of a symbol. In the tomb's coloring, chiseled reliefs, and proportions Van Brunt thought he had found "one of the most expressive elegies ever written."[61]

These lines were published in mid-1861, shortly after the Civil War's first battles, but too early to anticipate the full scope of the impending tragedy. The aspect of Ware and Van Brunt's Memorial Hall that resonated most with their spirit was the Memorial Transept that gave the building its name, which commemorated 136 Harvard alumni and students who died serving with the Union army. Inside, restrained Gothic Revival ornamentation, executed in black walnut and jarringly proportioned, set a darkly reserved tone that contrasted starkly with the buildings ebullient, polychromatic brick exterior. But the transept's most striking feature was the row of twenty-eight white marble plaques lining its four walls just above eye level. On the plaques were engraved the names of the deceased soldiers, three to six per plaque, organized by school, with class year, date of death, and battle (when known). The lettering on the memorial plaques, like that of the larger inscriptions arrayed above them, was colored a dark crimson, a color not yet identified with Harvard, that also enframed the white marble. The wooden trefoil arch around each interrupts a painted, stylized Greco-Roman entablature that seems to run continuously behind. Though the high wooden vaulting and the stained glass rose windows and surrounding tracery at either end accentuated a certain

2.8 Ware and Van Brunt, Memorial Hall, Harvard University, 1878. Memorial transept. Internet Archive via Alamy.

Gothic piety, the marbled row of plaques with lists of crimson-tinted names, as well as the expanse of blank wall above them, referred unmistakably to the façades of Labrouste's Bibliothèque Ste. Geneviève in Paris, completed in 1850.

Executed in a style that came to be known as Neo-Grèc for its free interpretation of Hellenic precedent, Labrouste's library is entirely clad on its piano nobile with a regular series of arched stone tablets on which were engraved, in blood-red lettering, the names of prominent authors, from Moses to Berzelius. These exterior lists corresponded in location to the interior book stacks that surrounded the great iron-vaulted reading room behind. The architectural historian Neil Levine has interpreted Labrouste's bibliographic façade, arranged in a tabloid format akin to newsprint, as a rejoinder to Victor Hugo's superordination of book to building— "This will kill that"—which already points toward a memorial function.[62]

The same year that Memorial Hall opened, 1877, Ware and Van Brunt completed an addition to Gore Hall, Harvard's first library (Richard Bond, 1841), making that Gothic Revival building the first in the country to include metal stacks to protect flammable books. A near contemporaneous description comes from Henry James who, in *The Bostonians* (1886), narrates a tour of the Harvard campus given by the feminist public speaker Verena Tarrant to Basil Ransom, her Mississippian suitor who had served in the Confederacy:

> The edifice [Gore Hall], a diminished copy of the chapel of King's College, at the greater Cambridge, is a rich and impressive institution; and as he [Ransom] stood there, in the bright, heated stillness, which seemed suffused with the odour of old print and old bindings, and looked up into the high, light vaults that hung over quiet book-laden galleries, alcoves and tables, and glazed cases where rarer treasures gleamed more vaguely, over busts of benefactors and portraits of worthies, bowed heads of working students and the gentle creak of passing messengers—as he took possession, in a comprehensive glance, of the wealth and wisdom of the place, he felt more than ever the soreness of an opportunity missed; but he abstained from expressing it (it was too deep for that), and in a moment Verena had introduced him to a young lady, a friend of hers, who, as she explained, was working on the catalogue, and whom she had asked for on entering the library, at a desk where another young lady was occupied. Miss Catching, the first-mentioned young lady, presented herself with promptness, offered Verena a low-toned but appreciative greeting, and, after a little, undertook to explain the mysteries of the catalogue, which consisted of a myriad little cards, disposed alphabetically in immense chests of drawers.[63]

Prior to the installation of electric lighting sometime in the 1880s, the "high, light vaults" Ransom admired were illuminated only by daylight, in silent remembrance of the 1764 fire in Harvard Hall that destroyed over five thousand books, which led to the exclusion of Gore Hall's "bright, heated stillness" from the incendiary gas light introduced to the campus in the 1850s.[64] The card catalogue, and the labor to which it corresponded (Miss Catching could have been a student of Louisa Tuthill's), were a sign of the building's modernity. But where the new card catalogue was a medium of scholarship, and hence belonged to the order of the university, the list of names at Memorial Hall, based on another, more monumental card catalogue, belonged to the order of the college. Harvard was a place, as James noted, where "benefactors" and "worthies" were well remembered in busts and building names. But his protagonists also bore witness to the more recent practice of commemorating the lives and actions of citizen-alumni in engraved lists.

The next stop on the campus tour for the faux-naïve Tarrant and her ex-Confederate suitor was Memorial Hall, where, James writes:

> Ransom and his companion wandered from one part of the building to another, and stayed their steps at several impressive points; but they lingered longest in the presence of the white, ranged tablets, each of which, in its proud, sad clearness, is inscribed with the name of a student-soldier. The effect of the place is singularly noble and solemn, and it is impossible to feel it without a lifting of the heart. . . .
>
> "It is very beautiful—but I think it is very dreadful!" This remark, from Verena, called back to the present. "It's a real sin to put up such a building, just to glorify a lot of bloodshed. If it wasn't so majestic, I would have pulled it down."[65]

As Reinhart Koselleck showed, modern war memorials are for the living, not the dead.[66] When colleges grew into universities, the corporate body lived on among the bodies of its members. Listing the dead reaffirmed that body's immortality. Into the 1890s campuses across the country struggled with how to commemorate those among them who lost their lives in what the Memorial Transept's central raised plaque called the "war for the preservation of the union." The Civil War would become the first modern conflict widely memorialized in lists like this.[67] As with the books in the library card catalogue, conjuring the corporate, collegiate body was becoming a matter of counting, name after name and line by line, in life and in death.

Van Brunt, an exponent of "love" (Greek lines) and "life" (the Romanesque), may have especially appreciated that the "majesty" of his eclectic building overcame Verena Tarrant's moral hesitation at the commemoration of mass bloodshed. No minimalist, he may also have appreciated James's prolix affect. Compare this scene to the words with which one critic commemorated Edgar Allan Poe one year after the poet's death in 1849:

> Briefly, [Poe] was what Napoleon named an ideologist—a man of ideas. He lived entirely apart from the solidities and realities of life: was an abstraction; thought, wrote, and dealt solely in abstractions. It is this which gives their peculiar feature to his writings. They have no color, but are in pure outline, delicately and accurately drawn, but altogether without the glow and pulse of humanity. His genius was mathematical, rather than pictorial or poetical. He demonstrates instead of painting. Selecting some quaint and abstruse theme, he proceeds to unfold it with the closeness, care, and demonstrative method of Euclid; and you have, to change the illustration, fireworks for fire; the appearance of water for water; and a great shadow in the place of an actual, moist, and thunder-bearing sky.[68]

Are the two so opposed, or has so much changed in thirty years? If Poe reduced the "glow and pulse of humanity" to "pure outline" as if writing from Plato's cave, had a new dialectic arisen from the killing fields listed on marble tablets at Harvard? Had not Van Brunt attempted to regain access, through the proliferation of post-Euclidean lineaments in Memorial Hall's Victorian excess, to the prewar world commemorated in the busts of "benefactors" and "worthies" lining Gore Hall? Despite Verena's reluctant, architecturally enabled accession to their presence, what were these lists but evidence of the futility of representation, the failure of the figural line to record the war's true, mathematical cost, enumerated here in series?

In 1897 West Point, which was much more evenly divided by the Southern states' secession, responded to the Civil War with a memorial of its own that

2.9 McKim, Mead & White, Battle Monument (Civil War Memorial), United States Military Academy at West Point, 1897. "The Work of Messrs. McKim, Mead & White," *Architectural Record* 20, no. 3 (September 1906): 268.

internalized the symbolic impasse recognized by Verena Tarrant: a freestanding Tuscan column designed by Stanford White of McKim, Mead & White, topped with a winged figure of Victory (later replaced by Fame), at the base of which were listed the names of 2,230 deceased members of the Union's Regular Army, differentiated by rank.[69] Although White's sober academicism contrasted with the predominantly Gothic Revival style of the West Point campus, it may be that commemorating the dead of mechanized warfare required something that presented the war's toll more dispassionately, with, as Poe's critic put it, the "closeness, care, and demonstrative method of Euclid." Despite appearances, Van Brunt (if not his academically more respectable partner, Ware) recognized the inversion, for whatever is elegiac in Memorial Hall is also mechanical.

What had changed since Poe's days of pining for "fair Greece" was the replacement, in limit cases like these, of poetic figures with lists as the bearers of cultural meaning. With Labrouste and even with Van Brunt despite himself, "Greek lines" were now matter-of-fact lines of text, alphanumeric lists made by humanists. During the Civil War, death became a matter of counting, and only recently have historians agreed upon an accurate tally of the bloodshed.[70] To this has now been added the problem of recovering the names of those on campus who had been subject to the war's chief catalyst, slavery, and reckoning with the legacy of those "benefactors" and "worthies" who maintained their brutal bondage. In the interim, notwithstanding Van Brunt's quest for a contour adequate to his times, the one-after-another iterations, of tablets and names without necessary end, adapted the "grammar of the machine" developed by engineers drawing Euclid to the commemorative temporalities of mechanization and of mechanized wars to come.

Part II
TEMPORALITIES

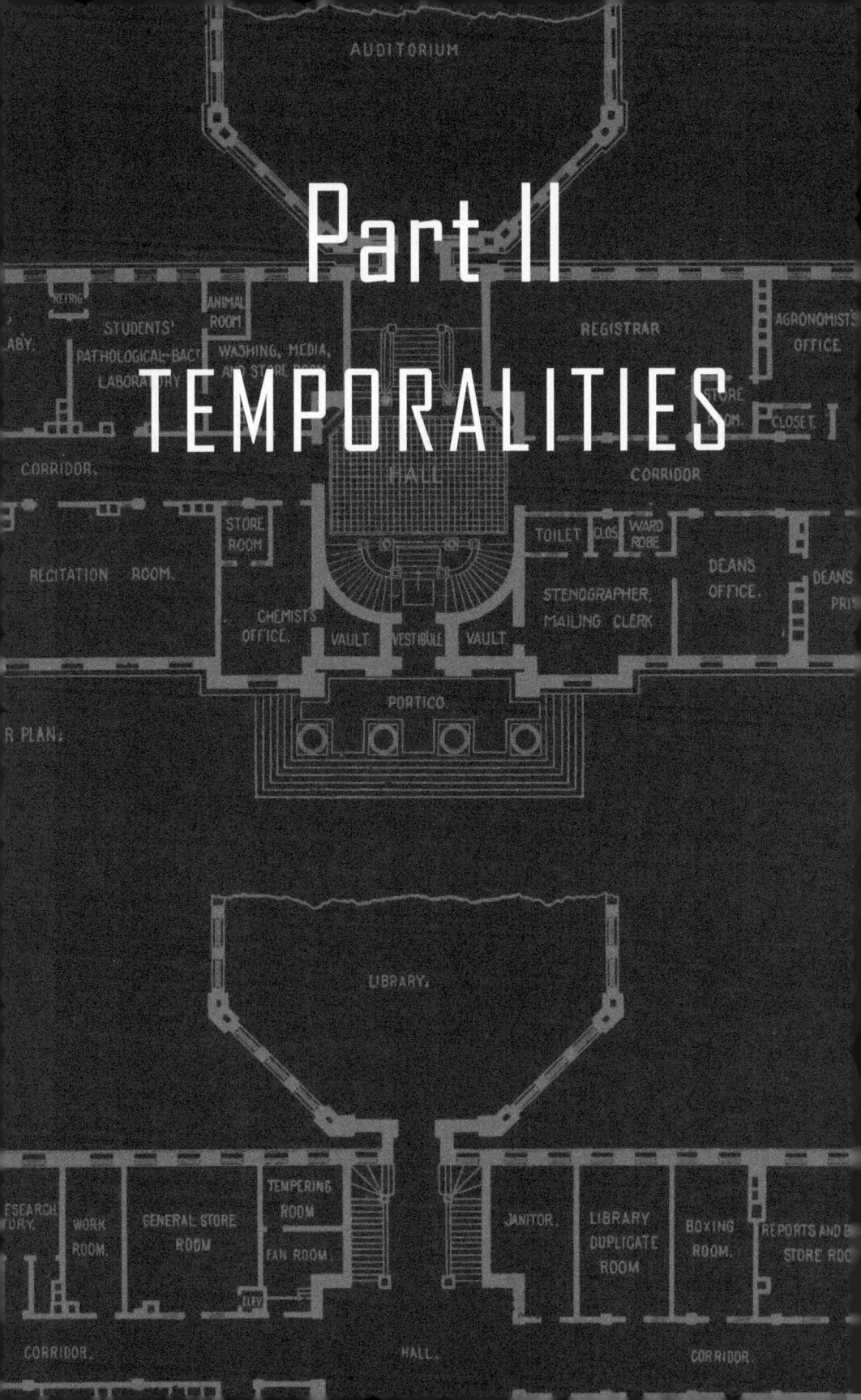

3

BRICKS AND STONES

Time-Based Media

A s access to higher education expanded in the later nineteenth century, and professional careers beckoned, classrooms became waiting rooms, and the rites of passage associated with college life split into specialized pathways. Personal growth, too, became a more inclusive project. But passage could also mean deferral; after graduation, the wait often became permanent and the path to societal change was often blocked, especially for women and more so for students of color. Change took time, yet time—waiting—was the enemy of change. In 1910, in a speech written for the ceremony marking the twenty-fifth anniversary of the founding of Bryn Mawr College but not delivered for lack of time, M. Carey Thomas, the college's second president, called for patience:

> We have come to believe that the power of a college to influence its students for good is vastly increased if it gathers them together for four impressionable years in the midst of beautiful surroundings in buildings built and furnished in accordance with the best architectural and decorative traditions and administered in accordance with the civilized traditions of well-bred households.[1]

Thomas's words reflect the common sense of bourgeois social reform to which women's colleges like Bryn Mawr belonged during the latter part of the nineteenth century. They also harbor temporalities less obviously associated with Historically Black Colleges and Universities (HBCUs). As time away, college and university education after the Civil War promised change to some white women and to a small percentage of those African Americans previously barred from entry to the halls of higher learning.

Seen in light of reformist traditions, Thomas's environmental determinism might seem belated.[2] Relatively new, however, was the assignment of a fixed timeframe for change—in this case, four years. Competing schedules regulated campuses of brick and stone, industrial capitalism's antechambers. The time-based renegotiation of femininity among the Northern bourgeoisie was linked dialectically to racial struggle in the post-Reconstruction South, within a changing division of domestic, industrial, and intellectual labor. In particular, a dynamic of advancement and deferral, rendered antithetically in brick and in stone, placed Northern women's colleges in unstated, differential tension with African American industrial education, as gender, race, and class intersected in learning environments around 1900.

Cottages and Corridors

Although coeducation and the first women's colleges date to the 1830s, during the two decades immediately following the Civil War philanthropists like the Quaker physician Joseph W. Taylor, who founded Bryn Mawr, and the industrialist Matthew Vassar, who founded Vassar College, provided the means by which middle- and upper-class white women joined white men in the collegiate sphere.[3] From the day it opened in 1885, Bryn Mawr combined socialization into what Thomas called "the civilized traditions of well-bred households" with a culture of scholarly research partly modeled on the recently founded Johns Hopkins University. Speaking alongside Thomas at the same anniversary event in 1910, Horace Howard Furness, a prominent Shakespearean at the University of Pennsylvania (and brother of the architect Frank Furness), was effusive in his praise of the college's effort to join liberal education with original scholarship:

> To these two high aims—Culture for all, Research for the few—this ground was dedicated, and they have been, from that hour, cherished and fostered by *one* all-pervading spirit, at the music of whose pleading voice the very stones have taken architectural shape and builded domes for learning, with corridors which will forever re-echo her immortal footsteps.[4]

Though there were many stones on the Bryn Mawr campus, there were no real domes to speak of, and what corridors there were—and there were many— ran longest through the dormitories rather than through the academic buildings. In their architectural expression, these dormitories—Radnor, Denbigh, Pembroke East and West, and Rockefeller Halls, completed between 1887 and 1904 to designs by the Philadelphia-based firm of Cope and Stewardson—are

3.1 Cope and Stewardson, Pembroke Hall East and West, Bryn Mawr College, 1894. Courtesy of Bryn Mawr College Special Collections.

among the earliest examples of what became known as Collegiate Gothic. Their temporality is one of preparation and withholding. Late instances of a transatlantic Gothic Revival with sources, in this case, in Tudor quadrangles at Cambridge and Oxford, the Bryn Mawr dormitories elicited a national and ecclesiastical pathos inseparable from the transplanted "stones of Venice" with which they were made.[5] Their corridors, however, had different origins.[6]

As Thomas pointed out in her remarks, "in 1880, it was not clearly understood that lecture rooms and students' living rooms should be in separate buildings, nor was it then fully recognized that young men or women should not be gathered together in great numbers under one roof."[7] With few exceptions, residential colleges initially combined teaching facilities with student (and sometimes faculty) living quarters in a single, large multipurpose building.[8] Several of the early women's colleges, including Vassar (founded in 1865) and Wellesley (founded in 1875) adhered to a variant on this model, also drawing on the example set by nineteenth-century female seminaries like Mount Holyoke, which was founded by Mary Lyon in 1837 and only chartered as a college in 1888.[9]

Deviating from this precedent, the Bryn Mawr trustees adapted the residential system developed at Smith College. Smith, which opened its doors in 1875, was among the first colleges—male, female, or in rare cases like Oberlin, coeducational—to group student living quarters separately from academic spaces.[10] In place of the single, phalanx-like multipurpose building that had become the norm elsewhere, students at Smith lived in domestically scaled "houses," or freestanding residential halls designed for up to fifty students. In these houses, each student was assigned a single-occupancy bedroom upstairs, and shared downstairs living and dining rooms with her housemates. The group was administratively and socioculturally conceived as a "family," with the bedrooms of the faculty resident and the "lady-in-charge" also located downstairs, near the single, central entrance hall for easy supervision. Later replicated at Wellesley, this became known as the "cottage system."[11]

Helen Lefkowitz Horowitz has shown that although female seminaries like Mount Holyoke were sometimes linked with male colleges like Amherst, "college men lived under far less supervision than seminary women." In many of the earlier multipurpose halls, the enforcement of formal rules was inhibited by multiple entrances and stairways, or by separate faculty living quarters, which made faculty supervision of students more difficult.[12] The supervisory paternalism that persisted in women's colleges stressed the enforcement of sexual norms, and life in the Smith cottages was no less rule-bound than that in the Mount Holyoke seminary. Bryn Mawr, however, downplayed this tutelary

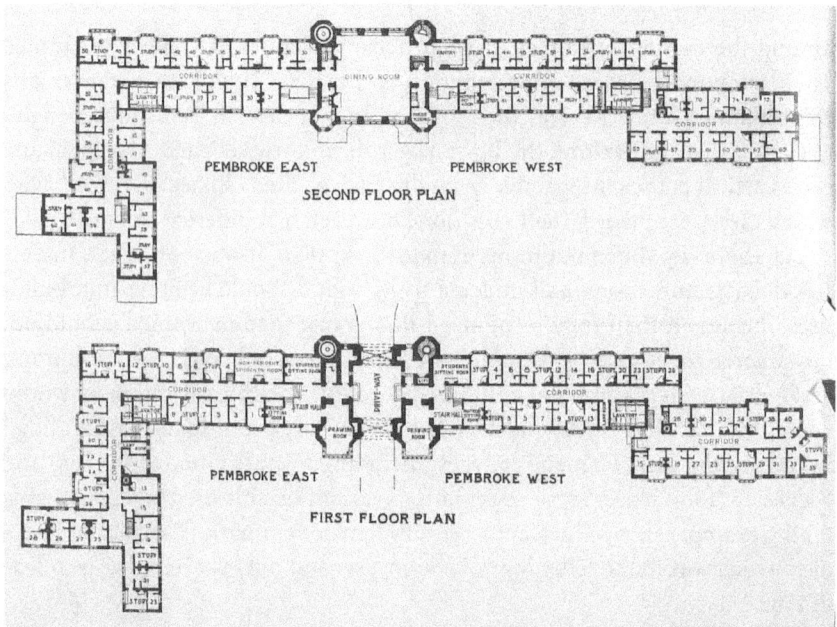

3.2 Cope and Stewardson, Pembroke Hall, Bryn Mawr College, 1894. First and second floor plans. Courtesy of Bryn Mawr College Special Collections.

domesticity by transferring the cottage back to the corridor, a social and supervisory unit derived from the multipurpose hall that had previously reached an apotheosis at Vassar. In the process, Bryn Mawr's corridors replaced Vassar's brick-housed, mechanized rituals with an artisanal stone reverie.

Schedules

Vassar's Main Building was designed in the Second Empire style by James Renwick Jr. and completed in 1865, in time to welcome the college's first students. Renwick, a self-taught architect and graduate of Columbia College, had recently designed Charity Hospital on Blackwell's (now Roosevelt) Island in New York based on a type codified earlier by French academicians, with an imposing central hall and two flanking, symmetrically disposed wings. With the encouragement of college benefactor Matthew Vassar's advisor, Milo P. Jewett, Renwick transferred that building's diagram to Vassar.[13] But rather than arranging rooms en suite, at Vassar Renwick also drew upon recent practices in the designs of hospitals and prisons, in which rooms were arranged along a wide, single-loaded corridor.[14]

A twelve-foot wide "exercise" corridor ranged along the full length of Vassar's Main Building's western (front) façade, turning the corner at right angles at the two flanking end pavilions. On each of the four main floors, sliding iron fire

3.3 James Renwick Jr., Main Building, Vassar College, 1865. Archives and Special Collections, Vassar College Library, Archives 08.05.02.

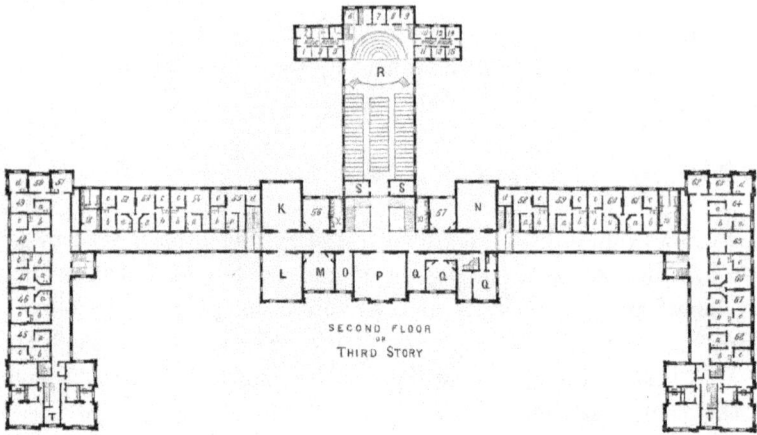

3.4 James Renwick Jr., Main Building, Vassar College, 1865. Second floor (third story) plan. John Benson Lossing, *Vassar College and Its Founder* (New York: C. A. Alvord, 1867), 125.

doors divided the corridor into five sections: a central administrative and teaching section with two residential sections disposed symmetrically to either side, along each of which ran suites of student rooms, with apartments for professors (who were known as "corridor teachers") located at the extremities of the two end pavilions and, as one early account put it, "commanding full view of the domain in charge."[15] Although the original design provided for single-room occupancy with only some of the rooms receiving natural light, in actuality a majority of students shared bedrooms.

The corridor was a unit of social life at Vassar at roughly the scale of Smith's cottages, with two pairs of residential compartments per floor overseen by a professor. Originally, each parlor around which suites of rooms clustered contained a printed students' manual that stipulated house rules, which the corridor teachers were charged with enforcing.[16] The manual also listed a prescribed daily schedule, as follows:

Rising	6.00 A.M.
Morning prayers	6.45
Breakfast	7.00
Arrangement of rooms	7.30
Silent time	7.40
Morning study hours	9.00–12.40
Dinner	1.00 P.M.

Recreation period	2.00–2.40
Afternoon study hours	2.45–5.45
Supper	6.00
Evening prayers followed by silent time	6.30
Evening study hour	8.00–9.00
Retiring	9.40–10.00[17]

Writing to her brother in 1866, Irene Anderson, one of Vassar's early students, reported on the details of this schedule. Having been summoned by the "breakfast bell," following the half-hour meal "we all get up at the ringing of Miss Lyman's bell, the Lady Principle [sic]," after which beds are made, following which comes the "silent hour" for Bible or prayer, after which, morning prayers at the chapel, which end just "ten minutes before the 1st bell rings for the first period." The morning was divided into four fifty-minute recitation periods separated by ten-minute intervals, with two more periods followed by an hour of recreation, an hour of chapel, an hour of study followed at nine o'clock by a twenty-minute "silent hour," then relaxation "until 15 minutes to 10 then the 'morning bell' rings, and at 10 O Clock precisely, the gas has to be extinguished all through the college."[18]

Miss Lyman was Hannah Lyman, the college's first administrative principal, author of the students' manual and superintendent of student life at Vassar. Her bell was, evidently, a handheld instrument with which she presided over meals in the dining room.[19] But as Anderson's letter testifies, that handheld bell was only one of several sources of auditory signals at Vassar. Other signals emanated daily from the messenger's room, located adjacent to the building's main entrance on the second (main) floor, "in which," according to a detailed early account, "is the only clock in the College, and by which all its prescribed internal movements are directed." The messenger's room thus combined clock, timetable, and the system of electromechanical bells into a daily, regulatory rhythm that also included spoken words, for "in it is also an annunciator, connected with various official apartments, by which right direction is given to answer a summons."[20] The corridors, then, were audiovisual instruments tied to the central clock. Looming large in students' lives and imaginations, in the recollections of alumnae, and in historical accounts, Miss Lyman was, from the perspective of the bells, but a unit in a spatiotemporal technics operated by a rather less memorable messenger.

In her letter home, Anderson also wrote of purchasing a blank book for the purpose of keeping a journal. Although that journal if it existed was lost, a number of student diaries and journals from the period testify to the linkup of the messenger's multimedia authority with the timekeeping practiced in daily journal entries. Among the diaries, commercially printed formats organized generally unremarkable content into the paginated rhythms of an imagined community of reader-writers. As Molly McCarthy has shown, commonplace diaries and day books kept a form of mechanical time that synchronized with, but also differed from, clock time.[21] Diary formats varied in length, from page-per-day to lines-per-day; in all cases, however, handwritten entries were practically limited to a maximum number of daily characters. The words of these diarists faithfully marked time. In 1876, Vassar student Frances Bromley began every daily page from January 1 through March 25 in her Standard Diary, "published for the trade" by the Cambridgeport Diary Company, with the phrase "A day when. . . ." The prevailing sense of repetition, anticipation, and deferral was marked especially by recursive entries like Bromley's on Monday, January 10, which reads: "A day when things don't begin."[22]

Bricks, Part 1

Bromley's Standard Diary competed commercially with the Excelsior Diary used in 1895 by Cornelia Raymond, class of 1883 and the daughter of Vassar's second president, John Howard Raymond.[23] Three decades prior, on the eve of his first sermon opening the college on September 23, 1865, an exhausted Raymond wrote to his wife Cornelia of:

> the sudden transmutation of this great lumbering pile of brick and mortar, which hung on my spirit like a mountainous millstone, into a palace of light and life. . . . On every side it sparkled like a diamond. The front windows open, you know, on the corridors, which were all ablaze with gas; the end and rear windows are in the young ladies' rooms, and of course were equally brilliant.[24]

The gaslight illuminating the corridors, which the schedule required to be extinguished each night at ten o'clock sharp, flickered from the twenty-five miles of pipes "for conveying gas, heat, water, and waste" running through the building's walls, along with the wiring for the electromechanical bells that governed the corridors' life.[25] But what was the edifice through which these networks threaded, this "great lumbering pile of brick and mortar" that disappeared into the night?

The joints between the Main Building's dull red bricks were pointed with black mortar, with bluestone water tables (linear projections) capping brick stringcourses, and bluestone door-and-window trim that accentuated a somber, monolithic form with slate mansard roofs, its silhouette balanced by day against the surrounding greenery.[26] In keeping with the building's diminished Second Empire idiom, corners were turned with brick pilasters, with Doric capitals also in brick except at the uppermost story, where a composite order was carved in bluestone. Most strikingly, the clusters of square, Doric columns marking the main entrance portico were also brick, with brick capitals and bases. These modest details distinguished Vassar's Main Building from Renwick's earlier Charity Hospital, where severe stone quoins turned the exterior corners. But the Main Building's details were more than an aesthetic upgrade of the asylum type transferred to a women's college. Like other decorative bits and pieces adorning countless asylums, prisons, and other seemingly utilitarian buildings across the century, these details evinced a representational impulse: recognition, if not fulfillment, of the need to signify.

On Vassar's opening day, a second academic building joined Renwick's "lumbering pile." This was the astronomical observatory, designed by chair of chemistry and physics Charles Farrar as part of the recruitment package offered to Maria Mitchell, a distinguished astronomer who had spent twenty years as a librarian in Nantucket, where she practiced astronomy with her schoolteacher father, William Mitchell. Of the original nine Vassar faculty members, Mitchell was the only one who did not live in the Main Building, taking up residence instead with her father in the observatory's north wing. Set on the crest of a rocky outcropping, the observatory was, like the Main Building, essentially a technical apparatus adorned with rudimentary classical ornamentation. With faint echoes of Thomas Jefferson's Monticello, three wings containing astronomical instruments pivoted symmetrically around a central octagonal hall shaped in solid brick and surmounted by a hemispherical rotunda, the wooden enclosure of which could be mechanically rotated its full circumference to access the celestial sphere. The telescope mounted beneath the dome contained the third largest lens in the country. To protect against metrical disturbances caused by even the slightest shaking or settling of its solid wooden floors, the instruments in each room sat on structurally isolated stone piers bearing directly on the bedrock below: a massive granite pier for the equatorial, Onondaga limestone shafts for the transit and meridian circle, white Westchester marble for the prime vertical, and mottled Dover marble for the astronomical clock and chronograph.[27]

The observatory was Mitchell's home, laboratory, and classroom. Students also remembered it as the scene of regular "dome parties" that she theatrically hosted.[28] In this and other ways, Mitchell allowed herself to be cast, deceptively, as a counterpart to Hannah Lyman, Vassar's "Lady Principal." Part teacher, part role model, and part comrade, Mitchell threw into relief the contradictions of the industrial-academic patriarchy that governed the early women's colleges. Before coming to Vassar she had achieved notoriety for observing an undiscovered comet, which became known as "Miss Mitchell's Comet," on which she published under her father's name in Benjamin Silliman's *American Journal of Science and Arts*.[29] Living in the observatory with her retired father, whose career hers already overshadowed, Mitchell introduced Vassar students to astronomy and its instruments while doing original science with them, on one occasion traveling with a group to Denver to observe a total solar eclipse.[30]

3.5 Charles Farrar, Maria Mitchell Observatory, Vassar College, 1865. Archives and Special Collections, Vassar College Library, Archives 08.06.08.

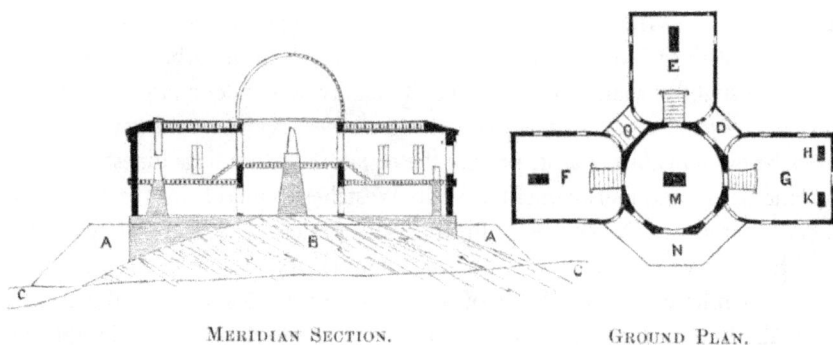

MERIDIAN SECTION.   GROUND PLAN.

3.6 Charles Farrar, Maria Mitchell Observatory, Vassar College, 1865. Section and plan. John Benson Lossing, *Vassar College and Its Founder* (New York: C. A. Alvord, 1867), 148.

To this mixture of social discipline, education, and research, brick was background. Although the observatory was completed before the Main Building, Farrar's designs followed Renwick's lead in exterior detailing. Plain brick pilasters marked rhythms and transitions on the façade, thinned and paired on the lower story and at corners. Innovative amateur mimicry at one level, the ornamentation signified at another. In itself, the material connoted little, save the associations with factories, hospitals, and other institutions from which the college needed to separate itself. But differentially, brick at Vassar also connoted negatively: it was not stone. At the uppermost, most distantly visible level of the Main Building, the central pilasters capped with carved stone capitals—the only stone carvings on the entire façade—reinforced the straining to signify, to mark the new institution with the faintest imprint of distinction. At Vassar, brick was always becoming stone, awkwardly leaning toward a less utilitarian, more erudite future, a future anchored in the past that could not be scheduled, only awaited. This anchoring was comparable to the manner in which the observatory's sensitive astronomical instruments were separated from the brick shell and anchored, in stone, to the Earth's firmament.

The bricks of Vassar's Main Building were machine-made and were laid by workers employed by the building contractor William Harlow. They may well have been drawn from the local brickmaking industry, with which Matthew Vassar's family had been involved.[31] The capacity of these bricks to bear meaning negatively was reinforced by the Main Building's forthright affinities with factories, asylums, and hospitals, as the college's ambivalent modernity shone through in its promissory qualities. Women were invited to join their male contemporaries as members of a growing intelligentsia, exemplified by a figure like Maria Mitchell hosting parties in her astronomer's dome. Even so, and despite the political activism of many students and faculty (including Mitchell) around women's rights, at Vassar women were asked symbolically to wait, to be patient. That was the function of the corridors, where young white women learned to submit to a time-based discipline invisibly related to that which governed the daily lives of Black women and men at the Tuskegee Institute in Alabama, but differently.

Bricks, Part 2

Via the ambivalence of materials like brick, women's colleges in the North entered into a dialectical relationship with Southern Black colleges and vocational institutes. At Vassar, factory-made brick connoted industrialization negatively. At the Tuskegee Institute in rural Alabama, hand-made brick connoted the same, but positively. In *Working with the Hands* (1904), his sequel to the autobiographical *Up from Slavery* (1901), Booker T. Washington, the founder of the Tuskegee Normal and Industrial Institute, described the practical instruction of students there in the arts of building. Since its inception, the Tuskegee campus had been largely student-built. Each new building presented an occasion for Washington's pedagogy of African American self-help, with faculty-guided student labor. With each new project, students

AT WORK IN THE SCHOOL'S BRICK-YARD
Getting a kiln ready to fire

3.7 "At Work in the School's Brick Yard" [Students preparing a kiln to fire bricks], Tuskegee Normal and Industrial Institute, n.d. [c. 1904]. Booker T. Washington, *Working with the Hands: Being a Sequel to "Up from Slavery" Covering the Author's Experiences in Industrial Training at Tuskegee* (New York: Doubleday, Page, 1904), n.p.

from the different "school industries" joined together; some began excavating the site, using wagons made by student wheelwrights, blacksmiths, and harness-makers, "the patterns and instructions [having] been given them on blackboards and in lectures":

> Then come the brick-makers, turning out 20,000 bricks a day in the school kilns. They know whether they have made good bricks when they see them handled, and put into the walls by the student masons. In the course for brick-masonry, there is practical demonstration the year round. All the brick work on the buildings of the school is done by students, under the supervision of the instructors. Plastering and repair work, both inside and outside of the buildings, is in charge [sic] of the Brickmasonry Division. The theory is taught in the class room, the practical test is always close at hand.[32]

The first building on the Tuskegee campus to be constructed in this manner was Alabama Hall, begun in 1883 using almost four hundred thousand bricks made by hand from clay drawn from a nearby ravine, with brickmaking

BUILDING A NEW DORMITORY

Students draw plans, dig foundations, make the brick, cut timber, which they saw and make into joists and frames.   The painting, plastering, plumbing and roofing are also done by the students under the direction of their instructors.

3.8 Students building Douglass Hall, Tuskegee Normal and Industrial Institute, n.d. [c. 1904]. From Booker T. Washington, *Working with the Hands: Being a Sequel to "Up from Slavery" Covering the Author's Experiences in Industrial Training at Tuskegee* (New York: Doubleday, Page, 1904), n.p.

machines being added at a later date.[33] Tuskegee had been coeducational since its founding as a normal school for teachers in 1881. By 1904, when Washington wrote, Alabama Hall was home to "many of the lady teachers and most of the girls."[34] Men and women studied literature, history, mathematics, and the natural sciences together in the institute's Academic Department. In the Department of Mechanical Industries, which admitted women only to its tailoring division, young men learned trades like brickmasonry, plastering, and carpentry. Most of the women at Tuskegee learned their trades, which included sewing, dressmaking, millinery, cooking, laundering, housekeeping, mattress making, and basketry, in the Department of Industries for Girls.[35]

In contrast to women's colleges like Vassar, there was little indication that these industrial activities included the transmission of cultural meaning through the fine arts. Although Washington hired Robert R. Taylor to teach architectural drawing in 1892, architectural design per se was not taught at Tuskegee until the late 1890s, when it was gradually integrated into the architectural and mechanical drawing curriculum.[36] In 1902 Taylor, who had graduated from the Massachusetts Institute of Technology as the nation's first academically trained Black architect, was appointed director of the Department of Mechanical Industries, by which time students of architectural drawing were required to undertake readings in the history of architecture in their third year.[37] Washington acknowledged the ambiguity when he emphasized that the three-year architectural drawing course "aims to give thorough instruction in drawing, building construction and design," adding that "in all cases, the general mechanical and artistic training is supplemented by the course of study in the Academic Department."[38] Reflecting this aim, the catalogue description of the Academic Department begins with an unattributed quotation, the words of which could well be Washington's:

> The laborer must not be regarded as a mere muscular machine, capable of greater productiveness; he is a man who thinks and feels and grows; he is a man responsive to ideals; he is a man for whom we seek wider spiritual margin. . . . It is good for Negroes in the New South to be artisans, not merely because like plows and hoes and horses they will be useful, but because, like men, they will live more wholesome lives.

The catalogue text continues: "The special business of the Academic Department is to enlarge the lives of men and women, but an enlarged life is essentially a more useful life."[39] The "enlarged life" of "wider spiritual margin" was the life of the mind, which remained vocational at Tuskegee to the extent that, in 1904, the Academic Department was devoted mostly to the training of teachers. Still, Tuskegee's vocationalism, which for Washington's critics like W. E. B. Du Bois reinforced a racialized division of labor, had within it an aporia. Regular movement between the divisions was encouraged among both faculty and students. From the brickyard to the construction site, building materials and the artisans who shaped them were, like college-educated humanists and their books, bearers of meaning. More than just a "muscular machine," at Tuskegee the young Black man whose parents and grandparents had recently risen, in Washington's words, "up from slavery," was a poet with his hands whose work with bricks made him a medium in two senses: an intermediary within the industrial system, and a spiritual channel to the future, a clairvoyant.

"The Gates of Toil"

In principle, African American students at Tuskegee did not belong to what Du Bois called the "Talented Tenth" being trained in the classical humanities and the natural sciences at recently founded Black colleges and universities like Du Bois's alma mater, Fisk University. Living an "enlarged life" as more than a "muscular machine" therefore meant finding time and resources to study literature, history, and mathematics in Tuskegee's Academic Department, while learning a trade in the Department of Mechanical Industries. As Du Bois summarized the situation in the South in *The Souls of Black Folk* (1903), "in the midst, then, of the larger problem of Negro education sprang up the more practical question of work, the inevitable economic quandary that faces a people in the transition from slavery to freedom, and especially those who make the change amid hate and prejudice, lawlessness and ruthless competition." It was in this context, of fierce racism and fierce economic competition, that Du Bois assessed the rise of industrial education as "an answer of singular wisdom and timeliness." Alluding to Washington's program at Tuskegee, he recognized that "from the very first in nearly all the schools some attention had been given to training in handiwork, but now was this training first raised to a dignity that brought it in direct touch with the South's magnificent industrial development, and given an emphasis which reminded black folk that before the Temple of Knowledge swing the Gates of Toil."[40]

For Du Bois, Tuskegee was therefore a gateway, a passage leading elsewhere. Though aspiring to racially integrated education, Du Bois acknowledged, as did Washington, that in the aftermath of Reconstruction and the initial influx of white teachers from Northern states, African Americans in the South had been left largely to educate themselves. In the space of three decades, amid segregation exacerbated by racist laws and economic competition, Black educators and their white collaborators set up a parallel system of public grammar schools and secondary schools for the children of formerly enslaved parents and grandparents. Normal schools and industrial institutes like Tuskegee and the Hampton Institute trained schoolteachers as well as tradespersons; colleges trained the teachers' teachers. What Du Bois called the "Gates of Toil" erected in the industrial institutes marked the system's boundaries with the promise of self-sufficiency.

"Yet after all they are but gates," Du Bois continued:

and when turning our eyes from the temporary and the contingent in the Negro problem to the broader question of the permanent uplifting and civilization of black men in America, we have a right to inquire, as this enthusiasm for material advancement mounts to its height, if after all the industrial school is the final and sufficient answer in the training of the Negro race; and to ask gently, but in all sincerity, the ever-recurring query of the ages, Is not life more than meat, and the body more than raiment?[41]

Extending the Southern Black educational system to include colleges and universities meant, for Du Bois, exchanging temporary toil for permanent uplift. On the one hand he argued that, as "institutions to furnish teachers for the untaught," the thirty-four college-level institutions like the coeducational Fisk, Atlanta, and Howard, or indeed Spelman Seminary (later College, the country's first Black women's college), were necessary for the system to reproduce itself:

"Above the sneers of critics at the obvious defects of this procedure must ever stand its one crushing rejoinder: in a single generation they put thirty thousand black teachers in the South; they wiped out the illiteracy of the majority of the black people of the land, and they made Tuskegee possible."[42] On the other hand, "it was not enough that the teachers of teachers should be trained in technical normal methods; they must also, as far as possible, be broadminded, cultured men and women, to scatter civilization among a people whose ignorance was not simply of letters, but of life itself."[43] Recognizing the "gift" of the white, college-educated teachers who had helped establish these institutions, Du Bois conjured the spirit of Alma Mater, a keeper of homes:

> The colleges they founded were social settlements; homes where the best of the sons of the freedmen came in close and sympathetic touch with the best traditions of New England. They lived and ate together studied and worked, hoped and harkened in the dawning light. In actual formal content their curriculum was doubtless old-fashioned, but in educational power it was supreme, for it was the contact of living souls.[44]

Who were these "souls"? In one sense they were a statistic, the "Talented Tenth" represented metonymically by the one hundred African Americans who had graduated from Northern colleges and the five hundred from the Southern Black colleges between 1895 and 1900.[45] But these "souls" were also a social type. After graduating from Fisk in 1888 Du Bois, who was from New England, earned a second bachelor's degree in history from Harvard, then began graduate studies there in sociology, and attended the University of Berlin for two years before becoming the first African American to earn a PhD from Harvard in 1895. Two years later, after brief stints teaching at Wilberforce College and at the University of Pennsylvania, Du Bois joined the faculty of Atlanta University, where he supervised the sociology program and directed a series of annual Conferences for the Study of the Negro Problems, also known as the Atlanta Conferences. Converting a loosely constructed study program into an intellectual project, Du Bois extrapolated the sociological methods employed in his study of *The Philadelphia Negro* (1899) into a series of reports on various carefully defined aspects of Black life. Each report was based on data culled from printed questionnaires and surveys distributed to varying numbers of subjects, often with uneven response rates and other anomalies.[46] Of the sixteen publications of conference proceedings that Du Bois oversaw from 1897 to 1914, two are especially relevant here: the 1900 report on *The College-Bred Negro* and the 1902 report on *The Negro Artisan*.[47]

The first of the two, which surveyed approximately 1,200 African American graduates "of the colleges of the land," mentioned neither Tuskegee nor Hampton.[48] In addition to the few majority-white institutions that had graduated any

African Americans, thirty-four historically Black colleges were represented, from antebellum schools like Wilberforce, to Freedman's Bureau schools established after the Civil War like Howard, Fisk, and Atlanta, to a number of smaller ecclesiastical and land-grant institutions.[49] The report's system of classification was performative; it went beyond mere inventory to bring into view an ideal-typical figure, the "College-Bred Negro," in dialectical relation with the "Negro Artisan" studied two years later. The latter report reversed the teleology by asking the 1,300 skilled laborers it queried, mostly from Georgia, how they learned their trade, whether they attended trade school, if so where, and for how long.[50] Summarizing the development of Black vocational education, the report listed ninety-eight institutions that offered some form of such training. That a number of institutions, including Atlanta, appear on both lists, demonstrates the ambiguity inherent in the typological exercise, as well as actual curricular overlaps.[51]

Du Bois's epistemology was clearest when addressing the seemingly technical matter of income-generating student labor, which was the basis of many trade schools. Although even Tuskegee sold its bricks to local builders, this practice gradually became secondary. Acknowledging the economic motive, *The Negro Artisan* observes: "It is coming to be seen, however, in the education of the Negro as clearly as it has been seen in the education of youths the world over that it is the *boy* and not the material product that is the true object of education."[52] In *The Souls of Black Folk*, Du Bois spelled this out with respect to collegiate education: "The function of the Negro college, then, is clear: it must maintain the standards of popular education, it must seek the social regeneration of the Negro, and it must help in the solution of race contact and co-operation. And finally, beyond all this, it must develop men."[53] Shaped in significant part by his German experience, Du Bois's theory of education remained at this point a theory of *Bildung*, or personal growth.[54] He contrasted this "higher individualism which the centres of culture protect" and with it, a "loftier respect for the sovereign human soul that seeks to know itself and the world about it" to the mass-worship of "modern socialism."[55] Even in the dry empiricism of the reports, then, both artisan and collegian had souls. The problem for a sociology of race as well as for young African Americans living in slavery's shadow, was finding the time to bring them together.

At Tuskegee, time was money. Again there were bells, described here by Warren Logan, a member of the Tuskegee faculty:

> We do not find that the manual labor system interferes seriously with the studies. We believe that in the long run, it will be found far more of a help than a hindrance, through its influence upon character and habits of industry. Of course, it makes a busy day for students and teachers, from the rising bell at half past five, and the work bell calling some after breakfast to their work shops or

cotton fields and others to the fresh morning study hour, to the bell for "lights out" at half past nine at night, when the sleep of the laborer is sweet. A busy day, but Tuskegee has work to do and means to do it.[56]

Thus, where the sixteen-hour Vassar day included time for reflection and diary-keeping, the Tuskegee day balanced academic study with manual labor within the same timeframe. But as Black men and women "up from slavery" prepared for new roles as self-sufficient workers in an industrializing South, the economic role of white, college-educated women like the first generations to graduate from Vassar was less clear. Hence the turning inward, the timekeeping and the waiting recorded in diaries, where, as Frances Bromley succinctly put it, every day was, repetitively and paradigmatically, "A day when. . . ."

Bryn Mawr

A different but related temporality reigned at Bryn Mawr, where Collegiate Gothic dormitories had more to do with stone than with architectural style. By around 1906, at which point the Bryn Mawr campus had grown to include four dormitories and a library designed in a neo-Gothic idiom, numerous college and university administrators had been tempted to adorn their growing campuses with similar structures. Though it may seem that all of this belonged to a Gilded Age *Kunstwollen*, or artistic will, another, simpler explanation is that that these administrators and their constituents felt the need to assemble a collegiate iconography to which carved stone surfaces were especially well suited. Despite Ruskinian odes to artisanship and handwork, this was not because stone compensated for industrial abstraction, but—again—because collegiate life was for many a prelude to industrial life at home or at work.

In her remarks on the occasion of Bryn Mawr's twenty-fifth anniversary in 1910 with which we began, M. Carey Thomas pointed out the decision to employ a dormitory system but not to require students to perform domestic chores, as did other women's colleges like Wellesley or Vassar at the time.[57] But it was equally important that evidence of manual labor was clearly visible on the exterior of the dormitories. As Thomas said of her campus's Collegiate Gothic halls,

> The artistically uneven way in which the stones are built into the walls of our college buildings reproduces the long stretch of Pembroke wall laid by John Stewardson with his own hands which was photographed and copied by the stone masons in all our later buildings.[58]

American Collegiate Gothic was therefore stone remediated. This was not simply a matter of architects like Walter Cope and John Stewardson copying details or other stylistic attributes from photographs of other older buildings taken by them or by their patrons on their European travels, or from casts made after the fact, as Thomas also reported of Bryn Mawr's gargoyles, staircases, and dining room furniture.[59] Rather, at Bryn Mawr remediation entailed the photographic documentation of local "Germantown stone," a grey mica schist, laid by the architect's hand in imitation of other stone witnessed firsthand or seen in published photographs, as the basis for further stonemasonry on the site.[60] The effect was Ruskinian, but not only as a moral rebuke to the brick industrial architecture of New England, including Vassar's Main Building, or a marker of class privilege comparable to the rusticated stone surfaces designed for New England's leisured elites by the Boston architect Henry Hobson Richardson. Like the bricks at Vassar and antithetically at Tuskegee, the stones at Bryn Mawr belonged to a division of time and labor centered on the mixed subjectivity of the college student.

Most of Bryn Mawr's Gothic precedents dated from the English Tudor period, which Thomas and her peers regarded as the epitome of a cultural heritage to which new American institutions like theirs laid claim. Pembroke Hall, a pair of dormitories designed by Cope and Stewardson around a central gate and completed in 1894, invoked this heritage most explicitly. The castellated arched gateway, flanked on either side by the dormitory wings with double-loaded corridors, mimicked the gateway towers at Cambridge and Oxford.[61] Writing in 1904 of Cope and Stewardson's Gothic Revival "poetry" at Bryn Mawr, at the University of Pennsylvania, and at Princeton, the architect, cultural critic, and author of ghost stories Ralph Adams Cram exclaimed: "Looking round, one thinks back to Oxford and Cambridge and Winchester, and the subtle obsession of the ivied Old World, the call of inextinguishable race-memory enters in and blots out reason and analysis."[62] Cram's assessment of the firm's work, the most extensive at the time, was filled with such associations. Having already credited Cope and Stewardson for stirring "ethnic and racial memories," Cram credited the "Philadelphia School" with which he grouped them as "standing for nationality, ethnic continuity and for the impulses of Christian civilization." Of the firm's turreted, neo-Elizabethan Memorial Tower gateway at the University of Pennsylvania, commemorating the university's dead from the Spanish-American War, Cram avowed that, "American heroism harks back to British heroism; the blood shed before Manila or on San Juan Hill was the same blood that flowed at Bosworth Field, Flodden, and the Boyne. Therefore the British base of the design is indispensable, for such were the racial foundations." In a similar vein, Cope and Stewardson's Blair and Stafford Little Halls at Princeton were, for Cram, "poetic, collegiate, racial and logical."[63]

Although the objects of Cram's disdain were as much Irish Catholics in New England as African Americans in the South, and although he used terms like *race* more in the earlier, civilizational sense than in the sociobiological sense

3.9 Cope and Stewardson, Rockefeller Hall, Bryn Mawr College, 1904. Courtesy of Bryn Mawr College Special Collections.

of nineteenth-century scientific racism, Cram's discourse was inseparable from the latter as an expression of white, Protestant ethno-nationalism.[64] Contrasting neo-Gothic "poetry" cultivated by architects in Philadelphia with the neo-classical "logic" of architects in New York, Cram put his taxonomy on full display: "In a word, one holds by eternal law, the other by indestructible race fealty and religious continuity." On the one side was paganism and on the other Christianity, not unmixed but distinct.[65] In his later political writings, Cram would direct such arguments against industrial mass culture and the excess of democracy brought about—to his mind—by the universal franchise.[66] As Cram emphasized in his assessment of Cope and Stewardson, architectural style communicated properly Christian values through details copied from precedent like the Elizabethan quadrangles at Cambridge. But more fundamentally, it was architecture's very capacity to convey "poetic" continuity with a racial past over legalistic, orderly "logic" that Cram found most fully developed in the Collegiate Gothic.

This was race as an emotive category, something felt through artistic expression rather than described analytically. The question is not whether

3.10 Cope and Stewardson, Rockefeller Hall, Bryn Mawr College, n.d. [completed 1904]. Construction, with stonework. Courtesy of Bryn Mawr College Special Collections.

Cope, Stewardson, or their patrons, including M. Carey Thomas, intended for their work to transmit such feelings. Regardless, a sympathetic interpreter like Cram was able to attribute such qualities to it. At Bryn Mawr, the final Cope and Stewardson dormitory, Rockefeller Hall, was completed in 1904 after the premature deaths of both architects. Cram judged the hall, still under construction when he wrote, superior even to its predecessors. He reserved special praise for "that very wonderful flat-bedded stone that is such a striking evidence of the goodness of Providence in furnishing architects with miraculous means to good ends."[67] As at Pembroke, the dormitory's two wings met at an arched, turreted gateway that turned the campus's southwestern corner. Carved stone owls, which a contemporaneous state report described earnestly as "the symbol of Athene," adorned both arch and tower; a carved stone crest consisting of three owls on a gold and ermine field, adopted by the trustees in 1903 as the college's coat of arms, crowned the tower to complete the ensemble.[68]

Thus the Owl Gate, as the arched campus entrance became known, fulfilled the project of delivering meaning in stone that had begun a decade and a half

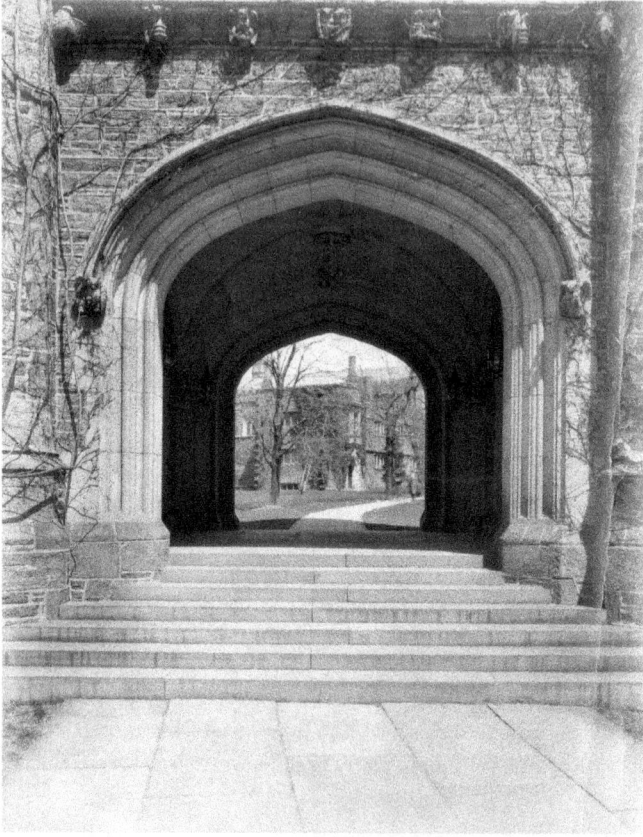

3.11 Cope and Stewardson, "Owl Gate," Rockefeller Hall, Bryn Mawr College, 1904. Courtesy of Bryn Mawr College Special Collections.

earlier. Visible allusion to popular Gothic chimeras notwithstanding, the message, reinforced in the new college motto, *Veritatem dilexi* ("I delight in truth"), was banal; these owls are also the source of the college's sporting mascot, that joined a menagerie of collegiate tigers (Princeton), bulldogs (Yale), lions (Columbia), and other assorted creatures. Rather, it is the medium here that matters, the complex of stone and brick and its discursive networks, through which the owls became recognizable as signifiers and the students themselves became owls. The dissonance of the two messages, devout, white Christian feeling for Cram and sporting pride for the Bryn Mawr collegians, should not deceive. As a differential medium, stone helped to bring an imagined community of gendered, racialized subjects into being. The owl signifies only that its substrate is not brick.

Four Years

Returning once more to Bryn Mawr president M. Carey Thomas speaking in 1910, what seems like a passing remark can now be contextualized. Thomas located the college's maximum influence in "four impressionable years in the midst of beautiful surroundings." When compared with temporalities at Vassar and Tuskegee, the metaphysics of waiting at Bryn Mawr situates collegiate time as a social medium in relation to the great new clock of the university.

In 1904, at the International Congress of Arts and Science at the Universal Exposition in St. Louis, Thomas had already mounted a lawyerly, social-scientific defense of the four-year collegiate experience.[69] Herself a Cornell alumna, Thomas was a medieval philologist with a PhD from the University of Zürich who had done additional graduate work at Leipzig, the Sorbonne, and Johns Hopkins. Her defense of the college responded to scrutiny from research universities, especially Harvard, which had introduced a system of elective coursework for undergraduates intended to prepare some number for graduate study by allowing undergraduate specialization as well as to encourage specialized scholarship among the faculty. Remarking on the frequent mixing of undergraduates and graduates in the diverse elective courses on offer, President Charles Eliot mused: "There is no telling where the College ends and the Graduate School begins."[70] Thomas replied with the counterexample of the "group system," a precursor to the system of majors and minors, which Bryn Mawr had adapted from Johns Hopkins as a means to ensure general training in "mental discipline" while allowing a limited number of elective courses and hence, a degree of specialization.[71] More troubling to her were efforts among university administrators like Eliot to reduce the time-to-degree for the Bachelor of Arts from four years to three, in order to lower the average age of matriculation to the graduate schools, some of which, like Harvard's law school, were beginning to require a BA for admission. Eliot had gradually implemented the three-year policy since assuming the Harvard presidency in 1869. Among his stated reasons was that Harvard graduates were having fewer children. Eliot attributed this decline to later marriage due to protracted professional education. In addition to increasing the quality of matriculants to the graduate schools, the possibility of a three-year degree, Eliot argued, lowered the average age of graduation and hence, of marriage and child-rearing among Harvard graduates.[72]

To refute Eliot's "fallacious" argument, Thomas cited the burgeoning literature on marriage rates, birth rates, and "race decline," including a privately published study on birth rates in Budapest with commentary by the race theorist Francis Galton. By 1900, this kind of statistical race thinking belonged to a hegemonic discourse of which Galton's eugenics was a limit case and to which Du Bois's advocacy of higher education for a "Talented Tenth" of African Americans was directly antithetical. In citing this literature, Thomas did not reject its underlying premise of racial decline. She only claimed that the literature showed that "the failure ... to reproduce" was not peculiar to Harvard graduates; rather, it "seems to be a characteristic of our American stock, and, above all, of our native Massachusetts stock, to which two thirds of Harvard graduates belong."[73] Nor was such race thinking anomalous to Thomas's own discourse. Her biographer Horowitz has documented Thomas's anti-Semitism, as well as her private disdain for Booker T. Washington. Bryn Mawr had an unspoken whites-only policy, and Thomas had withheld a scholarship to Jessie Fauset, a highly qualified Philadelphia-area Black student who went on to become a distinguished novelist and worked with Du Bois as the literary editor of *The Crisis*.[74] Thomas's claim that "the experience of seventy years has proved [the four-year college course] to be adapted to the needs of successive generations of college students" was calculated, if we take the orderly succession of generations as literally as she and Eliot stated it.[75] Expressing her firm conviction that "the college of the future will be coeducational," and advocating for the systematic recording of "educational statistics," Thomas concluded her defense with a rhetorical flourish: "The decline or advance of the race is the issue involved."[76] The old collegiate function of in loco parentis had become a population management program.

The Science of Time

Thomas made these arguments on the afternoon of Friday, September 23, 1904, as a contribution to Department 23 of the International Congress of Arts and Science on education. Joining her in a session dedicated to the undergraduate college was Bowdoin president William De Witt Hyde, who spoke of the all-around collegiate experience as "the best four years of one's life."[77] Their gathering was preceded by another that morning on secondary schools and followed the next day by a session on universities. The sixteen other sessions offered to attendees that Friday afternoon ranged from the History of Economics to "Mohammedism" to Private Law. Organized like a university, by discipline, with twenty-four departments under seven divisions, the congress crystallized a transatlantic metadiscourse on academic specialization. Comparing Bryn Mawr's curriculum to Harvard's, Thomas followed Eliot's priorities if not his conclusions in placing the threshold separating college from university on a sociobiological timeline.

The Congress of Arts and Science took place over six days in several recently completed buildings on the new Collegiate Gothic campus designed by Cope and Stewardson for Washington University in St. Louis. Its stated purpose was nothing less than "the unification of knowledge." This formulation reflected the synthetic epistemology advocated by Hugo Münsterberg, the Harvard psychologist who, together with the Chicago sociologist Albion W. Small, served as

3.12 Cope and Stewardson, Ridgley Hall, Washington University in St. Louis, 1904. Washington University Photographic Services Collection, Washington University Libraries, Department of Special Collections.

co-vice president of the congress and was most responsible for conceptualizing its aims. A plurality of the sections met in the Hall of International Congresses, which was later to become Washington University's Ridgley Library. In need of funds to complete the campus, university administrators had, in 1901, leased the new buildings and grounds to the Louisiana Purchase Exposition Company for the duration of the 1904 exposition, and committed to adding four more buildings, including the congress hall/library.[78]

In written remarks that accompanied drawings based on the firm's competition-winning campus plan, Cope and Stewardson explained how the design's temporality suited the "aesthetic ideal of a University": "Classic Architecture expresses completion, finality, perfection: Gothic Architecture expresses aspiration, growth, development."[79] The buildings' exterior walls were of Missouri red granite, explicitly chosen over pressed brick, with Indiana limestone trim. The contract with the stonecutter's union prohibited "machine worked" cornices and other trim; hence both granite and limestone were hand cut in the early buildings, with fine grooves "tooled" into the latter to enhance the effect. Spalls, or chipped stones discarded by others at the quarry, were incorporated into the walls, and a list of "Ten Commandments" instructed stonecutters in techniques related to stone proportions, distribution, orientation, and texture.[80]

On the matter of style for the campus, the Cope and Stewardson memorandum hewed closely to Cram, associating classical architecture with the "majesty of the law" and dead heroes, and affirming that "the Gothic has always, and will always, appeal to us as distinctly the style for a University, which, like a tree, must either grow or die."[81] Reviewing the results, however, Cram could not conceal his disappointment.[82] The St. Louis campus was, for him, a lesser model than was Bryn Mawr for the perpetuation of "race-memory" passed down through the Anglo-Protestant generations. On this deficiency, Cram may well have had the former Hall of International Congresses (Ridgley Library) especially in mind. Modeled on the west side of the Canterbury Quadrangle at St. John's College, Oxford, the library façade modified its source with Italian Renaissance detailing and a central, almost Baroque pavilion with superimposed classical orders and a segmented pediment.[83] With architectural style coded racially, such a dalliance with impurity would likely have been too much for Cram. Even so, Cram probably would have been reassured by the words Thomas spoke on the future Washington University campus; after all, she shared his devotion to the Collegiate Gothic and, as we have seen, to the orderly succession of the generations. But he may have found even more solace in the words of the German sociologist Max Weber, who spoke at the Congress two days before Thomas did.

As Andrew Zimmerman has explained, the publication of Weber's two-part "Protestant Ethic and the 'Spirit' of Capitalism," which connected Benjamin Franklin's celebrated adage "time is money" with the Protestant "calling," straddled its author's visit to the St. Louis Congress.[84] The 1904 exhibition celebrated the centenary of the Louisiana Purchase and hence, of westward settler-colonial expansion. In his contribution, on "The Rural Community," Weber detailed the decline of the landed nobility in Eastern Prussia and the appropriation of the feudal estates by capital, which, seeking "cheaper hands," imported landless "Slavonian" (i.e., mostly Polish Catholic) labor to replace the German peasants, many of whom migrated to cities or emigrated. This process, Weber argued, was a source of cultural conflict over the loss of rural tradition, which had been transmitted through the nobility.[85] Well aware that he was speaking in the Midwestern agricultural belt, Weber warned his American audience that, although the plentiful availability of "free land" in the United States had thus far prevented such conflict, the balance was fragile. The growing number of "negro farms" and the "migration from the country into the cities," he postulated, threatened to diminish wheat production. Furthermore, Weber argued, if "the expansive power of the Anglo-Saxon-German settlement of the rural districts and, besides, the number of children of the old, inborn population are on the wane, and if, at the same time, the enormous immigration of uncivilized elements from eastern Europe grows . . . a rural population might soon arise which could not be assimilated by the historically transmitted culture of this country." This population would, he concluded, "change forever the standard of the United States and would gradually form a community of a quite different type from the great creation of the Anglo-Saxon spirit."[86]

Weber admired Booker T. Washington's efforts to train "cheap hands" into industry at Tuskegee, which Weber and his wife Marianne visited on their return from St. Louis, even as he shared Washington's scorn for the culture of impoverished African Americans, and privately mocked Washington himself.[87] Zimmerman has shown how such exchanges shaped the imperial German milieu to which the Tuskegee Institute's experiments with colonial agriculture in Togo belonged, as did Weber's admiration for Du Bois, who attended the St. Louis Congress but did not speak. Weber knew Du Bois from the American sociologist's student days in Berlin and relied upon him for comparative data.[88] Contrary to the gist of Weber's St. Louis talk, it was not only in the medieval manor and its pious extension, the university, that "historically transmitted culture" was passed on through the generations. As Weber's language implied but his arguments belied, *Kultur*, or cultivation, was also a matter for fields, brickyards, and quarries, via the mediations of capital and its institutions, including universities, colleges, and vocational institutes.

A decade and a half later, lecturing at Munich University on the bureaucratization—or "Americanization"—of German academic life, Weber famously defined "Science as a Vocation."[89] Comparing the suspicion of intellectualization among the German youth of 1918 to the enthusiastic philosopher in Plato's parable of the cave who has broken his chains and turned toward the "truth of science," Weber complained that today, "the intellectual constructions of science constitute an unreal realm of artificial abstractions," whereas "here in life, in what for Plato was the play of shadows on the walls of the cave, genuine reality is pulsating; and the rest are derivatives of life, lifeless ghosts, and nothing else."[90] But the research universities of which Weber spoke were not mere instruments of disenchanted reason, their hallways stalked by "lifeless ghosts." In the United States around 1900, the collegiate hallways that led to those of the university marked intergenerational time, selecting whom to admit within the walls of their caves, and administering the time-based lessons of the media, like brick and stone, with which their walls were built. College had become preparatory; but its extension to women had also become a means by which to strengthen the chains of education conceived as cultivation, so that Anglo-Saxons of both sexes would remain in the cave just long enough to secure the future of their race, while others of their generation but not of their race prepared to tend fields, brickyards, factories, and households. To the extent that the training of these others postponed passage through what Du Bois called the "Gates of Toil" into the "Temple of Knowledge," it formed the vocational antithesis—and companion—to "science as a vocation."

4

SOURCES

A Political Ecology of Cultivation

T his chapter turns to research, in print and on the ground. By 1900, the recently established land-grant colleges and universities had become important sites for the cultivation of knowledge that, in many cases, began with the cultivation of land. Summarizing the origins of the land-grant institutions, the historian Allan Nevins called Simeon De Witt's 1819 pamphlet, *Considerations on the Necessity of Establishing an Agricultural College, and Having More of the Children of Wealthy Citizens Educated for the Profession of Farming*, which proposed a state agricultural college with a capacity for experimental research, "the first strong enunciation of the idea of agricultural colleges in America." In Nevins's telling, a sequence of reports, speeches, letters, articles, and legislative resolutions followed, leading to the establishment of the land-grant college and university system during the Civil War.[1]

De Witt based his proposal on existing precedents in Britain, France, Germany, and Russia. In a revealing footnote, Nevins ascribes the relative belatedness with which agricultural schools arose in the United States to the slowness of the older, Eastern states in moving toward mechanized farming, a process that occurred more rapidly in the Midwest. Nevins cites as his source the architectural historian Sigfried Giedion's 1948 "anonymous history," *Mechanization Takes Command*.[2] While Nevins is surely right in listing, after Giedion, the production of nearly 4,100 McCormick reapers in 1858 as one measure of differing rates of change, the feedback effect of Midwestern technological development on Eastern inertia had another, less determinate source, hinted at by the long run of grey technical literature on which Nevins draws. That is, the political economy and political ecology of the land-grant system rested upon the affordances of letterpress printing.[3] In this respect, it was the circulation of printed documents as much as it was mechanized production that took command as a medium of cultivation to which the land-grant universities were essential.

Print Agriculture

Controversies over the westward expansion of slavery were among the causes of the American Civil War, and the conquest and settlement of Western lands remained a governmental priority throughout the war years. Among the instruments for managing this expansion was the Homestead Act of 1862, which realized the aims of the earlier Free Soil movement by offering land grants for resettlement to any citizen who had not taken up arms against the Union. Also in 1862, the first Morrill Act made large tracts of land available to states and territories for the establishment of public colleges and universities "for the benefit of agriculture and the mechanic arts."[4] Often rendered in scrip, these land grants did not typically include sites for the campuses themselves. Rather, they were intended as capital for reinvestment or resale to provide funds for the enhancement of existing institutions or the establishment of new ones.

The resulting "land-grant" colleges and universities aimed, as the legislation put it, to "promote the liberal and practical education of the industrial classes."[5] The Jeffersonian yeoman farmer, who embodied the national compact between citizenship and landownership, became a student and a field researcher. As the needs of the incipient research infrastructure grew, the original land grants were supplemented by the Hatch Act of 1887, which awarded $15,000 annually to public colleges or universities toward the establishment or maintenance of "agricultural experiment stations." Among the requirements for funding was the publication of quarterly bulletins and annual reports, with a copy sent to each station as well as to local newspapers and to relevant government officials, and additionally to interested farmers "as far as the means of the station will permit."[6] Postage for circulating these documents would be free, while only a small percentage of the funds could be used toward the erection or repair of buildings. By 1893, the volume of reports and pamphlets issued by the experiment stations was such that, as one visiting German scholar put it, "340,000 people were on lists to receive 35 million pages of literature distributed *free of charge*."[7] The result was a circulating collection of printed material that construed its sources as resources to be analyzed and recirculated: "print agriculture" rather than print culture.

Pamphlets, bulletins, and reports produced by experiment stations and other research units fulfilled what Lisa Gitelman has called a "know-show" function.[8] They gathered information and circulated it among their networks in the land-grant system, which included other research units as well as field workers like farmers and engineers. In turn, these networks input new information. From the university's margins, and extending across state and national borders, this "paper knowledge" (Gitelman) remade the land-grant university's world in a manner that went well beyond the narrow geographies of what the intellectual historian Roger Chartier has called the "order of books."[9]

Harmony

Writing in July 1857, in the earliest of the notes in the *Grundrisse*, Karl Marx observed of the Philadelphian Henry Charles Carey that he was "the only original economist among the North Americans."[10] Carey, whose self-published four-volume treatise, *Principles of Political Economy*, appeared between 1837 and 1840 under the imprint of Carey, Lea & Blanchard, had inherited the printing house from his father, the Hamiltonian Irish nationalist, amateur economist, and friend of Benjamin Franklin, Mathew Carey. Marx was most likely referring to the younger Carey's later work, which included his 1851 *Harmony of Interests*.[11] The American's originality—and his error—lay, for Marx, in proposing that labor and capital tend toward what Carey called a "harmony of interests" in a closed national market, as manufacturing and agriculture industrialize. This, Marx pointed out, only displaces class conflict to the level of world trade: "The harmony of economic relations rests, according to Carey, on the harmonious cooperation of town and countryside, industry and agriculture." And yet, "with Carey the harmony of the bourgeois relations of production ends with the most complete disharmony of these relations on the grandest terrain where they appear, the world market, and in their grandest development, as the relations of producing nations."[12]

Carey was a protectionist who argued strenuously for tariffs limiting the access of English manufacturers to American raw materials. He also advocated Congressional support for scientific agriculture, particularly in the South as a means to render slavery obsolete. Carey's most regular vehicle for doing so was his friend John Skinner's influential farm journal, *The Plough, the Loom, and the Anvil*, which Carey had helped to found.[13] Self-educated through the printed works amid which he lived since childhood, Carey authored nine books (including two multivolume works) and dozens of pamphlets on political economy and related subjects. He summarized his doctrine of national self-sufficiency through progressive, technologically enhanced agricultural development in an early volume to which Marx could also have been referring, titled *The Past, the Present, and the Future* (1848), as follows:

The earth is a great machine, given to man to be fashioned to his purpose. The more he fashions it, the better it feeds him, because each step is but preparatory to a new one more productive than the last; requiring less labor and yielding larger return.[14]

Carey's thought was comparative; in this early work he reversed David Ricardo's law of decreasing land rent as cultivation proceeds from fertile to infertile land, with the implausible proposition that human settlement always begins on poorer soils and proceeds to richer ones. Carey illustrated this hypothesis with a dizzying survey that passed from the colonies of the New World, into modern Europe, through ancient Egypt, to modern India, to the Himalayan highlands, where he found the most rudimentary instance, "men in a state of barbarism," from which a line of civilizational development ascends as settlement descends, with increasing population, into the fertile valleys of the world's watercourses.[15]

Chiding Carey's "Yankee universality" ("France and China are equally close to him"), Marx admired his penchant for compiling statistics with "a catalogue-like erudition."[16] In the 1850s Carey, who was not an academic, doggedly put this erudition to work lobbying Congress to pass protective tariffs that, he argued, would discourage competition from England and other industrial nations. Among Carey's many correspondents in this effort was Justin Morrill, U.S. representative from Vermont and author of the Morrill Tariff of 1861, which was signed by another Carey correspondent, the outgoing President James Buchanan, shortly before Abraham Lincoln's inauguration.[17]

Carey's pamphleteering, by means of which he engaged other specialists in public polemics, was unusual only in its scale due surely to his lifelong involvement with a publishing industry undergoing rapid mechanization. Despite earning Marx's grudging admiration, Carey exerted comparatively little influence in academic circles. His most immediate predecessors were not scholars but other pamphleteers on political economy in the tradition of Alexander Hamilton, and his direct followers among the budding professoriate of economists numbered relatively few.[18] Carey's most immediate and perhaps most lasting effect on university discourse was, rather, through his worldly contacts, most notably the legislator Morrill and the Philadelphia ironmaster Joseph Wharton. A manufacturer of pig iron and later owner of Bethlehem Steel, Wharton became a prominent protectionist in his own right, taking care to ensure that the "right and duty of national self-protection" would be taught in the school that bore his name at the University of Pennsylvania, which he endowed in 1881.[19]

The case for Carey's influence on Morrill is more circumstantial.[20] The year after the successful passage of the tariff, Morrill authored another, equally well-known piece of legislation, which Lincoln signed into law as the Morrill

Land-Grant Act (or the Morrill Act) of 1862. While it does not appear that Carey lobbied directly for the measure, the connection between the land-grant legislation and the tariff becomes clear when triangulated with Carey's theory of economic development. In a diagram illustrating the third volume of his monumental *Principles of Social Science* (1859), Carey shows land value increasing with wages, as profits fall.[21] In this idealized scenario, settlement and cultivation lead to harmonious cooperation rather than to class conflict, as labor-saving technology supports an associational, vertically integrated mode of production, with increasing proximity of producers to consumers, and fewer intermediaries and profit-seeking brokers. In what is sometimes called Carey's "manure theory of soil improvement," productivity gains introduced by scientific agriculture, along with the movement of population from poorer to richer soils, compensate for capital investments and diminishing profits. Capital yields more rapid returns, while suppliers of raw materials benefit from the elimination of middlemen.[22] Enrichment of the soil thus equals social harmony, in a closed system threatened only by unrestricted trade. Further enrichment is achieved through education, opportunities for which increase with social concentration.

Again Carey's argument is comparative; he adduces cotton farmers in India buying back their product as overpriced British cloth as a signal instance of distant, unprotected labor, comparable to plantation slavery in the American South.[23] He also finds a similar pattern historically; where producers and consumers live and work in close proximity, as in Jean-Baptiste Colbert's France, "agriculture tends to become more of a science," whereas agriculture in the United States is such "that the yield of the land decreases; that the wheat culture is gradually receding towards the West; and that the power to maintain commerce with the world steadily declines."[24] If Carey's principal concern was the country's standing in the world economy, it follows that an educational system like that advocated by Morrill, dedicated to cultivating and disseminating the

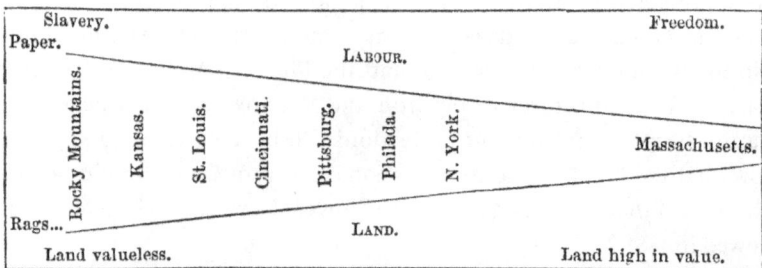

4.1 Henry Charles Carey, *Principles of Social Science*, vol. 3 (Philadelphia: J. B. Lippincott, 1859), diagram of land values, 187.

agricultural and manufacturing sciences, would be the domestic complement to the protectionist tariff.

In Carey's diagram, this logic leads to a peculiar correlation of space with time. At one level, the diagram graphs value relative to the time axis. But running down its middle is a dramatic spatial compression, from the sparsely settled frontier lands of the Rocky Mountains and the Midwest to densely settled and cultivated New England. As settlement density increases over time, so does the "harmony of interests" between capital and labor, mediated by technologically enhanced manure. Or, put differently, as the productivity of a given parcel of land increases with technical mediation, harmonious social relations follow. Carey's thesis was therefore the inverse of the "safety valve" theory of frontier settlement later developed by Wisconsin historian Frederick Jackson Turner, who was a vocal supporter of land-grant institutions. Rather than providing an outlet for excess urban labor, westward emigration was, for Carey, like free trade: a destabilizing factor in which progress from unproductive to productive soil, or from the mountains to Massachusetts, must always restart from scratch.

As conceived by a thinker like Carey, economic development and technological development were chained together in a mutually reinforcing relay. This relay entailed a sense of space and time for which going forward meant reaching backward, from the Rocky Mountain highlands toward New England's fertile, industrial river valleys, or, in Carey's imaginary, trans-historical world tour, from the Himalayan peaks to the ancient Nile delta. This was Massachusetts as Mesopotamia, a timeless civilizational pattern repeating across the land in a closed circuit, interrupted only by unscrupulous competition—"free trade"—from the outside.[25]

Fertilizer, Barley, Paper

The University of Wisconsin was not the only existing institution to be expanded under the Morrill Act, but it became among the largest and most influential. Founded in 1848, the same year that the territory of Wisconsin became a state, the university graduated two students in 1854. In 1866, a state act reorganized the university by providing for the teaching of agriculture and other "industrial arts," and a land grant was made on the basis of the Morrill Act.[26] At Wisconsin, the establishment of an agricultural experiment station preceded that of a college of agriculture. As William A. Henry, professor of agriculture and botany and the station's first director, recounted in his tenth annual report of 1893 (another printed booklet), the state act provided funds for the purchase of lands adjacent to the campus for an "experimental farm," and subsequent legislation provided the first research funds. In 1883, another round of state legislation provided for the establishment of an "experiment station" on the farm, funding for which was substantially increased in 1887 by the Hatch Act.[27]

Henry explained to farmers in his 1893 report that, previous reports now being "very difficult to obtain," the present report would be dedicated to summarizing the station's first decade:

> With this report in his library the farmer who has recently become interested in our station work and whose library lacks the back numbers will find in this volume, our tenth annual report, a good starting point, for his set.[28]

Recursively, Henry took care to explain the system of reports and bulletins, which had initially been provided for in the state legislation of 1881 and extended in 1883, with a subsequent appropriation providing funds for illustrations. Readers learn that the experimental farm's first report, published in 1881 and running seventy-eight pages, saw a print run of five thousand; the next, somewhat longer report ran to six thousand copies. The new legislation doubled this, requiring that twelve thousand copies be printed, and the first station report, in 1883, stretched the limits of the pamphlet format to 102 pages. By 1893, fifteen thousand copies of the annual report were printed, supplemented by the required quarterly bulletins, which ran from five thousand to twelve thousand copies each. The state further required that these publications be distributed free of charge to all interested residents—a provision also incorporated by Congress into the Hatch Act—and by 1893 the University of Wisconsin Agricultural Experiment Station had a mailing list of eight thousand.[29]

Notably for Carey's manure thesis, commercial fertilizers did not figure prominently in the tenth report's retrospective summaries, with only brief mention given to the analysis and application of artificial fertilizers and "land plasters" (ground gypsum). In the station's first annual report of 1883, however, Henry P. Armsby, professor of agricultural chemistry, did note that "as the fertility of the farming land of the state becomes gradually exhausted," the need for "outside aid" will rise. "Already," wrote Armsby, "the consumption of commercial fertilizers in the state is increasing and it will doubtless continue to increase."[30] By 1896, the station was analyzing licensed commercial fertilizers for sale per a new state law.[31]

In the interim, the bulletins and reports focused on the scientific production of manure, as when the 1886 report documented correspondence received from a "Wisconsin dairyman" inquiring into the most productive feed for cows utilized for this purpose. Henry's reply, given in *Hoard's Dairyman* and reproduced in the report, painstakingly compared local market values of different types of feed, corn, and bran, along with the chemical composition of the resulting manure, to the relative value and productivity of commercial fertilizers. In Wisconsin, bran proved superior, while in New Jersey, where the grain was in shorter supply, farmers paid over $1 million annually for fertilizers, for "their land has been so reduced and fertilizers so scarce that they are forced to pay these prices in order to raise good crops."[32] *Hoard's Dairyman*, published out of Fort Atkinson, Wisconsin, was among the thirty-five agricultural newspapers across the country, from San Francisco to New Orleans to Boston, with which the station exchanged printed materials. This geography, overlaid onto that of the nearly sixty experiment stations, agricultural colleges, and boards of agriculture nationally, and the many newspapers, granges, farmers institutes and individual farmers statewide, maps the media network to which the Wisconsin Agricultural Experiment Station belonged in 1885.

In his reply to the Wisconsin farmer, Henry also mentions data received from German experiment stations, a reminder that these networks were transnational from the start.[33] As he later noted, among the products on which the experiment station concentrated in its early years was Manshury barley. W. W. Daniells, the experimental farm's first director, had acquired seed from Dr. Herman Grunow, a Wisconsin farmer, who had brought it from Erfurt, Germany. In the first annual report (1883), Henry recounted the story in detail, confessing his own interest in determining the history of the grain's widespread Midwestern dissemination, which at the time was thought to have originated in Canada. This, too, was recorded in published correspondence between Henry, Grunow, and others.[34]

In unpublished records noted in the published account, Daniells had documented the seed's source as H. Grunow, Esq., of Mifflin, Wisconsin. In early 1884, Henry contacted Grunow, whose return correspondence, published in the report, confirmed that he had acquired the seed, which had proved to be "no. 1 for brewing purposes," from "Ferdinand Duehlke, of Erfurt, at present director of the Agricultural School at Potsdam, and gardener to the Emperor at Sans Souci [*sic*]" in the spring of 1861. Duehlke had obtained the barley from an unnamed "scientific traveler," who had encountered it in "the mountainous parts of Eastern Asia (Mandschurey [Manchuria]), about 1859." Grunow, who like his American colleagues practiced a variety of scientific agriculture for which progress depended upon recursive comparison, sent for more seed (presumably again to Erfurt) "to compare it with other kinds recommended for soil similar to ours, the two-rowed and six-rowed varieties from Peru, the Berbery, from Nepaul [*sic*], Australia, Spain, Denmark, England, the Chevalier, etc." Manshury proved superior to nearly all of these. In 1872 or thereabouts, Grunow sent a sample to the university's experimental farm.[35]

Not yet satisfied, Henry pursued the grain's trail further, into academic-governmental channels, discovering mention of "Mensury barley" in a report made to the United States Department of Agriculture by the Agricultural Department at the University of Washington in 1878. Again he inquired, and again he published the reply, from George B. Loring, U.S. Commissioner of Agriculture, who reported another pathway; the department had sold one hundred bushels of the barley to Mr. N. W. Dean of Madison, Wisconsin in March 1878. Given the timing of this transaction six years after Grunow's gift to the university, Henry concluded that Dean's "source of supply was the Experimental Farm."[36]

The name of the barley was also a matter of some confusion. In later correspondence, Grunow explained to Henry that in Germany it was called "Mandschurei" or "Mandschurey," to reflect the spelling of its purported area of origin on German maps. Grunow, aiming at the English "Manshoor," seems to have translated the name to "Manshury." Henry accepted the translation, which has since been replaced by Minnesota 6 or North Dakota 787, with or without changes to the underlying grain. But perhaps the most telling instance of renaming occurred when, as Henry notes, the grain became known locally as "university" barley, in recognition of its "source of supply."[37] Thus did Wisconsin's beer industry, which was founded largely by German immigrants beginning in the 1840s, register its debt to the experiment station complex, where epistemologies of linear development yielded to spatio-temporal recursivity.

Meanwhile, the networks were growing academic branches on the University of Wisconsin campus. Henry prefaced his second "brief history" of the experiment station, updated for the station's twentieth annual report of 1903, with a detailed description of Agriculture Hall, the building completed earlier that year to house the College of Agriculture.[38] As Henry recounts, early interest in a separate agricultural college led to the establishment of a "Short Course in Agriculture" in 1885, two years after the establishment of the experimental farm. In its first year, the course enrolled nineteen young men; by 1894, enrollment had grown to sixty-eight.

In 1889, the university reorganized to take advantage of provisions in the Hatch Act and created a College of Agriculture along with separate Colleges of Letters and Science, Mechanics and Engineering, and Law. In 1890, the new college added a "short" dairy course to the curriculum, with two students enrolled.[39] Dr. Stephen M. Babcock, an organic chemist trained in Göttingen, was among the course instructors. Babcock had recently developed a milk test that accurately measured the butterfat content of cow's milk, thus establishing pricing and productivity standards that proved crucial to the burgeoning Midwestern dairy industry. Widespread interest in the "Babcock milk test" contributed to an enrollment of seventy. "Here," writes Henry, "began the real enlargement of the College of Agriculture."[40]

At the time of reorganization in 1889, the college and experiment station had four buildings between them: two barns, a boarding house, and a combined dairy building and ice-house. By the end of 1891, the year that saw a dramatic increase in dairy students, a new dairy building had been erected on campus followed by a horticulture-physics building, a dairy barn, a horse barn, a dean's residence, and a number of minor structures. The dairy building was enlarged in 1901, with a central heating plant for the planned Agriculture Hall nearby.

4.2 John T. W. Jennings, Agriculture Hall, University of Wisconsin, 1903. *Twentieth Annual Report of the Agricultural Experiment Station of the University of Wisconsin for the Year Ending June 30, 1903* (Madison: Democrat Printing Co., 1904), frontis.

Agriculture Hall was designed by Wisconsin's first professionally trained campus architect, John T. W. Jennings, who positioned the staid Beaux-Arts monument at the top of a gentle, grand approach stair leading from Linden Drive at the campus's southern edge. The stair climbed toward a three-story Ionic portico, in Indiana limestone, which framed a comparatively modest entrance door. Three brick-clad stories with limestone trim sat atop a limestone-clad raised basement. The plan was straightforwardly symmetrical. Entry was at the basement level; on all four floors, a double-loaded corridor served offices, classrooms, and laboratories. The entry vestibule was flanked on either side by a curved stair leading upward to a large hall. The entry axis continued a half-story downward to an octagonal library located just behind the main volume. Above the library was a two-story octagonal auditorium.

Architecturally, the auditorium was the building's most distinctive feature, along with a sophisticated central heating system with forced-air ventilation ducts running upward to chimney vents from a brick plenum located directly below the basement's central hallway, through which ran electric, gas, water, and steam pipes, the latter connected to the central heating plant.[41] Five small, fireproof vaults were distributed throughout the building: two each on the basement and first floors, flanking the entry vestibule, and one in the same location on the second floor. We can infer from their construction that these vaults were meant for storing combustible objects of value, including paper. While not

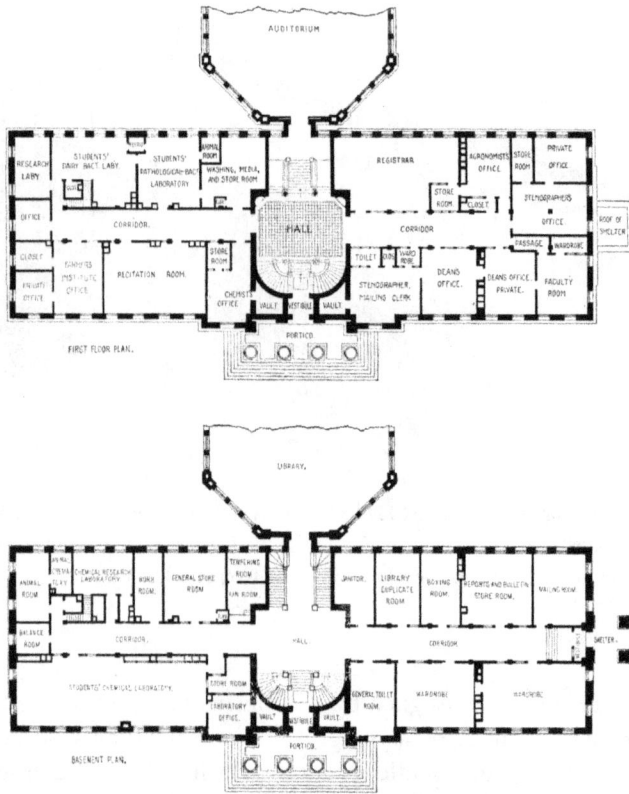

4.3 John T. W. Jennings, Agriculture Hall, University of Wisconsin, 1903. First floor plan and basement plan. William A. Henry, "The New Agricultural Building," *Twentieth Annual Report of the Agricultural Experiment Station of the University of Wisconsin for the Year Ending June 30, 1903* (Madison: Democrat Printing Co., 1904), 6, 8.

mentioning the vaults, Henry takes pains to point out the ample storage provided throughout the building, highlighting those spaces dedicated to the bulletin-and-report network: "The mailing room is located near the east entrance, which has a porte cochere, affording protection from storms in handling mail matter." Nearby, "there is a large room for the storage of extra bulletins and reports; also a room for duplicates from the library."[42]

Whether or not the vaults were actually used for archiving agricultural reports, bulletins, or other printed materials, their presence, along with that of the mail room, storage room, and porte-cochère, constitutes an interface with the network of print agriculture that testifies to that network's significance in tying farms and universities together. As Henry wrote, with the building's completion it was "hard to tell where the campus ends and the farm begins." Though he may have meant this in a visible, spatial sense, it applied even more so in a media-technological sense. According to the same 1903 report, the station distributed some "9,910,000 pages of printed matter in the form of reports and bulletins" the previous year. These included the "547 pages of printed matter, prepared by the workers of the Station," comprising seven bulletins and an annual report, in print runs ranging from ten thousand to fifty thousand each.[43] And, as paper went out, paper came in. Listing several out-of-print reports and bulletins from earlier years, Henry implored his readers to complete the relay:

> Friends of the Station who are not keeping files of our publications are earnestly urged to return to us any copies they may have of rare reports and bulletins. We will gladly pay a reasonable sum for any of the lacking numbers above noted. Readers should bear in mind that the documents asked for are Experiment Station bulletins and reports, and not bulletins of the Farmers' Institute, which is another branch of the Agricultural College.[44]

In this way, experiment station publications linked up with job printing, the postal system, railroads, and libraries, all of which linked up, in turn, with an agricultural apparatus that brought land, water, crops, universities, and government institutions into specific relation. By about 1910, when that system was fully functioning, its operators included researchers, technicians, administrators, students, field hands, bureaucrats, and farmers. Its poetics spoke, in the dry, technical language of the agricultural sciences, of unearthing the secrets of uncultivated lands to maximize their productivity. Though belonging to a national project derived from settler colonialism and linked with economic protectionism, this media complex was transnational. In one case, it extended well beyond the administrative borders of a state university in the American Southwest, first to the Nile delta and then to French West Africa. Knowledge drawn from one site was translated to another, and then to another, joining scientific agriculture with colonial administration.

Deserts and Rivers

In 1890, a board of regents appointed by the Arizona Territorial Legislature (Arizona did not gain statehood until 1912) established the Agricultural Experiment Station of the University of Arizona, with the help of funds provided by the Morrill Act and the Hatch Act. At that point, the new institution consisted of a single, still-unfinished building intended for a School of Mines on forty acres of desert land outside of Tucson, presided over by one professor, Frank A.

Gulley, who had been hired away from his previous post as director of the agricultural experiment station at the Texas Agricultural & Mechanical College. Fifteen acres were set aside for an experimental farm, with four thousand dollars of Hatch Act funding allocated for irrigation. At Gulley's recommendation, the experiment station quickly added five branches scattered throughout the territory and was made adjunct to a College of Agriculture. The following year, 1891, the long-planned School of Mines was added along with a preparatory department, and that fall, the University of Arizona, with a faculty of seven, opened its doors to thirty-two students, most of who were enrolled at the preparatory (i.e., precollegiate) level. What began as an agricultural experiment station distributed across five sites on about 122 acres of land, had become—on paper, at least—a university.[45]

Given the legislative priority accorded to the annual reports and quarterly bulletins of the experiment station, it is not too much to suggest that the University of Arizona was founded, to a considerable extent, first as an instrument for producing these bulletins, and only secondarily as an educational institution. As Gulley put it in the first bulletin, issued on December 1, 1890, although the university intended to use the station's agricultural research as the basis for teaching, in fact, "the question of what work the station should undertake, has received the careful consideration of the board of regents, who have been aided by the advice of persons from different sections of the Territory, who are interested in the development of the agricultural interests."[46]

What these "agricultural interests" were was a matter for the system's users—mainly farmers—to determine. In the second bulletin, issued on September 15, 1891 and dedicated to range grasses, Gulley's colleague, the botanist James W. Toumey, emphasized his willingness "to receive communications from all parts of the territory in regard to weeds, grasses or native plants of any kind." Toumey admonished his correspondents to accompany all letters with specimens, adding that

> In sending plants through the mails, wrap them securely in a newspaper, or better still, in oiled paper so that a minimum of air will reach them.
>
> Send flower and fruit if possible and if not too large, the entire plant, including root.[47]

Thus the archive took up its material. By the third bulletin of October 1891, on "Irrigation in Arizona," the researchers were asking readers, including representatives of "canal and reservoir companies," to send information on extant irrigation systems, including water levels and rates of flow, for tabulation and platting purposes.[48] The station formalized the process in the following issue, on "Water and Water Analysis," by reserving its right to "use and publish in the interests of the Territory any results so obtained" through correspondence with readers, who were given technical instructions for sending water for analysis (again free of charge): one gallon for irrigation water, two gallons for town water.[49]

In 1894, following a dispute over the allocation of faculty time to teaching rather than research, Frank Gulley resigned as director of the Arizona experiment station.[50] After several years of turmoil, Robert H. Forbes, a professor of chemistry hired several years earlier, was appointed in 1898 to take his place.[51] By that time, the experiment station had issued thirty bulletins and reports, included several authored by Forbes on sugar beets, soils, canaigre (a plant used in tanning), and the mesquite tree. Notably, the botanist Toumey's 1898 bulletin on the date palm, a species native to North Africa, provided detailed information on the partly successful importation of numerous seedlings from Egypt to Arizona, including correspondence with U.S. government officials and local growers.[52] Gripped by an agricultural orientalism that saw a scientifically managed Colorado River as a modern Egyptian Nile, Forbes devoted a considerable portion of his time as director of the experiment stations to developing a domestic date palm industry. This began in 1899 with the acquisition of fifteen

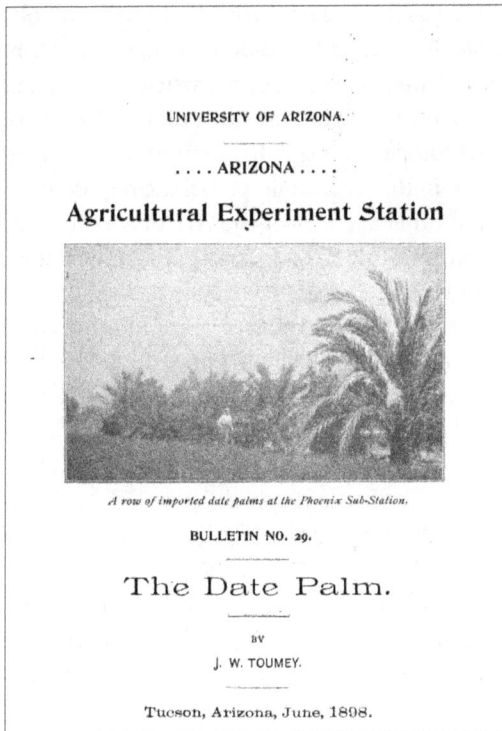

UNIVERSITY OF ARIZONA.

.... ARIZONA ....

Agricultural Experiment Station

A row of imported date palms at the Phoenix Sub-Station.

BULLETIN NO. 29.

The Date Palm.

BY

J. W. TOUMEY.

Tucson, Arizona, June, 1898.

4.4 James W. Toumey, "The Date Palm," *Arizona Agricultural Experiment Station, Bulletin,* no. 29 (15 June 1898), cover.

acres near Tempe for the cultivation of imported date palms in collaboration with the U.S. Department of Agriculture, and it ended almost twenty years later with Forbes's departure from the university to take up a position as scientific advisor to the Société Sultanienne d'Agriculture in Cairo in 1918.[53]

Although the agronomy of the date palm was Forbes's point of entry into the Cairene agricultural scene, cotton was his destination. His assignment in Cairo was to direct the Société's agricultural experiment work, which included extensive travel to observe extant practices, and the importation of over eight hundred plant varieties from Arizona and elsewhere in the American Southwest for experimentation. Forbes published some of his findings in the *Sultanic Agricultural Society Technical Section Bulletin*, and, after four years, made recommendations for further development in a detailed report that he submitted prior to his departure.[54]

This work secured for Forbes another appointment as an agricultural expert, now for the French Compagnie Générale des Colonies, as chief engineer of agronomic studies in the French Soudan (Mali), a position that he held until 1926. Working mainly out of Ségou (Segu) on the banks of the Niger River, Forbes spent four years managing the colonial administration of cotton production in the Niger basin. He summarized his work and observations there in a series of internal memos, in correspondence, in a published report to the French government, as well as in subsequent articles, only occasionally allowing his casual racism to show through.[55] In 1924, *Les Annales Coloniales* recorded in detail Forbes's work comparing the cultivation of several varieties of Egyptian and American cotton in the deltaic and predeltaic regions of the Niger basin.[56]

The bulletins and other records of the Arizona experiment stations were collected in the libraries of numerous land-grant universities and many others, in the offices of federal and state agricultural agencies, and in the offices and homes of the various researchers, farmers, and other correspondents who helped make these bulletins possible in the first place. The documents also cultivated a set of sources that they helped convert into resources, in the lands and waters that stretched across the territory and then state of Arizona, haunted by ancient Egyptian ghosts in the form of date palms from the Nile delta. All of these sources became the basis of Forbes's later work in Egypt and in French West Africa, which took him next to Haiti, as an agricultural advisor to the American occupation there, and then back to Arizona, where he sought to apply his extensive experience in the management of agricultural resources as a member of the Arizona House of Representatives. In each site the archive grew as new reports were published. But its extremities were already connected when Forbes fastidiously collected ancient knowledge and modern plants from North Africa to help cultivate the Arizona desert.

In 1901, anticipating a Southwestern cotton industry of which the date palm was an avatar, Forbes had compared the Colorado River to the Nile well before having seen, touched, or tested the latter's waters, when he wrote in the forty-fourth bulletin of the Arizona Agricultural Experiment Station that:

> When the Colorado is understood and utilized as successfully as is its greater and better known parallel, it will be recognized as the American Nile, the creator of a new country for the irrigator, and Mother of an Occidental Egypt.[57]

In fact, the reverse was also true. In the hands of the agricultural apparatus to which Forbes belonged, the Nile and the Niger became just a little like the Colorado. The two African rivers and their surrounding landscapes were important loci of colonial and protocolonial governance, via the Egyptian and French West African cotton industries, including the varieties of American cotton and other material transplanted by Forbes and his colleagues.[58] Despite Forbes's

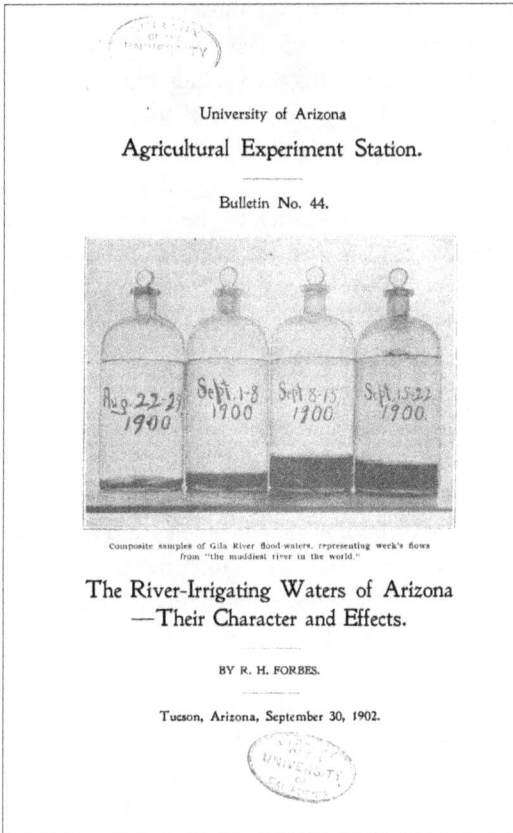

4.5 Robert H. Forbes, "The River Irrigating Waters of Arizona—Their Character and Effects," *Arizona Agricultural Experiment Station, Bulletin*, no. 44 (30 September 1902), cover.

efforts, and closer to the West African experience, a comparable industry did not take root in Arizona until much later. Nevertheless, the experiment station bulletins and their authors contributed to the work of governing at another level, wherein the "homogeneous, empty time"—and space—of modernization were anything but that.[59] Gathering data by correspondence, organizing and disseminating it as knowledge, the bulletins formed a relay that helped to define what later became known as "development." For this relay, going forward meant reaching back in both space and time, from the Colorado River to the ancient Nile, then back to the Nile and beyond.[60] Only then did the knowledge gathered in technical bulletins truly circulate, remorselessly building the epistemic ground from which resources grew.

Oil and Water

Toward the end of the posthumously published *Capital*, volume 3, Marx (or his editor, Friedrich Engels) began the chapter on "Building Site Rent, Rent in Mining, Price of Land" by explaining the partnership of landowners and capital in the exploitation of wage labor. "One part of society," he wrote, "thus exacts tribute from another for the permission to inhabit the earth, as landed property in general assigns the landlord the privilege of exploiting the terrestrial body, the bowels of the earth, the air, and thereby the maintenance and development of life." At pains to distinguish land (or ground) rent from profit on capital investment in dwelling, cultivation, or extraction while showing their interdependence, Marx again invoked Henry Carey if only to dismiss the American economist's "goodwill" in conflating the two.[61] Marx was referring to Carey's argument that land values increase with wages as profits on capital decline, thus harmonizing the interests of landlord and worker. Earlier in the same volume, Marx (or Engels) cited Carey's account of this process in *The Past, the Present, and the Future*, to show the contrary: that, although the value of land tends to increase due to growing technological efficiencies and enhancements, the bulk of such gains accrues to capitalist and landlord, not to wage labor. As contracts expire, the landlord incorporates the enhancements into future rents, and thus "sells [or rents] not merely the land but the improved land."[62] The same applies to lands bearing mineral resources as these are made accessible.

For his understanding of scientific agriculture Marx relied heavily on the work of the German organic chemist Justus von Liebig, who was also an important reference for Carey and who provided an influential model for the first generation of chemists and agronomists in the land-grant colleges and universities.[63] Although neither made extensive reference to William Stanley Jevons's *The Coal Question* (1865), which warned of the imminent depletion of Britain's coal reserves, Marx and Carey agreed that resource exhaustion, most commonly by the degradation of soil, represented an important ecological limit to the otherwise limitless cycle of extraction. Where Carey recommended protectionist tariffs, Marx saw class conflict.[64] In this context, the remediation of linear time we have observed in Carey's economics, Wisconsin's barley circuit, and Forbes's agricultural orientalism applies to the revaluation of land through the discovery and description of untapped subterranean resources.

The University of Texas at Austin was not a federal land-grant institution. Opened in 1881 in the aftermath of Reconstruction, the university did not receive funding through the Morrill legislation, which went instead to the Agricultural and Mechanical College of Texas (Texas AMC, later Texas A&M), founded in 1871 near Bryan, Texas. Both institutions were racially segregated until the mid-twentieth century, but where Texas AMC served a mainly rural population, the coeducational University of Texas drew many of its students from an entrepreneurial middle class that grew dramatically with the Texas oil boom that began in the early 1900s.[65]

The Texas Agricultural Experiment Station was founded at AMC in 1887 with funds provided by the Hatch Act. In 1901, the state legislature provided for the establishment of a comparable institution at the University of Texas devoted to the study and cultivation of mineral resources, the Texas Mineral Survey, under the direction of the geologist William B. Phillips. As with the agricultural experiment stations, a significant proportion of the survey's resources were devoted to compiling, publishing, and circulating printed reports. Like his Wisconsin colleagues, Phillips kept count of the volume of paper passing through the survey's offices. In the 1901–1902 academic year, the over twelve thousand items distributed from the survey offices in the university's Main Building comprised two bulletins, miscellaneous reprints, and over 2,800 letters. The first of the bulletins, nearly four thousand copies of which were distributed free of charge in the fall of 1901, was titled *Texas Petroleum*.[66]

According to Phillips, demand for *Texas Petroleum* was so great that the survey ran out of copies. The bulletin told the story of the state's still nascent oil industry, from the first few hundred barrels coming out of the ground annually around 1895, to eight hundred thousand by 1900. More than once, landowners or their agents discovered oil while in search of water, which was of special concern for agriculturalists in the region and the subject of other university reports. In the fall of 1890, for example, future University of Texas president Col. William L. Prather struck oil while boring for water on his farm in Waco, the first hint of petroleum in that part of the state. In 1894, Major Alexander Beaton did the same in nearby Corsicana, which was to become one of the state's two largest oil fields.[67] The search for oil in the area around Beaumont began in 1892 when, according to the bulletin, Patillo Higgins "seems to have organized the Gladys City Oil, Gas and Manufacturing Company and to have succeeded in interesting capital in the enterprise."[68] The ensuing discovery would develop

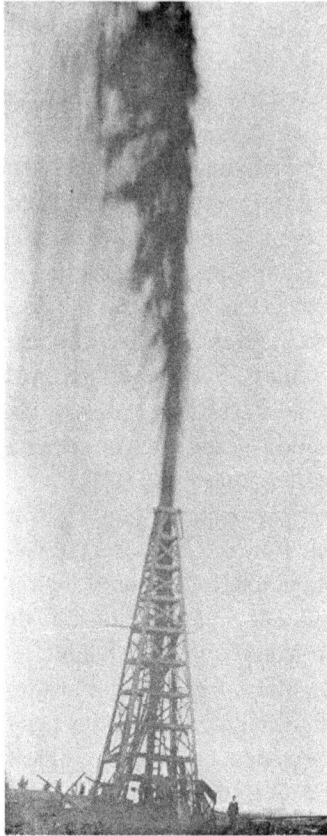

4.6 Lucas Well, Spindletop Oil Field, Beaumont, Texas. From William B. Phillips, *Texas Petroleum: Bulletin of the University of Texas, no. 5; The University of Texas Mineral Survey Bulletin, no. 1, July 1901* (Austin: University of Texas, 1901), n.p.

into the state's largest and most famous oil field, Spindletop. Under contract to the mining and mechanical engineer Anthony F. Lucas, Hamill Brothers of Corsicana drilled the first well of significance there, which erupted in a dramatic gusher on January 10, 1901, the capacity of which was estimated at seventy-five thousand barrels a day.[69]

Texas Petroleum reports that Corsicana oil lay in the Cretaceous subterranean stratum; the oil at Spindletop (Beaumont) was found in the Tertiary, several hundred feet below. Costs of drilling at Beaumont were higher, owing partly to the geology. Even then, they were "out of all proportion" when compared with Corsicana, where significant capital had already been invested in a high-capacity refinery. Economics permeates the bulletin's technical focus, such as when Phillips points out the drop in oil prices with the opening of the

Beaumont field.[70] In addition to quantifying the amount of crude found thus far within what Phillips called the "oil horizons" delimited by geological strata, the bulletin also includes a series of tables providing detailed information on the depth and geology of several wells at Corsicana. Each well is listed by landowner—Walton Farm, County Poor Farm, and Presley Well (Town Lot)— all of which were drilled by the Southern Oil Company, providing a microcosmic portrait of the relation of capital and landlord discussed by Marx and Carey several decades earlier with respect to agriculture. Labor is absent from the story Phillips tells in *Texas Petroleum*; in its place, detailed accounts of the geology and of the drilling equipment, exploration, and capital investment are accompanied by site-specific chemical analyses of the petroleum itself.

According to *Texas Petroleum*, the oil found at Beaumont was very close in composition to that coming out of the largest source of oil in world markets at the time, the Russian oil fields in Baku on the "Apsheron" (Absheron) Peninsula. At Baku, however, government ownership of the land limited the rent charged to investors, with leases usually requiring "minimum" royalty payments.[71] In comparison, the report quotes at length from another report, made by Benjamin F. Hill of the United States Geological Survey, on the discovery of oil beneath "grazing and rice lands" around Beaumont and Spindletop Heights. A "fever heat" immediately followed the discovery, when "many unwise investments were made," in the aftermath of which six companies operated a total of fourteen wells in the Spindletop area. Hill reports, however, that "a great number of companies have purchased small tracts of land" in the area, with a total of about three hundred derricks erected in various states of operation.[72] All of this occurred in a period of about six months, with pipelines, pumping stations, and storage tanks erected in anticipation of the flow, and shipping companies preparing the infrastructure for worldwide distribution inaugurated by the departure of three thousand barrels from Port Arthur on March 22, 1901. Most companies leased the land on which they drilled; a few owned it outright, but many paid well above market rents to land speculators, with barren lands fetching between five and one hundred times their value prior to the discovery of oil. Dozens of wells had been named and inventoried, some keeping records sufficiently detailed for geologists to begin mapping the new, subterranean frontier.

Against this frenzied backdrop, the geological analyses of the substrata, accompanied by detailed chemical analyses of the oil pumped out, form a prelude to the bulletin's prophetic concluding chapter, on "The Utilization of Petroleum as Fuel." In 1899, the United States was second only to Russia in oil production. Still, U.S. exports amounted to only about 5 percent of total production. The United Kingdom was the best customer for refined petroleum (naphtha), with France by far the leading importer of crude. Texas was only the seventh largest supplier, well behind Ohio, Pennsylvania, West Virginia, and other states with more developed oil industries.[73] The United States was not to become a net importer of oil until a century later. But even in these early years, such details show how the knowledge gathered in bulletins like *Texas Petroleum*, with thousands of copies circulating among universities, government agencies, and industry, mediated the dialectics of ground rent and capital investment elucidated by Marx. A subterranean connection born of technical bulletins and reports may help to explain, then, the transfer over the next century of the contradictions of development, free trade, and protectionism that Marx discerned in Carey's writings, from the domain of agriculture to that of energy.

Lost Time

At certain points in the network, however, the trail goes cold. The remediation of linear time we have followed, where feedback loops reached out and back at various levels to sustain the ideologies and the realities of economic development, met an impasse when it came to processing all the paper. New systems had to be devised and new timelines set out. This entailed a technics of catalogues and metadata premised on further expansion. As knowledge grew, so did its storage, but not without entropic data loss.[74]

Two decades before Wisconsin farmers began using commercial fertilizer, date palms began arriving in Arizona, or oil was struck in Texas, the young bibliographer and librarian Melvil Dewey boasted of the numerical classification system for "Cataloguing and Arranging the Books and Pamphlets of a Library" that he had recently worked out at Amherst College:

> These class numbers applied to pamphlets have proved specially satisfactory. The number is written on the upper left corner and the pamphlets are arranged either in pamphlet cases with the books on the same subject or on special shelves divided every decimeter by perpendicular sections. As each pamphlet is examined when received into the library, it is the work of a single moment to pencil on its class number. There is no expense whatever incurred, and yet the entire pamphlet resources of the library on any subject can be produced almost instantly. The immense advantages of this plan over those in common use, both in economy and usefulness, will be appreciated by every librarian caring for a pamphlet collection.[75]

The presence of pamphlets in Dewey's subtitle and as an exemplary instance of his system's efficiency testifies to their importance for librarians at the time. Wayne Wiegand has shown how Dewey synthesized such techniques, drawn from a miscellany of sources, with a conservative Anglo-Saxonism derived from the classical project of mental discipline. The first level, or "class," to which

Dewey assigned a given document reproduced the associated hierarchy of knowledge, which passed by then through the Hegelian system, with philosophy as a master discourse.[76]

Shortly after Henry Carey's death in 1879, approximately three thousand pamphlets from Carey's personal library arrived at the University of Pennsylvania. The university did not have adequate resources or personnel even to pencil a single number on the corner of each pamphlet and record that number with the document's title in an index. Along with a similar collection donated by the Philadelphia ironmaster Stephen Colwell, Carey's pamphlet collection, the bulk of which treated antebellum political economy and thus served as an archive for his writings, languished for at least a decade, most probably in College Hall where the university library had been housed. In 1891 the pamphlets, some of which may have been prebound, were most likely moved along with the books to the new library building designed by the Philadelphia architect Frank Furness, which opened in February of that year. Melvil Dewey and his associate, Harvard librarian Justin Winsor, had advised Furness and the library committee headed by Furness's brother, the Shakespeare scholar Horace Howard Furness, on the organization of the new library, which adopted Dewey's classification system for its expanded catalogue.[77]

Anticipating the difficulty of dealing with bulk items, Dewey had suggested that uncatalogued pamphlets be treated like books.[78] At some point, the remaining pamphlets in the Carey collection were bound into volumes, which received DDC call numbers like 330.8 P753 v.275. In the Dewey system, the first number (330) designated a "sub-section" or subset (Political Economy) of a general subject class (Sociology, 300), the number following the decimal designated in this case format (Polygraphy, or a collection), with the subsequent alphanumerics supplying further information related to order of accession, followed in this case by a volume number.[79] Cataloguers would have recorded the bound volumes in the new catalogue room on the ground floor of the building. Then, they would have inserted the cards into a two-way catalogue file with space for one million entries, which was fitted into the arched openings that separated that room from the main reading room and was thus accessible to readers from one side and cataloguers from the other.[80]

The Furness library belongs to a sequence of academic libraries that, in the United States, begins with Henry Van Brunt and William Ware's extension to Harvard's Gore Hall (1841), with its fireproof iron bookstacks, and runs through Henry Hobson Richardson's rough-hewn Billings Memorial Library at the University of Vermont (1886), with a significant debt also to Henri Labrouste's Bibliothèque Nationale in Paris (1875).[81] Furness's division of the library into three main functional zones was compatible with Dewey's drive to rationalize the process of cataloguing and storage. It was also replicable, as Dewey showed when he advised the University of Toronto on designs for a new library the

4.7 Frank Furness, University of Pennsylvania Library, 1891. *Proceedings at the Opening of the Library of the University of Pennsylvania, February 7, 1891* (Philadelphia: University of Pennsylvania Press, 1891), frontis.

following year that were remarkably similar.[82] Furness's main innovation, adapted from Richardson, was to treat each of the building's three sections in a distinct manner: a grand, apsidal space for the reading room; side and rear service areas for librarians; and behind, a greenhouse-like, theoretically extendable iron-and-glass shed for the books.

An early plan for a different site shows a gear-like ring of teaching alcoves for professors rotating around the circumference of the reading room and flattening out along the side wall to become a series of book-lined cubicles for the cataloguers, in a jarringly figural ode to mechanization. Clad in luminous red brick, the library as built also recalls the more somber red brick factories built in the preceding decades in the industrial Northeast, with their dissonant mixtures of Victorian ornament and utilitarian straightforwardness in massing and internal layout. Underlining the allusion, Furness fitted his building with a host of quasi-industrial equipment, including gear- and sprocket-like window trimmings and a custom-designed, three-story iron bookstack. Coupled with the utilitarian plan, these built-in bits of machinery encourage the interpretation of the building as a site of production.[83]

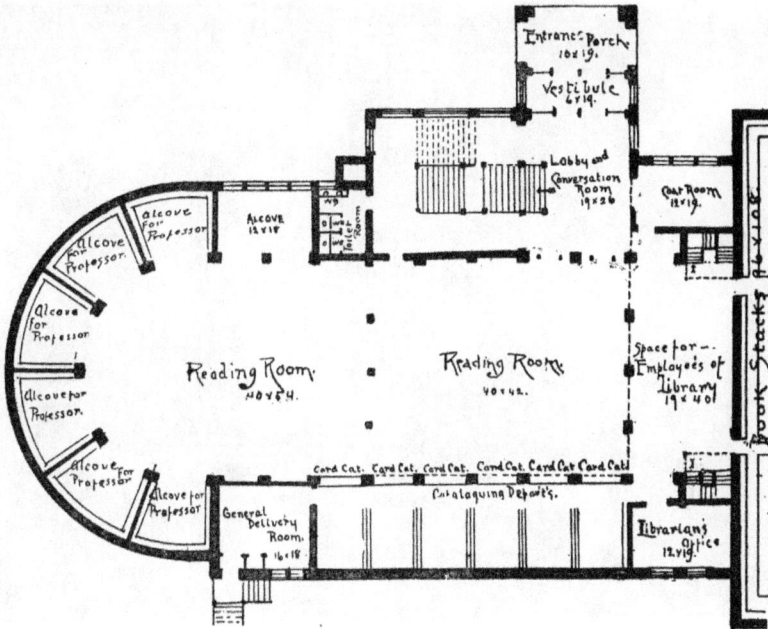

PLAN OF THE MAIN LIBRARY FLOOR.

4.8 Frank Furness, University of Pennsylvania Library, preliminary plan for a different site, main floor, 1888. Talcott Williams, "Plans for the Library Building of the University of Pennsylvania," *Library Journal* 13, no. 8 (August 1888): 241.

But the library's tripartite plan, with distinct components for data processing, transmission, and storage, made it as much an informatic device as a mechanical one. With its efficient cataloguing system for assigning metadata like addresses (DDC numbers), its extendable bookstacks, and its generous accommodations for reading and teaching, the library was designed to alleviate an informational deluge brought on by the mechanization of print, the growth of scholarship, and the expansion of the university. As such, it belonged to a much longer tradition within textual culture dating back several centuries devoted to managing the problem of, as Ann Blair has put it, "too much to know."[84] But what was uncatalogued and therefore unknown to the library's users is just as important. Centered on the bound volume, the Pennsylvania library system had difficulty processing printed knowledge that was not contained in books.

Although academic and public libraries successfully catalogued and stored countless pamphlets, bulletins, and reports using the DDC or other systems,

4.9 Frank Furness, University of Pennsylvania Library, 1891. Reading room. *Proceedings at the Opening of the Library of the University of Pennsylvania, February 7, 1891* (Philadelphia: University of Pennsylvania Press, 1891), n.p.

many of which now reside online, for over a century the Carey collection has remained in bibliographic limbo.[85] Though the bound volumes were catalogued and their contents matched to the volume number, the pamphlets were never individually indexed. This made the pamphlets into what library science calls a (partly) hidden collection, an undiscovered, ghostly presence held in storage without sufficient metadata to allow easy access and use by readers. At some point, the pamphlets were accessioned to the special collections center in the Van Pelt Library, which opened in 1962, which is where they are today. In many ways, the University of Pennsylvania library, and with it, the many other research libraries built on university campuses during the period, heralded a new chapter in the era of the book. But the partly hidden pamphlets suggest that the building may well also belong to a less illustrious though no less important lineage. As the examples of scientific agriculture and oil exploration show, by 1900 whole areas of technical knowledge had developed out of other, more easily produced, read, and circulated forms of printed media, like the bulletins and reports moving in and out of the academy's margins, for which the pamphlets collected by Carey were both precursors and resources. The significance of these old formats adapted to new needs lies not only in their ever-growing presence in the catalogue or on the shelves but in the unassigned numbers and unoccupied addresses, which bear modest witness to a subtle, almost imperceptible rescaling of knowledge into smaller, more agile units circulating in feedback loops that have long reached across the earth and under its surface, at scales at once expansive and compressed, that the order of books could not quite match.

INTERLUDE, c. 1900

During the later nineteenth century, as colleges became universities, the paradigmatic liberal individual was reborn in the plural—as a dataset, a collection of measurable characteristics. Faculty gradually became middle management, and students, grade point averages. When, in 1893 and based on recent census data, Frederick Jackson Turner, professor of American history at the University of Wisconsin, announced the closing of the American frontier, he inaugurated a vast literature around what has since become known as the "frontier thesis."[1] Turner argued that for a century or so after the nation's founding, Anglo-American colonial settlement on Western and other "frontier" lands continuously renewed a democratic ethos at risk of corruption in urban areas, by offering a "safety valve" in the form of "free land," resources, and opportunity. By 1890, that frontier had closed.[2] Although it has been discussed mainly in political, economic, and historical terms, Turner's thesis and the myth it reproduced depended upon and utilized technical procedures that differed significantly from Thomas Jefferson's dumbwaiters and the Republic of Letters that they served.

The nation was now a statistical body, as was the university's body corporate. The biopolitics of Turner's closed frontier were just as different from those of Jefferson's dumbwaiters as were its infrastructures. Variations on the topological and quantitative principle of "separate but equal"—codified in the Jim Crow South but practiced far more widely—reproduced upstairs-downstairs, inside-outside hierarchies. Correspondingly, the socioeconomic problem became one of locating and counting. What was produced where? In what quantity? By whom? These were the essential questions asked and answered by the 1893 World's Columbian Exposition in Chicago, where Turner announced his thesis. Like the thesis itself, such questions were enabled by a media complex of which the fair was only part.[3] Like the railroads that formed another of its elements, that complex governed more through information-based, infrastructural control than by sovereign discipline.[4] Also like the railroads and like the fair itself, a mediapolitics of territorial enclosure reoriented academic knowledge toward the interpretation of technologically produced symbols.

Symbolic Machines

To advance his thesis, Turner cited what he called the "significant words" of Robert P. Porter, superintendent of the 1890 census:

> Up to and including 1880 the country had a frontier of settlement, but at present the unsettled area has been so broken by isolated bodies of settlement that there can hardly be said to be a frontier line. In the discussion of its extent, its westward movement, etc. it can not, therefore, any longer have a place in the census reports.[5]

Porter's words appeared originally in an 1891 Census Bureau bulletin alongside a map showing areas of settlement in varying densities and demographics, including what the census tables called "Civilized Indians" among other nonwhite populations.[6] Anything less than two persons per square mile was considered unsettled. Visible among the many pockets of conquest west of the Mississippi River, and adding density elsewhere, were college and university campuses and the towns that grew up around them, particularly the land-grant institutions supported by the first Morrill Act of 1862.[7]

Reflecting increased government investment in social statistics and the large quantities of information that these required, the 1890 census was the first to use automated data processing, in the form of punched cards and the machines to encode and read them developed for this purpose by the engineer and entrepreneur Herman Hollerith. Data collected on each individual counted by the census were recorded on one punched card.[8] These vital statistics were gathered in household questionnaires and then individualized. A key advantage of the Hollerith system was that cards could easily be sorted to represent geographic areas at different scales, from "enumeration district" to county to state, in bundled data sets.[9] The first of four automated counts made for the 1890 census tabulated race, sex, nativity, and place of domicile.[10] Based on this information, the "frontier line," if it ever was a line at all, disappeared into the difference between one dataset ("settled") and another ("unsettled"), as the settler colony became a database.[11]

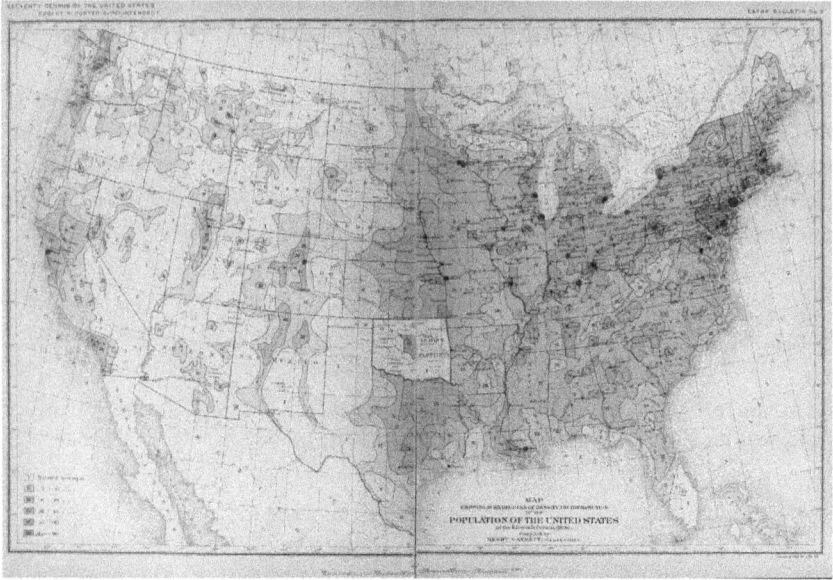

I.1 *Map Showing in Six Degrees of Density the Population of the United States at the Eleventh Census (1890)*, compiled by Henry Gannett. Robert P. Porter, "Distribution of Population According to Density: 1890," *Extra Census Bulletin*, no. 2 (20 April 1891): 6–7.

The entire process was extra-academic; the data were governmental and the machines were commercial. Hollerith, who had studied at the Columbia College School of Mines, was a businessman. Nonetheless, in 1888 he requested that Columbia award him a PhD "for the studies in which he has been engaged since he graduated, in connection with the tabulating system which has been adopted by the U.S. government."[12] An exception was made and a degree duly awarded. Hollerith's PhD, which was among the first awarded by the university, acknowledged a growing dependence of academic knowledge on commercial hardware. The early card punches and readers were succeeded by tabulating machines and automated calculators designed and manufactured by the Computing-Tabulating-Recording Company (CTR), which was incorporated in 1911 when Hollerith's company merged with several others. In 1924, CTR was renamed International Business Machines (IBM).[13]

Floating Signifiers

Turner presented his influential account of a threshold for primitive accumulation at a meeting of the American History Association held at the World's

Congress Auxiliary Building in Chicago (shortly thereafter, the Art Institute), immediately adjacent to the World's Columbian Exposition. Specially arranged as an "auxiliary congress," the meeting of historians was timed to coincide with the fair's run.[14] The exposition, on the fourth centennial of Christopher Columbus's arrival, celebrated the bloody conquest of Indigenous populations and the alchemical conversion of raw materials into capital. Against this backdrop, Turner argued that westward territorial expansion had halted at the Pacific Coast and land was no longer "free." Though, as he put it, the frontier had never been a "tabula rasa," each stage of advancement had offered a "gate of escape from the bondage of the past."[15] For Turner this was democracy at its purest, a form of cooperative individualism that now required other outlets to grow. Making this argument at a time of severe economic distress and agrarian discontent, Turner understood the United States, perhaps for the first time, as what the historian Martin Sklar much later called a "developing country."[16]

The centerpiece of the 1893 exposition was an ensemble of buildings designed in a Beaux-Arts manner by a consortium of architects led by the Chicago-based Daniel Burnham. The White City, so called because of its uniform white plaster staff façades, was a hymn to the money economy. Its massive exhibition buildings floated atop concrete "rafts" on unstable soil.[17] Despite the efforts of the planners to project a unified image, the exposition's rampant iconography did not cohere. Mixed messages proliferated, in architecture, sculpture, painting, photography, and various literary forms. Above all, the cacophony of signs exhibited an underlying need for a new signifying infrastructure, a new system of meaning, which Turner succinctly provided with his frontier thesis.

Arranged as a sort of campus, most of the fair's individual buildings repeated the architectural formula of a neoclassical portico backed up by a utilitarian shed. Among these, frontier symbols concentrated most densely in two adjacent structures, the Agriculture Building and the Mines and Mining Building. Dedicated to the Roman goddess Ceres, the Agriculture Building was designed by the New York firm of McKim, Mead & White, led by Charles F. McKim, who also served as an informal artistic advisor on the exposition's overall design. From the outside the building resembled a distended, heavily ornamented Renaissance palazzo that, in its sheer breadth and like many of its companions, eluded pictorial grasp. Inside the steel-and-glass shed, two sky-lit axes divided products from every state in the nation, its territories, and numerous other countries into four quadrants. At the center of the main façade was a circular entrance vestibule, covered by a 130-foot-high dome atop which stood an enigmatic master signifier: "Diana on her airy perch, turning to every breeze."[18] McKim's partner, Stanford White, had commissioned the sculptor Augustus Saint-Gaudens to produce an eighteen-foot gilded, sheet copper figure of the Roman goddess to serve as a weather vane atop Madison Square Garden in New York. Too large and too heavy for the urban leisure palace, the Diana sculpture was replaced with a smaller, lighter version. The original, detached from its already vague association with sport, was relocated to Chicago, where some exposition visitors may have recognized Diana's association with the hunt. But more likely, the giant, distant figure was the sign of a sign, a placeholder for something anticipated but not yet named.

Immediately adjacent was the Mines and Mining Building, designed in a deformed neo-Romanesque manner by the Chicago architect Solon Spencer Beman to exhibit mining industries and their equipment, as well as the corresponding ores, minerals, and precious metals.[19] Inside were, among other things, displays of Mexican and African gold amid which, in keeping with the fair's overall racial-ethnographic economy, "the Zulus washed diamonds before a continuous *queue* of people."[20] Their iconological partner, prominently placed before materials from the Montana mines, was the *Silver Queen* (or *Justice*). Modeled after a popular actress, the nine-foot figure was cast in sterling silver and stood

I.2 R. H. Parks, *The Silver Queen*, Montana exhibit, Mines and Mining Building, World's Columbian Exposition, Chicago, 1893. *Photographs of the World's Fair: An Elaborate Collection of Photographs of the Buildings, Grounds and Exhibits of the World's Columbian Exposition with a Special Description of the Famous Midway Plaisance* (Jersey City, NJ: Eureka Publishing/The Werner Co, 1894), 97.

on a two-foot diameter silver sphere atop a gold plinth, holding a scale "equi-poised with silver and gold coins, showing the sentiment of Montanians [*sic*] on the silver question."[21] Thus, in the midst of the 1893 economic crisis, the vicious political debate over two competing financial destinies for frontier capitalism, gold-silver convertibility (bimetallism) or a universal gold standard, was symbol-ically resolved in a placid balance, with silver anachronistically on top.[22]

Calculation

Lurking within Turner's thesis and on exhibit in Chicago was therefore a need prompted by the money economy for meaningful symbols. No less importantly, Turner's use of the 1890 census entailed a mediapolitics of number. Governing was calculation, and freedom was a matter of access to statistics, which meant access to the technics of research. W. E. B. Du Bois's early statistical attempt to erase the color line with the "Talented Tenth" was its dialectical partner.[23] But the abstractions of the money economy and the numbers circulating in the new research universities did not merely supersede the earthy values of an artisanal, precommodified past. In Friedrich Nietzsche's language, abstrac-tion was "transvaluation." Or, to put it differently, myth did not go the way of the frontier; rather, the mythic character of the frontier was remediated by its alleged disappearance. As dramatized by the *Silver Queen*'s straining for sig-nification and by the floating White City itself, financial capitalism was a sys-tem for the manufacture of meaning. Like money itself, these materially heavy, semantically weightless symbols testified to what the German sociologist Georg Simmel called, in 1900 and without having set foot on the North American continent, "the calculating character of modern times."[24]

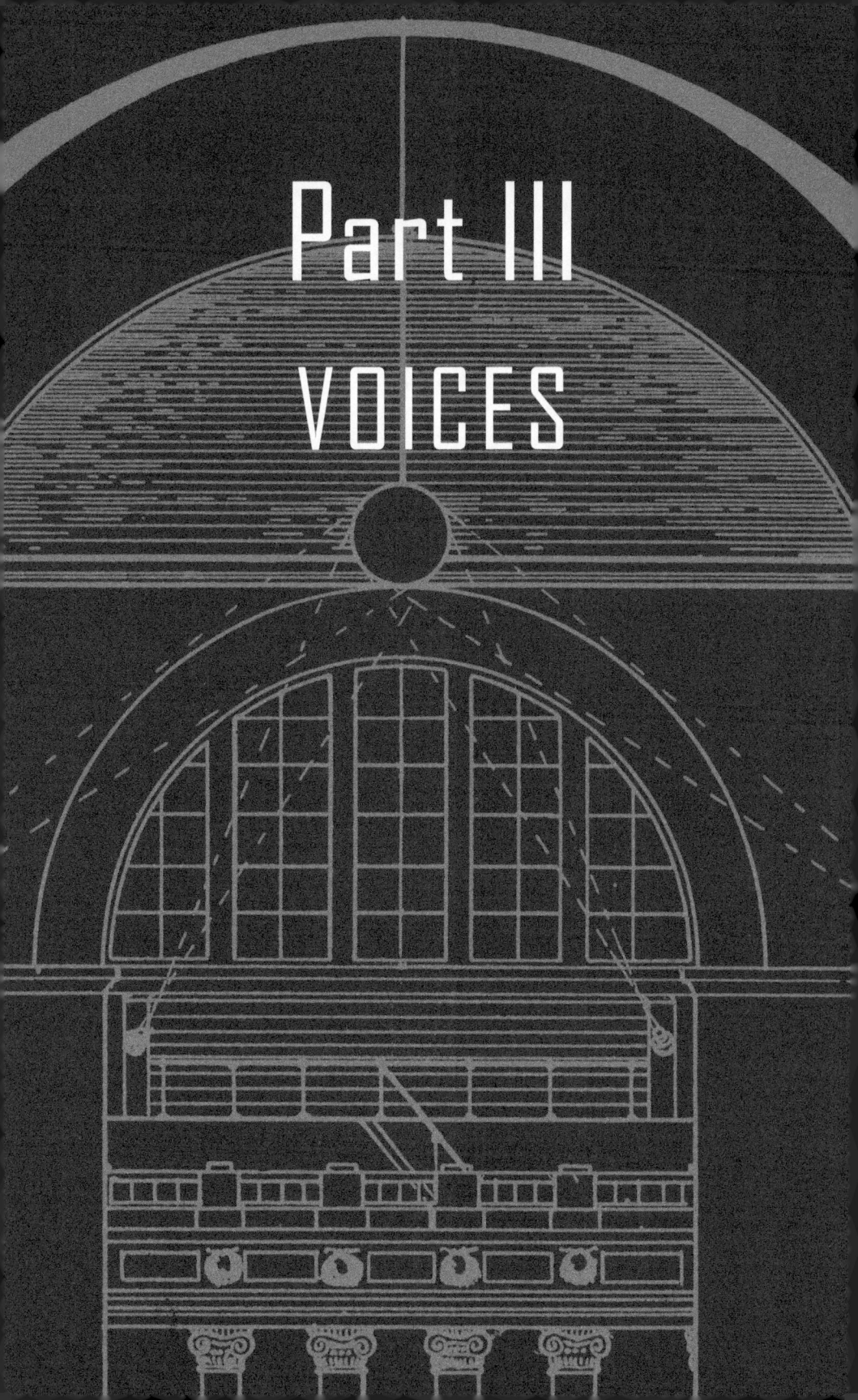

Part III
VOICES

5

DIFFUSE ILLUMINATION

The Silence of the Universal

I f Thomas Jefferson and other representatives of the liberal order owed
something to the Lockean proposition that natural rights are ideas,
or universals that float free from any particular material arrangement,
he and others also needed someplace material in which to have such ideas.[1]
In Jefferson's view, to know and to actualize the natural rights of life, liberty,
and property (or "the pursuit of happiness," in Jefferson's version) one needed
a liberal education. For which were required books, light, and silence. In this
chapter, we will follow a dialectics of silence and illumination in two reading
rooms in two libraries over the course of about a century, first at the University
of Virginia and then at Columbia University. From library to library, we will
see enlightenment made literal in a spectacle of silent research. A postcolonial
coda shows the translation of words associated with these two rooms from one
speaking situation to another, where tensions between embodied, democratic
citizenship and free-floating universality become more apparent.

The Diffusion of Knowledge

By 1820, visibly silent reading had become so basic to the democratic Republic
of Letters that Jefferson provided spaces in his Monticello home into which he
or his guests could withdraw without entirely leaving the company of others.
Like the conversation in the Monticello dining room, which, as we saw in the
prologue, was serviced by dumbwaiters designed to prevent enslaved persons

from interrupting or overhearing, these reading spaces were serviced by silence-producing mechanisms of several kinds.[2] As we also saw, that sphere, which we can only call public in a limited sense, was given its best description in 1779, when Jefferson proposed unsuccessfully a bill for the general "diffusion of knowledge" through a system of public education, from primary school to college.

At the outset of Jefferson's presidency in 1801, Monticello's collections far outnumbered those of the new Library of Congress, whose 740 volumes were stored in the north wing of the incomplete Capitol Building in Washington, DC. This is where the architect Benjamin Latrobe found them when he began work on that building in 1803. Latrobe's designs for more suitable quarters made little difference, though, when on August 24, 1814 the half-rebuilt north wing

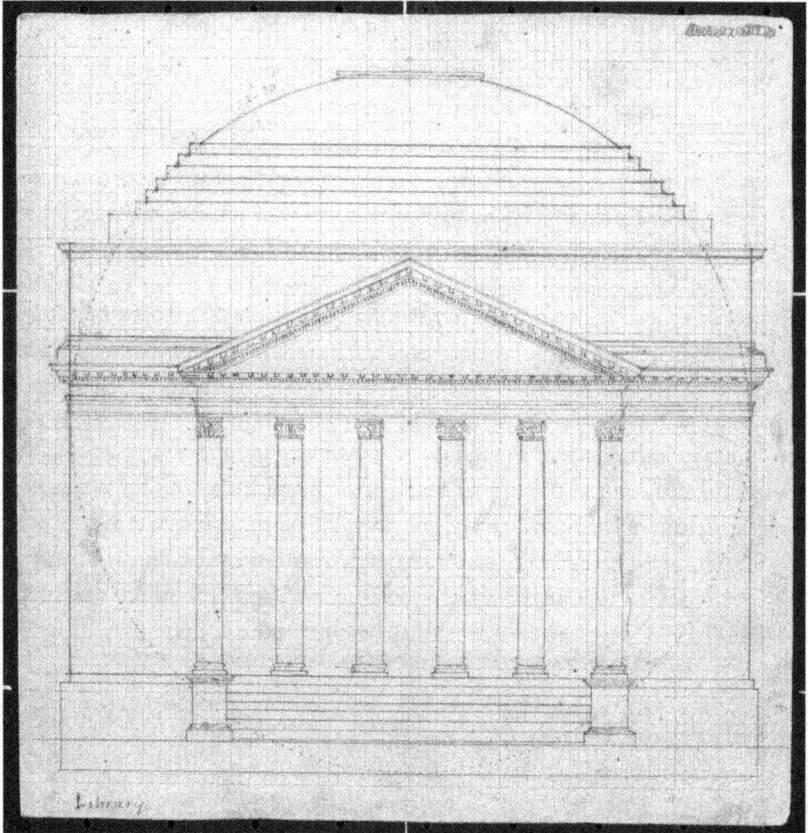

5.1 Thomas Jefferson, Library Rotunda, University of Virginia, 1819 (completed 1826). Elevation. Thomas Jefferson Papers, Albert and Shirley Small Special Collections Library, University of Virginia.

and its books burned along with the rest of the building, set ablaze by advancing British troops.³ And so in 1815, as if he had been preparing since the fire at his Shadwell home to literalize the bond between nation-building and books, and in need of funds to settle longstanding debts including those incurred with the construction of Monticello, Jefferson sold his second private library to Congress to replace the burned volumes.⁴

It was during this period, as he again rebuilt his Monticello library, that Jefferson worked with Joseph Cabell and others to found Central College (the former Albemarle Academy), which later became the University of Virginia in Charlottesville. Jefferson, a self-taught architect, designed the campus as a lesson in modified architectural classicism that framed a modified classical curriculum. In keeping with the neo-Palladianism common at the time, Jefferson modeled his central Rotunda after the one in Rome, which he had never visited. Like most of Jefferson's buildings and not unusually for the period, the Virginia Rotunda was largely designed from books.⁵

More precisely, through Jefferson and other intermediaries, overlapping media systems—books, libraries, legal documents, and letters—interacted to form to the new campus. Another source for the Virginia library was Jefferson's correspondence during the summer of 1817 with both architects of the Capitol Building in Washington to that point, William Thornton and Latrobe. The three-way correspondence is punctuated by the rhythms and delays of postal delivery, out of which Jefferson pieced together the layout of what he called an "academical village." His earliest design shows nine pavilions to house professors of different subjects arranged in an extendable U-shape around an open space. After selecting a site for the college, and with significant input from Latrobe, he developed these into model works of architecture, like little Monticellos with domestic libraries to match, separated by banks of student dormitories distributed along the two long sides of a U-shaped colonnade. Between them was a great, south-facing terraced lawn that overlooked the surrounding landscape.⁶

Prior to the enabling legislation and in response to Jefferson's initial description and sketch plan for the campus, Latrobe had suggested in an epistolary sketch a central, domed rotunda dividing the U in half. Jefferson soon incorporated such a building into the terraced plan that he was in the process of laying out on site. Seemingly ambivalent about his initial layout's symmetry, Jefferson marked the central position with a building but did not distinguish it from the others in the serially differentiated, open-ended pavilion system. Latrobe's suggestion resolved this ambivalence by introducing a hierarchy of building types. It is unclear exactly when the central building became a library. But it is clear that its authors expected its architectural harmonies to bind the composition together by resolving the formal and functional differences among the pavilions themselves. On the aesthetic *and*

5.2 Benjamin H. Latrobe to Thomas Jefferson, July 24, 1817, with sketch showing proposed revisions to University of Virginia site plan and elevation. Thomas Jefferson Papers at The Library of Congress, Manuscript Division.

on the epistemological plane, the library centerpiece sought to coordinate and to integrate potentially competing claims on intellectual authority. Differences among types of knowledge were reinforced by the architecture: a distinct neo-Palladian pavilion for each faculty. At the apex, the library's domed reading room stood ready to produce the reflective silence necessary to synthesize these differences in order to administer the natural right to govern oneself.

From the day the University of Virginia opened in 1825, the still-incomplete library Rotunda was the most celebrated technical feature of the new campus. Schematically, the Virginia library and its university were founded on behalf of an imagined subject inscribed into Denis Diderot and Jean

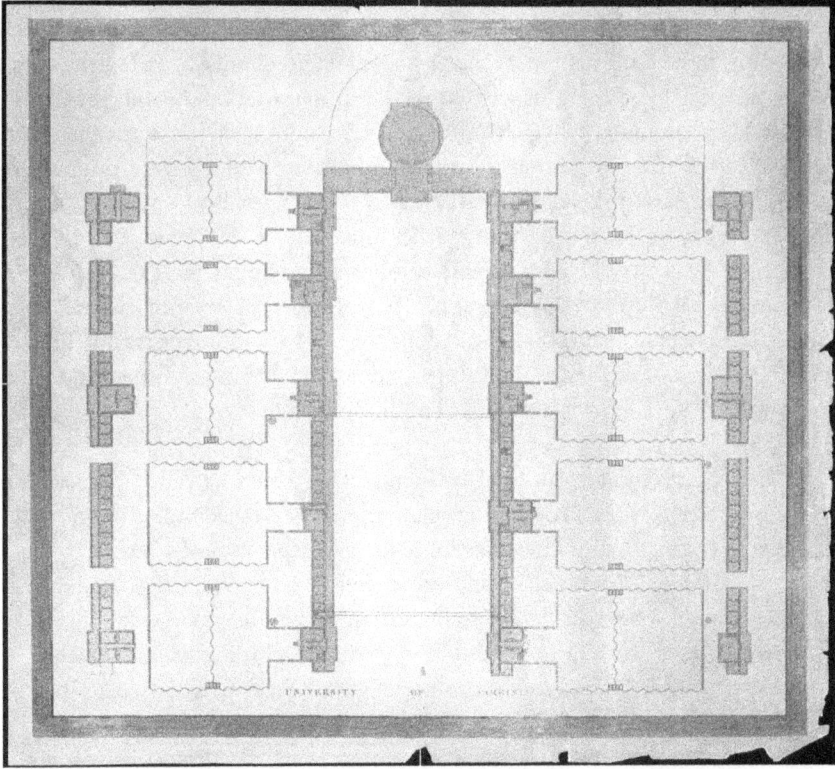

5.3 Thomas Jefferson, University of Virginia, 1826. Site plan of the university by Peter Maverick, 1825, based on John Neilson's drawing, 1822. Albert and Shirley Small Special Collections Library, University of Virginia.

Le Rond d'Alembert's encyclopedic "tree of knowledge," with its branches springing from an axial spine of liberal sovereignty. Jefferson owned a copy of the *Encyclopédie* (1751–1772), and it is reasonable to count him among its subjects as well as its readers.[7] However, as the particularities of knowing subjects became the focus of the human sciences, and the natural sciences challenged the moral and epistemological authority of philosophy and religion, each branch of knowledge began to take on explanatory powers of its own, somewhat independent of the others. Correspondingly, the claim on universality moved gradually from a subject from whose mind the tree of knowledge grew, to an intersubjective system of disciplines balanced against one another, as in the Virginia campus plan. Integrating these disciplines into a sovereign body was a task for scholars sitting quietly in libraries, reading.

Silent Reading

According to one influential account, the practice of silent reading became common with the spacing of written words in manuscripts during the European twelfth century; the inscription or transcription of those manuscripts generally took place in scholastic monasteries where books were chained to tables. By the early nineteenth century, silent reading had extended in different degrees to the European bourgeoisie and working classes, and to a lesser extent, the peasantry.[8] North America followed a similar pattern. Yet as we have already seen, colleges in Jefferson's day were noisy places, not least because knowledge was also reproduced out loud in the recitation rooms integrated into the phalanx-like central buildings around which most colleges were still organized. In 1810, Jefferson proposed a solution:

> I consider the common plan, followed in this country, but not in others, of making one large & expensive building as unfortunately erroneous. it is infinitely better to erect a small and separate lodge for each separate professorship, with only a hall below for his class, and two chambers above for himself; joining these lodges by barracks for a certain portion of the students opening into a covered way to give a dry communication between all the schools. the whole of these arranged around an open square of grass & trees would make it, what it should be in fact, an academical village, instead of a large & common den of noise, of filth, & of fetid air. It would afford that quiet retirement so friendly to study, and lessen the dangers of fire, infection & tumult.[9]

The pavilions comprising the academical village would help to discipline rowdy students in the double sense of the term, bringing them under the supervision of specialists within each branch of learning, in class and at the dinner table, while also clearly separating those branches into distinct areas of study. As built, on the ground floor of each pavilion in recitation rooms immediately adjacent to dining rooms, professors or tutors would read aloud from or reference canonical texts. Students recited passages from memory or, more rarely, responded to semi-Socratic questioning. The rote procedure later led one Harvard graduate to complain that recitations were more commonly "heard" than "taught."[10] Since Virginia students could borrow books from the main library only with written permission from their professors, and although the houses had smaller libraries of their own, silent reading was done mainly where most of the books were kept, in the central library Rotunda.[11]

Jefferson personally ordered almost seven thousand of these books, many from Europe, and oversaw the arrival of the first shipments during the last months of his life.[12] Unfortunately, the books circulated at a rate much faster than the space to house them could be prepared. In February of 1826, Jefferson complained to his friend James Madison about all the boxes piling up, lamenting that "not one of these can be opened, until the Bookroom is completely finished, and all the shelves ready to receive their charge directly from the boxes as they shall be opened."[13] Jefferson died that summer; the books were only unboxed and the library only opened later that fall. The missed connection testifies to the phatic nature of reading and writing, which must repeatedly overcome or forestall interruption, including unopened books, unopened boxes, and unopened buildings.

Raised above the lawn with two floors of paired, ovoid meeting and lecture rooms below, the library reading room consisted of a wooden dome with glazed oculus covering an open space ringed with curved reading tables. These stood in front of a circumferential mezzanine supported by pairs of regularly spaced wooden columns in a composite Ionic-Corinthian order. Wooden bookshelves lined the perimeter wall on both the main level and the mezzanine. Vertical windows punctuated the Rotunda's brick drum at regular intervals on both porch and reading room levels. Painted white, the room's interior surfaces would have been washed on most days with soft daylight. Though he made no real recommendations for the Rotunda interior, on the evidence of his manipulations of daylight in the Baltimore Cathedral and later at the United States Capitol, we can infer that Latrobe would have considered the illumination of the reading room a matter of inducing a feeling of transcendence. Jefferson seems instead to have conceived of this space as a technical device.[14]

Architecturally, Jefferson's unrealized design for the interior of the dome modified the French architect Étienne-Louis Boullée's well-known project for an idealized spherical cenotaph for Isaac Newton. Boullée's unbuilt planetarium was an apotheosis of his "architecture of shadows," inspiration for which, he claimed, was provided by a moonlit walk in the woods.[15] In contrast, Jefferson's early plans would have transformed the Virginia Rotunda's more modest interior into a theater of measurement and calculation. The scheme was Newtonian in that it was mechanistic, but it lacked Boullée's sublime melancholia. In his notebooks, Jefferson described a device for installing a system of moveable gilt stars on the dome's interior surface. The stars would be positioned on a blue interior surface by means of a pivoting arc that would accurately plot their position onto the dome's curvature at any given time in the night sky based on printed astronomical charts. Balanced by a rope-and-pulley system operated by students, a professor would then pivot from star to star in a saddle astride an oak boom, lecturing.[16] Had it been constructed, the device would have converted the dome into a teaching planetarium through a read-write mechanism that translated two-dimensional information, recorded in the charts, into a three-dimensional model of the celestial sphere on the dome's interior surface.

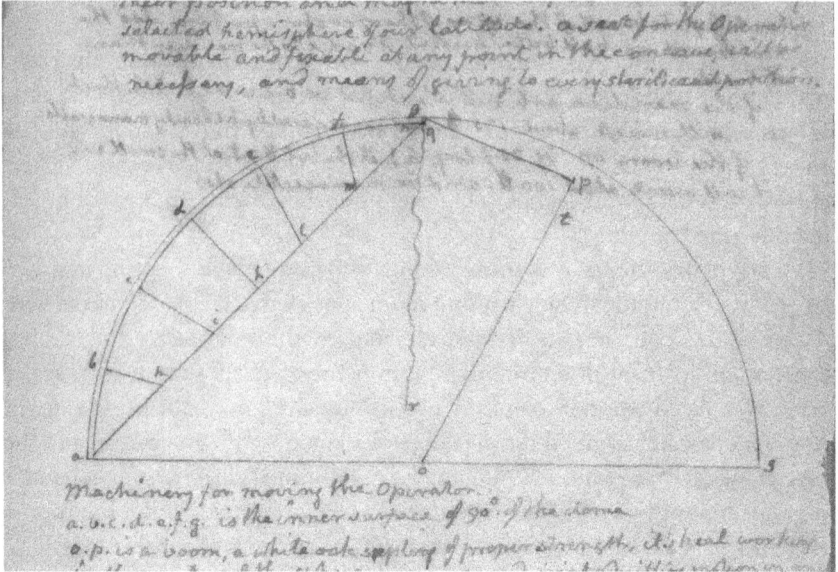

5.4 Thomas Jefferson, Proposed device for mapping astronomical charts onto the Rotunda ceiling, University of Virginia (unrealized). Pocket memorandum book, 1819. Page 2, recto. Thomas Jefferson Papers, Albert and Shirley Small Special Collections Library, University of Virginia.

As conceived by Jefferson, the dome also contained another piece of hardware that, when it was installed after his death, resembled the dumbwaiters in the Monticello dining room. In 1825 Jefferson drew up annotated specifications for a clock and bell to organize the university's daily rhythms. These were to be affixed to the pediment of the Rotunda's portico, facing the Lawn. The specifications called for a bell that could be heard "with certainty" for one and a half miles, and "*generally* be heard at a distance of 2 miles, because this will ensure it's being *always* heard in Charlottesville."[17] A bell, in other words, addressed to the landscape over which the University of Virginia presided with its outward facing Lawn.

The weights for the six-foot, two-inch diameter clock, with hour hand only, were suspended on ropes running down a five-foot diameter cylindrical void formed out of the brick poché on one side of the portico; the ropes for ringing the bell ran down an identical void on the other side.[18] Beginning around 1868, those bell ropes were pulled on the hour by Henry Martin, who by his own account was born into slavery at Monticello on July 4, 1826, the day of Jefferson's death. After the Civil War, Martin was hired as a bell ringer and janitor for the Rotunda, where he rang the university bell until

5.5 Henry Martin, in the University of Virginia Rotunda, n.d. Albert and Shirley Small Special Collections Library, University of Virginia.

his retirement in 1909.[19] The tones that Martin and his predecessors struck as they pulled on ropes to awaken students and professors at dawn, and to mark the hours of the recitations, lectures, and demonstrations through the day, did not exactly break the silence of those reading in the library bookroom which, in Jefferson's original plan, would have modeled the silence of the stars. Rather, the ringing bell *produced* that silence, by organizing it into hour-long temporal units around which a liberal education dedicated to the idea of universal, natural rights and self-governance could be built. The bell, the system of labor on which its ringing was based, and the system of knowledge practiced in the pavilions and in the library, also silenced the bell's ringers, such that they and their particular lives remain largely unknown to us today.

Gas and Electric

Following the fire that destroyed the first Library of Congress and prompted Jefferson to donate his books, Latrobe and his successor, Charles Bulfinch, renovated the U.S. Capitol Building in Washington. Between 1818 and 1823, Bulfinch added a double-shelled wooden dome atop the empty central rotunda, as well as a reading room for the library in the building's new west wing where, in 1825, most of the books survived a small fire caused by a lighted candle.[20] In 1847, the Capitol rotunda became a laboratory of sorts. Calls from architects and politicians for gas lighting, as well as the shattered glass from a chandelier collapsing in 1840 under the weight of seventy-eight whale oil lamps in the House chamber, led to the appointment of the gas entrepreneur James Crutchett to propose alternatives. His solution for the new rotunda involved installing a ninety-two-foot mast supporting a twenty-foot tall glass and gilded iron gas lantern, six feet in diameter. Due to safety concerns, however, the device was removed after less than a year in operation.[21]

This abortive effort parallels the appearance of gaslight in homes, meeting rooms, and streets during the 1840s and 1850s. But an overheated chimney flue, not gaslight, was evidently the cause of the fire on December 24, 1851 that once again destroyed the Library of Congress reading room located in the Capitol Building and along with it, about thirty-five thousand of the now fifty-five thousand–volume collection, including two-thirds of the original Jefferson holdings. Rebuilt two years later by the architect Thomas U. Walter, the library became the first major interior in the country to be covered by an iron roof.[22] The rebuilding also extended the Capitol rotunda to a significantly greater height, which was accentuated by a triumphal recessed fresco—*The Apotheosis of George Washington* by Constantino Brumidi. Visible through an ocular aperture and illuminated indirectly by a system of mirrors by day and hundreds of gas jets by night, its figures appeared to float above the inner shell.[23]

This phantasmagoric use of gaslight and mirrors accompanied the rationalized, "disenchanted night" spread by the new infrastructure of illumination during the mid-to-late nineteenth century in North America and in Europe.[24] The University of Virginia partially achieved a gaslit campus by 1857, and by the outset of the Civil War, both the university and the town were serviced by the Charlottesville and University Gas Light Company. As late as March 1894, gaslight was still the main alternative to daylight on the Virginia campus, and the university's board of visitors was still only discussing the possibility of installing electrical wiring.[25] So it must have been that the electrical wiring shown in an engraving of a burned out library Rotunda on the front page of the *Richmond Dispatch* on October 29, 1895 was relatively new.[26]

What the *Dispatch* called the "calamity of Sunday" resulted in the ruination of the Rotunda and the loss of about forty-five thousand of the Virginia library's fifty-three thousand volumes. A fire had started in the southwest corner of the

5.6 Thomas Ustick Walter, United States Capitol, Washington, DC, revised dome design, 1858. Section. Architect of the Capitol.

5.7 "Ruins of the Rotunda," *Richmond Dispatch* (October 29, 1895), 1.

5.8 Thomas Jefferson, Library Rotunda, University of Virginia, fire of October 27, 1895. Photograph by Rufus W. Holsinger. University of Virginia Visual History Collection, Albert and Shirley Small Special Collections Library, University of Virginia.

Annex, a 105-foot long addition to the rear of the library designed by Jefferson's apprentice, Robert Mills, and completed in 1854. It was Henry Martin who rang the bell to sound the alarm.[27]

The Rotunda annex contained classrooms for law, engineering, physical sciences, and modern languages, as well as a laboratory and machine shops, and a large public hall capable of seating 1,200 persons facing an oversize replica of Raphael's *School of Athens* by the French copyist, Paul Balze, behind its stage. With the differentiation of the natural sciences as disciplines requiring professional expertise, and with the development of the German research model, lecture-style demonstrations often with the use of technical apparatuses had become more common. By 1850, large lecture halls were needed to accommodate these more theatrical forms of pedagogy.[28] Aside from the now-demolished anatomy theater that Jefferson designed off to the side of the western range, the Rotunda annex provided the university's first purpose-built laboratory facilities and housed its first such lecture hall.[29]

The formal awkwardness of Mills's annex indicates the difficulties of integrating these new practices into the existing Virginia campus, with its two pairs of small elliptical lecture rooms tucked neatly into the Rotunda's base. Mills was known for his expertise in fireproof construction, but budget limitations

THE PUBLIC HALL OF THE UNIVERSITY OF VA.

5.9 Robert Mills, Rotunda Annex, University of Virginia, 1854. Lecture hall decorated for Thomas Jefferson's birthday, 1867, with the university's first copy of Raphael's *School of Athens* by Paul Balze (1854, rear). Albert and Shirley Small Special Collections Library, University of Virginia.

precluded its use. The fire's actual cause was never discovered with certainty, although initial speculation pointed to the electrical wiring used to illuminate the new teaching and research spaces.[30]

The *Richmond Dispatch* and university records are sprinkled with near-immediate calls to rebuild the Rotunda. Most of these exhibit a preference for reconstruction faithful to the original.[31] Following several inconclusive studies along these lines by the Louisville architect Harry P. McDonald, in January of 1896 the board of visitors engaged the New York architectural firm of McKim, Mead & White to rebuild the library and to add an ensemble of new buildings to house the lecture hall, physics laboratories, engineering shops, and classrooms.[32] By this time, Charles F. McKim had nearly completed his designs for a monumental library rotunda as the centerpiece for Columbia University's new campus in Upper Manhattan, which partly followed his partner Stanford White's designs for a similar building for New York University.[33] Though both New York projects' obvious borrowings from Jefferson's design have been widely noted, the differences are equally relevant.

During the process of rebuilding, Virginia borrowed from Columbia as Columbia borrowed from Virginia, beginning with the electric lighting fixtures installed on the library reading room tables, which were nearly identical in both rotundas. In his design for the rebuilt Virginia library, White aggrandized that building's relatively modest reading room, ringing the interior in a giant Corinthian order.[34] At the other end of the Lawn, White's new site plan enlarged and added to the lecture halls and other teaching spaces formerly contained in the annex in a collection of three buildings symmetrically arranged in axial counterpoint to the reconstructed Rotunda. Behind these a new, dynamo-equipped, fireproof boiler plant with electrical equipment was also added to provide heat and electricity to the new and existing buildings at a safe distance away from the books.

On the inside of the new ensemble's centerpiece, Cabell Hall, a university committee commissioned a replacement of the original replica of Raphael's *School of Athens* from George Breck, a painter working at the American Academy in Rome, to hang behind the stage of the building's central 1,500-seat auditorium. The American Academy was born out of the 1893 Chicago World's Columbian Exposition and gave cultural heft to the unabashed imperialism of the "American Renaissance."[35] Its presence in this circuit indicates the scale of the change. The indoor amphitheater in which the new painting hung faced the reconstructed Rotunda at the opposite end of the Lawn, projecting a daylit vision of classical education back onto the campus, and turning its back on the heating plant and other indicators of the university's modernity.

Behind the heating plant that was behind Cabell Hall, and just below the horizon of the pastoral, Jeffersonian vista framed by the Lawn but now blocked by the new buildings, was a neighborhood called Canada, populated mainly by formerly enslaved persons and their descendants, many of whom worked at the university and some of whose enslaved ancestors probably built the original campus.[36] Although White argued that the new buildings be placed so as not to block the vista from the Lawn, the Virginia board of visitors insisted that the view, now cluttered by the shacks of Canada, be closed off.[37] To complete the involution, a system of brick-vaulted tunnels was extended from the boiler plant behind Cabell Hall back toward the Lawn, to supply steam heat to the pavilions, dormitories, and Rotunda.[38] These vaults are the direct descendants of Monticello's dependencies, or service passageways for slaves, which ran under the main house.[39] At Monticello, the dependencies emerged from the ground as wings extending into the landscape to frame a view that, as it happened, looked back obliquely toward the University of Virginia. On the Virginia campus, they were buried and the view was blocked as mechanization took command.

5.10 Stanford White of McKim, Mead & White, University of Virginia, Cabell Hall (Academic Building), 1898. Auditorium, with the university's second copy of Raphael's *School of Athens* by George Breck (1902). Photograph by Rufus W. Holsinger, March 16, 1914. University of Virginia Grounds Views, Albert and Shirley Small Special Collections Library, University of Virginia.

From Sunlight to Moonlight

Jefferson's case, in which a political leader and statesman became rector of a new university that he had cofounded and designed, is as atypical as is the Virginia campus itself. Even so, McKim reinterpreted Jefferson's diagram in his designs for Columbia's campus in Upper Manhattan, which gave monumental form to the widespread establishment of research universities in the United States. Laid out by McKim in a Beaux-Arts manner that recalled the Virginia

5.11 Charles F. McKim of McKim, Mead & White, Low Memorial Library, Columbia University, 1897. Rare Book & Manuscript Library, Columbia University.

plan, the new Columbia campus, too, centered on a domed library surrounded by symmetrically disposed, departmentally differentiated academic pavilions that resembled freestanding Renaissance palazzi. The conversion of existing colleges into universities, and the founding of new research institutions, began in earnest during the 1870s based partly on German precedent. But it was more through the everyday work of institutionalized research than through the afterlife of Romantic idealism that the German model was translated, with significant differences, into the American context.

By the early 1900s, university-based research at Johns Hopkins, Columbia, Harvard, Clark and elsewhere had formed an intimate alliance with industrial and finance capital. Critics like Thorstein Veblen worried that the principles of business "will, by force of habit, in good part reassert themselves as indispensable and conclusive in the conduct of the affairs of learning."[40] Veblen argued that education had taken on a "dispassionate" and "mechanistic complexion," to the degree that all knowledge, including that which (according to him) had been the purview of subjective individuals since the days of the medieval schoolmen, tended now to be cast in the "dry light of science," "sterilized," and stored in a "cool, dry place."[41] Seen this way, the genealogy we have been following might seem to trace the decaying arc of Enlightenment, as paper-based liberal individualism stored in bourgeois libraries repeatedly burns, only to be reconstituted in ever more instrumental forms until we arrive at the massive, fireproof shell of Columbia's Low Memorial Library, designed by McKim and opened in 1897. By pledging $1 million toward its completion, Seth Low, Columbia's president, gained the right to name the new library after his father, Abiel Abbot Low, a New York merchant whose wealth derived largely from the tea and opium trade with China.[42] Nevertheless, this story of darkness and ruination—in which Minerva's owl flies only at dusk—presupposes at its origin the impossibly bright light of an idealized Mediterranean sun.

The anxious, twice-over reproduction of Raphael's *School of Athens* on Virginia's campus showing philosophers, mathematicians, and scientists gathered within a daylit monument records the changes. In 1850, the installation of the first copy, following Jefferson's reinterpretation of the classical architectural canon in the campus, reflected an ambivalence regarding European antiquity within American pedagogy. In "The American Scholar," an address delivered at Harvard University in 1837, Ralph Waldo Emerson stretched out the tensions between a refined Hellenism and a romantic naturalism, or quiet, reflective knowledge versus a life of unmediated action, almost to a point of no return. The year before, Emerson had described himself awash in the dedifferentiated thrall of the New England wilderness, becoming a "transparent eye-ball" through which only there, and not in Cambridge, "the currents of the Universal Being" could circulate.[43] Speaking to the Harvard students, the classically trained philosopher-poet implicitly rejected the intermediations that Jefferson had attempted when he proposed converting the luminous night sky into a mechanical teaching device inside the Virginia dome. For, as Emerson saw it, "meek young men grow up in libraries, believing it their duty to accept the views which Cicero, which Locke, which Bacon, have given; forgetful that Cicero, Locke, and Bacon were only young men in libraries when they wrote these books."[44] According to Emerson, to tap into the "currents of the Universal Being," young men had to step out of their introversion into the wild world to become transparent eyeballs.

Emerson called this new type of scholar a "university of knowledges" who was one with the new nation, a kind of universal soul finally able to turn away from "the courtly muses of Europe" and toward a theology of the frontier embryonically present in the Virginia annex's lecture halls and laboratories.[45] During the century's course as a gendered, racialized embodiment of the nation, Emerson's imagined scholar was sundered by the Civil War, torn apart by the political resistance to Reconstruction, and again by techno-economic expansion. This broken "university of knowledges" was subsequently reassembled and professionalized in new lecture halls like the one at Virginia in which the second copy of Raphael's painting was installed. By which time the academic disciplines had been enshrined in scholarly associations and scrupulously codified in textbooks, like the *Text-Book of Physics* coauthored in 1908 by the Columbia physicist William Hallock.[46]

Like hundreds before him who assisted in the founding or development of such universities in the United States, Hallock had done his graduate work in Germany, earning a PhD in physics at Würzburg in 1881. He then went on to an almost archetypal career in scientific manifest destiny at the nation's new institutions, working as a physicist at the United States Geological Survey (founded in 1879), serving as a professor of chemistry and toxicology at the National College of Pharmacy (founded in 1871), and running the astrophysical laboratory at the Smithsonian Institution (founded somewhat earlier, in 1846).[47]

In 1898, Hallock, then an associate professor of physics at Columbia and later dean of the faculty of pure science, published a modest article titled "Diffused Illumination" in the engineering journal *Progressive Age* (a journal previously known as *The Gas Age*). The article described a new system for the indirect, electric lighting of interior spaces that Hallock had devised to illuminate the domed reading room of the monumental library rotunda at the center of Columbia's new campus, which had opened the year before. Hallock began his account with a poetic summary of the recent history of artificial lighting that emphasized the desirability of "a mild, diffused illumination, without glare, without sharp shadows, and yet with abundance of light." He asked: "Is not the dense shade of the forest much to be preferred to the blazing sunshine? Is not the room with its heavy curtains a pleasanter place to read, to write or to do a thousand things rather than the open sunshine? In the grove or in the room we have plenty of light, but no glare nor sharp shadows."[48] Explaining the physiological benefits of such lighting, Hallock pointed out that dimness strains the eyes, while sharp contrast wearies them. There were, however, problems with the usual solutions. The use of "myriad points of light" confronted eyeglass wearers with "tantalizing reflections"; incandescent electric lights in clear globes yielded "various after images"; while frosted globes reduced efficiency by 40 to 50 percent.[49]

As an alternative, Hallock offered what he called "the general illumination of Columbia University Library," achieved by suspending a seven-foot diameter opaque sphere painted a dull white in the center of the rotunda reading room on a nearly invisible one-quarter inch steel cable. Describing the mysteriously suspended sphere, the physicist exclaimed that "to all appearances it floats in the air. Even by day this seeming giant pearl, seen against the dark blue of the interior of the dome possesses a unique beauty."[50] That was the daytime version. At dusk, eight automatic focusing, arc-light Criterion

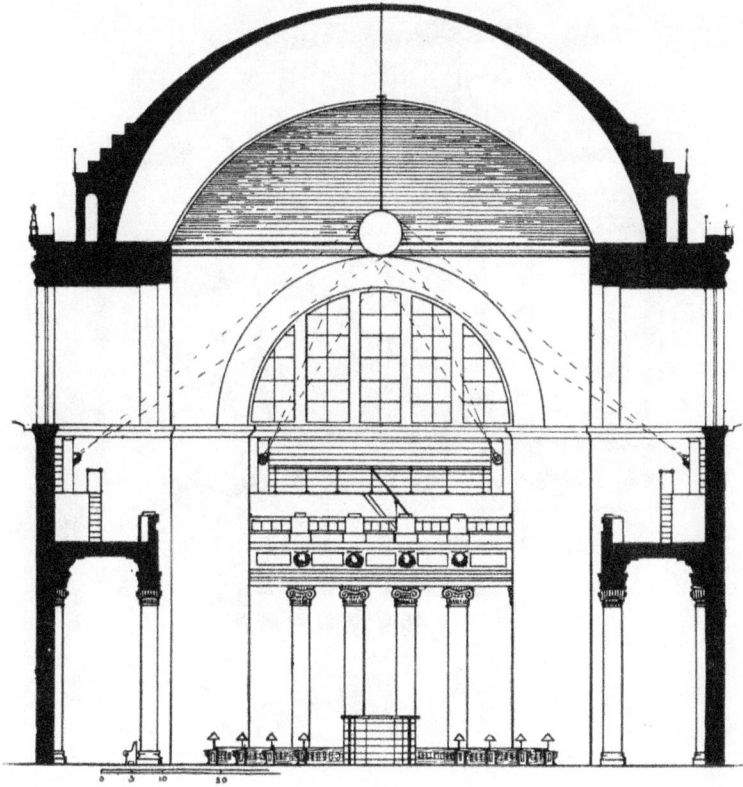

5.12 William Hallock and Charles F. McKim, illumination of main reading room, Low Memorial Library, Columbia University, c. 1897. Section. "Columbia's Artificial Moon," *Scientific American* 78, no. 15 (April 9, 1898), 229.

projectors manufactured by the J. B. Colt Company (manufacturers of Colt revolvers and early cinema projectors) located on the second floor balconies, projected their electrical light onto it such that "the whole sphere seems to glow with a pale diffused light."[51] Hallock emphasized that this light was not required for reading, as the room's concentrically arranged tables were provided with individual reading lamps. Rather, it was "needed for architectural effects of light and shade and to dispel the gloomy shadows of the upper dome."[52] Such effects were required, in other words, mainly to dispel the remnants of Boullée's "architecture of shadows," with its dark intimations of the sublime, to make way for what was quite exactly conceived as an architecture *without* shadows.

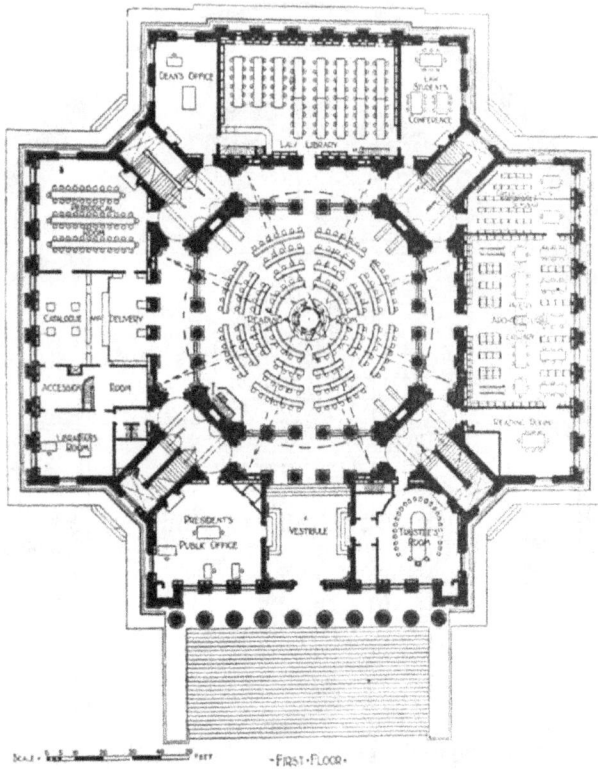

5.13 William Hallock and Charles F. McKim, illumination of main reading room, Low Memorial Library, Columbia University, c. 1897. "Plan Showing Position of Lamps, Dome, and Globe." From Hallock, "Diffused Illumination," *Progressive Age* 16, no. 3 (March 1, 1898), 109.

As the editorial introduction to Hallock's article explained:

> The dome is dark blue in color, shading to lighter tints toward its horizon, and has a dull surface preventing all undesirable reflections. Notwithstanding all precautions, a slight shadow of the globe is cast upon the dome, surrounded by a faint, luminous halo; this is probably due to lateral reflection from dust particles in the air, which are sufficient at times to make the projected rays visible from below, even though no dusting or sweeping is permitted in the library, but all cleaning is done with damp cloths.[53]

What Hallock's editor called "artificial moonlight" measured .01 to .02 footcandles at floor level, or "about equal to the illumination of a horizontal surface when the moon has climbed half way to our meridian."[54]

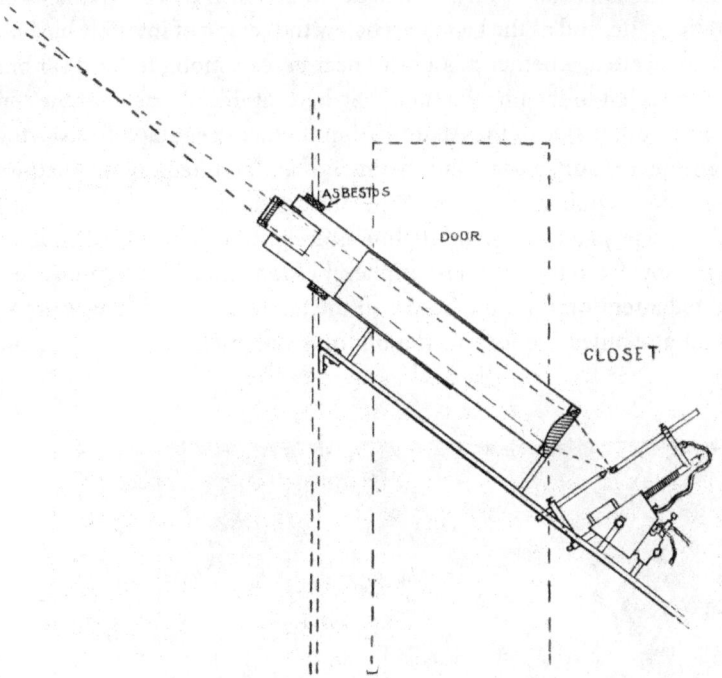

5.14 William Hallock and Charles F. McKim, illumination of main reading room, Low Memorial Library, Columbia University, c. 1897. Section of projector apparatus. "Columbia's Artificial Moon," *Scientific American* 78, no. 15 (April 9, 1898), 229.

Surrounding the main reading room were classrooms, offices, and departmental libraries, including the double height Avery Architectural Library above and the law library on the ground floor, and an array of multipurpose lecture rooms of different sizes on the third level. According to university librarian George H. Baker, these upper floor lecture rooms immediately became "a source of noise, which has distracted, to some extent, from the quiet desirable in the reading room," a situation only partly mitigated by the installation of corridor doors and "other devices."[55]

Intermedially, whether Baker realized it or not, Hallock's artificial moon was among the "other devices" designed to manage readers' attention. To describe the glowing sphere's luminosity, and despite the residual shadows and other optical interference caused by nontransparent, dusty air stirred up by restless readers or noncompliant cleaners, and as if to drown out by sheer luminous will any ambient noise from the lectures above, Hallock resorted to an unrestrained poetics: "The effect is beautiful in the extreme. The surface seems translucent and the light seems to come from a certain depth within and to make the whole glow with warm life, and as the ball floats below the ceiling of invisible blue it is impossible to locate it; whether it is a pearl near us, or a moon in the clear blue sky miles away is left to the imagination."[56] So here, at the other end of the century and on the other side of the Atlantic from Boullée's cenotaph for Newton, the sun became a moon, and what remained of an "architecture of shadows" was diffused into a cool, mild light to dispel the darkness.

Optically and physiologically, this light was designed to eliminate distracting glare and shadow from the reader's peripheral vision and thus to direct silent, uninterrupted attention onto the books on the tables below. A contemporary account that attributes the idea to the building's architect, Charles McKim,

5.15 Charles F. McKim of McKim, Mead & White, Low Memorial Library, Columbia University, n.d. [c. 1897]. Reading room dome with illuminated "moon." Rare Book & Manuscript Library, Columbia University.

elaborates on the aesthetic character of this "moonlight." McKim's colleague Frederick Parsell Hill describes the trial-and-error experiments on which the moon was based, which involved fabricating a large wooden sphere and covering it with different finishes—white paint, tinfoil, and even a projected photographic slide of the moon itself. Such experiments with the interaction of media yielded unexpected results. It was discovered that projecting a two-dimensional photograph of the moon's surface onto the three-dimensional surface of the sphere compensated for photographic foreshortening and allowed the markings on the moon's visible face to be seen in their "correct" position, which enabled the unnamed physicist conducting the experiment (most probably Hallock) to "get some side views of the moon." Successful as it was in remediating the distortions of another medium, however, the multiprojector attempt at verisimilitude failed to produce moonlight. The unfiltered light of the arc lamps replaced the lunar photograph, and the moon's surface was abstracted into a dull, "dingy" white and suspended in place.[57]

The lunar surface held a fascination for early astronomical photographers, and so the use of such images is not surprising.[58] But what mattered most for Hallock and McKim was not the moon's imagery but its glow. Though Columbia's lighting fixture was technically an optical medium, it also operated acoustically to manage attention and produce the imagined effect of an ambient, moonlit silence by which to read. In fact, Hallock's specialty was not optics but acoustics, an area in which he also sought practical pedagogical application.

"Voice-Production"

Prior to and during his collaboration with McKim, Hallock was engaged in another collaboration, with the physician Floyd S. Muckey, on what the pair called "Rational, Scientific Voice-Production."[59] Comparing the human vocal chords to a string instrument (rather than a reed instrument, a common comparison at the time), Hallock and Muckey sought to break down the voice into its constituent overtones, or harmonics, which are the higher tones that overlay the fundamental due to differential rates of vibration, as in a guitar string. Their larger aim was "to discover the proper mechanism for voice-production either for singing or for speaking," for the purposes of instruction as well as further research.[60] Hallock, who at the time was lecturing at Columbia on "The Undulatory Theory of Light" as well as on "Modes of Designing and Constructing Apparatuses," devised a mechanism for visualizing the overtones.[61] Attaching several spherical Helmholz resonators to a Koenig manometric capsule, in which a flame reflected in a rotating mirror changes height due to changes in resonance in the attached chambers, Hallock photographically recorded the periodicities of the flickering flames as sawtooth lines, in a continuous exposure

5.16 William Hallock and Floyd S. Muckey, apparatus for visualizing the human voice, with capsules, camera, and plate, and flames reflected in mirror. William Hallock and Floyd S. Muckey, *Voice-Production and Analysis* (New York: Looker-on Press, 1897), fig 5. This was the same apparatus documented in Hallock and Muckey, "Rational, Scientific Voice-Production," *Werner's Magazine* 18, no. 1 (January 1896), 1–10.

akin to Étienne Jules-Marey's chronophotography. Describing their approach as "*photographing the quality* of the tone," and coincident with other forms of acoustical "writing" that had been developed since the advent of the gramophone, Hallock and Muckey were certain: "Photography will not lie."[62]

Two years after Hallock's death in 1913, and at the behest of Solomon Henry Clark, associate professor in the University of Chicago's Department of Public Speaking, Muckey converted their work into a training manual titled *The Natural Method of Voice Production in Speech and Song*. Muckey's and Hallock's efforts to "rationalize" the human voice, which sought to exploit the underutilized physiological equivalent of a mechanical resonator, claimed to enable professional singers, orators, preachers, lecturers, university professors, schoolteachers, or students to read and reproduce a specific sound quality.[63] With photographic certainty, Hallock's apparatus trained these potential speakers to read visual traces of their voice, in order to regulate its "quality" by eliminating physiological interference from poorly utilized vocal equipment. In this, the apparatus complemented the pedagogy of Columbia's artificial moon. As public speaking became a science worthy of university study by figures like Hallock, Muckey, and Clark, every reader of library books became a potential speaker in need of a public, "rationalized" voice.

Not coincidentally, Hallock favorably compared the lighting levels achieved in the Columbia reading room to those in the domed reading room of the new Library of Congress, designed primarily by Paul J. Pelz and completed that same year (1897), which is known today as the Thomas Jefferson Building.[64] Having outgrown its quarters in the U.S. Capitol, the Library of Congress gained a building of its own to accommodate its recently assumed function as a library of record for all copyrighted documents. "Let all other libraries be exclusive," wrote Librarian of Congress Ainsworth Rand Spofford in 1878, "but let the library of the nation be inclusive, and contain all the literature of the nation, to be handed down to the men of the future."[65] Restating the point, he suggested that "in a republic which rests upon the popular intelligence, and one of whose cardinal glories is its literature, a great national collection of books, while formed primarily for the legislative and judicial branches of the government, ought to be utilized by a far wider circle of readers."[66] As Hallock's voice-production device implied, this was also to be a wider circle of public speakers. But his comparison overlooked an important distinction. Where admission to Columbia's library was restricted, admission to the new Library of Congress, in principle if not in practice, was not. The comparison, which connects elite knowledge with popular literacy, also measures the difference between universalized publics and the particularities of democratic citizenship.

Speaking Readers

In the aftermath of the Civil War and Reconstruction, many of Spofford's new readers were also, in principle, newly enfranchised voters. When the new Library of Congress opened, the circle of citizen-voters was still limited to men, and the civil rights of Black men and women were profoundly attenuated by "separate but equal" schools and "separate but equal" public libraries, or library entrances.[67] Similar contradictions pervaded elite universities. Although Harvard College graduated its first Black student, Richard Theodor Greener, in 1870, and in 1895 W. E. B. Du Bois became the first African American to earn a Harvard PhD, and James Dickson Carr became the first Black Columbia Law School graduate in 1896, these individuals were in a disproportionate minority that was not balanced by over seventy-five Black colleges and universities that had been founded by the turn of the century. During the late nineteenth century, U.S. universities also began to admit small numbers of international students, mostly male and mostly at the graduate level, a minority of whom were

5.17 Charles F. McKim of McKim, Mead & White, Low Memorial Library, Columbia University, n.d. [c. 1897]. Interior of reading room, with desks, desk lighting, and readers. Rare Book & Manuscript Library, Columbia University.

nonwhite and non-European.[68] The graduate schools of these newly founded, expanded, or refounded universities were therefore an important if limited channel for expanding the circle of readers around 1900.

This was the context in which Bhimrao R. Ambedkar enrolled as a graduate student in Columbia's political science department from 1913 to 1916, where, by all available accounts, he probably spent more time than most reading under the relatively new Low Library dome and possibly under its moon.[69] Ambedkar's example allows us to reconstruct some of the tensions governing the American university environment in the early twentieth century, as recorded in the educational philosophy of one of his Columbia professors, John Dewey, and at a greater distance, in the afterlife of Jefferson's political philosophy.

Ambedkar was a Dalit, or an impoverished member of India's "untouchable" caste, and a graduate of Bombay's elite Elphinstone College on a scholarship provided by Sayajirao Gaekwad, the Maharaja of Baroda. Gaekwad, who also sponsored Ambedkar's education at Columbia, had brought an admiration of the American educational system, along with several American educators and librarians, back to India with him from his visit to the Chicago World's Columbian Exposition in 1893.[70] At Columbia in 1915 Ambedkar submitted an economics MA thesis and in 1916, a second one, under the mentorship of Edwin Seligman, a progressive tax economist, cofounder with Dewey of the American Association of University Professors (AAUP), and friend of the Indian nationalist, Lala Lajpat Rai. The following year, Ambedkar departed for London, where he began work on a doctorate at the London School of Economics. Called back to India by his sponsor, Ambedkar embarked in August 1917 from Marseilles, sending his books and other belongings by separate passage in the care of Thomas Cook & Son. In another constitutive interruption, the steamer carrying his belongings was torpedoed and sunk in the Mediterranean; Ambedkar's library, consisting of some two thousand books, was gone, as was his second Columbia thesis.[71]

Upon his return to India, Ambedkar endured the daily humiliations of a Dalit lawyer working among caste Hindus in Baroda, to become a prominent voice for Dalit political rights and soon, an economics professor in Bombay's Sydenham College, where colleagues nonetheless objected to his drinking water from the staff water pot.[72] In 1920, Ambedkar returned to London to complete his studies; the missing Columbia MA thesis, which he intended as the basis for his PhD dissertation, required that he start from scratch. Thus on February 16, 1922, Ambedkar wrote to his Columbia mentor Seligman, that "having lost my manuscript of the original thesis when the steamer was torpedoed on my way back to India in 1917 I have written a new thesis entitled 'The Stabilization of the Indian Exchange' which I hope with your permission to submit for the PhD at Columbia."[73] Before doing so, Ambedkar earned another master's degree at the London School of Economics and a PhD at the University of London. In 1927, Ambedkar was finally awarded a Columbia PhD based on his published work and formally admitted into the discipline of economics.[74]

Equipped quite redundantly then, with three master's degrees and two PhDs from elite British and American institutions, later that same year Ambedkar spoke before the Bombay legislature against the caste and class hierarchies by which Bombay University was governed. He argued that merely holding examinations and conferring degrees was "a very narrow view of the University. One of the fundamental functions of the University, as I understand it, is to provide facilities for bringing the highest education to the doors of the needy and the poor." Specifically, Ambedkar argued for the reservation of seats in the university senate for "backward communities," or members of the lower castes. In 1927 in Bombay,

Ambedkar continued: "Sir, I look upon the University primarily as a machinery, whereby educational facilities are provided to all those who are intellectually capable of using those facilities to the best advantage, but who cannot avail themselves of those facilities for want of funds or for other handicaps in life."[75]

For Ambedkar, then, the university was an urbanizing machine that would welcome rural Dalits and other oppressed groups into its halls, with universal suffrage. The difficulty, however, lay not only in a misleading opposition of urban cosmopolitanism to rural communalism that distinguishes Ambedkar's vision of the university and its territory from the more pastoral but no less idealized vision laid out by Jefferson a century and a half earlier. The difficulty lay also in the contradictory imbrications of caste and nation in India, which had led Mohandas K. Gandhi, seeking national unity above all else, to found a Dalit rights organization with no Dalits on its governing board, to support Dalit higher education only as vocational education on the model of Booker T. Washington, and to ask of a Christian missionary preaching to Dalits: "Would you preach the Gospel to a cow?"[76] Whether in India or in the United States, when it came to nation-building, universality had its limits. As political ideals, universal suffrage and universal literacy collapsed the social particularities of caste and class. These particularities structured Ambedkar's efforts, like those of his teacher John Dewey but also differently, to ground democratic citizenship in a perpetual, public pedagogy.

Of the two thousand or so books Ambedkar acquired in New York, most of which were lost in the Mediterranean, Dewey's *Democracy and Education*, published in 1916 (the year Ambedkar departed for London), was among the few that seems to have made the trip to India intact.[77] We can presume this due in part to the many direct quotes and paraphrases from it that Arun Mukherjee has traced in Ambedkar's subsequent writings and speeches, since it is unlikely that he could have acquired an edition at the time in India. Among these references is one in Ambedkar's most widely read work, "The Annihilation of Caste," which is the text of a speech on the injustice of religious traditions that was written but, for political reasons, not delivered in 1936:

Professor John Dewey, who was my teacher and to whom I owe so much, has said:

"Every society gets encumbered with what is trivial, with dead wood from the past, and with what is positively perverse . . . As a society becomes more enlightened, it realizes that it is responsible *not* to transmit and conserve the whole of its existing achievements, but only such as make for a better future society."[78]

These words, with which Ambedkar urged Indians to abandon the injustices of caste, appear in Dewey's book under the section heading of "The School as a Special Environment." There, Dewey argued that "we never educate directly, but indirectly by means of the environment." He construed the school as a machine-environment that stores and communicates a finite amount of written information: "Roughly speaking [schools] come into existence when social traditions are so complex that a considerable part of the social store is committed to writing and transmitted through written symbols. . . . In addition, the written form tends to select and record matters which are comparatively foreign to everyday life." Like Spofford's national library but structurally limited rather than unlimited in scope, "the achievements accumulated from generation to generation are deposited in it though some of them have fallen temporarily out of use. Consequently as soon as a community depends to any considerable extent upon what lies beyond its own territory and its own immediate generation, it must rely upon the set agency of schools to insure adequate transmission of all its resources."[79] The school-as-library thus serves as an interface through which generations transmit relevant information to their successors, always with a surplus but never indiscriminately.

For Dewey, enlightened universalism therefore meant selective, useful knowledge, not universal knowledge. To gauge usefulness, he charged the "school environment" with balancing the heterogeneous particularities of the "social environment." A founding board member of the National Association for the Advancement of Colored People (NAACP) as well as a cofounder of the AAUP, Dewey wrote from within his own horizon of experience, as his philosophy required him to do: "There is in a country like our own a variety of races, religious affiliations, economic divisions. Inside the modern city, in spite of its nominal political unity, there are probably more communities, more differing customs, traditions, aspirations, and forms of government or control, than existed in an entire continent at an earlier epoch." All of which was magnified by the new infrastructures of "commerce, transportation, intercommunication, and emigration."

Thus:

It is this situation which has, perhaps more than any one cause, forced the demand for an educational institution which shall provide something like a homogeneous and balanced environment for the young. . . . The intermingling in the school of youth of different races, differing religions, and unlike customs [Dewey does not refer to gender or class] creates for all a new and broader environment. Common subject matter accustoms all to a unity of outlook upon a broader horizon than is visible to the members of any group while it is isolated.[80]

When in "The Annihilation of Caste" he quoted Dewey on the removal of historical "dead wood," Ambedkar displaced with an ellipsis a contextualizing sentence, in which Dewey argued that "the school has the duty of omitting such things [as dead wood] from the environment which it supplies." Restored to the passage, the sentence confirms that Dewey's educational philosophy is a matter of eliminating potentially burdensome, dissonant excess to produce a "homogeneous and balanced environment" that brings "common subject matter" into a "unity of outlook." His ideal school both presupposed and prepared students for participation in formal democracy. Thus conceived, the school was a context-specific editing device for balancing the countervailing forces of what Dewey called "associated life" in a pluralist society. Ambedkar turned this presupposition into a rights claim for formal participation in democratic procedures as such.

Ambedkar did so by coupling Dewey's thesis with a selective claim on the universal, on behalf of—though not directly by—the excluded particular. In Dewey's text, the school—primary education, but also education in general— produces the conditions necessary for pluralistic unity by leaving behind its historical remainder as so much "dead wood." As transcribed by Ambedkar, this "dead wood" refers to the allegedly ageless, ahistorical caste system, which had explicitly to be acknowledged and overturned—"burned"—rather than simply filtered out by the nationalist project.[81] This paradoxical form of unification particularized the universal in a manner that is inadmissible to Dewey and to liberal individualism more generally, by virtue of the history of the educational system to which he and it belonged. That system, from Jefferson onwards, presupposed a republic of speaking readers equipped a priori by their institutions to discriminate among commensurable propositions, while consigning the incommensurables of slavery and other forms of oppression and exclusion to an extracurricular division of labor, the scope of which was international, as we can now see from Ambedkar's historical experience. From the library Rotunda at Virginia and the pedagogical public sphere in which Jeffersonian universalism was produced, to Columbia's moonlit dome, where Ambedkar may well have sat reading Dewey, democracy was a matter of maintaining silence and illumination for specific readers and their specific voices. Ambedkar's use of Dewey turned this dialectic of silence and illumination on its head.

Just prior to independence, in 1947, as the Nehru government's first law minister, Ambedkar chaired the committee that wrote the Indian Constitution, a role that that gained him general recognition as the Constitution's chief author (or at least, its "architect") and has earned him periodic if inexact comparison to Thomas Jefferson.[82] Along with universal suffrage, that Constitution provided for reservations, or designated parliamentary seats, for Dalits and other oppressed groups, though without the separate electorate to protect against Hindu majoritarianism that Ambedkar had sought in an important dispute with Gandhi.

In the discussion following his final speech before the Indian Constituent Assembly in 1949, Ambedkar defended the new Constitution while pointing out its contradictions in perpetuating caste and class-based oppression: "In politics we will have equality and in social and economic life we will have inequality." Replying to absolutist critics and noting the relative ease with which the document could be amended, Ambedkar paraphrased a passage from Jefferson arguing against a permanent, unalterable law in which "the earth belongs to the dead and not the living."[83] The paraphrase is from a letter of 1816, although Jefferson's argument dates to 1789, in a famous letter to Madison written from Paris two years after the drafting of the American Constitution and during the process of its amendment. There Jefferson advocated the abolition—we can also say the "burning"—of fiscal debt from one generation to the next. Through an actuarial mathematics, he proposed that debts, whether individual or national, ought by natural right of property only extend the length of an average human lifespan, since *"the earth belongs in usufruct to the living."*[84] Peter Onuf has pointed out that the institution of chattel slavery contravened this reasoning. Slaveowners like Jefferson exercised direct influence through ownership over successive generations of enslaved persons, which sometimes included their own children, like the children born as Jefferson's slaves to Sally Hemings, the enslaved woman at Monticello with whom he maintained a long sexual relationship. This, says Onuf, "was the complete antithesis of everything Jefferson said he stood for."[85] A century later, Ambedkar began working through contradictions like these, until he arrived at the strategy of burning "dead wood" passed down through the generations and written into their laws, in order that voices that rarely echo through university libraries may be heard.

By claiming the heritage of Western liberal democracy from Jefferson to Dewey while inverting its structure of exclusion, Ambedkar sought but did not gain universal recognition for a historical singularity that, in turn, sought its own particular abolition. This was not a language game; it was a life-and-death game of silence, illumination, and speech. Its founding conflict turned on the question of who can play. Still, to call such conflicts contradictions, or to describe their logic as merely antithetical, risks reducing their material specificity to a vague idealization. Paper burns. Its force, which is also the force of its law, requires not only fireproofing but also silence bathed in light, so that a governing body may quietly read and quietly learn to speak, generation upon generation. This possibility, which exists on a plane *below* that of political speech and of political writing, is constituted by the dissonant noises that it eliminates as well as the public voices that it enables. Silence thereby grounds the democratic and pedagogical order of letters. To call this order universal, in the sense that it speaks to all and for all, is also to acknowledge the myriad and different ways in which it, by definition, does not.

6

THE DIALECTIC OF THE UNIVERSITY

His Master's Voice

Uring the 1980s, a dispute arose on and around campuses in the United States over efforts to expand or modify the Western canon of literary and philosophical works, especially in undergraduate curricula. This chapter revises that dispute's terms. Among the statements that defined this particular battle in the era's culture wars was Allan Bloom's *The Closing of the American Mind: How Higher Education Has Failed Democracy and Impoverished the Souls of Today's Students* (1987), which argued stridently against reform and in favor of a curriculum based on "great books." Bloom's crusade, which found allies among conservative policymakers, drew criticism from many sides.[1] Although the debate is often cast in terms of elite versus popular knowledge, frequently overlooked are its roots in curricular and extra-curricular projects earlier in the century to establish and to codify a literary and philosophical canon adapted to the protocols of mass culture. This took place against a background in which collegiate learning competed with scholarly research for priority and prestige in the nation's universities and in the academic public sphere.

The Western canon was not high-cultural metaphysics institutionalized. It was a prosaic, technical product of what Max Horkheimer and Theodor W. Adorno called in 1944 the "culture industry."[2] List-making was among that industry's techniques for consolidating authority; the undergraduate seminar was another. In academic skirmishes that later became culture wars, lists of books on syllabi, and the seminar tables around which those books were discussed, came together in a media complex dedicated to the production and reproduction of sovereign voices.

Mouths, Ears, Hands

During the first three months of 1872, a twenty-seven-year-old professor of classical philology delivered five lectures before the Öffentliche Akademische Gesellschaft (or Public Academy) at the University of Basel. In the last of his lectures, Friedrich Nietzsche offered this definition of the modern university: "One speaking mouth plus many ears and half as many writing hands: that is the academic system as seen from the outside—the educational machinery of the university in action."[3] In Nietzsche's university, a newfound zone of academic freedom separated professor and audience; but, as he pointedly remarked to his European listeners, standing behind it all, at some "discreet distance," was the state, to remind all concerned "that *it* is the aim, the purpose, the essence of this whole strange process of speaking and listening."[4]

Nietzsche and his extramural audience were bound together by a continental university system that reflected the Prussian reforms begun around 1810, by which universities became knowledge-seeking instruments of the new nation-states, reorganized around the kind of primary research the young philologist was doing in Basel as he prepared to publish his first book, *The Birth of Tragedy* (1872).[5] But even in translation, we can hear the indignation in Nietzsche's voice at what he took to be servitude masked as freedom, administered at a distance by feeble, sycophantic bureaucrats, guardians of a national culture dedicated to nothing more than their (and its) self-preservation.

In the United States, the authority that stood at a "discreet distance" from the speaking and writing machine of the university in the latter nineteenth century was less the state than the church. True, the small denominational colleges founded during the colonial period began rapidly expanding, in the 1870s, into larger research universities, largely but not entirely on the German model.[6] And yes, these East Coast institutions were joined by a cohort of new colleges and universities stretching to the Pacific coast, ranging from the secular, state-funded land-grant institutions established during the Civil War, to privately funded research institutions such as Johns Hopkins University, which opened in 1876. But in general, and although federal, state, and municipal bodies were central in establishing and governing the land grants and administering educational legitimacy, the church—or rather, this or that Protestant denomination with ties to business—still watched from a "discreet distance" over colleges and universities in the United States, as ears and hands recorded spoken words in the new lecture halls and seminar rooms built on religious foundations.

Voices

During the years of Nietzsche's professorship at Basel a small American college encountered financial difficulties. That college had been founded on borrowed money in 1857 under the auspices of the Baptist church and with an overly optimistic name: the University of Chicago. Unable to pay its mortgage debts, the college entered foreclosure and ceased doing business in 1886. But universities are rarely founded only once; they tend to be refounded, repeatedly. So it was with the University of Chicago. In 1885, a number of the original college's constituents attempted a rescue operation that proposed starting afresh in Chicago's Morgan Park suburb. In the wake of the original failure, the group, who were active within the American Baptist Education Society, had turned their attention to educational outreach, from preparatory schools to academies to colleges, in order to compete with other, more established denominations prevalent in the Western and Midwestern states, principally Congregationalists and Methodists. A Baptist college located in Chicago would serve as the fulcrum for such a regional strategy.[7]

Unable to raise sufficient funds locally, the Chicago Baptists sought out their denomination's wealthiest member, the New York businessman and founder of Standard Oil, John D. Rockefeller. By this time, Rockefeller had embarked on what would become a major philanthropic career. The Baptist church and, specifically, Baptist education were among his causes. Competing proposals for universities and seminaries in New York and Washington led the Chicago group to build consensus within the education society by scaling down their plans to include only a college that could, but did not necessarily have to, evolve into a graduate institution over time. After much cajoling from the Chicagoans and their intermediaries, Rockefeller provided the endowment on the condition that the group raise a comparable amount toward land and buildings. This condition was largely met in early 1890 when the department store magnate Marshall Field, himself a Presbyterian, donated land in the city's Hyde Park neighborhood.

With some reluctance, the Yale philologist and theologian William Rainey Harper accepted the presidency of the new University of Chicago, which was formally incorporated on September 10, 1890, with Rockefeller as the first of six signatories. Henry Ives Cobb designed a campus plan, and construction began in 1891. Although not formally a Baptist institution, the new university's articles of incorporation required that two-thirds of the trustees, as well as the president, be Baptist church members. But ecclesiastical affiliations can be deceptive; deep in the infrastructures of knowledge, secular and religious modes frequently coincide. When they do, old stories about the lucid gaze of enlightenment or about the progressively clarified voice of reason are inadequate if not simply wrong.[8] The same goes for the Weberian schema that defines European modernity as the Protestant calling sublimated into managerial capitalism.

Consider the sound that travels between speaking mouths and listening ears, leaving aside for the moment the equally important cultural technique of students taking notes. As the historian of American Christianity Leigh Eric Schmidt reminds us, the traditional association of Protestantism with audition—along the lines of Luther's famous claim, "The ears alone are the organs of a Christian"—perpetuates a division of the aural from the ocular that hides many acoustical affinities among Protestantism, Catholicism, and, to a lesser degree, other monotheisms.[9] Schmidt points out at length that, as in Europe, the American nineteenth century saw numerous efforts to demystify belief in prophetic or oracular revelation by simulating its effects in mechanical speaking machines, including phonographs. As he shows, these "oracles of reason" had the paradoxical consequence of materializing the very voices they sought to dispel. The paradox reached an apotheosis of sorts in the mid-twentieth century when, Schmidt informs us, the Danish art historian Frederik Poulsen, an authority on Delphi who had done his graduate work at Göttingen, fitted a chiseled oracular bust with a speaking tube and used his own voice to reproduce "god's voice," thus replacing what he called the "religious fraud" of speaking statues with the self-described "powerful and strange" voice of professorial reason.[10] Relatedly, in Chicago, a dialectic among textual and aural modes arose when, in a university founded on Protestant belief, ears hearing voices and responding to calls hooked up with hands writing lists, eyes reading them, and mouths speaking around tables, in an intermedial circuit. What had been sorted into distinct media platforms with the invention of specialized fields like acoustics began to split and combine. The result was an intermedial feedback loop, a series of media antinomies by which knowledge was defined and disseminated.[11]

Reverberation

We already get a hint of what was to come from the new University of Chicago president. In a lecture delivered to students sometime before 1904 and later published in a slim volume titled *Religion and the Higher Life*, Harper succinctly stated his own views on religion with a simple command: "The sum and substance of the Christian faith is found in two words, 'Follow me.' "[12] These words were not spoken in a university chapel, and the original lack of emphasis on such a building was consistent with Harper's theological convictions, which downplayed symbolic ritual in favor of Bible study, which Harper sought to place at the center of both academic and nonacademic life.[13] We can surmise, then, that in the early years of this religiously affiliated university, which at that point was really a coeducational college charged with the moral education of its students, "follow me" meant, in essence: listen, take notes, read, and exercise practical religious and moral judgment in the conduct of everyday affairs. For Harper and many of his faculty, this was perfectly compatible with scientific rationality.[14]

Despite the Baptist origins and the Baptist money, then, and although Cobb's plan included a centrally located Collegiate Gothic chapel, none was built during the first three decades of the University of Chicago's existence. Harper's own priority was a library, which was finally built in 1912 to designs by Shepley, Rutan & Coolidge as a memorial to Harper himself. Although from the beginning students at the new university were required to attend daily chapel, the lack of a dedicated space of sufficient size made this difficult. For a time, chapel was held in Cobb Hall, but already by 1897 a "provisional solution" had to be devised whereby each division of the university would meet once a week for morning assembly, which included brief religious services. Upon its completion in 1903, Leon Mandel Hall became the site for the largest of these assemblies.[15]

Mandel Hall was designed by Shepley, Rutan & Coolidge as part of an ensemble known as the Tower Group, located at the northeast corner of the original set of quadrangles and partly funded by an 1895 Rockefeller gift.[16] In 1903 the hall hosted the debut concert of the Chicago Symphony Orchestra and immediately became an important venue for performances of all kinds, including "orchestra concerts, dramatic performances, lectures, educational conferences, oratorical conferences, intercollegiate debates, athletic mass meetings, daily chapel assemblies, Sunday preaching services, the University Convocations, and other assemblies almost without number."[17] Laying the cornerstone for Mandel Hall, Harper reportedly said of the campus's first chapel in Cobb Hall that the latter could no longer accommodate "one third of the students"; hence the need for a replacement. University historian Thomas Goodspeed later observed that Harper's presidential successor, Harry Pratt Judson, could have said the same about Mandel Hall twenty-five years hence: "Remaining most useful for all ordinary demands on it, for great occasions it [Mandel Hall] was outgrown, and the University waited for the Chapel provided for it in the Founder's last gift, which would be commodious and beautiful, capable of meeting the religious and other needs of the growing University."[18]

Following Harper's death in 1906, Rockefeller was the prime mover behind a dedicated chapel building. Having already given approximately $25 million to the university, in 1910 he made a final gift of $10 million, of which he stipulated that at least $1.5 million be used for the construction and furnishing of a university chapel.[19] In his letter of designation, Rockefeller pointedly asserted that the chapel would confirm that "the University in its ideal, is dominated by the spirit of religion, all its departments are inspired by the religious feeling, and all its work is directed to the highest ends."[20] These words were visible on the chapel's dedication plaque when the building opened on October 28, 1928. The truth they spoke, however, was primarily audible, rather than visible, in the chapel itself.

6.1 Bertram Grosvenor Goodhue Associates and Mayers, Murray, and Phillip, University of Chicago Chapel, 1928. Exterior from southwest. Chicago Architectural Photographing Co. E. Donald Robb, "The University of Chicago Chapel," *Architecture* 59, no. 4 (April 1929), 220.

The historian of religion George M. Marsden has designated Harper's University of Chicago as the "high-water mark of liberal Protestant university building in which Christianity played an explicit role."[21] In contrast, and with palpable regret, Marsden describes the Rockefeller Memorial Chapel, completed twenty years later, as "one of the clearest cases of a building erected in memory of a fading religious spirit."[22] The chapel's rote symbolism, coupled with the university's loosening of formal religious ties and rituals (despite Rockefeller's wishes) and the prominence of Chicago faculty in the sciences and social sciences might lead us to agree with this assessment if certain technical details did not suggest otherwise.

In 1918, with the Rockefeller funds in hand, Judson selected the New York-based architect Bertram Grosvenor Goodhue to execute the chapel commission. The idiom was to be Gothic Revival, in reference to European cathedrals (which Goodhue studied closely) and in keeping with existing campus buildings designed mainly by Cobb and by Charles Allerton Coolidge. Following Goodhue's sudden death in 1924, work on the chapel was completed by the successor firm of Mayers, Murray & Phillip. Much can be said about the resulting building's location near the campus threshold, its monumental scale (it was to be the university's tallest building to date), its stony exterior, and its stripped-down Gothic proportions and detailing. But here we shall concentrate on an aspect of the building's interior that articulates what had become of the speaking and listening machine that drew Nietzsche's ire, as it was reformatted in newly founded research institutions like the University of Chicago.

In 1926, Floyd R. Watson, a professor of physics at the University of Illinois/Urbana who had gained prominence in the new field of acoustic science, together with his colleague from that university's architecture department, James M. White, were engaged by the University of Chicago to study the acoustical treatment of the chapel interior proposed by the Goodhue firm.

Photograph Showing Interesting Texture Obtainable with Akoustolith Plaster
Stone & Webster Investment Offices, Boston, Mass.

6.2 R. Guastavino Company, Akoustolith Plaster, detail. *Sweet's Architectural Catalogue 1927–1928* (New York: F.W. Dodge, 1927), A16.

The architects' designs called for an unspecified amount of acoustic tile in the vaulted ceiling and what was known as Akoustolith plaster on the walls.[23] The Guastavino Company, which had been collaborating with Goodhue since his earlier partnership with Ralph Adams Cram, were to supply the tile and the acoustic plaster.[24]

At this point the most significant acoustic issue for churches, auditoria, and lecture halls was the overlap of sounds and blending of words due to reverberation. The definitive solution, which included an equation and a new unit of measure (the sabin), had been developed in the 1910s by Wallace C. Sabine, the physicist pioneer of acoustic science whom Goodhue had introduced to Raphael Guastavino in 1911, and with whom Goodhue collaborated until

6.3 Bertram Grosvenor Goodhue Associates and Mayers, Murray and Phillip, University of Chicago Chapel, 1928. Nave looking toward the chancel. Chicago Architectural Photographing Co. Eccles Donald Robb, "The University of Chicago Chapel," *Architecture* 59, no 4 (April 1929), 221.

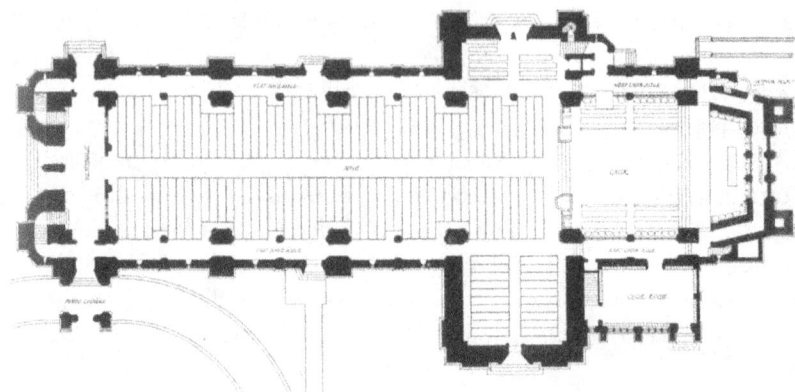

6.4 Bertram Grosvenor Goodhue Associates and Mayers, Murray and Phillip, University of Chicago Chapel, 1928. Plan. Eccles Donald Robb, "The University of Chicago Chapel," *Architecture* 59, no. 4 (April 1929), 219.

Sabine's death in 1919.[25] Sabine was a strict empiricist; he began his acoustical work with modifications to the auditorium in Harvard's newly constructed Fogg Art Museum in 1895 and achieved nationwide notoriety through his collaboration with Charles F. McKim on Boston Symphony Hall in 1900. Goodhue may have consulted Sabine while developing the initial designs for the chapel; in any event, he was intimately familiar with Sabine's approach. Watson and White's assessment also conformed with that approach by recommending that a total of thirty-two thousand square feet of sound-absorbing plaster and tiles be installed on the ceiling and the side walls. They were confident that such an acoustical treatment, combined with the correct placement and enclosure of the organ, would render the music performed in the chapel with what they called "the quality of excellence desired." The acousticians were less certain, however, about the spoken voice.[26]

The report prompted Lyman R. Flook, the university official in charge of the project, to ask his architects with some impatience whether anything could be done about "improving the acoustics for speaking."[27] Armed with another acoustical report by Paul E. Sabine, the late Wallace Sabine's cousin and successor, the architects suggested using Guastavino's proprietary Akoustolith tile on the ceiling vaults and either Akoustolith plaster or Sabinite, a competing product from US Gypsum, on the walls of the nave as well as in the transept and the tower. In the event, Sabinite won out over Akoustolith and the recommendations were carried out.[28] Not incidentally, the design also called for hard (nonabsorbent) plaster in the choir and aisle walls in the south gallery, as well as behind the organ.[29]

6.5 Bertram Grosvenor Goodhue Associates and Mayers, Murray and Phillip, University of Chicago Chapel, 1928. Organ bay from transept. Chicago Architectural Photographing Co. Eccles Donald Robb, "The University of Chicago Chapel," *Architecture* 59, no. 4 (April 1929), 225.

A few months before the Rockefeller Memorial Chapel opened in 1928, Watson summarized the latest thinking on reverberation in auditoria as follows:

> Conditions must be created by which the speaker, as he begins to talk, will find an immediate reinforcement of his voice without any effort on his part, so that he is given the confidence that comes with the assurance that his speech is at its best and that it is reaching its auditors.[30]

Shortly thereafter Watson found that the acoustics in the chapel satisfied these new criteria—through the subtle distinction, we can assume, between acoustically treated and untreated surfaces. Having tested the completed space with colleagues six days before it opened, he wrote to the building supervisor Flook that "when a speaker occupied the pulpit, he found a comforting reinforcement of his voice from the adjacent stone column that allowed him to 'hear himself,' and thus adjust his speech for best effect."[31] As Emily Thompson confirms with reference to Watson's writings, this reflected a change in acoustical thinking. Earlier, Watson's and Sabine's criteria for perfect auditorium acoustics had been limited to the experience of the *audience*; by the time Watson evaluated the results of his work at Rockefeller Chapel, his criteria had enlarged to include the auditory experience of the *speaker* as well. In doing so, it divided the one from the other and the voice from itself.[32]

In her study of the early-twentieth-century American soundscape, Thompson argues that the engineered dampening of reverberation prior to the advent of electroacoustics yielded a quintessentially modern product: discrete sounds rationalized into serial units.[33] Though she notes the change in Watson's thinking and practice to allow speakers or performers to hear their own voices in space, she possibly underestimates its consequences. For, contrary to Thompson's model, at Chicago's Rockefeller Chapel what was established was not—or, was not *only*—calculated, noise-free communication between speaking mouths and listening ears. It was also a doubled-up psycho-acoustic space built around a short circuit made possible by the calculated absence of sound-absorbing materials near the pulpit and the lectern, which localized rapid reverberation (or what Watson called "reinforcement") around the speaker. Outside this reverberant circuit, the audience, in principle, heard the speaker's voice as a series of deadened, mechanical sounds. While inside the circuit, the speaker, who was assumed to be male, severed from his audience like Nietzsche's professor, heard himself speaking as the sound returned from around and behind him.[34] The acoustics of Rockefeller Chapel therefore split the speaking voice in two: the serial voice of reason audible in the pews, and the subtly reverberant voice of a displaced, sublimated god, a master standing at some "discreet distance" and listening to himself, in a technical diagram that would become axiomatic for academic auditoria and lecture halls until microphones took over.[35]

Tables

In apparent contrast, as William Clark has shown, the format of the modern research seminar developed out of the intimacy of early modern professorial tables (or student boarding arrangements), collegia, and learned societies, mainly in Germany (with deeper roots in seminary-like Protestant convictoria), as well as out of the tutorial systems at Oxford and Cambridge. By the end of the eighteenth century, these philologically oriented research seminars began receiving state support, initially as separate institutions and then in universities, as they proliferated during the ensuing decades as a primary research environment along with the scientific laboratory. By and large retaining the formality of the earlier collegia, the German research seminar was, Clark argues, an important vehicle for the enactment and cultivation of academic charisma, albeit through the regular presentation of individually argued papers as disputational lessons rather than through informal conversation.[36] By the late nineteenth century, seminar- and laboratory-based research had begun also to predominate in the newly founded or reorganized American universities, where it retained what Clark calls its "cultic aspects."[37] Only later was the seminar transformed in the United States into a pedagogical instrument devoted to teaching undergraduates how to read books. We can understand, then, how Nietzsche took the universities of his time and place to be organized around the listening-writing assemblage of "one speaking mouth" and "many ears" associated with the specialized lecture or formal disputation. In humanities seminars at the University of Chicago and elsewhere that aimed to broaden undergraduate minds, however, speaking mouths multiplied and assembled around an infrastructure that doubled up the master's voice into a genial dialogue.

Rockefeller Memorial Chapel opened in October 1928. On the morning of November 19, 1929, Robert Maynard Hutchins gave his first speech from the chapel's pulpit as he assumed the presidency of the University of Chicago.[38] The following month, Hutchins recruited Mortimer J. Adler from Columbia University to join Chicago's philosophy department. Adler, a metaphysician with Aristotelian and Thomist leanings, was received coolly by his new colleagues, a number of who were distinguished pragmatists and social philosophers.[39] Adler had been among the first students and later, tutors, in the general honors undergraduate curriculum at Columbia, which was initiated in 1921 by John Erskine, a noted professor of English literature. Hutchins, stimulated by a prior meeting with Adler in which they discussed the course, brought him in to institute something similar in the undergraduate curriculum at Chicago to offset what Hutchins regarded as excessive specialization in the graduate schools.

The Columbia general honors course was a two-year seminar in which advanced undergraduates would read a comprehensive selection of canonical works in Western philosophy, literature, and science under the guidance of nonexpert tutors, led by Erskine, whose own expertise was in Elizabethan literature. As Erskine later wrote, somewhat disingenuously, he merely wanted the students "to read great books, the best sellers of ancient times, as spontaneously as they would read current best sellers," at the rate of a book a week, and "form their opinions at once in a free-for-all discussion."[40] Following on a two-year stint in Europe in which he helped set up and run a temporary university in the French town of Beaume for American soldiers on deployment, Erskine regarded the project as a welcome return to earlier efforts to persuade his colleagues to teach classic works in this manner.[41] But in its format, the honors course reiterated the administrative imagination that guided Erskine's activities during the war. For the Columbia general honors course was, above all and like the "great books" courses at Chicago that followed it, a list.

Recounting prewar faculty club debates on the matter, Erskine reproduced a letter from a dismayed colleague, who, fearing the end of "true scholarship at Columbia College," argued for depth over breadth, in the conviction that "it is better that a man should get to know ten authors well in his last two years of college, than that he should learn the names of the eighty-four men presented to him on this list."[42] Unlike undergraduates at Chicago, those at Columbia were universally male, and decades would pass before the gender and racial uniformity of such lists ("eighty-four [white] men") would be openly contested. Instead, around 1920, Erskine's lists, and Adler's after him, were mainly reactions against what these educators perceived as the laissez-faire system of elective courses adopted at Harvard and elsewhere around the turn of the century. The seminar format of the course also departed from tradition. The class met weekly for two hours on Wednesday evenings, a deliberate deviation from the norm of three fifty-minute sessions per week. Class sizes were limited to twenty-five or thirty students per section, by application.

Adler recalls that the inaugural seminar with Erskine was held around a "large oval table," a detail that is generally overlooked in discussions about the formation of literary canons.[43] Seated at this table, the form of which lacked a "head," were approximately twenty-five speaking mouths and twenty-five pairs of ears, plus those of the professors. Professors plural, since in their definitive form Columbia's general honors sections were taught in pairs. When Adler graduated from student to preceptor in general honors, his teaching partner was the poet and professor of English Mark van Doren, who, according to Adler, asked the first question in the first class: "What is the ruling passion in the *Iliad*?"[44] Van Doren then "went around the table soliciting proposals from every member of the group," demonstrating that with a good opening question, "you can call on everyone in rapid succession to try his hand at answering it, and then, with a wide variety of answers on the table, you can play one against the other to carry the discussion forward." Failing that, the format provided another option, wherein, as Adler advised:

> The second leader can always intervene to try his hand at asking the same question in still another way to make it more intelligible; or as frequently happens, he can correct his partner's failure to understand someone else's response to the last question. Listening with the inner ear to answers is even more difficult than asking good questions.[45]

Cultivated amateurism was preferred over professional expertise since, as Adler complained, "most professionals teach by telling; amateurs, among whom

Socrates was a paragon, teach by questioning."[46] The seminar therefore trained its teachers in a distinct set of pedagogical techniques: posing calculated questions, going rapidly around the table, putting responses "on the table," listening with the "inner ear." To reinforce the dialogic premise, exams were oral rather than written. These techniques worked together to make knowledge that was strictly tabular in character, in two senses. Such knowledge centered on the seminar table—in its primordial oval form at Columbia and in countless cognate forms elsewhere—and also on the list. Moreover, eliciting responses from students around tables required an inner ear sensitive to resonance, pitch, tone, and timbre. Like the speaker-hearer at the lecture podium, but for different reasons, this new form of professorial attention was quite literally doubled up, so that it could listen and learn from its own leading questions. All of which was set into motion by an administrative imagination that fed off of lists meant to replace the book-a-week reading of modern best sellers with what Erskine's course called "Classics of Western Civilization." This, in order to avoid the stenographic abyss of the lecture, in which, as Adler drily observed, "the notes of the teacher become the notes of the student without passing through the minds of either."[47]

What seemed a hermeneutic exercise was therefore a logistical procedure. In one of several reflexive turns, Adler's most widely read work was the 1940 bestseller, *How to Read a Book*, which grew out of the pedagogy he brought to Chicago. But in 1927, just prior to meeting Hutchins, he had also published *Dialectic*, a rambling quarrel with empiricism that he regarded as a semisecular counterpart to St. Thomas Aquinas's *Summa Theologica*.[48] Adler's "summa dialectica," as he called it, takes its title to mean conversational or argumentative thinking in general, thus assimilating (or reducing) the "Hegelian dialectic"—in those days an academic "catch-word of disapproval or praise"—to the Platonic/Socratic dialogue as treated by Aristotle, and the scholastic summa, or disputed question. From Georg Wilhelm Friedrich Hegel, whom Adler later admitted he was able to read only with difficulty and without conviction, Adler derived only the conclusion that "the mind can converse or dispute with itself"; hence, "what is required formally for dialectic is not two actually diverse minds, but rather an actual diversity or duality, an opposition or conflict" even "within the borders of a single mind."[49] Adler's book thereby recoded the format of the Columbia undergraduate honors seminar, with its paired professors, into the language of philosophy. The recoding itself was confused. What mattered more was that the institutional authority of philosophy, and more specifically, metaphysics, could now be summoned in the name of curricular reform. This was most likely how Hutchins saw the matter when he hired Adler to join the University of Chicago faculty.

The pair began by planning a two-year honors seminar on "great books" based on Erskine's list, which they would teach together for twenty first-year students chosen from a pool of eighty applicants. The class was assigned a special room, again with an oval table as a centerpiece and a stage. The discussions followed the same book-per-week format, and again the exams were oral rather than written.[50] At one point, after a dinner-table disagreement with Hutchins and Adler regarding the untranslatability of the great books into a common language (in this case, English), which ended with a whack on the head to Adler, Gertrude Stein visited the seminar to lead the discussion on Homer's *Odyssey*.[51] Within five years, the Adler-Hutchins seminar had become a talisman for what was by then known as the "great books movement," which stood as proxy for one side of a rancorous university-wide (and eventually, nationwide) dispute about curricular and institutional priorities.[52]

Among that dispute's most visible performances was a debate between Adler and the physiologist Anton J. Carlson, a prominent and outspoken empiricist, which took place in Mandel Hall on February 9, 1934. Tickets were sold, Adler reports, and "departments bought boxes for faculty to view the event, as if it were going to be a bullfight that should be seen from a vantage point."[53] Adler's prepared remarks were met by a challenge from Carlson to defend comments on education, philosophy, and science excerpted from various Hutchins

6.6 Mortimer Adler (right center) and Milton Mayer (left center) teaching the great books seminar at the University of Chicago, as shown in "Worst Kind of Troublemaker," cover story on Robert M. Hutchins, *Time* (November 21, 1949), 58. Myron Davis, The LIFE Picture Collection, Getty Images.

speeches. Adler complied, much to his own satisfaction. But the sociologist Edward Shils, who was in the audience that day and who regarded Adler as an intransigent bully, was unimpressed, describing the event as a "shabby performance" by both, "a vaudeville show, not an intellectual debate."[54]

Beyond intellectual malfeasance, Shils accused Adler of attaching, in his work at Chicago, a "theological penumbra" to Hutchins's proposals, worsened by an anti-Socratic, imperious disposition. He remembers hearing Adler for the first time in a seminar discussion on "Systematic Social Science," held in the Social Science Research Building in the 1930s, in "one of the more offensive academic performances I have seen." There, Shils found Adler speaking in a "domineering tone" and "slapp[ing] the table repeatedly and resoundingly with his palm to add weight to his declarations."[55] Likewise for the great books seminar, about which students were so enthusiastic that Shils wanted to see for himself. Visiting a class, he encountered "as harsh a piece of academic browbeating of a student as I have ever witnessed, carried out by Mortimer Adler. Table slapping was as much a part of the technique of interpretation of texts as it had been part of the techniques of exposition of 'systematic social science.' "[56]

Though the Hutchins-Adler reforms suffered a mixed reception, one notable outcome of the table slapping was *The Great Books of the Western World*, a fifty-four volume collection published by Encyclopaedia Britannica and the University of Chicago in 1952, edited by Adler and Hutchins. In 1947 Hutchins and William Benton, a former University of Chicago vice president who had become proprietor of Encyclopaedia Britannica in a joint venture with the university, established the Great Books Foundation for the purpose of promoting great books reading groups—extramural seminars—across the United States. These seminars were organized and conducted locally around tables in public libraries, schools, colleges, churches, and other public and private settings. Adler supplied a "Manual for Great Books Discussion Leaders" and traveled across the country to meet with library administrators to spread the word, and by 1953 a nationwide survey conducted by the foundation recorded a total of 1,176 such groups, with an average size of fourteen participants.[57] That is, by the time *The Great Books of the Western World* was published, the "great books" were more than a list; they were a system.[58]

The operating manual for this system was given by Adler and his coeditor William Gorman in their two-volume guide to the *Great Books* set, titled, *The Great Ideas: A Syntopicon of Great Books of the Western World*. Adler and Gorman began their syntopicon by claiming that the set was "something more than a collection of books"; rather it constituted a "unity" or a "certain kind of whole that can and should be read as such."[59] In lieu of the five years typically required by reading groups to work through the full list, which ran from Homer to Freud, the syntopicon provided a means of following short, thematic pathways through the set—a list of lists, bound together by indices, cross-references, and keywords.

The definitive list of great books to be included in the collection had been compiled in 1943–1944 by an advisory board consisting of Adler, Hutchins, Erskine, Van Doren, and a number of other prominent exponents of the larger project. Using criteria formulated by Hutchins, the board unanimously agreed on thirty-two essential authors (most of whom were on Erskine's original Columbia list). They later expanded the list to sixty-five and, finally, to seventy-four, with a total of 443 individual works. Midway through this process, the board made another list, of "100 rubrics representing the great objects, ideas, arts, sciences, and questions presented, expounded, and discussed," in order to furnish further criteria for inclusion.[60] Whether as feedback extrapolated from essential works, or as a tautology, this list eventually settled in at 102 "great ideas," from "Angel" to "World," and became the organizing matrix for Adler's and Gorman's syntopicon.

Behind the list of great ideas was an index of references to each in the collected books. This secondary list was compiled by two groups working in Chicago and Annapolis, home to St. John's College, which had been reorganized around the great books curriculum in 1937. As the group of indexers grew from ten to forty, it was consolidated in a former fraternity house on the Chicago campus (nicknamed Index House), along with seventy-five clerks.[61] Early on, a number of these indexers, few if any of whom possessed specialized knowledge, were tasked with breaking down classical Greek thought as a test case, an exercise that yielded a list of 1,003 key terms. That list, in turn, became the main source for the list of 102 "great ideas." A *Life* magazine feature on the index explained the domestic arrangements by which all of this was achieved, centered on:

> a staff of indexers whose job it was to read and reread two or three authors apiece until they know them perfectly. After a couple of years the indexers began to think like their authors and even to assume their names. From her window every morning Mrs. Freud would wave to Aristotle as he bicycled to work. Near her would sit St. Thomas Aquinas, who liked to work 36 hours at a stretch and relax by playing the horses. Kant was a man who had written his college thesis on "Misspellings in Old Southern Cookbooks."[62]

The fruits of their labors were recorded on over 150,000 index cards filed under the relevant ideas, in alphabetical order. From these, Adler wrote capsule introductions to each idea, a task he compared, again somewhat tautologically, to "writing 102 books."[63]

The Great Books of the Western World begins with a volume written by Hutchins entitled *The Great Conversation*, a title that should be taken literally. Although Hutchins strains to define "Western society" as progress toward "the

6.7 "The 102 Great Ideas: Scholars Complete a Monumental Catalog." The caption reads: "The Indexers pose with the file of Great Ideas. At sides stand editors [Mortimer] Adler (left) and [William] Gorman (right). Each file drawer contains index references to a Great Idea. In center are the works of the 71 authors which constitute the Great Books." *Life* 24, no. 4 (January 26, 1948), 92–93. George Skadding, The LIFE Picture Collection, Getty Images.

Civilization of the Dialogue," we should read, in place of that society, the under-graduate honors seminar gathered around an oval table at the University of Chicago; or, for that matter, the conversation, in the Index House, between Mrs. Freud, Aristotle, Aquinas, and Kant. That conversation's subject matter and scope are tabulated in the syntopicon itself, which comprises volumes 2 and 3 of the *Great Books* set. Its 102 chapters, each an alphabetically listed "great idea," are in turn broken into five parts: introduction, outline of topics, references, cross-references, and additional readings. The total adds up to approximately three thousand subtopics, with six to seventy-six per idea, and 163,000 references, with 284 to 7,065 references per idea. These are typically followed by shorter lists of cross-references pointing to other entries, as well as a list of additional readings beyond those in the set. The two volumes conclude with an alphabetical inventory of 1,800 terms, an index to the index by which the reader might locate specific subtopics without having to peruse the entire list.[64] In a majestically, manically reflexive gesture, this inventory is preceded by an exhaustive eighty-page appendix on "The Principles and Methods of Syntopical Construction."[65]

Dialectics 1

In the syntopicon entry under "Dialectic," Adler rehearses, in the studied, didactic language of general education, his anti-Hegelian model of a balanced give-and-take among opposing propositions. Textual references to Hegel, listed with other authors, are restricted to loosely connected passages in *The Philosophy of Right* and *The Philosophy of History*, which together comprise volume 46 of *The Great Books of the Western World*. Just as table slapping had no place in Adler's pedagogical philosophy (though apparently it did in his actual pedagogy), the selections allowed him to underplay, in passing, the unruly asymmetries and hierarchies that haunt the Hegelian dialectic, in favor of a duly oppositional but comparatively placid, contemplative "dialogue" with oneself or with others.

The entry on "Dialectic" also lists Hegel's *Phenomenology of Mind* (or *Phenomenology of Spirit*) as additional reading. *Great Books* readers who sought out that work would have found there a detailed exemplification of the fundamental asymmetry of Hegel's "struggle for recognition," in the dialectic of "lordship" and "bondage," commonly referred to as "master" and "slave." In place of the neat, balanced sequence of thesis, antithesis, and synthesis that Adler preferred to see in Hegel, recognition entails a life-and-death struggle between two "unequal and opposed" beings: "one is the independent consciousness whose essential nature is to be for itself, the other is the dependent consciousness whose essential nature is simply to live or be for another. The former is lord, the other is bondsman."[66] The dialectic of the lecture and the seminar does not mirror this relation (far from it) or resolve master/slave into a progressive, synthetic movement. Instead, this particular dialectic doubles it up.

Dialectics 2

Seventeen years after Adler's Hegel took his modest place in *The Great Books of the Western World*, on the other side of the Atlantic and in the midst of student revolts, the psychoanalyst Jacques Lacan explained to the audience of his seminar how the "discourse of the master," derived from Hegel's dialectic, transformed into the "discourse of the university." Lacan's audience sat in a lecture hall at the Parisian École de droit (School of Law) in the fall of 1969, watching and listening as Lacan drew symbols on the blackboard—$S1$, $S2$, the barred S, (*objet petit*) *a*— in four different algebraic combinations, while complaining on one occasion that the red chalk with which he was provided might prove to be illegible.

The first of these combinations denoted the "master's discourse," which, according to Lacan, is philosophy itself. By *discourse* Lacan meant not only enunciation but the social bond forged through signification: "Even before [philosophy] began talking about this alone, that is before it called it by its name—at least in Hegel it stands out, and is quite specially illustrated by him."[67] Acutely aware of the contested setting in which he spoke (the University of Paris, to which the École de droit belonged, was shortly to be disbanded and reorganized), Lacan designated as "knowledge" the product of that discourse—not the knowledge of philosophers per se, but rather, on the one hand, signification in general, and on the other (and more specifically), the "know-how" (savoir-faire) of enslaved or otherwise oppressed persons. For as Hegel pointed out, the lord depends upon, rather than simply dominates, the bondsman, materially but also as consciousness, in a primary inequality, "one [the lord] being only *recognized*, the other [the bondsman] only *recognizing*." This relation undergoes dialectical reversal "only when each is for the other what the other is for it."[68] But the reversal can never be complete, insofar as the bondsman's relation to his work is sociotechnologically mediated by power. To the extent that "what he [the bondsman] does is really the action of the lord," the asymmetry holds, and "the outcome is a recognition that is one-sided and unequal."[69] Hence, for Lacan, the principle of philosophy is one of "theft, abduction, stealing slavery of its knowledge, through the maneuvers of the master."[70]

In the algebraic formula that denotes the "discourse of the master," the master signifier S_1 (God, the King, the Absolute) occupies the dominant position. Its illegitimate product, acquired at the expense of the slave but not without remainder or surplus enjoyment (jouissance), is knowledge, S_2. During his fall 1969 lectures, to which he gave the title "Psychoanalysis Upside Down" (*La psychanalyse à l'envers*), Lacan explained and repeatedly drew three other formulae that derived from this "discourse of the master," two of which he readily named as the "discourse of the hysteric" and the "discourse of the analyst." About the fourth he was more cagey, withholding its name at the beginning and later referring to it only as "the one capped by the U" (just as the first was capped by an "M") before naming it outright. In this formula, the dominant position is occupied by S_2, knowledge, "not knowledge of everything [*savoir-tout*] . . . but all-knowing [*tout savoir*]. Understand this as being nothing other than knowledge, which in ordinary language is called the bureaucracy."[71] This bureaucratic or technocratic knowledge, occupying the position formerly held by the master, designates what Lacan called the "discourse of the university."

The product of the bureaucracy (which in Lacan's France as in Nietzsche's Germany or Switzerland we can take as a state bureaucracy) and, hence, of the university is the student, "object a," a "surplus value," but also a gap or void open to jouissance. Lacan explained this in a 1969 guest lecture at the experimental university at Vincennes, which had been established in response to student demands for reform the previous year. As he spoke, Lacan was interrupted by an audience member: "Who are you kidding? The University discourse is in the credit points." To which Lacan responded, "You are the product of the university, and you prove that you are the surplus value, even if only in this respect. . . . You come here to gain credit points for yourselves. You leave stamped 'credit points.' "[72]

Somewhat later in the same dialogue, if we can call it that (and, despite its many voices and interruptions, we must), another speaker, or perhaps the same one, asks,

> I wonder why this amphitheater is packed full with 800 people. It is true that you are a good clown, famous, and that you have come here to speak. A comrade also spoke for ten minutes to say that groups [*groupuscules*] were unable to get themselves out of the university. And everyone, recognizing that there is nothing to be said, is speaking but saying nothing. So, if there is nothing to say, nothing to know, nothing to do, why are so many people here? And, Lacan, why do you stay?

To which Lacan eventually replies:

> If you had a bit of patience, and if you really wanted our impromptus to continue, I would tell you that, always, the revolutionary aspiration has only a single possible outcome—of ending up as a master's discourse. This is what experience has proved.
>
> What you aspire to as revolutionaries is a master. You will get one.[73]

Lacan had just pointed out that, for him, the paradigmatic society in which "it is precisely the university that occupies the driving seat" was the Soviet Union.[74] He could just as well have looked in the other direction, toward the United States, where, the following year, Senator J. William Fulbright would add "academic" to outgoing President Dwight D. Eisenhower's earlier warnings about a "military-industrial complex."[75] But a detail in Hegel, not mentioned by Lacan in his lectures (or, for that matter, by Adler in his books), suggests that this analysis has its limitations. "The lord relates himself mediately to the bondsman," writes Hegel, "through a being [*Seyn/Sein*] that is independent, for it is just this which holds the bondsman in bondage; it is his chain [*Kette*] from which he could not break free in the struggle, thus proving himself to be dependent, to possess his independence in thinghood [*Dingheit*]."[76] The bondsman works on this being but does not master it, and so we are encouraged to understand the term to refer to the products of his coerced labor or to labor in general. But Hegel, consciously or not, is more specific: the being is a chain, a piece of infrastructure, a bond.

For the master-slave dialectic to become a dialogue among equals, as Adler wished, this bond would have to become a bridge. That, in the end, was the function of the oval seminar table: a leveling device that would presumably put teachers and students on the same plane. But both epistemologically and historically, Adler's table slapping was symptomatic of the technical impossi-bility of such a leveling. Whereas, at the edge of the Chicago campus stood the chapel, the function of which was not so much to convert the resonant voice of God into the dry voice of Reason but to double these up into a new kind of fold wherein the speaker listened to his own voice reverberate around him even as others heard reasoned argument. So, too, though in the obverse for the seminar, where pairs of professors—or, in the case of Chicago, an exiled professor of philosophy and the president of the university—listened to one another and to their students with "inner ears" finely tuned to pick up the slightest, most subtle signal in the ambient noise of the "great conversation," even as they knew that conversation to be, in its infrastructural reality, a self-authorizing, self-repro-ducing system of lists. This was the dialectic around which the "discourse of the university" was built.

As the Cold War university became a theater of technoscience, it may seem to have reiterated Nietzsche's speaking, listening, and writing machine, per-haps now without teachers, only knowledge systems, but still subservient to the power and interests of the state and of capital. But what of the humanistic intentions of the parallel system called the "great books" and associated ensem-bles? Is this just another instance of the bureaucratization of knowledge and of its commercialization as mass media? After all, more than just recording the voices of dead white men, these lists also *elicited* speech, in the form of an ongoing "great conversation," a sort of perpetual seminar that was meant to compensate, in its intimacy, for the abstraction of the lecture. And what of the political theology of the lecture hall, with its genealogical ties to the chapel? Are not the doubled-up acoustics of the lecture and the flat, oval architecture of the seminar table propped up by reading lists and indices one and the same thing: a chain, or bond, that binds students and teachers alike to the imperious dialectic, in which lord and bondsman are replaced by sovereign knowledge and its products, including enlightened readers of great books?

Minds, Closed and Open

In 1987, Allan Bloom, a political philosopher and alumnus of the University of Chicago during Adler's tenure there, defended what he called the "cultiva-tion" of enlightened readers, or reasoning truth seekers. Bloom only mentioned Adler once in his paean to the "good old Great Books approach," *The Clos-ing of the American Mind*, in connection with the philosopher-editor's "busi-ness genius" which, recognizing an "American" belief in equal access, "made a roaring success out of the Great Books."[77] Adler took offense, less it seems to the faint praise than to Bloom's indifference to his early work with Hutchins, the chronology of which Adler recounted. But most important to Adler was Bloom's inversion of his and Hutchins's project.[78] Where Adler and Hutchins saw the university as a platform for the practical democratization of knowledge, Bloom saw the "contemplative life" embodied even in Chicago's "fake Gothic buildings" as a necessarily aristocratic counterpoint to the intellectual tyrannies of a democratic society.[79] Yet, seen in light of the above excursus on Hegel, via Lacan, at a deeper level both projects for shaping the "American mind" stood firmly on the side of mastery—one popular, the other elite.

Bloom excoriated the indiscriminate "openness" of a cultural relativism that, he felt, had overtaken the pursuit of invariant moral truths. Access to these truths, and not unconditional respect for variable cultural values, ought to be the aim of a liberal education. "Culture is a cave," Bloom wrote, referring to Plato's allegory. Under the relativist sign of openness to all traditions, including insular, ethnocentric ones, "culture, hence closedness, reigns supreme. Openness to closedness is what we teach."[80] Not disagreeing with the criticism, Adler replied that, whether due to ignorance or to the willful neglect of six decades of prior work, Bloom's version of the great books remedy was just as dogmatic—and antidemocratic—as the totalitarian passivity he caricatured. Adler traced the difference to what happens around tables in classrooms. The search for truth, Adler emphasized, was riddled with contradictions, even among great books. Only a "dialectical" approach, such as that which he practiced around the seminar table with Hutchins, was capable of determining on which of the two opposing sides the truth lay. Rather than a dialectic Bloom was proposing a doctrine, and doctrine, Adler suggested, ought to be reserved for the interpretation of sacred texts, if that.[81] But as we have seen, Adler's "dialectic" was no less doctrinal, if not in defense of singular moral-philosophical authority, then in its adherence to the technical protocols by which such authority was produced and reproduced.

For, knowledge does not only entail the elimination of noise from the speaking system; it also entails the recapture of that noise as a signal, sent back to the speaker who is also a listener, in a feedback loop that, more often than not, has sought to restore the university's imagined soul. Not necessarily by building chapels but by echoing "his master's voice," the voice of a charismatic, secular god that reverberates only in his own ears.[82] This activity finds its counterpart in a gathering of readers speaking, listening, and interrupting one another around a seminar table. Together, they constitute the discourse—and the dialectic—of the university. Not only as a machine for the production of instrumental knowledge, in both its useful and its exploitative aspects, or for the production of critical knowledge, but as a machine for producing soulful, sovereign humans. These humans are moralizing agents, not of reason or unreason but of the performative chain or bond itself, reproduced in lists and consolidated around tables. It is in this sense that we can describe the university as a media system, the architecture of which forms the equipment through which their voices can still be heard.

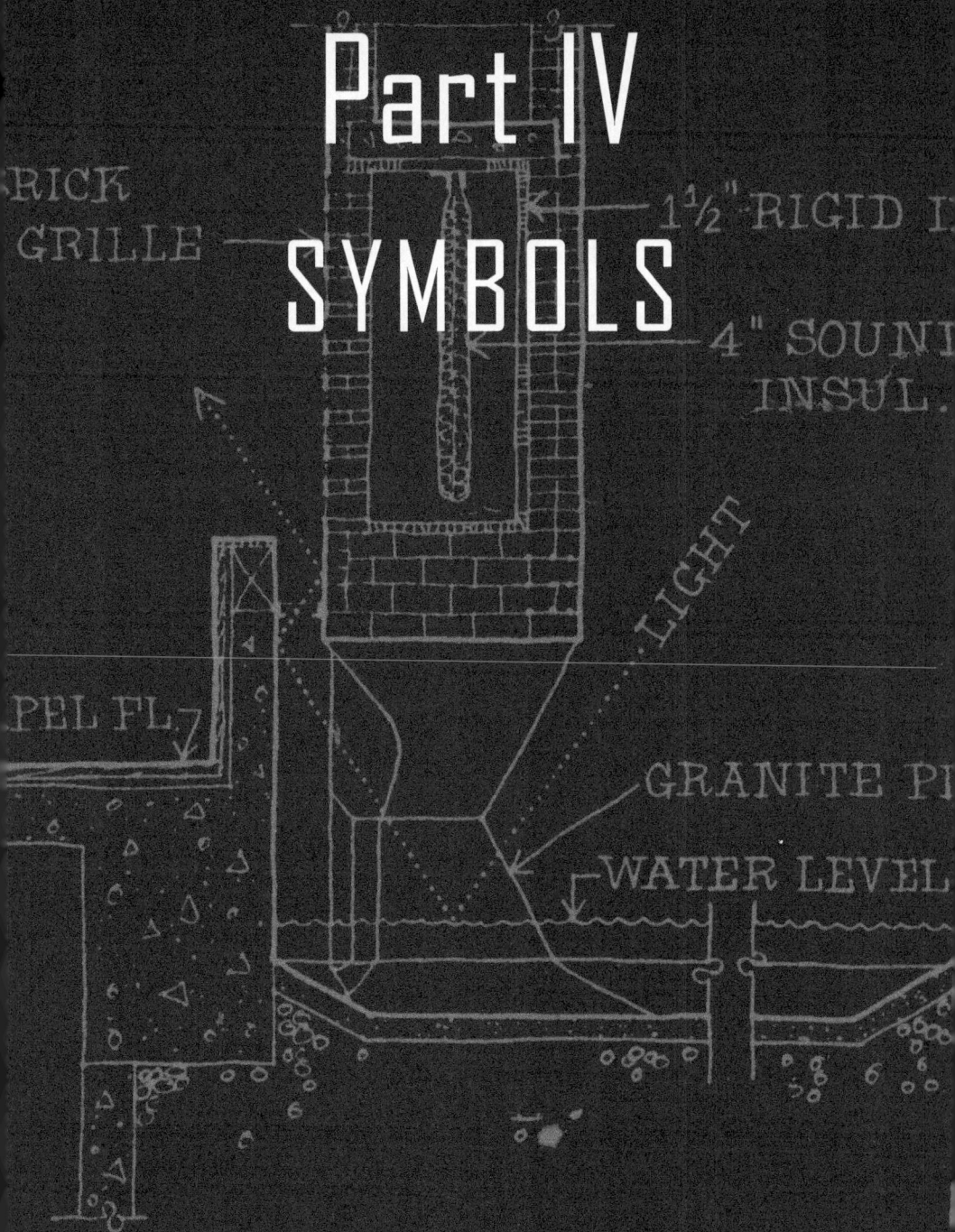

Part IV
SYMBOLS

7

FRONTIER AS SYMBOLIC FORM

The American frontier was a myth, used to justify the genocidal slaughter of Indigenous peoples and the forcible expropriation of land and resources.[1] As we glimpsed in the interlude, the frontier was also a *symbolic form*, a cognitive infrastructure from which that myth arose, activated by its users in a corresponding iconography. Unsurprisingly then, its vanishing into the Pacific horizon precipitated an iconographic crisis.

In 1927, the art historian Erwin Panofsky adapted Ernst Cassirer's sweeping "philosophy of symbolic forms" to the much narrower example of linear perspective.[2] But as Panofsky wrote, in the western United States (and, in a different manner, in the European colonies) a displaced territorial horizon, or frontier, had already begun to yield a new spatiality, with new categories, that unsettled this pictorial or mirror theory of representation. Lewis Mumford was on the right track when he wrote a few years later that, along with railroads and telegraphy, firearms were quintessentially metallic "space-annihilating" mechanisms born of the mines, while the "rational conquest of the environment by means of machines is fundamentally the work of the woodman."[3] Mumford showed how the literature, painting, and architecture of what he called the "Brown Decades" (the Gilded Age) had begun to yield a new iconography.[4] Its instruments were, in Mumford's terminology, "neotechnic" rather than "paleotechnic."

Recorded in the 1890 census by Herman Hollerith's calculating machines, the displaced frontier was, in short, a measurement bearing new symbols. This chapter follows the interplay of myth, symbol, and technics from East to West, beginning around 1875 in the New England quarries and ending in the 1960s on the campus of the University of California, Berkeley.

Axes, Rifles, and Stone

In a commencement speech delivered at Indiana University in 1910, Frederick Jackson Turner, the author of the frontier thesis, proposed that "the test tube and the microscope are needed rather than ax and rifle" in a "new ideal of conquest."[5] The heraldry of axes and rifles spoke to and glorified the violence inherent in putting Turner's "pioneer ideals"—which drew on the earlier doctrine of "manifest destiny"—into practice. Like many of his peers, Turner identified the Indigenous peoples colonized by Europeans and Anglo-Americans with a savagery akin to the wildness of an untamed nature, to which his choice of symbols bore witness: the ax for the forest and the rifle for the aboriginal. In the 1910 speech, Turner reiterated that the "safety valve" had finally been closed, and a transition was under way. "The times call for educated leaders," he said of the new land-grant state universities with their agriculture schools and schools of applied science. In these, "scientific farming must increase the yield of the field, scientific forestry must economize the woodlands, scientific experiment and construction by chemist, physicist, biologist and engineer must be applied to all of nature's forces in our complex modern society."[6] As the new symbols of test tubes and microscopes indicated, the frontier had not been erased but rather, *displaced* into the university.

Playing on the double meaning of the German term for both farmer and maker, Mumford quipped in *Sticks and Stones* (1924) that "architecture begins historically when the *Bauer* who plants becomes the *Bauer* who builds."[7] In his view, the Boston architect Henry Hobson Richardson was a builder whose works symbolically restored the ecological harmonies disrupted by industrial capitalism. Such restoration belonged to a more comprehensive geotechnical "renewal of the landscape" foreseen by figures such as the polymath geographer George Perkins Marsh, and modeled by Richardson's frequent collaborator, the landscape planner and social reformer Frederick Law Olmsted. As Mumford put it in 1931:

> For the pioneer, the land existed to be acquired, to be devoured, to be gutted out, to serve for a hasty turnover of profit. The conception that each man had a legal right to do as he would with his own far outbalanced any sense of the common weal. George Perkins Marsh was the first man to sense the destruction that was being wrought, to weigh its appalling losses, and to point out an intelligent course of action.[8]

Mumford credited Marsh, among others, with supplying the intellectual rudiments for ecological renewal in the form of "reparations to nature," the chief
practitioner of which would become, in Mumford's view, the "experimental
farmer and landscape planner" Olmsted.[9] Marsh mapped a sweeping geography that showed the frontier system's exhaustion of uncultivated wilderness,
and of woodlands in particular. Olmsted inserted public parks and university
campuses into this system, which activated the vanishing frontier as a symbolic
form in the sense discussed above.

Marsh's signal contribution to this discourse was *Man and Nature; Or, Physical Geography as Modified by Human Action*, which first appeared in 1864. In
his prefatory remarks, Marsh aimed at nothing less than "to indicate the character and, approximately, the extent of the changes produced by human action
in the physical conditions of the globe we inhabit," to show their dangers as well
as the possibility of remediating their effects, all while maintaining humankind's
preeminence as a species.[10] Marsh led a capacious life as a lawyer, politician,
diplomat, linguist, and sometime lecturer that compares to Mumford's in range
of interests, as well as in the half-in, half-out relationships that both maintained,
during different eras, with academic institutions.[11] Marsh also had an extensive
library, begun when a student at Dartmouth College and ultimately numbering
some twelve thousand volumes, in which he held most of the items listed in the
bibliography.[12]

"He treated man as an active geological agent," said Mumford of Marsh.[13]
Claiming that human activity had visibly transformed the ecosphere, Marsh
brought geography and ecology into contact with the human sciences well
before either of those two domains had been sorted into stable disciplines.[14]
Although he mentions Marsh's well-stocked personal library, Mumford does
not mention the fact that Richardson had designed a building to house Marsh's
books at the University of Vermont. The Billings Memorial Library, begun in
1883 and completed in 1885, was among Richardson's last works. Contemporaneous with the series of suburban railroad stations the architect designed for
the Boston & Albany Railroad and other lines, the Billings Library connects the
university with the cultural geography of these railroads via a series of public
libraries that Richardson designed more or less simultaneously, beginning with
the Oliver Ames Free Library in North Easton, Massachusetts.[15]

Located in its benefactor's hometown, the Oliver Ames Free Library was a
companion to the Oakes and Oliver Ames Monument in Albany County, Wyoming (1879–1882). Oakes Ames, a railroad executive and Republican congress-
man, had been censured in 1873 by the House of Representatives for his role in
the Crédit Mobilier scandal for offering undervalued Union Pacific Railroad
stock to fellow congressmen to cover up a complex fraudulent billing scheme.
As the head of the Crédit Mobilier construction company, Ames oversaw the

7.1 Henry Hobson Richardson and Augustus Saint-Gaudens, Ames Monument, Albany County, Wyoming, 1882. Photograph by J. E. Stimson, Neg. 2853. J. E. Stimson Collection, Wyoming State Archives.

financing and construction of the railroad, which, when it met the Central Pacific Railroad at Promontory Point, Utah in 1869, formed the eastern portion of the first transcontinental line. His son Oliver served for a time as Union Pacific's president.[16] The Ames family commissioned Richardson to design the memorial partly to rehabilitate the reputation of the elder Ames, and partly to mark the family's role in westward expansion. The same year, the children of Oakes Ames commissioned Richardson to design the Oakes Ames Memorial Hall (1879–1881), also in North Easton.[17]

Placed at the highest point on the Union Pacific rail line, the Ames Monument in Wyoming is a sixty-foot high monolith of rough-hewn ashlar granite quarried from nearby Reed's Rock, extending to a tetrahedral quasi-pyramid at the top. On opposite faces are stone bas-relief portraits of the two Ameses by Augustus Saint-Gaudens, with whom Richardson frequently worked. Seen from a moving train, the monument must have seemed a piece of Wyoming's geology exposed by the elements. Seen in a book or discussed in speeches, it added the miner's pick and shovel to Turner's symbolic ax and rifle in the networks of frontier discourse.[18]

The Ames fortune did not begin with railroads but with the Ames Shovel Company of North Easton, in which Oakes and Oliver were partners.

7.2 Henry Hobson Richardson, Billings Memorial Library, University of Vermont, 1885. Detroit Publishing Co., 1902. Library of Congress Prints and Photographs Division.

The company, which exhibited at the 1893 Chicago world's fair, manufactured shovels used in the construction of railroads, in the California gold mines, and (by Abraham Lincoln's order) by the Union army during Civil War.[19] Its tools were therefore vivid symbols of what Turner called "conquest," and profits derived from their manufacture and sale were recirculated as finance capital in institutions like Crédit Mobilier. The railroads, which also connected Eastern mills, factories, and forges to Midwestern mines and from there, westward, furnished the tracks. Such networks, with the Ames monument at one of their nodal points, trace the reciprocity that Turner emphasized when he observed the impact of westward expansion on Eastern industry and culture, most notably by the railroads and the fortunes they made, of which the Carnegie public libraries are another important example.[20]

Richardson's Billings Memorial Library at the University of Vermont belongs to these networks. Frederick P. Billings was a Vermont lawyer who had become wealthy representing mining companies and their investors in land claims in northern California; he would later become president of the Northern Pacific Railway, in recognition of which that line's westernmost railhead was named

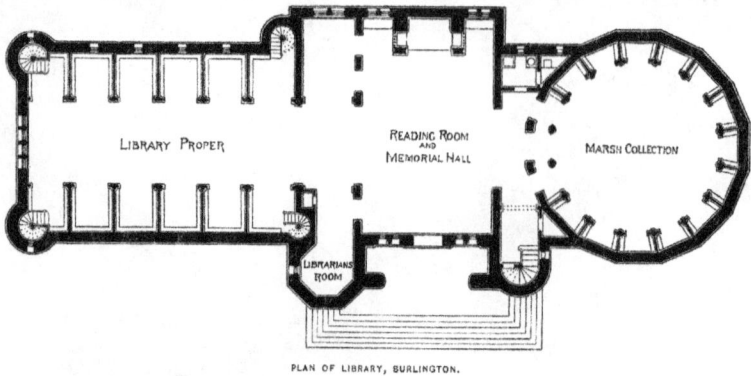

PLAN OF LIBRARY, BURLINGTON.

7.3 Henry Hobson Richardson, Billings Memorial Library, University of Vermont, 1885. Plan, main floor. Marina Griswold Van Rensselaer, *Henry Hobson Richardson and His Works* (Boston, New York: Houghton, Mifflin, 1888), 79.

Billings, Montana.[21] Billings had long admired Marsh's political career and was an avid reader of his writings. So much so that Billings purchased Marsh's childhood home in Woodstock, Vermont, where he set up a model farm. Late in life, Marsh had sought but failed to auction his library to supplement his dwindling finances. Shortly after Marsh's death in 1882, Billings approached University of Vermont president Matthew Buckham with an offer to purchase the library for the university and erect a "fireproof library building" to house it along with the rest of the university's collections. The pair selected Richardson as the library's architect, most likely on the strength of his public library designs.[22]

The floor plan of the Billings Library, which opened in 1885, adapted that of Richardson's earlier Winn Memorial Library in Woburn, Massachusetts (1876–1879) on a larger scale. A dimly gaslit central reading room (Billings was apparently nervous about the fire hazard posed by electric wiring) separated a polyhedral volume housing the Marsh collection from the remainder of the university collections, which were arranged in serial alcoves at the other end of the building. A monochrome exterior of quarry-faced ashlar stone was composed of typical Richardsonian elements like the "Syrian" entrance arch first used at Woburn.[23] With the exception of the uniformly brick-clad Sever Hall at Harvard, Richardson's previous academic and library buildings had all featured multihued brickwork or stone masonry, so the monochrome was something of an unexplained departure. Whatever the architect's intentions, its exterior treatment aligns the Billings Library with the monolithic, monochromatic Ames Memorial. Though both were made from locally quarried stone, memorial and library stand on the threshold of what Mumford decried as the industrialization of the quarries and their integration into the continental railroad system, which permitted near-replica fragments of the Chicago World Exposition's White City to be erected from Indiana limestone and Vermont marble in civic and institutional buildings across the country.

The specifications for the Billings Library called for the exterior ashlar walls to be of Kibbe stone, a dark red sandstone quarried from a site owned by the building contractor, Norcross Brothers, in East Longmeadow, Massachusetts, in the Connecticut River Valley. At some point, an alternative, lighter-hued sandstone from a neighboring quarry not owned by Norcross was proposed as a cost-saving measure for certain cut stone on the façade, but rejected.[24] Richardson worked with Norcross Brothers on most of his later buildings, and it is possible that he specified their stone out of professional loyalty as much as to maintain the façade's monolithic qualities. Regardless, the Norcross and other nearby quarries were hardly local in the sense suggested by Mumford. According to one government report, by the mid-1880s Norcross were "the largest shippers of stone from East Longmeadow, having last year loaded 115,000 cubic feet of brownstone for building purposes on about 900 freight cars," destined for building sites as far away as St. Louis, or, in the case of the neighbor whose stone was rejected, Chicago.[25]

In addition to his professional ties to Norcross, Richardson worked with Olmsted on a number of these Massachusetts projects, including the Oakes Ames Memorial Hall.[26] The pair had been collaborating since the early 1870s, not long after Olmsted returned to the East Coast from California, where he had spent two years managing the gold mines on the Mariposa Estate in the foothills of the Sierra Nevada Mountains. That estate, previously known as Rancho Mariposa, had for some time been the subject of an infamous ownership battle among frontier networks. The dispute began with contested land claims after the signing of the Treaty of Guadalupe Hidalgo in 1848 to end the Mexican-American War, by which the United States annexed California and a large portion of the Southwest territories. Though the treaty recognized existing land ownership by Mexican nationals and offered them U.S. citizenship, the verification requirements established by the Land Law of 1851 favored Anglo-American squatters who had settled on those lands and had begun extracting resources from them.[27]

Many of these squatters were subsistence farmers or, in the case of northern California, individual prospectors who flowed in from the East and Midwest during the gold rush. Others were land speculators, including the future California senator John C. Frémont, who purchased the Mariposa Estate in 1847 from the former governor of Alta California, Juan B. Alvarado. Gold was discovered there in 1849, and Frémont was unable to prevent mines from being set up by prospectors, who then claimed title on the basis of improvements. The disputed claims were eventually settled in Frémont's favor before the U.S.

Supreme Court, where Frémont was represented by Frederick Billings, the future benefactor of the Billings Library. But Frémont had borrowed heavily against the land, and his creditors—including Billings—repossessed a significant portion, which they sold to a group of New York investors. These investors then hired Olmsted to manage the property, and it was Billings who accompanied Olmsted to the mines upon his arrival in 1863.[28]

Despite Olmsted's managerial improvements, the yield from the Mariposa mines fell well short of expectations, stock in the mining company plummeted, and Olmsted left for San Francisco. During this time, and—as Mumford noted—the same year (1864) that Marsh's *Man and Nature* was published, the federal government ceded the Yosemite Valley and the Mariposa Grove of Big Trees, not far from the mines, to California in perpetuity as public parks. Olmsted was appointed to the state commission charged with establishing these parks, and in 1865 he presented a report detailing his proposals.[29] The following year, Olmsted completed a study for the grounds of the College of California, which was to be relocated from a site in downtown Oakland to nearby lands recently acquired by the college trustees from landowners who had purchased them from the owner of another contested Mexican land grant.

This journey to the California mines via Olmsted not only finds Billings, patron of the University of Vermont library, on the country's Western frontier; it maps a mineral geography that coincided with the disappearing woodlands charted by Marsh during the same period. Unlike the iron extracted from Midwestern mines to make axes, rifles, or shovels, precious metals from California and its vicinity circulated as gold and silver coins, or as other evanescent signifiers like that manifesto of bimetallism at the Chicago World Exposition, Montana's *Silver Queen*. In the White City, these value-representing metals met staff plaster façades in place of quarried stone. Elsewhere, in only apparent contradistinction, buildings like the Billings Library emerged from quarries linked to railroads linked, in turn, to quarried stone monuments that commemorated the financial practices of their managers. In this shadow play, "man" and "nature" did battle first with axes, rifles, and shovels, then with test tubes and microscopes.

Mining in Plato's Cave

Ralph Waldo Emerson, whom Mumford was quick to identify as the battle's first philosopher, said of Plato's dialectic that it brought together the opposed forces of unity and difference. The former belonged to nature and the latter to the human intellect, of which Periclean Athens was an apotheosis. Of the Athenian artists, Emerson wrote:

> They cut the Penticlean marble as if it were snow, and their perfect works in architecture and sculpture seemed things of course, not more difficult than the

completion of a new ship at the Medford yards or new mills at Lowell. These things are in course, and may be taken for granted. The Roman legion, Byzantine legislation, English trade, the saloons [sic] of Versailles, the cafés of Paris, the steam-mill, steamboat, steam-coach, may all be seen in perspective; the town-meeting, the ballot-box, the newspaper and cheap press.[30]

Emerson made these observations in 1849 in his series on "representative men," almost half a century before the Chicago World Exposition, at the time of the California gold rush and a few years before H. H. Richardson entered Harvard, Emerson's alma mater. In his essay on Plato, among the chief benefits Emerson attributed to the "cheap press" were the new translations in the London publisher Henry G. Bohn's Serial Library, which first appeared in 1848. Prompted by this popular series, Emerson appended to his essay a bulletin, titled "Plato: New Readings," in which he found the Greek philosopher "studying the state in the citizen and the citizen in the state; and leaving it doubtful whether he exhibited the Republic as an allegory on the education of the private soul."[31] Had they pursued this allusion, Emerson's readers would have found this version of Plato's cave in the "new literal translation" of the *Republic* published by Bohn:

> Behold men, as it were, in an underground cave-like dwelling, having its entrance open towards the light and extending through the whole cave,—and within it persons, who from childhood upwards have had chains on their legs and their necks, so as, while abiding there, to have the power of looking forward only, but not to turn round their heads by reason of their chains, their light coming from a fire that burns above and afar off, and behind them.[32]

Those who leave the cave and come to know the realm of ideas must return and govern.[33] By Emerson's time, the separation of campus from town had become an accepted model nationwide to ensure that "good" young men might cross the threshold and be trained to govern as free individuals, without "chains on their legs and necks." Rising out of the mines, forests, and fields, edifices like the Billings Library brought "nature" into the university, but only as a new realm of shadows. Connection and separation, unity and difference, cascaded from campus to city, from New England to the Western shores. Mumford cautioned: Do not take Emerson's Platonism "to mean that he lived in a perpetual cloud-world." Yes, it was a withdrawal, "but it was a withdrawal of water into a reservoir, or of grain into a bin, so that they might be available later, if they could not be distributed at once."[34] The realm of ideas, in other words, was a technical realm, and the Billings Library was among its grain silos. Located on the campus of a land-grant university, the library turned the frontier inside-out. Archetypally free individuals withdrew into this dimly lit, artificial cave, where, with the help of an ecologist's books presented to them by a land claims lawyer, they learned to manage the landscape from which its stones were hewn.

From Emerson to Turner, then, the threshold that separated the governors from the governed was that of the frontier as symbolic form, by which democracy allegedly underwent perpetual renewal. Caroline Winterer has described a "drift toward idealism in American thought" in both American and English universities after 1870, represented by figures like the Harvard philosopher Josiah Royce, who dedicated his own, occasionally critical history of the Californian conquest to his mother, "a California pioneer."[35] We have been tracking the material infrastructures of that idealism—the architecture, so to speak, of the cave itself. This architecture includes what Emerson called the "cheap press" and its "literal translations," as well as the railroads and their monuments, along with the mines and other caves out of which the new research universities were built.

The University of California, Berkeley, and Land

Marsh's *Man and Nature* began with an epigraph from a sermon by Horace Bushnell regarding "man's" inestimable dominion over the earth.[36] It was Bushnell who, at the behest of the trustees of the recently founded College of California (formerly the Contra Costa Academy), a nondenominational Protestant institution in Oakland, led the search for a new site for the college in 1856. Frederick P. Billings of Vermont's Billings Library was among those trustees. After initially rejecting Bushnell's suggestions, in 1857 the group began acquiring land in the area north of Oakland around Strawberry Creek from a number of settlers through a variety of means, including purchase, deed, and donation.[37] The acreage, which had previously been inhabited by the Indigenous Ohlone (or Costanoan) people, was part of Rancho San Antonio, a nineteen-thousand-acre land grant made by the Spanish crown in 1820 to Luis María Peralta, who deeded the land to his sons in 1842.[38]

The native inhabitants had been violently conscripted into forced labor or driven off by Spanish colonists, who, with their administrative techniques and their rifles, produced California *as land*—that is, as property that could be granted, in the form of ranchos and missions. Frémont and others followed with the outright slaughter of Indigenous peoples.[39] The Land Law of 1851 effectively alienated that land, *as property*, by specifying that landholding be verified against the claims of squatters, which required the original landowners and their lawyers to seek documentation as far away as Mexico City. Law firms nominally representing Mexican or Mexican American landowners to verify their claims would often manipulate paperwork in favor of the white squatters.[40]

In the case of the Peralta holdings, though an 1856 Supreme Court decision affirmed the family's claim, financial difficulties related to legal costs, taxes, and theft forced Vicente and José Domingo Peralta to sell off nearly all the land

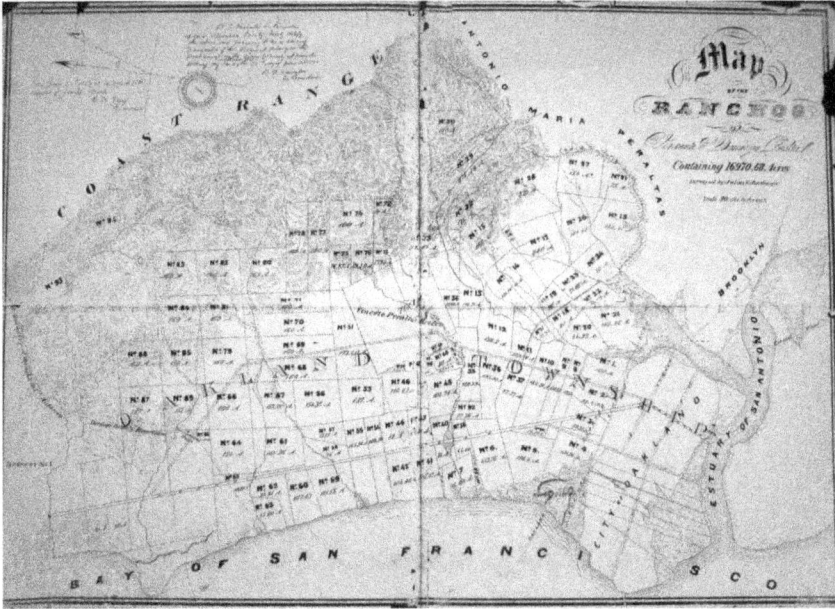

7.4 Julius Kellersberger, map of Rancho San Antonio, 1854. University Archives, Bancroft Library, University of California, Berkeley.

to Anglo-American settlers beginning in 1850.[41] Among the buyers was the "Forty-Niner" John C. Hays.[42] In 1854 Hays, who by then had been appointed U.S. surveyor general for California, commissioned the Swiss cartographer Julius Kellersberger to produce a definitive ownership survey of the property.[43] The Kellersberger map subdivided Rancho San Antonio into eighty-eight geometrically regular plots. The site selected by the trustees for the College of California was located in the area of plot 81, on land owned by Hays and his partner John Caperton. In 1857, Hays and Caperton sold the southernmost three-eighths of that plot to a pair of college trustees. A number of other transactions followed, and a parcel of significant size was assembled.[44]

About a decade later, in 1866, the trustees invited Olmsted, recently arrived from Mariposa, to propose a plan for the college's newly acquired lands. Rejecting an earlier proposal to concentrate college buildings on the uphill side of a landscaped park, Olmsted argued in frontier language that "scholars should be prepared to lead, not to follow reluctantly after, the advancing line of civilization." His plan provided for an intermediate environment, between what he called the "real life" of the city and the "rustic" countryside.[45] Olmsted proposed to devote a good portion of the land to individual home sites for professors and others.[46] These houses would form the core of a residential neighborhood

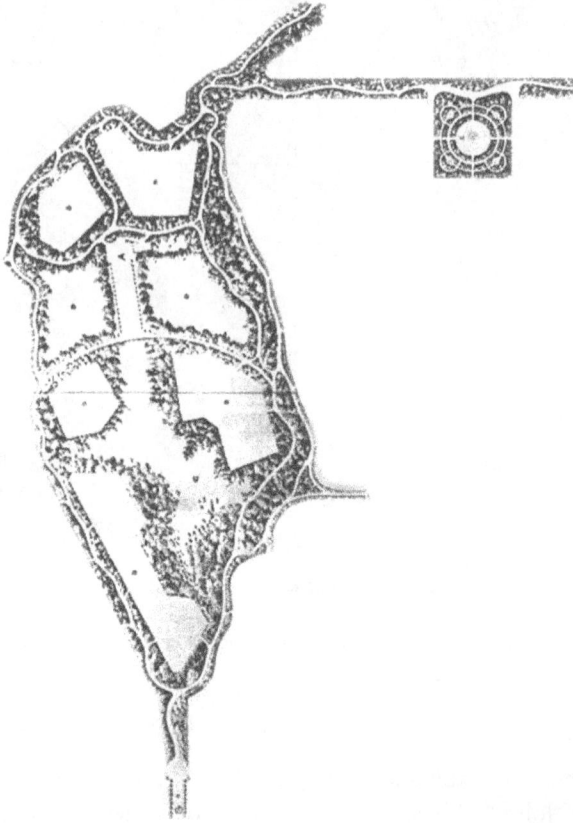

7.5 Frederick Law Olmsted, plan for the College of California, 1865. University Archives, Bancroft Library, University of California, Berkeley.

around the college buildings, which would cluster around a central, artificial glade culminating at its westward end in an architectonic terrace with views to the Golden Gate, the strait that separates the isthmus of San Francisco from the Marin peninsula and, on clear days, frames the Pacific horizon.

In their planning the college trustees, Frederick Billings among them, sought a new name for the town that would host their relocated institution. A naming committee was formed to which Olmsted made numerous suggestions, mostly based on landscape features or on the Spanish past but also including "Billings" and "Bushnell," all of which were rejected.[47] The committee eventually recommended "Peralta." But, during a visit to college lands in May of 1866, an apparently unsatisfied Billings, standing on a rocky outcropping on plot 81 and gazing out toward the Golden Gate, was reportedly moved to recall George Berkeley's well-worn phrase, "Westward the course of empire takes its way," from the Irish bishop's *Verses on the Prospect of Planting Arts and Learning in America* of 1728. From this Billings proposed "Berkeley." Thus the town, and later the university, received its name from a lawyer of the mines and of the land, and an idealist philosopher.[48]

The Olmsted plan remained on paper; the homestead sites went largely unsold, and the trustees, unable to raise sufficient funds and facing mounting debt, sought alternatives. Recognizing that the land-grant system offered a potential resolution to their financial difficulties, they urged that a recently chartered Agricultural, Mining, and Mechanical Arts College, which many had opposed for its solely vocational scope, be combined with their own institution of arts and letters into a new state university. Legislation to this effect was passed in 1868, and the College of California lands and its debt were transferred to the University of California.[49]

The Berkeley Campus Plan

In 1870, the architect David Farquharson loosely adapted aspects of the Olmsted plan into a grouping of six buildings in a French Second Empire style, three of which were realized and one of which still stands.[50] Farquharson's plan proved serviceable for about twenty-five years, but at the turn of the century it was replaced by a much longer-term plan that projected a monumental campus—a western White City—that became the definitive basis for growth. This plan, which was named after its principal benefactor, the mining heiress Phoebe Apperson Hearst, resulted from a palimpsest of authorship, though it is generally attributed to John Galen Howard, who served as UC Berkeley's supervising architect from 1901 to 1924. It began with the "International Competition for the Phebe [*sic*] Hearst Architectural Plan of the University of California," which required entrants to arrange twenty-eight new buildings including, among other things, a "room for animals for toxicological experiments" and "vivisection rooms," clearly orienting the university toward laboratory-based scientific research.[51] While the competition results were not built as projected, the grandiose plan, its publication, and worldwide commentary formed a media system passing through one building that *was* built. This was the Hearst Memorial Mining Building, on which the University of California at Berkeley was, in effect, precariously refounded.

Hearst had recently taken control of her late husband Senator George Hearst's mining and land interests, which included the Homestake gold mine in South Dakota, the Anaconda copper mine in Montana, and one million acres of land on which existed a number of significant ranches and farms.[52] Having been active in civic philanthropy for some time before her husband's death in 1891, Hearst now expanded that activity considerably, beginning with the endowment of five scholarships for women at the coeducational University of California.[53] Managed by his mother, the inheritance also financed William Randolph Hearst's newspaper empire, through which he would become a "representative man" of the "cheap press." By 1895, Phoebe Hearst had already proposed to fund a new building for the department of mining at the university as a memorial to her late husband. At the behest of the university president, Martin Kellogg, the architect Bernard Maybeck produced designs in a twenty-four hour charrette to secure the Hearst bequest.[54]

Maybeck, together with the prominent San Francisco attorney and California regent Jacob Reinstein, proposed that Hearst support an international design competition for an entirely new campus, to which she agreed, pledging to fund "a comprehensive and permanent plan" such that money would be no object.[55] Led by Maybeck (by now operating out of Paris) in late 1897 the organizers announced to potential competitors that: "In fact it is a city that is to be created—a City of Learning—in which there is to be no sordid or inharmonious feature."[56] The brief envisioned a kind of utopia which, given the prevailing Beaux-Arts ethos, was clearly to be rendered in a classical manner. As in the extension of the University of Virginia campus by McKim, Mead & White then under way, this "City of Learning" harked back to a philosophical School of Athens. But as with the overscaled Diana atop that firm's agriculture building at the Chicago World Exposition, an orientation toward an imagined classical past arose not out of nostalgia but from the new signifying systems of industrial capitalism and their redrawn frontiers.

When the final judging for the two-stage Berkeley competition concluded in 1900, first place went to the Beaux-Arts trained Parisian, Emile Bénard, an academic architect with an uneven career who had won the Prix de Rome in 1867.[57] After an unsettling trip to northern California, Bénard revised his neo-Baroque plan—which cast Berkeley as "Roma"—but was unable to come to terms with the group overseeing the process led by Hearst and by Kellogg's successor, university president Benjamin Ide Wheeler. Disillusioned, Hearst fired Bénard, and she and Wheeler turned to the New York-based architect John Galen Howard, who had placed fourth in the competition, to revise the plans and supervise construction of the new campus.[58]

The resulting master plan was among other things a fundraising instrument. From its inception, the University of California relied on a combination of state tax revenues, relatively meager tuition income, and private philanthropy to cover its operating and capital expenses. By leveraging the initial Hearst bequest for a single building into a grandiose hallucination, the plan had the practical effect of reconfiguring the university as a locus of symbolic capital. This is one reason that Bénard's relative indifference to actual site conditions was not an obstacle to the initial selection of his scheme. His original proposal was widely publicized not in spite of its fantastical unrealizability but because of it. More

7.6 Emile Bénard, Phoebe Apperson Hearst Architectural Competition, University of California, Berkeley, new project, 1900. Campus plan. University Archives, Bancroft Library, University of California, Berkeley.

than a public relations coup, however, this plan and the entire "City of Learning" that it conjured repositioned the University of California around 1900 at a real and symbolic threshold within a changing academic-industrial landscape.

Horizons, Inner and Outer

All three versions of the original Bénard plan were organized around a major east-west axis crossed by two minor north-south axes, with a series of monumental courts. The plan's pivot was what the architect had already labeled the mining building. Howard's revisions anticipated this building's construction, along with an administrative building, California Hall. To reduce the amount of expensive grading, Howard dedicated his initial efforts to pragmatic adjustments in siting the two buildings. Pointing out that Bénard's plan would have required the mining building to traverse a seven-foot slope from one corner to the other, Howard proposed shifting the overall plan's major, east-west axis on which that building was located. Bénard had terminated that axis at University Avenue, aligning his Acropolis-like "City of Learning" with the actual city, of which it would have formed an aloof, monumental precinct. Howard's reorientation turned the axis approximately 7.5 degrees counterclockwise, toward the southwest, distinguishing campus from city more decisively and aligning the main axis directly with the Golden Gate.

This seemingly minor adjustment reproduced an important feature of the Olmsted plan: a mirror-like identification with the open horizon, framed by the Golden Gate.[59] But where Olmsted's picturesque arrangement sought

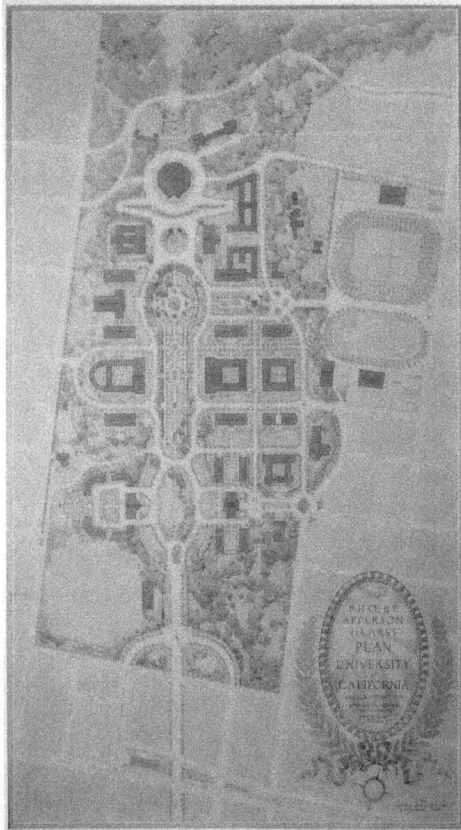

7.7 John Galen Howard, Phoebe Apperson Hearst Plan, University of California, Berkeley, 1914. With rotated east-west axis. Environmental Design Archives, College of Environmental Design, University of California, Berkeley.

quasi-continuity with the unbuilt city and its still bucolic setting by downplaying the formality of the axis, Howard reorganized the entire campus around it. Not only did the reorientation allow the buildings to settle more easily into the hillside, it shifted the implied horizon of the campus from the city of Berkeley to a relocated national frontier. With the new phase of imperialism inaugurated by the Spanish-American War of 1898, "manifest destiny's" threshold had overspilled its continental boundaries and reached the Pacific islands. Whereas, from within the more immediate horizon of the projected mining building, it was clear enough that, in order that further riches could be extracted from already conquered lands, resources now had to pass through the "test tube and the microscope," as Turner would later put it. Completed in 1907, the Hearst Memorial Mining Building was therefore a memorial both to an individual career devoted to the first phase of accumulation in the American West and to territorial expansion itself. As that expansion moved outward, into a new imperial phase, it also moved inward, converting mines, farms, and ranches into laboratories, and submitting their products and processes to academic study.

Architecturally, the mining building stood abreast the Golden Gate axis, its main, limestone-clad southern façade penetrated by three overscaled Roman arches, within which sat freestanding pairs of Ionic columns supporting entablatures disengaged from the building's mass. Inside, immediately behind the arches, was a two-story atrium covered by three low, domed skylights on Guastavino tiled vaults. The walls were of simple, solemn brickwork, with a

7.8 John Galen Howard, Hearst Memorial Mining Building, University of California, Berkeley, 1907. "The New University of California," *Architectural Record* 23, no. 4 (April 1908), 283.

plaque dedicating the building to George Hearst. The architect Howard, who had described the profession of mining as "a ruthless assault upon the bowels of the world, a contest with the crudest and most rudimentary forces," designed this space as a museum for the mining industry—a kind of world exhibition in miniature, with displays comparable to those at the Chicago World Exposition.[60] Perpendicular to the atrium and stretching deep back into the building was a three-story skylit mining laboratory, surrounded by galleries that gave access to teaching, research, and administrative spaces. Where the adjacent lobby commemorated earlier phases of resource extraction, this laboratory was an inward-looking, heterotopic theater of applied technical research. As much a stage as a workspace, its performances—boring, drilling, hoisting, ventilating—were visible to students and faculty moving about the upper galleries in their

7.9 John Galen Howard, Hearst Memorial Mining Building, University of California, Berkeley, 1907. Mining laboratory. "The New University of California," *Architectural Record* 23, no. 4 (April 1908), 287.

daily routines. Behind and around it were more machines and more laboratories: a three-story high ore crushing tower, smelting laboratories, assaying laboratories, forges, and a gold and silver mill for separating out the precious metals.[61]

Because in any case the future needs of a science of mines were largely unknown, Howard designed the overall building as a shell with maximum interior "elasticity." Interior walls were removable and, most dramatically, the exhaust chimneys around which laboratory work was done were isolated down to the foundations, so that they might be replaced, removed, or relocated without damage to the surrounding structure. The Hearst Memorial Mining Building was the first purpose-built facility of its type, though by this point there were a number of new scientific laboratories in the United States and in Europe.[62] Some, like the Jefferson Physical Laboratory completed at Harvard in 1884, had already tectonically isolated interior laboratory spaces in order to ensure optimum experimental conditions.[63] In a comparable fashion, the Hearst building isolated materials, phenomena, and techniques associated with an external, geographic frontier, folding that frontier inward, beyond its territorial limits and toward the seemingly limitless horizons of scientific and technological research.

The Multiversity at the "Endless Frontier"

Prior to designing and overseeing construction of the mining building, Howard also realized two other buildings projected in the Hearst plan. The first was the president's house, partially completed and in use initially as classrooms by 1901; the second was California Hall, partially completed and used for both teaching and administration by 1905. Howard also designed the Hearst Greek Theater, funded by William Randolph Hearst and located on a hillside site to the east of the mining building, as an outdoor amphitheater based on the Theater of Dionysus in Athens but for an audience of ten thousand.[64] Additionally, he designed a southern entry portal for the campus, Sather Gate, completed in 1910 to commemorate Peder Sather, a banker and College of California trustee.

The gate frames the southern end of the main north-south axis, which runs perpendicular to the major east-west axis. While the latter axis passes through the Golden Gate, Sather Gate marks the point where the north-south axis rotates off the city grid, at Telegraph Avenue, as part of the overall rotation described above. A central, densely ornamented bronze arch bearing the gate's name spans between stone-and-concrete piers, flanked by two smaller portals with electric globes atop each of the piers.[65] Crowning the arch on both sides is a bronze star, its rays contained within an oval medallion, below which is inscribed the university motto: *Fiat Lux* ("Let There Be Light"). Facing two directions at once, the gate and its emblem marked a border that distinguished

7.10 John Galen Howard, Sather Gate, University of California, Berkeley. Study, 1908. University Archives, Bancroft Library, University of California, Berkeley.

the students and faculty of the university from the citizens of Berkeley and of California, drawing a virtual line for each to cross in order to become the other.

In the following decades, the University of California quickly outgrew this and other boundaries established by the Hearst plan and its underlying property map. By 1948, what began as a single campus had become a statewide system consisting of four main campuses, at Berkeley, Davis, Los Angeles, and Santa Barbara, which were joined by seven state colleges, a maritime academy, and fifty-five junior colleges. That year, a document known as the Strayer Report surveyed the system's needs and, for the first time, drafted a statewide master plan for its growth.[66] In 1951, the university administration also expanded, adding two chancellors under President Robert Gordon Sproul, at Los Angeles and at Berkeley. Clark Kerr, a professor of industrial relations who went on to become university president, was the first chancellor of the Berkeley campus.[67] His and Sproul's offices were located in a confident Beaux-Arts structure designed by the architect Arthur Brown Jr., which sat on land immediately outside Sather Gate on the west side of Telegraph Avenue. In 1966 the building, which had been completed in 1940, would be rededicated as Sproul Hall.

The midcentury also saw the deep immersion of universities in extramural, government-funded wartime research. One notable outcome was *Science, the Endless Frontier*, a federal report authored in 1945 by the MIT engineer and director of the U.S. Office of Scientific Research and Development Vannevar

Bush, which proposed to make permanent Washington's massive wartime support for scientific research and led to the establishment of the National Science Foundation.[68] Technological and symbolic evidence of recursively "endless" frontiers also became available at around the same time on the Berkeley campus, on what was once plot 82 on the Kellersberger map. There, in 1940, Brown designed a large, round industrial shed for a fifth-generation cyclotron, or electromagnetic particle accelerator, to support work at Berkeley's Radiation Laboratory by its director, the nuclear physicist Ernest O. Lawrence and his colleague J. Robert Oppenheimer, among others. Brown located the cyclotron shed on the crest of the hill that bounded the easternmost edge of the campus, directly aligned with Howard's (and Olmsted's) skewed Golden Gate axis. Like Jefferson's Rotunda library at Virginia but porchless, with a ring of windows at the upper rim of its crypto-classical drum, the cyclotron building sat astride the axis but did not gaze westward toward the horizon. Instead, as the Hearst Memorial Mining Building had already begun to do, the simple round shed directed attention intensely inward.[69]

In 1940, explaining the decision to fund Lawrence's cyclotron, Raymond B. Fosdick, president of the Rockefeller Foundation, compared it with another Rockefeller-funded scientific instrument elsewhere in California, the Hale Telescope then nearing completion at the Palomar Observatory. Promising that "the new telescope will explore the outer reaches of the universe, the realm of the infinite; the new cyclotron will probe the inner reaches of the universe, the

7.11 Arthur Brown Jr. with Ernest O. Lawrence, Cyclotron Building, University of California, Berkeley, 1940. Lawrence Berkeley National Laboratories.

realm of the infinitesimal," Fosdick made what amounted to a case for a new iconography at the extremes of science's "endless frontier." In the space of about thirty years, Turner's symbolic hand-held laboratory equipment (test tubes and microscopes) had become, in the otherwise grey language of administration, 200-inch diameter telescopes and 184-inch cyclotrons:

> The real case for building a great cyclotron rests upon its ability to make accessible a new infinitesimal world—the interior of atomic nuclei, with all the possibilities of fresh knowledge that may there reside. It is an adventure in pure discovery, motivated by the unconquerable exploring urge within the mind of man.
>
> In this sense, therefore, the new cyclotron is more than an instrument of research. Like the 200-inch telescope, it is a mighty symbol, a token of man's hunger for knowledge, an emblem of the undiscourageable search for truth which is the noblest expression of the human spirit.[70]

In the event, the components of the cyclotron were repurposed for work on the Manhattan Project, and the instrument was not completed until after the war, at which point it entered the symbolic order of the Cold War.

At the Second World War's outset, on the pretense of protecting military secrets and on the heels of an attempt (with which Oppenheimer was involved) to unionize researchers at the Radiation Laboratory, the Board of Regents of the University of California established a policy barring members of the Communist Party from its faculty. Oppenheimer, who went on to head the wartime laboratory at Los Alamos but became an outspoken opponent of the hydrogen bomb, came to represent the suspicions and ambivalences that this and other such proscriptions entailed. In 1949, on the basis of his leftist sympathies, Oppenheimer was called to testify before the House Committee on Un-American Activities, and in 1954, during McCarthyism's twilight, the Atomic Energy Commission revoked his security clearance based partly on his earlier testimony.[71]

Also in 1949, by which time Oppenheimer had left to head the Institute for Advanced Study in Princeton, the regents of the University of California required all returning faculty to sign an anti-Communist loyalty oath. Thirty-one faculty who refused to sign were eventually fired. Among these non-signers was the German-Jewish medievalist Ernst Kantorowicz, a self-described conservative and a leading faculty voice against the oath.[72] Kantorowicz wrote in protest that the central issue was not an ideological one, as no bona fide Communists were identified, but rather, one of "obedience," "discipline," and "conformity" to a commercial order that did not distinguish between public servants, such as professors, and service workers, such as janitors.[73] In a line of thought he would develop in The King's Two Bodies (1957) with respect to late medieval oaths, Kantorowicz distinguished the limited sovereignty of the regents from the more extensive sovereignty of the faculty.[74] As "public officers, or officers of a public institution and public trust," faculty (and their students), not the regents, constituted the university. Hiring and firing without the consent of this self-governing academic body, and without just academic cause, would therefore not merely violate the faculty's abstract academic freedoms; it "would mean an infringement from without upon their own body corporate."[75]

Forced to leave Berkeley, Kantorowicz joined the faculty at the Institute for Advanced Study at the invitation of his former colleague Oppenheimer. Among his closest friends there was the German-Jewish émigré art historian Erwin Panofsky.[76] In the preface to his book on medieval political theology, Kantorowicz, who was sparing in his contemporary references, cited Ernst Cassirer's last, posthumous work, *The Myth of the State* (1946), which restated the German philosopher's previous arguments in the language of politics.[77] Earlier, Kantorowicz had aimed his remarks on the Berkeley loyalty oath, which were informed by his knowledge of the medieval *universitas*, not at what Cassirer called "the substance of myth" but rather, at what the German philosopher called the "function" of myth "in man's social and cultural life."[78] We might thereby read Kantorowicz's account of the "king's two bodies" as a study in "symbolic form" that maps onto the university's internal and external frontiers, including the distinction he awkwardly drew between professors and janitors in defense of the academic "body corporate."

For at least two decades at Berkeley, that body bore the scars of a functioning myth that confused the consent to be governed with loyalty to the governors. These scars still mark the ground just south of Sather Gate where the architect Arthur Brown Jr., in an expansion plan for the campus, had earlier identified a number of possible building sites, including the blocks that adjoined the gate on either side of the Telegraph Avenue, in the area of the old homestead association. On one side of this zone, Brown's plan showed the building that would become Sproul Hall, on the other, its axially mirrored, nonidentical twin.[79] A student union was later proposed for this second site and completed in 1961 to designs by Vernon De Mars, Donald Hardison, and Lawrence Halprin. During this time, University of California president Clark Kerr had considered designating the one-block extension of Telegraph Avenue between the two buildings as a "free speech island," and the city transferred the land to the university for this purpose. But after Kerr issued new rules that loosened restrictions on students regarding intramural political speech, the "free speech island" was abandoned.[80]

By then the Berkeley campus had become the central node in what Kerr called, in an influential series of lectures published in 1963 as *The Uses of the University*, a "multiversity." An extensive statewide system of higher education, with a half-billion dollar budget and forty thousand employees, the multiversity had "operations in over a hundred locations, counting campuses, experiment

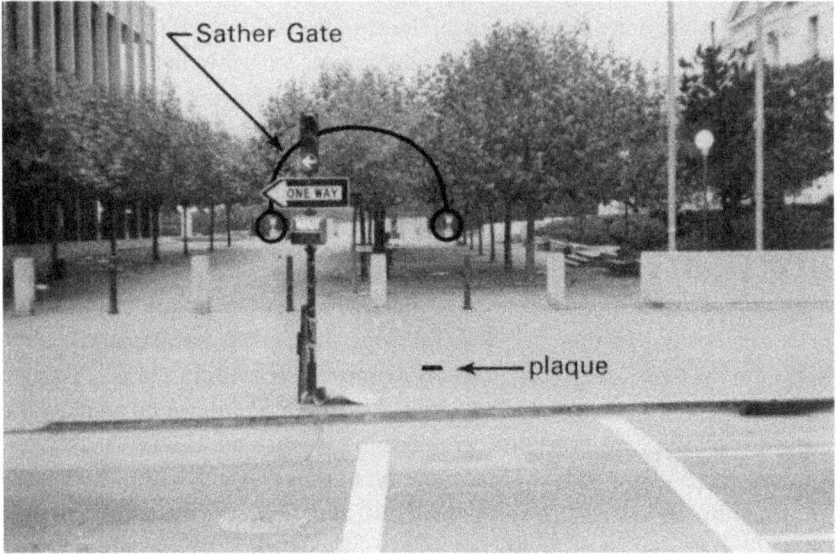

7.12 "Free speech" zone near Sather Gate with plaque marking university property, University of California, Berkeley, n.d. Photograph by John Lofland and Lyn Lofland, as annotated in Max Heirich, *The Spiral of Conflict: Berkeley, 1964* (New York: Columbia University Press, 1971), frontis.

stations, agricultural and urban extension centers, and projects abroad involving more than fifty countries."[81] Updating a celebrated remark by University of Chicago president Robert M. Hutchins, and in a travesty of Kantorowicz's "body corporate," Kerr half-joked that the new multiversity was made up of "a series of faculty entrepreneurs held together by a common grievance over parking."[82] A few years prior, Columbia provost Jacques Barzun had summoned the metaphor of a civic-minded "House of Intellect" to defend traditional learning against the narrow, scientistic pedantry he found in midcentury academic and public life. Divided between "substance" and "shadow," Barzun's "House" was lettered, in the strict sense that its imagined residents were alphabetized readers of Western languages.[83] In this, the "House of Intellect" was in no small measure an idealization of Columbia's undergraduate humanities curriculum, with which Barzun was identified. Describing Barzun's "House" as "inward looking," Kerr responded to it with a "City of Intellect," which he called an "Ideopolis." Unlike the Hearst plan's "City of Learning," wrenched apart from the actual city to survey the horizon from a distance, Kerr's "City of Intellect" embraced what he called the "conflict between internal and external dynamics" with no clearly established campus gates to prevent industry from "reach[ing] into a university laboratory to extract the newest ideas."[84] Singling out the recently founded

Stanford Research Institute as an instance of the university reciprocating, Kerr described the region from Boston to Washington as one such "Ideopolis." This region, where a century earlier, quarried sandstone linked libraries with mines, had just recently been described by the geographer Jean Gottmann as a sprawling, urban-suburban "Megalopolis."[85]

Free Speech

In mid-September 1964, as that year's bitter presidential contest neared its end, Berkeley administrators decided to enforce a ban on political advocacy on university property, principally in the area that would have been the "free speech island": the half-in, half-out zone between Sproul Hall and the student union, just outside Sather Gate at Bancroft Way. Student organizations objected, and the administration issued rules that allowed limited activity by permit only. In response, several groups, including Students for a Democratic Society and the Congress of Racial Equality, defied the ban and set up unauthorized tables in front of the gate, outside the old campus but on university property, using the boundary marked by the gate to assert performatively their rights as citizens to political speech, but within the formal bounds of the symbolically boundless multiversity. Eight violators were summoned to the dean of students office. There, they presented a petition signed by five hundred others demanding that any punishment be extended to all signatories. When the administration refused, about one hundred and fifty students commenced a three-day sit-in in Sproul Hall.[86]

That night, Berkeley chancellor Edward W. Strong issued a statement: "Some students demand on-campus solicitation of funds and planning and recruitment of off-campus social and political action. The University cannot allow its facilities to be so used without endangering its future as an independent educational institution."[87] The paradoxical implication being that, in the long shadow of McCarthyism, the price of academic freedom was political isolation. At the sit-in, Mario Savio, a twenty-one-year old philosophy student from New York and spokesperson for what became known as the Free Speech Movement (FSM), who had spent that summer organizing for civil rights in Mississippi, responded by referring to Kerr's "multiversity" as a "machine" producing human capital for industry that had been jammed by the students' actions.[88] Positionally, Savio and his colleagues enacted the contested right to speak politically *inside* that machine. But, insofar as they exploited the inside-outside zone between gate and sidewalk, their speech was also positioned, and conditioned, by the symbolic form defined by the misalignment of gates, axes, property lines, and frontiers, and the media complex of maps, laws, and campus plans that we have been following.[89] On campus, the protesting bodies corporate were

7.13 Mario Savio (standing on car roof) speaking in protest against the arrest of Jack Weinberg, University of California, Berkeley, October 1, 1964. Photograph by Don Kechley. University Archives, Bancroft Library, University of California, Berkeley.

students; off campus, they were citizens; in the threshold zone between gate and sidewalk, they were split.

The day after the sit-in, demonstrators set up tables at the steps of Sproul Hall, and the campus police arrested a non-Berkeley activist, Jack Weinberg, placing him in a police car within the protest zone. Students blockaded the car; Savio climbed atop it, shoeless, and spoke again, as did a string of others. In one of many links to earlier conflicts, among the speakers was Bettina Aptheker, an FSM Steering Committee member and frequent coauthor of its pamphlets whose father, the historian Herbert Aptheker, was a blacklisted Communist Party member.[90]

The sit-in ended, and two months of demonstrations and negotiations followed. In late 1964, after another impasse, Savio inaugurated a mass occupation of Sproul Hall with a speech on the steps that drew on Kerr's reference to a "knowledge industry." As Savio put it,

> There's a time when the operation of the machine becomes so odious, makes you so sick at heart, that you can't take part; you can't even passively take part. And you've got to put your bodies upon the gears and upon the wheels, upon the levers, upon all the apparatus, and you've got to make it stop.[91]

Another sit-in commenced; some eight hundred students were arrested, jailed overnight, and then released on bail. A few days later, Kerr led a university-wide meeting in John Galen Howard's (and William Randolph Hearst's) outdoor Greek Theater. Excluded from the program, Savio mounted the stage, was escorted off, and then was allowed to speak. Negotiations and demonstrations continued, teaching assistants went on strike, and the faculty voted to oppose the administration's position. Finally, in early 1965, the Berkeley administration issued new guidelines permitting political speech and advocacy in the contested zone and elsewhere.

Two conflicting accounts of the relation between political speech and academic freedom emerged from Berkeley faculty in the aftermath of the Free Speech Movement. One emphasized the educational function of the university

7.14 Free Speech Movement protestors marching through Sather Gate, University of California, Berkeley, November 20, 1964. Photograph by Don Kechley. University Archives, Bancroft Library, University of California, Berkeley.

as a space apart and argued that in politicizing that space the student protestors had violated its special trust and its special freedoms. The other emphasized continuities between campus and city and the permeability of boundaries, arguing that academic freedom and the freedom to speak politically were effectively the same.[92] In urging his fellow students to "put [their] bodies upon the gears" and bring the multiversity to a halt, Savio distinguished between machine-like bodies and human bodies, declaring that "this machine, this factory, this multiversity here, its parts are human beings."[93] But this very same human machine embodied a boundary problem of a different kind, one that, again, functioned as a symbolic form.

The multiversity had two bodies, the "body corporate" of the universitas and the material body of the "machine," each of which now doubled-up in turn. Symbolically and practically, these bodies split along two axes, one that passed through the Golden Gate, another that passed through Sather Gate. The first axis linked libraries and laboratories with mines, quarries, and land claims, and later, cyclotrons with bombs; the second axis linked the academic body with the civic body. Along the first axis, the "machine" was sovereign—a mythic, immortal "crown" served by crypto-royal regents, chancellors, and presidents, and embodied in the new infrastructures of knowledge; along the second axis, the body corporate was sovereign, materialized as both polis and universitas in the speaking bodies assembled at the gate. In neither case, however, was the multiversity a mere knowledge factory; nor was it a city or a house, whether of learning or of intellect. Rather, it was a frontier, a technopoetic, signifying system that limited what could be said, who could say it, and where it could be said. The machine's ancestors—the protagonists of Turner's frontier thesis—had remapped the territory in a manner that, step by step, located the university at series of thresholds, where the question of whether one did one's speaking and acting from the inside or the outside was resolved only provisionally. In 1964 and thereafter, speech acts that tested the machine's boundaries disclosed a simple maxim governing its two bodies: stop speaking, and you are free to speak.

8

TECHNOPOESIS

Human Capital and the Spirit of Research

B y the mid-twentieth century, while the formal study of poetics remained confined to the arts and humanities, the natural sciences had long been understood as an important source of meaningful symbols. In particular, the making of meaning became a preoccupation among scientists whose moral certitude had been compromised by the contribution of scientific and technological knowledge to unprecedented violence. In this chapter, we will consider two instances, one at the Massachusetts Institute of Technology (MIT) and the other at Stanford University, in which university administrators called on the humanities to reestablish moral order. The result was, on the one hand, a renewed alliance of secular knowledge with theology, and on the other, a technologically mediated conception of the human subject as both a symbol and an interpreter of symbols ready to rejoin industry as a form of capital.

Following the intensification of interdisciplinary research in the natural and social sciences during the Second World War, another problem facing both scientists and administrators was keeping it all together. Government laboratories, private think tanks, and corporate research centers joined forces to overcome academic compartmentalization. Humanists, summoned as spiritual advisors, worked earnestly to rebuild the war-sundered, overspecialized soul of "man." On the science side, the mathematician Norbert Wiener put it like this:

A man may be a topologist or an acoustician or a coleopterist. He will be filled with the jargon of his field, and will know all its literature, and all its ramifications, but, more frequently than not, he will regard the next subject as belonging to his colleague three doors down the corridor, and will consider any interest in it on his own part as an unwarrantable breach of privacy.[1]

The challenge, as Wiener and many others saw it, was more than just one of putting these isolated individuals into conversation. It was to develop a new science, a master discourse capable of synthesizing diverse forms of knowledge into an organic whole devoted to nothing less than, as Wiener put it in 1950, the "human use of human beings."[2]

Corridors, an Auditorium, and a Chapel

Norbert Wiener's office was located in the Department of Mathematics at the Massachusetts Institute of Technology, in Building 2, on the southeastern branch of that campus's "infinite corridor." Running along the transverse, east-west axis of William Welles Bosworth's 1913 Beaux-Arts adaptation of John R.

8.1 William Welles Bosworth, Massachusetts Institute of Technology, 1913. Aerial view. Photograph by Leslie Jones, c. 1930. Courtesy of the Boston Public Library, Leslie Jones Collection.

Freeman's rationalist plan for the MIT campus, the double-loaded corridor lined by offices, classrooms, and laboratories was by that time fed by several perpendicular branches, including the two original wings that embraced a central lawn facing the Charles River. Like its predecessor at the University of Virginia, MIT's central rotunda housed a library, but one that sat abreast the transverse corridor, which opens onto Massachusetts Avenue through a monumental side porch surmounted by a second dome added by Bosworth in 1939. In other words, the neoclassical figure facing the river was skewered by the corridor system.[3]

Wiener, "the original absent-minded professor," was known to wander these corridors frequently, dropping in on colleagues with an inquisitive "What's new?"[4] By 1955, had he exited through the side porch and crossed Massachusetts Avenue, Wiener would have encountered two recently completed buildings. Diagonally opposite, sitting askew to the corridor axis was the new Kresge Auditorium. Its thin concrete roof traced out an eighth of a sphere, in a fractional echo of Bosworth's two domes across the street. More immediately on the left, set further in from the wide lawn, was the new MIT chapel, a small brick cylinder sitting in asymmetrical counterpoint.

8.2 Eero Saarinen and Associates, MIT Chapel and Kresge Auditorium, Massachusetts Institute of Technology, 1955. Photograph by Balthazar Korab. Balthazar Korab collection of photographs showing Eero Saarinen architecture, Library of Congress, Prints and Photographs Division.

The chapel-and-auditorium ensemble was designed by Eero Saarinen and Associates and completed in 1955.

Inside the chapel, an undulating brick surface moves in and out of the reflected light thrown up by the water passing beneath the low circumferential arches supporting the cylinder, their irregularity matched by that of the interior undulations. The result is a subtle, double pulsation: the rippling walls rhythmically blocking and releasing the indirect uplighting, offset by the gentle movement of the water itself. A single, circular skylight accents the white

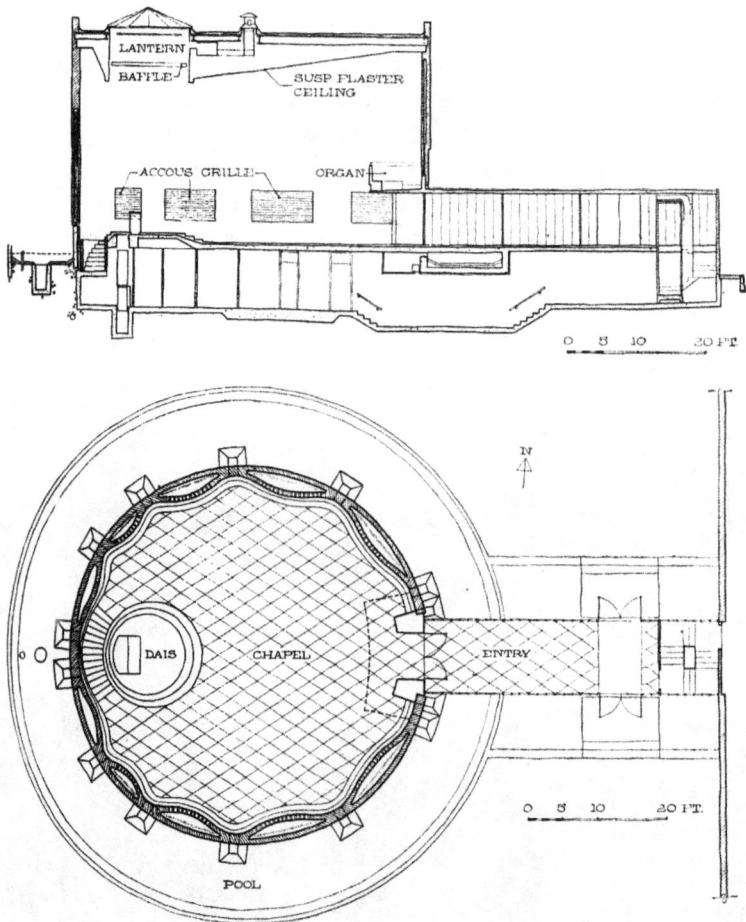

8.3 Eero Saarinen and Associates, MIT Chapel, Massachusetts Institute of Technology, 1955. Plan and section. "Buildings in the Round: MIT Completes Its Cylindrical Chapel and Domed Auditorium by Architect Eero Saarinen," *Architectural Forum* 104, no. 1 (January 1956), 119.

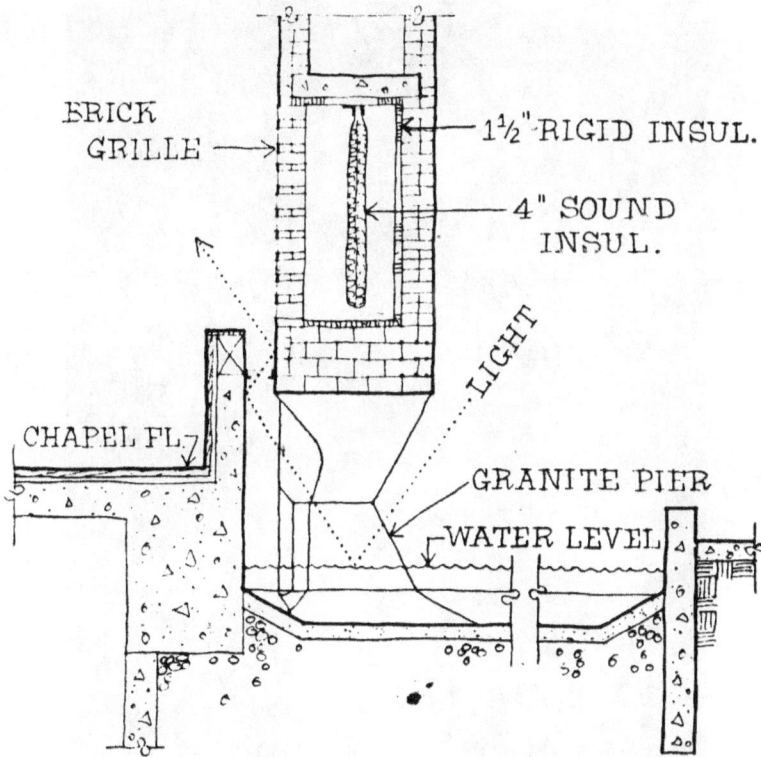

8.4 Eero Saarinen and Associates, MIT Chapel, Massachusetts Institute of Technology, 1955. Lighting detail at base. "Buildings in the Round: MIT Completes Its Cylindrical Chapel and Domed Auditorium by Architect Eero Saarinen," *Architectural Forum* 104, no. 1 (January 1956), 119.

marble altar, its light passing through a horizontal baffle and reflecting off a metal filigree screen behind, picking up a gentle flicker as it bounces off the screen. The varying wall thickness allows natural light to enter mysteriously from below through the gap between two sets of curves, the vertical exterior arches and the horizontal interior undulations. From the day it opened just off the corridors of "big science," this little theater of illumination emanated a soft spirituality that extended well beyond the confines of established religion.

Already in 1938 Bosworth, the architect of the MIT campus, had projected a chapel on Memorial Drive. To the two domes of the central academic complex, Bosworth's design would have added a third neoclassical domed structure.[5] In the event, the modernist brick chapel came late to MIT, almost as an after-thought rather than as the fulfillment of a preordained plan. Where the auditorium lobby opens onto the surrounding plaza with a transparent skin stretching

8.5 Eero Saarinen and Associates, MIT Chapel, Massachusetts Institute of Technology, 1955. Interior. Photograph by Ezra Stoller. © Ezra Stoller/Esto.

down from the concrete roof shell, the chapel is separated from the plaza by a narrow, circular moat, across which spans an enclosed entry passerelle that connects the cylinder to a small rectangular service wing. Ultimately, the formal and symbolic relationship between these two otherwise distinct architectural types, the secular auditorium and the interdenominational chapel, is unresolved.

In the second, 1954 edition of his popularization of cybernetics, *The Human Use of Human Beings*, Wiener warned that "*what is used as an element in a machine, is in fact an element in the machine.*" It mattered little whether societal decisions were entrusted to "machines of metal, or to those machines of flesh and blood which are bureaus and vast laboratories and armies and corporations," since neither was asking the right questions.[6] Even so, Wiener may not have fully understood how exploring the "human use of human beings" was becoming a major preoccupation for the very same "machines of flesh and blood" that concerned him.

A Convocation

On March 31, 1949, the architectural historian John Ely Burchard, dean of humanities, presided over a two-day convocation to celebrate the inauguration of MIT's tenth president, James R. Killian. The ceremony began with an invocation addressed to the "God of our fathers" delivered by Everett M. Baker, a Unitarian minister and MIT's dean of students.[7] In itself this was not unusual, though it does remind us of the religious origins of higher education in the United States. More notable was the convocation's subject matter, which explored "the social implications of scientific progress." Burchard's annotated publication of the proceedings reveals a bias, not limited to its editor, toward "spiritual" matters as these impinged upon scientific and technological research and education, particularly in the aftermath of world war.

The MIT presidential inaugural of 1949 was shaded by humanistic overtones, which can be readily if not fully explained as a response to wartime traumas. Since its inception in the 1860s, MIT had made little room in its curriculum for moral philosophy, which proposed a universal ethics compatible with Christianity. Nor was a curricular or cultural role originally allotted to the newly defined "humanities," which by the turn of the century had emerged out of classical learning to supplant religious doctrine as a core component of the modern liberal curriculum.[8] Only in 1932 was a division of humanities created at MIT, with its mandate gradually expanded in the 1940s as faculty and administrators began to plan the institute's postwar mission. The war was a turning point, and in 1947 a Committee on Educational Survey was set up to reevaluate curricular priorities in "a new era emerging from social upheaval and the disasters" brought on by the conflict.[9] Recognizing that "the world of 1940 is not the world of 1950," the committee observed in their report, which appeared in December 1949 (nine months after Killian's inauguration) that "the release of nuclear energy is having a profound effect upon the course of human events, but other forces are also at work on society. They were beginning to modify our way of life long before the atomic bomb."[10] As a corrective, the report recommended broadening the institute's curriculum especially at the undergraduate level, to require more thorough exposure to nonspecialized knowledge, particularly in the humanities.[11]

As the report noted, steps already taken in this direction by the administration of Karl T. Compton, president from 1930 to 1948, were interrupted by the war. A broadened educational mission at MIT would, the report's authors concluded, entail greater leadership in three primary areas in addition to engineering: the natural sciences, the humanities and social sciences, and architecture and planning.[12] More specifically, they recommended establishing a fourth school alongside the schools of engineering, science, and architecture and planning: a school of humanities and social science. The new school would be an integrated academic unit supporting both undergraduate and graduate education based on current offerings in economics and other social sciences, history, modern languages and literature, and (perhaps incongruously) business and engineering administration.[13]

"The Flame of Christian Ethics"

By the time of Killian's 1949 inaugural Burchard, already dean of humanities, was poised to become dean of the institute's new school of humanities and social studies, which was formally established in December 1950 on equal footing with the scientific and professional schools. The convocation's keynote speaker, Winston Churchill, even went so far as to note Burchard's visibly anomalous position at a technical institute. Addressing an aside to Compton, the institute's outgoing president, Churchill declared: "How right you are, Dr. Compton, in this great Institution of technical study and achievement, to keep a Dean of Humanities and give him so commanding a part to play in your discussions! No technical knowledge can outweigh knowledge of the humanities in the gaining of which philosophy and history walk hand in hand."[14] Warning that "the problems of victory may be even more baffling than those of defeat," Churchill exhorted his listeners to remember, "however much the conditions change, the supreme question is how we live and grow and bloom and die, and how far each human life conforms to standards which are not wholly related to space or time." Tying postwar success to spiritual awakening, Churchill emphasized that

> I speak not only to those who enjoy the blessings and consolation of revealed religion, but also to those who face the mysteries of human destiny alone. I say that the flame of Christian ethics is still our highest guide. To guard and cherish it is our first interest, both spiritually and materially. The fulfillment of Spiritual duty in our daily life is vital to our survival.[15]

Churchill's remarks were apparently not lost on MIT's administrators, including its new president. Over the next few years, in the planning for what would become the Kresge Auditorium and the chapel, Killian repeatedly cited Churchill's phrase, "the flame of Christian ethics," to situate the chapel in the institutional context for which it was conceived. Churchill had connected the dots in advance by associating the presence of a dean of humanities at a technical institute with the need to attend to the "spiritual duty" of all citizens in a nuclear age. In the Rockwell Cage in March 1949, Churchill devoted the remainder of his speech to politics, building in crescendo to a characteristically dramatic mise-en-scène: "I must not conceal from you tonight the truth as I see it. It is certain that Europe would have been communized like Czechoslovakia, and London under bombardment some time ago but for the deterrence of the Atomic Bomb in the hands of the United States."[16] Just four months before the first successful Soviet atomic test, what Burchard called the "mushroom cloud of 1945" cast its shadow over the entire event.[17] And there was no one in the room more suited than MIT's dean of humanities to meet its challenges on a campus newly populated with returning war veterans, whose general education would now be extended toward those spiritual matters that scientists and engineers, on their own, had been judged incapable of addressing.

A Meeting House and a Village Church

In 1950, the MIT administration applied to the Kresge Foundation "in support of a program in Development of Citizenship and Christian Character."[18] The Foundation, based in Detroit under the leadership of the entrepreneur Sebastian S. Kresge, was well known for its commitment to religious and educational institutions.[19] The MIT application proposed a "Kresge School of Human Relations, which would enrich the existing program of technological education by increased emphasis on humanities, social sciences, character building activities, and religion."[20] Former president Karl Compton's cover letter referred to the 1949 report by the Committee on Educational Survey, which was then under internal review and had not yet been made public. He summarized the report's arguments, including its recommendation for a new school of humanities and social sciences, and indicated that although some of the material needs for such an initiative were addressed by MIT's development campaign, substantially greater funding would be required to support professorships, library acquisitions, and an "Auditorium-Chapel building."[21]

The application listed four initiatives drawn from MIT's earlier efforts to reassess its curriculum and needs: enhanced resources to continue the scientific research concentrated by the war; the opening of a new library (the Hayden Memorial Library, designed by Voorhees, Walker, Foley, and Smith, and supported by the Charles Hayden Foundation) and the founding of the division of humanities; increased endowment; and improvements in student life and extracurricular activities. This framework formed the basis for a $20 million development effort, which Compton admitted was more successful in raising funds from industrial sources in expectation of a technological "quid pro quo," than in garnering support for the "spiritual" components of the long-term program.[22]

The application proposed that the Kresge Foundation especially consider supporting those activities dedicated to "Education for Better Character and Citizenship" through a combination of (1) formal study within the new school of human relations, (2) endowed lectures similar to those currently arranged by Burchard on an ad hoc basis as dean of humanities, and (3) extracurricular activities, including religious ones. Specific request was made for an auditorium-chapel with an estimated seating capacity of 1,200. Plans were also mentioned for separating the smaller chapel (seating approximately one hundred) from the larger auditorium "which, though less distinctively religious in atmosphere, could be used for larger religious gatherings with some advantage of common facilities."[23]

On July 1, 1950 Killian announced a $1.5 million grant from the Kresge Foundation for a "meeting house," an image first conjured by dean of students Everett Baker, dedicated to public gatherings and religious convocations.[24] In the meantime, Burchard prepared plans for a school of humanities and social sciences. He summarized the details in a memorandum that joined Baker's figure of the "meeting house" with a "village church," the chapel. Adding a jurisdictional distinction, Burchard's proposed school of humanities would be responsible for the curricular dimensions of the enhanced spiritual education of MIT students, including courses in comparative religion, leaving the administration of extracurricular activities, including those of the chapel, to the dean of students (a post that Baker vacated in 1950).[25] The results of the Kresge grant application, however, left Burchard's new school empty-handed, since the entire $1.5 million grant was devoted to the construction of what would eventually become the auditorium and chapel. Both secular and religious in nature, these extracurricular activities were meant to fulfill the initial program of enhanced spiritual education.

Killian frequently invoked this "meeting house" image in reference to the auditorium, describing it at the dedication ceremony for the two buildings in 1955 as a "house of many uses" where "men and women went to worship God, to hold their town meetings, and to further their cultural and civic interests."[26] In requesting that Burchard plan that ceremony, Killian expressed his hopes that the dedication could call attention to "the humanistic aspects of our program," adding that he "would like to see us build on the concept of the meeting-house, where the community comes together to transact its business, to develop its solidarity, and to enrich its intellectual life."[27]

About a year later, Burchard's event-planning subcommittee recorded an internal debate: "Is the dedication going to stress dependence on the creator, on a power greater than man, or not? The related question is: If we do not stress this dependence, do we silently affirm the opposite? Do we silently say that humanism is the answer?" In returning to the idea of "the auditorium as the New England Meeting House" and "the chapel as the one building on campus in scale with man" (both attributed to Killian), the subcommittee attempted to resolve the issue by synthesizing the opposition of theology to secular humanism into a higher unity.[28] Just as the imaginary of the New England meeting house conjured the village church, so did the auditorium (which would eventually receive a plaque describing it as a "meeting house") require the chapel to complete its meaning. Correspondingly, just as the intimate scale and inwardness of Saarinen's chapel, juxtaposed with the monumental academic buildings across the street, reconcile the human individual with an encompassing deity, the "meeting house" extrapolated a community of individual souls out of the anonymous corridors of big science. Coupled with the auditorium and read into the discourse around the humanities and social sciences at the institute, MIT's little chapel illuminated, softly and indirectly, a sacred humanism.

Like the 1949 presidential convocation, the 1955 dedication ceremony for the auditorium and chapel was framed in religious terms. It began with an invocation by Rabbi Herman Pollack, advisor to the MIT Hillel Foundation, was punctuated by an affirmation by the Reverend Theodore P. Ferris, rector of Trinity Church, Boston, and ended with a benediction delivered by Father Edward J. Nugent, chaplain to the Technology Catholic Club.[29] If this combination emphasized the ostensibly nondenominational (i.e., Judeo-Christian) program for the chapel (particularly resonant in the aftermath of the Holocaust), it also suppressed the dissonance spanning the ambiguous space that separated Saarinen's brick cylinder from the concrete-domed auditorium. This was the seeming difference between secular and religious symbolization and between the gathering of secular communities in the auditorium and the gathering of religious ones in the chapel. This dissonance shadowed both buildings. Saarinen's site planning attempted to resolve it by staging, unsuccessfully, a compositional equilibrium in which the two elements would hang suspended, and the dedication ceremony replayed the discrepancy between them in each of its parts.

Killian's repeated citation of Churchill's 1949 speech exemplified the dilemma. In remarks that were printed in the dedication pamphlet, it was as if Killian, who had managed MIT's wartime activities, and whose presidency had been inaugurated with the symbolic, moral authority that Churchill's name bore after the war, was calling upon the full force of that authority when he again cited Churchill's phrase, "the flame of Christian ethics." Paradoxically, Killian did this not only to stress MIT's nondenominational character but also to name a principle that "has lighted the institution throughout its history and given it direction and spirit. As a consequence we have a community held together by a humane and tolerant spirit of mediation, reconciliation and reverence for the individual, a community governed by a passion for truth, freedom of inquiry and a preoccupation with ideal aims." This was a community that lived and let live, an interfaith community of professionals, public servants, and artists. "These," Killian wrote in the dedication pamphlet, "are the spiritual bonds that hold together our society of scholars. Our developing spiritual program, to be valid, must embrace them, exalt them and be consonant with the environment they have created."[30]

Flash!

This was the same society of scholars, overseen by Killian, whose wartime work Burchard loyally documented in a 1948 publication.[31] Among that society's members was Harold (Doc) Edgerton, an electrical engineer who refined the art and science of stroboscopic photography, which broke down visible motion into a single-frame sequence of micromovements to evaluate the performance of machines. Killian, an MIT graduate with a degree in business administration, became fascinated with Edgerton's work in the early 1930s, and he wrote the introduction to Edgerton's first book, *Flash! Seeing the Unseen by Ultra High-Speed Photography* (1939). During the war, with Killian's support, Edgerton worked with the U.S. Army Air Force to develop a powerful xenon flash and related technologies to illuminate night landscapes from the very high altitudes necessary for reconnaissance planes to monitor enemy troop movements out of range of antiaircraft fire.[32] Burchard pointed out that Edgerton and his MIT colleagues were prepared to contribute militarily not because their work was inherently instrumental but because, on the contrary, "as free men in a free institution they had been permitted to proceed on projects which caught their imagination without any insistence on the part of their superiors that they be able to forecast a pay-off."[33]

The pay-off for Edgerton came in 1947 when, together with two former MIT graduate students and collaborators on the wartime research, he set up the consulting firm of Edgerton, Germeshausen, and Grier to contract with the Atomic Energy Commission on the design of firing mechanisms for atomic bomb tests by adapting the high-speed photography techniques that they had developed during the war. Prior to the firm's incorporation, the military contracted with MIT for their work. But after the war, the MIT administration, seeking to rebalance sponsored research with educational autonomy (another subject of the 1949 curricular report), had begun to recommend that faculty take on such work independently rather than through the institute, leading to the formation of the independent firm.[34] The result was not only Edgerton's high-speed "rapatronic" photographs of what we can call "the mushroom cloud of 1952" (the hydrogen bomb) taken at Eniwetok Atoll but also the firing mechanism for the bomb itself.

Rather than dismembering the academic community idealized by Killian into a cadre of guns for hire, this work and the images it yielded did just the opposite. It united the sacred with the secular under the sign of the bomb. Photographically sharpened electric light had already become a medium of engineering in Edgerton's laboratory, which was located along a stretch of the "infinite corridor" in Building 7 that was later renamed "Strobe Alley." The same methods yielded an optics of awe, recording the flash that had evidently caused one of the bomb's designers, J. Robert Oppenheimer, to recall Hindu scripture upon witnessing the first atomic test: "Now I am become Death, the destroyer of worlds!"[35] Awe here means not only humility in the face of unprecedented technological violence but also the reaction of a self-admiring "I," the supra-human

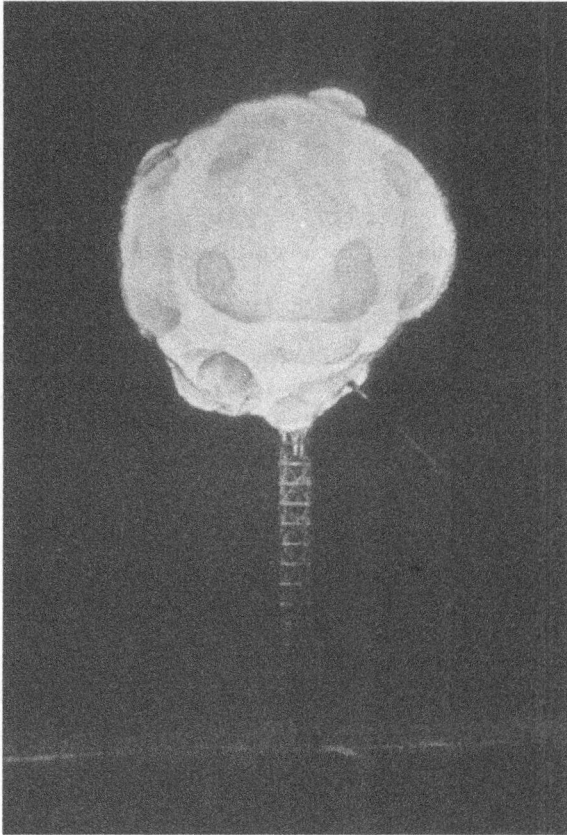

8.6 Harold Eugene Edgerton, Micro-second photograph of an atomic bomb explosion in progress, early 1950s. Edgerton and and James R. Killian, Jr., *Flash! Seeing the Unseen by Ultra-Speed Photography*, 2nd rev. ed. (Boston: Charles T. Branford, 1954), 55. Copyright 2010 MIT. Courtesy the MIT Museum.

scientist-artist, dialectically compatible with the awestruck humility solicited by soft natural light in the MIT chapel. Edgerton and Killian affirmed as much when they included in the second, 1954 edition of *Flash!* a photograph of an atomic bomb explosion. In the space of two microseconds burst forth a nuclear sublime.[36] The problem for this media complex was not too little spirituality but too much.

Acoustics, Cool and Warm

In addition to modulating the lighting, an important purpose of the irregular brick undulations on the MIT chapel's interior was acoustic. The building's nondenominational mandate gave priority to individual spiritual experience over group worship. The circular form emphasized this by maximizing personal intimacy with the abstracted altar bathed in diffuse light, while the undulations dispersed the inherent acoustical focus of the brick cylinder into a polycentric ambience, and built-in brick "grilles" backed with sound insulation controlled reverberation.[37] "The challenge," as its architect Saarinen put it, "was to create an atmosphere conducive to individual prayer . . . not derived from a particular religion but from basic spiritual feelings." Softening the light, the walls, and the sound created what he called an "other-worldly sense."[38] This softening was met in the auditorium by a pronounced focusing and sharpening, both visually and acoustically.

Kresge Auditorium's form placed visual focus on the stage and on the speaker's rostrum. Its clamshell profile was, however, especially challenging acoustically. The building contained two halls, the smaller one nestled under the larger, wedged underneath the concrete dome. On the inside of the 1,238-seat main

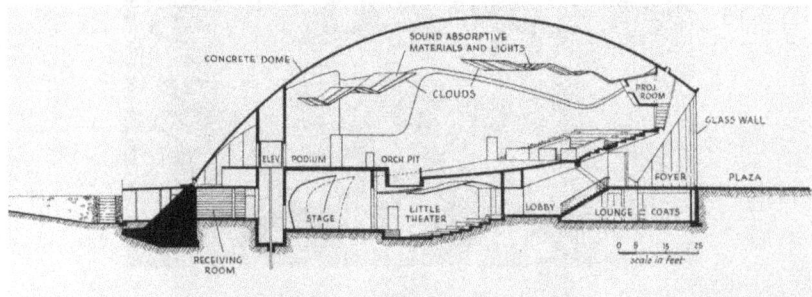

8.7 Eero Saarinen and Associates, Kresge Auditorium, Massachusetts Institute of Technology, 1955. Section. Beverly Dudley, "Structures—Spherical and Cylindrical," *Technology Review* 57, no. 2 (June 1955), 393.

hall there was no suspended ceiling, only clusters of sound-reflecting panels nicknamed "acoustic clouds," which hung directly from the interior surface of the thin concrete shell. By reducing the reverberation time in the hall, these plaster clouds sharpened the sound coming from the stage, an effect that was most conducive to an individual speaker or a solo musical performer. Leo Beranek, whose firm acted as acoustical consultants on the project, pointed out that musically, while ideal for small ensembles, the auditorium was "not sufficiently reverberant for symphonic music of the Romantic style."[39]

Writing in *Architectural Record*, Edward Weeks, editor of *The Atlantic*, said much the same: "The single voice and the solo instrument are beautifully accentuated, but it is still a question of how true a blend we shall get from the full orchestra."[40] Favoring the musical equivalent of Baroque mathematics over Romantic Sturm und Drang, and optimized for the individual voice, the auditorium aimed at providing each auditor with an identical, maximally rationalized experience that was equal and opposite to the diffuse relativism of the chapel. It was also materially cool. Weeks complained that "while there is plenty of light in the Kresge auditorium, there is precious little warmth to be felt in this great glass cage," and wondered whether, were the audience presented with the choice on a winter evening's intermission of "continuing with a difficult play or concert or going home to an open fire," the fireplace might prevail.[41]

But a preemptive synthesis was already under way. Chapel and auditorium shared a commitment to individuation. Weeks's observation that the auditorium's overall "bleakness" alienated audience members "as if even the individual had been insulated" might seem a standard indictment of architectural modernism's impersonal, mass-produced neutrality. But hints of something different were also visible in the main hall's 1,238 seats, which were upholstered in three different colors distributed with apparent randomness, in a proleptic pixelization of the "mass" of mass culture. More telling was the built-in audiovisual equipment that connected the auditorium with WGBH, the Boston area's public television station. In sync with the "tolerant" intimacy of the chapel, the WGBH viewer was the auditorium's ideal subject, a reasoning individual freely choosing to tune in at a distance. Weeks even noted the potential "warmth" generated by the variety of programs on offer in the auditorium, relayed to him in written detail by his friend Burchard, from Christmas carols to avant-garde theater. Encouraged, Weeks exclaimed: "Who says scientists aren't human?"[42]

Human Capital

On December 9, 1958, Lewis Mumford joined Norbert Wiener, the physicist Bernard Feld, and the sociologist Daniel Lerner at a colloquium in MIT's Kresge Auditorium sponsored by the MIT literary magazine, *Tangent*, called

"A Moratorium on Technology." Mumford was a frequent guest at MIT. He served as a visiting faculty member there from 1957 to 1958, and returned on at least one occasion in 1966 to speak on "The Missing Dimensions," or what his hosts, the MIT Society for Social Responsibility in Science, called "The Human Use of Human Beings at MIT."[43] An outspoken critic of what he considered to be the dehumanizing perils of the Cold War military-industrial complex and a tireless advocate of humanistic education, Mumford, who was in the main an autodidact, consistently supported educational reforms, especially at the high school and college levels, that he believed would inoculate citizens against the myth of technics.

Underlying this myth, and despite the Eurocentric category of "civilization" to which Mumford linked it in his work, was a postulate regarding the techno-poesis of human subjectivity, which attributed the making of subjects to the making of meaning through technical objects and systems. Toward the end of *Technics and Civilization* (1934) Mumford asked: "What sort of man comes out of modern technics?"[44] The question's formulation was indicative. Adapting the terminology of his mentor Patrick Geddes, Mumford argued that the emergent "neotechnic" era in which he wrote was characterized by what he called an "electricity-and-alloy complex," to be distinguished from the paleotechnic "coal-and-iron complex" that immediately preceded it, and from the eotechnic "water-and-wood complex" before that.[45] Though Mumford eschewed Marxist language, running through the details of his account was capital. In Mumford's view, each technical complex also yielded a specific form of human subjectivity adapted to a changing material environment. He sought to allay concerns over technological determinism with, in essence, a soft environmental determinism. Contrary to Mumford's prophecy, however, rewriting his question as "What sort of subject comes out of the electricity-and-alloy complex?" yields the same answer we found at MIT: a human.

A "New Key"

In a lecture titled "The Making of Men," delivered on May 8, 1943 as the keynote presentation at "Humanities in the War and the Post War World," a conference at Stanford University, Mumford observed that:

> Mrs. Susanne K. Langer's recent brilliant book, *Philosophy in a New Key*, indicates how a penetrating study of the semantic and aesthetic problems, in their interactions, opens up vistas on nearly every part of our higher culture and establishes, not only the fundamental value of the symbolic functions, but also the relative autonomy of all man's higher activities.[46]

Mumford was speaking as a recently hired omnibus professor of humanities at Stanford's new school of humanities, which was celebrating its first anniversary with the conference. Susanne Langer, whose *Philosophy in a New Key* had appeared two years earlier, and who had studied with Alfred North Whitehead at Harvard while she was enrolled at Radcliffe College, was among the first women professionally trained in philosophy in the United States. In the work Mumford cited, Langer argued that Western thought had struck a "new key" related to questions of symbolization. This included the symbolic lexicon employed by logical positivism as well as the interpretation of dream symbols by psychoanalysis, both of which had recently come to the fore among philosophers of mind and their colleagues in the human sciences.[47]

Langer's book was read widely by those who, like Mumford, advocated a renewed humanism across the arts and culture to counter the technologically enhanced barbarism of the Second World War and the apocalyptic mushroom cloud hanging over the Cold War. But more than a mere messenger of this new humanism, Langer was a philosopher of its techniques. Although her "new key" alluded explicitly to musical pitch, Mumford did not miss the figure's symbolic flexibility. As he argued in his speech, "semantics, aesthetics, logic, philosophy, and religion," the humanist's answer to science and engineering, "are as essential to us as algebra, geometry, and calculus are in the analysis of nature. These normative studies provide a key for understanding the arts and the humanities." The problem, Mumford continued, was that "we try to open too many doors for the student without giving him this key, whereas if he spent sufficient time on the key, we could leave it to the student himself to open more doors than we can hope even to hold ajar for him."[48]

Converting Langer's "key" from a musical to a mechanical one, Mumford substituted a strangely instrumental view of education—providing a "key for understanding the arts and the humanities"—in place of Langer's subtle aesthetic philosophy addressed to the abstruse signifiers emanating from scientific instruments. Here is Langer:

> With the advance of mathematical techniques in physics, the tangible results of experiment have become less and less spectacular; on the other hand, their *significance* has grown in inverse proportion. The men in the laboratory have departed so far from the old forms of experimentation—typified by Galileo's weights and Franklin's kite—that they cannot be said to observe the actual objects of their curiosity at all; instead, they are watching index needles, revolving drums, and sensitive plates.[49]

These physicists practiced what Langer called "symbolic transformation," or the translation of sensory data acquired from electromechanical media into meaningful knowledge by converting obscure technical signs into symbols. As she put it, when the "shivers and wiggles of our apparatus" are interpreted scientifically, "the problem of observation is all but eclipsed by the problem of *meaning*."[50] Langer's most immediate resource was Ernst Cassirer's philosophy of symbolic forms, which, as we have already noted, was elaborated with respect to the visual and spatial arts by the art historian Erwin Panofsky. Mumford, who knew Cassirer's work, later listed Langer alongside the German philosopher and his foremost American interpreter, Wilbert Marshall Urban, as leading thinkers on "man's propensity to symbolize his experience."[51] At Stanford in 1944, in an internal memorandum on "teaching and the arts," Mumford also recommended that the university recruit "an art historian of the range and ability of Panovsky [*sic*] at Princeton."[52] Instead, Stanford hired Panofsky's son, the physicist Wolfgang Panofsky.

By the time Mumford wrote, the Panofsky family had emigrated to the United States where, in 1935, Erwin joined the faculty at Princeton's Institute for Advanced Study. It was at Panofsky's urging that Oppenheimer, who had assumed the institute directorship in 1947, offered refuge to his former Berkeley colleague, Ernst Kantorowicz, after Kantorowicz refused to sign the University of California's anti-Communist loyalty oath. That same year, 1951, Panofsky's son Wolfgang, who was by then a physicist at Berkeley and who signed the oath but (by his own account) remained troubled by it, decided to leave Berkeley to join the Stanford physics department. A decade later, Wolfgang Panofsky became the first director of the Stanford Linear Accelerator Center.[53] This turn of events situates Langer's problem of "symbolic transformation," taken up by Mumford as a de facto program for the wartime humanities at Stanford, within an epistemic context bracketed by the work of the two Panofskys: the Stanford Linear Accelerator and its sociotechnical instrumentation as symbolic form.

"Steeples of Excellence"

In 1942 Mumford, joined at Stanford by two newly recruited assistants, had begun a three-year appointment as professor of humanities. Although his main lecture course, "The Nature of Man," was mostly an exercise in mythmaking around figures like "man" and "civilization" already characteristic of his writings, Langer's book made at least one reading list under the heading "Nature and Function of Language." Mumford's course was based on the book he was then writing, which would appear in 1944 as *The Condition of Man*, the completion of which was the reason he most frequently gave for leaving Stanford prematurely earlier that year.[54]

But already during wartime Mumford recognized the diminished institutional role to which the humanities were consigned. At Stanford that story begins around 1939, when Frederick Terman was appointed head of electrical engineering. Terman, along with his colleagues David Webster, William Hansen, and Russell Varian, as well as a cohort of graduate students that included William Hewlett (later of Hewlett Packard), was involved in research on tube electronics and high frequency, high energy microwave generation.[55] The outcome of this work was the klystron tube, also known as the "Stanford klystron," a high-power microwave vacuum tube that became a key component in aircraft and ground-based radar and radio communications systems during the war, with a staggering range of military, medical, and commercial applications thereafter. A signifier as potent as Edgerton's stroboscopic photographs, the Stanford klystron was also the first building block with which Terman would, as an academic administrator, erect the symbols that came to define his singular contribution to the neoliberal research university.

The klystron tube combined a device invented by Hansen known as a rhumbatron with the technique of "electron bunching" (projecting electrons in wave clusters rather than as a continuous beam) developed by Varian. By 1938, Hansen and other members of the Stanford physics department had contracted with the Sperry Gyroscope Company to develop the technology for military and commercial applications, and in 1939 Terman, Varian and his

8.8 Stanford "Model A" Klystron, n.d. Stanford Historical Photograph Collection, Department of Special Collections and University Archives, Stanford University Libraries.

brother Sigurd, and their colleagues in electrical engineering contracted with a subsidiary of International Telephone and Telegraph (IT&T) to do the same. Also in 1939, the Stanford klystron made its public debut in a series of military tests for a blind-landing radar system.[56] In 1947 the Varian brothers, who had left Stanford during the war to continue their work with Sperry on the East Coast, returned to Palo Alto to found Varian Associates, a firm built around the commercial manufacture of klystrons that would achieve mythic status in the university-industry nexus around which Silicon Valley developed.[57]

The klystron tube was therefore a critical component in the media systems, including radar, radio, and television, that dominated the midcentury Euro-American technosphere until the advent of solid-state electronics. Like the multiply-patented knowledge from which it arose, the tube was also a commodity that helped to reorganize the political economy of education and research at Stanford and well beyond. But equally important, as its classical name evoking waves lapping a beach suggests, the klystron was a symbol, a unit of meaning emanating from the military-industrial media complex and subject to interpretation in Langer's "new key."

While at Stanford, Mumford was asked by the university's then president, Donald Tressider, a school of humanities supporter, to work with him on an ambitious reorganization of the university that included plans for a "general college" dedicated to liberal education close to Mumford's own interests.[58] Lacking confidence, however, that sufficient faculty backing existed for such an initiative, and disappointed by the resistance he had encountered at the school of humanities, Mumford left Stanford in the spring of 1944. Three years later, Tressider died unexpectedly and his successor Wallace Sterling, a historian at the Hoover Institution, came quickly to favor Terman's entrepreneurial style. In 1955, Sterling appointed Terman provost of the University, an appointment that enabled Terman to continue the symbol-building he had begun with the klystron tube.

Terman's tenure as provost was marked by vigorous efforts to remake the university around specialized areas of expertise and international prestige by building what he called "steeples of excellence," often with the help of "salary splitting," or the sharing of expenses with government or industry, especially in the natural sciences and engineering. Looking only at this, and at the reassimilation of the school of humanities in 1948, it is easy to conclude that the humanities at Stanford were forced into the shadows of a well-funded "big science" willing to offer its services to corporate capital and to the U.S. military, which in many ways is true.[59] But this conclusion overlooks the overtly humanistic—we should even say with Mumford and with Langer, symbolic—functions of the media complex for which the klystron tube stands.

In 1947 or thereabouts Mumford, concerned that Stanford would fall prey to suburban scatter, advised Tressider to reinforce Frederick Law Olmsted's original vision for the campus as what Mumford called "a concentrated urban group in a permanent rural setting."[60] Mumford may have known of the Stanford Research Institute (SRI), which had just been founded under Terman's guidance as dean of engineering to support commercial enterprise stemming from salary-splitting "excellence" and located in nearby Menlo Park. With Varian Associates as its first tenant, the SRI established a precedent for tech-campus sprawl across the valley in the decades to follow.[61] But in recommending that "wherever University land abuts on other property a green belt should be established," Mumford did not foresee that the green land surrounding Stanford would house a "steeple" of a very different sort.[62]

During his tenure as provost, Terman was instrumental in securing Atomic Energy Commission (AEC) funds for the Stanford Linear Accelerator Center (SLAC). In 1961, Congress authorized construction and Wolfgang Panofsky, who had been heavily involved in the planning, became (as he put it) director "by default."[63] The project had begun with William Hansen, one of the designers of the klystron tube, a technology that made the unprecedentedly large linear electron accelerator conceivable and was crucial to its feasibility. Completed in 1966, the two-mile linear accelerator nestled discreetly into the foothills west of the main Stanford campus.[64] The prestige and funding that came with SLAC, as well as the science that it uniquely supported, secured for the Stanford physics department virtual preeminence among the many "steeples of excellence" that Terman erected as provost. Its basis in electrical engineering did something similar for that department by straddling the boundary between the two fields. Research became a matter of release from the classroom, pending the availability of unpredictable "beam time" on the device. Pure versus applied science—which had triangulated into a prewar race for patentable knowledge—became a matter of titles and appointments to the physics department or to SLAC, which had its own faculty; and scientific priorities and the allocation of beam time became a matter of balancing the interests of Stanford faculty with those of scientists based elsewhere, to whom the AEC funding agreement gave rights of access. In short, SLAC was a half-in, half-out institution at the edge of the Stanford campus, one that neither belonged entirely to the university nor to government.[65]

At first glance, SLAC seems to have little to do with the elder Panofsky's theory of symbolic form. But the klystron-dependent linear accelerator did yield symbols readable only by steeple-dwelling experts, successors to those physicists Langer had earlier observed "watching index needles, revolving drums, and sensitive plates."[66] In this way, blended into Stanford's hills, SLAC—itself a symbol—became a piece of signifying infrastructure that positioned its readers as "human," including entrepreneurial administrators like Terman and entrepreneurial engineers of "symbolic transformation" like Wolfgang Panofsky, the physicist son of an art historian.

8.9 Stanford Linear Accelerator Center (SLAC), Stanford University, c. 1966. Stanford University, Office of Development, Photographs, Department of Special Collections and University Archives, Stanford University Libraries.

8.10 Completed beamline at Stanford Linear Accelerator, June 1965. Photo by Richard Muffley, courtesy of SLAC National Accelerator Laboratory, Archives History & Records Office, Muffley Collection.

"The Archives of Contemporary Chaos"

In his later works, Mumford stridently denounced what he called the military-industrial "megamachine," or "pentagon of power." The humanism that drove his attempts to reform the Stanford curriculum now raged against what Mumford took to be a dehumanizing "myth of the machine."[67] But these terms deceive; what Norbert Wiener called "the human use of human beings," or the domestication of cybernetics, was not antithetical to technics but a product of it. Mumford already struggled with this around 1950 when he foresaw "post-historic man," reduced to base physiological functions, lifelessly worshipping a "cybernetic god."[68] Conceiving of humanity as primordially sociotechnical, Mumford's dilemma was one of untying the knots that bound society to the machinery of war. This, he believed, could only be accomplished by restoring collective human agency to an automated world. Which may be why, upon arriving at Stanford in 1942, Mumford misread that university's new monument to the liberal individual:

> It is fitting that a first essay toward the profound educational reorientation that is needed should be undertaken by Stanford University, precisely at this moment of tension and difficulty. Dominating the campus at Stanford is the new Hoover Tower with its great library that ranges over the entire field of the first World War and its aftermath—the archives of contemporary chaos.

Accordingly since, Mumford continues:

> No part of the present transformation is entirely automatic; and nothing that is worth achieving will be done by automatons. The need for whole men and women is the greatest of our needs.
> The School of Humanities accepts the challenge implicitly thrown down by the Hoover Library.[69]

The semi-independent Hoover Institution on War, Revolution and Peace at Stanford University centered on a library begun by Herbert Hoover in 1919 to preserve historical materials imperiled by conflict.[70] In 1941 the library, which had grown substantially, moved into the newly completed Hoover Tower, designed by Arthur Brown Jr. (architect of the Berkeley cyclotron building), under President Ray Lyman Wilbur and with Hoover's patronage. The Hoover Tower stood off the main campus axis, at the threshold of what was planned as a second, east quadrangle, occupying what would have been that quadrangle's courtyard. To gauge the building's prominence on the low-lying campus skyline, architect, client, and patron studied photomontages showing a wooden model superimposed onto views of the Stanford campus. Like the adjacent neo-Romanesque main quadrangle, planned by Henry Hobson Richardson's successor firm,

8.11 Arthur Brown Jr., Hoover Library Tower, Stanford University, 1941. Photograph by Jean Moulin © Moulin Studios.

Shepley, Rutan & Coolidge, the tower's vaguely Mission styling, which borrowed visual motifs from the twelfth-century Old Cathedral tower in Salamanca, bore just enough resemblance to Iberian precedent to associate the Stanford campus with an imperial, long vanished New Spain.[71]

The Hoover Tower's most striking external feature was its blank square shaft, fluted on each side by four deep pilasters culminating in three pairs of rounded arched windows that transitioned to the domed cupola. The blankness indicated the building's main function; it was, as Mumford said, an archive, a library housing an extraordinary collection of rare books, papers, manuscripts, and ephemera associated with war, peace, and revolt around the world. A massive vertical storage vault, the Hoover Tower stood as a reminder, as Mumford intuited, that the past always threatened to become prelude.

By the mid-1960s, the institution had evolved from an archive to a think tank. The library continued to collect rare publications, just as the archive collected the papers of revolutionaries, revolutionary governments, and prominent American politicians, among others.[72] Drawing on these resources, and on substantial independent support bolstered by Hoover's considerable fundraising capacity, the Hoover Institution acquired during these years a reputation as a bastion of anticommunism, reflecting its founder and namesake's outspoken views. The many prominent conservatives who joined as fellows and associates suggest that the reputation was deserved. Mumford's enthusiastic embrace of the tower's message, however, cannot be explained as a mere failure to read the obvious signs that, already in the 1940s, distinguished one political ideology from another. Rather, he misread the symbols.

Like the interplay between MIT's auditorium and chapel but at a greater distance, the Hoover Tower was offset against Stanford's other prominent monument, the Memorial Church, which sat deep within the main quadrangle terminating the central campus axis. The church's architect, Charles Allerton Coolidge, also drew on the Old Cathedral of Salamanca for the bell tower that hovered above the crossing, its central clock marking that axis. The 1906 earthquake that destroyed the Stanford library, gymnasium, and entrance gates damaged the church and collapsed the tower, which was not rebuilt when the church was restored.[73] In that sense, the Hoover Tower commemorated the vanished church tower, with a library and archive marking historical time, and a belfry equipped with a new set of bells.

During the 1960s, the Hoover Institution became a frequent target of faculty and student protests against the U.S.-led conflict in Vietnam. On one occasion in 1969, the institution's president, W. Glenn Campbell, found himself face-to-face with antiwar protestors led by English professor Bruce Franklin demanding access on the tower's steps. Campbell, realizing that the protestors had left a lone microphone on the steps, seized the device and began lecturing his audience, in a travesty of Mario Savio speaking on the steps of Berkeley's Sproul Hall (also designed by Hoover's architect, Arthur Brown).[74] But this microphonic performance was a distraction. The institution did not sit on the Cold War's front lines, and Campbell was no law-and-order Savio. Mumford was more correct than he knew; the Hoover Institution began gathering the "archives of contemporary chaos" as it became, in later decades, a premier site for the study of *homo oeconomicus*—less Mumford's soulless, automated "post-historic man," than liberalism's "economic man" reborn, a human being in the fullest sense, an animated, soulful figure whom Michel Foucault later described, aptly, as an "entrepreneur of himself."[75]

By the 1970s, the Hoover Institution's library had begun compiling an archive of neoliberal economic theory, to be stored behind its blind walls and among its relocated archival holdings, and recorded in its catalogue.[76] Philip Mirowski has shown how, during the 1950s and 1960s, liberal economics became what he calls a "cyborg science." By this Mirowski means mainly the computer-driven, probabilistic calculus of market optimization, game theory, risk analysis, and systems modeling undertaken by the University of Chicago's Cowles Commission and at the extra-academic RAND Corporation.[77] Comparatively little of this work was done at Stanford, and next to none at Hoover. The institution's holdings at the time were still primarily political and cultural, not economic, and Stanford even counted on its faculty one of very few Marxist economists in the U.S. academy, Paul A. Baran.[78] But quietly, the Hoover Library would soon store documents that recorded the birth of the entrepreneurial cyborg's rationally acting, self-governing, human soul.

This occurred slowly and discreetly. In 1980 the Mont Pèlerin Society, neoliberalism's vanguard organization, held its general meeting at the Hoover Institution, the first in North America since Princeton in 1958, when Campbell, an economist, had joined the society. Within a decade, the library's collections included the papers of the Austrian economist Friedrich von Hayek and those of his American counterpart, Milton Friedman, as well as the papers of other prominent Mont Pèlerin members.[79] Those collections were later joined in the Hoover Library by the papers of the society itself.

Another iconoclastic episode from the late 1960s anticipated the new archive's significance. Peter Duignan, a longtime fellow, recalls how antiwar protesters damaged the Hoover Library card catalogue, tearing out cards and pouring honey and red ink over its drawers.[80] Intentionally or not, the protestors' actions touched, if only barely, a principal tenet of the brutal Pax Americana memorialized in the Hoover Institution's devotion to the study of "War, Revolution and Peace": that political calculation, like that which drove the Vietnam policy of U.S. Secretary of Defense Robert McNamara's "Whiz Kids," and economic calculation, like that which would shortly animate Friedman's "Chicago Boys" in Chile, constituted the cybernetic subject as a human being.[81] These calmly reasoning "kids" and "boys" were experts in the game of power-knowledge whose gendered, racialized bodies—overwhelmingly white and overwhelmingly male—disappeared into the media complex of card catalogues, computers, and risk-managed calculations in which they worked. Regardless of party affiliation, the Hoover Institution's "fellows" were their brethren.[82] The spirit that united them was not religious. It was corporate, an esprit de corps. This was the new universitas, a spiritual body born of technics that stored its genetic code behind blank walls in a looming campus tower.[83] Frederick Terman's "steeples of excellence" had found their symbolic form.

As Susanne Langer taught Lewis Mumford, the "human" in the humanities converted signs into symbols, the output of a will to know. The cyborg science of homo oeconomicus conceived those signs not as the product of an inhuman machine but of all-too-human capital—a sensing, thinking, calculating being. What Langer called "symbolic transformation" was not necessarily premised, therefore, on the spectacular visibility of military-industrial technology. As Langer pointed out, symbolic transformation had already acquired a "new key," a cognitive training with new technical infrastructures. The data generated by these infrastructures awaited a cadre of humanist-experts to give it meaning within a new social order. There, at science's "endless frontier," stood homo oeconomicus as a symbolic analyst in the fullest sense, governed by a form of instrumental reason that operationalized the "human use of human beings." Crypto-theological "steeples" cultivated such analysts and their myths, as academics became entrepreneurs; and the Hoover Tower became a chapel to the cybernetic gods, a storage device in a mediapolitical economy—and a political theology—of knowledge. The science archived there restored to capital its human spirit, as the university's steeple dwellers became the subjects and objects of a technopoesis inseparable from that sought by Mumford, Langer, and the humanists at MIT: symbols rising from the megamachine.

EPILOGUE, c. 2000

I ntroducing this book, I cited a textual excerpt from the archives of Columbia University. Having written most of the book on or near the Columbia campus, I have found that the fragments gathered there, though unique in some ways and privileged in many others, still have much to teach. So to summarize my arguments and reflect on their implications, I want briefly to return to that campus once more. When, in the mid-1930s, Columbia moved its books from Low Memorial Library to South Hall (later Butler Library), which now stood opposite across the great plaza, it was not obvious what use could be made of the Low rotunda. Gradually, the building filled with administrative offices, to such an extent that Columbia faculty and staff now refer to the university's central administration as Low Library. As if on cue, this emptied-out edifice of learning, on whose steps sits Daniel Chester French's photogenic *Alma Mater*, offers early, material evidence of what Bill Readings elegiacally called, in the last century's final decade, the "university in ruins."[1]

An inflated descendant of the twice-built library Rotunda at the University of Virginia modeled on Hadrian's pantheistic Roman temple, Low Memorial Library was slowly transformed from an awkward monument to books to an even more awkward monument to administration. But, as the foregoing chapters have reminded us, the university that was "ruined" was an imperial one. In its heyday, Columbia's library-Pantheon evoked Edgar Allan Poe's "grandeur that was Rome." Before that, enslaved labor helped build and maintain its archetype in Thomas Jefferson's "academical" Roman villa/village, where the poet studied. The technics of mastery and subordination exemplified in the prologue

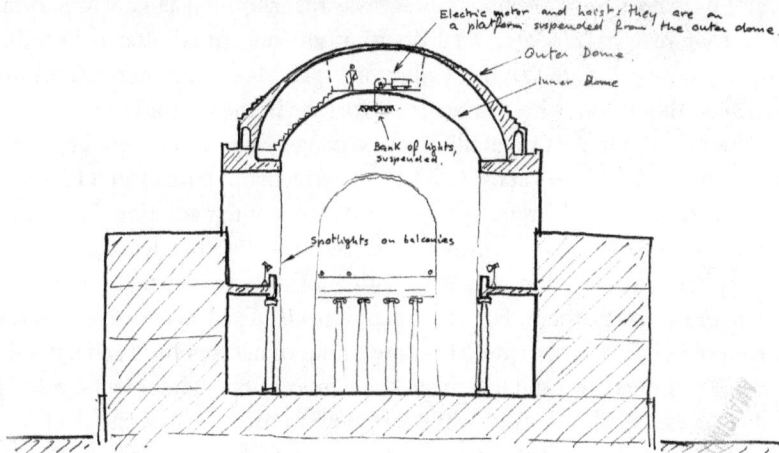

E.1 "Current System for Illumination of Rotunda," Low Memorial Library, Columbia University, n.d. Rare Book & Manuscript Library, Columbia University.

and repeated in several chapters explain how media, broadly construed, organized these situations.

An anonymous sketch from the Columbia archives describes the Low rotunda's lighting as it probably was on April 17, 1980, when Jacques Derrida spoke under the dome about Immanuel Kant's *Conflict of the Faculties*, in a two-day conference that marked the centenary of Columbia's Graduate School of Arts and Sciences. At some point, the place occupied by William Hallock's glowing moon (chapter 5), long gone, had been taken by a ring of lights on a motorized hoist suspended from the dome's inner shell, supplemented by spotlights on the balconies.[2] Taking his cue from the occasion, Derrida pointed out in his talk under the dome that the founding of a university reproduces the boundary problem structuring Kant's essay. The modern university requires the combined resources of reason, cultivated in the "lower," inward-looking philosophical faculty, and those of governmental authority to which the "higher," outward-looking professional faculties are devoted. In Kant's account, which turns on an antagonism between disinterested and interested knowledge, these faculties are otherwise opposed.[3]

As literally as possible, we have reconsidered the modern university's material foundations. Running through these are networks of all sorts, including but hardly limited to the electrical networks that brought—and continue to bring—light into our libraries and now to our "personal" reading, writing, viewing, recording, listening, and speaking devices. In 1895, as Hallock tapped into these networks to turn them into moonlight, his university rebuilt itself on a new campus, where the Columbia Library was reconstituted as Low Memorial Library. That year, by pledging a substantial portion of his inherited wealth toward its completion, Seth Low, Columbia's president, commemorated his father, Abiel Abbot Low, who had made his fortune in the tea trade with China, where opium was frequently a medium of exchange. Even as it secured the university's core mission, Low's act was therefore extracurricular, as Derrida would have had us recognize. The renaming was also an act of remediation that linked up one set of historical forces, visible in the sequence of libraries, domes, and lighting systems we found in chapter 5, with another set running underneath, between, and through them. For this other, less visible complex of forces, the modern research university would become a kind of necropolis, a collection of lapidary monuments to capital bearing the names of benefactors who mostly lived their lives outside its walls, while commemorating the lives and deaths of others in its memorials, its libraries, and its archives (chapters 2, 3, 4, 7, 8).

It would therefore be wise to learn to see the networks that still cast a steady, faint glow on our ever more fragile, flammable books, as the "corporate university," whose birth we witnessed in chapter 1, transmutes into the "global university," whose birth we glimpsed in chapter 4. Even before the nation's colleges became universities, American capital reached from New York to Shanghai, and before that, from Charlottesville to slave ports on the West African coast and back. Recognizing this should at least allow us to navigate, whether by moonlight or by the stars, the currents running beneath technological events that we sometimes misrecognize as determinant but which are instead closer to what Fernand Braudel described as "crests of foam that the tides of history carry on their strong backs."[4] In this and many other respects, the cool, equivocal light now coming from our books courtesy of corporations in partnership with university libraries may only be the afterglow, or perhaps the rekindling, of William Hallock's little moon and Thomas Jefferson's celestial sphere—knowledge balanced on the backs of slaves and served with Chinese tea.

In the introduction, we also asked whether the university is, despite it all, the last remaining utopia in a neoliberal, antidemocratic world. Yes or no, today's university is certainly among our most distinct heterotopias. Michel Foucault likened heterotopias, or "other spaces," to mirrors.[5] Like that other classic heterotopia, the modern factory, a university—any university—is a special kind of mirror. Even in the humanities, and even in college, its function is not limited to reflection. For the modern university is also a site of production, a "knowledge factory" as the Berkeley students called it (chapter 7). As if to close the circle, in 1980 Foucault became a visiting faculty member at Berkeley. In 1983, in what were to be his final public lectures there, Foucault spoke on the subject of *parrhesia*, which he translated as "free speech," or speech that oscillates between truth-telling and unconstrained opinion. Parrhesia can take the form of mindless chatter, or it can speak truth to power at considerable personal risk, not least because truth-telling and critique occupy unstable ground.[6] Whether or not he chose this subject specifically for that locale, where the Free Speech Movement began, Foucault was surely aware of its historical implications.

When we connect this task of the university—truth-telling—to the university's boundary-drawing functions, we also approach its symbolic form. Border, threshold, gate; these infrastructural lines are instruments of both separation and sanctuary. They distinguish insides from outsides for study and reflection; but they also let the outside in and the inside out. As we saw in the interlude, and especially in chapters 4 and 7, vast landscapes fold inward along their frontiers, extracting resources, knowledge, and value from the Earth and from its inhabitants. With each fold, the mirror reappears. Before its vanishing point, as Foucault demonstrated in his study of the human sciences, once stood a sovereign subject, doubled-up but visibly present.[7] The tensions we found joining American *Bildung* with industrial-capitalist development in chapters 1 and 2 already pulled that sovereign's offspring—liberal democratic subjects, young and white and male—in several competing directions; by the time we arrive at MIT and Stanford in the aftermath of the Second World War (chapter 8), those subjects have been replaced by a cadre of neoliberal entrepreneurs of the self, to adapt Foucault's prescient expression.

This does not mean that human beings have lacked agency at any step along the way. Colleges and universities in the United States have suffered from no shortage of sovereigns, whether trustees, presidents, professors, students, or administrators. In the vast majority of cases we have considered these were, again, mostly white, mostly male, and mostly bourgeois. Even those exceptions considered in chapter 3 were determined by this norm, as race and gender intertwined differently with class. Agency, however, is rarely individual. Like the project of corporate personhood, the most effective action on U.S. campuses has been collective. Students, joined sometimes by their teachers, have regularly risen to contest hegemonic discourse and its dark alliances (chapters 7, 8). Other teachers and other students have reproduced that discourse daily, in a manner that harks back to the disciplined recitations we have considered from several angles (chapters 1 and 2). Others still have sat around tables, or stood before lecterns, to speak with the confidence endowed by generations of lists (chapter 6). With each repetition, a fragile line separates the renewal of precious knowledge from fiercely durable power.

The same applies to the search for meaning. Erwin Panofsky said of linear perspective that it was twice victorious. First, humanist perspective marked an end to antique theocracy; second, it inaugurated modern "anthropocracy," the reign of the human sciences and their secular universals.[8] Panofsky may have been only half right. On the Stanford campus, we have found engineers building crypto-theological "steeples of excellence," and in the process making humans into symbolic analysts, even in the linear accelerator where Panofsky's son Wolfgang worked. As we have seen at MIT, the "endless frontier" of techno-scientific discovery also anchored a soft humanist theocracy (chapter 8). Over the course of two centuries, as individuals divided into datasets, it has become steadily more difficult to find the proper place of human beings amid these topologies. Where to look? In the laboratory? In the dormitory? In the chapel?

The 1980 Columbia conference at which Derrida spoke was titled "Languages of Knowledge and of Inquiry." Though the theme clearly alluded to the "linguistic turn" then under way in the humanities and in the qualitative social sciences, several natural scientists were also among the speakers. (The philosopher Julia Kristeva was the only woman.) The two panels that preceded Derrida's evening keynote took place in Avery Hall's Wood Auditorium. The afternoon concluded with a talk by D. Raj Reddy, a computer scientist from Carnegie Mellon University, on "Knowledge Structures in Machines."[9] Reddy had just founded the Robotics Institute at Carnegie Mellon; at the time, he was working on machine perception at the human-to-machine interface. That year, Reddy also published a book chapter on "Machine Models of Speech Perception," in which he discussed two poetically named speech recognition systems, HEARSAY and Harpy. Reddy argued that machine speech perception could be distinguished from human speech perception, and should be designed and studied accordingly.[10] Like his predecessor Norbert Wiener and many of Wiener's colleagues, Reddy's work with robots therefore retained more from the metaphysics of Western humanism (chapters 6 and 8) than did Derrida reading one of that tradition's central texts.

Around the same time, Donna Haraway had begun theorizing the cybernetic organism, or "cyborg," as what historians of science call an "epistemic thing."[11] But for Reddy, robotics was not quite yet a "cyborg science" (to borrow from Philip Mirowski, chapter 8). Haraway's 1985 "Manifesto for Cyborgs" argued for an emancipatory socialist-feminist analysis of inhuman technics. The networks she traced led from computer science classrooms in southern California to electronics factories in Southeast Asia. I have tried to locate the cyborg's kin in Cold War think tanks like the Hoover Institution but also to recognize that figure's ancestry in the early classical colleges, in nineteenth century women's colleges, and in the division of labor among historically Black colleges, research universities, and technical institutes (chapters 1, 3, 8). These institutions all did their work at the human-machine interface. Reaching back across the epochal break that so many have assigned to the mid-twentieth century, their history is a feedback channel through which the dehumanizations and the rehumanizations required by liberal and neoliberal reason have met.

Of the genealogies documented in this book, the most immediate for many readers may be the one that begins in chapter 1. There, around 1800, we witnessed the affective organization of student bodies as corporate persons bound by love to Alma Mater and to their curriculum by "mental discipline." Around 2000, descendants of those bodies linked up with photographic faces printed, then scanned, then "born digital" in college "facebooks." The corporate person that eventually took that name, Facebook, was born in a college dormitory as a facial recognition system that trained humans to see onscreen "friends" and eventually, therefore, enemies.[12]

As we have repeatedly seen, all media are social. "Social media" merely reverse the premises of the Turing test, an "imitation game" in which a human receiver is asked to compare signals coming from a machine with signals coming from another human being, to test the machine's "intelligence." Since Alan Turing proposed it in 1950, most of the interest in that test has centered on the machine. Rarely has it been asked: What kind of human being mistakes signals coming from a machine for those coming from another human?[13] This kind of question could well have been asked in 1980 of D. Raj Reddy, the Carnegie Mellon computer scientist, when he spoke in Columbia's Avery Hall: Is a voice that can be understood by a machine still a human voice? Or, the question can be put to Facebook and other corporate persons today: What kind of "user" looks at a screen and sees a friend? At these interfaces, which derive in different degrees from the ones we have followed above, a corporate body born in college and trained in university classrooms and laboratories secures its immortality. The studied adolescence cultivated on Silicon Valley campuses, where college never ends, belongs to a technics of eternal youth, the maintenance of which is the social function of social media. In this way, we return to where we began, looking at ourselves—and others—in and through our knowledge worlds, in and through our machines.

NOTES

Introduction: Knowledge and Technics

1. "The Sixteenth Annual Meeting of the Midwest Modern Language Association," *Bulletin of the Midwest Modern Language Association* 7, no. 2 (Autumn 1974): 41.
2. Fredric R. Jameson, "Beyond the Cave: Demystifying the Ideology of Modernism," *Bulletin of the Midwest Modern Language Association* 8, no. 1 (Spring 1975): 1–20; Edward W. Said, "The Text, the World, the Critic," *Bulletin of the Midwest Modern Language Association* 8, no. 2 (Autumn 1975): 1–23.
3. On the qualification and disqualification of subjects, see the debate between Jacques Derrida and Michel Foucault over Foucault's *Folie et déraison: Histoire de la folie à l'âge classique* (Paris: Plon, 1961). Derrida, "Cogito and the History of Madness" in *Writing and Difference*, trans. Alan Bass (Chicago: University of Chicago Press, 1978), 31–63; to which Foucault replied with "My Body, This Paper, This Fire," trans. Geoff Bennington, in *Aesthetics, Method, and Epistemology: Essential Works of Foucault 1954-1984*, vol. 2, ed. James D. Faubion (New York: New Press, 1998), 394–417. See also Foucault, "Reply to Derrida" in *History of Madness*, ed. Jean Khalfa, trans. Jonathan Murphy and Jean Khalfa (New York: Routledge, 2006), 575–590.
4. Edward W. Said, undated notes. Edward W. Said Papers, Rare Book & Manuscript Library, Columbia University; "Midwest MLA Worldliness Conference—The Text, the World, and the Critic, 1974," Box 111, Folder 21; and Said, *Beginnings: Intention and Method* (New York: Columbia University Press, 1985).
5. Edward W. Said, "The World, the Text, and the Critic," chap. 1 in *The World, the Text, and the Critic* (Cambridge, MA: Harvard University Press, 1983), 31–53. A typescript with title page from 1982 reveals that the book's original title was *Criticism Between Culture and System*. Said Papers, Box 57, Folder 1.
6. "Sixteenth Annual Meeting of the Midwest Modern Language Association," 41.
7. Gerald L. Bruns to Edward W. Said, 20 February 1974. Said Papers, Box 111, Folder 21.

8. Gerald L. Bruns, "Opening Session: 'The Worldliness of Literary Criticism,' " Sixteenth
    Annual Meeting of the Midwest Modern Language Association, October 31–November 2,
    1974, Chase-Park Plaza Hotel, St. Louis, Missouri, 1–2. Said Papers, Box 111, Folder 21. Said
    cites from Paul Ricoeur, "What Is a Text? Explanation and Interpretation," as reproduced
    in David Rasmussen, *Mythic-Symbolic Language and Philosophical Anthropology: A Con-
    structive Interpretation of the Thought of Paul Ricoeur* (The Hague: Nijhoff, 1971), 138.
9. "Professional Notes and Comment," *PMLA* 85, no. 3 (May 1970): 564.
10. "Sixteenth Annual Meeting of the Midwest Modern Language Association," 35.
11. Said, "The Text, the World, the Critic," 2.
12. Said, "The Text, the World, the Critic," 2.
13. Said, "The Text, the World, the Critic," 2–3.
14. This modifies John Guillory, "Genesis of the Media Concept," *Critical Inquiry* 36, no. 2
    (Winter 2010): 321–361. My approach is closer to Peter Becker and William Clark,
    eds., *Little Tools of Knowledge: Historical Essays on Academic and Bureaucratic Prac-
    tices* (Ann Arbor: University of Michigan Press, 2001). See in particular the editors'
    introduction, 1–34.
15. "Sixteenth Annual Meeting of the Midwest Modern Language Association," 61.
16. Fredric Jameson, *The Prison-House of Language: A Critical Account of Structuralism
    and Russian Formalism* (Princeton, NJ: Princeton University Press, 1972).
17. The media theorist Walter J. Ong responded to the Derrida seminar chaired by Spivak.
    "Sixteenth Annual Meeting of the Midwest Modern Language Association," 61.
18. For example, see Tim Hecker, "Glenn Gould, the Vanishing Performer and the Ambiv-
    alence of the Studio," *Leonardo Music Journal* 18 (2008): 77–83. More generally, see
    Emily Thompson, *The Soundscape of Modernity: Architectural Acoustics and the Culture
    of Listening in America, 1900–1933* (Cambridge, MA: MIT Press, 2002); and Jonathan
    Sterne, *The Audible Past: Cultural Origins of Sound Reproduction* (Durham, NC: Duke
    University Press, 2003). Compare to Said, "Remembrance of Things Played: Presence
    and Memory in the Pianist's Art," in *Reflections on Exile and Other Essays* (Cambridge,
    MA: Harvard University Press, 2000), 216–229.
19. "Sixteenth Annual Meeting of the Midwest Modern Language Association," 48.
20. Friedrich A. Kittler, *Discourse Networks, 1800 / 1900*, trans. Michael Metteer, with Chris
    Cullens (Redwood City, CA: Stanford University Press, 1990), 25–69. On maternal
    alphabetization, see Patricia Crain, *The Story of A: The Alphabetization of America from
    "The New England Primer" to "The Scarlet Letter"* (Redwood City, CA: Stanford Uni-
    versity Press, 2000), 103–140. On preliterate "primary orality," see Walter J. Ong, *Orality
    and Literacy: The Technologizing of the Word* (New York: Methuen, 1982), 5–15.
21. Friedrich A. Kittler, *Aufschreibesysteme 1800 / 1900* (Munich: Fink, 1985).
22. Immanuel Kant, *The Conflict of the Faculties* [1798], trans. Mary J. Gregor (New York:
    Abaris, 1979), 31–61.
23. The Chase Hotel, designed by Preston J. Bradshaw, opened in 1922. The Park Plaza
    Hotel, designed by Laurence O. Schopp and Edwin J. Bauman, opened in 1930.
24. The 1971 MMLA report lists the venue of the planned conference for 1974 as the Detroit
    Hilton. Carl H. Klaus, "Report of the Midwest Modern Language Association," *PMLA*
    86, no. 4 (September 1971): 602. On the history of the Detroit Hilton, formerly the
    Statler Hotel, see Dan Austin, "Statler Hotel," Historic Detroit, accessed June 23, 2020,
    http://www.historicdetroit.org/building/statler-hotel/.
25. Jack Grone, "One St. Louis Condo Is Worth More than Whole City Neighborhoods, *Citi-
    lab*, April 3, 2018, https://www.citylab.com/equity/2018/04/one-st-louis-condo-tower-is
    -worth-more-than-whole-city-neighborhoods/556157/.

26. Edward W. Said, handwritten notes on Statler Inn stationery, Cornell University, Ithaca, New York, 2pp, n.d. Said Papers, Box 111, Folder 21.

27. Brian Larkin, "Circulating Empires: Colonial Authority and the Immoral, Subversive Problem of American Film," in *Globalizing American Studies*, ed. Brian T. Edwards and Dilip Parameshwar Gaonkar (Chicago: University of Chicago Press, 2010), 155–183.

28. Kant, *Conflict of the Faculties*, 61–213.

29. Among the most relevant general works are James Axtell, *Wisdom's Workshop: The Rise of the Modern University* (Princeton, NJ: Princeton University Press, 2016); William Clark, *Academic Charisma and the Origins of the Research University* (Chicago: University of Chicago Press, 2006); Roger L. Geiger, *The History of American Higher Education: Learning and Culture from the Founding to World War II* (Princeton, NJ: Princeton University Press, 2015); Geiger, *Research & Relevant Knowledge: American Research Universities Since World War II*, 2nd ed. (New Brunswick, NJ: Transaction Publishers, 2008); Geiger, *To Advance Knowledge: The Growth of American Research Universities, 1900–1940* (New York: Oxford University Press, 1986); George M. Marsden, *The Soul of the American University: From Protestant Establishment to Established Nonbelief* (New York: Oxford University Press, 1994); Bill Readings, *The University in Ruins* (Cambridge, MA: Harvard University Press, 1996); Julie A. Reuben, *The Making of the Modern University: Intellectual Transformation and the Marginalization of Morality* (Chicago: University of Chicago Press, 1996); John R. Thelin, *A History of American Higher Education* (Baltimore, MD: Johns Hopkins University Press, 2004); Laurence R. Veysey, *The Emergence of the American University* (Chicago: University of Chicago Press, 1965); and Chad Wellmon, *Organizing Enlightenment: Information Overload and the Invention of the Modern Research University* (Baltimore:, MD Johns Hopkins University Press, 2015). See also the primary texts, with commentary, collected in Louis Menand, Paul Reitter, and Chad Wellmon, eds. *The Rise of the Research University: A Sourcebook* (Chicago: University of Chicago Press, 2017). For context, see the essays collected in Alexandra Oleson and Sanborn C. Brown, eds., *The Pursuit of Knowledge in the Early American Republic: American Scientific and Learned Societies from Colonial Times to the Civil War* (Baltimore, MD: Johns Hopkins University Press, 1976); and in Alexandra Oleson and John Voss, eds., *The Organization of Knowledge in Modern America, 1860–1920* (Baltimore, MD: Johns Hopkins University Press, 1979).

30. Clark, *Academic Charisma*, 339–476. See also Pierre Bourdieu, *Homo Academicus*, trans. Peter Collier (Redwood City, CA: Stanford University Press, 1988).

31. On Said's persona in relation to his work, see H. Aram Veeser, *Edward Said: The Charisma of Criticism* (New York: Routledge, 2010).

32. Said, "The Text, the World, the Critic," 17.

33. Stefano Harney and Fred Moten, *The Undercommons: Fugitive Planning & Black Study* (Wivenhoe, NY: Minor Compositions, 2013), 22–43.

34. Said, *Reflections on Exile*, xi.

35. Craig Steven Wilder, *Ebony & Ivy: Race, Slavery, and the Troubled History of America's Universities* (New York: Bloomsbury, 2013); and Alfred L. Brophy, *University, Court, & Slave: Pro-Slavery Thought in Southern Colleges & Courts & the Coming Civil War* (New York: Oxford University Press, 2016).

36. Gayatri Chakravorty Spivak, "Explanation and Culture: Marginalia," *Humanities in Society* 2, no. 3 (1979): 201–221. Reprinted in Spivak, *In Other Worlds: Essays in Cultural Politics* (New York: Routledge, 1988), 103–117, quotation 108–109.

37. Said, "The Text, the World, the Critic," 22. This comparison is present from the essay's first draft.

38. Gayatri Chakravorty Spivak, "Reading the World: Literary Studies in the 80s," *College English* 43, no. 7 (November 1981): 675–676.

39. Spivak, "Reading the World," 671.

40. On the German university system, see Charles E. McClelland, *State, Society and University in Germany 1700–1914* (New York: Cambridge University Press, 1980). For relevant comparisons and connections, see Walter Rüegg, ed., *A History of the University in Europe*, vol. 3, *Universities in the Nineteenth and Early Twentieth Centuries (1800–1945)* (New York: Cambridge University Press, 2004), especially Edward Shils and John Roberts, "The Diffusion of European Models Outside of Europe: North America," 164–177. See also Sheldon Rothblatt and Björn Wittrock, eds., *The European and American University Since 1800* (New York: Cambridge University Press, 1993).

41. Martin J. Sklar, *The United States as a Developing Country: Studies in U.S. History in the Progressive Era and the 1920s* (Cambridge: Cambridge University Press, 1992).

42. On the earlier, extramural "republic of letters" in the United States, see Michael Warner, *The Letters of the Republic: Publication and the Public Sphere in Eighteenth-Century America* (Cambridge, MA: Harvard University Press, 1990); and on "print culture" and nation building, Trish Loughran, *The Republic in Print: Print Culture in the Age of U.S. Nation Building, 1770–1870* (New York: Columbia University Press, 2007). See also Anthony Grafton, *Worlds Made by Words: Scholarship and Community in the Modern West* (Cambridge, MA: Harvard University Press, 2009).

43. Christopher Newfield, *Ivy and Industry: Business and the Making of the American University, 1880–1980* (Durham, NC: Duke University Press, 2003), especially 59–62. See also Paul Reitter and Chad Wellmon, "Field of Dreams: Public Higher Education in the United States," *Los Angeles Review of Books*, December 13, 2016, https://lareviewofbooks.org/article/field-of-dreams-public-higher-education-in-the-united-states/#!.

44. Cornelia Vismann, "Cultural Techniques and Sovereignty," *Theory, Culture & Society* 30, no. 6 (2013): 83. As Bernhard Siegert has put it, the study of cultural techniques "moves ontology into the domain of ontic operations." Siegert, *Cultural Techniques: Grids, Filters, Doors, and Other Articulations of the Real*, trans. Geoffrey Winthrop-Young (New York: Fordham University Press, 2015), 9.

45. Cornelia Vismann, *Files: Law and Media Technology*, trans. Geoffrey Winthrop-Young (Redwood City, CA: Stanford University Press, 2008); Bernhard Siegert, *Relays: Literature as an Epoch of the Postal System*, trans. Kevin Repp (Redwood City, CA: Stanford University Press, 1999); and Siegert, *Cultural Techniques*.

46. John Durham Peters, *The Marvelous Clouds: Toward a Philosophy of Elemental Media* (Chicago: University of Chicago Press, 2015), 29–30, 140–145.

47. Friedrich Kittler, "Universities: Wet, Hard, Soft, and Harder," *Critical Inquiry* 31, no. 1 (Autumn 2004): 251.

48. Vismann, "Cultural Techniques and Sovereignty," 84.

49. Jean-Jacques Rousseau, *Discourse on the Origin and Foundations of Inequality Among Men* [1755], trans. Peter Constantine, in *The Essential Writings of Rousseau*, ed. Leo Damrosch (New York: Modern Library, 2013), 50.

50. Siegert, *Cultural Techniques*, 14; on "door logic," 192–205; on corrals and calendars as techniques of hominization, 9.

51. Siegert, *Cultural Techniques*, 10. See also John Harwood, "On Wires; or, Metals and Modernity Reconsidered," *Grey Room* 69 (Fall 2017): 108–136.

52. On *dispositifs*, or apparatuses, see Michel Foucault, in conversation with Alain Grosrichard, Gerard Wajeman, Jacques-Alain Miller, Guy Le Gaufey, Dominique Celas, Gerard Miller, Catherine Millot, Jocelyne Livi, and Judith Miller, "The Confession of

the Flesh," in *Power/Knowledge: Selected Interviews and Other Writings*, ed. Colin Gordon (London: Harvester Press, 1980), 194–195.

53. David Wellbery, foreword to Kittler, *Discourse Networks*, xii–xxx.

54. On media archaeology, see Wolfgang Ernst, *Digital Memory and the Archive*, ed. Jussi Parikka (Minneapolis: University of Minnesota Press, 2013), esp. 37–73, as well as Parikka's introduction, 1–22, and "Media-Archaeology as a Transatlantic Bridge, " 23–31. See also Parikka, *What Is Media Archaeology?* (Malden, MA: Polity, 2012); and John Harwood, *The Interface: IBM and the Transformation of Corporate Design* (Minneapolis: University of Minnesota Press, 2011).

55. Peters, *Marvelous Clouds*, 33.

56. Jameson, "Beyond the Cave," 19–20; emphasis in original. Jameson also mentions Mumford, via Gilles Deleuze and Félix Guattari's *Anti-Oedipus*.

57. Jameson cites the Penguin edition of Plato's *Republic*, translated by Desmond Lee (New York: Penguin, 1955), 278–279.

58. Cardinal John Henry Newman, *The Idea of the University* (London: Longmans, Green, 1852). See also Abraham Flexner, *Universities: American, English, German* (New York: Oxford University Press, 1930).

59. Said, "The Text, the World, the Critic," 22.

60. Said, *The World, the Text, and the Critic*, 53. The reference to Arnold and Nietzsche first appears in a handwritten annotations to Edward W. Said, "The Text, the World, the Critic," 37, an undated typescript interleaved with an undated first draft of the book. Said Papers, Box 56, Folder 12.

61. Michel Foucault, "Nietzsche, Genealogy, History," trans. Donald F. Brouchard and Sherry Simon, in *Foucault: Aesthetics, Method, and Epistemology*, 369–391.

62. See for example Andrew Delbanco, *College: What It Was, Is, and Should Be* (Princeton, NJ: Princeton University Press, 2012); Frank Donogue, *The Last Professors: The Corporate University and the Fate of the Humanities* (New York: Fordham University Press, 2008); Andrew Hacker and Claudia Dreifus, *Higher Education? How Colleges Are Wasting Our Money and Failing Our Kids—and What We Can Do About It* (New York: St. Martin's Griffin, 2010); and Mark C. Taylor, *Crisis on Campus: A Bold Plan for Reforming Our Colleges and Universities* (New York: Alfred A. Knopf, 2010). See also the essays collected in Akeel Bilgrami and Jonathan R. Cole. eds., *Who's Afraid of Academic Freedom?* (New York: Columbia University Press, 2015); and Joan Wallach Scott, "The Conundrum of Equality," in *Gender and the Politics of History*, 30th Anniversary ed. (New York: Columbia University Press, 2018), 199–215.

63. See for example Derek Bok, *Higher Education in America* (Princeton, NJ: Princeton University Press, 2016); Jonathan R. Cole, *Toward a More Perfect University* (New York: Public Affairs, 2016); Cole, *The Great American University: Its Rise to Preeminence, Its Indispensable National Role, Why It Must Be Protected* (New York: Public Affairs, 2009). Christopher Newfield mounts a sober defense of public universities in *Unmaking the Public University: The Forty-Year Assault on the Middle Class* (Cambridge, MA: Harvard University Press, 2008); and *The Great Mistake: How We Wrecked Public Universities and How We Can Fix Them* (Baltimore: Johns Hopkins University Press, 2016).

64. See Wendy Brown, *Undoing the Demos: Neoliberalism's Stealth Revolution* (Brooklyn, NY: Zone Books, 2015).

65. Domenico Losurdo, *Liberalism: A Counter-History*, trans. Gregory Elliott (New York: Verso, 2011).

66. The slogans are from Marshall McLuhan, *Understanding Media: The Extensions of Man* (New York: McGraw-Hill, 1964), 7ff, and Friedrich A. Kittler, *Gramophone, Film,*

Typewriter, trans. Geoffrey Winthrop-Young and Michael Wutz (Redwood City, CA: Stanford University Press, 1999), xxxix, respectively.

67. The two most relevant touchstones for these ideas in Foucault's work are *The Archaeology of Knowledge and the Discourse on Language*, trans. A. M. Sheridan Smith (New York: Pantheon, 1972), and "Nietzsche, Genealogy, History," which originally appeared in 1969 and 1971, respectively..

68. The definitive history of campus architecture in the United States remains Paul Venable Turner, *Campus: An American Planning Tradition* (New York: Architectural History Foundation/Cambridge, MA: MIT Press, 1984). On the later twentieth century, see Stefan Muthesius, *The Postwar University: Utopianist Campus and College* (New Haven, CT: Yale University Press, 2000).

69. This, and the concept of a "media complex," builds on my argument in *The Organizational Complex: Architecture, Media, and Corporate Space* (Cambridge, MA: MIT Press, 2003). My formulation is also close to Weihong Bao's "mediating environment" in Bao, *Fiery Cinema: The Emergence of an Affective Medium in China, 1915–1945* (Minneapolis: University of Minnesota Press, 2015), 7ff.

70. Stefan Andriopoulos, *Possessed: Hypnotic Crimes, Corporate Fiction, and the Invention of Cinema*, trans. Peter Jansen and Stefan Andriopoulos (Chicago: University of Chicago Press, 2008), esp. 42–65.

71. See for example the essays collected in Rothblatt and Witrock, *The European and American University Since 1800*. See also Axtell, *Wisdom's Workshop*; Geiger, *The History of American Higher Education*; Veysey, *The Emergence of the American University*; and Rüegg, *A History of the University in Europe*, vol. 3. On the Humboldtian model, see Wellmon, *Organizing Enlightenment*.

72. Lisa Gitelman, *Paper Knowledge: Toward a Media History of Documents* (Durham, NC: Duke University Press, 2014).

73. Antonio Gramsci, "[War of Position and War of Manoeuvre]," "War of Position and War of Manoeuvre or Frontal War," and "Transition from the War of Manoeuvre (and from Frontal Attack) to the War of Position in the Political Field as Well," in *The Gramsci Reader: Selected Writings 1916–1935*, ed. David Forgacs (New York: New York University Press, 2000), 225–230; Donna Haraway, "A Cyborg Manifesto: Science, Technology, and Socialist Feminism in the Late Twentieth Century," in *Simians, Cyborgs, and Women: The Reinvention of Nature* (New York: Routledge, 1991), 150. See also Paul N. Edwards, "Border Wars: The Science and Politics of Artificial Intelligence," *Radical America* 19, no. 6 (November–December 1985): 39–50.

74. Kant, *Conflict of the Faculties*, 59–61; emphasis in original.

75. I am referring to Actor-Network-Theory (ANT) developed by Bruno Latour and others, as in Latour, *Reassembling the Social: An Introduction to Actor-Network-Theory* (New York: Oxford University Press, 2005), and to the work of Michel Foucault cited above.

Prologue, c. 1800

1. Thomas Jefferson, "A Bill for the More General Diffusion of Knowledge, 18 June 1779," *Founders Online*, National Archives, https://founders.archives.gov/documents/Jefferson /01-02-02-0132-0004-0079. Also in Julian P. Boyd, ed., *The Papers of Thomas Jefferson*, vol. 2, *1777–18 June 1779* (Princeton, NJ: Princeton University Press, 1950), 526–535.

2. Roy J. Honeywell, *The Educational Work of Thomas Jefferson* (Cambridge, MA: Harvard University Press, 1931), 7–25.

3. At roughly the same time Jefferson also introduced another bill to amend the constitution of the college, proposing to disestablish its ties to the Church of England, secularize the curriculum, and add professorships. This bill, too, was never adopted, although Jefferson was able to implement some changes after being elected governor in 1779. Honeywell, *Educational Work of Thomas Jefferson*, 54–56.

4. Honeywell, *Educational Work of Thomas Jefferson*, 62–65; and Thomas Jefferson, "A Bill for Establishing a System of Public Education," Gilder Lehrman Collection, Gilder Lehrman Institute of American History, October 24, 1817, https://www.gilderlehrman.org /collections/3559e0cb-b176-4d09-8084-254597147910.

5. Jefferson, "A Bill for the More General Diffusion of Knowledge."

6. Universal public education was not formally enacted in the Commonwealth until a new state constitution was adopted during Reconstruction. On public education prior to the Civil War, see A. J. Morrison, *The Beginnings of Public Education in Virginia, 1776–1860: Study of Secondary Schools in Relation to the State Literary Fund* (Richmond: David Bottom, Superintendent of Public Printing, 1917), 7–16.

7. Sarah N. Randolph, *The Domestic Life of Thomas Jefferson, Compiled from Family Letters and Reminiscences* (New York: Harper, 1871), 43.

8. Tafuri is referring sarcastically to the travesties of the classical language and of Enlightenment rationality in American architectural postmodernism. Manfredo Tafuri, "Les cendres de Jefferson," *Architecture d'aujourd'hui* 186 (August–September 1976): 53–72; revised and reprinted as "The Ashes of Jefferson" in Tafuri, *The Sphere and the Labyrinth: Avant-Gardes and Architecture from Piranesi to the 1970s*, trans. Pelligrino d'Acierno and Robert Connolly (Cambridge: MIT Press, 1987), 291–303.

9. On Jefferson's efforts to avoid publication, see Douglas L. Wilson, "Jefferson and the Republic of Letters," in *Jeffersonian Legacies*, ed. Peter S. Onuf (Charlottesville: University Press of Virginia, 1993), 50–76. On the relationship between Jefferson's books and his architecture, see Richard Guy Wilson, "Thomas Jefferson's 'Bibliomanie' and Architecture," in *American Architects and Their Books to 1848*, ed. Kenneth Hafertepe and James F. O'Gorman (Amherst, MA: University of Massachusetts Press, 2001), 57–72.

10. Max Horkheimer and Theodor W. Adorno, *Dialectic of Enlightenment: Philosophical Fragments*, trans. Edmund Jephcott (Stanford: Stanford University Press, 2002), 35–62.

11. On the dumbwaiters at Monticello, see Susan R. Stein, *The Worlds of Thomas Jefferson at Monticello* (New York: Harry N. Abrams, 1993), 60–61, 282–283. On Jefferson's likely encounter with the dumbwaiters at the Café Mécanique, a popular restaurant at the recently transformed Palais Royal, see the editorial note in Thomas Jefferson, *Jefferson's Memorandum Books: Accounts, with Legal Records and Miscellany, 1767–1826*, vol. 1, ed. James A. Bear, and Lucia Stanton (Princeton, NJ: Princeton University Press, 1997), 562–563 n91. See also Howard C. Rice, *Thomas Jefferson's Paris* (Princeton, NJ: Princeton University Press, 1976), 14–18. Markus Krajewski has interpreted Jefferson's devices as intermediary, hybridized "servants" belonging to a media history of "quasi-objects." Krajewski, *The Server: A Media History from the Present to the Baroque*, trans. Ilinca Iurascu (New Haven, CT: Yale University Press, 2018), 255–259. In his otherwise compelling genealogy of media-technological service, Krajewski refers to the enslaved persons at Monticello as "domestics" (*Domestiken*), or representatives of the category "servant" (*Diener*), rather than as slaves.

12. "Dumbwaiters," Thomas Jefferson Foundation, *The Thomas Jefferson Encyclopedia*, accessed June 27, 2020, https://www.monticello.org/site/research-and-collections/dumbwaiters.

13. Immanuel Kant, "An Answer to the Question: What Is Enlightenment?" [1784], trans. James Schmidt, in *What Is Enlightenment?: Eighteenth-Century Answers and Twentieth-Century Questions*, ed. James Schmidt (Berkeley: University of California Press, 1996), 63.

14. Margaret Bayard Smith, *The First Forty Years of Washington Society, Portrayed by the Family Letters of Mrs. Samuel Harrison Smith (Margaret Bayard)*, ed. Gaillard Hunt (New York: Scribner, 1906), 387–388.

15. Information on the provenance of standalone dumbwaiters at Monticello is available from "Dumbwaiters," Thomas Jefferson Foundation.

16. Isaac Jefferson, *Memoirs of a Monticello Slave, Dictated to Charles Campbell in the 1840s by Isaac, One of Thomas Jefferson's Slaves* (Charlottesville: University of Virginia Press, 1951), 27. The lives of enslaved persons at Monticello are documented in Lucia Stanton, *"Those Who Labor for My Happiness": Slavery at Thomas Jefferson's Monticello* (Charlottesville: University of Virginia Press, 2012). See also Annette Gordon-Reed, *Thomas Jefferson and Sally Hemings: An American Controversy* (Charlottesville: University of Virginia Press, 1997) and Gordon-Reed, *The Hemingses of Monticello: An American Family* (New York: Norton, 2008).

1. Student Bodies and Corporate Persons

1. Pauline Maier, "The Revolutionary Origins of the American Corporation," *William and Mary Quarterly* 50, no. 1 (January 1993): 53–58.

2. Ernst H. Kantorowicz, *The King's Two Bodies: A Study in Medieval Political Theology* (Princeton, NJ: Princeton University Press, 1957), 5, also 302ff, 314ff.

3. Maier, "Revolutionary Origins," 56–57. On corporate charters, see Oscar Handlin and Mary F. Handlin, "Origins of the American Business Corporation," *Journal of Economic History*, 5, no. 1 (May 1945): 1–23.

4. Charter of Dartmouth College, signed December 18, 1769 [copy], 4–5; Records of the Dartmouth College Trustees, 1770–2004; Series 25454, Box 2115, Bound Meeting Minutes 1770–1812, Rauner Special Collections Library, Dartmouth College. A transcript is available online at https://www.dartmouth.edu/~library/rauner/dartmouth/dc-charter .html. Ten years later, at a meeting of the board of trustees, a committee was formed "to enquire into the civil rights of this college as conveyed in the charter." Meeting of the Trustees, August 31, 1779, Bound Meeting Minutes, Vol. 1, 49. Rauner Manuscript DA-1, Series 25454, Meeting Files of the Board of Trustees, 1770–2002, Box 9296, Rauner Special Collections Library, Dartmouth College.

5. Leon Burr Richardson, *History of Dartmouth College* (Hanover, NH: Dartmouth College Publications, 1932), 79–84, 101–102. On Indigenous enrollments, James Axtell, *The European and the Indian: Essays in the Enthnohistory of Colonial North America* (New York: Oxford University Press, 1981), 108. On Indian schools, including Wheelock's, see also Craig Steven Wilder, *Ebony & Ivy: Race, Slavery, and the Troubled History of America's Universities* (New York: Bloomsbury, 2013), 162–179.

6. For a detailed study of the Dartmouth case, see Francis N. Stites, *Private Interest and Public Gain: The Dartmouth College Case, 1819* (Amherst: University of Massachusetts Press, 1972). The "contracts clause" is found in Article I, Section 10 of the U.S. Constitution.

7. On the Fourteenth Amendment and corporate rights, see Adam Winkler, *We the Corporations: How American Businesses Won Their Civil Rights* (New York: Liveright, 2018). 113–160.

8. Southern Railway Co. v. Greene, 216 US 400. 1909. https://www.loc.gov/item /usrep216400/. For historical summaries, see Joshua Barkan, *Corporate Sovereignty: Law and Government under Capitalism* (Minneapolis: University of Minnesota Press, 2013), 65–86; and Martin J. Sklar, *The Corporate Reconstruction of American Capitalism,*

1890–1916: The Market, The Law, and Politics (New York: Cambridge University Press, 1988), 49–53.

9. A representative treatment of corporate personhood as fiction is I. Maurice Wormser, *Disregard of the Corporate Fiction and Allied Corporation Problems* (New York: Baker, Voorhis, 1927). Winkler surveys this history in *We the Corporations*, 3–70. For more detail, see also Suzanna Kim Ripken, *Corporate Personhood* (New York: Cambridge University Press, 2019), 21–57. Joshua Barkan argues that corporate personhood constitutes a Foucauldian *dispositif*, or apparatus: *Corporate Sovereignty*, 76–86. On corporate personhood and architecture, see John Harwood, "Corporate Abstraction," *Perspecta* 46 (2013): 218–243.

10. Webster is said to have continued: "I know not how others may feel . . . but for myself, when I see my *Alma Mater* surrounded, like Caesar in the senate house by those who are reiterating stab upon stab, I would not for this right hand have her say to me, '*et tu quoque, mi fili?*' ['And thou too, my son?'']," John W. Black, "Webster's Peroration in the Dartmouth College Case," *Quarterly Journal of Speech* 23 (December 1937): 639. Also in *Daniel Webster, "The Completest Man": Documents from the Daniel Webster Papers*, ed. Kenneth E. Shewmaker (Hanover, NH: Dartmouth College/University Press, 1990), 145; and Winkler, *We the Corporations*, 83. For the complete text of Webster's argument before the court, which does not include the peroration, see *The Great Speeches and Orations of Daniel Webster, with an Essay on Daniel Webster as a Master of English Style*, ed. Edwin P. Whipple (Boston: Little Brown, 1894), 1–24; and *The Writings of Daniel Webster*, vol. 10 (Boston: Little, Brown, 1903), 194–233. For a description of the trial, see Winkler, *We the Corporations*, 75–84. The quotation may be an approximation of Webster's words, which have nonetheless become part of the oratorical canon. On the evidence see Black, "Webster's Peroration in the Dartmouth College Case," 636–642. My argument does not depend on the peroration's exact wording, only its principal affect, which Black confirms through analysis of extant documentation and its context.

11. Joseph Story, quoted in Maurice Glen Baxter, *Daniel Webster & the Supreme Court* (Amherst: University of Massachusetts Press, 1966), 84–85. Chauncey Allen Goodrich, quoted in Black, "Webster's Peroration," 639.

12. Dartmouth College v. Woodward., 17 US 4 Wheat. 518. 1819. https://www.loc.gov/item/usrep017518/. On Marshall's reasoning, see Winkler, *We the Corporations*, 84–88.

13. Francis Lane Childs, "A Dartmouth History Lesson for Freshmen," *Dartmouth Alumni Magazine* (December 1957), http://www.dartmouth.edu/~library/rauner/dartmouth/dartmouth_history.html. On the Dartmouth student body during Webster's time, see Robert V. Remini, *Daniel Webster: The Man and His Time* (New York: Norton, 1997), 44.

14. On this building type, see Paul Venable Turner, *Campus: An American Planning Tradition* (New York: Architectural History Foundation/Cambridge, MA: MIT Press, 1984), 8–53; and Carla Yanni, *Living on Campus: An Architectural History of the American Dormitory* (Minneapolis: University of Minnesota Press, 2019), 33–53. The college also made use of the top story of another building, since demolished, known as Rowley Hall. John King Lord, *A History of Dartmouth College* (Concord, NH: Rumford Press, 1913), 122; and Bryant Franklin Tolles, *Architecture and Academe: College Buildings in New England Before 1860* (Hanover, NH: University Press of New England, 2011), 51–58.

15. The entirely wooden original, which contained sixteen dormitory rooms plus a kitchen and a meeting room, was completed in 1791 and was most likely designed by master builder Peter Harrison, with the aid of drawings by the housewright William Gamble and the assistance of the carpenter Comfort Sever. Dartmouth professor Bezaleel Woodward oversaw the construction. Tolles, *Architecture and Academe*, 54–56.

16. Remini, *Daniel Webster*, 43–46. See also Herbert Darling Foster, "Webster and Choate in College: The Dartmouth Curriculum 1796–1819," [typescript of an article that
appeared in the *Dartmouth Alumni Magazine*, April–May 1927], 9. Rauner Special Collections Library, Dartmouth College; Dartmouth College History, LD 1442.F6. Ephraim
Smedley, a Dartmouth student who died two years before graduating, in 1791, gives in
his diary a matter-of-fact account of the workload. "Diary of Ephraim Smedley, Class
of 1793, 1789–1791" [typescript], 4–8. Rauner Special Collections Library, Dartmouth
College; Dartmouth Hall, MS 789558.
17. Remini, *Daniel Webster*, 55–56.
18. This version of the building lasted until another fire, in 1855, necessitated total reconstruction within the original walls. On Latrobe's designs, see Paul Norton, "Benjamin
Henry Latrobe's Nassau Hall," in *Nassau Hall, 1756–1956*, ed. Henry Lyttleton Savage
(Princeton, NJ: Princeton University Press, 1956), 27–38.
19. Michel Foucault, *Discipline and Punish: The Birth of the Prison*, trans. Alan Sheridan
(New York: Pantheon Books, 1977), 266–267.
20. Paul Norton, "Robert Smith's Nassau Hall and President's House," in Savage, ed., *Nassau
Hall, 1756–1956*, 16. On the early layout of the Princeton campus, see Turner, *Campus*,
47–50.
21. Foucault, *Discipline and Punish*, 141–154; cf. Giorgio Agamben, "What Is an Apparatus?"
in *What Is an Apparatus and Other Essays*, trans. David Kishik and Stefan Pedatella
(Redwood City, CA: Stanford University Press, 2009), 1–24; and Roberto Esposito, "The
Dispositif of the Person," *Law, Culture, and the Humanities* 8, no. 1 (2012): 17–30.
22. Foucault, *Discipline and Punish*, 135–169, esp. 155–156.
23. Thomas Jefferson Wertenbaker, *Princeton, 1746–1896* (Princeton, NJ: Princeton University Press, 1946), 155.
24. Wertenbaker, *Princeton, 1746–1896*, 156.
25. Wertenbaker, *Princeton, 1746–1896*, 156–157.
26. Wertenbaker, *Princeton, 1746–1896*, 157.
27. Wertenbaker, *Princeton, 1746–1896*, 167.
28. Wertenbaker, *Princeton, 1746–1896*, 158. On the rebellions at Harvard, see Samuel Eliot
Morison, *Three Centuries of Harvard 1636–1936* (Cambridge, MA: Harvard University
Press, 1946), 230–231; and Corydon Ireland, "Harvard's Long-Ago Student Risings," *Harvard Gazette*, April 19, 2012, https://news.harvard.edu/gazette/story/2012/04/harvards
-long-ago-student-risings/. Similar events at Yale are described below.
29. *Reports on the Course of Instruction in Yale College by a Committee of the Corporation and
the Academical Faculty* (New Haven, CT: Hezekiah Howe, 1828), 7; emphasis in original.
30. *Reports on the Course of Instruction in Yale College*, 9; emphasis in original.
31. Wertenbaker, *Princeton, 1746–1896*, 158.
32. Charles W. Kent, "Poe's Student Days at the University of Virginia," *Bookman* 44, no. 5
(January 1917): 520.
33. On Poe's experience, Edgar Allan Poe, "Letter From Edgar Allan Poe to John Allan, 1831
December 15," Poe Collection, University of Virginia Library, December 15, 1831, search.
lib.virginia.edu/catalog/uva-lib:501856.
34. Arthur Hobson Quinn, *Edgar Allan Poe: A Critical Biography* [1941] (Baltimore: Johns
Hopkins University Press, 1998), 110–111. See also Kenneth Silverman, *Edgar A. Poe:
Mournful and Never-Ending Remembrance* (New York: Harper Collins, 1991), 29–36.
35. Edgar Allan Poe, "To Helen," in *Poems by Edgar A. Poe*, 2nd ed. (New York: Elam Bliss, 1831),
39. By 1841, Poe had changed these lines to read: "To the glory that was Greece / And the
grandeur that was Rome." For a contextualization, see Quinn, *Edgar Allan Poe*, 177–179.

36. See, for example, Darlene Harbour Unrue, "Edgar Allan Poe: The Romantic as Classi-cist," *International Journal of the Classical Tradition*, 1, no. 4 (Spring 1995): 112–119.

37. Lewis Mumford, *Sticks and Stones: A Study of American Architecture and Civilization* (New York: Boni & Liveright, 1924), 68.

38. Lewis Mumford, *The Golden Day: A Study in American Experience and Culture* (New York: Boni & Liveright, 1926), 76. On Poe's media practices, see John Tresch, " 'Matter No More': Edgar Allan Poe and the Paradoxes of Materialism," *Critical Inquiry* 42 (Sum-mer 2016): 865–898.

39. Edgar Allan Poe, "The Domain of Arnheim" [1847] in *The Works of the Late Edgar Allan Poe, with Notices of His Life and Genius*, ed. N. P. Willis, J. R. Lowell, and R. W. Griswold, vol. 1, *Tales* (New York: J. S Redfield, Clinton Hall, 1850), 402–403.

40. Mumford, *The Golden Day*, 280–281.

41. Mumford, *Sticks and Stones*, 90.

42. Foucault, *Discipline and Punish*, 293–308. On Haviland's prison designs, see Norman B. Johnston, "John Haviland, Jailor to the World," *Journal of the Society of Architectural Historians* 23, no. 2 (May 1964): 101–105.

43. Leonard Bacon, "The Corporation," in *Yale College; A Sketch of Its History: with Notices of Its Several Departments, Instructors, and Benefactors Together with Some Account of Student Life and Amusements by Various Authors*, ed. William L. Kingsley, vol. 1 (New York: Henry Holt, 1879), 163.

44. Bacon, "The Corporation," 163–171, quotation from the Yale charter, 164.

45. Jurgen Herbst, *From Crisis to Crisis: American College Government 1636–1819* (Cam-bridge, MA: Harvard University Press, 1982), 42–54.

46. Bacon, "The Corporation," 163–164. See also George Wilson Pierson, *The Founding of Yale: The Legend of the Forty Folios* (New Haven, CT: Yale University Press, 1988). The broader context is treated in Herbst, *From Crisis to Crisis*.

47. Bacon, "The Corporation," 172; on the completion and naming of the building, 173–175.

48. Bacon, "The Corporation," 171–172. William L. Kingsley supplies further details on the controversy over location, including the erection of the new building at New Haven with advice on the "architectonic part of the building" from Connecticut Governor Gurdon Saltonstall, in "Historical Sketch," in Kingsley, *Yale College*, 31–48.

49. George Dudley Seymour, "Henry Caner, 1680–1731, Master Carpenter, Builder of the First Yale College Building, 1718, and of the Rector's House, 1722," *Old-Time New England: The Bulletin of the Society for the Preservation of New England Antiquities* 15, no. 3 (January 1925): 99–124.

50. Franklin Bowditch Dexter, *Biographical Sketches of the Graduates of Yale College with Annals of the College History*, vol. 1, *October 1701–May 1745* (New York: Henry Holt, 1885), 198, cited also in Seymour, "Henry Caner," 105.

51. Seymour, "Henry Caner," on bell-ringing, 109; on windows, citing Edwards, 113.

52. Bacon, "The Corporation," 175; on the original rules governing the rectorship, 164–165.

53. Philip Lee, "The Curious Life of *In Loco Parentis* at American Universities," *Higher Education Review* 8 (2011): 67; Lee cites Gilman's address, which can be found in *Addresses at the Inauguration of Daniel C. Gilman as President of the Johns Hopkins University, Baltimore, February 22, 1876* (Baltimore: John Murphy, 1876), 15–64; on in loco parentis, 32. William Blackstone refers to the relation of tutor or schoolmaster to the child as one of in loco parentis. *Blackstone's Commentaries on the Laws of England* [1765–1770], ed. Wayne Morrison, book 1, chapter 16, (London: Cavendish, 2001), [453], 348.

54. On Clap's tenure, see Kingsley, "Historical Sketch," in Kingsley, *Yale College*, 63–93.

55. The charter further stipulated that this body

> shall hereafter be called and known by the NAME of the PRESIDENT AND FEL-
> LOWS OF YALE COLLEGE in NEW HAVEN, and by that same Name they and
> their Successors shall and may have perpetual Succession, and shall and may be
> Persons capable in the Law to plead and be impleaded, Defend and be Defended
> and answer and be answered unto, and also to have take possess acquire purchase
> or otherwise Receive Lands Teneaments Hereditaments Goods Chattels or other
> Estates and the Same Lands Teneaments Hereditaments Goods Chattels or other
> Estates to grant Demise Lease Use Manage or Improve for ye Good and Benefit
> of ye Sd COLLEGE according to the Tenor of ye Donation & their Discretion.

> "Charter of Yale College May [1745]; By the Governor and Company of his Majes-
> ties Colony of Connecticut in New England in America," in Yale University, *The Yale
> Corporation: Charter and Legislation; Printed for the President and Fellows* (New Haven:
> Yale University, 1976), 9.

56. "Charter of Yale College May [1745]," 10–11.
57. This arrangement was precipitated by a legislative report that spoke to extramural inter-
    est in loosening the college's classical curriculum. The 1792 report is quoted in Kingsley,
    "Historical Sketch," 109, on Union Hall, (later South College), 110. See also Bacon,
    "The Corporation," 180–182. A series of related amendments to the charter and other
    legislative acts followed. In 1872, the state officials were replaced by six alumni. The full
    text of this and earlier legislation is available in Yale University, *Yale Corporation*, 12–20.
58. Jurgen Herbst, "The Yale Report of 1828," *International Journal of the Classical Tradition*
    11, no. 2 (Fall 2004): 214.
59. On the context and interpretations of the Yale Report, see Melvin I. Urofsky, "Reforms
    and Response: The Yale Report of 1828," *History of Education Quarterly* 5, no. 1 (March
    1965): 53–67; and Herbst, "The Yale Report of 1828."
60. Kingsley, "Historical Sketch," in Kingsley, *Yale College*, 133.
61. As quoted in Kingsley, "Historical Sketch," in Kingsley, *Yale College*, 137. This seemingly
    benign request probably referred to *An Elementary Treatise on Conic Sections, Spheri-
    cal Geometry, and Spherical Trigonometry* (1824), authored by Olmsted's predecessor,
    the recently deceased Matthew Dutton. John C. Schwab, "The Yale College Curriculum
    1701–1901," *Educational Review* 22 (June 1901): 10. On Olmsted, see "Denison Olmsted,"
    in Franklin Bowditch Dexter, *Biographical Sketches of the Graduates of Yale College*, vol. 6,
    September, 1805–September, 1815 (New Haven, CT: Yale University Press, 1912), 592–600.
62. Kingsley, "Historical Sketch," in Kingsley, *Yale College*, 138.
63. On the Yale Report as the "basis for the modernization of the college curriculum during
    the nineteenth century," see Herbst, "The Yale Report of 1828," 214.
64. *Reports on the Course of Instruction in Yale College*, 7; emphasis in original.
65. *Reports on the Course of Instruction in Yale College*, 6; emphasis in original.
66. The full passage reads:

> Those branches of study should be prescribed, and those modes of instruction
> adopted, which are best calculated to teach the art of fixing the attention, direct-
> ing the train of thought, analyzing a subject proposed for investigation; follow-
> ing, with accurate discrimination, the course of argument; balancing nicely the
> evidence presented to the judgment; awakening, elevating, and controlling the
> imagination; arranging, with skill, the treasures which memory gathers; rousing
> and guiding the powers of genius.

> *Reports on the Course of Instruction in Yale College*, 7.

67. *Reports on the Course of Instruction in Yale College*, 8.
68. *Reports on the Course of Instruction in Yale College*, 35.
69. *Reports on the Course of Instruction in Yale College*, 36.
70. Caroline Winterer, *The Culture of Classicism: Ancient Greece and Rome in American Intellectual Life 1780–1910* (Baltimore: Johns Hopkins University Press, 2002), 48.
71. G. P. Brooks, "The Faculty Psychology of Thomas Reid," *Journal of the History of the Behavioral Sciences* 12 (1976): 65–77. Also, Dabney Townsend, "Thomas Reid and the Theory of Taste," *Journal of Aesthetics and Art Criticism* 61, no. 4 (Autumn 2003): 341–351.
72. Thomas Reid, "Of Taste," in *Essays on the Intellectual Powers of Man: Abridged. With Notes and Illustrations from Sir William Hamilton and Others*, ed. James Walker (Cambridge, MA: John Bartlett, 1850), 429.
73. Reid, "Of Taste," 439; emphasis in original.
74. Reid, "Of Taste," 440; emphasis in original.
75. Reid, "Of Taste," 443.
76. Frederick Rudolph, *Curriculum: A History of the American Undergraduate Course of Study Since 1636* (San Francisco: Josey-Bass, 1977), 75–79.
77. "Rumford Professor," in *Report of a Committee of the Overseers of Harvard College, January 6, 1825* (Cambridge, MA: University Press/Hilliard and Metcalf, 1825), 39.
78. Jacob Bigelow, *Elements of Technology, Taken Chiefly from a Course of Lectures at Cambridge on the Application of the Sciences to the Useful Arts Now Published for the Use of Seminaries and Students* (Boston: Hilliard, Gray, Little, and Wilkins, 1829), 1; emphasis in original.
79. Bigelow, *Elements of Technology*, 3.
80. *Reports on the Course of Instruction in Yale College*, 35–36.
81. Bruce A. Kimball, *Orators & Philosophers: A History of the Idea of Liberal Education* (New York: Teachers College Press, 1986).
82. "Original Papers in Relation to a Course on Liberal Education," *American Journal of Science and Arts*, 15 (January 1829): 297–351.
83. Benjamin Silliman, "Remarks by the Editor," in "Original Papers," 297. On Silliman's contributions to the report, see Urofsky, "Reforms and Response," 58.
84. The passage reads as follows:

    Educated in this way, besides the advantages of mental discipline which have been already mentioned, [the student] enlarges the circle of his thoughts, finds in his superior information, new means of benefiting or influencing others, and his mind is thus far liberalized by liberal knowledge. . . . It is on the same grounds, that the use and necessity of classical literature in a liberal education may be defended.

    Reports on the Course of Instruction in Yale College, 32–34.
85. Chandos Michael Brown, *Benjamin Silliman: A Life in the Young Republic* (Princeton, NJ: Princeton University Press, 1989), 127. According to a report compiled by the Amistad Committee on the occasion of Yale's tercentennial in 2001, Silliman's family were the largest slave owners in Fairfield County, and his own education at Yale was partly financed through the sale of enslaved persons from the estate that he later managed while a Yale faculty member, even as Silliman expressed increasing sympathy for the abolitionist cause. See the entry on "Benjamin Silliman" in Antony Dugdale, J. J. Fueser, and J. Celso de Castro Alves, *Yale, Slavery & Abolition* (New Haven, CT: Amistad Committee, 2001) 14–16, http://www.yaleslavery.org/Resources/summ.html.
86. Brown, *Benjamin Silliman*, 115–118; on Silliman's early lectures, including enrollments and fees, 134–140.

87. Brooks Mather Kelley, *Yale: A History* (New Haven, CT: Yale University Press, 1974), 137.

88. George W. Pierson, *A Yale Book of Numbers: Historical Statistics of the College and University 1701–1976* (New Haven, CT: Yale University, 1983), 530–531, 535.

89. Kingsley, "Historical Sketch," 143–144.

90. Kingsley, "Historical Sketch," 143.

91. Benjamin Cardozo, Berkey v. Third Avenue Railway Co. 244 NY 602 (1927). Winkler summarizes the discourse of "piercing the corporate veil" in *We the Corporations*, 55ff. See also Robert B. Thompson, "Piercing the Corporate Veil: An Empirical Study," *Cornell Law Review* 75, issue 5 (July 1992): 1036–1074.

92. I. Maurice Wormser, "Piercing the Veil of Corporate Entity," *Columbia Law Review* 12 (1912): 496–518. Reprinted in Wormser, *Disregard of the Corporate Fiction*, 42–85.

93. I. Maurice Wormser, "Disregard of the Corporate Fiction—When and Why," *Columbia Law Review* 23 (December 1923): 702–715. Cited from Wormser, *Disregard of the Corporate Fiction*, 5.

94. Wormser, *Disregard of the Corporate Fiction*, 10; quotation, 3.

95. Wormser, *Disregard of the Corporate Fiction*, 19–20.

96. Wormser, *Disregard of the Corporate Fiction*, 30; on fraudulent corporate fictions, 40–41.

97. Stefan Andriopoulos, *Possessed: Hypnotic Crimes, Corporate Fiction, and the Invention of Cinema*, trans. Peter Jansen and Stefan Andriopoulos (Chicago: University of Chicago Press, 2008), 42–65.

98. The doctrine of "veil piercing" also weakened legal protections in cases where the injustice of the law was at issue; Wormser, *Disregard of the Corporate Fiction*, 26–27. On the performativity of gender, see Judith Butler, *Gender Trouble: Feminism and the Subversion of Identity* (New York: Routledge, 1990).

99. John Dewey, "The Historic Background of Corporate Legal Personality," *Yale Law Journal* 35, no. 6 (April 1926): 661.

2. Greek Lines: The Geometry of Thought

1. Louisa Caroline Tuthill, *History of Architecture from the Earliest Times; Its Present Condition in Europe and the United States; with a Biography of Eminent Architects and a Glossary of Architectural Terms* (Philadelphia: Lindsay and Blakiston, 1848), frontis, title page.

2. Sarah Allaback, "The Writings of Louisa Tuthill: Cultivating Architectural Taste in Nineteenth-Century America" (PhD diss. MIT, 1993), 66–110. See also Allaback, "Louisa Tuthill, Ithiel Town, and the Beginnings of Architectural History Writing in America," in *American Architects and Their Books to 1848*, ed. Kenneth Hafertepe and James F. O'Gorman (Amherst: University of Massachusetts Press, 2001), 199–215. For the later academic context, see Gwendolyn Wright and Janet Parks, eds., *The History of History in American Schools of Architecture 1865–1975* (New York: Temple Hoyne Buell Center for the Study of American Architecture, Columbia University/Princeton Architectural Press, 1990).

3. Tuthill, *History of Architecture*, viii.

4. The American Institute of Architects (AIA) was founded in New York in 1836. Although mechanics institutes had trained students in architectural drafting, design, and even history since the 1820s, aspiring architects commonly apprenticed in offices. William Ware established the first university program of professional studies in architecture at the Massachusetts Institute of Technology (MIT) in 1868. Mary Woods, *From Craft to*

Profession: The Practice of Architecture in Nineteenth-Century America (Berkeley: University of California Press, 1999), 28–30, 66–71. As Michael J. Lewis has shown, polytechnics led in the establishment of college-level architectural education. Lewis, "The Battle Between Polytechnic and Beaux-Arts in the American University," in *Architecture School: Three Centuries of Educating Architects in North America*, ed. Joan Ockman (Cambridge, MA: MIT Press, 2012), 66–89. For a history prior to 1860, see Dell Upton, "Defining the Profession," in Ockman, *Architecture School*, 36–65.

5. Tuthill, *History of Architecture*, ix.

6. Tuthill, *History of Architecture*, iii.

7. Tuthill, *History of Architecture*, v.

8. On two important architectural pattern books from the period, see Kenneth Hafertepe, "*The Country Builder's Assistant*: Text and Context," and Michael J. Lewis, "Owen Biddle and *The Young Carpenter's Assistant*," both in Hafertepe and O'Gorman, *American Architects*, 129–148 and 149–162.

9. On Tuthill's education and social context, see Allaback, "Writings of Louisa Tuthill," 14–65.

10. Allaback, "Louisa Tuthill, Ithiel Town, and the Beginnings," 205–208.

11. Tuthill, *History of Architecture*, 19. On the linear narratives typical of early architectural surveys like Tuthill's, see Petra Brouwer, "Handbook," in *The Printed and the Built: Architecture, Print Culture, and Public Debate in the Nineteenth Century*, ed. Mari Hvattum and Anne Hultzsch (London: Bloomsbury, 2018), 211–217. Other such handbooks included Thomas Talbot Bury, *Rudimentary Architecture* (London: John Weale, 1849); James Fergusson, *The Illustrated Handbook of Architecture* (London: John Murray, 1855); Wilhelm Lübke, *Geschichte der Architektur* (Leipzig: Emil Graul, 1855); and Franz Kugler, *Geschichte der Baukunst*, 3 vols. (Stuttgart: Ebner & Seubert, 1856–1873). Elsewhere, Brouwer has emphasized affinities between these handbooks and works of natural history, such as Charles Lyell's *Principles of Geology* (1830–1833). Brouwer, " 'Book Constructors': Architectural History Writing in the Nineteenth Century" (unpublished paper, Architecture of Science and the Humanities Workshop, National Institute for Advanced Study in the Humanities and Social Sciences, Amsterdam, May 2019).

12. Tuthill, *History of Architecture*, 20–21.

13. Tuthill, *History of Architecture*, 82.

14. Clara Erskine Clement [Waters], *An Outline History of Architecture for Beginners and Students, with Complete Indexes and Numerous Illustrations* (New York: White, Stokes & Allen, 1886), 46.

15. Allaback, "Writings of Louisa Tuthill," 42–47.

16. Louisa Tuthill, *I Will Be a Lady* (Boston: Crosby and Nichols, 1844), *I Will Be a Gentleman* (Boston: Crosby and Nichols, 1845), and *The Boarding School Girl* (Boston: Crosby and Nichols, 1848). For a complete bibliography of Tuthill's writings, see Allaback, "Writings of Louisa Tuthill," 189–191.

17. Caroline Winterer, *The Culture of Classicism: Ancient Greece and Rome in American Intellectual Life, 1780–1910* (Baltimore: Johns Hopkins University Press, 2002). On German philhellenic scholarship across the arts, see Suzanne L. Marchand, *Down from Olympus: Archaeology and Philhellenism in Germany, 1750–1970* (Princeton, NJ: Princeton University Press, 1996).

18. Nathalie Sinclair, *The History of the Geometry Curriculum in the United States* (Charlotte, NC: Information Age, 2008), 18.

19. Winterer, *Culture of Classicism*, 82.

20. On the teaching of Euclid in early American colleges, see Alva Walker Stamper, *A History of the Teaching of Elementary Geometry* (New York: Teachers College/Columbia

University, 1909), 96–100. See also Sinclair, *History of the Geometry Curriculum*, 14–18. On classical virtue, see J. G. A. Pocock, *The Machiavellian Moment: Florentine Political Thought and the Atlantic Republican Tradition* (Princeton, NJ: Princeton University Press, 1975), 506–552.

21. Thomas Jefferson, *Notes on the State of Virginia* [1785] (New York: Penguin, 1999), 146.

22. Henry Van Brunt, "Greek Lines," part 1, *Atlantic Monthly* 7, no. 44 (June 1861): 654–668, and "Greek Lines," part 2, *Atlantic Monthly* 8, no. 45 (July 1861): 76–88.

23. Van Brunt, "Greek Lines," part 2, 82.

24. Van Brunt, "Greek Lines," part 2, 87.

25. Friedrich Nietzsche, *The Birth of Tragedy* [1872] in *The Birth of Tragedy and Other Writings*, ed. Raymond Geuss and Ronald Speirs, trans. Ronald Speirs (Cambridge: Cambridge University Press, 1999), 1–116.

26. Van Brunt, "Greek Lines," part 1, 662.

27. Henry Van Brunt Diary (manuscript), vol. 1, March 13, 1852, n.p. Avery Library Classics Collection, Columbia University.

28. Harvard University, *Sixteenth Annual Report of the President of Harvard University to the Overseers on The State of the Institution for the Academic Year 1840–41* (Cambridge, MA: Thomas G. Wells, 1842), ii.

29. Van Brunt Diary, vol. 1, March 19, 1852, n.p.

30. Van Brunt diary vol. 2, September 12, 1852.

31. William A. Coles, introduction to *Architecture and Society: Selected Essays of Henry Van Brunt* (Cambridge, MA; Belknap Press of Harvard University Press, 1969), 3.

32. John Bullock, ed., *The History and Rudiments of Architecture; for the Use of Architects, Builders, Draughtsmen, Machinists, Engineers and Mechanics* (New York: Stringer & Townsend, 1853). Bullock's professions are listed in Bullock, *The American Cottage Builder: A Series of Designs, Plans, and Specifications from $200 to $20,000 for Homes for the People* (New York: Stringer & Townsend, 1854).

33. For an overview of architectural publishing in the United States at the time, see Kenneth Hafertepe and James F. O'Gorman, "Introduction: Architects and Their Books, 1840–1915," in *American Architects and Their Books to 1840–1915* (Amherst: University of Massachusetts Press, 2007), xv–xxii. Earlier data is available in Helen Park, *A List of Architectural Books Available in America before the Revolution*, 2nd rev. ed., (Los Angeles: Hennessey & Ingalls, 1973). See also Henry-Russell Hitchcock, *American Architectural Books: A List of Books, Portfolios, and Pamphlets on Architecture and Related Subjects Published in America Before 1895* (Minneapolis: University of Minnesota Press, 1946).

34. Louisa Caroline Tuthill, *History of Architecture*, viii. Tuthill is alluding to W. H. Leeds, "Modern Architecture and Architectural Study," *Foreign Quarterly Review* 7 no. 14 (April 1831): 432–461, which reviews Quatremère de Quincy's *Histoire de la Vie et des Ouvrages des plus célèbres Architectes du XIe Siècle jusqu'à la fin du XVIIe* (1830).

35. After reading *Uncle Tom's Cabin*, Van Brunt noted in his diary: "Mrs. Harriet Beecher Stowe is welcome to my admiration of her as an authoress; but as for her forms as a philanthropist, no true American, nor real lover of law, liberty & peace can envy her, or regard her in any other light but as a traitress to the holy cause of the country whose bosom has cherished her." Van Brunt Diary, vol. 3, March 1, 1853.

36. Harvard University, *Fourteenth Annual Report of the President of Harvard University to the Overseers on the State of the Institution for the Academic Year 1838–39* (Cambridge, MA: Folsom, Wells and Thurston, 1840), ii.

37. Benjamin Peirce, *An Elementary Treatise on Plane and Solid Geometry* (Boston: James Munroe, 1837), preface, iii; and Peirce, *An Elementary Treatise on Curves, Functions,*

and Forces, Volume First, Containing Analytic Geometry and the Differential Calculus (Boston: James Munroe, 1851), 163–212.

38. Raymond Clare Archibald, *Benjamin Peirce 1809–1880: Biographical Sketch and Bibliography* (Oberlin, OH: Mathematical Association of America, 1925), 8.

39. Simon Newcomb, quoted in Archibald, *Benjamin Peirce*, 13.

40. T. [Timothy] Walker, *Elements of Geometry with Practical Applications for the Use of Schools* (Boston: Richardson and Lord, 1829), xv; emphasis in original.

41. Of the many classical treatises reproduced in the early years of the printing press, Euclid's was among the latest, since printers had difficulty devising a technique for reproducing the figures set within the text. Thomas Heath, *The Thirteen Books of Euclid's Elements*, 2nd ed., vol. 1 (New York: Dover, 1956), 97. Heath reviews the translation and editions of Euclid into the nineteenth century.

42. Robert Simson's *The Elements of Euclid* (1756), printed in Philadelphia in 1803, and John Playfair's *Elements of Geometry* (1795), printed in the same city in 1806, were both available to mathematics teachers at the time. Florian Cajori, *The Teaching and History of Mathematics in the United States* (Washington, DC: Government Printing Office, 1890), 55. See also, Alva Walker Stamper, "A History of the Teaching of Elementary Geometry" (PhD diss., Columbia University, 1909), 99.

43. *Catalogue of Books in the Library of the Military Academy, August, 1822* (Newburgh, NY: Ward M. Gazlay, 1822), 17; also, Joe Albree, David C. Arney, and V. Frederick Rickey, *A Station Favorable to the Pursuits of Science: Primary Materials in the History of Mathematics at the United States Military Academy* (Providence, RI: American Mathematical Society, 1991), 13–14. For context and background, see Victoria Sanger, "L'influence et la genèse de l'enseignement du genie militaire à l'École de West Point," in *Les saviors de l'ingénieur militaire et l'édition de manuels, cours et cahiers 'd'exercises, 1751–1914*, ed. Émilie d'Orgeix and Isabelle Warmoes [conference proceedings] (Paris: Musée des Plans-Reliefs, 2013), 127–138. On Thayer's travels to France, see also Sidney Forman, *West Point: A History of the United States Military Academy* (New York: Columbia University Press, 1950), 41–43. On Ticknor, Everett, and others, see Winterer, *Culture of Classicism*, 52.

44. Edward D. Mansfield, "The Military Academy at West Point," *American Journal of Education* 13 (March 1863), 32.

45. Mansfield, "Military Academy at West Point," 31–33. See also Cajori, *Teaching and History of Mathematics*, 114–123; on Crozet's introduction of blackboards, 116–117. See also Peggy Aldrich Kidwell, Amy Ackerberg-Hastings, and David Lindsay Roberts, *Tools of American Mathematics Teaching, 1800–2000* (Baltimore and Washington, DC: Johns Hopkins University Press/Smithsonian Institution, 2008), 24–26. On West Point, see V. Frederick Rickey and Amy Shell-Gellasch, "Mathematics Education at West Point: The First Hundred Years," Mathematical Association of America, July 2010, https://www.maa.org/press/periodicals/convergence/mathematics-education-at-west-point-the-first-hundred-years-introduction. On Crozet at West Point, see also Robert F. Hunter and Edwin L. Dooley, Jr., *Claudius Crozet: French Engineer in America 1790–1864* (Charlottesville: University of Virginia Press, 1989), 18–30.

46. [Charles Davies], in A. M. Legendre, *Elements of Geometry and Trigonometry; with Notes, Revised and Altered for the Use of the Military at West Point*, trans. David Brewster, ed. Charles Davies (New York: James Ryan, 1828); preface to the American edition, iv. Davies added the reference to "the method of Euclid" in an 1834 edition. These comments also appear in later editions.

47. [John Farrar], in A. M. Legendre, *Elements of Geometry: Translated from the French for the Use of the Students of the University in Cambridge, N.E.*, trans. John Farrar

(Cambridge, MA: Hilliard and Metcalf, 1819), 4; and [Davies], in Legendre, *Elements of Geometry and Trigonometry*, 6.

48. Charles Davies, *Elements of Geometry and Trigonometry from the Works of A. M. Legendre* (New York: A. S. Barnes, 1862), iii.

49. On Davies and "mental discipline," see Amy K. Ackerberg-Hastings, "Mathematics Is a Gentleman's Art: Analysis and Synthesis in American College Geometry Teaching, 1790–1840" (PhD diss., Iowa State University, 2000), 254–262. For a summary, see Kidwell, Ackerberg-Hastings, and Roberts, *Tools of American Mathematics Teaching*, 10–20. See also Davies, *The Logic and Utility of Mathematics, with the Best Methods of Instruction Explained and Illustrated* (New York: A. S. Barnes, 1850), 28–29.

50. Edward W. Stevens, *The Grammar of the Machine: Technical Literacy and Early Industrial Expansion in the United States* (New Haven, CT: Yale University Press, 1995). On the use of blackboards, see Cajori, *Teaching and History of Mathematics*, 120.

51. Stevens, *Grammar of the Machine*, 97; also, 133–147. For a related account of an "occultist" approach to drawing in Germany around 1900, see Zeynep Çelik Alexander, *Kinaesthetic Knowing: Aesthetics, Epistemology, Modern Design* (Chicago: University of Chicago Press, 2017), 131–165.

52. On the interplay of "analytic" and "synthetic" models for mathematics education, see Ackerberg-Hastings, "Mathematics Is a Gentleman's Art," passim.

53. Palmer C. Ricketts, *History of Rensselaer Polytechnic Institute* (New York: John Wiley, 1914), 99. Already in 1841, a prospective student reported to Amos Eaton that he had mastered nearly all of Davies's Legendre. Stevens, *Grammar of the Machine*, 155. Given the textbook's popularity, it was no doubt in use well before that.

54. Stephen Van Rensselaer to Rev. Dr. Blatchford, November 5, 1824, adopted as the Constitution of the Rensselaer School. *The Constitution and Laws of Rensselaer School in Troy, New York Adopted by the Board of Trustees, March 11, 1825* (Troy, NY: Tuttle and Richards, 1825), 6; emphasis in original. Prior to the establishment of the Rensselaer School, formal training in engineering was limited to cadets at the Military Academy at West Point. Peter Lundgren, "Engineering Education in Europe and the USA, 1750–1930: The Rise to Dominance of School Culture and the Engineering Professions," *Annals of Science* 47 (1990): 33–75, esp. 52–55.

55. On the influence of Pestalozzi, see Stevens, *Grammar of the Machine*, 172. On the "Rensselaerean plan" (or what Stevens calls the "Rensselaerean system"), 151–152; see also Ricketts, *History of Rensselaer Polytechnic Institute*, 49, and on "Repeaters," 97–98. The reorganization of Rensselaer as a polytechnic began in 1849 under B. Franklin Greene in partial emulation of French and German models. Lundgren, "Engineering Education," 52–55; and William E. Wickenden, *A Comparative Study of Engineering Education in the United States and in Europe, Bulletin No. 16 of the Investigation of Engineering Education* (Lancaster, PA: Society for the Promotion of Engineering Education, 1929), 63–64.

56. Kidwell, Ackerberg-Hastings, and Roberts, *Tools of American Mathematics Teaching*, 31–33. On related forms of visual pedagogy in Germany, see Alexander, *Kinaesthetic Knowing*, 131–165; and on primitivism and visual pedagogy in the "industrial arts," see Ginger Nolan, *Weltgeist/Wildegeist: The Savage Inside 'World History,'* " *Grey Room* 64 (Summer 2016): 40–63.

57. Van Brunt, "Greek Lines," Part 1, 659. The transcription of the Ancient Greek is Van Brunt's.

58. Van Brunt, "Greek Lines," part 1, 662.

59. Van Brunt, "Greek Lines," part 2, 87.

60. Van Brunt, "Greek Lines," part 2, 86; emphasis in original.

61. Van Brunt, "Greek Lines," part 2, 86–87. On Constant-Dufeux, see Ralph Ghoche, "Simon-Claude Constant-Dufeux and the Symbolic Interpretation of Architectural Origins in 19th-Century France," *Architectural Histories* 6, no. 1 (2018): 1–14.

62. Neil Levine, "The Book and the Building: Hugo's Theory of Architecture and Labrouste's Bibliothèque Ste.-Geneviève," in *The Beaux-Arts and Nineteenth-Century French Architecture*, ed. Robin Middleton (Cambridge, MA: MIT Press, 1982), 138–173.

63. Henry James, *The Bostonians* (London: Macmillan, 1886), 240.

64. The Harvard University website cites Holworthy Hall as getting "the first gas lights in the yard" in 1855; "Historical Facts," Harvard University (website), accessed July 1, 2020, http://www.harvard.edu/historical-facts.

65. James, *The Bostonians*, 242.

66. Reinhart Koselleck, "War Memorials: Identity Formations of the Survivors," trans. Todd Presner, in *The Practice of Conceptual History: Timing History, Spacing Concepts* (Redwood City, CA: Stanford University Press, 2002), 285–325. Koselleck interprets the requirement by the Northern states during the U.S. Civil War that every dead Union soldier be commemorated individually as an indication of the "democratization of death," 317–318.

67. In the United States, historians generally date the commemoration of war dead in lists to the Civil War, and in Europe to the First World War. Graham Oliver, "Naming the Dead, Writing the Individual: Classical Traditions and Commemorative Practices in the Nineteenth and Twentieth Centuries," in *Cultures of Commemoration: War Memorials, Ancient and Modern*, ed. Polly Low, Graham Oliver, and P. J. Rhodes (New York: Oxford University Press, 2012), 113–134. A related practice was the annual observance of Memorial Day, which began in 1868. David W. Blight, "Decoration Days: The Origins of Memorial Day in North and South," in *The Memory of the Civil War in American Culture*, ed. Alice Fahs and Joan Waugh (Chapel Hill, NC: The University of North Carolina Press, 2004), 94–129. Among the precursors to lists of the dead on Civil War monuments were the casualty lists published in newspapers following major battles, and the "Rolls of Honor" published by most Northern states. Often, casualties were initially deduced from "muster rolls" completed by officers prior to each battle. Drew Gilpin Faust, *This Republic of Suffering: Death and the American Civil War* (New York: Knopf, 2008), 104–106, 254–255. See also Faust, " 'Numbers on Top of Numbers': Counting the Civil War Dead," *Journal of Military History* 70, no. 4 (October 2006): 995–1009.

68. [Everet A. or George L. Duyckinck?] "Poe's Works," *Literary World* 6, no. 156 (January 26, 1850): 81. Review of N. P. Willis, J. R. Lowell, and R. W. Griswold, eds., *The Works of the Late Edgar Allan Poe: With Notices of His Life and Genius*, vols. 1 and 2 (New York: J. S. Redfield, 1850).

69. Charles W. Larned, *On the History of the Battle Monument at West Point* (West Point, NY: Devinne Press, 1898), 1–18; for the list of names, 113–193; for the numbers, 194–196; also Forman, *West Point*, 130–131. On the monument's design, see Mosette Broderick, *Triumverate: McKim, Mead & White: Art, Architecture, Scandal, and Class in America's Gilded Age* (New York: Knopf Doubleday, 2010), 352–354.

70. Until recently, the most widely accepted count of Civil War dead among Union soldiers was 360,222 (Faust, *This Republic of Suffering*, 255). To this were added approximately 258,000 Confederate deaths, for a total of 618,222. In 2011, the demographic historian J. David Hacker used census data to revise this count to at least 750,000 and perhaps as high as 850,000. Guy Gugliotta, "New Estimate Raises Civil War Death Toll," *New York Times*, April 2, 2012, https://www.nytimes.com/2012/04/03/science/civil-war-toll-up-by-20-percent-in-new-estimate.html; and J. David Hacker, "A Census-Based Count of the Civil War Dead," *Civil War History* 57, no. 4 (December 2011): 307–348.

3. Bricks and Stones: Time-Based Media

1. M. Carey Thomas, "Closing Address," in Bryn Mawr College, *Bryn Mawr College Twenty-Fifth Anniversary, October Twenty-First and Twenty-Second, 1910* (Bryn Mawr, PA: 1910), 49. The ceremony's proceedings note that due to the "lateness of the hour" Thomas was only able to deliver a single paragraph of her speech (42).

2. On social reform and architecture in the nineteenth century, see Dolores Hayden, *The Grand Domestic Revolution: A History of Feminist Designs for American Homes, Neighborhoods, and Cities* (Cambridge, MA: MIT Press, 1981); Carla Yanni, *The Architecture of Madness: Insane Asylums in the United States* (Minneapolis: University of Minnesota Press, 2007); and Irene Cheng, "Race and Architectural Geometry: Thomas Jefferson's Octagons," *J19: Journal of Nineteenth-Century Americanists* 3, no. 1 (Spring 2015): 121–130.

3. On the history of women's colleges in the United States, see Helen Lefkowitz Horowitz, *Alma Mater: Design and Experience in the Women's Colleges from Their Nineteenth-Century Beginnings to the 1930s*, 2nd ed. (Amherst: University of Massachusetts Press, 1993).

4. Horace Howard Furness, "Address," in Bryn Mawr College, *Bryn Mawr College Twenty-Fifth Anniversary*, 41.

5. On Collegiate Gothic, see Michael J. Lewis, *The Gothic Revival* (London: Thames & Hudson, 2002), 185–189. The reference is to John Ruskin, *The Stones of Venice* [1851–1853] (New York: Da Capo, 1985). On the Collegiate Gothic dormitories at Bryn Mawr, see George E. Thomas, "The Architecture of the Bryn Mawr Campus," *Architecture, Grounds, and History* 5 (1978): http://repository.brynmawr.edu/facilities_history/5; and Michelle Osborn, "The Making of the Early Bryn Mawr Campus (Parts I–II)," *Bryn Mawr Now* 2, nos. 1–2 (September-November 1974): https://repository.brynmawr.edu/facilities_history/6/.

6. On the architectural history of corridors, see Mark Jarzombek, "Corridor Spaces," *Critical Inquiry* 36 (Summer 2010): 728–770; and Robin Evans, "Figures, Doors, and Passages," *Architectural Design* 4 (1978): 267–278; on corridors as "service" media, see Markus Krajewski, *The Server: A Media History from the Present to the Baroque*, trans. Ilinca Iurascu (New Haven, CT: Yale University Press, 2018), esp. 66–73.

7. M. Carey Thomas, "Closing Address," 45.

8. Paul Venable Turner, *Campus: An American Planning Tradition* (Cambridge, MA: MIT Press, 1984), 17–51.

9. Horowitz, *Alma Mater*, 9–55.

10. Horowitz, *Alma Mater*, 69–81, 105–133; on Oberlin, see Carla Yanni, *Living on Campus: An Architectural History of the American Dormitory* (Minneapolis: University of Minnesota Press, 2019), 79–116.

11. Horowitz, *Alma Mater*, 77–78; on Wellesley, 87–90.

12. Horowitz, *Alma Matter*, 21–24; quotation, 22.

13. Vassar also expressed admiration for the [Thomas] Guy's Hospital in London. Rosalie Thorne McKenna, "James Renwick, Jr. and the Second Empire Style in the United States," *Magazine of Art* 44, no. 3 (March 1951): 97–101; Horowitz, *Alma Mater*, 28–35.

14. On Renwick, see McKenna, "James Renwick, Jr.," 97–101. The asylum type—usually with double-loaded corridors—to which Renwick's building is related was known as the "Kirkbride plan." See Yanni, *Architecture of Madness*, 51–78; on its relation to Vassar, 95–97.

15. John Benson Lossing, *Vassar College and Its Founder* (New York: C. A. Alvord, 1867), 113ff. On "corridor teachers" and residential occupancy, Horowitz, *Alma Mater*, 35–39; quotation, 35.

16. Frances A. Wood, *Earliest Years at Vassar: Personal Recollections* (Poughkeepsie, NY: Vassar College Press, 1909), 29, 34–35.

17. Wood, *Earliest Years at Vassar*, 21. The schedule for 1867 is also described in Frances T. Marburg, "The Social Life of Vassar Students," *Vassar Miscellany*, special number (October 1915): 7.

18. Irene Anderson to Norton B. Anderson, October 10, 1866, 3–6; Vassar College Special Collections, 54115, Folder 64.2, Vassar College Digital Library, https://digitallibrary.vassar.edu/islandora/object/vassar%3A54115#page/1/mode/1up. Anderson attended recitations during four of the six periods, the other two being reserved for music practice.

19. Mary Harriott Norris, *The Golden Age of Vassar* (Poughkeepsie, NY: Vassar College, 1915), 20–21.

20. Lossing, *Vassar College*, 124.

21. Molly McCarthy, "The Diary and the Pocket-Watch: Rethinking Time in Nineteenth Century America," in *Controlling Time and Shaping the Self: Developments in Autobiographical Writing since the Sixteenth Century*, ed. Arianne Baggerman, Rudolf Dekker, and Michael Mascush (Leiden and Boston: Koninklijke Brill NV, 2011), 121–145. Also McCarthy, *The Accidental Diarist: A History of the Daily Planner in America* (Chicago: University of Chicago Press, 2013). On blank pages, blank books, and job printing during this period, see Lisa Gitelman, *Paper Knowledge: Toward a Media History of Documents* (Durham, NC: Duke University Press, 2014), 21–52.

22. Frances M. Bromley Diary, 1876. Vassar College Archives and Special Collections, Student Diaries, Box 122, VC Ex 1879. Vassar College Digital Library, https://digitallibrary.vassar.edu/islandora/object/vassar%3A2774#page/37/mode/1up. On the standardization of diaries, including the Excelsior Diary and the Standard Diary, and clock time, see McCarthy, *Accidental Diarist*, 153–200.

23. Raymond remained active at Vassar following her graduation in 1883. Cornelia M. Raymond Diary, 1895. Student Diaries, Box 122, VC 1883. Vassar College Digital Library, https://digitallibrary.vassar.edu/islandora/object/vassar%3A2762#page/1/mode/1up.

24. John Howard Raymond to Cornelia Raymond, September 23, 1865, reproduced in Adoniram Judson, *Life and Letters of John Howard Raymond, Late President of Vassar College* (New York: Fords, Howard & Hulbery, 1881), 559; also quoted in Horowitz, *Alma Mater*, 41.

25. Lossing, *Vassar College and Its Founder*, 115.

26. Lossing, *Vassar College and Its Founder*, 113. McKenna emphasizes the brick-against-trees color palate, "James Renwick, Jr.," 101.

27. Lossing, *Vassar College and Its Founder*, 148–149.

28. Renée Bergland, *Maria Mitchell and the Sexing of Science: An Astronomer Among the American Romantics* (Boston: Beacon Press, 2008), 195.

29. Maria Mitchell [as William Mitchell], "On the Comet of the 10th Month, (October 1st) 1847," *American Journal of Science and Arts* 5, no. 8 (May 1848): 83–85. Mitchell was also among the founding members and later president of the Association for the Advancement of Women (AAW, founded 1873), where she advocated for women's access to higher education, and in particular to science. Sally Gregory Kohlstedt, "Maria Mitchell: The Advancement of Women in Science," *New England Quarterly* 51, no. 1 (March 1978): 39–63.

30. Phebe Mitchell Kendall, *Maria Mitchell: Life, Letters, and Journals* (Boston: Lee and Shepard, 1896), 223–232.

31. Vassar contracted former mayor of Poughkeepsie William Harlow to oversee the construction. Rosalie Thorne McKenna, "Mr. Vassar's Consecrated Brick," *Vassar Quarterly* 35, no. 6 (June 1950): 5–9. Vassar's family had been involved in the brickmaking business,

and in the 1830s his brother Charles operated a brickyard very near what would become the Vassar campus. Edmund Platt, *The Eagle's History of Poughkeepsie from the Earliest Settlements, 1683–1905* (Poughkeepsie, NY: Platt & Platt, 1905), 136; and "The Rise and Fall of 'Brickyard Hill,'" Casperkill Watershed Oral History Project, Vassar College Environmental Research Institute, June 3, 2010, https://pages.vassar.edu/casperkill/the-rise -and-fall-of-brickyard-hill/. On brickmaking in the Northeast during the 1850s and 1860s, see I. B. Holley Jr., "The Mechanization of Brickmaking," *History of Technology* 50, no. 1 (January 2009): 82–102. One of the most important brickmaking machines was designed in 1852 by Richard VerValen, in Haverstraw, about forty miles south and across the Hudson River from Poughkeepsie. "BRICK! BRICK! BRICK!—THE BEST AND MOST" [advertisement], *Scientific American* 13, no. 10 (2 September 1865): 156; on the VerValen machine and brickmaking in Rockland County, see Daniel DeNoyelles, *Within These Gates* (Thiells, NY: [self-published], 1982), 9–15; further details in George V. Hutton, *The Great Hudson River Brick Industry: Commemorating Three and One Half Centuries of Brickmaking* (Fleischmanns, NY: Purple Mountain Press, 2003), 11–131. I am grateful to Ife Salema Vanable for calling my attention to the significance of Hudson Valley common brick during this period.

32. Booker T. Washington, *Working with the Hands: Being a Sequel to "Up from Slavery" Covering the Author's Experiences in Industrial Training at Tuskegee* (New York: Doubleday, 1904), 72–73.

33. By 1904 there were two brickyards on the Tuskegee grounds, with a brickmaking machine on each site. Robert R. Taylor to Booker T. Washington, March 5, 1904. Booker T. Washington Papers, Reel 445, Tuskegee University Archives. I am grateful to Tuskegee archivist Dana Chandler for guiding me to one of these former brickyard sites. On Tuskegee's first brickyard, and on the first wooden, horse-powered brickmaking machine (later replaced by the two mechanical devices), see *Tuskegee to Date* (Tuskegee, AL: Tuskegee Institute, 1915), 5. On brickmaking and brick masonry at Tuskegee, see for example *Tuskegee Normal and Industrial Institute, Tuskegee, Alabama: Catalogue 1897–97* (Tuskegee, AL: Normal School Steam Press, 1897), 78–79. On the early buildings at Tuskegee, see Ellen Weiss, *Robert R. Taylor and Tuskegee: An African American Architect Designs for Booker T. Washington* (Montgomery, AL: New South Books, 2012), 20–44. The institute's annual report for 1884 records four hundred thousand bricks made, most of which were used in the new building, with student labor going toward boarding expenses. *Third Annual Report of the Tuskegee Normal School for the Fiscal Year Ending August 31st, 1884* (Hampton, VA: Normal School Steam Press, 1885), 13.

34. *Twenty-Third Annual Catalogue of the Tuskegee Normal and Industrial Institute, Tuskegee, Alabama, 1903–1904* (Tuskegee, AL: Tuskegee Institute, [1904]), 15.

35. For details on industrial curricula for men and women, see *Twenty-Third Annual Catalogue*, 61–91.

36. Weiss, *Robert R. Taylor and Tuskegee*, 41–42, 47–52. Unlike at other historically Black institutions such as the Hampton Institute, the entirety of the Tuskegee faculty and administration were African American. Mary N. Woods, *From Craft to Profession: The Practice of Architecture in Nineteenth-Century America* (Berkeley: University of California Press, 1999), 73–75. Notably, Maura Lucking shows how technical drawing and construction functioned at Tuskegee as "object lessons." Lucking, "Technical Drawing as an Object Lesson at Tuskegee," in "American Artisan: Design and Race-Making in Industrial Education" (PhD diss., University of California, Los Angeles), in progress.

37. By 1902, architectural drawing was taught by W. Sidney Pittman and mechanical drawing was taught by Wallace A. Rayfield; *Twenty-Third Annual Catalogue*, 8; for the curriculum for architectural drawing, 77–79.

38. Washington, *Working with the Hands*, 77.

39. *Twenty-Third Annual Catalogue*, 23.

40. W. E. B. Du Bois, "Of the Training of Black Men," in *The Souls of Black Folk [1903]: Authoritative Text, Contexts, Criticism*, ed. Henry Louis Gates Jr. and Terri Hume Oliver (New York: W. W. Norton, 1999), 65.

41. Du Bois, "Of the Training of Black Men," 65.

42. Du Bois, "Of the Training of Black Men," 67.

43. Du Bois, "Of the Training of Black Men," 67.

44. Du Bois, "Of the Training of Black Men," 69.

45. Du Bois first used the expression the "Talented Tenth" in an earlier version of this chapter published in the *Atlantic Monthly* (September 1902): 287–297. The statistics given are his: Du Bois, "Of the Training of Black Men," 72. See also Du Bois, "The Talented Tenth," in Booker T. Washington et al., *The Negro Problem: A Series of Articles by Representative American Negroes of To-Day* (New York: James Pott & Co., 1903), 31–75.

46. Elliott M. Rudwick, "W. E. B. Du Bois and the Atlanta University Studies on the Negro," *Journal of Negro Education* 26, no. 4 (Autumn 1957): 466–476. See also Kimberly E. Nichols, "Atlanta Conferences for the Study of Negro Problems," in *Organizing Black America: An Encyclopedia of African American Associations*, ed. Nina Mjagkij (New York: Routledge, 2013), 72–73.

47. W. E. B. Du Bois, ed., *The College-Bred Negro: Report of a Social Study Made Under the Direction of Atlanta University; Together with the Proceedings of the Fifth Conference for the Study of the Negro Problems, Held at Atlanta University, May 29–30, 1900* (Atlanta, GA: Atlanta University Press, 1900); and Du Bois, ed. *The Negro Artisan: Report of a Social Study Made Under the Direction of Atlanta University; Together with the Proceedings of the Seventh Conference for the Study of the Negro Problems, Held at Atlanta University, on May 27, 1902* (Atlanta, GA: Atlanta University Press, 1902). Du Bois cites the report on "The College-Bred Negro" in "Of the Training of Black Men," 70. Du Bois also prepared striking visual materials based on his 1900 study of the "Georgia Negro" as part of the 1900 "American Negro" exhibit at the Exposition Universelle in Paris. Mabel O. Wilson, *Negro Building: Black Americans in the World of Fairs and Museums* (Berkeley: University of California Press, 2012), 107–112.

48. Du Bois, *College-Bred Negro*, 10–11. About 2,500 questionnaires were sent out, 1,252 were returned.

49. Du Bois, *College-Bred Negro*, 12–14. Around 1900, of the historically Black colleges and universities (HBCUs) Fisk, where Du Bois graduated in 1888, and Atlanta most closely approximated the Northern liberal arts model; Howard, with more graduate students than undergraduates, was the only "true" university. Roger L. Geiger, *The History of American Higher Education: Learning and Culture from the Founding to World War II* (Princeton, NJ: Princeton University Press, 2015), 467–472. Du Bois's first teaching appointment was at Wilberforce, where he taught classics and modern languages from 1894 to 1896. On the early HBCUs, see Bobby L. Lovett, *America's Historically Black Colleges and Universities: A Narrative History* (Macon, GA: Mercer University Press, 2011), 1–41.

50. Du Bois, *Negro Artisan*, 9.

51. Du Bois, *Negro Artisan*, 33–39.

52. Du Bois, *Negro Artisan*, 32.

53. Du Bois, "Of the Training of Black Men," 73.

54. Du Bois spent one and a half years in Germany, from fall 1892 to winter 1894, as a graduate student at the University of Berlin. W. E. B. Du Bois, *Dusk of Dawn* [1940], ed. Henry Louis Gates Jr. (New York: Oxford University Press, 2007), 23. On Du Bois's exposure

to German social thought, see Francis L. Broderick, "German Influence on the Scholarship of W. E. B. Du Bois," *Phylon Quarterly* 19, no. 4 (4th quarter, 1958): 367–371; and Kenneth D. Barkin, " 'Berlin Days,' 1892–1894: W. E. B. Du Bois and German Political Economy," *Boundary* 2 27, no. 3 (2000): 79–101.

55. Du Bois, "Of the Training of Black Men," 73. Speaking on behalf of Atlanta University ten years later, Du Bois extended his arguments to a "college-bred community." W. E. B. Du Bois, "The College-Bred Community," in *The Education of Black People: Ten Critiques, 1906–1960*, 2nd ed., ed. Herbert Apthekar (New York: Monthly Review Press, 2001), 49–59.

56. Warren Logan, "Life in and Around the School from a Teacher's Standpoint," in *Tuskegee Normal and Industrial School for Training Colored Teachers at Tuskegee, Alabama: Its Story and Its Songs*, ed. Helen W. Ludlow (Hampton, VA: Normal School Steam Press, 1884), 21.

57. Thomas, "Closing Address," 46.

58. Thomas, "Closing Address," 48. On the "random ashlar" of Pembroke's walls, see also William Emlyn Stewardson, "Cope and Stewardson: The Architects of a Philadelphia Renascence" (A.B. thesis, Princeton University, May 2, 1960), 65–66.

59. Thomas, "Closing Address," 48–49.

60. On the detailing of these dormitories, including the use of Germantown stone, see Stewardson, "Cope and Stewardson," 58–66.

61. The Cambridge type, which Bryn Mawr's Pembroke most clearly resembles, first took on its distinctive corner turrets at King Edward's Gate, Trinity College (1427), followed by Queens College two decades later. Examples from the Tudor period include Christ's College (1505), St. John's College (1510), the Great Gate at Trinity College (1518), and the Queen's Gate (1597). Robert Willis, *The Architectural History of the University of Cambridge, and of the Colleges of Cambridge and Eton*, ed. John Willis Clark, vol. 3, (Cambridge: Cambridge University Press, 1886), 284–296.

62. Ralph Adams Cram, "The Work of Messrs. Cope & Stewardson," *Architectural Record* 16, no. 5 (November 1904): 411.

63. Cram, "Work of Messrs. Cope & Stewardson," 411, 413, 417, 423.

64. On eighteenth-century racial and ethnological typologies, and the racial hierarchies claimed by later white supremacists, see George M. Frederickson, *Racism: A Short History* (Princeton, NJ: Princeton University Press, 2002), 49–95. Although white supremacist ideologies had circulated for centuries, prior to the nineteenth century race was most commonly understood in civilizational terms that referred to generational lineages. See, for example, Michael Banton, *The Idea of Race* (London: Tavistock Publications, 1977), 18–22. On race during the European eighteenth century, see Ivan Hannaford, *Race: The History of an Idea in the West* (Washington, DC: Woodrow Wilson Center Press, 1996), 187–233; on the passage from a "conflict among races" to a historico-biological discourse of degeneration, and then to "the rise of the race-state," 235–324. For the American context, see Thomas F. Gossett, *Race: The History of an Idea in America* (Dallas, TX: Southern Methodist University Press, 1963).

65. Cram, "Work of Messrs. Cope & Stewardson," 412–413.

66. Ralph Adams Cram, *End of Democracy* (Boston: Marshall Jones Company, 1937), 144.

67. Cram, "Work of Messrs. Cope & Stewardson," 418.

68. A detailed description of the gate's heraldry is given in "Biennial Report on Higher Education in Pennsylvania [1904]," *Official Documents Comprising the Department and Other Reports, Made to the Governor, Senate and House of Representatives of Pennsylvania*, vol. 9 (Harrisburg, PA: Harrisburg Publishing Company, State Printer, 1906), 604.

69. M. Carey Thomas, "The College," in *Congress of Arts and Science: Universal Exposition, St. Louis, 1904*, ed. Howard Jason Rogers, vol. 8 (Boston: Houghton, Mifflin, 1907), 133–150.

70. Charles Eliot, "President's Report," in *Annual Reports of the President and the Treasurer of Harvard College 1901–02* (Cambridge, MA: Harvard University, 1903), 23. On the introduction of the elective system at Harvard and elsewhere, see Frederick Rudolph, *Curriculum: A History of the American Undergraduate Course of Study since 1636* (San Francisco: Jossey-Bass, 1977), 135–138, 191–196. On the undergraduate "group system" at Johns Hopkins University in the 1880s, see John C. French, *A History of the University Founded by Johns Hopkins* (Baltimore, MD: Johns Hopkins Press, 1946), 66–68.

71. This also reflected Bryn Mawr's stated commitment to advanced scholarship at the collegiate level, while preserving the older project of molding the student according to classical ideals. Thomas, "The College," 146–147.

72. As Eliot put it in his 1901–1902 report, which Thomas cited, the six Harvard classes from 1872–1877 (early into Eliot's tenure) on which the university had kept "vital statistics" as a means of tracking its alumni "have by no means reproduced themselves." Eliot, "President's Report," 24–32.

73. Thomas, "The College," 142. Women's colleges were frequently viewed as delaying or preempting marriage. Patricia A. Palmieri, "From Republican Motherhood to Race Suicide: Arguments on the Higher Education of Women in the United States, 1820–1920," in *Educating Men and Women Together: Coeducation in a Changing World*, ed. Carol Lasser (Urbana: University of Illinois Press in conjunction with Oberlin College, 1987), 49–64.

74. Thomas arranged support for Fauset to attend Cornell instead. Helen Lefkowitz Horowitz, *The Power and Passion of M. Carey Thomas* (New York: Knopf, 1994), 340–343.

75. Thomas, "The College," 139.

76. Thomas, "The College," 147–148, 149, 150.

77. William De Witt Hyde, "The College," in Rogers, *Congress of Arts and Science*, vol. 8, 132. The schedule of the congress is given in *International Congress of Arts and Science, Universal Exposition, St. Louis, September 19–25, 1904: Programme and List of Speakers* (June 1904), 9–33.

78. Isaac S. Taylor, "Report Presented to David R. Francis, President of the Louisiana Purchase Exhibition," June 1905, 4–5. Isaac S. Taylor Papers, University Archives, Washington University in St. Louis, Box 1. See also, Ralph E. Morrow, *Washington University in St. Louis: A History* (St. Louis: Missouri Historical Society Press, 1996), 164–169.

79. Cope & Stewardson, Architects, "New Buildings for Washington University St. Louis: Explanation of Drawings," undated typescript, 3. Hilltop Campus Architectural Competition, 1899 Information Files, University Archives, Washington University in St. Louis, Box 1. Cope made these remarks to the Washington University Board of Trustees. Candace O'Connor, *Beginning a Great Work: Washington University in St. Louis, 1853–2003* (St. Louis, MO: Washington University in St. Louis, 2003), 87.

80. James P. Jamieson, *Intimate History of the Campus and Buildings of Washington University Saint Louis* (St. Louis: Mound City Press [private publication], 1941), 14–15. Washington University in St. Louis, University Archives. See also O'Connor, *Beginning a Great Work*, 87–88; and Stewardson, "Cope and Stewardson," 90–92.

81. Cope & Stewardson, Architects, "New Buildings," 4.

82. As Cram wrote of Cope and Stewardson's efforts at Washington University: "When a Greek drama has been translated into Latin, from this language into Italian, thence into Low Dutch, and so into English, there is not apt to be much in the original left, and it is hardly a good model to use as a basis for creative work." Cram, "Work of Messrs. Cope & Stewardson," 424.

83. Stewardson, "Cope and Stewardson," 92–93.

84. Andrew Zimmerman, *Alabama in Africa: Booker T. Washington, the German Empire, and the Globalization of the New South* (Princeton, NJ: Princeton University Press, 2010), 205–209.

85. Max Weber, "Relations of the Rural Community to Other Branches of Social Science," in *Congress of Arts and Science: Universal Exposition, St. Louis, 1904*, ed. Howard Jason Rogers, vol. 7 (Boston: Houghton Mifflin, 1906), 725–746.

86. Weber, "Relations of the Rural Community," 745.

87. Zimmerman, *Alabama in Africa*, 207–212.

88. Zimmerman, *Alabama in Africa*, esp. 100–111, 207–217. On Weber's racial theories, German colonialism in Africa, and the "internal colonization" of the Prussian Polish lands, see also Hollyamber Kennedy, "Modernism's Politics of Land: Settlement Colonialism and Migrant Mobility in the German Empire, from Prussian Poland to German Namibia, 1884–1918" (PhD diss., Columbia University, 2019).

89. Max Weber, "Science as a Vocation," in *From Max Weber: Essays in Sociology*, ed. and trans. H. H. Gerth and C. Wright Mills (New York: Routledge, 2009), 129–165.

90. Weber, "Science as a Vocation," 140–141.

4. Sources: A Political Ecology of Cultivation

1. Allan Nevins, *The State Universities and Democracy* (Urbana: University of Illinois Press, 1962), 13–16; quotation, 13.

2. Nevins (*State Universities and Democracy*, 15, n4) cites Sigfried Giedion, *Mechanization Takes Command: A Contribution to Anonymous History* (New York: Oxford University Press, 1948), 130–168.

3. The mechanization of letterpress printing advanced in the 1820s with the widespread use of stereotype plates. James N. Green, "The Rise of Book Publishing," in *A History of the Book in America*, ed. Robert A. Gross and Mary Kelley, vol. 2, *An Extensive Republic: Print, Culture, and Society in the New Nation, 1790–1840* (Chapel Hill: University of North Carolina Press/American Antiquarian Society, 2010), 113–118. For later developments, see Michael Winship, "Manufacturing and Book Production," in *A History of the Book in America*, ed. Scott E. Casper, Jeffrey D. Groves, Stephen W. Nissenbaum, and Michael Winship, vol. 3, *The Industrial Book, 1840–1880* (Chapel Hill: University of North Carolina Press/American Antiquarian Society, 2007), 42–48.

4. "An Act donating Public Lands to the several States and Territories which may provide Colleges for the Benefit of Agriculture and the Mechanic Arts [Morrill Act]," in *The Statutes at Large, Treaties, and Proclamations of the United States of America from December 5, 1859, to March 3, 1863*, ed. George P. Sanger, vol. 12 (Boston: Little, Brown, 1863), 503–505.

5. "Morrill Act," 504.

6. "An act to establish agricultural experiment stations in connection with the colleges established in several States under the provisions of an act approved July second, eighteen-hundred and sixty-two, and of the acts supplementary thereto [Hatch Act of 1887]," *Statutes at Large*, vol. 24, *Public Acts of the Forty-Ninth Congress* (1885–1887), 440–441.

7. Ferdinand Wohltmann, cited in Mark R. Finlay, "Transnational Exchanges of Agricultural Scientific Thought from the Morrill Act through the Hatch Act," in *Science as Service: Establishing and Reformulating American Land-Grant Universities, 1865–1930*,

ed. Alan Marcus (Tuscaloosa: University of Alabama Press, 2015), 50; emphasis in original.

8. Lisa Gitelman, *Paper Knowledge: Toward a Media History of Documents* (Durham, NC: Duke University Press, 2014), 1–5.

9. Roger Chartier, *The Order of Books: Readers, Authors, and Libraries in Europe Between the Fourteenth and Eighteenth Centuries*, trans. Lydia G. Cochrane (Redwood City, CA: Stanford University Press, 1994); also Robert Darnton, *The Business of Enlightenment: A Publishing History of the Encyclopédie 1775–1800* (Cambridge, MA: Harvard University Press, 1979), esp. 279.

10. Karl Marx, *Grundrisse: Foundations of the Critique of Political Economy (Rough Draft)* [1857–1858], trans. Martin Nicholas (New York: Penguin Books, 1993), 884.

11. Henry Charles Carey, *Harmony of Interests: Agricultural, Manufacturing, and Commercial* (Philadelphia: J. S. Skinner, 1851). John Bellamy Foster notes that by 1853, "Marx had read all of Carey's major works up to that date." *Marx's Ecology: Materialism and Nature* (New York: New York University Press, 2000), 285n29.

12. Marx, *Grundrisse*, 886.

13. William Elder, *A Memoir of Henry C. Carey, Read Before the Historical Society of Pennsylvania; Philadelphia, January 5, 1880* (Philadelphia: Henry Carey Baird, 1880), 27.

14. Henry Charles Carey, *The Past, The Present, and the Future* (Philadelphia: Carey & Hart, 1848), 95.

15. Carey, *The Past, The Present, and the Future*, 24–50.

16. Marx, *Grundrisse*, 888.

17. Carey's influence on Morrill is documented in Arnold W. Green, *Henry Charles Carey: Nineteenth Century Sociologist* (Philadelphia: University of Pennsylvania Press, 1951), 167, 189–191.

18. On Carey's status within the tradition of pamphleteers and lay authors of treatises on political economy, see A. D. H. Kaplan, *Henry Charles Carey: A Study in Economic Thought* (Baltimore, MD: Johns Hopkins Press, 1931), 18–28. On his academic influence, see Green, *Henry Charles Carey*, 172–204. Compare also Rodney Morrison, "Henry C. Carey and American Economic Development," *Transactions of the American Philosophical Society* 76, no. 3 (1986): i–ix, 1–91.

19. Green, *Henry Charles Carey*, 175–177. The quotation is from Wharton's agreement with the university, cited by Green, 177.

20. Nathan Sorber, "Creating Colleges of Science, Industry, and National Advancement: The Origins of the New England Land-Grant Colleges," in *The Land-Grant Colleges and the Reshaping of American Higher Education*, ed. Roger L. Geiger and Nathan M. Sorber (New Brunswick: Transaction, 2013), 55–56. On Carey's influence on Congressional debates during the 1850s, see Sarah T. Phillips, "Antebellum Agricultural Reform, Republican Ideology, and Sectional Tension," *Agricultural History* 74, no. 4 (Autumn 2000): 799–822. On Morrill (but with no mention of Carey), see also Coy F. Cross II, *Justin Smith Morrill: Father of the Land-Grant Colleges* (East Lansing: Michigan State University Press, 1999).

21. Henry Charles Carey, *Principles of Social Science*, vol. 3 (Philadelphia: J. B. Lippincott, 1859), 187.

22. James L. Huston, *Securing the Fruits of Labor: The American Concept of Wealth Distribution, 1765–1900* (Baton Rouge: Louisiana State University Press, 2015), 180–181. On Carey's diagram as a commodity map, see Michael Perelman, "Henry Carey's Political-Ecological Economics: An Introduction," *Organization & Environment* 12, no. 3 (September 1999): 286–288.

23. Carey, *Principles of Social Science*, vol. 3, 188.

24. Carey, *Principles of Social Science*, vol. 3, 321.

25. Carey writes of what his index calls the "inconsistencies" of "free-trade" as specifically those of the doctrine of laissez-faire. Carey, *Principles of Social Science*, vol. 3, 442–444. The quotation is from John Lalor, *Money and Morals: A Book for the Times* (London: John Chapman, 1852), 135–136. Initially a "free trader" himself, in the 1840s Carey began to adopt the protectionist position for which he became famous. Stephen Meardon, "Reciprocity and Henry C. Carey's Traverses on 'The Road to Perfect Freedom of Trade,' " *Journal of the History of Economic Thought* 33, no. 3 (September 2011): 307–333.

26. Alfred Charles True, *A History of Agricultural Education in the United States 1785–1925* (Washington, DC: United States Government Printing Office, 1929), 73–75. Also, Merle Curti and Vernon Carstensen, *The University of Wisconsin: A History, 1848–1925*, vol. 1 (Madison: University of Wisconsin Press, 1949), 296–326.

27. William A. Henry, "A Brief History of the Wisconsin Agricultural Experiment Station," in *Tenth Annual Report of the Agricultural Experiment Station of the University of Wisconsin for the Year Ending June 30, 1893* (Madison, WI: Democrat Printing, 1894), 3–6.

28. Henry, "Report of the Director," in *Tenth Annual Report*, 1.

29. William A. Henry, "A Brief History of the Wisconsin Agricultural Experiment Station," *Tenth Annual Report*, 5, 7–8. Details on the 1883 legislation are provided in "Laws Relative to the Experiment Station," in *First Annual Report of the Agricultural Experiment Station of the University of Wisconsin for the Year 1883* (Madison, WI: Democrat Printing, 1884), 5–6.

30. Henry P. Armsby, "Miscellaneous Chemical and Other Work," in *First Annual Report*, 80.

31. "Report of the Division of Feeding Stuffs and Fertilzers," in *Twentieth Annual Report of the Agricultural Experiment Station of the University of Wisconsin for the Year Ending June 30, 1903* (Madison, WI: Democrat Printing, 1904), 310–313.

32. William A. Henry, "Commercial Fertilizers—Bran and Corn Meal for Making Manure," in *Third Annual Report of the Agricultural Experiment Station of the University of Wisconsin for the Year 1885* (Madison, WI: Democrat Printing, 1886), 169–172.

33. "Report of the Officers of the Station," *Third Annual Report*, 5–8. Henry mentions the study of cow manure by "the German Experiment Stations" in "Commercial Fertilizers," 170–171.

34. William A. Henry, "Manshury Barley: An Account of Its Introduction and Dissemination," in *First Annual Report*, 17–21.

35. Henry, "Manshury Barley," 18–19.

36. Henry, "Manshury Barley," 19.

37. Henry, "Manshury Barley," 20–21. Further information on the dissemination of Manchurian barley in the United States is available in Christopher Martin Cumo, *The Ongoing Columbian Exchange: Stories of Biological and Economic Transfer in World History* (Santa Barbara, CA: ABC-CLIO, 2015), 22–23.

38. William A. Henry, "The New Agricultural Building," in *Twentieth Annual Report*, 7–12.

39. William A. Henry, "A Brief History of the Agricultural College and Agricultural Experiment Station of the University of Wisconsin," in *Twentieth Annual Report*, 20–23.

40. Henry, "Brief History of the Agricultural College," 23.

41. A detailed description, with plans, is provided in Henry, "New Agricultural Building," 6–12. Further detail is given in United States Department of the Interior National Park

Service, National Register of Historic Places Inventory—Nomination Form, "Agriculture Hall," submitted January 30, 1985. University Archives Record Group, University
of Wisconsin-Madison Archives, Madison, Wisconsin. National Register of Historic
Places-UW-Madison Properties, binder prepared by Daniel Einstein, February 11, 2004.

42. Henry, "New Agricultural Building," 11.

43. Henry, "Report of the Director," in *Twentieth Annual Report*, 4–5.

44. Henry, "Report of the Director," in *Twentieth Annual Report*, 5.

45. Richard A. Haney Jr., *College of Agriculture: A Century of Discovery* (Tucson: University
of Arizona, 1985), 5–19. The early history of the University of Arizona is also given in
Estelle Lutrell, "History of the University of Arizona 1885-1926, Supplementary Data
1936-1947," unpublished typescript, Estelle Lutrell Papers, University of Arizona Libraries, Special Collections, AZ 055, Box 1.

46. Frank A. Gulley, "Arizona Agricultural Experiment Station," *Arizona Agricultural
Experiment Station, Bulletin*, no. 1 (December 1, 1890): n.p.

47. James W. Toumey, "Notice," *Arizona Agricultural Experiment Station, Bulletin*, no. 2
(September 15, 1891): frontis.

48. Vasa E. Stolbrand, "Announcement," *Arizona Agricultural Experiment Station, Bulletin*,
no. 3 (October 1891): 15.

49. "Water and Water Analysis," *Arizona Agricultural Experiment Station, Bulletin*, no. 4
(November 1891): 1–3.

50. Haney, *College of Agriculture*, 23–28.

51. Haney, *College of Agriculture*, 37–38.

52. James W. Toumey, "The Date Palm," *Arizona Agricultural Experiment Station, Bulletin*,
no. 29 (June 15, 1898): 102–149.

53. On the Tempe date palm orchard, Haney, *College of Agriculture*, 38; Charles C. Col-
ley, *The Century of Robert H. Forbes* (Tucson: Arizona Historical Society, 1977), 18. On
Forbes's departure for Egypt, Haney, *College of Agriculture*, 97; Colley, *Century of Robert
H. Forbes*, 34–36.

54. Colley, *Century of Robert H. Forbes*, 37–52.

55. Robert H. Forbes, *Le Coton dans la vallée moyenne du Niger, Essais du culture, 1923-24*
(Paris: Gouvernement Générale de l'Afrique Occidentale Française, Service General de
Textiles et de l'Hydraulique Agricole, 1926). Forbes described the villagers he observed in
his travels in West Africa as "a complex semicivilization." Forbes, "The Black Man's Industries," *Geographical Review* 23, no. 2 (April 1933): 246–247. Colley cites Forbes's extensive
correspondence, his diaries, and his reports in *Century of Robert H. Forbes*, 53–74.

56. "La production du coton en Afrique Occidentale Française: La culture des cotonniers
égyptiens et américains," *Les Annales Coloniales* (November 4, 1924): 1–5. In 1929 the
French engineer Émile Bélime, Forbes's immediate successor in Ségou, also cited
Forbes's work comparing environmental effects on cotton in the United States and
French West Africa. Bélime, "La situation actuelle de la culture cotonnière en A.O.F.,"
Revue de botanique appliquée et d' agriculture tropicale 9 (1929): 14. On Forbes and
Bélime in Ségou: Colley, *Century of Robert H. Forbes*, 95. In 1921 Bélime had proposed
a vast irrigation scheme for French Soudan that included the reclamation of 460,000
hectares for cotton cultivation, with the aim of reducing the dependence of the French
textile industry on the United States as a source of cotton. By 1945, partial implementa-
tion of the project entailed the forced settlement of at least thirty thousand people from
across French West Africa. The project's "monumental failure" to produce a reliable cotton crop has been partly attributed to the inability of French agronomists to develop a
strain of cotton suited to the region's ecology. Jean Filipovich, "Destined to Fail: Forced

Settlement at the *Office du Niger, 1926–1945*," *Journal of African History* 42, no. 2 (2001): 239–260; On Bélime's irrigation scheme, see also Monica M. van Beusekom, "Disjunctures in Theory and Practice: Making Sense of Change in Agricultural Development at the *Office du Niger, 1920–1960*," *Journal of African History* 41, no. 1 (2000): 79–99.

57. Robert H. Forbes, "Colorado River Waters," in "The River-Irrigating Waters of Arizona—Their Character and Effects," *University of Arizona Agricultural Experiment Station Bulletin,* no. 44 (September 30, 1902): 206.

58. Forbes began his experiments comparing Egyptian, American, and indigenous varieties in the Niger River Valley in 1923. Richard L. Roberts, *Two Worlds of Cotton: Colonialism and the Regional Economy in the French Soudan, 1800–1946* (Redwood City, CA: Stanford University Press, 1996), 146–147. As Roberts explains, the French program of "cotton colonialism" was based on an analogy with the cultivation of irrigated cotton in the Nile Valley where Forbes had also worked, 118–144.

59. Walter Benjamin, "On the Concept of History" [1940], trans. Harry Zohn, in *Walter Benjamin: Selected Writings*, vol. 4, *1938–1940*, ed. Howard Eiland and Michael W. Jennings (Cambridge, MA: Harvard University Press, 2003), 395.

60. Timothy Mitchell has contributed key concepts to the study of colonial political economy and postcolonial "development," most especially regarding the "techno-politics" of expert knowledge. Mitchell, *Rule of Experts: Egypt, Techno-Politics, Modernity* (Berkeley: University of California Press, 2002), esp. 19–53. On Barak has shown how the Nile has also been an important site for peasant struggles over the control of time and temporality in relation to infrastructural systems. Barak, *On Time: Technology and Temporality in Modern Egypt* (Berkeley: University of California Press, 2013), 193–200.

61. Karl Marx, *Capital*, vol. 3, *The Process of Capitalist Production as a Whole*, ed. Frederick Engels (New York: International Publishers, 1967), 773–774.

62. Marx, *Capital*, vol. 3, 619–620. Engels, in an editor's note, cites Carey's *The Past, the Present, and the Future*, 129–131.

63. On Marx reading Liebig, Foster, *Marx's Ecology*, 155ff. On the reception of Liebig's work in the United States, Margaret W. Rossiter, *The Emergence of Agricultural Science: Justus Liebig and the Americans, 1840–1880* (New Haven, CT: Yale University Press, 1975).

64. Foster, *Marx's Ecology*, 152–154, 285n29.

65. On racial segregation at Texas A&M, see "In Fulfillment of a Dream: African-Americans at Texas A&M University," Texas A&M University library (website), accessed July 8, 2020, https://archiveexhibits.library.tamu.edu/africanamerican/chronology/index.html; for the University of Texas at Austin, see "The History of Integration at the University of Texas Austin: Timeline," Division of Diversity and Community Engagement, University of Texas (website), accessed July 8, 2020, http://diversity.utexas.edu/integration/timeline/.

66. William B. Phillips, "Mineral Survey," *University of Texas Bulletin*, no. 14: *Annual Report of the President and Faculties of the University of Texas to the Board of Regents for the Session of 1901–1902* (Austin: Von Boeckman, Schutze & Co, 1902), 78–79.

67. William B. Phillips, *Texas Petroleum: Bulletin of the University of Texas*, no. 5: *The University of Texas Mineral Survey Bulletin No. 1, July 1901* (Austin: University of Texas, 1901), 5–6.

68. Phillips, *Texas Petroleum*, 7.

69. Phillips, *Texas Petroleum*, 8.

70. Phillips, *Texas Petroleum*, 37–39.

71. Phillips, *Texas Petroleum*, 63–64.

72. Phillips, *Texas Petroleum*, 64–65.

73. Phillips, *Texas Petroleum*, 89–90.

74. On catalogues and data loss, see Markus Krajewski, *Paper Machines: About Cards & Catalogs, 1548-1929*, trans. Peter Krapp (Cambridge, MA: MIT Press, 2011).

75. Melvil Dewey, *A Classification and Subject Index for Cataloguing and Arranging the Books and Pamphlets of a Library* (Amherst, MA: [Printed by Case, Lockwood & Brainard Co., Hartford, CT], 1876), 9.

76. Wayne A. Wiegand, "The 'Amherst Method': The Origins of the Dewey Decimal Classification Scheme," *Libraries & Culture* 33, no. 2 (Spring 1998): 175-194. Pamphlets that have been cited as possible sources for Dewey's system are Charles C. Jewett, *A Plan for Stereotyping Catalogues by Separate Titles, and for Forming a General Stereotyped Catalogue of Public Libraries in the United States* (Washington, DC: American Association for the Advancement of Science, 1851); Nathaniel B. Shurtleff, *A Decimal System for the Arrangement and Administration of Libraries* (Boston: [Privately Printed], 1856); and a report on decimal classification by William Phipps Blake prepared in 1873 for the United States Centennial Exposition in Philadelphia of 1876. Wiegand shows Shurtleff's pamphlet to be the most directly influential, rejecting arguments made in favor of the Blake report by John Maass, "Who Invented Dewey's Classification?" *Wilson Library Bulletin* 47, no. 4 (December 1972): 335-341.

77. Horace Howard Furness (Chairman of the Library Committee), "Remarks," *Proceedings at the Opening of the Library of the University of Pennsylvania; 7th of February, 1891* (Philadelphia: University of Pennsylvania Press, 1891), 7. The early history of the University of Pennsylvania library is given in Charles W. David, "The University Library in 1886," *Library Chronicle of the Friends of the University of Pennsylvania Library* 18, no. 2 (Summer 1952): 72-76; and Paul H. Mosher, "University of Pennsylvania Libraries," in *International Dictionary of Library Histories*, ed. David H. Stam (New York: Routledge, 2016), 884-889. On Dewey's role in planning the University of Pennsylvania library, see George E. Thomas, " 'The Happy Employment of Means to Ends': Frank Furness's Library of the University of Pennsylvania and the Industrial Culture of Philadelphia," *Pennsylvania Magazine of History and Biography* 126, no. 2 (April 2001): 249-272. A detailed account of the original specifications for the library, including fittings as built, was published in Melvil Dewey's *Library Journal*: Talcott Williams, "Plans for the Library Building of Pennsylvania," *Library Journal* 13, no. 8 (August 1888): 237-243. See also Edward Potts Cheyney, *History of the University of Pennsylvania, 1740-1940* (Philadelphia: University of Pennsylvania Press, 1940), 322-324; David B. Brownlee and George Thomas, *Building America's First University: An Historical and Architectural Guide to the University of Pennsylvania* (Philadelphia: University of Pennsylvania Press, 1999), 159-163; George E. Thomas, Michael J. Lewis, and Jeffrey A. Cohen, *Frank Furness: The Complete Works* (Princeton, NJ: Princeton Architectural Press, 1991), passim.; James F. O'Gorman, *The Architecture of Frank Furness* (Philadelphia: Philadelphia Museum of Art, 1973), 64, 164-171; Thomas, "Frank Furness: The Poetry of the Present," in *University of Pennsylvania Library: Frank Furness*, ed. Edward R. Bosley (London: Phaidon, 1996), 4-24; and Michael J. Lewis, *Frank Furness: Architecture and the Violent Mind* (New York: Norton, 2001), 176-187. See also Lewis, "Frank Furness and the Expandable Library," *Journal of the Society of Architectural Historians* 77, no. 2 (June 2018): 138-145.

78. "The uncatalogued pamphlets treating of any subject bear the same class number and are arranged on the shelves immediately after the books of each section." Dewey, *A Classification and Subject Index*, 7.

79. This level of detail extended to the digit following the decimal is only given in the second edition of Dewey's system, published in 1885 and in subsequent editions. Melvil Dewey, *Relativ Index for Arranging Cataloging and Indexing Public and Private Libraries*

and for Pamflets, Clippings, Notes, Scrap Books, Index Rerums, Etc., 2nd ed., revised and greatly enlarged (Boston: Library Bureau, 1885), 121. The Pennsylvania catalogues therefore appear to have used this or later editions. Dewey and his colleagues at the Library Bureau, the company he founded in 1876, regularly issued updated editions of this Relativ Index, the spelling of which, like that of *pamflet*, reflected his efforts at lexical economy.

80. On the two-way catalogue see Thomas, " 'Happy Employment of Means to Ends,' " 255n15. Although such a piece does not appear in the sales catalogues of Dewey's company from 1890, 1893, or 1894, it is possible that the Library Bureau may have manufactured this as a custom item, a service that the bureau did offer. See for example, *Classified Illustrated Catalogue of the Library Bureau: A Handbook of Office Fittings and Supplies* (Boston: Library Bureau, 1893), 23. On the importance of library supplies and other hardware to Dewey's system and its successors, see Krajewski, *Paper Machines*, 87–106.

81. For an architectural history, see David Kaser, "The American Academic Library Building, 1870–1890," *Journal of Library History (1974–1987)* 21, no. 1 (Winter 1986): 60–71; and Kaser, *The Evolution of the American Academic Library Building* (Lanham, MD: Scarecrow Press, 1997).

82. The University of Toronto library (1892), designed by D. B. Dick beginning in 1891 with Dewey and Charles Ammi Cutter as consultants, exhibited many organizational features resembling those of the Pennsylvania library, which opened earlier that year. Robert H. Blackburn, "Dewey and Cutter as Building Consultants," *Library Quarterly: Information, Community, Policy* 58, no. 4 (October 1988): 377–384.

83. A detailed interpretation of the building as a site of production is given in Thomas, " 'Happy Employment of Means to Ends.' "

84. Ann M. Blair, *Too Much to Know: Managing Scholarly Information before the Modern Age* (New Haven, CT: Yale University Press, 2010). See also Chad Wellmon, *Organizing Enlightenment: Information Overload and the Invention of the Modern Research University* (Baltimore, MD: Johns Hopkins University Press, 2015).

85. Ariel Ron, "A Lost Gem? Uncovering the Carey-Colwell Library," Unique at Penn (University of Pennsylvania Library blog), September 4, 2013, https://uniqueatpenn.wordpress.com/2013/09/04/a-lost-gem-uncovering-the-carey-colwell-library/.

Interlude, c. 1900

1. Kerwin Lee Klein has reviewed the literature around the Turner thesis in *Frontiers of Historical Imagination: Narrating the European Conquest of Native America, 1890–1990* (Berkeley: University of California Press, 1997). See also Henry Nash Smith, *Virgin Land: The American West as Symbol and Myth* (Cambridge, MA: Harvard University Press, 1950); Richard Hofstadter, *The Age of Reform: From Bryan to F.D.R.* (New York: Vintage, 1955); Leo Marx, *The Machine in the Garden: Technology and the Pastoral Ideal in America* (New York: Oxford University Press, 1965); Hofstadter and Seymour Martin Lipset, eds., *Turner and the Sociology of the Frontier* (New York: Basic, 1968); David W. Noble, *Historians Against History: The Frontier Thesis and the National Covenant in American Historical Writing Since 1830* (Minneapolis: University of Minnesota Press, 1965); and Ray Allen Billington, *The Genesis of the Frontier Thesis: A Study in Historical Creativity* (San Marino, CA: Huntington Library, 1971).

2. Frederick Jackson Turner, "The Significance of the Frontier in American History," in *Report of the American Historical Association for the Year 1893* (Washington, DC: United

States Government Printing Office, 1894), 199–227. Reprinted in Turner, *The Frontier in American History* (New York: H. Holt, 1920), 1–38. The term "free land" refers to the provisions of the 1862 Homestead Act, which granted 160 acres of public lands, mostly in the Midwest and the West, to any citizen who had lived on that land for at least five years.

3. Compare, for example, Tony Bennett, "The Exhibitionary Complex," *New Formations* 4 (Spring 1988): 73–102.

4. James R. Beniger, *The Control Revolution: Technological and Economic Origins of the Information Society* (Cambridge, MA: Harvard University Press, 1986), esp. 390–425. This anticipates the periodization in Gilles Deleuze, "Postscript on Control Societies" [1990], trans. Martin Joughin, in *Negotiations 1972–1990* (New York: Columbia University Press, 1995), 177–182.

5. Robert P. Porter, "Distribution of Population According to Density: 1890," *Extra Census Bulletin*, no. 2 (April 20, 1891): 4. Turner quotes from this bulletin without citation in "Significance of the Frontier," 13.

6. The map is found in Porter, "Distribution of Population," 6–7. The Census Bureau lists nonwhite populations in "Table 8—The Colored Population Classified as Blacks, Mulattoes, Quadroons, Octoroons, Chinese, Japanese, and Civilized Indians, by States and Territories: 1890," in Robert P. Porter, *Compendium of the Eleventh Census: 1890* (Washington, DC: Government Printing Office, 1892), 470.

7. The Morrill Act of 1862 provided for large quantities of public land scrip allocated by the federal government, which individual states could utilize as capital to develop new or existing public colleges and universities. The University of Wisconsin, where Turner taught from 1890–1910, was an early land-grant institution. On the Morrill Act, see Edward Danforth Eddy Jr., *Colleges for Our Land and Time: The Land-Grant Idea in American Education* (New York: Harper, 1956), 23–45.

8. Emerson W. Pugh, *Building IBM: Shaping an Industry and Its Technology* (Cambridge, MA: MIT Press, 1995), 1–18. See also Fielding H. Garrison, M.D., *John Shaw Billings: A Memoir* (New York: G. P. Putnam's Sons, 1915), 343.

9. Leon E. Truesdell, *The Development of Punch Card Tabulation in the Bureau of the Census 1890–1940* (Washington, DC: United States Government Printing Office, 1965), 57–60.

10. Truesdell, *Development of Punch Card Tabulation*, 64–69. Data gathered in the 1890 census included place of domicile (by "enumeration district"), family structure and composition, race, age, marital status, place of birth (state or country), parental heritage, citizenship, years of U.S. domicile, occupation and employment status, health, literacy and education, English-language proficiency, and military service, the last three of which were new to this census.

11. Billington argues for the importance of the Census Bureau's statistical cartography to Turner in formulating his thesis, and in particular to visualizing the "frontier line," in *Genesis of the Frontier Thesis*, 108–116.

12. Minutes of the Faculty of the School of Mines, Columbia University, April 3, 1890, quoted in Geoffrey D. Austrian, *Herman Hollerith: Forgotten Giant of Information Processing* (New York: Columbia University Press, 1982), 56. Hollerith had also had a brief stint teaching mechanical engineering at the Massachusetts Institute of Technology.

13. Pugh, *Building IBM*, 23–28. Also Charles J. Bashe, Lyle R. Johnson, John H. Palmer, and Emerson W. Pugh, *IBM's Early Computers* (Cambridge, MA: MIT Press, 1986), 1–33. Columbia granted Hollerith a PhD in political science in 1890, technically (it seems) on the basis of an article describing his system published the previous year. Robert A. McCaughey, *Stand, Columbia: A History of Columbia University in the City of New York,*

1754–2004 (New York: Columbia University Press, 2003), 394; Herman Hollerith, "An Electric Tabulating System," *[Columbia College] School of Mines Quarterly: Journal of Applied Science* 10, no. 16 (April 1889): 238–255. Frank da Cruz has documented additional details on Hollerith's association with Columbia at "Columbia University Computing History," http://www.columbia.edu/cu/computinghistory/#early, including an annotated excerpt of Hollerith's article: http://www.columbia.edu/cu/computinghistory/hh/index.html.

14. For the details of the conference, see Billington, *Genesis of the Frontier Thesis*, 156–170.

15. Turner, "Significance of the Frontier in American History," 34.

16. Martin J. Sklar, *The United States as a Developing Country: Studies in U.S. History in the Progressive Era and the 1920s* (New York: Cambridge University Press, 1992). On the World's Columbian Exposition as consolidation, see Alan Trachtenberg, *The Incorporation of America: Culture and Society in the Gilded Age* (New York: Hill and Wang, 1982), 208–234; on the urban fair's relation to agrarian life, see William Cronon, *Nature's Metropolis: Chicago and the Great West* (New York: Norton, 1991), 341–369.

17. For a detailed account of the 1893 Chicago exposition in relation to the imperial imagination, see Robert Rydell, *All the World's a Fair: Visons of Empire at the American International Expositions 1876–1916* (Chicago: University of Chicago Press, 1984), 38–71. Diana Martinez has shown how Burnham used technical practices developed for the Chicago exposition, including the concrete "raft" foundation, in his replanning of Manila under American imperial rule. See Martinez, "Concrete Colonialism: Architecture, Urbanism, Infrastructure, and the American Colonial Project in the Philippines" (PhD diss., Columbia University, 2017).

18. Photo caption, "The Agricultural Building," *The World's Columbian Exposition Reproduced* (Chicago: Rand, McNally & Co., 1894), n.p.

19. The building's dimensions are given as 700 ft. x 350 ft. in Norman Bolotin and Christine Laing, *The World's Columbian Exposition: The Chicago World's Fair of 1893* (Washington, DC: Preservation Press, 1992).

20. Photo caption, N. D. Thompson Publishing Co., *The Dream City: a Portfolio of Photographic Views of the World's Columbian Exposition*, Educational Art Series 1, nos. 1–17 (St. Louis: N. D. Thompson, [weekly] 1893), "The Mines and Mining Building," Portfolio 2, Plate 13.

21. "Mining at the Columbian Exposition," *Engineering and Mining Journal* 56, no. 8 (August 19, 1893): 187. The gold was lent by the Spotted Horse Mine in Maiden, Montana, and the silver by Montana's "free silver" ex-governor Samuel Hauser and the mining entrepreneur William A. Clark. The sculptor was R. H. Parks. Details on the statue, referred to as *Justice*, are also given in Rossiter Johnson, *A History of the World's Columbian Exposition Held in Chicago in 1893; by Authority of the Board of Directors* (New York: D. Appleton, 1897), 159.

22. Elsewhere in the same building another "Silver Queen" statue by sculptor Hiram L. Johnson represented a mining company in Aspen, Colorado. See the captioned photo of "The Silver Queen," in N. D. Thompson Publishing Co., *The Dream City*. Portfolio 7, Plate 16.

23. W. E. B. Du Bois, "The Talented Tenth," in Booker T. Washington et al., *The Negro Problem: A Series of Articles by Representative American Negroes of To-Day* (New York: James Pott, 1903), 31–75. On the "Talented Tenth" as a political strategy, see Manning Marable, *W. E. B. Du Bois: Black Radical Democrat*, 2nd ed. (Boulder, CO: Paradigm, 2005), 50–51.

24. Georg Simmel, *Philosophie des Geldes* (Leipzig: Verlag von Duncker & Humblot, 1900), xv. The second edition from 1907 is translated as *The Philosophy of Money* [1907], 2nd enlarged ed., ed. David Frisby, trans. Tom Bottomore and David Frisby (New York: Routledge, 1978).

5. Diffuse Illumination: The Silence of the Universal

1. Rejecting the common doctrine that "Men have in native *Ideas*, and original Characters stamped upon their Minds," John Locke wrote: "Let us then suppose the Mind to be, as we say, white Paper, void of all Characters, without any *Ideas*. . . ." Locke, *An Essay Concerning Human Understanding* [1689] (Oxford: Clarendon Press, 1975), book II, chapter 1, 104. Among the other material artifacts that make their way into Locke's epistemology are "Imprinted truths" (49), an "empty Cabinet," (55), a "Looking-glass" (112), mirrors (118), a "Presence-room" (121), and drawn "Pictures" (152).
2. On the dumbwaiters at Monticello, see the prologue. On the "master and slave" performance there, and on the spaces for withdrawal and degrees of privacy, see Peter S. Onuf and Annette Gordon-Reed, "Jefferson's Spaces [Review Essay]," *Early American Literature* 48, no. 3 (2013): 762–764.
3. William C. Allen, *History of the United States Capitol: A Chronicle of Design, Construction, and Politics* (Washington, DC: United States Government Printing Office, 2001), 98.
4. On Jefferson's debt, see Herbert Sloan, *Principle and Interest: Thomas Jefferson and the Problem of Debt* (New York: Oxford University Press, 1995). On the sale of the library, see Richard B. Bernstein, *Thomas Jefferson* (New York: Oxford University Press, 2003), 178.
5. Mary N. Woods, "Thomas Jefferson and the University of Virginia: Planning the Academic Village," *Journal of the Society of Architectural Historians* 44, no. 3 (October 1985): 266–283; Buford Pickens, "Mr. Jefferson as a Revolutionary Architect," *Journal of the Society of Architectural Historians* 34, no. 4 (December 1975): 257–279; and Richard Guy Wilson, ed., *Thomas Jefferson's Academical Village: The Creation of an Architectural Masterpiece*, rev. ed. (Charlottesville: University of Virginia Press, 2009). On Jefferson's use of Giacomo Leoni's 1721 edition of Palladio's *Quattro Libri*, Pickens, 272, and Woods, 268.
6. The design and construction sequence is described in detail in Joseph M. Lasala, Patricia C. Sherwood, and Richard Guy Wilson, "Architecture for Education," in Wilson, *Thomas Jefferson's Academical Village*, 1–54. On the Jefferson, Latrobe, and Thornton correspondence, 13–22.
7. According to Robert Darnton, Jefferson placed an order for the Lucca edition of Diderot and D'Alembert's *Encyclopédie* in 1781 "for the use of the Public," based on an advertisement in the *Virginia Gazette*. The price was 15,068 pounds of tobacco. He also sought a copy for his own use, which he does not seem to have obtained until his stay in Paris from 1784 to 1789. Robert Darnton, *The Business of Enlightenment: A Publishing History of the Encyclopédie 1775–1800* (Cambridge, MA: Belknap Press of Harvard University Press, 1979), 318–319. Later, Jefferson also contributed to and revised articles for the *Encyclopédie Méthodique*. Charles B. Sanford, *Thomas Jefferson and His Library: A Study of His Literary Interests and of the Religious Attitudes Revealed by Relevant Titles in His Library* (Hamden, CT: Archon, 1977), 24–25, 53. Also, George B. Watts, "Thomas Jefferson, the 'Encyclopédie' and the 'Encyclopédie Méthodique,' " *French Review* 38, no. 3 (January 1965): 318–325. On Jefferson's reading practices, see also Barry Bergdoll, "Books, Buildings, and the Spaces of Democracy: Jefferson's Library from Paris

to Washington," in Lloyd DeWitt and Corey Parker, eds., *Thomas Jefferson, Architect: Palladian Models, Democratic Principles, and the Conflict of Ideals* (Norfolk: Chrysler Museum of Art/New Haven, CT: Yale University Press, 2019), 65–79.

8. On silent reading, see Paul Saenger, *Space Between Words: The Origins of Silent Reading* (Redwood City, CA: Stanford University Press, 1997). On the dissemination of reading practices, see Reinhard Wittmann, "Was there a Reading Revolution at the End of the Eighteenth Century?" and Martyn Lyons, "New Readers in the Nineteenth Century: Women, Children, Workers," in *A History of Reading in the West*, ed. Giglielmo Cavallo and Roger Chartier, trans. Lydia G. Cochrane (Amherst, MA: University of Massachusetts Press, 1999), 284–312 and 313–344.

9. "Thomas Jefferson to the Trustees of the Lottery for East Tennessee College, 6 May 1810," *Founders Online*, National Archives, https://founders.archives.gov/documents/Jefferson/03-02-02-0322. Also in J. Jefferson Looney, ed., *The Papers of Thomas Jefferson, Retirement Series*, vol. 2, *16 November 1809 to 11 August 1810* (Princeton, NJ: Princeton University Press, 2005), 365–366.

10. John S. Brubacher and Willis Rudy, *Higher Education in Transition: A History of American Colleges and Universities, 1636–1976*, 3rd enlarged ed. (New York: Harper & Row, 1976), 86. The authors provide a useful summary of the recitation method, 84–88.

11. On the early borrowing practices at the University of Virginia, see Harry Clemons, *The University of Virginia Library 1825–1950: Story of a Jeffersonian Foundation* (Charlottesville: University of Virginia Press, 1954), 14–15. On reading practices in antebellum college libraries, see James Axtell, *Wisdom's Workshop: The Rise of the Modern University* (Princeton, NJ: Princeton University Press, 2016), 207–220.

12. Sanford, *Thomas Jefferson and His Library*, 45.

13. "Thomas Jefferson to James Madison, 17 February 1826," *Founders Online*, National Archives, https://founders.archives.gov/documents/Jefferson/98-01-02-5912.

14. Silvio A. Bedini, *Thomas Jefferson and His Copying Machines* (Charlottesville: University of Virginia Press, 1984).

15. Étienne-Louis Boullée, *Architecture: Essai sur l'art*, ed. Jean-Marie Pérouse de Montclos (Paris: Hermann, 1968), 136; on the "architecture of shadows," 156. On the lighting of Boullée's cenotaph, see Pérouse de Montclos, *Etienne-Louis Boullée* (Paris: Flammarion, 1994), 151. Richard Etlin suggests the possible use of fireworks as a light source, in Etlin, *The Architecture of Death: The Transformation of the Cemetery in Eighteenth-Century Paris* (Cambridge, MA: MIT Press, 1984), 130.

16. Thomas Jefferson, "Notes and Specifications," Pocket memorandum book, University of Virginia, dated July 18, 1819, page 2 recto and verso. Albert and Shirley Small Special Collections Library, University of Virginia, The Thomas Jefferson Papers, AD. 1 vol. #38–163, http://ead.lib.virginia.edu/vivaxtf/view?docId=uva-sc/viu00007.xml#series1, images N318pg2r, N318pg2v; and Douglas J. Harnsberger, "Elevating Jefferson's High-Flying Vision for His Last Delorme Dome Project at the University of Virginia," in *The Founding of Thomas Jefferson's University*, ed. John A. Ragosta, Peter S. Onuf, and Andrew J. O'Shaughnessy (Charlottesville: University of Virginia Press, 2019), 115–125.

17. Thomas Jefferson to Joseph Coolidge, April 12, 1825, cited in Office of the Architect, University of Virginia, *Rotunda Historic Structure Report*, 38, emphasis in original, https://officearchitect.virginia.edu/index.php/documents/item/127-rotunda-historic-structure-report.

18. The clock assemblage, which was fabricated by the noted Boston clockmaker Simon Willard, arrived and was installed in 1827. The bell, possibly also fabricated by Willard, arrived from Boston in 1827. *Rotunda Historic Structure Report*, 37–39, 47. See also

Philip Alexander Bruce, *History of the University of Virginia, 1819–1919*, vol. 1 (New York: Macmillan, 1920), 274–275.

19. Details on Henry Martin's life are available at "Henry Martin," President's Commission on Slavery and the University, University of Virginia, accessed July 12, 2020, http://slavery .virginia.edu/henry-martin/; and "A Brief History of Free People of Color and UVA," President's Commission on Slavery and the University, University of Virginia, accessed July 12, 2020, http://slavery.virginia.edu/a-brief-history-of-free-people-of-color-and-uva/.

20. Allen, *History of the United States Capitol*, 144–167. Also, Harold Kirker, *The Architecture of Charles Bulfinch* (Cambridge, MA: Harvard University Press, 1969), 321–333.

21. Allen, *History of the United States Capitol*, 178–180.

22. Allen, *History of the United States Capitol*, 206.

23. Allen, *History of the United States Capitol*, 322, 338–339.

24. Wolfgang Schivelbusch, *Disenchanted Night: The Industrialization of Light in the Nineteenth Century*, trans. Angela Davies (Berkeley: University of California Press, 1988).

25. Jefferson's correspondence indicates that he had considered the possibility of installing gaslight on the campus. Jefferson to Hartwell Cocke, May 20, 1826, Thomas Jefferson Papers, Special Collections, University of Virginia Library, Draft #7254-b, https://search .lib.virginia.edu/catalog/u2642758#?#view-u2642758&c=0&m=0&s=0&cv=88&xywh =-273%2C-409%2C5441%2C6719. At its February 1857 meeting, the board of visitors resolved "to contract with the Charlottesville and University Gas Company for the fitting up within the University of such gas fixtures as in their judgement [*sic*] will be sufficient for the uses of the institution." "Board of Visitors Minutes, February 13, 1857," University of Virginia Library, http://xtf.lib.virginia.edu/xtf/view?docId=2006_06%2 FuvaGenText%2Ftei%2Fbov_18570211.xml&chunk.id=d3&query=gas, 38.

By February, the board was confirming gas prices, "Board of Visitors Minutes, June 25, 1857," University of Virginia Library, http://xtf.lib.virginia.edu/xtf/view?docId=2006_06 /uvaGenText/tei/bov_18570625.xml&chunk.id=d3&toc.id=&brand=default, 56.

At the March 1894 meeting of the board of visitors "Profr [William M.] Thornton's suggestion & Estimate for an Electric plant for lighting etc." was noted but tabled. 374. "Board of Visitors Minutes, March 16, 1894," University of Virginia Library, http://xtf.lib.virginia .edu/xtf/view?docId=2006_06/uvaGenText/tei/bov_18940316.xml;brand=default, 374. A map made by Kaigiro Sugino in September 1895 shows gas lines entering the chemical laboratory and the infirmary, both outside the Lawn. These lines were also used for walkway lighting. Kaigiro Sugino, "1895 Map of the University of Virginia," Jefferson's University . . . the Early Life, University of Virginia, September 1895, http://juel.iath.virginia .edu/node/432. I am grateful to Garth Anderson, resource center manager at the University of Virginia, for calling this map to my attention.

26. "Calamity of Sunday: Main Building at the University Burned," *Richmond Dispatch* October 29, 1895, 1.

27. Philip Alexander Bruce, *History of the University of Virginia, 1819–1919: The Lengthened Shadow of One Man*, vol. 4 (New York: Macmillan, 1921), 254.

28. On the lecture as a mode of instruction during the nineteenth century, see Brubacher and Rudy, *Higher Education in Transition*, 88–90. On its medieval links with the agonistic disputation and on the modern return of professorial voice as academic charisma, see William Clark, *Academic Charisma and the Origins of the Research University* (Chicago: University of Chicago Press, 2006), 68–92, and 398–432. On the interdependence of secular and evangelical speech, see Michael Warner "The Preacher's Footing," in *This Is Enlightenment*, ed. Clifford Siskin and William Warner (Chicago: University of Chicago Press, 2010), 368–383.

29. On Mills's annex, see Rhodri Windsor Liscombe, *Altogether American: Robert Mills Architect and Engineer, 1781–1855* (New York: Oxford University Press, 1994), 282–284; William B. O'Neal, *Pictorial History of the University of Virginia* (Charlottesville: University of Virginia Press, 1968), 54–55.

30. A sketch wiring plan of the Rotunda (apparently now lost), was prepared for submission to the investigating committee, "It Must Be Rebuilt," *Richmond Dispatch*, November 6, 1895, 3.

31. For example: "It Must Be Rebuilt," 1–3; "Their Mixed Orders: The Architecture of the University Buildings" and "Mr. Massey's Views," *Richmond Dispatch*, November 6, 1895, 3; and "Have Need for All: What the New Plans Are," *Richmond Dispatch*, January 15, 1896, 6. A building committee was formed at a board of visitors meeting about a week after the fire, with specific recommendations regarding "heating, lighting, and ventilation," which in the old building were inadequately solved, as well as a new "academical building," "physical laboratories," an "engineering building," and a "law building," all of which were expected to follow "classical types of design" and be located "so as to create a harmonious combination with the original Jeffersonian group." "Board of Visitors Minutes, November 4, 1895," University of Virginia Library, http://xtf.lib.virginia.edu/xtf/view?docId=2006_06/uvaGenText/tei/bov_18951104.xml, 1–11.

32. Leland M. Roth, *McKim, Mead & White Architects* (New York: Harper & Row, 1983), 195–199.

33. Beginning in the early 1890s, Columbia College began planning a move from its campus in Midtown Manhattan at Madison Avenue at Forty-Ninth Street, to a new uptown campus in Morningside Heights at Broadway at 116th Street, designed by Charles F. McKim of McKim, Mead & White. In 1896, Columbia College formally became Columbia University in the City of New York, and the new campus opened in October 1897. For a detailed history of the planning of Columbia's Morningside Heights campus, see Barry Bergdoll, "The Genesis and Legacy of McKim, Mead & White's Master Plan for Columbia University," in *Mastering McKim's Plan: Columbia's First Century on Morningside Heights*, ed. Barry Bergdoll and Janet Parks (New York: Miriam and Ira D. Wallach Art Gallery, Columbia University in the City of New York, 1997), 17–76; as well as Andrew S. Dolkart, *Morningside Heights: A History of Its Architecture & Development* (New York: Columbia University Press, 1998), 103–155.

34. The decision to rebuild the reading room as a single large room was apparently made by the board of visitors in consultation with White. Roth, *McKim, Mead & White Architects*, 197, and 398n55. Details on the redesigned rotunda, along with the new buildings at the south end of the lawn—the "academical building" (with a "public hall"), a "mechanical laboratory," a "physical laboratory," and a boiler plant—are already given in "The University," *Richmond Dispatch*, May 31, 1896, 10.

35. A committee commissioned the painting from Breck in 1900, and it was installed in 1902. For background, see American Academy in Rome, *The American Academy in Rome* (New York: DeVinne Press, 1904). Details on the Breck commission are given in James Mercer Garnett, "A History of the University of Virginia," in *University of Virginia: Its History, Influence, Equipment and Characteristics*, ed. Paul Brandon Barringer, James Mercer Garnett, and Roswell Page, vol. 1 (New York: Lewis Publishing, 1904), 241.

36. "Brief History of Free People of Color and UVA."

37. On the siting of Cabell Hall on its auditorium, see Lasala, Sherwood, and Wilson, "Architecture for Education," 76–77. On the Canada neighborhood in Charlottesville, see "Brief History of Free People of Color and UVA."

38. An early report on the proposed new buildings refers to a planned structure for "boilers for the heating and electric-lighting apparatus." "Work of Restoring: Plans for the

Erection of the New University Buildings," *Richmond Dispatch*, March 29, 1896, 1. Records from 1900 refer to an appropriation of funds "for the erection of an electric plant and to extend its steam heating apparatus," and board minutes from 1901 record an expense "for extending the steam heating system to the buildings on West Lawn," "Board of Visitors Minutes, June 11, 1900," University of Virginia Library, http://xtf .lib.virginia.edu/xtf/view?docId=2006_06/uvaGenText/tei/bov_19000611.xml&chunk .id=d3&toc.id=&brand=default, 372; and "Board of Visitors Minutes, June 10, 1901," University of Virginia Library, http://xtf.lib.virginia.edu/xtf/view?docId=2006_06/uva GenText/tei/bov_19010610.xml&chunk.id=d3&toc.id=&brand=default, 410.

39. On service functions at Monticello, including the "agency" of dumbwaiters and dependencies in concealing service, see Markus Krajewski, *The Server: A Media History from the Present to the Baroque*, trans. Ilinca Iurascu (New Haven, CT: Yale University Press, 2018), 257–258, 288–289. On the campus architecture and slavery, including the role of enslaved persons in constructing the campus and the use of cellars beneath campus buildings as dwellings and workspaces for enslaved persons, see Louis P. Nelson, "The Architecture of Democracy in a Landscape of Slavery," in DeWitt and Parker, *Thomas Jefferson, Architect*, 98–118.

40. Thorstein Veblen, *The Higher Learning in America: A Memorandum on the Conduct of Universities by Business Men* (New York: B. W. Huebsch, 1918), 6–7; see also Christopher Newfield, *Ivy and Industry: Business and the Making of the American University* (Durham, NC: Duke University Press, 2003).

41. Veblen, *Higher Learning in America*, 7.

42. At the May 6, 1895 board meeting at which it was announced, Low's bequest was followed minutes later by trustee William C. Schermerhorn's gift of $300,000 for an academic building to be erected in his name. Bergdoll, "Genesis and Legacy," 49. On Abiel Abbot Low, A. A. Low & Brothers, and the tea and opium trade with China, see Conrad Edick Wright, "Merchants and Mandarins: New York and the Early China Trade," in *New York and the China Trade*, ed. David Sanctuary Howard (New York: New York Historical Society, 1984), 48–49; John R. Haddad, *America's First Adventure in China: Trade, Treaties, and Salvation* (Philadelphia: Temple University Press, 2013), 168–171; also Dolkart, *Morningside Heights*, 108, 404n168; and William G. Low, *A. A. Low & Brothers' Fleet of Clipper Ships*, 2nd ed. (n.p., 1922).

43. Ralph Waldo Emerson, *Nature* (Boston: James Munroe, 1836), 13.

44. Ralph Waldo Emerson, *An Oration Delivered Before the Phi Beta Kappa Society at Cambridge, August 31, 1837* ["The American Scholar"], 2nd ed. (Boston: James Munroe, 1838), 10. On Emerson and the classical tradition, see Caroline Winterer, *The Culture of Classicism: Ancient Greece and Rome in American Intellectual Life, 1780–1910* (Baltimore: Johns Hopkins University Press, 2002), 66–68.

45. Emerson, *An Oration Delivered*, 30–31.

46. Wilmer Alexander Duff, ed., *A Text-Book of Physics* (Philadelphia: P. Blakiston's Son, 1908).

47. Hallock joined the Columbia faculty as associate professor of physics in 1892, which is the position he held while assisting McKim on the rotunda lighting, rising to the position of dean of the faculty of pure sciences in 1906. "Prof. William Hallock," *School of Mines Quarterly* 34, no. 4 (July 1913): 420. The Smithsonian's Astrophysical Observatory was set up in 1891. Although unmentioned in the early histories, the astrophysical laboratory apparently run by Hallock may have been a precursor. G. Brown Goode, *An Account of the Smithsonian Institution, Its Origin, History, Objects and Achievements* (Washington, DC: [n.p.] 1895), 38–39; Samuel Pierpont Langley, "The Astrophysical Laboratory," in *The Smithsonian Institution, 1846–1896: The History of Its First Half-Century*, ed. George Brown Goode (Washington, DC: De Vinne Press, 1896): 419–442; and Bessie Zaban

Jones, *Lighthouse in the Skies: The Smithsonian Astrophysical Observatory; Background and History 1846–1955* (Washington, DC: Smithsonian Institution, 1965).

48. William Hallock, "Diffused Illumination," *Progressive Age* 16, no. 3 (1 March 1898): 107.

49. Hallock, "Diffused Illumination," 107.

50. Hallock, "Diffused Illumination," 108.

51. Hallock, "Diffused Illumination," 108. Although Dolkart indicates uncertainty as to whether the projectors were ever installed (*Morningside Heights*, 149, 406n206), circular holes for the projector lenses remain visible in the wooden casework provided for them. The illumination system is described as functioning in "Columbia University," *Scientific American* 78, no. 13 (March 26, 1898): 202. A subsequent article in the same publication confirms that the "moon" did operate. Describing the installation in greater detail, that article reports that "the sphere was built in the summer of 1897, tried once in December, and at the present time [April 1898] is to be seen every Friday evening between the hours of 5 and 7, for the life of the carbons [the arc light electrodes] is but 2.5 hours. The large reading room is not used at night, and the 'moon' shines but for the accommodation of visitors at the present time. It is as yet in somewhat of an experimental stage of development, but will later on be used regularly." Diagrams illustrating the positioning and angle of the projectors accompany the text, which also describes their focusing mechanism and the process of testing each lamp prior to operation and documents the results of photometric tests made of the lighting levels. These measurements match those described by Hallock. "Columbia's Artificial Moon," *Scientific American* 78, no. 15 (April 9, 1898): 229–230, quotation 229. The information provided in this article, including illustrations, was subsequently reproduced in "The Artificial Moon at Columbia University," *English Mechanic and World of Science*, no. 1728 (May 6, 1898): 261.

52. Hallock, "Diffused Illumination," 109.

53. [E. C. Brown], "Artificial Moonlight," *Progressive Age* 16, no. 3 (March 1, 1898): 92.

54. [E. C. Brown], "Artificial Moonlight," 92.

55. George H. Baker, "Report of the Librarian," in Columbia University, Office of the President, *Ninth Annual Report of President Low to the Trustees, October 3, 1898* (New York: Columbia University, 1898), 282. On the background and development of the Columbia library, see Winifred B. Linderman, "History of the Columbia University Library, 1876–1926" (PhD diss., Columbia University, 1959).

56. Hallock, "Diffused Illumination," 109.

57. Frederick Parsell Hill, *Charles F. McKim, the Man* (Francestown, NH: M. Jones, 1950), 21–22. Hill relates that initially, four "search-lights," one from each gallery, shone on the sphere, but colored light appeared at the intersection of their light waves. To remedy this, four more lights were added and the light redistributed across the sphere's surface, causing the light waves to overlap and eliminating the optical interference. In 1895, Hallock delivered a lecture on "photographic optics." "Calendar," *Columbia Daily Spectator* 36, no. 4 (April 10, 1895): 66.

58. John Lankford, "The Impact of Photography on Astronomy," in *The General History of Astronomy*, ed. Owen Gingerich, vol. 4, *Astrophysics and Twentieth Century Astronomy to 1950*, part A (Cambridge, MA: Harvard University Press, 1984): 16–39. See also Daniel Norman, "The Development of Astronomical Photography," *Osiris* 5 (1938): 560–594; and Beth Saunders, "Mapping the Moon," in *Apollo's Muse: The Moon in the Age of Photography*, ed. Mia Fineman and Beth Saunders (New York: Metropolitian Museum of Art, 2019), 16–69, on Rutherfurd, 24.

59. William Hallock and Floyd S. Muckey, "Rational, Scientific Voice-Production," *Werner's Magazine* 18, no. 1 (January 1896): 1–10.

60. Hallock and Muckey, "Rational, Scientific Voice-Production," 10.

61. In the academic year 1896–1897, Hallock offered lecture courses in the Department of Physics on "Modes of Designing and Constructing Apparatus" and the "Undulatory Theory of Light." Columbia University, Office of the President, *Eighth Annual Report of President Low to the Trustees, October 4, 1897* (New York: Columbia University, 1898), 207–208.

62. Hallock and Muckey, "Rational, Scientific Voice-Production," 9, 1; emphasis in original. A summary of contemporary techniques, including the Koenig manometric flame (but not including Hallock's adaptation), is given in Dayton Clarence Miller, *The Science of Musical Sounds* (New York: Macmillan, 1916), 70–91. On the history of acoustical writing, see Thomas Y. Levin, "Tones from Out of Nowhere: Rudolph Pfenninger and the Archaeology of Synthetic Sound," *Grey Room* 12 (Summer 2003): 32–79.

63. Floyd S. Muckey, *The Natural Method of Voice Production in Speech and Song* (New York: Charles Scribner's Sons, 1915). See also "The Result of Eighteen Years of Research Work in Voice-Production and Voice-Analysis—William Hallock (Prof. Physics, Columbia University, New York, NY) and Floyd Muckey, MD (New York, NY)," *Journal of Laryngology, Rhinology, and Otology* 28, no. 1 (January 1913): 40–41. Clark is listed as the sole faculty member in the Department of Elocution in the *University of Chicago Annual Register July 1892–July 1893* (Chicago: University of Chicago Press, 1896), 95. The Department of Public Speaking first appears in the *University of Chicago Annual Register July 1895–July 1896* (Chicago: University of Chicago Press, 1896), 187. By 1916 the department had been relocated to the divinity school; *University of Chicago Annual Register covering the Academic Year Ending June 30, 1917* (Chicago: University of Chicago Press, 1917), 325. See also F. M. Blanchard, "Department of Public Speaking," *School Review* 13, no. 1 (January 1905): 75–76.

64. Hallock, "Diffused Illumination," 109. Pelz won the design competition for the new Library of Congress with his partner John L. Smithmeyer in 1873. Smithmeyer took over the project but was dismissed in 1888. Pelz, who is generally credited with the building's overall design, returned but was dismissed in 1892. The engineer and superintendent of construction Bernard Green and the architect Edward Pearce Casey are generally credited with the design of the building's interiors. The building opened on November 1, 1897, shortly after the opening of Columbia's new library. John Y. Cole, "Struggle for a Structure: Ainsworth Rand Spofford and a New Building for the Library of Congress," in *The Art and Architecture of the Thomas Jefferson Building*, ed. John Y. Cole and Henry Hope Reed (Washington, DC: Norton/Library of Congress, 1997), 30–63.

65. A. R. [Ainsworth Rand] Spofford, "The Government Library at Washington," *International Review* 5 (November 1878): 765–766.

66. Spofford, "The Government Library at Washington," 769. On "print culture" prior to the Civil War, see Trish Loughran, *The Republic in Print: Print Culture in the Age of U.S. Nation Building, 1770–1870* (New York: Columbia University Press, 2007).

67. See, for example, Stephen Cresswell, "The Last Days of Jim Crow in Southern Libraries," *Libraries & Culture* 31, nos. 3–4 (Summer 1996): 557–573.

68. Graduate schools were also points of entry for women. For example, although Columbia College did not admit women until 1987, Winifred Edgerton became the first woman to receive a graduate degree at Columbia in 1886. Robert A. McCaughey, *Stand, Columbia: A History of Columbia University in the City of New York, 1754–2004* (New York: Columbia University Press, 2003), 164–165. Although McCaughey states that Edgerton's PhD was in astronomy, it was in mathematics. Judy Green and Jeanne LaDuke, "Women in the American Mathematical Community: The Pre-1940 PhD's," *Mathematical Intelligencer* 9,

no. 1 (1987): 13. On international students: Teresa Brawner Bevis and Christopher J. Lucas, *International Students in American Colleges and Universities: A History* (New York: Palgrave Macmillan, 2007). At Columbia, Pixley ka Isaka Seme, a Black South African and cofounder of the African National Congress, graduated with a Bachelor of Arts in 1906. "Pixley ka Isaka Seme," Columbia 250, accessed July 12, 2020, http://c250.columbia.edu /c250_celebrates/remarkable_columbians/pixley_ka_isakka_seme.html.

69. Ambedkar enrolled as a student in the faculty of political science, which had just recently moved out of Low Library. Nonetheless, he probably spent a good deal of time there: "His college colleagues related afterwards with pride how Ambedkar seized every possible hour for his study for which he said he'd been given a life's opportunity." Dhananjay Keer, *Dr. Ambedkar: Life and Mission* (Bombay: Popular Prakashan, 1954), 28. In the academic year 1913–1914, the first year of Ambedkar's enrollment, he was one of three Indian students in the faculty of political science, and six Indians overall. There were a total of 191 international graduate students enrolled that year at Columbia (about 5.4 percent of the total) and twenty undergraduates (about 2.1 percent), or 4.7 percent of the total student population, from twenty-eight countries other than the United States, mostly from Europe, though the largest number (fifty-one) were from China. "Report of the Registrar," Table XI, in Columbia University in the City of New York, *Annual Reports of the President and Treasurer to the Trustees with Accompanying Documents for the Year Ending June 30, 1914* (New York: Columbia University, 1914), 233.

70. Daniel Immerwahr, "Caste or Colony? Indianizing Race in the United States," *Modern Intellectual History* 4, no. 2 (2007): 278.

71. Keer, *Dr. Ambedkar*, 30–32.

72. Keer, *Dr. Ambedkar*, 39.

73. B. R. Ambedkar to Edwin Seligman, February 16, 1922. Edwin Seligman Papers, Rare Book & Manuscript Library, Columbia University, http://www.columbia.edu/itc/mealac /pritchett/00ambedkar/timeline/1920s.html.

74. Bhimrao R. Ambedkar, *The Evolution of Provincial Finance in British India: A Study in the Provincial Decentralization of Imperial Finance* (London: P. S. King & Son, 1925). In the copy in the Columbia Libraries collection, above the publisher's imprint on the title page, is pasted: "Submitted in partial fulfillment of the requirements of the degree of Doctor of Philosophy in the Faculty of Political Science, Columbia University, in the City of New York."

75. Ambedkar, quoted in Arun P. Mukherjee, "B. R. Ambedkar, John Dewey, and the Meaning of Democracy," *New Literary History* 40, no. 2 (Spring 2009): 357.

76. Immerwahr, "Caste or Colony?" 286–287.

77. In Ambedkhar's personal library, which is kept at Siddhartha College, Mumbai, Dewey's *Education and Democracy* is among the books that bear Ambedkhar's signature. I am grateful to Dr. Varsha Ayyer of the Tata Institute of Social Sciences for her assistance in confirming this information, and to Sheldon Pollock for making the connection.

78. Bhimrao R. Ambedkhar, "Annhilation of Caste" [1936], in *The Essential Writings of B. R. Ambedkar*, ed. Valerian Rodrigues (New Delhi: Oxford University Press, 2002), 303. Ambedkar is citing John Dewey, *Democracy and Education: An Introduction to the Philosophy of Education* (New York: Macmillan, 1916), 24. Ellipsis in Ambedkar's original text. Mukherjee has reconstructed textually Ambedkar's many direct and indirect borrowings from Dewey and from *Democracy and Education* in particular, with special attention to Ambedkar's frequent use of the term *endosmosis*, a term originating with Henri Bergson and then William James, which Dewey borrowed to describe the permeability of social boundaries and fluid relations among groups in democracy. "The Annhilation of Caste"

was to be delivered at the annual conference of the Jat Pat Todak Mandal (Organiza-
tion for the Destruction of Caste) in Lahore in 1936. The Hindu organizers objected to
Ambedkar's treatment of the Vedas, or Hindu scriptures, and the speech was canceled.
Mukherjee, "B.R. Ambedkar, John Dewey," 345–370. See also K. N. Kadam, "Dr. Ambed-
kar's Philosophy of Emancipation and the Impact of John Dewey," in *The Meaning of
Ambedkarite Conversion to Buddhism and Other Essays* (Mumbai: Popular Prakashan,
1997), 1–33. Kadam suggests that Ambedkar had been planning to write a book on
Dewey. Mukherjee also refers to a newspaper article in which Ambedkar is quoted tell-
ing friends that he could cite Dewey's lectures verbatim. That article is quoted in Dinkar
Khabde, *Dr. Ambedkar and Western Thinkers* (Pune: Sugava Prakashan, 1989), 42.

79. Dewey, *Democracy and Education*, 22–23.
80. Dewey, *Democracy and Education*, 25–26.
81. K. N. Kadam has argued that Ambedkar's use of Dewey possibly also refers here to the
burning of the Manu Smriti [the Laws of Manu, or Manusmriti, an ancient Hindu text that
established the caste system] by Dalits in 1927. Kadam, "Dr. Ambedkar's Philosophy," 7.
82. For example, Surendra Shrirang Dhaktode, *Thomas Jefferson and Dr. B. R. Ambedkar: A
Comparative Study* (Mumbai: Bhashya Prakashan, 2017).
83. Bhimrao R. Ambedkar, Speech before the Parliament of India, November 25, 1949,
"Third Reading of the Draft Constitution," in *Dr. Babasaheb Ambedkar, Writings and
Speeches*, vol. 13, ed. Vasant Moon (Bombay: Education Department, Government of
Maharastra, 1994), 1216, 1211.
84. "Thomas Jefferson to William Plumer, 21 July 1816," *Founders Online*, National Archives,
https://founders.archives.gov/?q=jefferson%20to%20plumer%201816&s
=1111311111&sa=&r=5&sr=; also in J. Jefferson Looney, ed., *The Papers of Thomas Jefferson,
Retirement Series*, vol. 10, *May 1816 to 18 January 1817* (Princeton, NJ: Princeton University
Press, 2013), 260–161. The earlier quotation is in "Thomas Jefferson to James Madison, 6
September 1789," *Founders Online*, National Archives, https://founders.archives.gov/?q
=jefferson%20to%20madison%20usufruct&s=1111311111&sa=&r=1&sr=; also in Charles F.
Hobson and Robert A. Rutland, eds., *The Papers of James Madison*, vol. 12, *2 March 1789–20
January 1790 and Supplement 24 October 1775–24 January 1789* (Charlottesville: University
of Virginia Press, 1979), 382–388.
85. Peter S. Onuf, *The Mind of Thomas Jefferson* (Charlottesville: University of Virginia
Press, 2007), 217. On Jefferson's exchange with Madison and his ambivalence regard-
ing personal and public debt related to his own financial indebtedness, see Herbert
Sloan, "The Earth Belongs in Usufruct to the Living," in *Jeffersonian Legacies*, ed.
Peter S. Onuf (Charlottesville: University of Virginia Press, 1993), 281–315; as well as
Sloan, *Principle and Interest: Thomas Jefferson and the Problem of Debt* (New York:
Oxford University Press, 1995). On debt, land, and sovereignty in Jefferson's writ-
ings, see also Arindam Dutta, "Mammoths, Inc.: Nature, Architecture, and the Debt,
Part 1," The Aggregate Website, accessed July 12, 2020, http://we-aggregate.org/piece
/mammoths-inc-nature-architecture-and-the-debt-part-1. On Jefferson and Hemings:
Annette Gordon-Reed, *Thomas Jefferson and Sally Hemings: An American Controversy*
(Charlottesville: University of Virginia Press, 1997); and Gordon-Reed, *The Hemingses
of Monticello: An American Family* (New York: Norton, 2008). Historical accounts
and DNA evidence have established that Jefferson fathered at least six children with
Sally Hemings, who was born into slavery at Monticello in 1773, accompanied Jeffer-
son and his daughter Maria to Paris from 1787 to 1789, and was freed sometime after
Jefferson's death in 1826. On their relationship and the evidence of Jefferson's paternity,
"Thomas Jefferson and Sally Hemings: A Brief Account," Thomas Jefferson Foundation,

accessed July 12, 2020, https://www.monticello.org/thomas-jefferson/jefferson-slavery /thomas-jefferson-and-sally-hemings-a-brief-account/; and "Report of the Research Committee on Thomas Jefferson and Sally Hemings," Thomas Jefferson Foundation, January 2000, https://www.monticello.org/thomas-jefferson/jefferson-slavery/thomas -jefferson-and-sally-hemings-a-brief-account/research-report-on-jefferson-and-hemings/.

6. The Dialectic of the University: His Master's Voice

1. Allan Bloom, *The Closing of the American Mind: How Higher Education Has Failed Democracy and Impoverished the Souls of Today's Students* (New York: Simon and Schuster, 1987); and in reply, Lawrence W. Levine, *The Opening of the American Mind: Canons, Culture, and History* (Boston: Beacon Press, 1996). On the culture wars debates, see Andrew Hartman, *A War for the Soul of America: A History of the Culture Wars* (Chicago: University of Chicago Press, 2015), 222–252, and on the related history wars, 253–284.

2. Max Horkheimer and Theodor W. Adorno, *Dialectic of Enlightenment: Philosophical Fragments*, trans. Edmund Jephcott (Redwood City, CA: Stanford University Press, 2002), 94–136.

3. Friedrich Nietzsche, *Anti-Education: On the Future of Our Educational Institutions*, ed. Paul Reitter and Chad Wellmon, trans. Damion Searls (New York: New York Review Books, 2016), lecture 5, March 23, 1872, 75–76. For background on Nietzsche's appointment at Basel and on German debates, see Reitter and Wellmon's introduction, vii–xxv.

4. Nietzsche, *Anti-Education*, 75–76.

5. On Nietzsche's *The Birth of Tragedy* and the interplay of Apollonian and Dionysian knowledge in relation to "academic voices," see William Clark, *Academic Charisma and the Origins of the Research University* (Chicago: University of Chicago Press, 2006), 398–432; and on the international dissemination of the Prussian (or Hanoverian-Prussian) model, 435–476.

6. For an overview, see Laurence R. Veysey, *The Emergence of the American University* (Chicago: University of Chicago Press, 1965), esp. 121–179; and Roger L. Geiger, *To Advance Knowledge: The Growth of American Research Universities 1900–1940* (New York: Oxford University Press, 1986), 1–57. See also Geiger, *The History of American Higher Education: Learning and Culture from the Founding to World War II* (Princeton, NJ: Princeton University Press, 2015), 316–363. John R. Thelin emphasizes university ties to industry in *A History of Higher Education* (Baltimore, MD: Johns Hopkins University Press, 2004), 110–154. On the German universities, see also Charles E. McClelland, *State, Society, and University in Germany 1700–1914* (New York: Cambridge University Press, 1980), esp. 239–340.

7. Richard J. Storr, *Harper's University: The Beginnings* (Chicago: University of Chicago Press, 1966), 13–17.

8. This includes Horkheimer and Adorno's *Dialectic of Enlightenment*. A noteworthy alternative is Veit Erlmann, *Reason and Resonance: A History of Modern Aurality* (New York: Zone Books, 2010), esp. 185–216, 307–342. On "enlightenment" as a concept, see Caroline Winterer, *American Enlightenments: Pursuing Happiness in the Age of Reason* (New Haven, CT: Yale University Press, 2016).

9. Leigh Eric Schmidt, *Hearing Things: Religion, Illusion, and the American Enlightenment* (Cambridge, MA: Harvard University Press, 2000), 13.

10. Schmidt, *Hearing Things*, 134. Schmidt quotes from Frederik Poulsen, "Talking, Weeping, and Bleeding Statues," *Acta Archaeologica* 16 (1945): 178–195. On the mechanico-acoustic "oracles of reason," see Schmidt, 78–134.

11. This circuit is related to Friedrich A. Kittler's description of the university as a "writing-down system" (*Aufschreibesystem*) or "discourse network." See Friedrich A. Kittler, *Discourse Networks: 1800/1900*, trans. Michael Metteer, with Chris Cullens (Redwood City, CA: Stanford University Press, 1990), esp. 368. See also Friedrich A. Kittler, "Universities: Wet, Hard, Soft, and Harder," *Critical Inquiry* 31, no. 1 (Autumn 2004): 244–255.

12. William Rainey Harper, *Religion and the Higher Life* (Chicago: University of Chicago Press, 1904), 107.

13. See, in particular Storr, *Harper's University*, 57–64.

14. Beginning in 1896, juniors and seniors were required to attend weekly chapel, with faculty participation. George E. Vincent, "The Junior Colleges," *The President's Report, University of Chicago, July 1892–July 1902* (Chicago: University of Chicago Press, 1903), 115.

15. Thomas Wakefield Goodspeed, *A History of the University of Chicago, Founded by John D. Rockefeller: The First Quarter-Century* (Chicago: University of Chicago Press, 1916), 450.

16. Goodspeed, *A History of the University of Chicago*, 347.

17. Goodspeed, *A History of the University of Chicago*, 348.

18. Goodspeed, *A History of the University of Chicago*, 348.

19. Jean F. Block, *The Uses of Gothic: Planning and Building the Campus of the University of Chicago, 1892–1932* (Chicago: University of Chicago Library, 1983), 152.

20. John D. Rockefeller to the President and Trustees of the University of Chicago, December 13, 1910, quoted in "The University of Chicago Statement of the Chapel Fund," February 9, 1924, University of Chicago Department of Buildings and Grounds. Records, Box 26, Folder 14, Special Collections Research Center, University of Chicago Library. Hereinafter referred to as University of Chicago Department of Buildings and Grounds Records.

21. George M. Marsden, *The Soul of the American University: From Protestant Establishment to Established Nonbelief* (New York: Oxford University Press, 1994), 265.

22. Marsden, *Soul of the American University*, 246.

23. Based on a maximum audience of 1,600 persons, Watson and White's preliminary estimate showed that the interior would require nine thousand square feet of acoustic tile and twenty thousand square feet of Akoustalith plaster. F. R. Watson to L. R. Flook, July 3, 1926, University of Chicago Department of Buildings and Grounds Records, Box 27, Folder 7.

24. The Guastavino Company proposed replacing their proprietary Rumford acoustic ceiling tile with cast Akoustalith plaster due to the unreliable color variations in the clay used in manufacturing the tile. O. H. Murray to L. R. Flook, July 30, 1926, University of Chicago Department of Buildings and Grounds Records, Box 27, Folder 7.

25. Emily Thompson, *The Soundscape of Modernity: Architectural Acoustics and the Culture of Listening in America, 1900–1933* (Cambridge: MIT Press, 2002), esp. 70–74 on the ties between Sabine, Goodhue, and Guastavino. Goodhue and Guastavino first used Sabine's Rumford tile for the vaulting of St. Thomas Church in New York, completed in 1913. Richard Oliver, *Bertram Grosvenor Goodhue* (New York: Architectural History Foundation/Cambridge, MA: MIT Press), 65, 254n32.

26. "The sound of the speaker's voice proceeds outward in all directions, with only a small part of it going directly to the audience and the reflected sound, which usually reinforces the direct sound, is largely diffused and broken up by the distant, irregular surfaces." F. R. Watson to L. R. Flook, August 4, 1926, in University of Chicago Department of Buildings and Grounds Records, Box 27, Folder 7.

27. L. R. Flook to Bertram Grosvenor Goodhue Associates, August 20, 1926, University of Chicago Department of Buildings and Grounds Records, Box 27, Folder 7. Shortly thereafter Flook again wrote to the Goodhue office on behalf of the building committee to indicate its opposition to replacing the original Rumford tile with cast Akoustolith, which they felt to be an inferior product. A representative of the Guastavino Company replied, on Goodhue office letterhead, affirming the permanence of the cast Akoustolith and its advantages in regard to coloration. R. Guastavino Company to L. R. Flook, August 26, 1926, in University of Chicago Department of Buildings and Grounds Records, Box 27, Folder 7.

28. F. R. Watson to L. R. Flook, October 22, 1928, in University of Chicago Department of Buildings and Grounds Records, Box 27, Folder 7; and L. R. Flook to Rev. Clement Noenig, January 7, 1929, in University of Chicago Department of Buildings and Grounds Records, Box 27, Folder 7.

29. Francis Mayers to University of Chicago, September 22, 1926, University of Chicago Department of Buildings and Grounds Records, Box 27, Folder 7.

30. Floyd R. Watson, "Ideal Auditorium Acoustics," *Journal of the American Institute of Architects*, July 1928, 9–10. Watson delivered this address to the American Institute of Architects annual convention in May 1928.

31. Watson to Flook, October 22, 1928.

32. Watson lists the "Conditions for Perfect Acoustics" in *Acoustics of Buildings, Including Acoustics of Auditoriums and Soundproof Rooms*, 3rd ed. (New York: John Wiley, 1941), 11–12. Thompson notes Watson's tendency, in the mid-1920s, "to conceptualize the concert hall as a combination of two different rooms, one for performers and another for auditors." She writes that, in Watson's ideal, the stage would remain " 'live' or reflective" while the audience is wrapped in what amounts to a "reverberation-muffling blanket." The result was "a concert hall that provided a sound similar to that beginning to be heard via electroacoustic technologies in the home," thus reinforcing "the physical separation of music producers from consumers." Thompson, *Soundscape of Modernity*, 251–252.

33. Thompson, *Soundscape of Modernity*, 3.

34. In a revised version of his "Ideal Auditorium Acoustics," Watson observed, "Some years ago, on reading a number of published accounts of various investigations on acoustics and comparing the results, the author was led to two conclusions: first, that practically all the acoustic defects in auditoriums are due to reflected sound; and second, that speakers and musicians are aided by nearby reflecting surfaces." Insisting that this counterintuitive arrangement is not contradictory, Watson adds that, "particularly when it is equipped with a stage that has reflecting surfaces," the outdoor theater is a model. He goes on to repeat his earlier conclusion, that "from this conception, to obtain ideal acoustic conditions in an indoor auditorium, it would be necessary to follow two rules:"

    1. Provide a stage with suitable reflecting surfaces so that performers can "hear themselves."
    2. Design the auditorium or listening so that the reflected sound will be reduced to be compatible with outdoor conditions.

    Watson, *Acoustics of Buildings*, 50.

    Referring to Harold Burris-Meyer, "The Control of Acoustic Conditions on the Concert Stage," *Journal of the Acoustical Society of America* 12 (January 1941): 335–337, Watson goes on to argue that comparable results may be achieved electroacoustically, 63.

35. On the parallel development of electroacoustics from around 1900, see Thompson, *Soundscape of Modernity*, 229–293.
36. Clark, *Academic Charisma*, 141–182. On the persistence of the disputational model, see in particular 172–179. On genealogical ties between the history seminar and the scientific laboratory, as well as on these as sites for the performance of normative gender roles, see Bonnie G. Smith, "Gender and the Practices of Scientific History: The Seminar and Archival Research in the Nineteenth Century," *American Historical Review* 100, no. 4 (October 1995): 1150–1176.
37. Clark, *Academic Charisma*, 181.
38. Mary Ann Dzuback, *Robert M. Hutchins: Portrait of an Educator* (Chicago: University of Chicago Press, 1991), 82.
39. Senior among these figures were James R. Tufts and George Herbert Mead. The coming unrest was foreshadowed, perhaps, by the fact that Adler's initial salary exceeded all but Tufts's by a significant margin, indicating a tension between departmental and presidential prerogatives. Dzuback, *Robert M. Hutchins*, 95.
40. John Erskine, *The Memory of Certain Persons* (Philadelphia: J. B. Lippincott, 1947), 343. The history of the Columbia College core curriculum, which was formalized in the mid-1930s and of which Erskine's general honors course was an immediate precursor, is summarized in Robert A. McCaughey, *Stand, Columbia: A History of Columbia University in the City of New York, 1754–2004* (New York: Columbia University Press, 2003), 285–299. McCaughey emphasizes tensions between faculty who, like Mark Van Doren and Jacques Barzun, remained more closely associated with Columbia College and taught regularly in the undergraduate core and those university researchers who preferred to teach graduate students. Notably, the two groups were separated spatially; those who taught undergraduates did so in Hamilton Hall, while the researchers did their work in Philosophy Hall, Fayerweather Hall, and other university buildings north of 116th Street. See also Lionel Trilling, "The Van Amringe and Keppel Eras," and Justus Buchler, "Reconstruction in the Liberal Arts," in *A History of Columbia College on Morningside*, ed. Dwight C. Miner (New York: Columbia University Press, 1954), 14–47 and 48–135, respectively.
41. Erskine, *Memory of Certain Persons*, 311–337.
42. Undated letter from an unnamed author to Dean Frederick P. Keppel, in John Erskine, *My Life as a Teacher* (Philadelphia: J. B. Lippincott, 1948), 168. At Columbia, the list of books was initially provisional and was subject to monthly modification in consultation with faculty colleagues.
43. Mortimer J. Adler, *Philosopher at Large: An Intellectual Autobiography* (New York: Macmillan, 1977), 55. Adler's title for the chapter in which this detail appears is "Book Lists without End."
44. Although he never formally graduated from Columbia (having failed to complete the physical education requirement), in 1923 Adler entered graduate school there without a diploma, earning his PhD in 1929. At the same time (1923) he became a preceptor in the general honors course with Mark Van Doren.
45. Adler, *Philosopher at Large*, 57.
46. Adler, *Philosopher at Large*, 58.
47. Adler, *Philosopher at Large*, 68. Already at Columbia, Adler had immersed himself in resolving the seemingly interminable disputes over the legitimacy of Erskine's original list, which actually numbered fifty-two authors and more than a hundred works. In 1925 Adler expanded the list to 176. By 1927, balloting and debate among faculty had reduced it to seventy-six. This was basically the list around which Adler and Hutchins built the

"great books" course at the University of Chicago when they began teaching an undergraduate honors seminar together in 1930.

48. A few years prior, having been "excommunicated" from Columbia's philosophy department and moved over to psychology, Adler presented a paper at a philosophy conference titled "God and the Psychologists." The paper, according to Adler, opposed the "man-centered thinker" of pragmatist philosophy—the model for which, John Dewey, sat in the audience—to the "God-centered thinker," or metaphysician, in the person of George Santayana (or, more tendentiously, Adler himself). The psychologists of his title were principally the new behaviorists, led by John B. Watson, who had studied under Dewey. As Adler read his paper, it seems, Dewey became visibly annoyed, "pounded the arms of his chair, stood up, and walked out of the room muttering that he did not intend to sit around listening to someone tell him how to think about God." Adler, *Philosopher at Large*, 49. At the time, Dewey's name was virtually synonymous with the dominant philosophical and social-scientific orientation at the University of Chicago when Hutchins, the son of a Presbyterian minister, arrived, followed by Adler, a Jewish devotee of Aquinas.

49. Mortimer J. Adler, *Dialectic* (New York: Harcourt, Brace, 1927), 10–11. Adler acknowledges his antipathy to Hegel in *Philosopher at Large*, 156.

50. Dzuback, *Robert M. Hutchins*, 101–102.

51. Adler, *Philosopher at Large*, 139–140. For a "media theory of tableware" in the symbolic economy of dinner, see Bernhard Siegert, "Eating Animals—Eating God—Eating Man: Variations on the Last Supper, or the Cultural Techniques of Communion," in *Cultural Techniques: Grids, Filters, Doors, and Other Articulations of the Real*, trans. Geoffrey Winthrop-Young (New York: Fordham University Press, 2015), 33–52. Stein's unruly slap can be interpreted as an interruption of that economy, especially in light of Adler's seminar-table slapping, mentioned below. Anthony Grafton also reports on the family dinner table as a zone of edifying conversation now "gone the way of the Edsel." Grafton's evident nostalgia for the "serious talk of serious people about serious things" around dinner tables risks misconstrual, however, as uncritically invested in the social relations reproduced there. Grafton, "The Public Intellectual and the Private Sphere: Arendt and Eichmann at the Dinner Table," in *Worlds Made by Words: Scholarship and Community in the Modern West* (Cambridge, MA: Harvard University Press, 2009), 271–287, quotations 286.

52. In his 1930 New Plan, which designated the undergraduate college as custodian of general education, Hutchins proposed reorganizing the university into four separate divisions—humanities, social sciences, physical sciences, and biological sciences—with the college separated out as a fifth, each with its own faculty. The plan was supported by key members of the senior faculty and was accepted by the trustees. See Dzuback, *Robert M. Hutchins*, 109–112. Hutchins's educational philosophy at the time is documented in Robert Maynard Hutchins, *The Higher Learning in America* (New Haven, CT: Yale University Press, 1936).

53. Adler, *Philosopher at Large*, 164.

54. Edward Shils, "Robert Maynard Hutchins," *American Scholar* 59, no. 2 (Spring 1990): 216.

55. Shils, "Robert Maynard Hutchins," 214–215. Adler later acknowledged his embarrassment at the "brashness of my performance" in the seminar, in which "I lectured my elders, allowing no time for questions or discussion." Adler, *Philosopher at Large*, 153.

56. Shils, "Robert Maynard Hutchins," 217.

57. *Great Books Under Discussion: A Report on the Program in 1953* (Chicago: Great Books Foundation, 1954).

58. The 1953 report contains 129 tables based on a questionnaire returned by 4,791 participants, recording extensive data on the program, from the gender, ages, and occupations of participants, to meeting arrangements, "Patterns of Leadership," and "Leader Training," to the books themselves. The questionnaire tabulates the books in terms of the reactions from readers: "too long," "too brief for effective discussion," with rankings by genre according to degrees of difficulty and enjoyment." *Great Books Under Discussion*, 105.

59. Mortimer J. Adler, preface to Mortimer J. Adler and William Gorman, *The Great Ideas: A Syntopicon of Great Books of the Western World*, vol. 1, in *Great Books of the Western World*, ed. Robert Maynard Hutchins, vol. 2 (Chicago: Encyclopaedia Britannica, 1952), xi.

60. Tim Lacy, *The Dream of a Democratic Culture: Mortimer J. Adler and the Great Books Idea* (New York: Palgrave Macmillan, 2013), 49–51.

61. Lacy, *Dream of a Democratic Culture*, 51.

62. "The 102 Great Ideas: Scholars Complete a Monumental Catalog," *Life*, January 26, 1948, 92.

63. Lacy, *Dream of a Democratic Culture*, 52; and Adler, *Philosopher at Large*, 248–250.

64. Adler, preface to *The Great Ideas*, xiii–xxi. This, the second part of the preface, is titled "The Structure of the Syntopicon."

65. Mortimer J. Adler and William Gorman, "The Principles and Methods of Syntopical Construction," in *The Great Ideas: A Syntopicon of Great Books of the Western World*, vol. 2, in *Great Books of the Western World*, ed. Robert Maynard Hutchins, vol. 3 (Chicago: Encyclopaedia Britannica, 1952), 1219–1299.

66. Georg Wilhelm Friedrich Hegel, *Phenomenology of Spirit*, trans. A. V. Miller (New York: Oxford University Press, 1977), 115. On the historicity of this relation, see Susan Buck-Morss, *Hegel, Haiti, and Universal History* (Pittsburgh, PA: University of Pittsburgh Press, 2009); and Andrew Cole, "What Hegel's Master/Slave Dialectic Really Means," *Journal of Medieval and Early Modern Studies* 34, no. 3 (Fall 2004): 577–610. Cole makes a persuasive case for locating Hegel's model in feudalism and hence for conceiving the dialectic as one of "lordship" and "bondage." I retain the terms *master* and *slave*, used influentially by Alexandre Kojève, to point to the more recent discourse.

67. Jacques Lacan, *The Other Side of Psychoanalysis*, trans. Russell Grigg (New York: Norton, 2007), 20.

68. Hegel, *Phenomenology of Spirit*, 112–113.

69. Hegel, *Phenomenology of Spirit*, 116.

70. Lacan, *The Other Side of Psychoanalysis*, 21.

71. Lacan, *The Other Side of Psychoanalysis*, 31.

72. Lacan, *The Other Side of Psychoanalysis*, 201.

73. Lacan, *The Other Side of Psychoanalysis*, 207.

74. Lacan, *The Other Side of Psychoanalysis*, 206.

75. J. William Fulbright, "The War and Its Effects: The Military-Industrial-Academic Complex," in *Super-State: Readings in the Military-Industrial Complex*, ed. Herbert I. Schiller (Urbana: University of Illinois, 1970), 171–178.

76. Hegel, *Phenomenology of Spirit*, 115. The German original is Georg Wilhelm Friedrich Hegel, *System der Wissenschaft. Erster Theil: Die Phänomenologie des Geistes* (Bamberg: Joseph Anton Goebhardt, 1807), 122; available at: http://www.deutschestextarchiv.de /book/show/hegel_phaenomenologie_1807.

77. Bloom, *Closing of the American Mind*, 344, 54.

78. Mortimer Adler, "Great Books, Democracy, and Truth," *Educational Studies* 19, no. 3 (Fall/Winter 1988): 290–302, later included in Adler, *Reforming Education: The Opening of the American Mind* (New York: Macmillan, 1988). According to Adler, as a graduate student at the University of Chicago under Leo Strauss, Bloom taught the great books

in the university's extension course that Adler had helped establish, called "The Basic Program for the Liberal Education for Adults" (292).

79. Bloom, *Closing of the American Mind*, 243–245, 246–256.

80. Bloom, *Closing of the American Mind*, 38–39.

81. Adler, "Great Books, Democracy, and Truth," 291–298.

82. *His Master's Voice* is the title of a painting made by Francis Barraud in 1898. It shows a dog named Nipper listening intently to his dead master's voice (that of Barraud's brother) on an Edison-Bell cylinder phonograph. In 1899, Barraud modified the painting to show a Berliner disc gramophone in place of the phonograph. In 1900 the painting became the trademark of the Gramophone Company and, shortly thereafter in the United States, the Victor Talking Machine Company. Media theory has had much to say about Nipper, the dog shown listening to the gramophone in Barraud's painting. See, for example, Theodor W. Adorno, "The Curves of the Needle," trans. Thomas Y. Levin, *October* 55 (Winter 1990): 54; Friedrich A. Kittler, *Gramophone, Film, Typewriter*, trans. Geoffrey Winthrop-Young and Michael Wutz (Redwood City, CA: Stanford University Press, 1999), 69; John Durham Peters, *Speaking into the Air: A History of the Idea of Communication* (Chicago: University of Chicago Press, 1999), 161–163; and Jonathan Sterne, *The Audible Past: Cultural Origins of Sound Reproduction* (Durham, NC: Duke University Press, 2003), 301–307. "His Master's Voice" is also the title of a 1968 work of science fiction by the Polish writer Stanisław Lem, which sardonically follows the technocratic discourse of the university beyond the campus in a latter-day Manhattan Project—code name: His Master's Voice—devoted to decrypting a possible message received from intelligent beings elsewhere in the universe. Of the message, Lem writes, "It was conceived as a voice whose echo would return—once it was heard and understood." Stanisław Lem, *His Master's Voice*, trans. Michael Kandel (Evanston: Northwestern University Press, 1983), 195.

7. Frontier as Symbolic Form

1. On land and conquest in the West, see Patricia Nelson Limerick, *The Legacy of Conquest: The Unbroken Past of the American West* (New York: Norton, 1987), esp. 55–77. In addition to the literature on Turner's frontier thesis cited in the interlude, see Greg Grandin, *The End of the Myth: From the Frontier to the Border Wall in the Mind of America* (New York: Metropolitan Books / Henry Holt and Co., 2019).

2. Erwin Panofsky, *Perspective as Symbolic Form*, trans. Christopher S. Wood (New York: Zone Books, 1991), originally published as "Die Perspektive als 'symbolische Form,' " *Vorträge der Bibliothek Warburg 1924–1925* (Leipzig and Berlin, 1927): 258–330. Only one of the three volumes of Cassirer's treatise had appeared by this time, as Ernst Cassirer, *Philosophie der symbolischen Formen, Erster Teil: Die Sprache* (Berlin: Bruno Cassirer, 1923), on language. The others are *Philosophie der symbolischen Formen, Zweiter Teil: Das mythische Denken* (Berlin: Bruno Cassirer, 1925), on myth; and *Philosophie der symbolischen Formen, Dritter Teil: Phänomenologie der Erkenntnis* (Berlin: Bruno Cassirer, 1929), on mathematical and scientific knowledge.

3. Lewis Mumford, *Technics and Civilization* (New York: Harcourt Brace, 1934), 88–89, 77.

4. On late nineteenth century American literary culture, Lewis Mumford, *The Golden Day: A Study in American Experience and Culture* (New York: Boni and Liveright, 1926) and on artistic culture, including architecture, Mumford, *The Brown Decades: A Study of the Arts in America 1865–1895* (New York: Harcourt Brace, 1931).

5. Frederick Jackson Turner, "Pioneer Ideals and the State University," in *The Frontier in American History* (New York: H. Holt, 1920), 284. Turner characterized the state university as a miner who "sinks deep shafts through the social strata to find the gold of real ability in the underlying rock of the masses" (283), which he repeated at another commencement address, delivered at the University of Washington in 1914 and anthologized in the same volume as "The West and American Ideals," 292. On the frontier myth, see also Henry Nash Smith, *Virgin Land: The American West as Symbol and Myth* (Cambridge, MA: Harvard University Press, 1950), vii.

6. Turner, "Pioneer Ideals and the State University," 284.

7. Lewis Mumford, *Sticks and Stones: A Study of American Architecture and Civilization* (New York: Boni and Liveright, 1924), 209.

8. Mumford, *Brown Decades*, 72.

9. Mumford, *Brown Decades*, 79.

10. George Perkins Marsh, *Man and Nature; Or, Physical Geography as Modified by Human Action* (New York: Charles Scribner, 1864), v. One of Turner's biographers, Allan G. Bogue, citing the research of Turner's student Fulmer Mood into his teacher's sources, suggests Marsh's book as context for Turner's later argument. In Bogue, *Frederick Jackson Turner: Strange Roads Going Down* (Norman: University of Oklahoma Press, 1998), 110.

11. Marsh was a frequent speaker on college and university campuses, and in the winter of 1858–1859 he delivered a series of lectures on the English language at Columbia College, which were later published. David Lowenthal, *George Perkins Marsh: Prophet of Conservation* (Seattle: University of Washington Press, 2003), 197–201.

12. As discussed below, the University of Vermont acquired Marsh's library in 1883; The University of Vermont, *Catalogue of the Library of George P. Marsh* (Burlington, VT: Free Press Association, 1892), v–viii.

13. University of Vermont, *Catalogue of the Library of George P. Marsh*, 76.

14. It is noteworthy, for example, that the American Association of Geographers was not founded until 1904. On the institutionalization of the academic disciplines in the United States during the latter two decades of the nineteenth century, see Roger L. Geiger, *To Advance Knowledge: The Growth of American Research Universities, 1900–1940* (New York: Oxford University Press, 1986), 20–30.

15. See for example Mumford, *Brown Decades*, 119, and Margaret Henderson Floyd, *Henry Hobson Richardson: A Genius for Architecture* (New York: Monacelli Press, 1997), 189–200.

16. On the genesis of the Ames Memorial commission, see James F. O'Gorman, *H. H. Richardson: Architectural Forms for an American Society* (Chicago: University of Chicago Press, 1987), 95–97. Also: O'Gorman, "Man-Made Mountain: 'Gathering and Governing' in H. H. Richardson's Design for the Ames Monument in Wyoming," in *The Railroad in American Art: Representations of Technological Change*, ed. Susan Danly and Leo Marx (Cambridge, MA: MIT Press, 1988), 113–126.

17. During these same years, Richardson also designed several commercial buildings in Boston for Frederick L. Ames, as well as the rustic Gate Lodge at Langwater, the Ames estate (1880–1881), and the Old Colony Railroad Station in North Easton (1881–1884). Floyd, *Henry Hobson Richardson*, 176–189. An early overview of Richardson's career and work is given in Mariana Griswold [Schuyler] van Rensselaer, *Henry Hobson Richardson and His Works* (Boston: Houghton Mifflin, 1888). For individual projects, see Jeffrey Karl Osner, *H. H. Richardson: Complete Architectural Works* (Cambridge, MA: MIT Press, 1982).

18. As one of the speakers at the dedication of Oakes Ames Memorial Hall said, "Remembering the part which spade and shovel play in civilizing the earth, an honest implement of this kind seems to be a fit emblem of progress." Judge Thomas Russell, as recorded in

Oakes Ames: A Memoir; With an Account of the Dedication of Oakes Ames Memorial Hall at North Easton, Mass., November 17, 1881 (Cambridge, MA: Riverside Press, 1883), 69.

19. The display of Ames shovels and other tools is noted in Rossiter Johnson, *A History of the World's Columbian Exposition Held in Chicago in 1893; by Authority of the Board of Directors* (New York: D. Appleton, 1897), 318.

20. On the Carnegie libraries, including Richardson's influence, see Abigail A. Van Slyck, *Free to All: Carnegie Libraries & American Culture* (Chicago: University of Chicago Press, 1995); On Richardson's libraries, see Kenneth A. Breisch, *Henry Hobson Richardson and the Small Public Library in America: A Study in Typology* (Cambridge, MA: MIT Press, 1997).

21. Billings, like Richardson, belonged to the world described by Noam Maggor in *Brahmin Capitalism: Frontiers of Wealth and Populism in America's First Gilded Age* (Cambridge, MA: Harvard University Press, 2017).

22. Billings also donated funds for the library, insisting that "the need of the University for a fire-proof building, which has been pressing for so many years, can no longer be put aside." Frederick P. Billings to Matthew H. Buckham, March 15, 1883. University of Vermont Special Collections, Group 25: Libraries, Box 33. It seems that Richardson's ability to deliver a fireproof building was among the conditions for the commission. Billings to Buckham, May 25, 1883. University of Vermont Special Collections, Group 25: Libraries, Box 33. On Billings's early admiration of Marsh, see Robin W. Winks, *Frederick Billings: A Life* (Berkeley: University of California Press, 1991), 25; on his purchase of the Marsh family estate, 297–301; on the origins of the Billings Library, including the hiring of Richardson, 303–305. On Marsh's library, see also Lowenthal, *George Perkins Marsh*, 364–365.

23. In an unpublished typescript on the university's history, Joseph L. Hills reports on the interior lighting, including Billings's concerns about fire and his insistence that "electricity should not be used." Hills, "Typescript History of University of Vermont Campus 1800–1947," n.d., 42. University of Vermont Special Collections, J. L. Hills Papers, Folder 1B. Henry-Russell Hitchcock suggests that Richardson derived the "Syrian" arch detail from Charles-Jean-Melchior de Vogüé's *Syrie Centrale: Architecture civile et religieuse du Ier au VIIer siècle* (1865), a copy of which Richardson held in his personal library. Hitchcock, *The Architecture of H. H. Richardson and His Times* (New York: Museum of Modern Art, 1936), 101, 181.

24. Office of Henry Hobson Richardson, "Specification: Burlington Library, Burlington, Vermont [Richardson, Henry Hobson, Billings Library]," n.d., n.p. [11–12]. University of Vermont Special Collections, Records Group 25: Libraries, Box 42, Folder "Library: Billings." In the specification, "local stone" is crossed out to read "Kibbe stone." The proposal for alternative cut stone is found in Richardson, "To Reduce the Cost" n.d., n.p. [2]. University of Vermont Special Collections, Records Group 25: Libraries, Box 42, Folder "Library: Billings." The rejected cost reduction reads: "Cut stone to be from the Saulsburg quarry—medium stone—instead of Kibbe." On the East Longmeadow quarries, see Benjamin Kendall Emerson, *Geology of Old Hampshire County, Massachusetts: Comprising Franklin, Hampshire, and Hampden Counties* (Washington, DC: United States Government Printing Office, 1898), 391–393. Erik Carver has shown how the acquisition of stone quarries by the vertically organized Norcross construction firm belonged to an integration of architectural and technical knowledge into far-reaching knowledge networks. Carver, "Ordering Modernity: How Nineteenth Century Architectural Classicists Built a Techno-Cultural System" (PhD diss., Columbia University, in progress). Relatively early on, Buckham consulted with Billings on the choice of stone,

sending him a sample of unknown origin. Matthew H. Buckham to Frederick Billings, March 20, 1883. Billings Family Archives, Series 1, Manuscripts, Box A 10c, Folder 395.

25. Emerson, *Geology of Old Hampshire County*, 391–392.

26. Francis R. Kowsky, "The Veil of Nature: H. H. Richardson and Frederick Law Olmsted," in *H. H. Richardson: The Architect, His Peers, and Their Era*, ed. Maureen Meister (Cambridge, MA: MIT Press, 1999), 54–75.

27. Mining claims were often complicated by the fact that unlike U.S. law, Mexican law did not necessarily grant mineral rights to land claimants, an obstacle that John C. Frémont and his representatives had to overcome, since the estate was originally established as a Mexican land grant. W. W. Robinson, *Land in California: The Story of Mission Lands, Ranchos, Squatters, Mining Claims, Railroad Grants, Land Scrip, Homesteads* (Berkeley: University of California Press, 1948), 143–145.

28. Laura Wood Roper, *FLO: A Biography of Frederick Law Olmsted* (Baltimore, MD: Johns Hopkins University Press, 1973), 233–243.

29. Mumford, *Brown Decades*, 78. Olmsted's report is discussed in Roper, *FLO*, 271–288.

30. Ralph Waldo Emerson, "Plato; Or, the Philosopher," in *Representative Men: Seven Lectures* (Boston: Phillips, Samson, 1850), 56–57. On Emerson reading Plato, and on the "dialectic" of the one and the many (or unity and difference), see Russell B. Goodman, *American Philosophy Before Pragmatism* (New York: Oxford University Press, 2015), 151–153, 185–186.

31. Ralph Waldo Emerson, "Plato: New Readings," in *Representative Men*, 84–85.

32. Plato, *The Republic*, book 7, in *The Works of Plato: A New and Literal Version, Chiefly from the Text of Stallbaum*, trans. Henry Davis, vol. 2 (London: Henry G. Bohn, 1849), 202.

33. As Emerson put it, "the fine which the good, refusing to govern, ought to pay, is, to be governed by a worse man." Emerson, "Plato: New Readings," 86.

34. Mumford, *Golden Day*, 100.

35. Caroline Winterer, *The Culture of Classicism: Ancient Greece and Rome in American Intellectual Life 1780–1910* (Baltimore, MD: Johns Hopkins University Press, 2002), 123; and Josiah Royce, *California, From the Conquest in 1846 to the Second Vigilance Committee in San Francisco: A Study in American Character* (Boston: Houghton Mifflin, 1886).

36. The quotation, which is from Bushnell's sermon on "The Power of an Endless Life," reads: "Not all the winds, and storms, and earthquakes, and seas, and seasons of the world, have done so much to revolutionize the earth as MAN, the power of an endless life, has done the day he came forth upon it, and received dominion over it." Marsh, *Man and Nature*, title page.

37. Verne A. Stadtman, *The University of California 1868–1968* (New York: McGraw-Hill, 1970), 12–14.

38. On the prior Ohlone (formerly known as Costanoan) inhabitation of what became the Berkeley lands, see George A. Pettitt, *Berkeley: The Town and Gown of It* (Berkeley, CA: Howell North Books, 1973), 9–19. Two entries in Phil McArdle, ed. *Exactly Opposite the Golden Gate: Essays on Berkeley's History 1845–1945* (Berkeley, CA: Berkeley Historical Society, 1983) add some details: McArdle, "The Costanoan Indians, " 35–38, and Trish Hawthorne, "Mortar Rock Park," 42–45. On the Peralta land grant, see J. N. Bowman, "The Peraltas and Their Houses," *California Historical Quarterly* 30, no. 3 (September 1951): 217–231.

39. The deadly conquest of the California Indians by Spanish and later Mexican colonists, and more systematically after them by U.S. settlers, is detailed in Benjamin Madley, *An American Genocide: The United States and the California Indian Catastrophe, 1846–1873* (New Haven, CT: Yale University Press, 2016). Madley describes the massacre of

hundreds of Wintu natives by the band of colonists led by John Frémont in 1846 as "the prelude to hundreds of similar massacres and ultimately an American genocide," 47. Other, less immediately violent but no less effective colonial techniques included a longstanding administrative cartography. Bernhard Siegert, "*Pasajeros a Indias*: Registers and Biographical Writings as Cultural Techniques of Subject Constitution (Spain, Sixteenth Century)," in *Cultural Techniques: Grids, Filters, Doors, and Other Articulations of the Real*, trans. Geoffrey Winthrop-Young (Fordham: Fordham University Press, 2015), 82–96.

40. On the relationship between Californios (Mexican or Mexican American Californians) and American land claims lawyers, including Billings's law partner, Henry W. Halleck, see Leonard Pitt, *The Decline of the Californios: The Social History of the Spanish-Speaking Californians, 1846–1890* (Berkeley: University of California Press, 1966), 91–97.

41. United States v. Peralta et al, 60 US 19 How. 1856, https://www.loc.gov/item/usrep060343/. A detailed account of the legal conflicts over Chicana/Chicano land claims in California, Texas, and the southwest territories during this period is given in Guadalupe T. Luna, "Chicana/Chicano Land Tenure in the Agrarian Domain: On the Edge of a 'Naked Knife,' " *Michigan Journal of Race and Law* 4, no. 38 (Fall 1998): 39–144, with reference to boundary disputes including the Peralta case on 115–117. On the California Land Commission, which was set up to adjudicate these claims, see Robinson, *Land in California*, 91–109.

42. William Warren Ferrier, *Berkeley, California: The Story of the Evolution of a Hamlet into a City of Culture and Commerce* (Berkeley: [Published by the Author], 1933), 29. On the sale of the Peralta lands more generally, see Pettitt, *Berkeley*, 18–20; as well as two entries in McArdle, ed., *Exactly Opposite the Golden Gate*: McArdle, "The Peralta Land Grant," 46–50, and Edward Staniford, "Domingo Peralta," 51–56.

43. On Kellersberger, see Jack J. Studer, "Julius Kellersberger: A Swiss as Surveyor and City Planner in California, 1851–1857," *California Historical Society Quarterly* 47, no. 1 (March 1968): 3–14.

44. Ferrier, *Berkeley, California*, 75; and William Warren Ferrier, *Origin and Development of the University of California* (Berkeley, CA: Sather Gate Bookshop, 1930), 195.

45. Olmsted, Vaux & Company, *Report upon a Projected Improvement of the Estate of the College of California, at Berkeley, near Oakland* (New York: W. C. Bryant, 1866), 4.

46. Olmsted's plan may have been partly based on the extant College Homestead Association, which had been established in 1864 for a site contiguous to the college property, to the south. S. H. Willey, College of California, *Articles of Agreement of the Homestead Association Together with a Water Report and Map by the Engineer and a Series of College Papers* (San Francisco: Towne and Bacon, 1865).

47. Ferrier, *Origin and Development*, 238–241.

48. Ferrier, *Origin and Development*, 244–245. Numerous other accounts repeat versions of this story, among them Winks, *Frederick Billings*, 92–93; Stadtman, *University of California*, 14; and Writer's Program of the Works Projects Administration, *Berkeley: The First Seventy-Five Years* (Berkeley, CA: The Gillick Press, 1941), 5–7. On the overall transition from college to university, see Stadtman, *University of California*, 4–49.

49. Ferrier, *Origin and Development*, 256–275.

50. Stadtman, *University of California*, 42–43.

51. Phoebe Hearst Architectural Plan for the University of California, *The International Competition for the Phoebe Hearst Architectural Plan for the University of California* (San Francisco: Trustees of the Phoebe A. Hearst Architectural Plan for the University of California, 1899), 29.

52. Kathryn P. Hearst, "Phoebe Apperson Hearst: The Making of an Upper-Class Woman, 1842–1919" (PhD diss., Columbia University, 2005), 284.

53. Hearst, "Phoebe Apperson Hearst," 295.

54. Hearst, "Phoebe Apperson Hearst," 295–296. See also Loren W. Partridge, *John Galen Howard and the Berkeley Campus: Beaux-Arts Architecture in the "Athens of the West"* (Berkeley, CA: Berkeley Architectural Heritage Association, 1978), 11. Sally B. Woodbridge also suggests that Hearst had already been considering the memorial, in *John Galen Howard and the University of California: The Design of a Great Public Campus* (Berkeley: University of California Press, 2002), 27. On Maybeck's work on the campus plan, including his own proposed plan of 1896, see Kenneth H. Cardwell, *Bernard Maybeck: Artisan, Architect, Artist* (Santa Barbara, CA: Peregrine Smith, 1977), 37–43; and Cardwell and Wm. C. Hays, "Fifty Years from Now," *California Monthly* 44 (April 1954): 20–26.

55. Phoebe Apperson Hearst, letter to the University of California Board of Regents, October 24, 1896, cited in *The International Competition*, 6. The international scope of the competition, the first round of which was coordinated out of Antwerp, is reflected in the printing of this document's text in four languages: English, French, German, and Italian.

56. Phoebe Hearst Architectural Plan for the University of California, *The International Competition*, 8–10. For details on the competition brief, see *University of California, Berkeley, Programme for an International Competition for the Phebe Hearst Architectural Plan of the University of California* (Berkeley, CA: [Trustees of the Phebe Hearst Architectural Plan of the University of California], 1897). The preliminary program was released on August 31, 1897, the final on December 3, 1897.

57. For a detailed reconstruction of the competition process, see Roy Lowe, *A Western Acropolis of Learning: The University of California in 1897* (Berkeley: Center for Studies in Higher Education and Institute of Governmental Studies, University of California, Berkeley, 1996).

58. Woodbridge, *John Galen Howard*, 39–59.

59. In 1874, Olmsted wrote to William Hammond Hall, the chief surveyor and superintendent of Golden Gate Park who had also consulted on the early planning of the Berkeley campus, that: "There was an axial line in my plan extending from near the centre of the property toward the Golden Gate. There is a similar line in yours I think, but if so I doubt the two lines correspond. Your line I judge is laid along the middle of a knoll or spur; mine through an adjoining valley. If so there is an obvious difference of motive between the two plans." "Frederick Law Olmsted to William Hammond Hall, March 23, 1874," in *The Papers of Frederick Law Olmsted*, ed. Charles E. Beveridge, Carolyn F. Hoffman, Kenneth Hawkins, and Tina Hummel, vol. 7, *Parks, Politics, and Patronage, 1874–1882* (Baltimore, MD: Johns Hopkins University Press, 2007), 50.

60. Howard wrote in 1902: "The profession of mining has to do with the very body and bone of Earth; its process is a ruthless assault on the bowels of the world, a contest with the crudest and most rudimentary forces. There is about it something essentially elementary, something primordial; and its expression in Architecture must, to be true, have something of the rude, the Cyclopean." John Galen Howard, "The Hearst Memorial Building for the College of Mining," *University of California Magazine* 8, no. 6 (October 1902): 288. University Archives, Bancroft Library, University of California at Berkeley, John Galen Howard Records at the University of California Berkeley, 1874–1954, Box 17, Folder 335.

61. From 1909 to 1915, the university register gave detailed technical descriptions of the mining building. "The Hearst Memorial Mining Building," *University of California*

Register 1907-08-09 (Berkeley, CA: University Press, 1909), 462–466. For an early architectural analysis of the new campus buildings, including the mining building, see Herbert Croly, "The New University of California," *Architectural Record* 23, no. 4 (April 4, 1908): 269–293.

62. In preparation for the design and with funding from Hearst, Howard traveled with Samuel B. Cristy, dean of the College of Mines, across the country and in Europe to visit "all existing mining schools of importance, in order that no element of fitness might be overlooked." John Galen Howard, in University of California, *Dedication of the Hearst Memorial Mining Building: Samuel Benedict Cristy, Thomas A. Rickard, William Randolph Hearst* (Berkeley, CA: University Press, 1907), 6. University Archives, Bancroft Library, University of California at Berkeley, John Galen Howard Records at the University of California Berkeley, 1874–1954, Box 17, Folder 335. See also Woodbridge, *John Galen Howard*, 80–84.

63. To minimize interference with sensitive measurements from vibration, the central core of the research wing of Harvard University's Jefferson Physical Laboratory was built on a separate foundation, and its walls were also isolated from the rest of the structure. To the extent possible, ferromagnetic materials were eliminated from the fixtures, pipes, and furnishings in this part of the building for the study of the Earth's magnetic field. The result was imperfect; the building's bricks turned out to possess a faint magnetic charge, and the soil underneath was less stable than hoped. "The Jefferson Physical Laboratory: A Note on Its Early Days," Centennial Celebration, May 4, 1984, Harvard University. Pamphlet. Harvard University Special Collections, General Information by and about Jefferson Physical Laboratory, HUB 1466.2, Box 18. Further detail in John Trowbridge, "The Jefferson Physical Laboratory," *Science* 5, no. 111 (March 20, 1885): 229–231.

64. On the Hearst Greek Theater, see Woodbridge, *John Galen Howard*, 59–61.

65. On Howard's work on the Berkeley campus during this period, including the Hearst Memorial Mining Building and Sather Gate, see Woodbridge, *John Galen Howard*, 74–111.

66. John Aubrey Douglass, *The California Idea and American Higher Education: 1850 to the 1960 Master Plan* (Redwood City, CA: Stanford University Press, 2000), 184–194. See also Monroe E. Deutsch, Aubrey A. Douglass, and George Drayton Strayer, *A Report of a Survey of the Needs of California in Higher Education*. Report to the Liason Committee of the Regents of the University of California and the State Board of Education (March 1, 1948).

67. Stadtman, *University of California*, 356–358.

68. Vannevar Bush, *Science—The Endless Frontier* (Washington, DC: United States Government Printing Office, 1945). Bush's title borrows from a letter addressed to him from President Franklin Delano Roosevelt on November 17, 1944, which is reproduced in the report, in which Roosevelt declared: "New frontiers of the mind are before us, and if they are pioneered with the same vision, boldness, and drive with which we have waged this war we can create a fuller and more fruitful employment and a fuller and more fruitful life" (vii).

    On the role of Bush's report in the establishment of the National Science Foundation, see Daniel J. Kevles, "The National Science Foundation and the Debate over Postwar Research Policy, 1942–1945: A Political Interpretation of *Science—The Endless Frontier*," *Isis* 68, no. 1 (March 1977): 4–26.

69. On Brown's design for the cyclotron building, see Jeffrey T. Tilman, *Arthur Brown Jr. Progressive Classicist* (New York: Institute of Classical Architecture/Norton, 2006), 228–230. The main Berkeley campus ultimately came to occupy most of plots 69, 70, 71, 79, 80, 81, and 82 of the Kellersberger map.

70. Raymond B. Fosdick, *The Rockefeller Foundation: President's Review for 1940* (New York: Rockefeller Foundation, 1940), 37, 42–43. Writing to Edsel Ford in an effort to raise funds for its construction, Lawrence's colleague David Morris described the cyclotron as "an instrument which will enlarge the frontier of science almost beyond belief." Morris, quoted in J. L. Heilbron and Robert W. Seidel, *Lawrence and His Laboratory: A History of the Lawrence Berkeley Laboratory*, vol. 1 (Berkeley: University of California Press, 1989), 474.

71. On Oppenheimer, the Radiation Laboratory, and the House Committee on Un-American Activities investigations, see Ellen W. Strecker, *No Ivory Tower: McCarthyism and the Universities* (New York: Oxford University Press, 1986), 130–142. On Oppenheimer's testimony, see Nuel Pharr Davis, *Lawrence and Oppenheimer* (New York: Da Capo, 1986), 283–284; on the 1954 security hearing resulting in his dismissal, 337–351.

72. For an overview of the Berkeley loyalty oath controversy in context, see Strecker, *No Ivory Tower*, 117–125. Detail on the process is given in David P. Gardner, *The California Oath Controversy* (Berkeley: University of California Press, 1967). On Kantorowicz's role in publicly opposing the oath and his eventual dismissal, see Robert E. Lerner, *Ernst Kantorowicz: A Life* (Princeton, NJ: Princeton University Press, 2017), 312–328. An account by Berkeley faculty is given in George R. Stewart in collaboration with other professors of the University of California, *The Year of the Oath: The Fight for Academic Freedom at the University of California* (Garden City, NY: Doubleday, 1950). Historical background on academic loyalty oaths during the First World War is given in Richard Hofstadter and Walter P. Metzger, *The Development of Academic Freedom in the United States* (New York: Columbia University Press, 1955), 495–506.

73. Ernst H. Kantorowicz, *The Fundamental Issue: Documents and Marginal Notes on the University of California Loyalty Oath* (San Francisco: Parker Printing, 1950), 10–18. Kantorowicz seized on the professors-versus-janitors comparison made in a public meeting by California regent Sydney Ehrman, a proponent of the oath, 14–15.

74. On the medieval loyalty oath and the *universitas*, see Kantorowicz, *The King's Two Bodies: A Study in Medieval Political Theology* (Princeton, NJ: Princeton University Press, 1957), 358–372.

75. Kantorowicz, *The Fundamental Issue*, 18.

76. Though he was Jewish, Kantorowicz had been associated with nationalist cultural politics in Weimar, Germany, which prompted Panofsky initially to oppose the appointment. Kantorowicz's role in the loyalty oath controversy was an important factor in persuading Panofsky to support him. At the Institute, Kantorowicz and Panofsky became close personally and intellectually. Lerner, *Ernst Kantorowicz*, 330–332, 335.

77. Kantorowicz, *King's Two Bodies*, ix.

78. Ernst Cassirer, *The Myth of the State* (New Haven, CT: Yale University Press, 1946), 34.

79. Tilman, *Arthur Brown Jr.*, 230–231.

80. On the reconfiguration of the area around Sproul Hall and the design and construction of the student union, see Clare Robinson, "Architecture in Support of Citizenry: Vernon DeMars and the Berkeley Student Union," *Journal of Architectural Education* 70, no. 2 (2016): 236–246. On the political geography of the urban space in question, see also Don Mitchell, *The Right to the City: Social Justice and the Fight for Public Space* (New York: Guilford Press, 2003), 86–92.

81. Clark Kerr, *The Uses of the University* (Cambridge, MA: Harvard University Press, 1963), 7.

82. Kerr, *Uses of the University*, 20. The remark that universities were "a collection of disparate interests held together by a common plumbing system" is usually attributed to

University of Chicago president Robert Maynard Hutchins. George M. Marsden, *The Soul of the American University: From Protestant Establishment to Established Nonbelief* (New York: Oxford University Press, 1994), 340.

83. Jacques Barzun, *The House of Intellect* (New York: Harper, 1959), 14. On alphabeticization, Barzun writes: "The alphabet is a fundamental form to bear in mind while discussing the decay of Intellect, because intellectual work here defined presupposes the concentration and continuity, the self-awareness and articulate precision, which can only be achieved through some firm record of fluent thought; that is, Intellect presupposes Literacy," (5–6). Acknowledging that "it is true that Intellect as I am defining it belongs to the Western tradition," Barzun scolds Lewis Mumford for an anti-Western "Orientalism" in the latter's book on Toynbee (25–26).

84. Kerr, *Uses of the University*, 93–94.

85. Kerr, *Uses of the University*, 89–90; Jean Gottmann, *Megalopolis: The Urbanized Northeastern Seaboard of the United States* (Cambridge, MA: MIT Press, 1961).

86. Seymour Martin Lipset and Sheldon S. Wolin, eds., *The Berkeley Student Revolt: Facts and Interpretations* (New York: Anchor Books/Doubleday, 1965), 99–109; quotation on 109. A detailed account of these events is also given in Max Heirich, *The Beginning: Berkeley 1964* (New York: Columbia University Press, 1968).

87. Edward W. Strong, quoted in Lipset and Wolin, *Berkeley Student Revolt*, 109–110.

88. "We won't operate according to the way the parts of this machine should operate, and the machine started to go out of commission. But the remedy is the same! In the case of a regular machine, you throw the parts out! And that's what they decided to do. That's what the statement says. They're on indefinite suspension." Mario Savio, "Speech at the Sit-In, Sproul Hall, 30 September 1964," in *The Essential Mario Savio: Speeches and Writings that Changed America*, ed. Robert Cohen (Berkeley: University of California Press, 2014), 115.

89. Heirich lists spatial conditions as among the contextual factors "structuring the conflict." Heirich, *The Beginning*, 17–24. Don Mitchell offers a related but more complex argument, on the "geography of free speech," in *Right to the City*, 81–105.

90. Later, Aptheker recalled that "it was men who dominated our meetings and discussions. Women did most of the clerical work and fund-raising and provided food." She suggested that ridicule and contempt from men on the New Left were an important impetus for the organized women's movement that followed and "became a significant experience in our understandings of the extent to which patriarchal conventions and male supremacy cut across boundaries of race, ethnicity, and class." Bettina Aptheker, "Gender Politics and the FSM: A Meditation on Women and Freedom of Speech," in *The Free Speech Movement: Reflections on Berkeley in the 1960s*, ed. Robert Cohen (Berkeley: University of California Press, 2002), 131, 133.

91. Mario Savio, " 'Bodies upon the Gears' Speech at FSM Rally, Sproul Hall Steps, 2 December 1964," in *Essential Mario Savio*, 188. Kerr used the expression "knowledge industry" in *Uses of the University*, 87.

92. These two possibilities are summarized in two responses by Berkeley faculty to the Free Speech Movement, in Lipset and Wolin, *Berkeley Student Revolt*—the first, in Sidney Hook, "Academic Freedom and the Rights of Students," 432–442; and the second, in Jacobus Ten Broek, Norman Jacobsen, and Sheldon S. Wolin, "Academic Freedom and Student Political Activity," 443–452.

93. Savio, "Speech at the Sit-In, Sproul Hall, September 30, 1964," in *Essential Mario Savio*, 115.

8. Technopoesis: Human Capital and the Spirit of Research

1. Norbert Wiener, *Cybernetics: Or Control and Communication in the Animal and the Machine* (Cambridge, MA: Technology Press, 1948), 8.
2. Norbert Wiener, *The Human Use of Human Beings: Cybernetics and Society* (Boston: Houghton Mifflin, 1950). On the history of this problem, see Peter Galison, "The Americanization of Unity," *Daedalus* 127, no. 1 (Winter 1998): 45–71.
3. On the design of the MIT campus, see Mark Jarzombek, *Designing MIT: Bosworth's New Tech* (Boston: Northeastern University Press, 2004). On the double-loaded corridor as a new imaginary, see also Jarzombek, "Corridor Spaces," *Critical Inquiry* 36, no. 4 (Summer 2010): 728–770.
4. Larry Hardesty, "The Original Absent-Minded Professor," *MIT Technology Review*, June 21, 2011, https://www.technologyreview.com/s/424363/the-original-absent-minded-professor/.
5. Jarzombek, *Designing MIT*, 112.
6. Norbert Wiener, *The Human Use of Human Beings: Cybernetics and Society*, 2nd rev. ed. (Garden City, NY: Doubleday, 1954), 185–186; emphasis in original. The first edition is cited above.
7. John Ely Burchard, ed. *Mid-Century: The Social Implications of Scientific Progress* (Cambridge, MA: Technology Press and MIT, 1950), 3.
8. On moral philosophy and higher education in the American colonies and early republic, see George M. Marsden, *The Soul of the American University: From Protestant Establishment to Established Nonbelief* (New York: Oxford University Press, 1994), 50–64. On the role of the humanities, see Jon H. Roberts and James Turner, *The Sacred and the Secular University* (Princeton, NJ: Princeton University Press, 2000), 75ff.
9. Ronald H. Robnett, C. Richard Soderberg, Julias A. Stratton, John R. Loofbourow, and Warren K. Lewis, *Report of the Committee on Educational Survey to the Faculty of the Massachusetts Institute of Technology* (Cambridge, MA: Technology Press, 1949), 3.
10. Robnett et al., *Report of the Committee on Educational Survey*, 4.
11. As the report puts it:

   > In the past [during which vocational training was unduly emphasized], the humanities have necessarily been service fields concerned primarily with instruction at the elementary level. Now, however, there is a growing concern with human and social problems, an increased awareness of the interplay between science and technology on the one hand and the conduct of human affairs on the other, and an awakened realization of the fruitfulness of the techniques of the natural sciences in the study of human and social problems. We believe that these trends now make possible the development of the humanities and social sciences at advanced professional levels in the environment of a technological institution.

   Robnett et al., *Report of the Committee on Educational Survey*, 27.
12. Although architecture had been taught at MIT since 1865, the first half of the twentieth century suffered from what the report politely calls an "emphasis" on the "aesthetic" that alienated the curriculum from an institutional milieu dominated by engineering. Robnett et al., *Report of the Committee on Educational Survey*, 42.
13. Robnett et al., *Report of the Committee on Educational Survey*, 40–44.
14. Winston Churchill, "The Twentieth Century," in Burchard, *Mid-Century*, 60–61. In his otherwise enthusiastic annotations to the transcription, Burchard regretfully noted that most newspaper accounts of the speech had concentrated on Churchill's subsequent

remarks on nuclear armament rather than on the importance of humanistic knowledge. Another footnote adds that, the editor having "carelessly left his recording machines at home," the transcript provided is as reported the following morning in *The Boston Herald* rather than verbatim (60–61n42, 75n61).

15. Churchill, "The Twentieth Century," 62–63.
16. Churchill, "The Twentieth Century," 67.
17. John Ely Burchard, opening remarks before the Mid-Century Convocation on the Social Implications of Twentieth Century Progress, in Burchard, *Mid-Century*, 6.
18. "An Application to the Kresge Foundation from the Massachusetts Institute of Technology in Support of a Program in Development of Citizenship and Christian Character," April 11, 1950; Institute Archives, Massachusetts Institute of Technology (Hereafter: MIT Archives) AC004, Box 131, Folder 12.
19. An internal MIT document summarizes the purpose of the Kresge Foundation as being the "promotion of eleemosynary, philanthropic and charitable means of any and all of the means of human progress, whether they be for the benefit of religious, charitable, benevolent or educational institutions or public benefaction of whatever name or nature." In "The Kresge Foundation," n.d.; MIT Archives AC004, Box 131, Folder 12. Killian had apparently first approached Kresge's son, who served as the foundation's vice president, in personal correspondence in late 1949, James R. Killian to Stanley S. Kresge, November 7, 1949, MIT Archives AC004, Box 131, Folder 4.
20. Karl T. Compton to the Trustees of the Kresge Foundation (cover letter to Kresge application), April 11, 1950, MIT Archives AC004, Box 131, Folder 12.
21. Compton to the Trustees of the Kresge Foundation.
22. "Enclosure to Application to the Kresge Foundation from The Massachusetts Institute of Technology (Statement of Background and Details)," 8; MIT Archives AC004, Box 131, Folder 12.
23. "Enclosure to Application to the Kresge Foundation," 21.
24. News Service, Massachusetts Institute of Technology, "For Release in the Morning Papers of July 1, 1950," MIT Archives AC004, Box 131, Folder 12. Baker proposed the "meeting house" figure in a memorandum, Everett M. Baker, "Specifications for Auditorium-Chapel for M.I.T.," July 17, 1950, MIT Archives AC004, Box 131, Folder 5. Although the Kresge proposal suggested two separate buildings, Baker's memo still contemplated a single building but now with a separate entrance for the chapel, 4.
25. John E. Burchard, "Objectives of M.I.T. School of Humanities," June 2, 1950, MIT Archives AC004, Box 131, Folder 12.
26. Press Release, "Full Text of an Address Prepared by James R. Killian, Jr., President of the Massachusetts Institute of Technology, for Delivery at the Dedication of the Kresge Auditorium and M.I.T. Chapel at 3:30 O'clock on Sunday Afternoon, May 8," May 9, 1955, 6; MIT Archives AC004, Box 131, Folder 8.
27. James R. Killian to John E. Burchard, August 14, 1953, MIT Archives AC004, Box 131, Folder 6.
28. Subcommittee on Actual Dedication Ceremony for Chapel and Auditorium, Meeting minutes, July 23, 1954, MIT Archives, Box 131, Folder 7.
29. "Dedication of the Kresge Auditorium and the M.I.T. Chapel, Massachusetts Institute of Technology, May 8, 1955," Karl T. Compton and James R. Killian Administrations (1930–1959), Records, 1930–1959; MIT Archives AC004, Box 131, Folder 10.
30. James R. Killian, "Our Religious Program," in "Dedication of the Kresge Auditorium and the M.I.T. Chapel," n.p.
31. John E. Burchard, *Q.E.D: M.I.T. in World War II* (New York: Wiley, 1948).

32. Jimena Canales, "Harold E. 'Doc' Edgerton and His Laboratory Notebooks," *Aperture* 211 (Summer 2013): 72–73. On Edgerton's wartime work, see Burchard, *Q.E.D.*, 196–204. See also Harold E. Edgerton and James R. Killian Jr., *Flash! Seeing the Unseen by Ultra High-Speed Photography* (Boston: Hale, Cushman & Flint, 1939), 2nd ed. (Boston: Charles T. Branford, 1954).

33. Burchard, *Q.E.D.*, 204.

34. The contract with the AEC is explained in Karl L. Wildes and Nilo A. Lindgren, *A Century of Electrical Engineering and Computer Science at MIT, 1882–1982* (Cambridge, MA: MIT Press, 1985), 152–153. See also Julius A. Stratton, "Harold Eugene Edgerton (April 6, 1903–January 4, 1990)," *Proceedings of the American Philosophical Society* 135, no. 3 (1991): 447–448; and "EG&G the Company: 1947 Onwards," available at Edgerton Digital Collections (EDC) Project, accessed July 16, 2020, http://edgerton-digital-collections.org/docs-life/egg-the-company.

35. In a 1965 television documentary on NBC, *The Decision to Drop the Bomb*, prod. Fred Freed, Oppenheimer recalled thinking these words from the Bhagavad Gita as he witnessed the atomic explosion at the Trinity test site on July 16, 1945. James A. Hijiya, "The *Gita* of Robert Oppenheimer," *Proceedings of the American Philosophical Society* 144, no. 2 (June 2000): 123–125.

36. Edgerton and Killian, *Flash!* 2nd rev. ed., 55. Also, Canales, "Harold E. 'Doc' Edgerton," 73. On atomic testing and the aesthetics of the sublime, see David E. Nye, *American Technological Sublime* (Cambridge, MA: MIT Press, 1994), 225–234.

37. "Buildings in the Round: MIT Completes Its Cylindrical Chapel and Domed Auditorium by Architect Eero Saarinen," *Architectural Forum* 104, no. 1 (January 1956): 117.

38. Eero Saarinen, "Auditorium and Chapel, Massachusetts Institute of Technology, Cambridge, Mass.," Eero Saarinen Papers, Yale University Manuscripts and Archives, Box 28, Folder 121.

39. Leo L. Beranek, *Music, Acoustics & Architecture* (New York: John Wiley, 1962), 105. Beranek also quoted from an acoustical analysis of the auditorium made by Klaus Liepmann, MIT director of music, in 1959: "The tone is clear and clean, and while the reverberation period might seem somewhat short for the repertoire of the Romantics when they employ a big orchestra, this very clarity turns out to be a decided advantage when it comes to solo recitals, chamber music, and music of the Baroque" (108).

40. Edward Weeks, "The Opal on the Charles," *Architectural Record* 118, no. 1 (July 1955): 133.

41. Weeks, "Opal on the Charles," 135–137.

42. Weeks, "Opal on the Charles," 137.

43. "A Moratorium on Technology [1958]," announcement; MIT Society for Social Responsibility in Science memorandum, 6 January 1966; and "Lewis Mumford, 'The Missing Dimensions: The Human Use of Human Beings at MIT,' " seminar announcement, all in Lewis Mumford Papers, Kislak Center for Special Collections, Rare Books and Manuscripts, University of Pennsylvania. Box 184, Folder 8102.

44. Lewis Mumford, *Technics and Civilization* (New York: Harcourt Brace, 1934), 359.

45. Mumford, *Technics and Civilization*, 110.

46. Lewis Mumford, "The Making of Men," in *The Humanities Look Ahead: Report of the First Annual Conference Held by the Stanford School of Humanities*, ed. Henry Hoyt Hudson (Redwood City, CA: Stanford University Press, 1943), 144.

47. On Langer, see Robert E. Innis, *Susanne Langer in Focus: The Symbolic Mind* (Indianapolis: Indiana University Press, 2009).

48. Mumford, "The Making of Men," 144.

49. Susanne K. Langer, *Philosophy in a New Key: A Study in the Symbolism of Reason, Rite, and Art* (Cambridge, MA: Harvard University Press, 1942), 20; emphasis in original.

50. Langer, *Philosophy in a New Key*, 21; emphasis in original.

51. Lewis Mumford, *Art and Technics* (New York: Columbia University Press, 1952), 22.

52. Lewis Mumford, "Memorandum on the Teaching of the Arts" [Stanford University], 10 April 1944, 4. Mumford Papers, University of Pennsylvania, Box 182, Folder 8071.

53. John David Jackson, "Panofsky Agonistes: The 1950 Loyalty Oath at Berkeley," *Physics Today* 62, no. 1 (January 2009): 41–47; and Wolfgang K. H. Panofsky, *Panofsky on Physics, Politics and Peace: Pief Remembers* (New York: Springer, 2007), 39–44.

54. Lewis Mumford, Undated bibliography, including entry on "The Nature and Function of Language," Mumford Papers, Box 182, Folder 8077. The collection also contains descriptions of Mumford's course, "The Nature of Man," Box 182, Folder 8075, Folder 8077.

55. C. Stewart Gillmor, *Fred Terman at Stanford: Building a Discipline, a University, and Silicon Valley* (Redwood City, CA: Stanford University Press, 2004), 140, 156–157.

56. Gillmor, *Fred Terman at Stanford*, 159–167.

57. Gillmor, *Fred Terman at Stanford*, 282–284; and Christophe Lécuyer, *Making Silicon Valley: Innovation and the Growth of High Tech* (Cambridge, MA: MIT Press, 2006), 89–128.

58. Lewis Mumford, Personalia, March 12, 1944, p. 2 and Random Note, April 20, 1944, pp. 1–2. Mumford Papers, Box 192, Folder 8239 and 8238. On Tressider's support for the school of humanities, see Edith R. Mirrielees, *Stanford: The Story of a University* (New York: G. B. Putnam, 1959), 241.

59. On Terman's "steeples of excellence" and Cold War science, see Rebecca S. Lowen, *Creating the Cold War University: The Transformation of Stanford* (Berkeley: University of California Press, 1997); Stuart W. Leslie, *The Cold War and American Science: The Military-Industrial-Academic Complex at MIT and Stanford* (New York: Columbia University Press, 1993); and Roger L. Geiger, *Research & Relevant Knowledge: American Universities Since World War II*, 2nd ed. (New Brunswick, NJ: Transaction, 2009). On Stanford and corporate influence, see Christophe Lécuyer, "What Do Universities Really Owe Industry? The Case of Solid State Electronics at Stanford," *Minerva* 43, no. 1 (March 2005): 51–71.

60. Lewis Mumford, "Memorandum on Planning I," n.d., 1. ("Memorandum on Planning II" is dated March 6, 1947. "Campus Planning," Buildings & Grounds, Stanford University Archives, Box 0220/2.

61. Margaret Pugh O'Mara, *Cities of Knowledge: Cold War Science and the Search for the Next Silicon Valley* (Princeton, NJ: Princeton University Press, 2005).

62. Mumford, "Memorandum on Planning I," 4.

63. Panofsky, *Panofsky on Physics*, 81–82.

64. Robert Moulton, "Physics, Power, and Politics: Fear and Loathing on the Electron Trail," *Sandstone & Tile* [Stanford Historical Society] 25, no. 1 (Winter 2001): 3–12; and Peter Galison, Bruce Hevly, and Rebecca Lowen, "Controlling the Monster: Stanford and the Growth of Physics Research, 1935–1962," in *Big Science: The Growth of Large-Scale Research*, ed. Peter Galison and Bruce Hevly (Redwood City, CA: Stanford University Press, 1992), 46–77.

65. Stuart W. Leslie and Bruce Hevly, "Steeple Building at Stanford: Electrical Engineering, Physics, and Microwave Research," *Proceedings of the IEEE* 73, no. 7 (July 1985): 1169–1180; Wolfgang Panofsky, "SLAC and Big Science: Stanford University," in Galison and Hevly, *Big Science*, 129–146.

66. The younger Panofsky gives the example of when, with the installation at SLAC of a large bubble chamber to record visual data, "pictorial images" recorded on film "suddenly transformed the laboratory to the world's most prolific producer of bubble-chamber film for a wide outside community." Panofsky, "SLAC and Big Science," 137.

67. Lewis Mumford, *The Myth of the Machine: Technics and Human Development* (New York: Harcourt Brace, 1967) and *The Myth of the Machine: The Pentagon of Power* (New York: Harcourt Brace Jovanovich, 1970).

68. Lewis Mumford, *The Transformations of Man* (New York: Collier, 1956), 130ff.

69. Lewis Mumford, "The School of Humanities at Stanford," in *The School of Humanities: A Description* [pamphlet] (Stanford University, 1942), 8–9. Mumford Papers, Box 112, Folder 6663.

70. On the early history of the Hoover Library, see J. Pearce Mitchell, *Stanford University 1916–1941* (Redwood City, CA: Stanford University, 1958), 18–22. For details on the library's collections, see Peter Duignan, "The Library of the Hoover Institution on War, Revolution and Peace: Part I, Origin and Growth," *Library History* 17, no. 1 (March 2001): 3–20; and Duignan, "The Library of the Hoover Institution on War, Revolution and Peace: Part II, The Campbell Years," *Library History* 17, no. 2 (July 2001): 107–118. Also, Duignan, ed., *The Library of the Hoover Institution on War, Revolution and Peace* (Stanford: Hoover Institution, 1985).

71. Prior to his appointment, Mumford spoke at the conference celebrating Stanford's fiftieth anniversary and the dedication of the Hoover Tower. *Stanford University Fiftieth Anniversary Celebration, Provisional Program, Commemoration Week, June 15–21, 1941.* Mumford Papers, Box 182, Folder 8073. For details on Brown's design for the Hoover Tower, see Jeffrey T. Tilman, *Arthur Brown Jr.: Progressive Classicist* (New York: Institute of Classical Architecture/Norton, 2006), 216–223. On the design of the Stanford University campus, Paul V. Turner, Marcia E. Vetroq, and Karen Weitze, *The Founders & the Architects: The Design of Stanford University* (Redwood City, CA: Department of Art, Stanford University, 1976), on the Hoover Tower, Paul V. Turner, "The Collaborative Design of Stanford University," in *The Founders & the Architects*, 94–96.

72. Detailed information on the Hoover Institution's collection policies is available in Duignan, ed., *The Library of the Hoover Institution.*

73. Turner, "The Collaborative Design of Stanford University," 42–57. Coolidge's former employer Richardson had also reinterpreted the Salamanca tower in Boston's Trinity Church and in an unsuccessful competition entry for the Albany Cathedral.

74. Campbell boasts of shaming the assembled protestors with reasoned argument. W. Glenn Campbell, *The Competition of Ideas: How My Colleagues and I Built the Hoover Institution* (Ottawa, IL: Jameson Books, 2000), 139–146. Also, Kenneth Lamott, "Right-Thinking Think Tank," *New York Times Magazine*, July 23, 1978, 16, 45, 48–49. Franklin, a tenured professor, was controversially discharged from Stanford after another protest.

75. Michel Foucault, *The Birth of Biopolitics: Lectures at the Collège de France 1978–1979*, ed. Michel Senellart, trans. Graham Burchell (New York: Palgrave Macmillan, 2008), 226.

76. By 1970, the Hoover Library catalogue had also been microfilmed in eighty-eight volumes. Duignan, "The Library of the Hoover Institution on War, Revolution and Peace: Part II," 110.

77. Philip Mirowski, *Machine Dreams: Economics Becomes a Cyborg Science* (New York: Cambridge University Press, 2002). Mirowski derives the concept of the cyborg, or cybernetic organism, from Donna Haraway, *Simians, Cyborgs, and Women: The Reinvention of Nature* (New York: Routledge, 1991). For a related history in the social sciences, see Jamie Cohen-Cole, *The Open Mind: Cold War Politics and the Sciences of Human Nature* (Chicago: University of Chicago Press, 2014), esp. chaps. 3 and 4. On the communicative environment as a zone of "democratic" interaction during the same period, see Fred Turner, *The Democratic Surround: Multimedia & American Liberalism from World War II to the Psychedelic Sixties* (Chicago: University of Chicago Press, 2013).

78. Baran, who was tenured, was also a target of anticommunist administrative measures at Stanford. Lowen, *Creating the Cold War University*, 205, 208.

79. Campbell, *The Competition of Ideas*, 43, 251–252, 256–257; and Duignan, ed., *The Library of the Hoover Institution*, 123. On the Mont Pèlerin Society, see the essays collected in Philip Mirowski and Dieter Plehwe, eds., *The Road from Mont Pèlerin: The Making of the Neoliberal Thought Collective* (Cambridge, MA: Harvard University Press, 2009).

80. Duignan, "The Library of the Hoover Institution: Part II," 110.

81. The "Whiz Kids" were a group of technical experts who brought the analytics-based management methods of "operations research" (OR) developed at the RAND Corporation to the U.S. Department of Defense under Defense Secretary Robert McNamara in the early 1960s. Mirowski, *Machine Dreams*, 188, 313; "The Pentagon's Whiz Kids," *Time Magazine* 80, issue 5 (August 3, 1962): 11. The "Chicago Boys" were a group of Chilean economists, most of who trained at the University of Chicago under Milton Friedman and Arnold Harberger, and who designed and oversaw the neoliberal economic policies implemented in Chile under General Augusto Pinochet after 1973. Juan-Gabriel Valdés, *Pinochet's Economists: The Chicago School in Chile* (New York: Cambridge University Press, 1995), 1–3; and from the Hoover Institution's discourse, Gary Becker, "What Latin America Owes to the 'Chicago Boys,' " *Hoover Digest*, no. 4 (October 30, 1997): https://www.hoover.org /research/what-latin-america-owes-chicago-boys, originally in *Business Week*, June 9, 1997. On the RAND Corporation and the U.S. Defense Department, see also S. M. Amadae, *Rationalizing Capitalist Democracy: The Cold War Origins of Rational Choice Liberalism* (Chicago: University of Chicago Press, 2003); and on the game-theoretical reasoning characteristic of neoliberal economic thought, see Amadae, *Prisoners of Reason: Game Theory and Neoliberal Political Economy* (New York: Cambridge University Press, 2015).

82. Although most of the Hoover Institution's early fellows were male, Rita Ricardo-Campbell was an important exception. In 1985, she remained one of two female senior fellows out of thirty-three. Duignan, ed., *The Library of the Hoover Institution*, 161.

83. For context, see Sheila Slaughter and Larry L. Leslie, *Academic Capitalism: Politics, Policies, and the Entrepreneurial University* (Baltimore, MD: Johns Hopkins University Press, 1997). See also Slaughter and Gary Rhoades, *Academic Capitalism and the New Economy: Markets, States, and Higher Education* (Baltimore, MD: Johns Hopkins University, 2004); and Brendan Cantwell and Ilkka Kauppinen, eds., *Academic Capitalism in the Age of Globalization* (Baltimore, MD: Johns Hopkins University Press, 2014).

Epilogue, c. 2000

1. Bill Readings, *The University in Ruins* (Cambridge, MA: Harvard University Press, 1996). In 1900, Daniel Chester French's *Alma Mater*, which sits midway up the monumental steps leading to the main entrance of Low Library, became the first sculpture accepted for installation on Columbia's new Morningside Heights campus. Barry Bergdoll, "The Genesis and Legacy of McKim, Mead & White's Master Plan for Columbia University," in *Mastering McKim's Plan: Columbia's First Century on Morningside Heights*, ed. Bergdoll and Janet Parks (New York: Miriam and Ira D. Wallach Art Gallery, Columbia University in the City of New York, 1997), 56.

2. "Current System for Illumination of Rotunda," n.d. Buildings and Grounds Collection, Columbia University, Rare Book & Manuscript Library, Columbia University. Box 11, Folder 1. The lighting system for the dome was most likely changed sometime during the 1960s. Christopher Gray, "Streetscapes / Morningside Heights: The Dome that

Crowned Columbia's Move North," *New York Times*, February 17, 2002, https://www
.nytimes.com/2002/02/17/realestate/streetscapes-morningside-heights-the-library-that
-crowned-columbia-s-move-north.html.

3. Jacques Derrida, "Mochlos; or, The Conflict of the Faculties," trans. Richard Rand and
    Amy Wigant, in *Logomachia: The Conflict of the Faculties*, ed. Rand (Lincoln: Univer-
    sity of Nebraska Press, 1992), 1–34.

4. Fernand Braudel, *The Mediterranean and the Mediterranean World in the Age of Phillip
    II*, vol. 1, trans. Siân Reynolds (New York: Harper & Row, 1972), 21.

5. Michel Foucault, "Of Other Spaces," trans. Jay Miskowiec, *Diacritics* 16, no. 1 (Spring
    1986): 22–27. Compare to Richard Rorty, *Philosophy and the Mirror of Nature* (Prince-
    ton, NJ: Princeton University Press, 1979).

6. Michel Foucault, "Discourse and Truth: The Problematization of *Parrhesia*: Six Lectures
    Given by Michel Foucault at the University of California at Berkeley, October–Novem-
    ber 1983," accessed August 21, 2020, https://foucault.info/parrhesia/.

7. Michel Foucault, *The Order of Things: An Archaeology of the Human Sciences* [1966]
    (New York: Pantheon, 1970), 3–16.

8. Erwin Panofsky, *Perspective As Symbolic Form*, trans. Christopher S. Wood (New York:
    Zone Books, 1991), 72.

9. "Languages of Knowledge and of Inquiry: A Conference on the Occasion of the Cen-
    tennial of the Graduate School of Arts and Sciences, Columbia University, April 17–18,
    1980," announcement in the *Columbia Daily Spectator* 104, no. 105 (April 14, 1980): 7.

10. Raj Reddy, "Machine Models of Speech Perception," in *Perception and Production of
    Fluent Speech*, ed. Ronald A. Cole (New York: Routledge, 1980), 215.

11. Donna Haraway, "A Cyborg Manifesto: Science, Technology, and Socialist Feminism
    in the Late Twentieth Century," in *Simians, Cyborgs, and Women: The Reinvention
    of Nature* (New York: Routledge, 1991), 149–181; first published as "A Manifesto for
    Cyborgs: Science, Technology, and Socialist Feminism in the 1980s," *Socialist Review*
    80 (1985): 65–107. On the concept of an "epistemic thing," see Hans-Jörg Rheinberger,
    Toward a History of Epistemic Things: Synthesizing Proteins in the Test Tube (Redwood
    City, CA: Stanford University Press, 1997).

12. In 2003, Mark A. Zuckerberg, class of 2006, hacked into the online "facebook," an index
    of residents at his Harvard University dormitory, Kirkland House, and began compiling
    the photographs available there and on other hacked Harvard dormitory facebooks on
    a new website, Facemash, which invited Zuckerberg's fellow undergraduates to, as the
    Harvard Crimson put it, "rate their peers" based on their "looks." Bari M. Schwartz, "Hot
    or Not? Website Briefly Judges Looks," *Harvard Crimson*, November 4, 2003, https://
    www.thecrimson.com/article/2003/11/4/hot-or-not-website-briefly-judges/?page=1.
    Surviving near expulsion, Zuckerberg followed this with thefacebook.com, Facebook's
    immediate precursor. The website included many Facemash elements minus the rating
    system, which was replaced by a function based on the website Friendster that, as the
    Crimson put it, allowed students to "create an online network of friends." Alan J. Tabak,
    "Hundreds Register for New Facebook Website," *Harvard Crimson*, February 9, 2004,
    https://www.thecrimson.com/article/2004/2/9/hundreds-register-for-new-facebook
    -website/; and Siva Vaidhyanathan, *Antisocial Media: How Facebook Disconnects Us and
    Undermines Democracy* (New York: Oxford University Press, 2018), 27–29.

13. Alan M. Turing, "Computing Machinery and Intelligence," *Mind* 59, no. 236 (1950):
    433–460. On the human interrogator in Turing's "imitation game," see Reinhold Mar-
    tin, *The Organizational Complex: Architecture, Media, and Corporate Space* (Cam-
    bridge, MA: MIT Press, 2003), 172–173.

SELECTED BIBLIOGRAPHY

Archives Consulted

Architectural Archives of the University of Pennsylvania
Avery Library Classics Collection, Columbia University
Billings Family Archives, Billings Farm and Museum
Environmental Design Archives, College of Environmental Design, University of California, Berkeley
Harvard University Special Collections
Institute Archives and Distinctive Collections, Massachusetts Institute of Technology
Kislak Center for Special Collections, Rare Books and Manuscripts, University of Pennsylvania
Rare Book & Manuscript Library, Columbia University
Rauner Special Collections Library, Dartmouth College
Special Collections Research Center, University of Chicago Library
Stanford University Archives
Tuskegee University Archives
University Archives, Bancroft Library, University of California at Berkeley
University Archives, Washington University in St. Louis
University of Arizona Libraries, Special Collections
University of Vermont Special Collections
University of Wisconsin-Madison Archives, Madison, Wisconsin
Yale University Manuscripts and Archives

Online Archives

Albert and Shirley Small Special Collections Library, University of Virginia
Bryn Mawr College Archives

Institute Archives and Special Collections, Rensselaer Polytechnic Institute
Princeton University Archives, Department of Special Collections, Princeton University Library
Thomas Jefferson Papers, Albert and Shirley Small Special Collections Library, University of Virginia
United States Library of Congress
Vassar College Archives and Special Collections

Published Sources

Ackerberg-Hastings, Amy K. "Mathematics Is a Gentleman's Art: Analysis and Synthesis in American College Geometry Teaching, 1790–1840." PhD diss., Iowa State University, 2000.
Adler, Mortimer J. *Dialectic*. New York: Harcourt, Brace, 1927.
Adler, Mortimer. "Great Books, Democracy, and Truth." *Educational Studies* 19, no. 3 (Fall/Winter 1988): 290–302.
Adler, Mortimer J. *Reforming Education: The Opening of the American Mind*. New York: Macmillan, 1988.
Adler, Mortimer J. *Philosopher at Large: An Intellectual Autobiography*. New York: Macmillan, 1977.
Adorno, Theodor W. "The Curves of the Needle." Trans. Thomas Y. Levin, *October* 55 (Winter 1990): 48–55.
Agamben, Giorgio. "What Is an Apparatus?" In *What Is an Apparatus and Other Essays*. Trans. David Kishik and Stefan Pedatella, 1–24. Redwood City, CA: Stanford University Press, 2009.
Albree, Joe, David C. Arney, and V. Frederick Rickey. *A Station Favorable to the Pursuits of Science: Primary Materials in the History of Mathematics at the United States Military Academy*. Providence, RI: American Mathematical Society, 1991.
Alexander, Zeynep Çelik. *Kinaesthetic Knowing: Aesthetics, Epistemology, Modern Design*. Chicago: University of Chicago Press, 2017.
Allaback, Sarah. "The Writings of Louisa Tuthill: Cultivating Architectural Taste in Nineteenth-Century America." PhD diss., Massachusetts Institute of Technology, 1993.
Allen, William C. *History of the United States Capitol: A Chronicle of Design, Construction, and Politics*. Washington, DC: United States Government Printing Office, 2001.
Amadae, S. M. *Prisoners of Reason: Game Theory and Neoliberal Political Economy*. New York: Cambridge University Press, 2015.
Amadae, S. M. *Rationalizing Capitalist Democracy: The Cold War Origins of Rational Choice Liberalism*. Chicago: University of Chicago Press, 2003.
Ambedkhar, Bhimrao R. "Annihilation of Caste" [1936]. In *The Essential Writings of B. R. Ambedkar*, ed. Valerian Rodrigues, 263–305. New Delhi: Oxford University Press, 2002.
Ambedkar, Bhimrao R. *Autobiographical Notes* (Pondicherry: Navayana, 2003).
Ambedkar, Bhimrao R. *The Evolution of Provincial Finance in British India: A Study in the Provincial Decentralization of Imperial Finance*. London: P. S. King & Son, 1925.
American Academy in Rome. *The American Academy in Rome*. New York: DeVinne, 1904.
Andriopoulos, Stefan. *Possessed: Hypnotic Crimes, Corporate Fiction, and the Invention of Cinema*. Trans. Peter Jansen and Stefan Andriopoulos. Chicago: University of Chicago Press, 2008.
Archibald, Raymond Clare. *Benjamin Peirce 1809–1880: Biographical Sketch and Bibliography*. Oberlin, OH: Mathematical Association of America, 1925.

Austrian, Geoffrey D. *Herman Hollerith: Forgotten Giant of Information Processing*. New York: Columbia University Press, 1982.

Axtell, James. *The European and the Indian: Essays in the Enthnohistory of Colonial North America*. New York: Oxford University Press, 1981.

Axtell, James. *Wisdom's Workshop: The Rise of the Modern University*. Princeton, NJ: Princeton University Press, 2016.

Baggerman, Arianne, Rudolf Dekker, and Michael Mascush, eds. *Controlling Time and Shaping the Self: Developments in Autobiographical Writing Since the Sixteenth Century*. Leiden: Koninklijke Brill NV, 2011.

Banton, Michael. *The Idea of Race*. London: Tavistock, 1977.

Bao, Weihong. *Fiery Cinema: The Emergence of an Affective Medium in China, 1915–1945*. Minneapolis: University of Minnesota Press, 2015.

Barak, On. *On Time: Technology and Temporality in Modern Egypt*. Berkeley: University of California Press, 2013.

Barkan, Joshua. *Corporate Sovereignty: Law and Government under Capitalism*. Minneapolis: University of Minnesota Press, 2013.

Barkin, Kenneth D. " 'Berlin Days,' 1892–1894: W. E. B. Du Bois and German Political Economy." *Boundary 2* 27, no. 3 (2000): 79–101.

Barringer, Paul Brandon, James Mercer Garnett, and Roswell Page, eds. *University of Virginia: Its History, Influence, Equipment and Characteristics*. 2 vols. New York: Lewis Publishing, 1904.

Barzun, Jacques. *The House of Intellect*. New York: Harper & Brothers, 1959.

Bashe, Charles J., Lyle R. Johnson, John H. Palmer, and Emerson W. Pugh. *IBM's Early Computers*. Cambridge, MA: MIT Press, 1986.

Baxter, Maurice Glen. *Daniel Webster & the Supreme Court*. Amherst: University of Massachusetts Press, 1966.

Becker, Gary. "What Latin America Owes to the 'Chicago Boys.' " *Hoover Digest*, no. 4 (October 30, 1997). https://www.hoover.org/research/what-latin-america-owes-chicago-boys.

Becker, Peter, and William Clark, eds. *Little Tools of Knowledge: Historical Essays on Academic and Bureaucratic Practices*. Ann Arbor: University of Michigan Press, 2001.

Bedini, Silvio A. *Thomas Jefferson and His Copying Machines*. Charlottesville: University of Virginia Press, 1984.

Bélime, Émile. "La situation actuelle de la culture cotonnière en A.O.F." *Revue de botanique appliquée et d' agriculture tropicale* 9 (1929): 3–15.

Beniger, James R. *The Control Revolution: Technological and Economic Origins of the Information Society*. Cambridge, MA: Harvard University Press, 1986.

Benjamin, Walter. "On the Concept of History" [1940]. Trans. Harry Zohn. In *Walter Benjamin: Selected Writings*. Vol. 4, *1938–1940*, ed. Howard Eiland and Michael W. Jennings, 389–400. Cambridge, MA: Harvard University Press, 2003.

Bennett, Tony. "The Exhibitionary Complex." *New Formations* 4 (Spring 1988): 73–102.

Beranek, Leo L. *Music, Acoustics & Architecture*. New York: John Wiley, 1962.

Bergdoll, Barry. "Books, Buildings, and the Spaces of Democracy: Jefferson's Library from Paris to Washington." In *Thomas Jefferson, Architect: Palladian Models, Democratic Principles, and the Conflict of Ideals*, ed. Lloyd DeWitt and Corey Piper, 65–79. Norfolk: Chrysler Museum of Art/New Haven, CT: Yale University Press, 2019.

Bergdoll, Barry, and Janet Parks, eds. *Mastering McKim's Plan: Columbia's First Century on Morningside Heights*. New York: Miriam and Ira D. Wallach Art Gallery, Columbia University in the City of New York, 1997.

Bergland, Renée. *Maria Mitchell and the Sexing of Science: An Astronomer among the American Romantics*. Boston: Beacon Press, 2008.

Bernstein, Richard B. *Thomas Jefferson*. New York: Oxford University Press, 2003.

Bevis, Teresa Brawner, and Christopher J. Lucas. *International Students in American Colleges and Universities: A History*. New York: Palgrave Macmillan, 2007.

Bigelow, Jacob. *Elements of Technology, Taken Chiefly from a Course of Lectures at Cambridge on the Application of the Sciences to the Useful Arts Now Published for the Use of Seminaries and Students*. Boston: Hilliard, Gray, Little, and Wilkins, 1829.

Bilgrami, Akeel, and Jonathan R. Cole. eds. *Who's Afraid of Academic Freedom?* New York: Columbia University Press, 2015.

Billington, Allen. *The Genesis of the Frontier Thesis: A Study in Historical Creativity*. San Marino, CA: Huntington Library, 1971.

Black, John W. "Webster's Peroration in the Dartmouth College Case." *Quarterly Journal of Speech* 23 (December 1937): 636–642.

Blackburn, Robert H. "Dewey and Cutter as Building Consultants." *Library Quarterly: Information, Community, Policy* 58, no. 4 (October 1988): 377–384.

Blair, Ann M. *Too Much to Know: Managing Scholarly Information before the Modern Age*. New Haven, CT: Yale University Press, 2010.

Blanchard, F. M. "Department of Public Speaking." *School Review* 13, no. 1 (January 1905): 75–76.

Bledstein, Burton J. *The Culture of Professionalism: The Middle Class and the Development of Higher Education in America*. New York: Norton, 1976.

Block, Jean F. *The Uses of Gothic: Planning and Building the Campus of the University of Chicago, 1892–1932*. Chicago: University of Chicago Library, 1983.

Bloom, Allan. *The Closing of the American Mind: How Higher Education Has Failed Democracy and Impoverished the Souls of Today's Students*. New York: Simon and Schuster, 1987.

Bogue, Allan G. *Frederick Jackson Turner: Strange Roads Going Down*. Norman: University of Oklahoma Press, 1998.

Bok, Derek. *Higher Education in America*. Princeton, NJ: Princeton University Press, 2016.

Bolotin, Norman, and Christine Laing. *The World's Columbian Exposition: The Chicago World's Fair of 1893*. Washington, DC: Preservation Press, 1992.

Bosley, Edward R. *University of Pennsylvania Library: Frank Furness*. London: Phaidon, 1996.

Boullée, Étienne-Louis. *Architecture: Essai sur l'art*. Ed. Jean-Marie Pérouse de Montclos. Paris: Hermann, 1968.

Bourdieu, Pierre. *Homo Academicus*, trans. Peter Collier. Redwood City, CA: Stanford University Press, 1988.

Bowman, J. N. "The Peraltas and Their Houses." *California Historical Quarterly* 30, no. 3 (September 1951): 217–231.

Braudel, Fernand. *The Mediterranean and the Mediterranean World in the Age of Phillip II*. 2 vols. Trans. Siân Reynolds. New York: Harper & Row, 1972.

Breisch, Kenneth A. *Henry Hobson Richardson and the Small Public Library in America: A Study in Typology*. Cambridge, MA: MIT Press, 1997.

Broderick, Francis L. "German Influence on the Scholarship of W. E. B. Du Bois." *Phylon Quarterly* 19, no. 4 (4th quarter, 1958): 367–371.

Broderick, Mosette. *Triumverate: McKim, Mead & White: Art, Architecture, Scandal, and Class in America's Gilded Age*. New York: Knopf Doubleday, 2010.

Brooks, G. P. "The Faculty Psychology of Thomas Reid." *Journal of the History of the Behavioral Sciences* 12 (1976): 65–77.

Brophy, Alfred L. *University, Court, & Slave: Pro-Slavery Thought in Southern Colleges & Courts & the Coming Civil War*. New York: Oxford University Press, 2016.

Brown, Bill, ed. *Things*. Chicago: University of Chicago Press, 2004.

Brown, Chandos Michael. *Benjamin Silliman: A Life in the Young Republic*. Princeton, NJ: Princeton University Press, 1989.

Brown, Wendy. *Undoing the Demos: Neoliberalism's Stealth Revolution*. Brooklyn, NY: Zone, 2015.

Brownlee, David B., and George Thomas. *Building America's First University: An Historical and Architectural Guide to the University of Pennsylvania*. Philadelphia: University of Pennsylvania Press, 1999.

Brubacher, John S., and Willis Rudy. *Higher Education in Transition: A History of American Colleges and Universities, 1636–1976*. 3rd enlarged ed. New York: Harper & Row, 1976.

Bruce, Philip Alexander. *History of the University of Virginia, 1819–1919: The Lengthened Shadow of One Man*. 5 vols. New York: Macmillan, 1921.

Buck-Morss, Susan. *Hegel, Haiti, and Universal History*. Pittsburgh, PA: University of Pittsburgh Press, 2009.

Bullock, John, ed. *The History and Rudiments of Architecture; for the Use of Architects, Builders, Draughtsmen, Machinists, Engineers and Mechanics*. New York: Stringer & Townsend, 1853.

Burchard, John E., ed. *Mid-Century: The Social Implications of Scientific Progress* Cambridge, MA: Technology Press and MIT, 1950.

Burchard, John E. *Q.E.D.: M.I.T. in World War II*. New York: Wiley, 1948.

Burris-Meyer, Harold. "The Control of Acoustic Conditions on the Concert Stage." *Journal of the Acoustical Society of America* 12 (January 1941): 335–337.

Bush, Vannevar. *Science—The Endless Frontier*. Washington, DC: United States Government Printing Office, 1945.

Butler, Judith. *Gender Trouble: Feminism and the Subversion of Identity*. New York: Routledge, 1990.

Cajori, Florian. *The Teaching and History of Mathematics in the United States*. Washington, DC: Government Printing Office, 1890.

Campbell, W. Glenn. *The Competition of Ideas: How My Colleagues and I Built the Hoover Institution*. Ottawa, IL: Jameson, 2000.

Canales, Jimena. "Harold E. 'Doc' Edgerton and His Laboratory Notebooks," *Aperture* 211 (Summer 2013): 72–73.

Cantwell, Brendan, and Ilkka Kauppinen, eds. *Academic Capitalism in the Age of Globalization*. Baltimore, MD: Johns Hopkins University Press, 2014.

Cardwell, Kenneth H. *Bernard Maybeck: Artisan, Architect, Artist*. Santa Barbara, CA: Peregrine Smith, 1977.

Carey, Henry Charles. *French and American Tariffs Compared; in a Series of Letters Addressed to Mons. Michel Chevalier*. Philadelphia: Collins Printer, 1861.

Carey, Henry Charles. *Harmony of Interests: Agricultural, Manufacturing, and Commercial*. Philadelphia: J. S. Skinner, 1851.

Carey, Henry Charles. *Letters to the President on the Foreign and Domestic Policy of the Union, and Its Effects, as Exhibited in the Condition of the People and the State*. Philadelphia: J. B. Lippincott, 1858.

Carey, Henry Charles. *The Past, The Present, and the Future*. Philadelphia: Carey & Hart, 1848.

Carey, Henry Charles. *Principles of Social Science*. 3 vols. Philadelphia: J. B. Lippincott, 1859.

Casper, Scott E., Jeffrey D. Groves, Stephen W. Nissenbaum, and Michael Winship, eds. *A History of the Book in America*. Vol. 3, *The Industrial Book, 1840–1880*. Chapel Hill: University of North Carolina Press/American Antiquarian Society, 2007.

Cassirer, Ernst. *The Myth of the State*. New Haven, CT: Yale University Press, 1946.

Cassirer, Ernst. *The Philosophy of Symbolic Forms*. Volume 1, *Language*. Trans. Ralph Mannheim. New Haven, CT: Yale University Press, 1955.

Cassirer, Ernst. *The Philosophy of Symbolic Forms*. Volume 2, *Mythical Thought*. Trans. Ralph Mannheim. New Haven, CT: Yale University Press, 1955.

Cassirer, Ernst. *The Philosophy of Symbolic Forms*. Volume 3, *The Phenomenology of Knowledge*. Trans. Ralph Mannheim. New Haven, CT: Yale University Press, 1957.

Cavallo, Giglielmo, and Roger Chartier, eds. *A History of Reading in the West*. Trans. Lydia G. Cochrane. Amherst: University of Massachusetts Press, 1999.

Chartier, Roger. *The Order of Books: Readers, Authors, and Libraries in Europe Between the Fourteenth and Eighteenth Centuries*. Trans. Lydia G. Cochrane. Redwood City, CA: Stanford University Press, 1994.

Cheng, Irene. "Race and Architectural Geometry: Thomas Jefferson's Octagons." *J19: Journal of Nineteenth-Century Americanists* 3, no. 1 (Spring 2015): 121–130.

Cheyney, Edward Potts. *History of the University of Pennsylvania, 1740–1940*. Philadelphia: University of Pennsylvania Press, 1940.

Clark, William. *Academic Charisma and the Origins of the Research University*. Chicago: University of Chicago Press, 2006.

Clement [Waters], Clara Erskine. *An Outline History of Architecture for Beginners and Students, with Complete Indexes and Numerous Illustrations*. New York: White, Stokes & Allen, 1886.

Clemons, Harry. *The University of Virginia Library 1825–1950: Story of a Jeffersonian Foundation*. Charlottesville: University of Virginia Press, 1954.

Cohen, Robert, ed. *The Free Speech Movement: Reflections on Berkeley in the 1960s*. Berkeley: University of California Press, 2002.

Cohen-Cole, Jamie. *The Open Mind: Cold War Politics and the Sciences of Human Nature*. Chicago: University of Chicago Press, 2014.

Cole, Andrew. "What Hegel's Master/Slave Dialectic Really Means." *Journal of Medieval and Early Modern Studies* 34, no. 3 (Fall 2004): 577–610.

Cole, Jonathan R. *The Great American University: Its Rise to Preeminence, Its Indispensable National Role, Why It Must Be Protected*. New York: Public Affairs, 2009.

Cole, Jonathan R. *Toward a More Perfect University*. New York: Public Affairs, 2016.

Cole, John Y. "Struggle for a Structure: Ainsworth Rand Spofford and a New Building for the Library of Congress." In *The Art and Architecture of the Thomas Jefferson Building*, ed. Cole and Henry Hope Reed, 30–63. Washington, DC: W.W. Norton/Library of Congress, 1997.

Coles, William, ed. *Architecture and Society: Selected Essays of Henry Van Brunt*, Cambridge, MA; Belknap Press, 1969.

Colley, Charles C. *The Century of Robert H. Forbes*. Tucson: Arizona Historical Society, 1977.

Crain, Patricia. *The Story of A: The Alphabetization of America from* The New England Primer *to* The Scarlet Letter. Redwood City, CA: Stanford University Press, 2000.

Cram, Ralph Adams. *End of Democracy*. Boston: Marshall Jones Company, 1937.

Cram, Ralph Adams. "The Work of Messrs. Cope & Stewardson." *Architectural Record* 16, no. 5 (November 1904): 407–438.

Cresswell, Stephen. "The Last Days of Jim Crow in Southern Libraries." *Libraries & Culture* 31, nos. 3–4 (Summer 1996): 557–573.

Croly, Herbert. "The New University of California." *Architectural Record* 23, no. 4 (April 4, 1908): 269–293.

Cronon, William. *Nature's Metropolis: Chicago and the Great West*. New York: W.W. Norton, 1991.

Cronon, William, George Miles, and Jay Gitlin, eds. *Under an Open Sky: Rethinking America's Western Past.* New York: Norton, 1992.

Cross, Coy F., II. *Justin Smith Morrill: Father of the Land-Grant Colleges.* East Lansing: Michigan State University Press, 1999.

Cumo, Christopher Martin. *The Ongoing Columbian Exchange: Stories of Biological and Economic Transfer in World History.* Santa Barbara, CA: ABC-CLIO, 2015.

Curti, Merle, and Vernon Carstensen. *The University of Wisconsin: A History, 1848–1925.* 2 vols. Madison: University of Wisconsin Press, 1949.

Danly, Susan, and Leo Marx, eds. *The Railroad in American Art: Representations of Technological Change.* Cambridge, MA: MIT Press, 1988.

Darnton, Robert. *The Business of Enlightenment: A Publishing History of the Encyclopédie 1775–1800.* Cambridge, MA: Harvard University Press, 1979.

David, Charles W. "The University Library in 1886." *Library Chronicle of the Friends of the University of Pennsylvania Library* 18, no. 2 (Summer 1952): 72–76.

Davies, Charles. *Elements of Geometry and Trigonometry from the Works of A. M. Legendre.* New York: A. S. Barnes, 1862.

Davies, Charles. *The Logic and Utility of Mathematics, with the Best Methods of Instruction Explained and Illustrated.* New York: A. S. Barnes, 1850.

Davis, Nuel Pharr. *Lawrence and Oppenheimer.* New York: Da Capo, 1986.

Delbanco, Andrew. *College: What It Was, Is, and Should Be.* Princeton, NJ: Princeton University Press, 2012.

Deleuze, Gilles. "Postscript on Control Societies." Trans. Martin Joughin. In *Negotiations 1972–1990,* 177–182. New York: Columbia University Press, 1995.

DeNoyelles, Daniel. *Within These Gates.* Thiells, NY: [self-published], 1982.

Derrida, Jacques. "Cogito and the History of Madness." In *Writing and Difference,* trans. Alan Bass, 31–63. Chicago: University of Chicago Press, 1978.

Derrida, Jacques. "Mochlos, or, The Conflict of the Faculties." Trans. Richard Rand and Amy Wygant. In *Logomachia: The Conflict of the Faculties,* ed. Richard Rand, 1–34. Lincoln: University of Nebraska Press, 1992.

Dewey, John. *Democracy and Education: An Introduction to the Philosophy of Education.* New York: Macmillan, 1916.

Dewey, John. "The Historic Background of Corporate Legal Personality." *Yale Law Journal* 35, no. 6 (April 1926): 655–673.

Dewey, Melvil. *A Classification and Subject Index for Cataloguing and Arranging the Books and Pamphlets of a Library.* Amherst, MA: [Printed by Case, Lockwood & Brainard, Hartford, CT], 1876.

Dewey, Melvil. *Relativ Index for Arranging Cataloging and Indexing Public and Private Libraries and for Pamflets, Clippings, Notes, Scrap Books, Index Rerums, Etc.* 2nd ed., revised and enlarged. Boston: Library Bureau, 1885.

DeWitt, Lloyd, and Corey Piper, eds. *Thomas Jefferson, Architect: Palladian Models, Democratic Principles, and the Conflict of Ideals.* Norfolk: Chrysler Museum of Art/New Haven, CT: Yale University Press, 2019.

Dexter, Franklin Bowditch. *Biographical Sketches of the Graduates of Yale College with Annals of the College History,* vol. 1, *October 1701–May 1745.* New York: Henry Holt, 1885.

Dexter, Franklin Bowditch. *Biographical Sketches of the Graduates of Yale College,* vol. 6, *September, 1805–September, 1815.* New Haven, CT: Yale University Press, 1912. Dhaktode, Surendra Shrirang. *Thomas Jefferson and Dr. B. R. Ambedkar: A Comparative Study.* Mumbai: Bhashya Prakashan, 2017.

Dolkart, Andrew. *Morningside Heights: A History of Its Architecture and Development*. New York: Columbia University Press, 2001.

Donogue, Frank. *The Last Professors: The Corporate University and the Fate of the Humanities*. New York: Fordham University Press, 2008.

Douglass, John Aubrey. *The California Idea and American Higher Education: 1850 to the 1960 Master Plan*. Redwood City, CA: Stanford University Press, 2000.

Du Bois, W. E. B., ed. *The College-Bred Negro: Report of a Social Study Made Under the Direction of Atlanta University; Together with the Proceedings of the Fifth Conference for the Study of the Negro Problems, Held at Atlanta University, May 29–30, 1900*. Atlanta, GA: Atlanta University Press, 1900.

Du Bois, W. E. B. *Dusk of Dawn*. Ed. Henry Louis Gates Jr. New York: Oxford University Press, 2007.

Du Bois, W. E. B. *The Education of Black People: Ten Critiques, 1906–1960*. 2nd ed. Ed. Herbert Apthekar. New York: Monthly Review Press, 2001.

Du Bois, W. E. B., ed. *The Negro Artisan: Report of a Social Study Made Under the Direction of Atlanta University; Together with the Proceedings of the Seventh Conference for the Study of the Negro Problems, Held at Atlanta University, on May 27, 1902*. Atlanta, GA: Atlanta University Press, 1902.

Du Bois, W. E. B. *The Souls of Black Folk: Authoritative Text, Contexts, Criticism*. Ed. Henry Louis Gates Jr. and Terri Hume Oliver. New York: Norton, 1999.

Duff, Wilmer Alexander, ed. *A Text-Book of Physics*. Philadelphia: P. Blakiston's Son, 1908.

Duignan, Peter, ed. *The Library of the Hoover Institution on War, Revolution and Peace*. Redwood City, CA: Hoover Institution, 1985.

Duignan, Peter. "The Library of the Hoover Institution on War, Revolution and Peace: Part I, Origin and Growth." *Library History* 17, no. 1 (March 2001): 3–20.

Duignan, Peter. "The Library of the Hoover Institution on War, Revolution and Peace: Part II, The Campbell Years." *Library History* 17, no. 2 (July 2001): 107–118.

Dutta, Arindam. "Mammoths, Inc.: Nature, Architecture, and the Debt, Part 1." The Aggregate Website. Accessed July 12, 2020. http://we-aggregate.org/piece/mammoths-inc-nature -architecture-and-the-debt-part-1.

Dzuback, Mary Ann. *Robert M. Hutchins: Portrait of an Educator*. Chicago: University of Chicago Press, 1991.

Eddy, Edward Danforth, Jr. *Colleges for Our Land and Time: The Land-Grant Idea in American Education*. New York: Harper, 1956.

Edgerton, Harold E. *Electronic Flash, Strobe*. New York: McGraw-Hill, 1970.

Edgerton, Harold E., and James R. Killian Jr. *Flash! The Unseen by Ultra High-Speed Photography*. Boston: Hale, Cushman & Flint, 1939.

Edgerton, Harold E., and James R. Killian Jr. *Flash! Seeing the Unseen by Ultra High-Speed Photography*. 2nd rev. ed. Boston: Charles T. Branford, 1954.

Edwards, Paul N. "Border Wars: The Science and Politics of Artificial Intelligence." *Radical America* 19, no. 6 (November–December 1985): 39–50.

Elder, William. *A Memoir of Henry C. Carey, Read Before the Historical Society of Pennsylvania; Philadelphia, January 5, 1880*. Philadelphia: Henry Carey Baird, 1880.

Emerson, Benjamin Kendall. *Geology of Old Hampshire County, Massachusetts: Comprising Franklin, Hampshire, and Hampden Counties*. Washington, DC: United States Government Printing Office, 1898.

Emerson, Ralph Waldo. *An Oration Delivered Before the Phi Beta Kappa Society at Cambridge, August 31, 1837* ["The American Scholar"]. 2nd ed. Boston: James Munroe, 1838.

Emerson, Ralph Waldo. *Nature*. Boston: James Munroe, 1836.

Emerson, Ralph Waldo. *Representative Men: Seven Lectures*. Boston: Phillips, Samson, 1850.

Emmerson, George S. *Engineering Education: A Social History*. New York: Crane, Russak, 1973.

Erlmann, Veit. *Reason and Resonance: A History of Modern Aurality*. New York: Zone, 2010.

Ernst, Wolfgang. *Digital Memory and the Archive*. Ed. Jussi Parikka. Minneapolis: University of Minnesota Press, 2013.

Erskine, John. *The Memory of Certain Persons*. Philadelphia: J. B. Lippincott, 1947.

Erskine, John. *My Life as a Teacher*. Philadelphia: J. B. Lippincott, 1948.

Esposito, Roberto. "The *Dispositif* of the Person." *Law, Culture, and the Humanities* 8, no. 1 (2012): 17–30.

Etlin, Richard. *The Architecture of Death: The Transformation of the Cemetery in Eighteenth-Century Paris*. Cambridge, MA: MIT Press, 1984.

Evans, Robin. "Figures, Doors, and Passages." *Architectural Design* 4 (1978): 267–278.

Fahs, Alice, and Joan Waugh, eds. *The Memory of the Civil War in American Culture*. Chapel Hill: University of North Carolina Press, 2004.

Faust, Drew Gilpin. " 'Numbers on Top of Numbers': Counting the Civil War Dead." *Journal of Military History* 70, no. 4 (October 2006): 995–1009.

Faust, Drew Gilpin. *This Republic of Suffering: Death and the American Civil War*. New York: Knopf, 2008.

Ferrier, William Warren. *Berkeley, California: The Story of the Evolution of a Hamlet into a City of Culture and Commerce*. Berkeley: [Published by the Author], 1933.

Ferrier, William Warren. *Origin and Development of the University of California*. Berkeley, CA: Sather Gate Bookshop, 1930.

Filipovich, Jean. "Destined to Fail: Forced Settlement at the *Office du Niger*, 1926–1945." *Journal of African History* 42, no. 2 (2001): 239–260.

Fineman, Mia, and Beth Saunders, eds. *Apollo's Muse: The Moon in the Age of Photography*. New York: Metropolitian Museum of Art, 2019.

Flexner, Abraham. *Universities: American, English, German*. New York: Oxford University Press, 1930.

Floyd, Margaret Henderson. *Henry Hobson Richardson: A Genius for Architecture*. New York: Monacelli Press, 1997.

Forbes, Robert H. "The Black Man's Industries." *Geographical Review* 23, no. 2 (April 1933): 230–247.

Forbes, Robert H. *Le Coton dans la vallée moyenne du Niger, Essais du culture, 1923–24*. Paris: Gouvernement Générale de l'Afrique Occidentale Française, Service General de Textiles et de l'Hydraulique Agricole, 1926.

Forman, Sidney. *West Point: A History of the United States Military Academy*. New York: Columbia University Press, 1950.

Foster, John Bellamy. *Marx's Ecology: Materialism and Nature*. New York: New York University Press, 2000.

Foucault, Michel. *The Archaeology of Knowledge and the Discourse on Language*. Trans. A. M. Sheridan Smith. New York: Pantheon, 1972.

Foucault, Michel. *The Birth of Biopolitics: Lectures at the Collège de France 1978–1979*. Ed. Michel Senellart. Trans. Graham Burchell. New York: Palgrave Macmillan, 2008.

Foucault, Michel. *Discipline and Punish: The Birth of the Prison*. Trans. Alan Sheridan. New York: Pantheon, 1977.

Foucault, Michel. "Discourse and Truth: The Problematization of *Parrhesia*: Six Lectures Given by Michel Foucault at the University of California at Berkeley, October-November 1983." https://www.foucault.info/parrhesia/.

Foucault, Michel. *History of Madness*. Ed. Jean Khalfa. Trans. Jonathan Murphy and Jean Khalfa. New York: Routledge, 2006.

Foucault, Michel. *Lectures on the Will to Know: Lectures at the Collège de France 1970–1971, and Oedipal Knowledge*. Ed. Daniel Defert. Trans. Graham Burchell. New York: Palgrave Macmillan, 2013.

Foucault, Michel. *Madness and Civilization: A History of Insanity in the Age of Reason*. Trans. Richard Howard. New York: Random House, 1965.

Foucault, Michel. "My Body, This Paper, This Fire," trans. Geoff Bennington. In *Aesthetics, Method, and Epistemology: Essential Works of Foucault 1954–1984*, vol. 2, ed. James D. Faubion, 394–417. New York: New Press, 1998.

Foucault, Michel. "Nietzsche, Genealogy, History," trans. Donald F. Brouchard and Sherry Simon. In *Michel Foucault: Aesthetics, Method, and Epistemology*, ed. James D. Faubion, 369–391. New York: New Press, 1991.

Foucault, Michel. *The Order of Things: An Archaeology of the Human Sciences*. New York: Pantheon, 1970.

Foucault, Michel. "Of Other Spaces." Trans. Jay Miskowiec. *Diacritics* 16, no. 1 (Spring 1986): 22–27.

Foucault, Michel, in conversation with Alain Grosrichard, Gerard Wajeman, Jacques-Alain Miller, Guy Le Gaufey, Dominique Celas, Gerard Miller, Catherine Millot, Jocelyne Livi, and Judith Miller. "The Confession of the Flesh." In *Power/Knowledge: Selected Interviews and Other Writings*, ed. Colin Gordon, 194–228. London: Harvester Press, 1980.

Frederickson, George M. *Racism: A Short History*. Princeton, NJ: Princeton University Press, 2002.

French, John C. *A History of the University Founded by Johns Hopkins*. Baltimore, MD: Johns Hopkins University Press, 1946.

Galison, Peter. "The Americanization of Unity." *Daedalus* 127, no. 1 (Winter 1998): 45–71.

Galison, Peter, and Bruce Hevly, eds. *Big Science: The Growth of Large-Scale Research*. Redwood City, CA: Stanford University Press, 1992.

Gardner, David P. *The California Oath Controversy*. Berkeley: University of California Press, 1967.

Garrison, Fielding H., M.D. *John Shaw Billings: A Memoir*. New York: G. P. Putnam's Sons, 1915.

Geiger, Roger L. *To Advance Knowledge: The Growth of American Research Universities, 1900–1940*. New York: Oxford University Press, 1986.

Geiger, Roger L. *The History of American Higher Education: Learning and Culture from the Founding to World War II*. Princeton, NJ: Princeton University Press, 2015.

Geiger, Roger L. *Research & Relevant Knowledge: American Research Universities Since World War II*. 2nd ed. New Brunswick, NJ: Transaction, 2008.

Geiger, Roger L., and Nathan M. Sorber, eds. *The Land-Grant Colleges and the Reshaping of American Higher Education*. New Brunswick: Transaction, 2013.

Geitz, Henry, Jürgen Heideking, and Jurgen Herbst. *German Influences on Education in the United States to 1917*. New York: Cambridge University Press/German Historical Institute, 1995.

Ghoche, Ralph. "Simon-Claude Constant-Dufeux and the Symbolic Interpretation of Architectural Origins in 19th-Century France." *Architectural Histories* 6, no. 1 (2018): 1–14.

Gideon, Sigfried. *Mechanization Takes Command: A Contribution to Anonymous History*. New York: Oxford University Press, 1948.

Gillmor, C. Stewart. *Fred Terman at Stanford: Building a Discipline, a University, and Silicon Valley*. Redwood City, CA: Stanford University Press, 2004.

Gingerich, Owen, ed. *The General History of Astronomy*, vol. 4, *Astrophysics and Twentieth Century Astronomy to 1950*, part A. Cambridge, MA: Harvard University Press, 1984.

Gitelman, Lisa. *Paper Knowledge: Toward a Media History of Documents*. Durham, NC: Duke University Press, 2014.

Goode, George Brown, ed. *The Smithsonian Institution, 1846–1896: The History of Its First Half-Century*. Washington, DC: De Vinne Press, 1896.Goodman, Russell B. *American Philosophy Before Pragmatism*. New York: Oxford University Press, 2015.

Gordon-Reed, Annette. *The Hemingses of Monticello: An American Family*. New York: Norton, 2008.

Gordon-Reed, Annette. *Thomas Jefferson and Sally Hemings: An American Controversy*. Charlottesville: University of Virginia Press, 1997.

Goode, G. Brown. *An Account of the Smithsonian Institution, Its Origin, History, Objects and Achievements*. Washington, DC: [n.p.], 1895.

Goodspeed, Thomas Wakefield. *A History of the University of Chicago, Founded by John D. Rockefeller: The First Quarter-Century*. Chicago: University of Chicago Press, 1916.

Gossett, Thomas F. *Race: The History of an Idea in America*. Dallas, TX: Southern Methodist University Press, 1963.

Gottmann, Jean. *Megalopolis: The Urbanized Northeastern Seaboard of the United States*. Cambridge, MA: MIT Press, 1961.

Grafton, Anthony. *Worlds Made by Words: Scholarship and Community in the Modern West*. Cambridge, MA: Harvard University Press, 2009.

Gramsci, Antonio. *The Gramsci Reader: Selected Writings, 1916–1935*, ed. David Forgacs. New York: New York University Press, 2000.

Grandin, Greg. *The End of the Myth: From the Frontier to the Border Wall in the Mind of America*. New York: Metropolitan/Henry Holt, 2019.

Grayson, Lawrence P. *The Making of an Engineer: An Illustrated History of Engineering Education in the United States and Canada*. New York: John Wiley, 1993.

Green, Arnold W. *Henry Charles Carey: Nineteenth Century Sociologist*. Philadelphia: University of Pennsylvania Press, 1951.

Green, Judy, and Jeanne LaDuke. "Women in the American Mathematical Community: The Pre-1940 PhD's." *Mathematical Intelligencer* 9, no. 1 (1987): 11–23.

Gross, Robert A., and Mary Kelley, eds. *A History of the Book in America*. Vol. 2, *An Extensive Republic: Print, Culture, and Society in the New Nation, 1790–1840*. Chapel Hill: University of North Carolina Press/American Antiquarian Society, 2010.

Guillory, John. "Genesis of the Media Concept." *Critical Inquiry* 36, no. 2 (Winter 2010): 321–361.

Gyure, Dale Allen. "The Heart of the University: A History of the Library as an Architectural Symbol of American Higher Education." *Winterthur Portfolio* 42, no. 2/3 (Summer/Autumn 2008): 107–132.

Hacker, Andrew, and Claudia Dreifus. *Higher Education? How Colleges Are Wasting Our Money and Failing Our Kids—and What We Can Do About It*. New York: St. Martin's Griffin, 2010.

Hacker, J. David. "A Census-Based Count of the Civil War Dead." *Civil War History* 57, no. 4 (December 2011): 307–348.

Haddad, John R. *America's First Adventure in China: Trade, Treaties, and Salvation*. Philadelphia: Temple University Press, 2013.

Hafertepe, Kenneth, and James F. O'Gorman, eds. *American Architects and Their Books to 1840–1915*. Amherst: University of Massachusetts Press, 2007.

Hafertepe, Kenneth, and James F. O'Gorman, eds. *American Architects and Their Books to 1848*. Amherst, MA: University of Massachusetts Press, 2001.

Hallock, William. "Diffused Illumination." *Progressive Age* 16, no. 3 (1 March 1898): 107–109.

Hallock, William, and Floyd S. Muckey. "Rational, Scientific Voice-Production." *Werner's Magazine* 18, no. 1 (January 1896): 1–10.

Handlin, Oscar, and Mary F. Handlin, "Origins of the American Business Corporation." *Journal of Economic History*, 5, no. 1 (May 1945): 1–23.

Haney, Richard A., Jr. *College of Agriculture: A Century of Discovery*. Tucson: University of Arizona, 1985.

Hannaford, Ivan. *Race: The History of an Idea in the West*. Washington, DC: Woodrow Wilson Center Press, 1996.

Haraway, Donna. "A Cyborg Manifesto: Science, Technology, and Socialist Feminism in the Late Twentieth Century." In *Simians, Cyborgs, and Women: The Reinvention of Nature*. New York: Routledge, 1991, 149–181.

Haraway, Donna. "A Manifesto for Cyborgs: Science, Technology, and Socialist Feminism in the 1980s." *Socialist Review* 80 (1985): 65–107.

Harney, Stefano, and Fred Moten. *The Undercommons: Fugitive Planning & Black Study*. Wivenhoe, NY: Minor Compositions, 2013.

Harper, William Rainey. *Religion and the Higher Life*. Chicago: University of Chicago Press, 1904.

Hartman, Andrew. *A War for the Soul of America: A History of the Culture Wars*. Chicago: University of Chicago Press, 2015.

Harwood, John. "Corporate Abstraction." *Perspecta* 46 (2013): 218–243.

Harwood, John. *The Interface: IBM and the Transformation of Corporate Design*. Minneapolis: University of Minnesota Press, 2011.

Harwood, John. "On Wires; or, Metals and Modernity Reconsidered." *Grey Room* 69 (Fall 2017): 108–136.

Hayden, Dolores. *The Grand Domestic Revolution; A History of Feminist Designs for American Homes, Neighborhoods, and Cities*. Cambridge, MA: MIT Press, 1981.

Hearst, Kathryn P. "Phoebe Apperson Hearst: The Making of an Upper-Class Woman, 1842–1919." PhD diss., Columbia University, 2005.

Heath, Thomas. *The Thirteen Books of Euclid's Elements*. 2nd ed., vol. 1. New York: Dover, 1956.

Hecker, Tim. "Glenn Gould, the Vanishing Performer, and the Ambivalence of the Studio." *Leonardo Music Journal* 18 (2008): 77–83.

Hegel, Georg Wilhelm Friedrich. *Phenomenology of Spirit*. Trans. A. V. Miller. New York: Oxford University Press, 1977.

Heilbron J. L., and Robert W. Seidel. *Lawrence and His Laboratory: A History of the Lawrence Berkeley Laboratory*. Vol. 1. Berkeley: University of California Press, 1989.

Heirich, Max. *The Beginning: Berkeley 1964*. New York: Columbia University Press, 1968.

Heirich, Max. *The Spiral of Conflict: Berkeley, 1964*. New York: Columbia University Press, 1971.

Herbst, Jurgen. *From Crisis to Crisis: American College Government 1636–1819*. Cambridge, MA: Harvard University Press, 1982.

Herbst, Jurgen. "The Yale Report of 1828." *International Journal of the Classical Tradition* 11, no. 2 (Fall 2004): 213–231.

Hijiya, James A. "The *Gita* of Robert Oppenheimer." *Proceedings of the American Philosophical Society* 144, no. 2 (June 2000): 123–167.

Hill, Frederick Parsell. *Charles F. McKim, the Man*. Francestown, NH: M. Jones, 1950.

Hitchcock, Henry-Russell. *American Architectural Books: A List of Books, Portfolios, and Pamphlets on Architecture and Related Subjects Published in America Before 1895*. Minneapolis: University of Minnesota Press, 1946.

Hitchcock, Henry-Russell. *The Architecture of H. H. Richardson and His Times*. New York: Museum of Modern Art, 1936.

Hofstadter, Richard. *The Age of Reform: From Bryan to F.D.R.* New York: Vintage, 1955.

Hofstadter, Richard, and Seymour Martin Lipset, eds. *Turner and the Sociology of the Frontier*. New York: Basic, 1968.

Hofstadter, Richard, and Walter P. Metzger. *The Development of Academic Freedom in the United States*. New York: Columbia University Press, 1955.

Hofstadter, Richard, and Wilson Smith, eds. *American Higher Education: A Documentary History*. 2 vols. (Chicago: University of Chicago Press, 1961).

Hollerith, Herman. "An Electric Tabulating System." *[Columbia College] School of Mines Quarterly: Journal of Applied Science* 10, no. 16 (April 1889): 238–255.

Holley, I. B., Jr. "The Mechanization of Brickmaking." *History of Technology* 50, no. 1 (January 2009): 82–102.

Holly, Michael Ann. *Panofsky and the Foundations of Art History*. Ithaca: Cornell University Press, 1984.

Honeywell, Roy J. *The Educational Work of Thomas Jefferson*. Cambridge, MA: Harvard University Press, 1931.

Horkheimer, Max, and Theodor W. Adorno. *Dialectic of Enlightenment: Philosophical Fragments*. Trans. Edmund Jephcott. Redwood City, CA: Stanford University Press, 2002.

Horowitz, Helen Lefkowitz. *Alma Mater: Design and Experience in the Women's Colleges from Their Nineteenth-Century Beginnings to the 1930s*. 2nd ed. Amherst: University of Massachusetts Press, 1993.

Horowitz, Helen Lefkowitz. *The Power and Passion of M. Carey Thomas*. New York: Knopf, 1994.

Howard, David Sanctuary, ed. *New York and the China Trade*. New York: New York Historical Society, 1984.

Hudson, Henry Hoyt, ed. *The Humanities Look Ahead: Report of the First Annual Conference Held by the Stanford School of Humanities*. Redwood City, CA: Stanford University Press, 1943.

Hughes, Thomas Parke. *Networks of Power: Electrification in Western Society, 1880–1930*. Baltimore, MD: Johns Hopkins University Press, 1983.

Hunter, Robert F., and Edwin L. Dooley, Jr. *Claudius Crozet: French Engineer in America 1790–1864*. Charlottesville: University of Virginia Press, 1989.

Huston, James L. *Securing the Fruits of Labor: The American Concept of Wealth Distribution, 1765–1900*. Baton Rouge: Louisiana State University Press, 2015.

Hutchins, Robert Maynard, ed. *Great Books of the Western World*. 54 vols. Chicago: Encyclopaedia Britannica, 1952.

Hutchins, Robert Maynard. *The Higher Learning in America*. New Haven, CT: Yale University Press, 1936.

Hutton, George V. *The Great Hudson River Brick Industry: Commemorating Three and One Half Centuries of Brickmaking*. Fleischmanns, NY: Purple Mountain Press, 2003.

Hvattum, Mari, and Anne Hultzsch, eds. *The Printed and the Built: Architecture, Print Culture, and Public Debate in the Nineteenth Century*. London: Bloomsbury, 2018.

Immerwahr, Daniel. "Caste or Colony? Indianizing Race in the United States." *Modern Intellectual History* 4, no. 2 (2007): 275–301.

Innis, Robert E. *Susanne Langer in Focus: The Symbolic Mind*. Indianapolis: Indiana University Press, 2009.

Jackson, John David. "Panofsky Agonistes: The 1950 Loyalty Oath at Berkeley." *Physics Today* 62, no. 1 (January 2009): 41–47.

James, Henry. *The Bostonians*. London: Macmillan, 1886.

Jameson, Fredric. "Beyond the Cave: Demystifying the Ideology of Modernism." *Bulletin of the Midwest Modern Language Association* 8, no. 1 (Spring 1975): 1–20.

Jameson, Fredric. *The Prison-House of Language: A Critical Account of Structuralism and Russian Formalism*. Princeton, NJ: Princeton University Press, 1972.

Jamieson, James P. *Intimate History of the Campus and Buildings of Washington University Saint Louis*. St. Louis: Mound City Press [private publication], 1941.

Jarzombek, Mark. "Corridor Spaces." *Critical Inquiry* 36 (Summer 2010): 728–770.

Jarzombek, Mark. *Designing MIT: Bosworth's New Tech*. Boston: Northeastern University Press, 2004.

Jefferson, Isaac. *Memoirs of a Monticello Slave, Dictated to Charles Campbell in the 1840s by Isaac, One of Thomas Jefferson's Slaves*. Charlottesville: University of Virginia Press, 1951.

Jefferson, Thomas. *Notes on the State of Virginia* [1785]. New York: Penguin, 1999.

Jencks, Christopher, and David Riesman. *The Academic Revolution*. New York: Doubleday, 1968.

Jewett, Charles C. *A Plan for Stereotyping Catalogues by Separate Titles, and for Forming a General Stereotyped Catalogue of Public Libraries in the United States*. Washington, DC: American Association for the Advancement of Science, 1851.

Johns, Adrian. *The Nature of the Book: Print and Knowledge in the Making*. Chicago: University of Chicago Press, 1998.

Johnson, Rossiter. *A History of the World's Columbian Exposition Held in Chicago in 1893; by Authority of the Board of Directors*. New York: D. Appleton, 1897.

Johnston, Norman B. "John Haviland, Jailor to the World." *Journal of the Society of Architectural Historians* 23, no. 2 (May 1964): 101–105.

Jones, Bessie Zaban. *Lighthouse in the Skies: The Smithsonian Astrophysical Observatory; Background and History 1846–1955*. Washington, DC: Smithsonian Institution, 1965.

Judson, Adoniram. *Life and Letters of John Howard Raymond, Late President of Vassar College*. New York: Fords, Howard & Hulbery, 1881.

Kadam, K. N. "Dr. Ambedkar's Philosophy of Emancipation and the Impact of John Dewey." In *The Meaning of Ambedkarite Conversion to Buddhism and Other Essays*, 1–33. Mumbai: Popular Prakashan, 1997.

Kant, Immanuel. "An Answer to the Question: What Is Enlightenment?" [1784]. In *What Is Enlightenment?: Eighteenth-Century Answers and Twentieth-Century Questions*, ed. and trans. James Schmidt, 58–64. Berkeley: University of California Press, 1996.

Kant, Immanuel. *The Conflict of the Faculties*. 1798. Trans. Mary J. Gregor. New York: Abaris, 1979.

Kantorowicz, Ernst H. *The Fundamental Issue: Documents and Marginal Notes on the University of California Loyalty Oath*. San Francisco: Parker Printing, 1950.

Kantorowicz, Ernst H. *The King's Two Bodies: A Study in Medieval Political Theology*. Princeton, NJ: Princeton University Press, 1957.

Kaplan, A. D. H. *Henry Charles Carey: A Study in Economic Thought*. Baltimore, MD: Johns Hopkins University Press, 1931.

Kaser, David. "The American Academic Library Building, 1870–1890." *Journal of Library History (1974–1987)* 21, no. 1 (Winter 1986): 60–71.

Kaser, David. *The Evolution of the American Academic Library Building*. Lanham, MD: Scarecrow Press, 1997.

Keer, Dhananjay. *Dr. Ambedkar: Life and Mission*. Bombay: Popular Prakashan, 1954.

Kelley, Brooks Mather. *Yale: A History*. New Haven, CT: Yale University Press, 1974.

Kendall, Phebe Mitchell. *Maria Mitchell: Life, Letters, and Journals*. Boston: Lee and Shepard, 1896.

Kennedy, Hollyamber. "Modernism's Politics of Land: Settlement Colonialism and Migrant Mobility in the German Empire, from Prussian Poland to German Namibia, 1884–1918." PhD diss., Columbia University, 2019.

Kent, Charles W. "Poe's Student Days at the University of Virginia." *Bookman* 44, no. 5 (January 1917): 517–525.

Kerr, Clark. *The Uses of the University.* Cambridge, MA: Harvard University Press, 1963.

Kevles, Daniel J. "The National Science Foundation and the Debate over Postwar Research Policy, 1942–1945: A Political Interpretation of *Science—The Endless Frontier.*" *Isis* 68, no. 1 (March 1977): 4–26.

Khabde, Dinkar. *Dr. Ambedkar and Western Thinkers.* Pune: Sugava Prakashan, 1989.

Kidwell, Peggy Aldrich, Amy Ackerberg-Hastings, and David Lindsay Roberts, *Tools of American Mathematics Teaching, 1800–2000.* Baltimore and Washington, DC: Johns Hopkins University Press/Smithsonian Institution, 2008.

Kimball, Bruce A. *Orators & Philosophers: A History of the Idea of Liberal Education.* New York: Teachers College Press, 1986.

Kingsley, William L., ed. *Yale College; A Sketch of Its History: with Notices of Its Several Departments, Instructors, and Benefactors Together with Some Account of Student Life and Amusements by Various Authors.* 2 vols. New York: Henry Holt, 1879.

Kirker, Harold. *The Architecture of Charles Bulfinch.* Cambridge, MA: Harvard University Press, 1969.

Kittler, Friedrich A. *Aufschreibesysteme 1800 / 1900.* Munich: Fink, 1985.

Kittler, Friedrich A. *Discourse Networks, 1800 / 1900.* Trans. Michael Metteer, with Chris Cullens. Redwood City, CA: Stanford University Press, 1990.

Kittler, Friedrich A. *Gramophone, Film, Typewriter.* Trans. Geoffrey Winthrop-Young and Michael Wutz. Redwood City, CA: Stanford University Press, 1999.

Kittler, Friedrich A. "Universities: Wet, Hard, Soft, and Harder." *Critical Inquiry* 31, no. 1 (Autumn 2004): 244–255.

Klein, Kerwin Lee. *Frontiers of Historical Imagination: Narrating the European Conquest of Native America, 1890–1990.* Berkeley: University of California Press, 1997.

Kohlstedt, Sally Gregory. "Maria Mitchell: The Advancement of Women in Science." *New England Quarterly* 51, no. 1 (March 1978): 39–63.

Koselleck, Reinhart. *The Practice of Conceptual History: Timing History, Spacing Concepts.* Redwood City, CA: Stanford University Press, 2002.

Krajewski, Markus. *The Server: A Media History from the Present to the Baroque,* trans. Ilinca Iurascu. New Haven, CT: Yale University Press, 2018.

Krajewski, Markus. *Paper Machines: About Cards & Catalogs, 1548–1929.* Trans. Peter Krapp. Cambridge, MA: MIT Press, 2011.

Lacan, Jacques. *The Other Side of Psychoanalysis.* Trans. Russell Grigg. New York: Norton, 2007.

Lacy, Tim. *The Dream of a Democratic Culture: Mortimer J. Adler and the Great Books Idea.* New York: Palgrave Macmillan, 2013.

Lalor, John. *Money and Morals: A Book for the Times.* London: John Chapman, 1852.

Lamott, Kenneth. "Right-Thinking Think Tank," *New York Times Magazine,* July 23, 1978, 16, 45, 48–49.

Langer, Susanne K. *Philosophy in a New Key: A Study in the Symbolism of Reason, Rite, and Art.* Cambridge, MA: Harvard University Press, 1942.

Larkin, Brian. "Circulating Empires: Colonial Authority and the Immoral, Subversive Problem of American Film." In *Globalizing American Studies,* ed. Brian T. Edwards and Dilip Parameshwar Gaonkar, 155–183. Chicago: University of Chicago Press, 2010.

Larned, Charles W. *On the History of the Battle Monument at West Point*. West Point, NY: Devinne Press, 1898.

Lasser, Carol, ed. *Educating Men and Women Together: Coeducation in a Changing World*. Urbana: University of Illinois Press in conjunction with Oberlin College, 1987.

Latour, Bruno. *Reassembling the Social: An Introduction to Actor-Network-Theory*. New York: Oxford University Press, 2005.

Latour, Bruno, and Steve Woolgar. *Laboratory Life: The Construction of Scientific Facts*. 2nd ed. Princeton, NJ: Princeton University Press, 1986.

Lécuyer, Christophe. *Making Silicon Valley: Innovation and the Growth of High Tech*. Cambridge, MA: MIT Press, 2006.

Lécuyer, Christophe. "What Do Universities Really Owe Industry? The Case of Solid State Electronics at Stanford." *Minerva* 43, no. 1 (March 2005): 51–71.

Lee, Philip. "The Curious Life of *In Loco Parentis* at American Universities." *Higher Education Review* 8 (2011): 65–90.

Legendre, A. M. *Elements of Geometry and Trigonometry*. 5th ed., ed. and adapted by Charles Davies, trans. David Brewster. New York: Wiley & Long, 1835.

Legendre, A. M. *Elements of Geometry and Trigonometry; with Notes, Revised and Altered for the Use of the Military at West Point*. 2nd ed., ed. and adapted by Charles Davies, trans. David Brewster. New York: Wiley & Long; Collins, Keene & Co., 1820.

Legendre, A. M. *Elements of Geometry: Translated from the French for the Use of the Students of the University in Cambridge, N.E.*, trans. John Farrar. Cambridge, MA: Hilliard and Metcalf, 1819.

Lem, Stanisław. *His Master's Voice*. Trans. Michael Kandel. Evanston, IL: Northwestern University Press, 1983.

Lerner, Robert E. *Ernst Kantorowicz: A Life*. Princeton, NJ: Princeton University Press, 2017.

Leslie, Stuart W. *The Cold War and American Science: The Military-Industrial-Academic Complex at MIT and Stanford*. New York: Columbia University Press, 1993.

Leslie, Stuart W., and Bruce Hevly. "Steeple Building at Stanford: Electrical Engineering, Physics, and Microwave Research." *Proceedings of the IEEE* 73, no. 7 (July 1985): 1169–1180.

Levin, Thomas Y. "Tones from Out of Nowhere: Rudolph Pfenninger and the Archaeology of Synthetic Sound." *Grey Room* 12 (Summer 2003): 32–79.

Levine, Lawrence W. *The Opening of the American Mind: Canons, Culture, and History*. Boston: Beacon Press, 1996.

Lewis, Michael J. *Frank Furness: Architecture and the Violent Mind*. New York: Norton, 2001.

Lewis, Michael J. "Frank Furness and the Expandable Library." *Journal of the Society of Architectural Historians* 77, no. 2 (June 2018): 138–145.

Lewis, Michael J. *The Gothic Revival*. London: Thames & Hudson, 2002.

Limerick, Patricia Nelson. *The Legacy of Conquest: The Unbroken Past of the American West*. New York: Norton, 1987.

Linderman, Winifred B. "History of the Columbia University Library, 1876–1926." PhD diss., Columbia University, 1959.

Lipset, Seymour Martin, and Sheldon S. Wolin, eds. *The Berkeley Student Revolt: Facts and Interpretations*. New York: Anchor/Doubleday, 1965.

Liscombe, Rhodri Windsor. *Altogether American: Robert Mills Architect and Engineer, 1781–1855*. New York: Oxford University Press, 1994. Locke, John. *An Essay Concerning Human Understanding* [1689]. Oxford: Clarendon Press, 1975.

Lord, John King. *A History of Dartmouth College*. Concord, NH: Rumford Press, 1913.

Lossing, John Benson. *Vassar College and Its Founder*. New York: C. A. Alvord, 1867.

Losurdo, Domenico. *Liberalism: A Counter-History*. Trans. Gregory Elliott. New York: Verso, 2011.

Loughran, Trish. *The Republic in Print: Print Culture in the Age of U.S. Nation Building, 1770–1870*. New York: Columbia University Press, 2007.

Lovett, Bobby L. *America's Historically Black Colleges and Universities: A Narrative History*. Macon, GA: Mercer University Press, 2011.

Low, Polly, Graham Oliver, and P. J. Rhodes, eds. *Cultures of Commemoration: War Memorials, Ancient and Modern*. New York: Oxford University Press, 2012.

Low, William G. *A. A. Low & Brothers' Fleet of Clipper Ships*. 2nd ed. n.p., 1922.

Lowe, Roy. *A Western Acropolis of Learning: The University of California in 1897*. Berkeley: Center for Studies in Higher Education and Institute of Governmental Studies, University of California, Berkeley, 1996.

Lowen, Rebecca S. *Creating the Cold War University: The Transformation of Stanford*. Berkeley: University of California Press, 1997.

Lowenthal, David. *George Perkins Marsh: Prophet of Conservation*. Seattle: University of Washington Press, 2003.

Ludlow, Helen W., ed. *Tuskegee Normal and Industrial School for Training Colored Teachers at Tuskegee, Alabama: Its Story and Its Songs*. Hampton, VA: Normal School Steam Press, 1884.

Luna, Guadalupe T. "Chicana/Chicano Land Tenure in the Agrarian Domain: On the Edge of a 'Naked Knife.' " *Michigan Journal of Race and Law* 4, no. 38 (Fall 1998): 39–144.

Lundgren, Peter. "Engineering Education in Europe and the USA, 1750–1930: The Rise to Dominance of School Culture and the Engineering Professions." *Annals of Science* 47 (1990): 33–75.

Lynch, Michael, and Steve Woolgar. *Representation in Scientific Practice*. Cambridge, MA: MIT Press, 1990.

Maass, John. "Who Invented Dewey's Classification?" *Wilson Library Bulletin* 47, no. 4 (December 1972): 335–341.

Maclean, John. *History of the College of New Jersey 1746–1854 (Two Volumes in One)*. New York: Arno Press, 1969.

Madley, Benjamin. *An American Genocide: The United States and the California Indian Catastrophe, 1846–1873*. New Haven, CT: Yale University Press, 2016.

Maggor, Noam. *Brahmin Capitalism: Frontiers of Wealth and Populism in America's First Gilded Age*. Cambridge, MA: Harvard University Press, 2017.

Maier, Pauline. "The Revolutionary Origins of the American Corporation." *William and Mary Quarterly* 50, no. 1 (January 1993): 51–84.

Mansfield, Edward D. "The Military Academy at West Point." *American Journal of Education* 13 (March 1863): 17–46.

Marable, Manning. *W. E. B. Du Bois: Black Radical Democrat*. 2nd ed. Boulder, CO: Paradigm, 2005.

Marburg, Frances T. "The Social Life of Vassar Students." *Vassar Miscellany*, special number (October 1, 1915): 3–39.

Marchand, Suzanne L. *Down from Olympus: Archaeology and Philhellenism in Germany, 1750–1970*. Princeton, NJ: Princeton University Press, 1996.

Marcus, Alan, ed. *Science as Service: Establishing and Reformulating American Land-Grant Universities, 1865–1930*. Tuscaloosa: University of Alabama Press, 2015.

Marsden, George M. *The Soul of the American University: From Protestant Establishment to Established Nonbelief*. New York: Oxford University Press, 1994.

Marsh, George Perkins. *Man and Nature; Or, Physical Geography as Modified by Human Action*. New York: Scribner, 1864.

Martin, Reinhold. *The Organizational Complex: Architecture, Media, and Corporate Space.* Cambridge, MA: MIT Press, 2003.

Martinez, Diana. "Concrete Colonialism: Architecture, Urbanism, Infrastructure, and the American Colonial Project in the Philippines." PhD diss., Columbia University, 2017.

Marx, Karl. *Capital.* Vol. 3, *The Process of Capitalist Production as a Whole,* ed. Frederick Engels. New York: International Publishers, 1967.

Marx, Karl. *Grundrisse: Foundations of the Critique of Political Economy (Rough Draft)* [1857–1858]. Trans. Martin Nicholas. New York: Penguin, 1993.

Marx, Leo. *The Machine in the Garden: Technology and the Pastoral Ideal in America.* New York: Oxford University Press, 1965.

McArdle, Phil, ed. *Exactly Opposite the Golden Gate: Essays on Berkeley's History 1845–1945.* Berkeley, CA: Berkeley Historical Society, 1983.

McCarthy, Molly. *The Accidental Diarist: A History of the Daily Planner in America.* Chicago: University of Chicago Press, 2013.

McCaughey, Robert A. *Stand, Columbia: A History of Columbia University in the City of New York, 1754–2004.* New York: Columbia University Press, 2003.

McClelland, Charles E. *State, Society and University in Germany 1700–1914.* New York: Cambridge University Press, 1980.

McKenna, Rosalie Thorne. "James Renwick, Jr. and the Second Empire Style in the United States." *Magazine of Art* 44, no. 3 (March 1951): 97–101.

McKenna, Rosalie Thorne. "Mr. Vassar's Consecrated Brick." *Vassar Quarterly* 35, no. 6 (June 1950): 5–9.

McLuhan, Marshall. *Understanding Media: The Extensions of Man.* New York: McGraw-Hill, 1964.

Meardon, Stephen. "Reciprocity and Henry C. Carey's Traverses on 'The Road to Perfect Freedom of Trade.'" *Journal of the History of Economic Thought* 33, no. 3 (September 2011): 307–333.

Meister, Maureen, ed. *H. H. Richardson: The Architect, His Peers, and Their Era.* Cambridge, MA: MIT Press, 1999.

Menand, Louis, Paul Reitter, and Chad Wellmon, eds. *The Rise of the Research University: A Sourcebook.* Chicago: University of Chicago Press, 2017.

Merritt, Raymond H. *Engineering in American Society 1850–1875.* Lexington: University Press of Kentucky, 1969.

Middleton, Robin, ed. *The Beaux-Arts and Nineteenth-Century French Architecture.* Cambridge, MA: MIT Press, 1982.

Miller, Dayton Clarence. *The Science of Musical Sounds.* New York: Macmillan, 1916.

Miner, Dwight C., ed. *A History of Columbia College on Morningside.* New York: Columbia University Press, 1954.

Mirowski, Philip. *Machine Dreams: Economics Becomes a Cyborg Science.* New York: Cambridge University Press, 2002.

Mirowski, Philip, and Dieter Plehwe, eds. *The Road from Mont Pèlerin: The Making of the Neoliberal Thought Collective.* Cambridge, MA: Harvard University Press, 2009.

Mirrielees, Edith R. *Stanford: The Story of a University.* New York: G.B. Putnam, 1959.

Mitchell, Don. *The Right to the City: Social Justice and the Fight for Public Space.* New York: Guilford Press, 2003.

Mitchell, J. Pearce. *Stanford University 1916–1941.* Redwood City, CA: Stanford University, 1958.

Mitchell, Maria [as William Mitchell]. "On the Comet of the 10th Month, (October 1st) 1847." *American Journal of Science and Arts* 5, no. 8 (May 1848): 83–85.Mitchell, Timothy.

Rule of Experts: Egypt, Techno-Politics, Modernity. Berkeley: University of California Press, 2002.

Mjagkij, Nina, ed. *Organizing Black America: An Encyclopedia of African American Associations.* New York: Routledge, 2013.

Morison, Samuel Eliot. *The Founding of Harvard College.* Cambridge, MA: Harvard University Press, 1935.

Morison, Samuel Eliot. *Three Centuries of Harvard 1636–1936.* Cambridge, MA: Harvard University Press, 1946.

Morrison, A. J. *The Beginnings of Public Education in Virginia, 1776–1860: Study of Secondary Schools in Relation to the State Literary Fund.* Richmond: David Bottom, Superintendent of Public Printing, 1917.

Morrison, Rodney. "Henry C. Carey and American Economic Development." *Transactions of the American Philosophical Society* 76, no. 3 (1986): i–ix, 1–91.

Mosher, Paul H. "University of Pennsylvania Libraries." In *International Dictionary of Library Histories,* ed. David H. Stam, 884–889. New York: Routledge, 2016.

Moulton, Robert. "Physics, Power, and Politics: Fear and Loathing on the Electron Trail." *Sandstone & Tile* [Stanford Historical Society] 25, no. 1 (Winter 2001): 3–12.

Mukherjee, Arun P. "B. R. Ambedkar, John Dewey, and the Meaning of Democracy." *New Literary History* 40, no. 2 (Spring 2009): 345–370.

Mumford, Lewis. *Art and Technics.* New York: Columbia University Press, 1952.

Mumford, Lewis. *The Brown Decades: A Study of the Arts in America 1865–1895.* New York: Harcourt Brace, 1931.

Mumford, Lewis. *The Golden Day: A Study in American Experience and Culture.* New York: Boni and Liveright, 1926.

Mumford, Lewis. *The Myth of the Machine: The Pentagon of Power.* New York: Harcourt Brace Jovanovich, 1970.

Mumford, Lewis. *The Myth of the Machine: Technics and Human Development.* New York: Harcourt Brace, 1967.

Mumford, Lewis. *Sticks and Stones: A Study of American Architecture and Civilization.* New York: Boni & Liveright, 1924.

Mumford, Lewis. *Technics and Civilization.* New York: Harcourt Brace, 1934.

Mumford, Lewis. *The Transformations of Man.* New York: Collier, 1956.

Muthesius, Stefan. *The Postwar University: Utopianist Campus and College.* New Haven, CT: Yale University Press, 2000.

Nelson, Louis P. "The Architecture of Democracy in a Landscape of Slavery." In *Thomas Jefferson, Architect: Palladian Models, Democratic Principles, and the Conflict of Ideals,* ed. Dewitt Lloyd and Corey Piper, 98–118. Norfolk: Chrysler Museum of Art/New Haven, CT: Yale University Press, 2019.

Nevins, Allan. *The State Universities and Democracy.* Urbana: University of Illinois Press, 1962.

Newfield, Christopher. *The Great Mistake: How We Wrecked Public Universities and How We Can Fix Them.* Baltimore, MD: Johns Hopkins University Press, 2016.

Newfield, Christopher. *Ivy and Industry: Business and the Making of the American University, 1880–1980.* Durham, NC: Duke University Press, 2003.

Newfield, Christopher. *Unmaking the Public University: The Forty-Year Assault on the Middle Class.* Cambridge, MA: Harvard University Press, 2008.

Newman, Cardinal John Henry. *The Idea of the University.* London: Longmans, Green, 1852.

Nietzsche, Friedrich. *Anti-Education: On the Future of Our Educational Institutions.* Ed. Paul Reitter and Chad Wellmon. Trans. Damion Searls. New York: New York Review Books, 2016.

Nietzsche, Friedrich. *The Birth of Tragedy*. In *The Birth of Tragedy and Other Writings*, ed. Raymond Geuss and Ronald Speirs, trans. Ronald Speirs, 1–116. Cambridge: Cambridge University Press, 1999.

Noble, David W. *Historians Against History: The Frontier Thesis and the National Covenant in American Historical Writing Since 1830*. Minneapolis: University of Minnesota Press, 1965.

Nolan, Ginger. "*Weltgeist/Wildegeist*: The Savage Inside 'World History.'" *Grey Room* 64 (Summer 2016): 40–63.

Norman, Daniel. "The Development of Astronomical Photography." *Osiris* 5 (1938): 560–594.

Norris, Mary Harriott. *The Golden Age of Vassar*. Poughkeepsie, NY: Vassar College, 1915.

Nye, David E. *American Technological Sublime*. Cambridge, MA: MIT Press, 1994.

Nye, David E. *Electrifying America: Social Meanings of a New Technology, 1880–1940*. Cambridge, MA: MIT Press, 1990.

Ockman, Joan, ed. *Architecture School: Three Centuries of Educating Architects in North America*. Cambridge, MA: MIT Press, 2012.

O'Connor, Candace. *Beginning a Great Work: Washington University in St. Louis, 1853–2003*. St. Louis, MO: Washington University in St. Louis, 2003.

O'Gorman, James F. *The Architecture of Frank Furness*. Philadelphia: Philadelphia Museum of Art, 1973.

O'Gorman, James F. *H. H. Richardson: Architectural Forms for an American Society*. Chicago: University of Chicago Press, 1987.

Oleson, Alexandra, and John Voss, eds. *The Organization of Knowledge in Modern America, 1860–1920*. Baltimore, MD: Johns Hopkins University Press, 1979.

Oliver, Richard. *Bertram Grosvenor Goodhue*. New York: Architectural History Foundation/ Cambridge, MA: MIT Press, 1983.

O'Mara, Margaret Pugh. *Cities of Knowledge: Cold War Science and the Search for the Next Silicon Valley*. Princeton, NJ: Princeton University Press, 2005.

O'Neal, William B. *Pictorial History of the University of Virginia*. Charlottesville: University of Virginia Press, 1968.

Ong, Walter J. *Orality and Literacy: The Technologizing of the Word*. New York: Methuen, 1982.

Onuf, Peter S., ed. *Jeffersonian Legacies*. Charlottesville: University of Virginia Press, 1993.

Onuf, Peter S. *The Mind of Thomas Jefferson*. Charlottesville: University of Virginia Press, 2007.

Onuf, Peter S., and Annette Gordon-Reed. "Jefferson's Spaces [Review Essay]." *Early American Literature* 48, no. 3 (2013): 765–769.

Osner, Jeffrey Karl. *H. H. Richardson: Complete Architectural Works*. Cambridge, MA: MIT Press, 1982.

Panofsky, Erwin. *Perspective as Symbolic Form*. Trans. Christopher S. Wood (New York: Zone, 1991.

Panofsky, Wolfgang K. H. *Panofsky on Physics, Politics and Peace: Pief Remembers*. New York: Springer, 2007.

Parikka, Jussi. *What Is Media Archaeology?* Malden, MA: Polity Press, 2012.

Park, Helen. *A List of Architectural Books Available in America before the Revolution*. 2nd rev. ed. Los Angeles: Hennessey & Ingalls, 1973.

Partridge, Loren W. *John Galen Howard and the Berkeley Campus: Beaux-Arts Architecture in the "Athens of the West."* Berkeley, CA: Berkeley Architectural Heritage Association, 1978.

Peirce, Benjamin. *An Elementary Treatise on Curves, Functions, and Forces, Volume First, Containing Analytic Geometry and the Differential Calculus.* Boston: James Munroe, 1851.

Peirce, Benjamin. *An Elementary Treatise on Plane and Solid Geometry.* Boston: James Munroe, 1837.

Perelman, Michael. "Henry Carey's Political-Ecological Economics: An Introduction." *Organization & Environment* 12, no. 3 (September 1999): 280–292.

Pérouse de Montclos, Jean-Marie. *Etienne-Louis Boullée.* Paris: Flammarion, 1994.

Peters, John Durham. *The Marvelous Clouds: Toward a Philosophy of Elemental Media.* Chicago: University of Chicago Press, 2015.

Peters, John Durham. *Speaking into the Air: A History of the Idea of Communication.* Chicago: University of Chicago Press, 1999.

Pettitt, George A. *Berkeley: The Town and Gown of It.* Berkeley, CA: Howell North, 1973.

Phillips, Sarah T. "Antebellum Agricultural Reform, Republican Ideology, and Sectional Tension." *Agricultural History* 74, no. 4 (Autumn 2000): 799–822.

Pickens, Buford. "Mr. Jefferson as a Revolutionary Architect." *Journal of the Society of Architectural Historians* 34, no. 4 (December 1975): 257–279.

Pierson, George Wilson. *The Founding of Yale: The Legend of the Forty Folios.* New Haven, CT: Yale University Press, 1988.

Pierson, George W. *A Yale Book of Numbers: Historical Statistics of the College and University 1701–1976.* New Haven, CT: Yale University, 1983.

Pitt, Leonard. *The Decline of the Californios: The Social History of the Spanish-Speaking Californians, 1846–1890.* Berkeley: University of California Press, 1966.

Plato, *The Republic.* Trans. Henry Davis. In *The Works of Plato: A New and Literal Version, Chiefly from the Text of Stallbaum,* vol. 2. London: Henry G. Bohn, 1849.

Plato. *The Republic.* Trans. Desmond Lee. New York: Penguin, 1955.

Platt, Edmund. *The Eagle's History of Poughkeepsie from the Earliest Settlements, 1683–1905.* Poughkeepsie, NY: Platt & Platt, 1905.

Pocock, J. G. A. *The Machiavellian Moment: Florentine Political Thought and the Atlantic Republican Tradition.* Princeton, NJ: Princeton University Press, 1975.

Poe, Edgar Allan. *Poems by Edgar A. Poe.* 2nd ed. New York: Elam Bliss, 1831.

Poulsen, Frederik. "Talking, Weeping, and Bleeding Statues." *Acta Archaeologica* 16 (1945): 178–195.

Pugh, Emerson W. *Building IBM: Shaping an Industry and Its Technology.* Cambridge, MA: MIT Press, 1995.

Quinn, Arthur Hobson. *Edgar Allan Poe: A Critical Biography.* Baltimore, MD: Johns Hopkins University Press, 1998.

Ragosta, John, A., Peter S. Onuf, and Andrew J. O'Shaughnessy, eds. *The Founding of Thomas Jefferson's University.* Charlottesville: University of Virginia Press, 2019.

Rand, Richard, ed. *Logomachia: The Conflict of the Faculties.* Lincoln: University of Nebraska Press, 1992.

Randolph, Sarah N. *The Domestic Life of Thomas Jefferson, Compiled from Family Letters and Reminiscences.* New York: Harper, 1871.

Readings, Bill. *The University in Ruins.* Cambridge, MA: Harvard University Press, 1996.

Reddy, Raj. "Machine Models of Speech Perception," in *Perception and Production of Fluent Speech,* ed. Ronald A. Cole. New York: Routledge, 1980.

Reid, Thomas. "Of Taste." In *Essays on the Intellectual Powers of Man,* ed. James Walker. Cambridge, MA: John Bartlett, 1850.

Remini, Robert V. *Daniel Webster: The Man and His Time.* New York: Norton, 1997.

Reuben, Julie A. *The Making of the Modern University: Intellectual Transformation and the Marginalization of Morality*. Chicago: University of Chicago Press, 1996.

Rheinberger, Hans-Jörg. *Toward a History of Epistemic Things: Synthesizing Proteins in the Test Tube*. Redwood City, CA: Stanford University Press, 1997.

Rice, Howard C. *Thomas Jefferson's Paris*. Princeton, NJ: Princeton University Press, 1976.

Richardson, Leon Burr. *History of Dartmouth College*. Hanover, NH: Dartmouth College Publications, 1932.

Ricketts, Palmer C. *History of Rensselaer Polytechnic Institute 1824–1914*. New York: John Wiley, 1914.

Rickey, V. Frederick and Amy Shell-Gellasch. "Mathematics Education at West Point: The First Hundred Years." Mathematical Association of America. July 2010. https://www.maa.org/press/periodicals/convergence/mathematics-education-at-west-point-the-first-hundred-years-introduction.

Ripken, Suzanna Kim. *Corporate Personhood*. New York: Cambridge University Press, 2019.

Roberts, Jon H., and James Turner. *The Sacred and the Secular University*. Princeton, NJ: Princeton University Press, 2000.

Roberts, Richard L. *Two Worlds of Cotton: Colonialism and the Regional Economy in the French Soudan, 1800–1946*. Redwood City, CA: Stanford University Press, 1996.

Robinson, Clare. "Architecture in Support of Citizenry: Vernon DeMars and the Berkeley Student Union." *Journal of Architectural Education* 70, no. 2 (2016): 236–246.

Robinson, W. W. *Land in California: The Story of Mission Lands, Ranchos, Squatters, Mining Claims, Railroad Grants, Land Scrip, Homesteads*. Berkeley: University of California Press, 1948.

Rogers, Howard Jason, ed. *Congress of Arts and Science: Universal Exposition, St. Louis, 1904*. 8 vols. Boston: Houghton, Mifflin, 1907.

Roper, Laura Wood. *FLO: A Biography of Frederick Law Olmsted*. Baltimore, MD: Johns Hopkins University Press, 1973.

Rorty, Richard. *Philosophy and the Mirror of Nature*. Princeton, NJ: Princeton University Press, 1979.

Rossiter, Margaret W. *The Emergence of Agricultural Science: Justus Liebig and the Americans, 1840–1880*. New Haven, CT: Yale University Press, 1975.

Roth, Leland M. *McKim, Mead & White Architects*. New York: Harper & Row, 1983.

Rothblatt, Sheldon, and Björn Wittrock, eds. *The European and American University Since 1800*. New York: Cambridge University Press, 1993.

Rousseau, Jean-Jacques. *The Essential Writings of Rousseau*. Ed. Leo Damrosch. New York: Modern Library, 2013.

Royce, Josiah. *California, From the Conquest in 1846 to the Second Vigilance Committee in San Francisco: A Study in American Character*. Boston: Houghton Mifflin, 1886.

Rudolph, Frederick. *The American College: A History*. New York: Vintage, 1965.

Rudolph, Frederick. *Curriculum: A History of the American Undergraduate Course of Study Since 1636*. San Francisco: Josey-Bass, 1977.

Rudwick, Elliott M. "W. E. B. Du Bois and the Atlanta University Studies on the Negro." *Journal of Negro Education* 26, no. 4 (Autumn 1957): 466–476.

Rüegg, Walter, ed. *A History of the University in Europe*. Vol. 3, *Universities in the Nineteenth and Early Twentieth Centuries (1800–1945)*. New York: Cambridge University Press, 2004.

Ruskin, John. *The Stones of Venice*. New York: Da Capo Press, 1985.

Rydell, Robert. *All the World's a Fair: Visons of Empire at the American International Expositions 1876–1916*. Chicago: University of Chicago Press, 1984.

Saenger, Paul. *Space Between Words: The Origins of Silent Reading*. Redwood City, CA: Stanford University Press, 1997.

Said, Edward W. *Beginnings: Intention and Method*. New York: Columbia University Press, 1985.

Said, Edward W. *Reflections on Exile and Other Essays*. Cambridge, MA: Harvard University Press, 2000.

Said, Edward W. "The Text, the World, the Critic." *Bulletin of the Midwest Modern Language Association* 8, no. 2 (Autumn 1975): 1–23.

Said, Edward W. *The World, the Text, and the Critic*. Cambridge, MA: Harvard University Press, 1983.

Sanford, Charles B. *Thomas Jefferson and His Library: A Study of His Literary Interests and of the Religious Attitudes Revealed by Relevant Titles in His Library*. Hamden, CT: Archon, 1977.

Sanger, Victoria. "L'influence et la genèse de l'enseignement du genie militaire à l'École de West Point." In *Les saviors de l'ingénieur militaire et l'édition de manuels, cours et cahiers d'exercices, 1751–1914*, ed. Émilie d'Orgeix and Isabelle Warmoes [conference proceedings], 127–138. Paris: Musée des Plans-Reliefs, 2013.

Savio, Mario. *The Essential Mario Savio: Speeches and Writings that Changed America*. Ed. Robert Cohen. Berkeley: University of California Press, 2014.

Schiller, Herbert I., ed. *Super-State: Readings in the Military-Industrial Complex*. Urbana: University of Illinois, 1970.

Schivelbusch, Wolfgang. *Disenchanted Night: The Industrialization of Light in the Nineteenth Century*. Trans. Angela Davies. Berkeley: University of California Press, 1988.

Schmidt, Leigh Eric. *Hearing Things: Religion, Illusion, and the American Enlightenment*. Cambridge, MA: Harvard University Press, 2000.

Schwab, John C. "The Yale College Curriculum 1701–1901." *Educational Review* 22 (June 1901): 1–17.

Scott, Joan Wallach. *Gender and the Politics of History*. 30th anniversary ed. New York: Columbia University Press, 2018.

Seymour, George Dudley. "Henry Caner, 1680–1731, Master Carpenter, Builder of the First Yale College Building, 1718, and of the Rector's House, 1722." *Old-Time New England: The Bulletin of the Society for the Preservation of New England Antiquities* 15, no. 3 (January 1925): 99–124.

Shils, Edward. "Robert Maynard Hutchins." *American Scholar* 59, no. 2 (Spring 1990): 211–235.

Shurtleff, Nathaniel B. *A Decimal System for the Arrangement and Administration of Libraries*. Boston: [Privately Printed], 1856.

Siegert, Bernhard. "Cultural Techniques: Or the End of the Intellectual Postwar Era in German Media Theory." *Theory, Culture & Society* 30, no. 6 (2013): 48–65.

Siegert, Bernhard. *Cultural Techniques: Grids, Filters, Doors, and Other Articulations of the Real*. Trans. Geoffrey Winthrop-Young. New York: Fordham University Press, 2015.

Siegert, Bernhard. *Relays: Literature as an Epoch of the Postal System*. Trans. Kevin Repp. Redwood City, CA: Stanford University Press, 1999.

Silverman, Kenneth. *Edgar A. Poe: Mournful and Never-Ending Remembrance*. New York: Harper Collins, 1991.

Simmel, Georg. *The Philosophy of Money* [1907]. 2nd enlarged ed. Ed. David Frisby. Trans. Tom Bottomore and David Frisby. New York: Routledge, 1978.

Sinclair, Nathalie. *The History of the Geometry Curriculum in the United States*. Charlotte, NC: Information Age, 2008.

Siskin, Clifford, and William Warner, eds. *This Is Enlightenment*. Chicago: University of Chicago Press, 2010.

Sklar, Martin J. *The Corporate Reconstruction of American Capitalism, 1890–1916: The Market, The Law, and Politics*. New York: Cambridge University Press, 1988.

Sklar, Martin J. *The United States as a Developing Country: Studies in U.S. History in the Progressive Era and the 1920s*. Cambridge: Cambridge University Press, 1992.

Slaughter, Sheila, and Larry L. Leslie. *Academic Capitalism: Politics, Policies, and the Entrepreneurial University*. Baltimore, MD: Johns Hopkins University Press, 1997.

Slaughter, Sheila, and Gary Rhoades. *Academic Capitalism and the New Economy: Markets, States, and Higher Education*. Baltimore, MD: Johns Hopkins University Press, 2004.

Sloan, Herbert. *Principle and Interest: Thomas Jefferson and the Problem of Debt*. New York: Oxford University Press, 1995.

Smith, Bonnie G. "Gender and the Practices of Scientific History: The Seminar and Archival Research in the Nineteenth Century." *American Historical Review* 100, no. 4 (October 1995): 1150–1176.

Smith, Henry Nash. *Virgin Land: The American West as Symbol and Myth*. Cambridge, MA: Harvard University Press, 1950.

Smith, Margaret Bayard. *The First Forty Years of Washington Society, Portrayed by the Family Letters of Mrs. Samuel Harrison Smith (Margaret Bayard)*. Ed. Gaillard Hunt. New York: Charles Scribner's Sons, 1906.

Snyder, Thomas D., ed. *120 Years of American Education: A Statistical Portrait*. Washington, DC: National Center for Education Statistics, U.S. Department of Education, 1993.

Spivak, Gayatri Chakravorty. "Explanation and Culture: Marginalia." *Humanities in Society* 2, no. 3 (1979): 201–221.

Spivak, Gayatri Chakravorty. *In Other Worlds: Essays in Cultural Politics*. New York: Routledge, 1988.

Spivak, Gayatri Chakravorty. "Reading the World: Literary Studies in the 80s." *College English* 43, no. 7 (November 1981): 671–679.

Spofford, A. R. [Ainsworth Rand]. "The Government Library at Washington." *International Review* 5 (November 1878): 754–769.

Stadtman, Verne A. *The University of California 1868–1968*. New York: McGraw-Hill, 1970.

Stamper, Alva Walker. *A History of the Teaching of Elementary Geometry*. New York: Teachers College/Columbia University, 1909.

Stamper, Alva Walker. "A History of the Teaching of Elementary Geometry." PhD diss., Columbia University, 1909.

Stanton, Lucia. *"Those Who Labor for My Happiness": Slavery at Thomas Jefferson's Monticello*. Charlottesville: University of Virginia Press, 2012.

Stein, Susan R. *The Worlds of Thomas Jefferson at Monticello*. New York: Harry N. Abrams, 1993.

Sterne, Jonathan. *The Audible Past: Cultural Origins of Sound Reproduction*. Durham, NC: Duke University Press, 2003.

Stevens, Edward W. *The Grammar of the Machine: Technical Literacy and Early Industrial Expansion in the United States*. New Haven, CT: Yale University Press, 1995.

Stewardson, William Emlyn. "Cope and Stewardson: The Architects of a Philadelphia Renascence." A. B. thesis, Princeton University, May 2, 1960.

Stewart, George R., in collaboration with other professors of the University of California. *The Year of the Oath: The Fight for Academic Freedom at the University of California*. Garden City, NY: Doubleday, 1950.

Stites, Francis N. *Private Interest and Public Gain: The Dartmouth College Case, 1819.* Amherst: University of Massachusetts Press, 1972.

Storr, Richard J. *Harper's University: The Beginnings.* Chicago: University of Chicago Press, 1966.

Stratton, Julius A. "Harold Eugene Edgerton (April 6, 1903–January 4, 1990)." *Proceedings of the American Philosophical Society* 135, no. 3 (1991): 447–448.

Strecker, Ellen W. *No Ivory Tower: McCarthyism and the Universities.* New York: Oxford University Press, 1986.

Studer, Jack J. "Julius Kellersberger: A Swiss as Surveyor and City Planner in California, 1851–1857." *California Historical Society Quarterly* 47, no. 1 (March 1968): 3–14.

Tafuri, Manfredo. "Les cendres de Jefferson." *Architecture d'aujourd'hui* 186 (August–September 1976): 53–72.

Tafuri, Manfredo. *The Sphere and the Labyrinth: Avant-Gardes and Architecture from Piranesi to the 1970s.* Trans. Pelligrino d'Acierno and Robert Connolly. Cambridge: MIT Press, 1987.

Taylor, Mark C. *Crisis on Campus: A Bold Plan for Reforming Our Colleges and Universities.* New York: Knopf, 2010.

Thelin, John R. *A History of American Higher Education.* Baltimore, MD: Johns Hopkins University Press, 2004.

Thomas, George E. " 'The Happy Employment of Means to Ends': Frank Furness's Library of the University of Pennsylvania and the Industrial Culture of Philadelphia." *Pennsylvania Magazine of History and Biography*, 126, no. 2 (April 2001): 249–272.

Thomas, George E., Michael J. Lewis, and Jeffrey A. Cohen. *Frank Furness: The Complete Works.* Princeton, NJ: Princeton Architectural Press, 1991.

Thompson, Emily. *The Soundscape of Modernity: Architectural Acoustics and the Culture of Listening in America, 1900–1933.* Cambridge, MA: MIT Press, 2002.

Thompson, Robert B. "Piercing the Corporate Veil: An Empirical Study." *Cornell Law Review* 75, issue 5 (July 1992): 1036–1074.

Tilman, Jeffrey T. *Arthur Brown Jr. Progressive Classicist.* New York: Institute of Classical Architecture/Norton, 2006.

Tolles, Bryant Franklin. *Architecture and Academe: College Buildings in New England Before 1860.* Hanover, NH: University Press of New England, 2011.

Townsend, Dabney. "Thomas Reid and the Theory of Taste." *The Journal of Aesthetics and Art Criticism* 61, no. 4 (Autumn 2003): 341–351.

Trachtenberg, Alan. *The Incorporation of America: Culture and Society in the Gilded Age.* New York: Hill and Wang, 1982.

Tresch, John. " 'Matter No More': Edgar Allan Poe and the Paradoxes of Materialism." *Critical Inquiry* 42 (Summer 2016): 865–898.

Tresch, John. *The Romantic Machine: Utopian Science and Technology after Napoleon.* Chicago: University of Chicago Press, 2012.

Trowbridge, John. "The Jefferson Physical Laboratory." *Science* 5, no. 111 (March 20, 1885): 229–231.

True, Alfred Charles. *A History of Agricultural Education in the United States 1785–1925.* Washington, DC: United States Government Printing Office, 1929.

Truesdell, Leon E. *The Development of Punch Card Tabulation in the Bureau of the Census 1890–1940.* Washington, DC: United States Government Printing Office, 1965.

Turing, Alan M. "Computing Machinery and Intelligence." *Mind* 59, no. 236 (1950): 433–460.

Turner, Fred. *The Democratic Surround: Multimedia & American Liberalism from World War II to the Psychedelic Sixties.* Chicago: University of Chicago Press, 2013.

Turner, Frederick Jackson. *The Frontier in American History*. New York: H. Holt, 1920.

Turner, Paul Venable. *Campus: An American Planning Tradition*. New York: Architectural History Foundation/Cambridge, MA: MIT Press, 1984.

Turner, Paul V., Marcia E. Vetroq, and Karen Weitze. *The Founders & the Architects: The Design of Stanford University*. Redwood City, CA: Department of Art, Stanford University, 1976.

Tuthill, Louisa Caroline. *History of Architecture from the Earliest Times; Its Present Condition in Europe and the United States; with a Biography of Eminent Architects and a Glossary of Architectural Terms*. Philadelphia: Lindsay and Blakiston, 1848.

Unrue, Darlene Harbour. "Edgar Allan Poe: The Romantic as Classicist." *International Journal of the Classical Tradition*, 1, no. 4 (Spring 1995): 112–119.

Upton, Dell. "Defining the Profession," In *Architecture School: Three Centuries of Educating Architects in North America*, ed. Joan Ockman, 36–65. Cambridge, MA: MIT Press, 2012.

Urofsky, Melvin I. "Reforms and Response: The Yale Report of 1828." *History of Education Quarterly* 5, no. 1 (March 1965): 53–67.

Vaidhyanathan, Siva. *Antisocial Media: How Facebook Disconnects Us and Undermines Democracy*. New York: Oxford University Press, 2018.

Valdés, Juan-Gabriel. *Pinochet's Economists: The Chicago School in Chile*. New York: Cambridge University Press, 1995.

Van Beusekom, Monica M. "Disjunctures in Theory and Practice: Making Sense of Change in Agricultural Development at the *Office du Niger*, 1920–1960." *Journal of African History* 41, no. 1 (2000): 79–99.

Van Brunt, Henry. "Greek Lines." Parts 1 and 2. *Atlantic Monthly* 7–8, nos. 44–45 (June–July 1861): 654–668; 76–88.

Van Rensselaer, Mariana Griswold [Schuyler]. *Henry Hobson Richardson and His Works*. Boston: Houghton Mifflin, 1888.

Van Slyck, Abigail A. *Free to All: Carnegie Libraries & American Culture*. Chicago: University of Chicago Press, 1995.

Veblen, Thorstein. *The Higher Learning in America: A Memorandum on the Conduct of Universities by Business Men*. New York: B. W. Huebsch, 1918.

Veeser, H. Aram. *Edward Said: The Charisma of Criticism*. New York: Routledge, 2010.

Veysey, Laurence R. *The Emergence of the American University*. Chicago: University of Chicago Press, 1965.

Vismann, Cornelia. "Cultural Techniques and Sovereignty." *Theory, Culture & Society* 30, no. 6 (2013): 83–93.

Vismann, Cornelia. *Files: Law and Media Technology*. Trans. Geoffrey Winthrop-Young. Redwood City, CA: Stanford University Press, 2008.

Walker, T. [Timothy]. *Elements of Geometry with Practical Applications for the Use of Schools*. Boston: Richardson and Lord, 1829

Warner, Michael. *The Letters of the Republic: Publication and the Public Sphere in Eighteenth-Century America*. Cambridge, MA: Harvard University Press, 1990.

Washington, Booker T. *Up from Slavery: An Autobiography*. New York: A. L. Burt, 1901.

Washington, Booker T. *Working with the Hands: Being a Sequel to "Up from Slavery" Covering the Author's Experiences in Industrial Training at Tuskegee*. New York: Doubleday, 1904.

Washington, Booker T., et al., *The Negro Problem: A Series of Articles by Representative American Negroes of To-Day*. New York: James Pott & Co., 1903.

Watson, Floyd R. *Acoustics of Buildings, Including Acoustics of Auditoriums and Soundproof Rooms*. 3rd ed. New York: John Wiley, 1941.

Watts, George B. "Thomas Jefferson, the 'Encyclopédie' and the 'Encyclopédie Méthodique.' " *French Review* 38, no. 3 (January 1965): 318–325.

Weber, Max. *From Max Weber: Essays in Sociology.* Ed. and trans. H. H. Gerth and C. Wright Mills. New York: Routledge, 2009.

Webster, Daniel. *Daniel Webster, "The Completest Man": Documents from the Daniel Webster Papers.* Ed. Kenneth E. Shewmaker. Hanover, NH: Dartmouth College/University Press, 1990.

Webster, Daniel. *The Great Speeches and Orations of Daniel Webster, with an Essay on Daniel Webster as a Master of English Style.* Ed. Edwin P. Whipple. Boston: Little Brown, 1894.

Webster, Daniel. *The Writings of Daniel Webster,* vol. 10. Boston: Little, Brown, 1903.

Weeks, Edward. "The Opal on the Charles." *Architectural Record* 118, no. 1 (July 1955): 131–137.

Weiss, Ellen. *Robert R. Taylor and Tuskegee: An African American Architect Designs for Booker T. Washington.* Montgomery, AL: New South, 2012.

Wellmon, Chad. *Organizing Enlightenment: Information Overload and the Invention of the Modern Research University.* Baltimore, MD: Johns Hopkins University Press, 2015.

Wertenbaker, Thomas Jefferson. *Princeton, 1746–1896.* Princeton, NJ: Princeton University Press, 1946.

Wickenden, William E. *A Comparative Study of Engineering Education in the United States and in Europe, Bulletin No. 16 of the Investigation of Engineering Education.* Lancaster, PA: Society for the Promotion of Engineering Education, 1929.

Wiegand, Wayne A. "The 'Amherst Method': The Origins of the Dewey Decimal Classification Scheme." *Libraries & Culture* 33, no. 2 (Spring 1998): 175–194.

Wiener, Norbert. *Cybernetics: Or Control and Communication in the Animal and the Machine.* Cambridge, MA: Technology Press, 1948.

Wiener, Norbert. *The Human Use of Human Beings: Cybernetics and Society.* Boston: Houghton Mifflin, 1950.

Wiener, Norbert. *The Human Use of Human Beings: Cybernetics and Society.* 2nd rev. ed. Garden City, NY: Doubleday, 1954.

Wilbur, Ray Lyman, ed. *The University and the Future of America.* Redwood City, CA: Stanford University Press, 1941.

Wilder, Craig Steven. *Ebony & Ivy: Race, Slavery, and the Troubled History of America's Universities.* New York: Bloomsbury, 2013.

Wildes, Karl L., and Nilo A. Lindgren, *A Century of Electrical Engineering and Computer Science at MIT, 1882–1982.* Cambridge, MA: MIT Press, 1985.

Williams, Talcott. "Plans for the Library Building of Pennsylvania." *Library Journal* 13, no. 8 (August 1888): 237–243.

Willis, N. P., J. R. Lowell, and R. W. Griswold, eds. *The Works of the Late Edgar Allan Poe, with Notices of His Life and Genius,* vols. 1 and 2. New York: J. S. Redfield, Clinton Hall, 1850.

Wilson, Mabel O. *Negro Building: Black Americans in the World of Fairs and Museums.* Berkeley: University of California Press, 2012.

Wilson, Richard Guy, ed. *Thomas Jefferson's Academical Village: The Creation of an Architectural Masterpiece.* Rev. ed. Charlottesville: University of Virginia Press, 2009.

Winkler, Adam. *We the Corporations: How American Businesses Won Their Civil Rights.* New York: Liveright, 2018.

Winks, Robin W. *Frederick Billings: A Life.* Berkeley: University of California Press, 1991.

Winterer, Caroline. *American Enlightenments: Pursuing Happiness in the Age of Reason.* New Haven, CT: Yale University Press, 2016.

Winterer, Caroline. *The Culture of Classicism: Ancient Greece and Rome in American Intellectual Life 1780–1910.* Baltimore, MD: Johns Hopkins University Press, 2002.

Winthrop-Young, Geoffrey. "Cultural Techniques: Preliminary Remarks." *Theory, Culture & Society* 30, no. 6 (2013): 3–19.

Wood, Frances A. *Earliest Years at Vassar: Personal Recollections*. Poughkeepsie, NY: Vassar College Press, 1909.

Woodbridge, Sally B. *John Galen Howard and the University of California: The Design of a Great Public Campus*. Berkeley: University of California Press, 2002.

Woods, Mary N. *From Craft to Profession: The Practice of Architecture in Nineteenth-Century America*. Berkeley: University of California Press, 1999.

Woods, Mary N. "Thomas Jefferson and the University of Virginia: Planning the Academic Village." *Journal of the Society of Architectural Historians* 44, no. 3 (October 1985): 266–283.

Wormser, I. Maurice. *Disregard of the Corporate Fiction and Allied Corporation Problems*. New York: Baker, Voorhis, 1927.

Wormser, I. Maurice. "Disregard of the Corporate Fiction—When and Why." *Columbia Law Review* 23 (December 1923): 702–715.

Wormser, I. Maurice. "Piercing the Veil of Corporate Entity." *Columbia Law Review* 12 (1912): 496–518.

Wright, Gwendolyn, and Janet Parks, eds. *The History of History in American Schools of Architecture 1865–1975*. New York: Temple Hoyne Buell Center for the Study of American Architecture, Columbia University/Princeton Architectural Press, 1990.

Writer's Program of the Works Projects Administration. *Berkeley: The First Seventy-Five Years*. Berkeley, CA: The Gillick Press, 1941.

Yale University, *The Yale Corporation: Charter and Legislation; Printed for the President and Fellows*. New Haven, CT: Yale University, 1976.

Yanni, Carla. *The Architecture of Madness: Insane Asylums in the United States*. Minneapolis: University of Minnesota Press, 2007.

Yanni, Carla. *Living on Campus: An Architectural History of the American Dormitory*. Minneapolis: University of Minnesota Press, 2019.

Zelliot, Eleanor. *From Untouchable to Dalit: Essays on the Ambedkar Movement*. New Delhi: Manhomar Publications, 1992.

Zimmerman, Andrew. *Alabama in Africa: Booker T. Washington, the German Empire, and the Globalization of the New South*. Princeton, NJ: Princeton University Press, 2010.

INDEX

Page numbers in *italics* refer to illustrations.

Academic Charisma and the Origins of the Research University (Clark), 7, 180, 181

academic freedom, 7, 14, 171, 217, 219, 221–22, 314n88

Ackerberg-Hastings, Amy, 64

acoustics: Akoustolith plaster, *176*, 177, 301n23; auditoria, 180, 236–37, *236*; 302n32, 302n34; Kresge Auditorium (MIT), 236–37, *236*, 317n39; MIT Chapel, 236; reverberation, 177, 179, 237, 301n32; Rockefeller Memorial Chapel (University of Chicago), 176–80, 301n23; Rumford tile, 301n23, 302n2n7

Actor-Network Theory (ANT), 262n75

Adler, Mortimer J., 181–86, *184*, *187*, 188, 191, 303n44, 303nn47–48, 304n55; Allan Bloom's inversion of his "great books" project, 191–92, 305n78; anti-Hegelian dialectic of, 183, 188; *Dialectic*, 183; *The Great Books of the Western World*, 185, 186–87; *The Great Ideas, a Syntopicon of Great Books of the Western* World, 185–87; *How to Read a Book*, 183; metaphysical/God-centered philosophy of, 304n48; psychology and, 304n48; table-slapping of, 185, 191

administration, colonial, 115, 118

Adorno, Theodor W., 24, 170

agency, 253

Agricultural and Mechanical College of Texas. *See* Texas AMC

Agricultural, Mining and Mechanical Arts College, California, 207

agriculture, 115; scientific, 106, 111, 115, 117–18, 120

Akoustolith plaster, *176*, 177, 178, 301n23, 302n27

Alembert, Jean Le Rond d': *Encyclopédie*, 142–43, 291n7

Alma Mater, 40, 92

Alma Mater (French), 250, 320n1

alphabetization, 314n83

Alvarado, Juan B., 201

amateurism, cultivated, 182–82

Ambedkar, Bhimrao R., 8, 164–69, 298n69; "The Annihilation of Caste," 166–67, 168, 299n78; on education, 165–66; Indian Constitution and, 168–69; John Dewey's influence on, 166, 167–68, 299n78, 299n81; as voice for Dalit political rights, 165, 168

American Academy in Rome, 152

American Association of Geographers, 307n14

American Association of University Professors (AAUP), 165, 167

American Baptist Education Society, 172
American History Association, 132–33
American Institute of Architects (AIA), 270n4
American Journal of Science and Arts, 48–49, 85
"American Scholar, The" (Emerson), 155
Ames, Frederick L., 307n17
Ames, Oakes, 198–99
Ames Shovel Company, 199
Amistad Committee, 269n85
Anderson, Irene, 83, 277n18
Andriopoulos, Stefan, 16, 51
"Annihilation of Caste, The" (Ambedkar), 166–67, 168, 299n78
anthropocracy, 253
Apotheosis of George Washington, The (Brumidi), 148
apparatuses. See *dispositifs*
Aptheker, Bettina, 220, 314n90
Aptheker, Herbert, 220
archē, 12
Archibald, Raymond Clare, 61
architecture, 5–6, 12, 13, 47, 196; as an academic discipline, 47–48, 56, 89, 270n4; coded racially, 95–96, 102; drawing and design, 89–90, 278nn36–37; history of, x–xi, 53–56, 59, 263n8; mathematics and, 66–67; profession of, 54; practical instruction in, 87, 89; texts on, 53–56, 58–60
architecture: styles, 68; Beaux-Arts, 113, 133, 153–54, 208; classical, 46, 46, 48, 55–56, 57; Collegiate Gothic, 79, 94–98, 99–102; Egyptian, 68; English Tudor, 95; Gothic Revival, 176; Greek, 67, 68; neoclassical, 53, 57, 96, 101, 102, 141; neo-Gothic, 96; Neo-Grèc, 70; neo-Palladian, 141, 142; neo-Romanesque, 134; Philadelphia School, 95; postmodernist, 263n8; Romanesque, 68–69; Second Empire, 81, 84, 207
Architecture: Part I, Ancient Architecture, 54
Armsby, Henry P., 110
Arnold, Matthew: *Culture and Anarchy*, 13, 261n60
Association for the Advancement of Women (AAW), 277n29
asylums, 85, 276n14
Atlanta Conferences, 92
Atlanta University, 92, 93, 279n49
auditoria, 232–33, 225, 236–37, 236; acoustics for, 180, 302n27, 302n34

Babcock, Stephen M., 112
Babcock milk test, 112
Bacon, Leonard, 38–39, 40
Baker, Everett M., 229, 232, 316n24
Baker, George H., 159
Baltimore Cathedral, 145
Balze, Paul: copy of Raphael's *School of Athens*, 150, *151*, 155
Banner, Peter: Lyceum Building (Yale), 49
Bao, Weihong, 262n69
Baran, Paul A., 248, 320n78
Barkan, Joshua, 265n9
barley, 111–12
Barraud, Francis: *His Master's Voice*, 306n82
Barzun, Jacques, 303n40: *House of Intellect*, 218–19, 314n83
Bauman, Edwin, J.: Park Plaza Hotel, 258n23
beam time, 243
Beaton, Alexander, 121
Beaumont, Texas, 121–22, 123
beauty, 44–45
Bélime, Émile, 285n56
bells, 83, 93, 146–47, 292n18
Bénard, Emile: University of California, Berkeley, 208–9, *209*, 210
Benton, William, 185
Beranek, Leo, 237, 317n39
Bergson, Henri, 298n78
Berkeley, George: *Verses on the Prospect of Planting Arts and Learning in America*, 206–7
Berkeley, California, 206–7
Bertram Grosvenor Goodhue Associates: Rockefeller Memorial Chapel (University of Chicago), 174–80, *175*, *177*, *178*, *179*, 302n27
"Beyond the Cave" (Jameson), 13
Bhagavad Gita, 235, 317n35
Bibliothèque Nationale, Paris, 125
Bibliothèque Ste. Geneviève, Paris, 70
Bigelow, Jacob, 45–48; on architecture, 46, 47; *Elements of Technology*, 46–48, 47; on science vs. useful arts, 46
Bildung, 12, 56, 93, 253
Billings, Frederick P., 199–200, 202, 206
bimetallism, 135, 202
Birth of Tragedy, The (Nietzsche), 13
birth rates, 99–100, 281n72
blackboards, 63, 64, 65
Blackstone, William, 267n53
Blair, Ann, 127
Blake, William Phipps, 287n76
Bloom, Allan: *The Closing of the American Mind*, 170, 191–92; his inversion of

Adler's "great books" project, 191–92, 305n78

Bogue, Allan G., 307n10

Bohn, Henry G., 203

Bohn's Library, 203

Bombay University, 165

bombs: atomic and hydrogen, 22, 231, 235–36, 235, 317n35; firing mechanisms for, 234

Bond, Richard: Gore Hall (Harvard), 71

books, 106, 127; classification of, 124–25, 127, 287n76, 287nn78–79; fragility of, 23, 71, 141; "great," 183–84; lists of, 170, 181–82, 183–84, 303n42, 303n47; mass marketing of, 203; Western canon, 170–71, 180–87

Borges, Jorge Luis: "The Library of Babel," 4

Boston & Albany Railroad, 197

Bostonians, The (James), 71–72

Bosworth, William Welles: Massachusetts Institute of Technology campus, 224–25, 227

boulevards: Paris, 57, 69

Boullée, Étienne-Louis: cenotaph, unbuilt, for Isaac Newton, 145

Bradshaw, Preston J.: Chase Hotel, 258n23

Brainard, John Gardiner Calkins: "Jerusalem," 55

Braudel, Fernand, 252

Bread and Butter Rebellion (Yale), 42

Breck, George: copy of Raphael's School of Athens, 152, 153, 294n35

bricks and brickmaking, 84, 86–90, 126, 226, 236, 277n31; handmade, 87–90, 88, 278n33

Bromley, Frances, 84, 94

Brown, Arthur, Jr., 217: Cyclotron Building (Berkeley), 215, 215; Hoover Library Tower (Stanford), 245–48, 245, 249; Sproul Hall (Berkeley), 214, 217

Brown University: University Hall, 35

Brumidi, Constantino: The Apotheosis of George Washington, 148

Bruns, Gerald, L., 2, 4

Bryn Mawr College, 77, 78, 94–98, 100, 276n1; Collegiate Gothic style, 94–98; corridors, 79, 80–81, 80; dormitories, 78–79, 79, 80–81, 80; Owl Gate, 97–98, 98; Pembroke Hall East and West, 78, 79, 80–81, 80, 95; Rockefeller Hall, 78, 96, 97–98, 97, 98

Buchanan, James, 107

Buckham, Matthew, 200

Bulfinch, Charles, 148

Bullock, John: The History and Rudiments of Architecture, 58–59, 59

Burchard, John Ely, 229, 231, 232–33, 234, 315n14

bureaucracy, 189

Burnham, Daniel, 133, 290n17

Bush, Vannevar: Science, the Endless Frontier, 214–15, 312n68

Bushnell, Horace, 204, 309n36

Byrne, Oliver, 62

Cabell, Joseph C., 22, 141

Café Mécanique, Paris, 25

calculus, 60–61, 64

calendars, 12

Californios, 201, 204

Cambridge, 95, 280n61

Cambridgeport Diary Corporation, 84

Campbell, W. Glenn, 247, 319n74

campuses, xi, 16–17, 35–38; separation from towns and countryside, 202, 203, 205, 210–11; See also specific universities

Canada (neighborhood), Charlottesville, Virginia, 152

Caner, Henry, 39–40

canon (Western), 170–71, 180–87

Caperton, John, 205

Capital (Marx), 120

capitalism, 21, 135, 196, 208

Cardozo, Benjamin, 50

Carey, Henry Charles, 106; on agriculture, 108–9; on dangers of free trade, 109, 284n25; Harmony of Interests, 106, 283n11; on land, economic development, and capital investment, 107, 108, 108, 109, 120–21;; his manure theory of soil improvement, 108, 110; pamphleteering of, 107; The Past, the Present, and the Future, The, 106–7, 120; Principles of Political Economy, 106; Principles of Social Science, 108; protectionism of, 106, 107, 108, 284n25; on resource exhaustion, 120–21; on tariffs, 106, 107, 108

Carey, Mathew, 106

Carey, Lea & Blanchard, 106

Carlson, Anton J., 184–85

Carr, James Dickson, 163

cartography, 310n39

Carver, Erik, 308n24

Casey, Edward Pearce: Library of Congress, 297n64

Cassirer, Ernst, 195, 240; The Myth of the State, 217

Central Pacific Railroad, 198

Centum Milla Fund, 49
chain (Hegel), 12, 14, 190–92
charisma: academic, 7–8, 181
Charity Hospital, Blackwell (Roosevelt)
   Island, 81, 85
Charles Hayden Foundation, 231
Charlottesville and University Gas Light
   Company, 148, 293n25
Chartier, Roger, 106
Chase-Park Plaza Hotel, St. Louis, 1, 6,
   258n23
chemistry, 49
"Chicago Boys," 248, 320n81
Choate, Charles Francis, 58
Christianity, 95, 96, 98, 102–3, 171, 172–74,
   175, 230–31, 233; association with the
   auditory, 173; See also religion
chronophotography, 162
Churchill, Winston, 230–31, 233
Civil War, 105; commemoration of deaths,
   69–70, 70, 72–74, 73, 95, 275nn66–67;
   deaths, number of, 74, 275n70
Clap, Thomas, 41
Clark, Solomon Henry, 162
Clark, William: Academic Charisma and
   the Origins of the Research University, 7,
   180, 181
Clark, William A., 290n21
clocks, 83, 146, 292n18
Closing of the American Mind, The (Bloom),
   170, 191–92
coal, 120
Coal Question, The (Jevons), 120
Cobb, Henry Ives: University of Chicago
   campus, 172, 176
Colbert, Burwell, 25
Cold War, 191, 216, 238, 239, 247
Cole, Andrew, 305n66
College-Bred Negro, The (Du Bois), 92–93,
   279nn47–49
College Homestead Association, 301n46
College of California, Oakland, 202, 204–6,
   206, 207, 310n46; See also University of
   California, Berkeley
College of New Jersey. See Princeton
   University
College of Rhode Island. See Brown
   University
College of William and Mary, 22, 263n3
colleges, x, 77, 99, 100, 103; agricultural, 104,
   105; coeducational, 79–80, 89, 100; group
   system, 99; land-grant, 104, 105; original
   scholarship at, 78, 281n71; teachers at,
   89, 91, 92; undergraduate specialization

at, 99; women's, 77–81, 87, 94, 103; See
   also Historically Black Colleges and
   Universities (HBCUs); universities
colleges, residential, 7, 14, 21, 30, 30–36,
   79, 80, 82; living quarters, 80–84,
   276nn13–14; misbehavior at, 33, 35,
   40, 144; multipurpose buildings of,
   33, 39–40, 79–81, 144
colonialism, 8, 18, 115, 286n58
Colorado River, 117, 118–19
Columbia University, 151, 153–54, 294n33;
   administrative offices, 250; Black
   graduate of Law School, first, 163; Low
   Memorial Library, 4, 151, 152, 154, 154,
   155–61, 157, 158, 159, 160, 164, 250, 251,
   251; undergraduate honors course/core
   curriculum, 181–82, 218, 303n40
Colwell, Stephen, 125
comets, 85
Compagnie Générale des Colonies, 118
Compendium of the Eleventh Census, 1890
   (Porter), 131, 289n6
Compton, Karl T., 229, 231
Computing-Tabulating Recording
   Company (CTR). See International
   Business Machines (IBM)
Condition of Man, The (Mumford), 240
Conferences for the Study of the Negro
   Problems. See Atlanta Conferences
Congress for Racial Equality, 219
Conic Sections Rebellion (Yale), 42
Considerations on the Necessity of
   Establishing an Agricultural College, and
   Having More of the Children of Wealthy
   Citizens Educated for the Profession of
   Farming (De Witt), 104
Constant-Dufeux, Simon-Claude, 69
Coolidge, Charles Allerton: Memorial
   Church (Stanford University), 247;
   University of Chicago, 174, 176
Cope, Walter, 94
Cope and Stewardson, 78–79, 95; Memorial
   Gate (Bryn Mawr), 95; Owl Gate (Bryn
   Mawr), 97–98, 98; Pembroke Hall East
   and West (Bryn Mawr), 78, 79, 80–81,
   80, 95; Ridgley Hall (Washington
   University), 101, 101, 102; Rockefeller
   Hall (Bryn Mawr), 78, 96, 97–98, 97,
   98; Washington University, St. Louis,
   campus, 100–102
"corporate veil," 50–51, 270n98
corporations, 29, 50–51; personhood of, 29,
   30–31, 38, 40–41, 50–51, 216–17, 253
corrals, 12

corridors, 79, *80*, 81–82, *82*, 87, 224–25, 276n14
Corsicana, Texas, 122–23
cottage system, 80
cotton, 118–19, 285n56, 286n58
Cram, Ralph Adams, 95–96, 102, 177, 281n82
Crédit Mobilier, 197–98
Cristy, Samuel B., 312n62
Crozet, Claudius, 62–63
Crutchett, James, 148
cultivation, 11–12, 103–4
cultural relativism, 192
cultural studies, 11–12
cultural techniques, 11, 12, 260n44
culture, 13, 14, 192
culture industry, 170
Culture of Classicism, The (Winterer), 44, 56, 204
curricula; classical vs. modern/scientific/ technological, 7, 9, 14, 36, 41–45, 46, 49, 56, 57, 65, 152, 218–19, 268n57, 268n66; military, 62–63; science and humanities, 229–34, 315n11; science vs. useful arts, 46, 49, 65, 269n84
Curves, Functions, and Forces (Peirce), 58
Cutter, Charles Ammi, 288n82
cybernetics, 228, 245, 254
"Cyborg Manifesto" (Haraway), 254
"cyborg science," 248
cyclotrons, 215–16, 313n70

Dalits, 165, 166, 299n81
Daniells, W. W., 111
Darling, Noyes, 41, 42
Dartmouth College, 30, 31, 33, 35, 264n4, 265n10, 266n16; Dartmouth Hall, 31, *32*, 35, 265n15; Rowley Hall, 265n14
data, 130–32, 135
data processing, 131–32; census and, 131–32, 289n6, 289nn10–11
"Date Palm, The" (Toumey), 117, *117*
Davies, Charles, 63–64, 65; *Elements of Geometry and Trigonometry* (Legendre), 63–64, *63*
Day, Jeremiah, 42, 43
Dean, N. W., 112
De Mars, Vernon: student union (Berkeley), 217
democracy, 21, 96, 133, 168, 169, 204
Democracy and Education (John Dewey), 166–68, 298n78
Derrida, Jacques, 12, 254; on Kant's *Conflict of the Faculties* and boundaries, 251
determinism, 238
Detroit Hilton, 6, 258n24

Dewey, John, 51, 165, 304n48; *Democracy and Education*, 166–68, 298n78; educational philosophy of, 164, 166–68; pragmatists/man-centered philosophy of, 304n48
Dewey, Melvil, 125–26; on classification of pamphlets, 124, 125, 287nn78–79; classification system of, 124–25, 287n76, 287nn78–79; lexical economy of, 288n79
De Witt, Simeon: *Considerations on the Necessity of Establishing an Agricultural College, and Having More of the Children of Wealthy Citizens Educated for the Profession of Farming*, 104
Dialectic (Adler), 183
dialectics, 15–16, 17, 18, 20, 188–91; Hegelian, 183, 188, 190; Mortimer Adler's anti-Hegelian, 183, 188, 190, 192; Plato's unity and difference, 202–3; syntopicon entry for, 188; textual and aural modes, 173
Diana (Saint-Gaudens), 133–34
diaries, daily, 58, 60, 83–84
Dick, D. B.: University of Toronto Library, 125–26, 288n82
Diderot, Denis: *Encyclopédie*, 142–43, 291n7
"Diffused Illumination" (Hallock), 156
dinners, 184, 304n51
disciplinary systems, 33
Discourse Networks (Kittler), 5
Discourse on the Origin and Foundations of Inequality among Men (Rousseau), 11
dispositifs, 12, 38, 265n9
"Domain of Arnheim, The" (Poe), 36–37
dormitories: Collegiate Gothic, 78–79, 94–98; corridors of, 79, *80*, 81–82, *82*, 87, 276n14
Du Bois, W. E. B., 8. 90, 92, 163, 279n49, 279n54; *The College-Bred Negro*, 92–93, 279nn47–49; Max Weber's admiration of, 103; *The Negro Artisan*, 92; *The Souls of Black Folks*, 91, 93; "Talented Tenth," 90, 92, 135, 279n45
Duehlke, Ferdinand, 111
Duignan, Peter, 248
dumbwaiters, 18, 23–26, *24*, 263n11
Dumont d'Urville, Jules, 69
Durand, Jean-Nicolas-Louis, 47

Eaton, Amos, 65, 274n53
École de droit, Paris, 188, 189
École des Beaux-Arts, Paris, 57–58
ecology, 197
economic man. See *homo oeconomicus* (economic man)

economic theory: neoliberal, 247–49
Edgerton, Harold Eugene, 234–35; *Flash!*, 234, 235, 236
Edgerton, Winifred, 297n68
Edgerton, Germeshausen, and Grier, 234
education: Baptist, 172; John Dewey's philosophy of, 166–68; use of failure and examinations at, 33, 58
education, higher: access to, 77–78, 103; African Americans and, 87–94, 99, 103; history of, ix–x, 10, 14–15, 41–50; international students and, 163–64, 298n69; liberal, 78, 139, 142–43, 192, 238–40; neoliberal, 15, 43, 241, 242, 249; W. E. B. Du Bois's theory of, 93; women and, 77–87, 94, 208, 281n73
education, public, 18, 21, 22–23, 263n6
education, technical/vocational, 57, 60, 64, 87–91, 93, 103
Edward W. Said Papers, 2, 6
Edwards, Jonathan, 40
Eero Saarinen and Associates: Kresge Auditorium (MIT), 225, 225, 227–28, 233, 236–37, 236, 317n39; MIT Chapel, 225–28, 225, 226, 227, 228, 233, 236, 237
Ehrman, Sydney, 313n73
Eisenhower, Dwight D., 190
electron bunching, 241
Elementary Treatise on Plane and Solid Geometry (Peirce), 60
Elements, The (Euclid), 57
Éléments de géométrie (Legendre), 61, 62–63, 63
Elements of Euclid, The (Simson), 62, 273n42
Elements of Geometry (Playfair), 62, 273n42
Elements of Geometry and Trigonometry (Legendre, adapted by Davies), 63–64, 63, 274n53
Elements of Geometry with Practical Applications (Walker), 61
Elements of Technology (Bigelow), 46–48, 47
Eliot, Charles, 99, 281n72
Ely, David, 49
Emerson, Ralph Waldo: "The American Scholar," 155; "Plato: New Readings" 203, 309n33; *Representative Men*, 202–3
empiricism, 183
enclosures, 12
Encyclopedia Britannica, 185
Encyclopédie (Diderot and D'Alembert), 142–43, 291n7
endosmosis, 298n78
Engels, Friedrich: *Capital*, 120

enslaved people, 23–24, 25–26, 139–40, 169, 189, 250, 263n11, 269n85, 295n39; *See also* slavery
Erskine, John, 181, 182, 186
etiquette manuals, 56
Euclid: *The Elements*, 57; *See also* geometry, Euclidean
Everett, Edward, 62
Excelsior Diary, 84
experimental stations, agricultural, 105, 109; circulation of pamphlets, bulletins, and reports of, 105–6, 109–12, 114–15, 116–17, 118–19
Extra Census Bulletin (Porter), 131, 132

Facebook, 255, 321n12
facial recognition systems, 255, 321n12
faculty psychology, 43, 44, 48
Fanon, Frantz, 7; *The Wretched of the Earth*, 8
farmers, 21, 196
farming, 104, 196
Farquharson, David, 207
Farrar, Charles: Maria Mitchell Observatory (Vassar), 85, 86
Farrar, John, 62, 64
Fauset, Jessie, 100, 281n74
Feld, Bernard, 237
Ferris, Theodore P., 233
fertilizers, 110–11
Field, Marshall, 172
figures, visual, 54, 56, 64, 65
firearms, 195
fires, 23, 71, 140–41, 148, 149, 150–51, 150
Fisk University, 279n49
Flash! (Edgerton), 234, 235, 236
Flook, Lyman R., 178, 179, 302n27
Forbes, Robert H., 117–18, 285n55; *The River Irrigating Waters of Arizona*, 118–19, 119
Fosdick, Raymond B., 215–16
Foucault, Michel, 12, 14, 16, 247, 253; on delinquency and failure, 33, 37; on *parrhesia* (free speech), 252–53
Franklin, Benjamin, 21
Franklin, Bruce, 247, 319n74
Free Speech Movement (FSM), 219, 221
Freeman, John R.: Massachusetts Institute of Technology campus, 224–25
Frémont, John C., 201, 204, 309n27, 310n39
French, Daniel Chester: *Alma Mater*, 250, 320n1
French Soudan (Mali): cotton production in, 118, 285n56, 286n58; irrigation of, 285n56

Friedman, Milton, 248, 320n81
Friendster, 321n12
frontier: displacement into the university, 196; tools of, 196, 198, 307n18; Western, 102, 133, 135, 195–96, 198, 199, 211
frontier thesis, 18, 109, 130, 131, 132–33, 289n11
Fulbright, J. William, 190
Furness, Frank: University of Pennsylvania Library, 125–29, *126*, *127*, *128*, 288n80
Furness, Horace Howard, 78, 125

Gaekwad, Sayajirao, 165
Galton, Francis, 99
Gamble, William, 265n15
Gandhi, Mohandas K., 166, 168
Gate Lodge (Langwater), North Easton, Massachusetts, 307n17
Geddes, Patrick, 238
gender, 18, 56, 314n90
genealogy, 14
genocide: Indigenous peoples, 133, 195, 204, 309n39
geography, 197
geometry, Euclidean: teaching of, 52, 56–57, 60–66, *66*, 273nn41–42, 273n46
Giedion, Sigfried: *Mechanization Takes Command*, 104
Gierke, Otto von, 29, 50, 51
Gilman, Daniel Coit, 40
Girard College for Orphans, Philadelphia: Girard Hall, 53, *53*
Gitelman, Lisa, 17, 105
Gladys City Oil, Gas and Manufacturing Company, 121
gold, 134, 135, 201, 202, 290n21
gold standard, 135
Golden Gate, 206, 210
Golden Gate Park, 311n59
Goodhue, Bertram Grosvenor: Rockefeller Memorial Chapel (University of Chicago), 174–80, *175*, *177*, *178*, *179*
Goodrich, Chauncey Allen, 31
Goodspeed, Thomas, 174
Gorman, William, 185, *187*
Gottmann, Jean, 219
Gould, Glenn, 3, 5
Grafton, Anthony, 304n51
Gramophone and Typewriter, Ltd. v. Stanley, 51
Gramophone Company, 305n82
gramophones, 306n82
Gramsci, Antonio, 19
grandeur, 44

grasses, 116
Great Books Foundation, 185; survey, 185, 305n58
great books movement, 184–85
Great Books of the Western World, The (Adler and Hutchins), 185, 186–87
Great Conversation, The (Hutchins), 186–87
Great Ideas, a Syntopicon of Great Books of the Western World, The (Adler and Gorman), 185–87
"Greek Lines" (Van Brunt), 57, 65, *68*
Green, Ashbel, 33, 35
Green, Bernard: Library of Congress, 297n64
Greene, B. Franklin, 274n55
Greener, Richard Theodor, 163
grey literature, 17, 128–29; circulation of, 104–5, 109–12, 114–15, 116–17, 118–19, 121–24
Grundrisse (Marx), 106, 107
Grunow, Herman, 111, 112
Guastavino, Raphael, 177
Guastavino Company, 177, 301n24; Akoustolith plaster, *176*, 177, 178, 301n23, 302n27
Gulley, Frank A., 115–16, 117
Guy's Hospital, London, 276n13

Hacker, J. David, 275n70
Hale Telescope, 215–16
Hall, William Hammond, 311n59
Hallock, William, 156, 295n47; "Diffused Illumination," 156; illumination of Low Memorial Library (Columbia), 156–61, *157*, *158*, *159*, *160*, 251, *251*, 252; *Text-Book of Physics*, 156; work on voice-production visualization, 161–63, *162*
Halprin, Lawrence: student union (Berkeley), 217
Hamill Brothers of Corsicana, 122
Hampton Institute, 91
handbooks, 54
Hansen, William, 241, 243
Haraway, Donna, 19; "Cyborg Manifesto," 254
Harberger, Arnold, 320n81
Hardison, Donald: student union (Berkeley), 217
Harlow, William, 87, 227n31
Harmony of Interests (Carey), 106, 283n11
Harper, William Rainey, 172, 173, 174; *Religion and Higher Life*, 173
Harrison, Peter, 265n15

Harvard University, 35, 45–48; alumni, 281n72; Black graduates of, 163; campus, 71; curricula, 45–48, 56, 60–61, 99, 182; gas lighting of, 71, 275n64; Gore Hall addition, 71, 125; Harvard Hall, 71; Holworthy Hall, 275n64; Jefferson Physical Laboratory, 213, 312n63; Lawrence Scientific School, 65; lecturing at, 46, 48; Massachusetts Hall, 36; Memorial Hall, 66–70, *67, 70,* 74; Van Brunt's curricula at, 58–60

Hatch Act of 1887, 105, 110, 115, 121

Hauser, Samuel, 290n21

Haviland, John: Tombs (prison), 37

Hay, David Ramsey, 57

Hayek, Friedrich von, 248

Hays, John C., 205

Hearst, George, 207, 212

Hearst, Phoebe Apperson, 207–8

Hearst, William Randolph, 208

Hegel, Georg Wilhelm Friedrich, 12, *12,* 14, 24–25, 183, 189; chain of, 12, 14, 190–92; *Phenomenology of Spirit,* 188; *The Philosophy of History,* 188; *The Philosophy of Right,* 188

Hemings, Sally, 25, 169, 299n85

Hemmings, John, 25

Henry, William, A., 109–12

heterotopias, 252

Hewlett, William, 241

Higgins, Patillo, 121

Hill, Benjamin F., 123

Hill, Frederick Parsell, 161, 296n57

Hills, Joseph L., 308n23

His Master's Voice (Barraud), 306n82

His Master's Voice (Lem), 306n82

Historically Black Colleges and Universities (HBCUs), 77–78, 87–94, 163, 278n36, 279nn47–49

History and Rudiments of Architecture, The, (Bullock) 58–59, *59*

History of Architecture from the Earliest Times (Tuthill), 53–56, 59

Hitchcock, Henry-Russell, 308n23

Hoard's Dairyman, 110, 111

Hogarth, William, 57

Hollerith, Herman, 131, 132, 289nn12–13

Homestead Act of 1862, 104, 289n2

homo oeconomicus (economic man), 247, 248, 249

Hoover, Herbert, 245

Hoover Institution on War, Revolution, and Peace, 245–48, 254; anti-Vietnam War protests and, 247; library collection and catalogue, 245, 247, 248, 319n76; as think tank, 247, 248

Horkheimer, Max, 24, 170

Horowitz, Helen Lefkowitz, 80, 100

hospitals, 81, 276nn13–14

House of Intellect (Barzun), 218–19, 314n83

How to Read a Book (Adler), 183

Howard, John Galen: Berkeley campus plan, 207, 208, 209–13; California House (Berkeley), 209, 213; Hearst Greek Theater (Berkeley), 213; Hearst Memorial Mining Building (Berkeley), 207, 211–12, *211, 212,* 215, 311nn61–62; on mining, 212, 311n60; president's house (Berkeley), 213; Sather Gate (Berkeley), 213–14, *214, 218*

Howard University, 279n49

Howe, Hezekiah, 54

Hugo, Victor, 70

human capital, 19, 219, 221–22, 223, 237–40, 248–49, 314n88

human subjectivity, 238, 255

Human Use of Human Beings, The (Wiener), 228–29

humanism, 57, 239, 254

humanities, 9, 19, 218, 223, 229–34, 238–40, 242, 245, 248, 254, 315n11

Hunt, Richard Morris, 57

Hutchins, Robert Maynard, 181, 218, 313n82; *The Great Conversation,* 186–86; *The Great Books of the Western World,* 185, 186–87

Hyde, William De Witt, 100

"Ideal Auditorium Acoustics" (Watson), 302n34

idealism, 204

ideas, 13, 14, 139, 203, 291n1, 390n33; "great" and the index to, 186–87, *187*

in loco parentis, 35, 40, 43, 100, 267n53

India: caste and nation unity, 166, 169; Constitution, 168–69

Indigenous peoples, 30, 133, 195, 196, 204, 309n39

individualism, 93, 133, 154–55, 168, 237

individuals, 21, 130, 192, 237, 238, 245

infrastructural media. *See* media complexes

infrastructure, ix, xi, 1, 3, 16, 19, 130, 133, 172, 181, 190, 195, 204, 222, 243, 249

intellectuals, 13–14

International Business Machines (IBM), 132

International Congress of Arts and Science, St. Louis, 99, 102

International Telephone and Telegraph (IT&T), 242
irrigation systems, 116

J. B. Colt Company, 157
James, Henry: *The Bostonians*, 71–72
James, William, 298n78
Jameson, Fredric R., 1, 4; "Beyond the Cave," 13
Jat Pat Todak Mandal, 299n78
Jefferson, Isaac, 25–26
Jefferson, Thomas, 21–26, 57, 139; on abolition of fiscal debt, 169; academical village of, 141, 144; book collection, 23, 140, 141; correspondence with William Thornton and Henry Latrobe, 141, *142*; destruction of his books at Shadwell, 23; Library Rotunda (University of Virginia), *140*, 141–42, 144–48, *146*, *147, 149, 150*, 294n31; Library Rotunda's bell and clock, 146–47, 292n18; plan for public education, 18, 21, 22–23, 140; proposal for mechanized astronomical device in Library Rotunda, 145, *146*, 155; on tyranny, 22; University of Virginia, 21, 22, 36–38, 141–42, *142, 143*, 146, 293n25; *See also* Monticello, Virginia
Jennings, John T. W.: Agriculture Hall (University of Wisconsin), 112, 113–14, *113, 114*, 284n41
"Jerusalem" (Brainard), 55
Jevons, William Stanley: *The Coal Question*, 120
Jewett, Milo P., 81
Johns Hopkins University, 78, 99
Johnson, Hiram L.: *The Silver Queen*, 290n22
journals, daily. *See* diaries, daily
Judson, Harry Pratt, 174,175
Jules-Marey, Étienne, 162

Kant, Immanuel, 5–6, 7, 19, 25, 252; Derrida on, 251
Kantorowicz, Ernst, 29, 216, 240, 313n73, 313n76; *The King's Two Bodies*, 216–17
Kellersberger, Julius, 205
Kellersberger map, 205, *205*, 215, 312n69
Kellogg, Martin, 208
Kerr, Clark, 214, 217–18, 221, 313n82; *The Uses of the University*, 217, 218–19
Killian, James R., 229, 230, 233–34
King's Two Bodies, The (Kantorowicz), 216–17
Kingsley, James L., 42, 43–44, 49

Kingsley, William Lathrop, 49, 50, 267n48
Kirkbride plan, 276n14
Kittler, Friedrich A., 5, 261n66; *Discourse Networks*, 5, 301n11
klystron tube. *See* Stanford klystron
knowledge, x, 5–6, 16, 17, 19, 21–22, 43–44, 100–101, 106, 142–43, 154–56, 166–67, 189, 192, 253; academic, 2, 132; bureaucratic/technocratic, 189; Jacques Lacan on, 189; library classification and management of, 124–25, 127–29, 287n76, 287nn78–79; mediapolitics of, 10, 12, 18; power-, 248
Kojève, Alexandre, 305n66
Koselleck, Reinhart, 72
Krajewski, Markus: *The Server*, 263n11
Kresge, Sebastian S., 231
Kresge Foundation, 231–32, 316n19
Kristeva, Julia, 254
Kulturtechniken. See cultural techniques
Kulturwissenschaften. See cultural studies

labor, 9, 12, 14, 23, 56, 59, 78, 90, 93–94, 95, 102, 106–107, 108–109, 120, 123, 168, 190, 250, 254; *See also* enslaved people
laboratories, 49, 181, 212–13
Labrouste, Henri, 57, 74: Bibliothèque Nationale, Paris, 125; Bibliothèque Ste. Geneviève, Paris, 70
Lacan, Jacques, 188; on the discourse of the university, 188, 189; "Psychoanalysis Upside Down," 189
land, 120–21, 124; annexation of California and Southwest territories, 201, 204–5, *205*; free, 102, 130, 133, 289n2; revaluation of, due to subterranean resources, 120–21; rural, 102; speculation on, 123, 201, 309n27; Western expansion, 105, 130, 133, 195, 196 (*see also* frontier thesis); *See also* property
land grants, 105, 131, 201, 202, 204, 309n27
Land Law of 1851, 201, 204
landscape, 196–97, 203
Langer, Susanne K.: *Philosophy in a New Key*, 238, 239–40, 248–49
languages: Greek and Latin, 33, 42, 43-44, 49, 50, 52, 56, 58
Larkin, Brian, 6
Latour, Bruno, 262n75
Latrobe, Benjamin Henry: Baltimore Cathedral, 145; correspondence with Thomas Jefferson, 141; Nassau Hall (Princeton), 33, *34*, 35; U.S. Capitol Building, 140, 145, 148

Lawrence, Ernest O., 215; Cyclotron
  Building (Berkeley), 215, *215*
lecture halls, 150, *151*
Leeds, William Henry: *Rudimentary
  Architecture*, 60
Legendre, Adrien-Marie: *Éléments de
  géometrie*, *61*, 62–63; *Elements of
  Geometry and Trigonometry*, 63–64, *63*,
  274n53
Lem, Stanisław: *His Master's Voice*, 306n82
Lerner, Daniel, 237
Levine, Neil, 70
Lewis, Michael J., 271n4
libraries, 70, 125–26; archives, 6, 245,
  246–48; card catalogues, 71, 125, 288n80,
  308n22; classification systems for,
  124–25, 127–29, 287n76, 287nn78–79;
  fireproof, 200; fires destroying books, 23,
  71, 140 –41, 148; public, 197, 199; stacks,
  71; Thomas Jefferson's, 23, 141, 148; *See
  also under specific universities*
Library Bureau, 288nn79–80
"Library of Babel, The" (Borges), 4
Library of Congress, 140–41, 148, 163,
  297n64; fires 140–41, 148; Thomas
  Jefferson's books at, 141, 148
Liebig, Justus von, 120
lighting, electric: Low Memorial Library
  (Columbia), 156–61, 296n57, *157*, *158*, *159*,
  160
lighting, gas, 148; Harvard, 71, 275n64; U.S.
  Capitol, 148; University of Vermont, 200;
  University of Virginia, 148; Vassar, 84
Lincoln, Abraham, 107
linear accelerators, 240, 243
lines: Greek, 57, 65, 74; Van Brunt's
  reanimation of, 68–69
listening, 173, 182
list-making, 170, 181–82, 185–86, 303n42,
  303n47
Locke, John, 139, 291n1
Logan, Warren, 93–94
lordship and bondage. *See* master and slave
Loring, George B., 111
Louisiana Purchase Exposition, St. Louis, 102;
  Hall of International Congresses, 101, 102
Louisiana Purchase Exposition Company,
  101
Low, Abiel Abbot, 155, 252
Low, Seth, 155, 252
Lucas, Anthony F., 122
Lucking, Maura, 278n36
Lyman, Hannah, 83
Lyon, Mary, 79

machines, 18, 37–38, 44–45, 47, 51, 64, 65,
  245, 249, 254–55
Madison, James, 62, 145, 169
Madison Square Garden, 133
"Making of Men, The" (Mumford), 238–40
male supremacy, 314n90
Mali. *See* French Soudan (Mali)
Man and Nature (Marsh), 197, 202, 204,
  307n10
Manila, Philippines, 290n17
Manu Smriti: burning of, 299n81
manure, 108, 110, 111
Mariposa Estate, Sierra Nevada Mountains,
  201–2, 309n27
Mariposa Grove of Big Trees, 201
marriage rates, 99, 281n73
Marsden, George M., 175
Marsh, George Perkins, 196–97, 200, 202,
  307n11; Frederick P. Billings's purchase
  of his childhood home, 200; Frederick
  P. Billings's purchase of his library, 200;
  library of, 197, 200, 307n12; *Man and
  Nature*, 197, 202, 204, 307n10
Marshall, John, 31, 50
Martin, Henry, 146–47, *147*, 150
Martinez, Diana, 290n17
Marx, Karl: *Capital*, 120; *Grundrisse*, 106,
  107; on Henry Charles Carey, 106, 120,
  283n11; on land, economic development,
  and capital investment, 120–24; on
  resource exhaustion, 120–21
mascots, 98
Massachusetts Institute of Technology
  (MIT), 65, 224–25, 229–37, 254, 270n4;
  Christian ethics and, 230–31, 233;
  Committee on Educational Survey, 229–30,
  231, 315n11; corridors, 224–25; Hayden
  Memorial Library, 231; humanities and
  social sciences curricula at, 229–34,
  315nn11–12; Kresge Auditorium, 225, *225*,
  227–28, 233, 236–37, *236*, 317n39; MIT
  Chapel, 225–28, *225*, *226*, *227*, *228*, 230,
  233, 236, 237; village church (theology)
  and meeting house (secularism
  humanism) at, 232–34; wartime work at,
  234–36
master and slave, 12, 14, 18, 22, 24–26, 188–
  92, 204, 250–51, 305n66
material complexes, 13, 251–52
materialism, 12; historical, 14
materiality, 14, 16, 48, 135, 139, 169, 222, 251–52
mathematics: as an academic discipline,
  65; teaching of, 49, 52, 56–58, 60–66,
  273nn41–42, 273n46

Maybeck, Bernard, 207
Mayer, Milton, *184*
Mayers, Murray, & Phillip: Rockefeller
    Memorial Chapel (University of
    Chicago), 174–80, *175*, *177*, *178*, *179*
McCarthy, Molly, 84
McCaughey, Robert A.: *Stand, Columbia*,
    303n40
McCormick reapers, 104
McDonald, Harry P., 151
McKim, Charles F., 133; Boston Symphony
    Hall, 178; Columbia University, 151,
    153–54, 294n33; Fogg Art Museum
    (Harvard), 178; Low Memorial Library
    (Columbia), 4, 151, 154, *154*, 156–61, *157*,
    158, *159*, *160*, *164*
McKim, Mead & White: Agriculture
    Building (World's Exposition), 133; Battle
    Monument (U.S. Military Academy),
    73–74, *74*; University of Virginia,
    151–52, *153*, 208, 294n34; *See also* McKim,
    Charles F.; White, Stanford
McLuhan, Marshall, 261n66
McNamara, Robert, 248, 320n81
Mead, George Herbert, 303n39
Mechanization Takes Command (Giedion),
    104
media, 2, 5, 11; history, xi, 11, 13, 14; slogans,
    16, 261n66; social, 255; theory, xi
media complexes, ix, 5, 12–13, 16, 19–20, 22,
    115, 131, 171, 219, 236, 242, 248, 251–52,
    262n69; definition of, 1–2
mediapolitics, 10, 11, 12, 13, 18, 20, 22, 131,
    135, 249
Megalopolis, 219
"megamachine," 245, 249;
Memorial Day, 275n67
memorization, 42, 45, 48, 50, 58, 60, 64, 65
mental discipline, 42, 64, 99, 124, 255,
    269n84
metaphysics, 183
Midwest Modern Language Association
    (MMLA), 1, 2–3
military technologies, 62, 214, 234–35,
    241–42
military-industrial complex, 190, 238, 245
Mills, Robert: Library Rotunda annex
    (University of Virginia), 150–51, *151*
mining, 120, 134, 199, 201, 202, 207, 211, 212,
    309n27, 311n60
Mirowski, Philip, 247–48
Mitchell, Maria, 85, 87
Mitchell, Timothy, 286n60
Mitchell, William, 85, 277n29

MMLA. *See* Midwest Modern Language
    Association (MMLA)
MMLA Bulletin, 1
modernity, x, 8, 10, 11, 15, 62, 172
money economy, 133, 135
Monge, Gaspard, 62
monocentrism, 13
Monroe, James, 62
Mont Pèlerin Society, 248
Monticello, Virginia: dining room, 23–26,
    24, 139–40; dumbwaiters, 18, 21, 22,
    23–26, *24*, 139–40, 152; reading spaces,
    139–40
monuments, funerary, 69–70
Mood, Fulmer, 307n10
Moor's Indian Charity School, 30
"Moratorium on Technology, A"
    (colloquium), 237–38
Morrill, Justin, 107
Morrill Act of 1862, 105, 107–8, 115, 131,
    289n7
Morrill Land-Grant Act of 1862. *See* Morrill
    Act of 1862
Morrill Tariff of 1861, 107
Morris, David, 313n70
Mount Holyoke, 79, 80
Muckey, Floyd S.: *The Natural Method of
    Voice Production in Speech and Song*, 162;
    work on voice-production visualization,
    161–63, *162*
Mukherjee, Arun P., 166, 298n78
multiversity, 217–19, 221–22
Mumford, Lewis, 11, 13, 36–38, 195, 237–38,
    245, 314n83; *The Condition of Man*, 240;
    on Edgar Allan Poe, 36–37; on Emerson's
    Platonism, 203; on firearms, 195; on
    humanity vs. machines, 37–38, 237–39,
    242; on the industrialization of quarries,
    200–201; "The Making of Men," 238–40;
    on the material environment, 238;
    "megamachine," 245, 249; on nature,
    195–97, 203; *Sticks and Stones*, 196;
    Technics and Civilization, 238
Münsterberg, Hugo, 100
Myth of the State (Cassirer), 217
myths, 217

National Association for the Advancement
    of Colored People (NAACP), 167
National Science Foundation, 215
*Natural Method of Voice Production in
    Speech and Song, The* (Muckey), 162
necropolis, 252
Negro Artisan, The (Du Bois), 92, 93

neoliberalism, 15, 19, 241, 247–249, 252
Nevins, Allan, 104
New York University, 151
Newcomb, Simon, 61
Newfield, Christopher, 10–11, 13
newsprint, 70
Newton, Isaac: Étienne-Louis Boullée's cenotaph for, 145
Nietzsche, Friedrich Wilhelm: *The Birth of Tragedy*, 13, 261n60; on dichotomy in classical studies, 57; on the modern university, 171, 181
Niger River, 118, 119
Nile River, 117, 118–19, 286n60
Nipper (dog), 306n82
Norcross Brothers, 201, 308n24
Northern Pacific Railway, 199–200
Norton, Charles Eliot, 58
Nugent, Edward J., 233

Oakes Ames Memorial Hall, North Easton, Massachusetts, 198, 201, 307n18
Oakes and Oliver Ames Monument, Albany County, Wyoming, 197, 198, *198*
Oberlin College, 79–80
oil and oil industry, 121–24; Baku, Russia, fields, 123; discovery of, 121–23; prices, 122–23; wells, 122–23
Old Colony Railroad Station, North Easton, Massachusetts, 307n17
Oliver Ames Free Library, North Easton, Massachusetts, 197
Olmsted, Denison, 42
Olmsted, Frederick Law, 196, 197, 201, 242–43; proposed plan for College of California, 202, 205–6, *206*, 207, 210–11, 310n46, 311n59
Ong, Walter J., 5, 258n17
Onuf, Peter, 169
operations research (OR), 320n81
opium trade, 155, 252
Oppenheimer, J. Robert, 215, 216, 217, 235, 240
oration, 48, 49: Daniel Webster's on Dartmouth, 31, 265n10
orders, classical, *47*, 58, *59*
Organization for the Destruction of Caste. *See* Jat Pat Todak Mandal
owls, carved, 97–98, *98*

pamphlets: classification of, 124–25, 127–29, 287n76, 287nn78–79; individually uncatalogued, 125, 127–29
Panofsky, Erwin, 195, 217, 240, 253, 313n76
Panofsky, Wolfgang, 240, 243, 254, 318n66

Park Plaza Hotel, St. Louis, 6, 258n23
Parks, R. H.: *The Silver Queen (Justice)*, 134–35, *134*, 202, 290n21
parks, public, 202
parrhesia (free speech), 252–53
Past, the Present, and the Future, The (Carey), 106–7
pedagogy, 43, 45–46, 48, 64, 65, 87–88, 150, 181–85, 191
Peirce, Benjamin, 60; *Curves, Functions, and Forces*, 58; *Elementary Treatise on Plane and Solid Geometry*, 60
Peirce, Charles Sanders, 51, 60, 64
Pelz, Paul J.: Library of Congress, 163, 297n64
Peralta, Jose Domingo, 204
Peralta, Luis María, 204
Peralta, Vicente, 204
perspective: linear, 195, 253
Pestalozzi, Johan, 65
Peters, John Durham, 11, 12–13
Phenomenology of Spirit (Hegel), 188
Phillips, William B., 121; *Texas Petroleum*, 121–24
philosophy, 44–45, 188–89, 238, 239–40, 248–49
Philosophy in a New Key (Langer), 238, 239–40, 248–49
Philosophy of History, The (Hegel), 188
Philosophy of Right, The (Hegel), 188
photography: stroboscopic, 234, *235*, 236
Pinochet, Augusto, 320n81
Pittman, W. Sidney, 278n37
Plato: allegory of the cave, 13, 16, 103, 192, 203–4; Ralph Waldo Emerson on, 203, 309n33
"Plato: New Readings" (Emerson), 203, 309n33
Playfair, John: *Elements of Geometry*, 62, 273n42
Plough, The Loom, and the Anvil, The, 106
Pocock, J. G. A., 57
Poe, Edgar Allan, 36–37, 72–73, 250; "The Domain of Arnheim," 36–37; "To Helen," 36, 38, 266n35
political economy, 106, 107, 108, 109, 120, 286n60
Pollack, Herman, 233
polytechnics, 65, 271n4
Porter, Robert P.: *Compendium of the Eleventh Census, 1890*, 131 289n6; *Extra Census Bulletin*, 131, *132*
postcolonial studies, 4
postmodernism, 4
Poulsen, Frederik, 173

power, x, 11, 12, 19, 20, 77, 92, 102, 108, 170, 173, 189, 191, 203, 245, 248, 253
Prather, William L., 121
press, popular, 203, 208
Princeton University, 33; campus, 33; Institute for Advanced Studies, 216, 217, 240; misbehavior at, 33, 35; Nassau Hall, 33, 34, 35, 266n18
Principles of Political Economy (Carey), 106
Principles of Social Science (Carey), 108
print culture, 17; "print agriculture" and, 105
printing, 105, 203, 282n3
prisons, 81
projectors: use of in Low Memorial Library (Columbia), 156–61, 159, 296n51, 296n57
property, 11–12, 19, 23, 120, 169, 204, 219; *See also* land
protectionism, 106, 107
"Protestant Ethic and the 'Spirit' of Capitalism" (Weber), 102–3
Protestantism. *See* Christianity
"Psychoanalysis Upside Down" (Lacan), 189
punch cards, 131

quarries, 200–201
questioning, 182–83

race, 18, 95–98, 99, 102–3, 280n64
radar systems, 242
Rai, Lala Lajpat, 165
railroads, 199, 201; stations, 197
Rancho San Antonio, 204, 205, 205
RAND Corporation, 248, 320n81
Raphael: *School of Athens*, 150, 155
Rayfield, Wallace A., 278n37
Raymond, Cornelia, 84, 277n23
Raymond, John Howard, 84
reading: silent, 21, 139–39, 144
Readings, Bill, 250
reasoning, 25, 43–44; abstract, 64–65; algebraic, 61–62, 64–65; deductive, 56–57, 61; inductive, 65
recitations, 31, 42, 45, 48, 50, 64, 144
Reddy, D. Raj, 254, 255
Reflections on Exile (Said), 8–9
Reid, Thomas, 44–45, 47
Reinstein, Jacob, 208
religion, 171, 172–80, 223–24, 226–28, 229, 230–34, 236, 237; *See also* Christianity
Religion and Higher Life (Harper), 173
Rensselaer Polytechnic Institute, 65, 66, 274nn53–55
Rensselaer School. *See* Rensselaer Polytechnic Institute

Rensselaerean plan, 65
Renwick, James, Jr., 81; Charity Hospital, Blackwell (Roosevelt) Island, 81, 85; Main Building (Vassar), 81–82, 81, 82, 84–85, 87, 95
Representative Men (Emerson), 202–3
Republic of Letters, 10, 21–23, 24–25, 60, 130–31, 139–40
research: experimental, 104, 215–16; laboratory-based, 181; silent, 139; wartime, 214–15
resource exhaustion, 120–21
revelations: prophetic, 173
rhumbatron, 241
Ricardo-Campbell, Rita, 320n82
Richardson, Henry Hobson, 13, 60, 95, 126, 196; Billings Memorial Library (University of Vermont), 125, 197, 199–201, 199, 200, 203, 308nn22–24; Gate Lodge (Langwater), North Easton, 307n17; Oakes Ames Memorial Hall, North Easton, 198, 201, 307n18; Oakes and Oliver Ames Memorial, Albany County, 197, 198, 198; Oliver Ames Free Library, North Easton, 197; Old Colony Railroad Station, North Easton, 307n17; "Syrian" arch detail, 200, 308n23; Winn Memorial Library, Woburn, 200
Ricoeur, Paul, 2, 8
River Irrigating Waters of Arizona, The (Forbes), 118–19, 119
Riyadh University, Saudi Arabia, 9–10
robotics, 254
Rockefeller, John D., 172, 174
Roosevelt, Franklin Delano, 312n68
Rousseau, Jean-Jacques: *Discourse on the Origin and Foundations of Inequality among Men*, 11
Royce, Josiah, 204
Rudimentary Architecture (Leeds), 60
Rumford tile, 301n25, 302n27
"Rural Community, The" (Weber), 102–3
Russell, Thomas, 307n18

Sabine, Paul E., 178
Sabine, Wallace C., 176–77; Boston Symphony Hall, 178; Fogg Art Museum (Harvard), 178
Sabinite (plaster), 178
Said, Edward W., 1, 4, 6, 7–9, 13–14, 17; *Reflections on Exile*, 8–9; "The World, the Text, and the Critic" and its iterations, 1, 2–5, 7–9, 13, 257n5, 259n37, 261n60

Saint-Gaudens, Augustus: bas-reliefs (Ames Memorial), 198; *Diana*, 133–34
salary splitting, 242, 243
Saltonstall, Gurdon, 267n48
Santa Clara County v. Southern Pacific Railroad Co., 30
Santayana, George, 304n48
Sather, Peder, 213
Savio, Mario, 219–22, *220*
Schermerhorn, William C., 295n42
Schinkel, Karl Friedrich, 57, 69
Schmidt, Leigh Eric, 173
School of Athens (Raphael), 150, 155
Schopp, Laurence O.: Park Plaza Hotel, 258n23
Science, the Endless Frontier (Bush), 214–15, 312n68
sculpture, 46
Seligman, Edwin, 165
seminars: German, 180, 181; listening-writing, 181; pedagogy of and dialogues at, 181, 182, 183, 190–91, 192; research, 180–81; tables of, 170, 182, *184*, 190–91; undergraduate, 170, 180, 181–85, 303n40
separate but equal, 130, 163
Server, The (Krajewski), 263n11
Sever, Comfort, 265n15
Shepley, Rutan & Coolidge, 246: University of Chicago, 174, 176
Shils, Edward, 185
Shippen, William: Nassau Hall (Princeton), 33, *34*, 35
shovels, 198, 199, 307n18
Shurtleff, Nathaniel B., 287n76
Siegert, Bernhard, 11, 12, 260n44
signification and signs, 18–19, 44, 98, 188–89, 199, 239–40, 241, 243, 248
Silliman, Benjamin, 42, 48, 54, 269nn84–85; *American Journal of Science and Arts*, 48–49, 85
silver, 134–35, 202, 290n21
Silver Queen, The (Johnson), 290n22
Silver Queen, The/Justice (Parks), 134–35, *134*, 202, 290n21
silver question, 135, 290n21
Simmel, Georg, 135
Simson, Robert: *The Elements of Euclid*, 62, 273n42
Skinner, John: *The Plough, The Loom, and the Anvil*, 106
Sklar, Martin, 133
slavery, 169; use of scientific agriculture as means to end, 106; westward expansion of, 105; *See also* enslaved people

Small, Albion W., 100
Smedley, Ephraim, 266n16
Smith, Margaret Bayard, 25
Smith, Robert: Nassau Hall (Princeton), 33, *34, 35*
Smith College, 79–80
Smithmeyer, John L., 297n64
Smithsonian Astrophysical Observatory, 295n47
social media. *See under* media
social reform, 77–78, 276n1
Sociéte Sultanienne d'Agriculture, Cairo, 118
Souls of Black Folks, The (Du Bois), 91, 93
Southern Oil Company, 123
Southern Railway Co. v. Greene, 30
Spanish-American War, 211; commemoration of deaths, 95
spatiality, 195
speech and speaking, 2, 3, 12, 18, 38, 173, 191, 252–53; acoustics for, 178, 179–80, 236–37, 301n26; free, 219–22; machine, 254; regulation of, 21, 23–25, 219–22; See also *parrhesia* (free speech); voices
Spencer, Solon, 134
Sperry Gyroscope Company, 241
Spindletop Oil Field, Beaumont, 122, *122*, 123
Spivak, Gayatri Chakravorty, 4, 9–10
Spofford, Ainsworth Rand, 163, 167
Spotted Horse Mine, Maiden, Montana, 290n21
Sproul, Robert Gordon, 214
squatters, 201, 204
St. John's College, Annapolis, 186
St. Thomas Aquinas: *Summa Theologica*, 183
St. Thomas Church, New York, 301n25
Stand, Columbia (McCaughey), 303n40
Standard Diary, 84
Stanford klystron, 241–42, *241*
Stanford Linear Accelerator Center (SLAC), 240, 243, *244*
Stanford Research Institute (SRI), 219, 243₂
Stanford University, 238–39, 240–43, 253–54; Hoover Library Tower, 245–48, *246*, 249; Memorial Church, 247
Stein, Gertrude, 184, 304n51
stereotype plates, 282n3
Sterling, Wallace, 242
Stevens, Edward W., 64
Stewardson, John, 94
Sticks and Stones (Mumford), 196
Stiles, Ezra, 41
stone and stonemasonry, 94–94, 97–98, 101–2, 200–201, 308n24

Story, Joseph, 31
Stowe, Harriet Beecher: *Uncle Tom's Cabin*, 60, 272n35
Strauss, Leo, 305n78
Strayer Plan, 214
Strong, Edward W., 219
students: Black, 87–94, 99, 103, 163; international, 163–64, 298n69; Lacan on, 189–90; love of university and, 31, 36, 50, 51, 255; misbehavior of, 31, 33, 35, 40, 42, 144; note-taking of, 173; political actions of, 219–22, 253; supervision of, 35, 40, 43, 100, 267n53; women, 71–87, 94, 103, 208, 281n73
Students for a Democratic Society, 219
sublime, 19, 44, 157, 236
Sugino, Kaigiro, 293n25
Summa Theologica (St. Thomas Aquinas), 183
symbolization, 98, 199, 239–43, 248, 254
syntopicon, 185–87
Syrie Centrale (Vogüé), 308n23

tables, seminar, 170, 182, 184, *184*, 190–91
Tafuri, Manfredo, 23, 263n8
"Talented Tenth" (Du Bois), 90, 92, 279n45
tariffs, 106, 107
taste, 43–48, 50, 52, 56
Taylor, Joseph W., 78
Taylor, Robert R., 89
tea trade, 155, 252
technē, 11, 12
technics, 11, 12, 14–16, 238, 245, 250–51, 254
Technics and Civilization (Mumford), 238
technopoesis, 222, 238, 249
telescopes, 215–16
Terman, Frederick, 241, 242
Texas AMC, 121: Texas Agricultural Experiment Station and its reports, 121–23
Texas Petroleum (Phillips), 121–24
Text-Book of Physics (Hallock), 156
textbooks, 54, 60, 65, 156; alphanumeric vs. textual-visual, 60–66; geometry, 60–66, 273nn41–42, 273n46; inscribed to women, 53, 60
Thatcher, Thomas A., 50
Thayer, Sylvanus, 62
theocracy, 252
think tanks, 247, 254
Thomas, M. Carey, 77, 78, 79, 94, 99–100, 102, 276n1, 281nn71–74; pamphlet collection of, 125, 128
Thompson, Emily, 180, 302n32

Thornton, William, 141, 293n25
thought, 25, 43–44, 183, 314n83; Greek, 186
Ticknor, George, 45, 62
Tilden, Samuel J., 50
time, 77, 79, 83–84, 93–94, 99, 100, 276n1, 286n60
timekeeping, 18, 83–84, 99
"To Helen" (Poe), 36, 38, 266n35
Tombs (prison), New York, 37
Toumey, James W., 116, 117; "The Date Palm," 117
Town, Ithiel, 55
transepts, 69–70
translations: Latin, 50
Treaty of Guadalupe Hidalgo (1848), 201
tree of knowledge, 143
Tressider, Donald, 242
Trustees of Dartmouth College v. Woodward, 30, 50
truths, 64, 192, 253
Tufts, James R., 303n39
Turing, Alan, 255
Turing test, 255
Turner, Frederick Jackson: frontier thesis of, 18, 109, 130 131, 132–33, 135, 196, 199, 289n11; pioneer ideals of, 196, 307n5, 307n10
Tuskegee Institute, 87–90, *88*, 89, 103; Academic Department, 89, 90; Alabama Hall, 88–89; architectural drawing and design at, 89, 278nn36–37; auditory signals at, 93–94; brickmaking at, 87–90, 277n33; Department of Industries for Girls, 89; Department of Mechanical Industries, 89–90; Douglass Hall, 89; experiments with colonial agriculture in Togo, 103; Max Weber's visit to, 103; training for trades, 89
Tuskegee Normal and Industrial Institute. *See* Tuskegee Institute
Tuthill, Louisa Caroline, 53–54; *History of Architecture from the Earliest Times*, 53–56, 59

U.S. Atomic Energy Commission, 216, 234, 243
U.S. Capitol Building, 140, 145, 148, *149*
U.S. Constitution: contracts clause, 30, 264n6
U.S. Department of Agriculture, 111
U.S. House Committee on Un-American Activities, 216
Uncle Tom's Cabin (Stowe), 60, 272n35
Union Pacific Railroad, 197

United States, 130–31; census, 131–32, 135, 289n6, 289nn10–11; as a developing country, 10, 133; population, 131, *132*; Western territorial expansion and conquest, 18, 21, 109, 130–31

United States Military Academy, West Point, 62–63, 73–74, 274n54; Battle Monument, 73–74, *73*

universality and universalism, x, 10, 15, 16, 166–67

universities, American, x, 8–10, 18, 19–20, 130, 192, 221–22, 250, 251, 252, 255; academic disciplines, specializations and compartmentalization, 65, 99, 100, 156, 197, 223–24, 242; academic freedom, 7, 14, 171, 217, 219, 221–22 314n88; academic knowledge, 2, 8, 132, 142–43; African Americans and, 87–94, 99, 103, 163; architecture and campuses of, xi, 16–17, 35–38, 94 (*see also under specific universities and institutions*); archives of, 6; benefactors of, 252; births, marriage, and "race decline" as related to, 99–100, 281nn72–74; boundaries and boundary problems of, x, 1, 6–7, 8–9, 10, 20, 214, 216–17, 217–22, 251, 253; Cold War and, 191, 238; collective action and, 219–22, *220, 221*, 247, 253, 314n88–90; colleges vs., ix, 78, 99–100; collegiate learning vs. scholarly research, 170; collegiate time, 77–78, 79, 83–84, 93–94, 99, 100, 276n1; commemoration of alumni, 71, 95; conflicts within, 19–20; as corporations/corporate persons, 14, 16–17, 31–45, 130, 216–17, 219, 222, 252, 253, 254, 314n88; decolonization of, 8; examinations at, 33, 58, 183; faculty sovereignty and, 216–17, 218; free speech and, 219–22, 314nn88–90; global, 252; graduate schools, 163–64, 297n68; history of, ix–x, 6, 7, 8, 14–17, 33, 90, 104, 252; human capital and, 219, 221–22, 223, 237–40, 248–49, 314n88; humanities and, 9, 19, 218, 223, 229–34, 238–40, 242, 245, 248, 254, 315n11; *in loco parentis* and, 35, 40, 43, 100, 267n53; industrial and financial capital and, 14–15, 154–55, 171, 218–19, 231–32, 242; international students and, 163–64, 298n69; land-grant/state, 104, 131, 196, 307n5; legal immortality of, 16–17, 72, 268n55; love for, 31, 36, 50, 51, 255; measurements of achievement at, 8; military research and, 214, 234–35, 241–42; modern, x, 6–7, 10,

65, 171, 251–52; Protestant church and, 171, 172–74; scientific research and, 243; separation of campuses from towns and countryside, 202, 203, 205, 210–11; tech-campus sprawl, 243; time-to-degree and, 99; undergraduate curricula at, 99, 170, 180–85, 303n40; universality and, x, 10, 15, 16; as a utopia, 8–9, 208, 252; Western canon and, 170–71, 181–87; women and, 77–87, 94, 208, 281n73; as a writing-down system, 173, 301n11; *See also* colleges; education, polytechnics; Historically Black Colleges and Universities (HBCUs); *See also specific universities and institutions*

University of Arizona, 116; Agricultural Experiment Station and its reports, 115–16, 118–19, 120; College of Agriculture, 116; School of Mines, 115, 116

University of California: expansion of, 214, 217–18; policy barring Communist Party members from faculty, 216; policy requiring faculty to sign loyalty oath, 216–17, 240, 313n73, 313n76

University of California, Berkeley, 207–22, 312n69; ban on political advocacy on university property, protests, free speech and 219–22, *220, 221*, 314n88–90; California Hall, 209, 213; campus plan, 207–13, *210*; Cyclotron Building, 215, *215*; Hearst Greek Theater, 213; Hearst Memorial Mining Building, 207, 211–12, *211, 212*, 215, 311nn61–62; Kellersberger map and, 205, *205*, 215, 312n69; Phoebe Apperson Hearst Architectural Competition for campus plan, 207, 208–9, *209*, 210, 311n55; president's house, 213; proposed "free speech" zone, 217, 219, *218*; Radiation Laboratory, 215, 216; Sather Gate, 213–14, *214, 218*, 219, *221*; sit-ins and building occupations at, 219–21; Sproul Hall, 214, 217, 220; student union, 217

University of Chicago, 172, 175; chapel attendance at, 174, 301n14; Cobb Hall, 174; Cowles Commission, 248; Leon Mandel Hall, 174; library, 174; philosophic and social-science orientation of, 304n48; Rockefeller Memorial Chapel, 174–80, *175, 177, 178, 179*, 181; Tower Group, 174; unrest at, 181, 303n39

University of Pennsylvania: Library, 125–28, *126, 127, 128*, 288n80; pamphlet

collection of, 125, 127–29; Van Pelt Library special collections, 128; Wharton School, 107, 283n19,
University of Texas at Austin, 121; Texas Mineral Survey, 121
University of Toronto: Library, 125–26, 288n82
University of Vermont: Billings Memorial Library, 125, 197, 199–201, *199, 200,* 203, 308nn22–24
University of Virginia, 21, 22, 36–38, 141–42, *142, 143,* 148, 150–52, 208, 293n25, 294n31, 294n34, 295n39; bell and clock, 146–47, 150, 292n18; Cabell Hall, 152, *152;* fire at, 148, *149,* 150–51, *150;* gas light, electricity and heating at, 148, *149,* 150–52, 293n25, 294n30, 294n38; Lawn, 21, 36, 141, 146, 152; Library Rotunda, *140,* 141–42, 144–48, *146, 147, 149,* 150–51, *150,* 294n31, 294n34; Library Rotunda annex, 150–51, *151; School of Athens* (copies), 150, *151,* 152, 294n35
University of Wisconsin, 109, 289n7; Agricultural Experiment Station and its reports, 109–12, 114–15; Agriculture Hall, 112, 113–15, *113, 114,* 284n41; College of Agriculture, 112; dairy course, 112; media network of, 111, 112, 115
Urban, Wilbert Marshall, 240
Uses of the University, The (Kerr), 217, 218–19
utilitarianism, 36, 37

Van Brunt, Henry, 57–60, 65–73, 74; Gore Hall addition (Harvard), 71, 125; "Greek Lines," 57, 65, *68;* on Harriet Beecher Stowe and *Uncle Tom's Cabin,* 60, 272n35; Memorial Hall (Harvard), 66–73, *67, 70,* 74; opinion of women, 60
Van Doren, Mark, 182, 186, 303n40, 303n44
Varian, Russell, 241
Varian, Sigurd, 242
Varian Associates, 242, 243
Vassar, Charles, 277n31
Vassar, Matthew, 78, 81; brickmaking business of, 87, 277n31
Vassar College, 78, 79, 81–87; auditory signals at, 83–84; bricks at, 84, 86–87, 277n31; corridor teachers, 82; corridors, 81–82, 82, 87; daily schedule, 82–84, 277n17; dome parties at, 85; gas light at, 84; Main Building, 81–82, *81, 82,* 84–85, 87, 95; Maria Mitchell Observatory, 85–87, *86*
Veblen, Thorstein, 154

Verses on the Prospect of Planting Arts and Learning in America (Berkeley), 206–7
VerValen, Richard, 277n31
Victor Talking Machine Company, 306n82
Vismann, Cornelia, 11
visual literacy, 54, 56, 64, 65
Vogüé, Charles-Jean-Melchoir: *Syrie Centrale,* 308n23
voices, 178, 180, 192, 301n26, 306n82; materializing of, 173; overtones/harmonics of, 161–63, *162; See also* speech and speaking
Voorhees, Walker, Foley and Smith: Hayden Memorial Library (MIT), 231

Walker, Timothy: *Elements of Geometry with Practical Applications,* 61
Walter, Thomas Ustick, 53: U.S. Capitol Building, 148, *149*
war memorials, 69–70, 72
Ware, William, 60, 66, 270n4; Gore Hall addition (Harvard), 71, 125; Memorial Hall (Harvard), 66–73, *67, 70,* 74
Washington University, St. Louis, 100–102, 281n82; Ridgley Hall, *101;* Ridgley Library, 101, 102
Washington, Booker T., 87–90, 91, 100, 103; *Working with the Hands,* 87, *88, 89*
water and water analysis, 116–17, 118–19, *119,* 121
Waters, Clara Erskine Clement, 55
Watson, Floyd R., 176, 178, 179–80, 302n32; "Ideal Auditorium Acoustics," 302n34
Watson, John B., 304n48
Weber, Max: admiration for W. E. B. Du Bois, 103; on bureaucratization of German academic life, 103; defining "science as vocation," 103; on immigration of eastern Europeans to the United States, 102–3; opinion of Book T. Washington and his efforts, 103; "Protestant Ethic and the 'Spirit' of Capitalism," 102–3; "The Rural Community," 102
Webster, Daniel, 31, 265n10
Webster, David, 241
Weeks, Edward, 237
Weinberg, Jack, 220
Wellesley College, 79, 80
West Point. *See* United States Military Academy, West Point
Western canon. *See* canon (Western)
WGBH, 237
Wharton, Joseph: Charles Henry Carey's influence on, 107

wheat, 102
Wheeler, Benjamin Ide, 208
Wheelock, Eleazor, 30
Wheelock, John, 30
White, James M., 176, 178
White, Stanford, 74, 33, 294n34; New York University, 151; University of Virginia, 151–52, 153, 294n34
Whitehead, Alfred North, 239
"Whiz Kids," 248, 320n81
Wiegand, Wayne A., 124, 287n76
Wiener, Norbert, 223, 224–25, 237, 245, 254; *The Human Use of Human Beings*, 228–29
Wilberforce College, 279n49
Wilbur, Ray Lyman, 245
Willard, Simon, 292n18
Williams, Elisha, 40
Winn Memorial Library, Woburn, Massachusetts, 200
Winsor, Justin, 125
Winterer, Caroline: *The Culture of Classicism*, 44, 56, 204
women's movement, 314n90
Woodward, Bezaleel, 265n15
Woolsey, Theodore D., 49
Working with the Hands (Washington), 87, 88, 89
"World, the Text, and the Critic, The" (Said), 1, 2–5, 7–9, 257n5
World's Columbian Exposition, Chicago, 131, 132–35, 202; Agriculture Building, 133; *Diana*, 133–34; Mines and Mining Building, 133, 134, *134*, 290n19; Montana exhibit, 134–35, *134*; "raft" foundation of, 133, 290n17; signs at, 133, 134; *The Silver Queen* (Johnson), 290n22; *The Silver Queen/Justice* (Parks), 134–35, *134*, 202, 290n21
worldliness, 2, 3, 4, 8, 9
Wormser, Maurice, 50
Wretched of the Earth, The (Fanon), 8
writing, 2, 3, 21

Yale, Elihu, 39
Yale Corporation, 35, 38–50, 268n55
Yale Report of 1828, 35, 42, 43–45, 48–49, 269n84; on classical architecture and sculpture, 46, 47
Yale University, 35, 49–50; Benjamin Silliman's lectures in chemistry at, 48–49; Bread and Butter Rebellion, 42; campus, 38–40; charter of, 41, 268n55, 268n57; Conic Sections Rebellion, 42; Connecticut Hall, 36; curricula at, 35, 42, 43–45, 48, 49; discipline at, 42; food boycott, 42; Joseph Bigelow's instruction at, 45–48; location of, 38, 267n48; Lyceum Building, 49; misbehavior at, 40, 42; presidency, 40–41; professorship in classical languages, 49; Union Hall, 41; Yale College, 39–40, *39*; *See also* Yale Corporation
Yosemite Valley, 202
youth, eternal, 255

Zimmerman, Andrew, 102, 103
Zuckerberg, Mark A., 321n12

GPSR Authorized Representative: Easy Access System Europe, Mustamäe tee 50, 10621 Tallinn, Estonia, gpsr.requests@easproject.com

www.ingramcontent.com/pod-product-compliance
Lightning Source LLC
Chambersburg PA
CBHW021846020426
42334CB00013B/205